W9-CCY-055

22.95

Fortas, A

Murphy, Bruce Allen

Fortas: the rise and ruin of a
Supreme Court justice

DEC 2 7 1988
JAN - 5 1989
JAN 1 7 1989
FEB 1 0 1989
MAR 7 - 1989
MAR 2 1 1989
APR, 3 -1989
AUG - 2 1989
JAN 1 1 1993

DEC   1988

FORTAS

FORTAS

THE RISE AND RUIN OF A SUPREME COURT JUSTICE

BRUCE ALLEN MURPHY

WILLIAM MORROW AND COMPANY, INC.

NEW YORK

Library of Congress Cataloging-in-Publication Data

Murphy, Bruce Allen.
    Fortas : the rise and ruin of a Supreme Court Justice.
    Bibliography: p.
    Includes index.
    1. Fortas, Abe.   2. Judges—United States—Biography.
I. Title.
KF8745.F65M87 1988   347.73'2634 [B] 88-1751
ISBN 0-688-05357-2   347.3073534 [B]

Printed in the United States of America

First Edition

1 2 3 4 5 6 7 8 9 10

BOOK DESIGN BY RICHARD ORIOLO

B
Fortas, A

For my children,
Emily and Geoffrey

CONTENTS

When an elevator car carrying lawyers,
judges and administrators was trapped between
floors in the Export-Import Bank on the way
to a meeting, [a man] opened the operator's
panel, pulled a lever, flicked a switch or
two and the car was once again on its way.
When his fellow passengers expressed their
astonishment, [Abe] Fortas replied with the
mock innocence he occasionally affected,
"It's really quite simple, for an insider."

–REX LEE, FORMER SOLICITOR GENERAL

I did not seek the post
of Justice of the Supreme
Court of the United States.
That was not part of my
life plan.

—ABE FORTAS

PROLOGUE

The man doing all the talking as he drove the big Lincoln convertible at breakneck speed over the Texas scrublands was not an old man at sixty-one, but he looked close to death. The pains in his chest, relieved more and more frequently by nitroglycerin pills, told him that his time was drawing to a close. Once this tall, floppy-eared giant of a man with the flowing white hair had held the most powerful political position in the world. But now, Lyndon Johnson's days were filled with decisions about his ranch in Stonewall, Texas, the library that was being built in his name on the University of Texas campus, and dictating his memoirs.

There were several things now on Johnson's mind as he spoke about his memoirs to an assistant who raced to keep up, using his own version of reporter's shorthand. In the middle of a monologue on the Kennedy assassination, the Warren Commission, and the protests in 1968, one subject came up that seemed almost totally out of context. It was about a friend, a dear friend, a man who had remained loyal right to the end. Johnson spoke about Abe Fortas, a man who, in his words, "was liberal and able and courageous, and would do what's good for the people." [1] But somewhere it had all gone wrong. Now, in this very private conversation, the former president tried to put all of his most sincere emotions into words. "When that phone rings at night in the White House it's always bad news," Johnson began. "So, I talked to a number of people that I knew and trusted. I talked to Abe Fortas. Abe Fortas is as good, fine, patriotic, and concerned a human as I ever knew. He has been victimized and it's terrible. We're cruel people. I made him take the justiceship. In that way, I ruined his life." [2]

"I ruined his life." Whether Johnson truly believed what he said

that day will never be known. But the truth was that he was absolutely correct. Once it had seemed so perfect that it was like the American dream—two old friends rising together from poverty to the absolute pinnacles of power in their respective professions, and one rewarding the other by changing his place in history. But instead it was really an American tragedy. Together the two men had risen to power, and together they fell from grace with history. And neither one of them really ever knew why.

I

DOUGLAS'S WHIZ KID

If it is true that some are born to lead and others are born to follow, then Abe Fortas was born to lead the leaders whom others would follow. But Fortas's rise to this lofty position was not an easy one. Later, he would be portrayed as the embodiment of the American Dream. To journalists he was "The Southern Smoothie Who Came East," and "The Jewish Immigrant's Son Who Worked His Way Up."[1] In fact, despite all of his talents, Fortas never could have done it alone. His ticket to the top involved not just what he could do on his own, but also what others could do for him. And there is no question that the central character in his constellation of early mentors was a man named William O. Douglas.

For a long time, it seemed unlikely that the two men would ever meet. Abe Fortas was born in the poor Jewish section of Memphis, Tennessee, on June 19, 1910, the youngest of five children of William Fortas and his wife, Ray Berson Fortas, two Orthodox Jews who had emigrated from England. Upon arriving in the United States, the elder

Fortas had moved his family directly to the sleepy southern city because it was the home of his older brother.

But realizing the dream of every immigrant to achieve a better life for his family was not easy. William Fortas scratched out a living at various times as a jeweler, shopkeeper, and pawnbroker, but his most lasting trade was as a cabinetmaker. Since the only housing he could afford was on Pontotoc Street, across an alley from the black area in town, the Fortas family was only one short rung up on the social ladder in the segregationist city. Abe Fortas would later recall his early years as being "as poor as you can imagine."[2] Still, as a young boy he was taught to manage on minimal resources. While Fortas was raised in the Orthodox Jewish faith, the family was too poor to afford streetcar fare, so it was necessary to walk the considerable distance to the religious school. In his early teens he would be asked to help the family finances by working nights at a local shoe store. It seems that the only luxury in young Abe's life came when his father, passing on his own love of music, insisted that the boy take violin lessons.

Being raised as a poor Orthodox Jewish boy was not the path normally leading to success in this city. "Memphis has always been Southern with a Western twist," an observer later wrote.[3] There was a small Jewish community, 6,000 out of a total population of 160,000, which had not quite been assimilated into the city's life. Memphis at the time was divided into sections—for the Jews, Scots, Irish, and of course the refined Protestant southern natives—with rival gangs of youths at one time raiding each other's territory. Schools let out and the young boys, those who had attended classes, would be seen terrorizing the Jewish shopkeepers. Eventually, thanks to one man, Rabbi Hardwig Peres, the Jewish community slowly began to become assimilated into the mainstream of Memphis life. Voted the city's most valued citizen by the readers of the *Memphis Press-Scimitar* in 1927, Peres was idolized for his efforts to convene in his office a weekly meeting of prominent Memphians for discussions on improvements in the city's social relations. The high esteem that the rabbi was held in throughout the city was easily recognizable. Years later, city folk would recall how Mrs. Fortas would frequently take her youngest son to various Jewish social gatherings in town and whisper to him, "See, that's Mr. Peres," holding the great man up as a model of what could be achieved by members of their faith.[4]

Nothing in Abe Fortas's physical appearance gave promise of great things to come. He was small and slightly built, with hands that struck people as being so delicate that they belonged on a china doll. He always looked younger than his years, with his smooth dark face and deep-set oversized hazel eyes, framed by two huge protruding ears that resembled saucers turned on their edges. People were struck by the young man's temperament. Disarmingly modest, with a rather sticky-sweet, quiet sense of politeness, Fortas appeared to be almost too serious. "I wish he'd laugh more," an associate later said.[5] It was not that he didn't have a sense of humor. But he resorted to a dry, puckish wit too sparingly for people to think of him as anything other than businesslike. He seemed to cut through life like a boat that slips through water without leaving a wake, and those ears missed nothing.

But if the outside of the boat was unprepossessing, the motor inside was high-powered. Like the children of other immigrants, Fortas looked for a way out of his childhood poverty, a path to a better life. Since education represented that ticket out, he set out to achieve in the public school system. Having come from working-class stock, though, he would not find it easy. His father had taught himself to read and write, while his mother remained illiterate all of her life. Abe, however, dazzled everyone with his intellectual capacity and his performance in the public schools. He seemed driven, on a mission to achieve. His brother Meyer recalled, "With Abe, it was study, study, study. He had a goal to attain."[6] And attain he did. It was in South Side High School that he began to show his incredible intellectual promise. After only three years in the school, he had amassed such extraordinary grades that he graduated at the tender age of fifteen with the second-highest average in his class.

But attending high school involves more than just earning grades. While young Abe did not automatically fit in socially because of his family background, he learned to cope in this environment. He captained the debate team, where achievement was judged on the merits of argumentation and evidence rather than his heritage. And by the age of thirteen, after his ability with the violin became professional enough, he formed his own jazz dance band, the Blue Melody Boys Band, earning eight dollars a night by playing at high school dances. The money he earned over the next few years would help to put him through the rest of his schooling. Just as valuable as the money, though, were the social skills he acquired, which would help the young Jew, now known around town as Fiddlin' Abe, gain entrée to various social events and would one day make him the life of dinner dances in Washington.

But even with all of his personal achievements, Fortas needed the help of others to go on. Had he been one of the children of the social elite in the city, he might have expected to attend an Ivy League college, or one of the fine southern schools such as Vanderbilt or the University of Virginia. However, being poor and Jewish, in the best of worlds Fortas could hope only to have the chance to commute from his home to a local college, Southwestern. And with his family's financial situation even that prospect seemed unlikely.

Were it not for the greatness of the man that Fortas had been taught from childhood to admire—Rabbi Hardwig Peres—he might have had to follow his father into carpentry, or perhaps continue to try to earn a living from music. After being forced to abandon his dream of a career in the law to raise his younger siblings, and then witnessing the death of his younger brother whom he had put through law school, Rabbi Peres created a scholarship fund in his brother's name and donated ten thousand dollars to the cause. This fund—the Israel H. Peres Memorial Scholarship—would make it possible for some poor Memphis child to attend Southwestern. It mattered little to Peres that this was a Presbyterian school; what was important was the education that was being offered. Appropriately, the first beneficiary of this new scholarship was Abe Fortas.[7] So, out of two aborted legal careers would one day come a third that was more fantastic than either of the two Peres brothers could have imagined.

Upon entering Southwestern in the fall of 1926, Fortas faced the same social problems that had dogged him in his early years. "He just really didn't fit into things," one of his professors later commented. "He was an outsider looking in."[8] Younger than nearly everyone else in the school, living at home, and one of only six Jews in the five-hundred-member student body, Abe found it hard to feel at home in the small, seventy-five-year-old, Presbyterian liberal arts college. Fortas had turned away from Judaism, and any other form of organized religion, during this period, becoming what some people labeled an agnostic. Whether this was a legitimate questioning of his religious views or an effort to fit into the new society around him is not known. But if his purpose was to join the college society, it did not help him assimilate into a school where daily Presbyterian chapel was required. The result was, one teacher recalled, "a strain of unhappiness about him. He took life very seriously on the whole."[9]

In spite of the obstacles—financial and social—Fortas once more achieved at an astonishing rate, gaining the admiration of students and teachers alike. He majored in both English and economics.[10] He also became a member of the college debate team, and his home in Memphis became a popular meeting place for friends who were anx-

ious to hone their debating skills. By his senior year, Fortas was elected president of the Quibblers' Forum, a forensic society. Beyond that,
he became a Renaissance man of sorts, joining and leading school
groups that fit his considerable talents. Because of his musical skills,
he was the director of the school's orchestra for two years. In addition,
he became assistant editor of *The Journal,* a literary magazine, and
served as president of two literary societies, Sigma Upsilon and the
Sophoclean Club, as well as a philosophical society called the Nitist
Club.

Even though he didn't leave his hometown to go to college, by his
own efforts Fortas was exposed to new ideas and ways of life. As
president of the Nitist Club, he had the privilege of inviting a speaker
to campus. Perhaps to show his "outsider" status by opening the door
for another outsider, he invited the leading local black minister to
speak on campus for the first time. It was "with a sense of shock" that
the young man realized that, even though he had played with the black
children in the alley behind his house before they were separated to go
to the city's segregated schools, this was the very first time he had
shaken a black man's hand. So he began to rethink his family's traditional southern segregationist views and started to see blacks as "entitled to rights and to decent regard from others."[11]

Fortas established the sort of academic record that once more would
give him some options. He graduated from Southwestern at age nineteen, first in his class, with highest honors in both English and economics. Because of these accomplishments, he became a member of
the honorary scholastic fraternity on campus, Alpha Theta Phi. While
in college, Fortas had decided on a career in law, not an unusual
choice for one with his great skills in writing and argumentation. But
more than that, law, like medicine, represented a classic avenue for
children of struggling immigrants to make it to the top.

In applying to two of the finest law schools of the day—Harvard
and Yale—Fortas could not have chosen two more divergent schools.
Harvard had an open admissions policy, requiring only a college degree from a recognized college or university, and admitted a class of
between five hundred and seven hundred, on the theory that a large
number could be flunked out after yielding the sort of tuition base
necessary to keep the school afloat. It is said that at Harvard on the
first day students were told to look at their peers to the right and to the
left, and told truthfully that "one of you will not be back next year."
As a result there was fantastically intense competition for grades.
Yale, on the other hand, admitted only 125 "highly selected" stu-

dents, giving them more individual attention, with the expectation that only a few would flunk out of the much smaller class.

More significant than the greater individual attention at Yale, though, was the fact that this law school was now embarked on a new and adventurous legal mission. Like most of the law schools at the time, Harvard's curriculum used the classic "case method" of study, examining law as it was "discovered" by judges in deciding cases. On the other hand, Yale's iconoclastic faculty, under the direction of a young dean, Robert Maynard Hutchins, had embarked on a search for "legal realism." This innovative "functional" approach examined the law as it was "made" by judges, employing the fruits of various behavioral, social, and even physical sciences. The effort to see how law actually operated in the real world had given birth to a new vital spirit at Yale.[12]

But as with everything else in Fortas's life, the road to law school was not an easy one. The young man's professors filled his file with the sort of recommendations that would seem to make him attractive to any professional school. "As far as scholastic records go, there is no one better in the class," one professor of philosophy wrote. "But it is in the part that he has played in stimulating others to think in a philosophical club we have, and in intercollegiate debate, that the extraordinary power of the man is seen. . . . As far as one can tell, he will be heard from some day."[13] However, the story goes that even with this stellar application file, Yale Law School was not convinced. His credentials were fine, but Southwestern was just too small, and produced too unknown a quantity, to risk a precious seat in the next class on the precocious émigré from the Jewish section of Memphis. So, the admissions committee asked Fortas to interview with a local attorney who had graduated from Yale Law School.[14] This attorney was only moderately impressed with Fortas's abilities, reporting to the school, "I would say that he would be capable of doing good, original work, particularly along research lines, and probably will wind up as an instructor and author, or in some kind of social welfare work."[15] After deliberating, the admissions committee decided to take a chance on the young man.

Since Harvard also admitted Fortas, he had a choice to make, but the fifty dollars more per month in the scholarship offer extended by Yale looked better to the poor boy from Memphis.[16] Beyond the money, though, the choice to attend Yale was probably the one best tailored to his experiences.[17] Coming from a somewhat less prestigious educational background with relatively weak student competition at

Southwestern, even a young man of Fortas's brilliance could have found the life-or-death competition at Harvard brutal. Moreover, rather than facing the anti-Semitic WASPish orientation of Cambridge, Massachusetts, he would meet the more open-minded, tolerant attitude in New Haven, Connecticut, which made it more comfortable for the few Jews in law school there. For Fortas, this gave him a chance to be judged for his brilliance rather than his family background.[18]

Fortas brought to Yale in the fall of 1930 all of the talents and work ethic that had made him successful in other levels of schooling, but the rise to the top of the heap took a little time. Since the law school's old building, Hendrie Hall, was not big enough to house all of its students, Fortas lived off campus for the first year. (For the last two he would live in the more spacious quarters in the newly completed Gothic law quadrangle called the Sterling Law Building.) To make his quarters more comfortable, he brought with him from Memphis a huge oak chaise longue he had made using the woodworking skills taught by his father, with wide arms on which one could write, allowing him to read and study in maximum comfort.[19] His days were filled with the rather dull, prescribed first-year classes in contracts, torts, property, civil procedure, commercial bank credit, legal bibliography and professional practice, jurisprudence, and criminal law.

No one worked harder that first year than the young man from Memphis. Thomas Emerson, that year's editor in chief of the law review, and himself one of the hardest working members of the third-year class, claimed that no matter when he came to school in the morning, Fortas was already seated at his favorite library table, where he would remain until after Emerson left the school late at night.[20] This intensive zeal for studying spoke volumes about Fortas's state of mind at the time. He was a driven young man—having come so far, and with so much further to go. When he arrived in New Haven, the odds seemed to be against him. He was poor, Jewish, the only representative of tiny Southwestern in the school, and at twenty the youngest member of the law school class. It seemed unlikely that he would fit in with his older, better-heeled classmates. So the only ticket to acceptance, not to mention to a successful career, came with the achievements that resulted from hard work.

Soon, though, as Fortas focused on his studies, the rewards of his labors followed as naturally as they had back in Memphis. As he worked, he achieved, and the honors came to him once more. His grades after the first year were high enough to make him one of the four first-year students awarded another year from the General Fund

Scholarship, which helped to pay the annual tuition and fees of $450. However, indicating the stiffer competition from his law school peers, all of the special scholarship prizes available for such accomplishments as the highest final-exam grades and the greatest proficiency in first-year moot court went to other students.[21]

It was in his second-year courses that Fortas began to show his true promise. In January of 1932, after a yearlong law journal writing competition in which students were required to write a series of one-page "Notes" and a ten-page "Comment," Fortas took the first prize.[22] This success brought something even more precious in March of that year—election to the coveted editor-in-chief position on the *Yale Law Journal*. It was the position that immediately marked him as one of the school's rising superstars.[23] Then Fortas justified the confidence of his colleagues by leading his second-year class in the annual examinations with an average of 81.8, an accomplishment that earned him the fifty-dollar Jewell Prize. Accordingly, the faculty had tapped Fortas as someone truly special, and awarded him the prestigious Eliza Townsend Parker Scholarship of over five hundred dollars for the following year, which was given to students "desiring to pursue graduate work with a view to becoming teachers of law."[24] Whether they did this to encourage him to think about teaching, or whether Fortas was talking at that time about teaching as a possible career, is not known. But the result was the same.

By now, Fortas had met and impressed the finest Yale Law School professors, men who molded his mind now and would shape his career options in the future. There was Walton Hamilton, an economist from the Brookings Institution teaching constitutional law, who epitomized the "legal realist" spirit of the school in that he did not have a law degree, yet was considered to be one of the most stimulating teachers in the school. Then there was Wes Sturges, who impressed everyone in his arbitration class with his lively Socratic questioning style and his ability to leave the class in a state of total confusion. Finally, there was the inimitable Thurman Arnold, who led classes in civil procedure. It mattered little what Arnold was formally charged with teaching, because it was the brilliance of his mind and his unique wit that entranced the students. An absentminded genius, Arnold would frequently bring his dog Duffy to class, and threaten to pose questions to the poor creature if the class did not shape up. All of these men taught Fortas to see the law more pragmatically, and to see legal decisions as instruments of the political designs of judges. So, rather than analyzing law as a series of inflexible rules that are the product of "discovery" through hours of study of legal materials, Fortas was taught to analyze law as a solution growing out of a variety of forces in society. This mandate to see legal work for its pragmatic or technical aspects, rather than being wedded to any particular ideology, would shape the young man's outlook for the rest of his career.[25]

Of all of these mentors, though, one man stood out above the rest in his importance for Abe Fortas's career—William O. Douglas. Here was a man who was clearly on his way to the top, and it surprised few when years later he became one of the greatest Supreme Court justices in history. But like Fortas, he first had many obstacles to overcome. Raised in poverty in Yakima, Washington, Douglas had dazzled people at nearby Whitman College, and then hitchhiked cross-country on the freight trains in the fall of 1922 to attend Columbia Law School, arriving with six cents in his pocket. After a sterling three years of legal study and a stint in private practice, he was invited back to Columbia to teach. In 1928, Robert Hutchins snatched him away for the Yale Law School faculty. When Hutchins left to become president of the University of Chicago the following year, he proclaimed that Douglas was "the most outstanding law professor" in the nation, and offered him the exorbitant sum of twenty thousand dollars to join his school. Instead, Douglas chose to stay at Yale after his salary was doubled to the school's maximum at the time of fifteen thousand dollars.[26]

In those early years, students complained that Douglas, while admittedly brilliant, was stylistically only a mediocre teacher. Instead, he made his reputation by reorganizing the teaching of the business management and finance courses along "functional" lines.[27] Then, seeing that Harvard Law School was unwilling to offer a joint curriculum with the university's business school, Douglas took advantage of the opportunity of creating such a program by marrying Yale Law School to the Harvard Business School. This innovative course of study, organized by Douglas in conjunction with Professor George Bates of Harvard Business, rose in importance during the Depression because of its ability to shed light on the causes of the economic problems of the time and offer solutions for the nation's recovery. Accordingly, Douglas's importance, as well as that of the students and assistants around him, also grew.

As Douglas undertook this massive curriculum revision, he began to look around for a promising student who might help create the enterprise, with the prospect of taking it over one day. And he found one in young Abe Fortas. Douglas held most of the students in the law school in very low esteem, thinking of them as "spoiled brats," descended from "eminent and at times disreputable characters" and anxious only to return home to take over Daddy's business. He saw himself as treating "the class as a lion tamer in the circus treats his wards."[28] And in his early years at Yale, his wards did not take well to the whip, deciding to visit the dean en masse in an unsuccessful effort to have him fired.

There was another side to Douglas, though, one that recognized true brilliance and responded to it. He had a practice of picking out a few prize students and sending them "into the markets, into the highways, into the back streets to find out how rules of law looked in operation."[29] And that was where Abe Fortas caught his eye. By reason of his performance in his first two years, Fortas was clearly recognized as one of the very best students in the school. And his performance in Douglas's Business Units III course on finance, which examined the legal problems in the accumulation of funds by modern businesses, gave the professor no reason to doubt that general assessment.

But there was more to the attraction than just Fortas's intellect. Other equally brilliant students in the school found themselves virtually ignored by Douglas. No doubt the background of the young man from Memphis made him particularly appealing to the professor. Here was a poor boy, struggling as Douglas had done to overcome his background, and achieving through brilliance rather than inherited family wealth. Here also was another outsider—by reason of his religion rather than the geographical hurdles that had faced Douglas—who was trying to overcome the disadvantage of not being one of the children of the Eastern Establishment. So Douglas picked him out from the rest as a man worth helping, not to mention a man who could help him. In a short time, he would be telling employers that Fortas was "by all odds one of the most outstanding men I have met in my nine years of teaching."[30]

Douglas's first step in overseeing Fortas's career came in the summer of 1932. As part of a continuing study he was doing on bankruptcy for Yale's Institute of Human Relations, Douglas had conceived a study of the overextension of consumer credit to workers in Chicago. Using what were called wage assignments, workers were obtaining credit by assigning their future earnings to merchants. The practice could be studied properly only by applying the lessons of sociology to the study of the operation of Illinois's laws governing such agreements. So Douglas selected Abe Fortas to do the study, and helped further by writing to friends in Chicago who could assist the young man's research.[31] It was the type of thing that a professor might do to ensure that a special student has an easier road to success, and Fortas made the most of his opportunity.

After pounding the hot streets of Chicago in the summer between his second and third years of law school to do the research, Fortas, with Douglas's help, wrote an important piece for the *Yale Law Journal*. In a mind-numbing compendium of "real world" statistics, containing all of the excellent scholarship but little of the eloquently stylish language that would one day be his trademark, Fortas displayed considerable sympathy for the "impecunious, propertyless workingman."[32] However, his reluctant conclusion was that "a contract is a contract," leaving employers in the difficult position of having to hold up paychecks to satisfy their workers' debts. After convincingly rejecting a proposed revision of the practice that would have required a spouse's consent before assigning future wages, Fortas recommended that the practice be abolished altogether.[33] The piece demonstrated to Douglas that his initial instincts to keep an eye on this young man had been correct. Later, Fortas's colleagues would call it "a spectacular achievement . . . a factual, functional, classically Yale piece of investigation at its statistical best."[34] And all this from a fellow who had just turned twenty-two years old.

In June 1933, Fortas graduated from Yale with another string of scholastic honors. While it was frequently later reported that Fortas had graduated first in his class, in fact his grades had slipped to the point that he graduated second in his class.[35] But the precise order of finish no longer really mattered. Yale now recognized the sheer brilliance of its young star. A colleague would later say, "He was the golden boy. . . . He was perhaps the most brilliant legal mind ever to come out of the Yale Law School."[36] Indeed, he was one of six out of the eighty-six male graduates (one woman had started with the class but did not graduate that June) awarded a *cum laude* degree.[37] And, he was also one of the nine men elected to the Order of the Coif, awarded to the top 10 percent of the class's graduates.

Even more valuable than all of these honors was the offer at graduation of a teaching job at Yale. Though the school was struggling financially in the middle of the Depression, Fortas was one of two men to receive a coveted two-thousand-dollar Sterling Teaching Fellowship for 1933–1934 at Yale Law School.[38] As it happened, the offer could not have been more valuable to the young man. Times were tough for everyone in the Depression, including lawyers. But jobs were especially scarce in the best New York firms for young law graduates who happened to be Jewish.[39] Despite his outstanding accomplishments, none of the recommendations given him by William O. Douglas for the finest law firms in New York had panned out. This was true even though one firm had indicated to Douglas that it could "create a vacancy" for a young man of "real first rate ability."[40]

But there was more involved here than just getting a job. The offer of a teaching fellowship from Yale held even greater importance for Fortas. A call back by the faculty to educate future generations of law students is perhaps the highest honor that a law school can give to one of its graduates. It would give Fortas the opportunity to reflect for a year while assessing other career options, and also indicating to future employers on his curriculum vitae that he was one of the truly elite Yale graduates. But, even more important from the standpoint of his future career, it gave Fortas even more opportunity to benefit from the backing of Professor William O. Douglas. For with the fellowship came the chance to work with Douglas in continuing the reorganization process of the corporation law courses in the school's curriculum.[41]

Since the teaching job did not start until September, Fortas searched around for something to tide him over through the summer. Once more, William O. Douglas helped out. Douglas was working on a book dealing with bankruptcy, and needed to have some work done on the same state wage-assignment laws that Fortas had investigated earlier. So he offered the young man four hundred dollars for a summer's worth of research on the topic, thinking that it would be far more help to him financially than intellectually.[42] However, before he could complete the work, an even better offer came along from one of Douglas's pals.[43]

Wes Sturges, one of Fortas's Yale law professors, had been temporarily drafted to work in Washington in the Legal Division of the Agricultural Adjustment Administration (AAA). This agency's job was to raise agricultural values to pre–First World War levels by balancing prices and production. Accordingly, it was empowered to draft trade agreements among farmers and the processors and distributors of agricultural products in hopes of achieving economic recovery through the use of voluntary crop reduction, production quotas on the final product, and fixed price levels at every stage of the process. These governing limits, all backed by government subsidies that were funded by taxes on the products at the processing stage, were to be set by the voluntary cooperation of the farmers and processors themselves in hearings arbitrated by lawyers in the AAA's Legal Division.[44]

Sturges had been brought to Washington to draft the agreements for the meat packers and the sugar industry. In the middle of the summer, quite likely at the suggestion of William O. Douglas, who had been inquiring about his own prospects in the AAA, Sturges arranged for Fortas to be brought down until school opened in order to serve as assistant to the general counsel for the agency, Jerome Frank. The young man had no special expertise, just a Yale law degree, a sterling set of credentials, and the right mentors.

At the age of twenty-three, then, Abe Fortas had become part of the crackerjack legal team assembled by Frank to implement this complicated law. This young group of lawyers drove George Peek, the agency's administrator, to distraction: "A plague of young lawyers settled on Washington. They all claimed to be friends of somebody or other, and mostly of Jerome Frank and Felix Frankfurter. They floated airily into offices, took desks, asked for papers, and found no end of things to be busy about. I never found out why they came, what they did, or why they left."[45] For Fortas, it was a great chance to make some important contacts and move up in the legal world. Here was another Jew, Frank, who was opening the door in government for other lawyers of his religious background who were finding it impossible to break through the exclusionary policies of the most prestigious law firms. It was not a role that Frank always relished, fearing an anti-Semitic backlash against his agency, but his rigid adherence to a policy of hiring the best available talent led him there.[46]

For Fortas, the chance to spend a few weeks in the center of the New Deal action before taking up the life of the intellectual in New Haven was a tremendous opportunity. When he arrived in the capital, the excitement and the feverish pace of the work seemed overwhelming. Unable even to unpack his bags, he was pressed into immediate service for three days and nights without sleep. Only then was he allowed to search for a place to live.[47] Eventually, he rented a three-story house on Thirty-fourth Street in Northwest Washington with Thomas Emerson, who was then working in the National Recovery Administration; Leon Keyserling, who was an administrative assistant to New York Senator Robert Wagner; Ambrose Doskow, a law clerk to Justice Benjamin Cardozo; and one or two other young members of the New Deal agencies.[48]

It was an exciting time to be in Washington. In the first hundred days of his new presidency in 1933, Franklin Delano Roosevelt had infused in the best young men and women a crusading spirit, as they joined the pilgrimage to Washington and fought to end the Depression. In better times these people would have been working in the nation's industries, law firms, universities, and elsewhere. Now they had answered the call from their president to help the nation. It was as if these young people believed that through hard work and ingenuity they could rewrite the rules, remake the social order, and bring about a recovery. There was a tremendous excitement and fervor, as they worked sixteen- to twenty-hour days, six days a week, in a desperate attempt to find the keys to economic recovery. Only young people could keep up with the pace, let alone be trusted to have the flexibility to propose and carry out new ideas. "Uncle Sam has grown twenty years younger. Here is a new type of man for a new age in politics," said one journalist. "They have tremendous enthusiasm, and are working with a fury which threatens many of them with nervous breakdown. Youth is in the saddle, riding hell-bent for victory or a fall."[49] And in profiling a number of prominent young whiz kids then serving with distinction in the New Deal bureaucracy, the same journalist argued that "one of the youngest and brightest of the bright young men" was twenty-three-year-old Abe Fortas of Memphis, Tennessee.

As one of the very few lawyers in the early days of the AAA, the young man had plenty to do.[50] Fortas was immediately put to work forging the marketing agreements governing the prices and production schedules in the canned cling peach industry, and drafting the "license" that made it all legally enforceable. To outsiders it seemed as if this would be the ultimate test of the young man's confidence in himself. He would come to work in the morning and waiting in the anteroom outside the hearing room where the arguments would be presented for his ruling on the new agreement would be distinguished men who were twice his age and were earning many times his salary. They were the presidents of the companies whose fate now lay with the rulings of the twenty-three-year-old Yale attorney.

But Fortas never wavered. As he worked, there developed a certain confidence that came with bending and breaking the old rules, and writing new rules to govern society.[51] In these efforts Fortas never struck people as one of those committed New Dealers, dedicated to the philosophy of liberalism espoused by Franklin D. Roosevelt. In fact, to many he did not seem to have any definable philosophy at all, political or otherwise. Instead, trained in the functional approach of Yale Law School, his *modus operandi* was a certain sense of pragmatism. Never mind the philosophy, give this man a problem and he would find the solution. It was simply a matter of applying what he had learned in books in New Haven to real life in Washington.

As the hearings went on, these prominent company executives from the peach industry came to like the young man. Because they respected his intellect, his knowledge of their industry, and his sense of fair play, his suggested codes setting prices and production quotas went through as written. Unlike most of the other lawyers in the division, Fortas showed an ability not just to cut through the maze of acrimonious arguments in negotiating compromise solutions, but also to convert all of the legalese in his decisions into language that the laymen in the room could comprehend. "Fortas can talk law in terms that the farmer and businessman can understand," one of his former professors said. "Why, that boy can pick peaches or irrigate a field with the Due Process clause of the Constitution."[52] This was not something he had been taught, though perhaps it had been honed by all of those years of trying to persuade less intelligent and no doubt religiously bigoted judges in school debate tournaments; it was an instinctive ability. And it was a talent that would serve him well through the years as he explained the world of legal jargon to a wider range of important people—from fellow bureaucrats to businesssmen and finally to a president of the United States.

As luck would have it, this initial assignment on canned cling peaches placed Fortas right in the middle of a major fight. After he completed the marketing license, it came under legal attack in California when one of the regulated companies, Calistan Packers, began producing and selling more than its allotted product quota, thereby undercutting the opposition. So Fortas and Thurman Arnold, who was also down for the summer from Yale Law School doing temporary consulting work for the AAA Legal Division, were sent out on a fancy Ford trimotor plane to California to defend the license in federal district court.[53] Their immediate goal was to secure an injunction preventing the company from selling the excess peaches. For the young men who had not yet tried a single case in court, it was a remarkable opportunity.

Since this was one of the earliest tests of the New Deal's agricultural recovery program, Arnold saw a chance for raising a great case dealing with the constitutionality of the AAA.[54] Could the government use its "taxation and spending" power to suspend the antitrust rules in the agricultural field, and exercise what had traditionally been state powers to regulate individual farm practices? By dealing with the broader mandate of the AAA act, rather than securing a judgment in this one case, the two men could aid the overall recovery effort, not to mention increase their own legal reputation. And the strategy worked. They were able to convince the district judge to uphold the AAA on every point.[55]

After this success, Fortas was assigned to fashion a code of prices and production quotas for the citrus fruit growers in Florida. However, before he could finish, the time came in September 1933 for him to return to teach at Yale. Since the heads of the citrus fruit industry had also come to respect Fortas's work, a delegation of them traveled to Washington to insist that Secretary of Agriculture Henry Wallace pressure Yale into granting the young man a one-term leave of absence to finish his work. It was a testament to Fortas's consummate negotiating skill that the normally contentious parties were so unanimous in their support of his work. So Yale gave him a one-term leave without pay, allowing him to stay in Washington and finish the agreement.[56]

Before he had to start the spring 1934 school term, though, there was time enough after the citrus growers' code had been finished for someone to raise a legal challenge to it in Florida. Two companies had refused to limit their production to stay within the assigned quotas. So Fortas was sent down to represent the AAA in court. Here Fortas was able to put into practice the skill he had begun to develop at Yale in working as second banana to the more experienced William O. Douglas.

The case was being tried by a lawyer from the Justice Department, James Lawrence Fly, and a Florida attorney named Francis Whitehair, representing the Florida citrus commission that had been set up by the AAA to enforce the new code. The two men continually fought over legal tactics and goals in the case. Whitehair wanted to defend the entire marketing system, while Fly sought to create a case on this one violation of the agreement, which could be challenged in front of the Supreme Court. Realizing that the case was unwinnable at the lower level because of the anti–New Deal bias of the supervising judge, Fortas argued that by compromising their goals and presenting the case on narrow procedural grounds, they could establish a strong enough record to uphold both the agreement and the overall agency in a higher court. The two men were persuaded by Fortas's advice, which was accompanied by a generous dose of verbal balm to soothe the tensions between them. Eventually, as the young man predicted, the record that the government's legal team built in losing at the lower court did lead to a victory on appeal.[57]

Once more, it was an impressive performance. Here was Fortas at age twenty-three convincing much older and more experienced attorneys to follow his advice. Thus he began on the road to becoming what one of his friends later called a ''lawyer's lawyer's lawyer''—the sort of fellow you called in when even the lawyers whom all of the other attorneys had called in when *they* were baffled proved unable to handle the case as well.[58]

Despite his impressive successes in the New Deal program, Fortas was contractually committed to return to New Haven in January 1934 to teach the spring term at Yale Law School. Once again, it was William O. Douglas who helped to ensure his success. Though Fortas was six years younger than the rest of an excellent crop of new professors in the school, Douglas was so impressed by his skills that he tapped him as his lieutenant in the revision of the corporate law curriculum.

The work was a major undertaking. Fortas helped to create the joint business-law curriculum with George E. Bates of the Harvard Business School, revamping the law school's courses to fit the program.[59] He redeveloped and taught Douglas's old Business Units III course on finance, which examined the problems of the "organization, valuation, promotion, and financing of business with emphasis on the Federal Securities Act of 1933."[60] In time, Douglas would also ask Fortas to reorganize the first-year course on marketing, which studied the legal and commercial problems involved in the purchase and sale aspects of wholesale and retail merchandising, and a second-year Business Units course called "Losses," which examined the legal devices for obtaining limited liability in organizing businesses. Years later, members of the Yale Law School administration were still citing this effort by the two men to stake out and reorganize these courses as a real contribution to improving Yale's overall status in the legal education community.[61]

But the effort also did much for the two men personally. With the Roosevelt administration in the process of instituting the largest financial reforms in the nation's history, a premium was placed on those lawyers who understood the law in this area. All of this put Fortas's mentor, Douglas, on the cutting edge of a central problem of the New Deal. Since Douglas was becoming one of the recognized experts in corporate finance, producing with the help of Fortas and others five casebooks and nine law review articles on the subject, it was inevitable that he would move into the forefront of the governmental action in the area. And what was good for William O. Douglas was also good for Abe Fortas.[62]

But it was not all work for the young professor at Yale. Douglas saw to it that Fortas was now included as part of the inner circle that was invited to his occasional poker games and other fun. He was also invited to Douglas's outdoor barbecues, where the absentminded chef was known to forget to put a grill on his barbecue pit and throw a valuable steak directly onto the charcoal. Douglas and Thurman Arnold had also established the Hunt Club, an elaborate game of hide and seek in which members, well under the influence of copious amounts of liquid refreshment, went searching late at night for the elusive snipe in the city's East Rock Park. Douglas was the Mattress Bearer and Arnold was the Flashlight Carrier. Fortas was brought in as an "apprentice" as the older men tried to make him into a Beater.[63] Then Fortas was included in their "get ahead" celebrity game, in which participants received points for having their names mentioned in newspapers of varying levels of prominence—ranging from a hundred points for mention in *The New York Times* editorial down to one point for simply being mentioned in someone else's speech.

As nice as this life was, though, when the school year ended in June there was little doubt where Fortas would spend his summer months. Though his teaching had been sufficiently impressive to advance him to the rank of assistant professor after only one semester, Fortas made it plain to the dean in accepting the offer that "if certain things develop there he is likely to ask his release."[64] And there was little doubt what those "certain things" might be. The dean had already noticed that his eyes "were somewhat turned toward Washington."[65]

Fortas's game plan was to resume work in Jerome Frank's Legal Division during the summer break before returning to Yale to teach. But, like all of the other bright and ambitious young attorneys in town, he was always on the prowl for a better offer, and one seemed on the horizon when, in July 1934, his mentor William O. Douglas was hired as one of the top staff people on the newly created Securities and Exchange Commission (SEC). The Securities and Exchange Act of 1934, which created the SEC, had established a set of regulations for the stock market, requiring the registration and full disclosure of all new securities traded on the market. In Section 211 of that law, Congress had charged the SEC with making a detailed study of businesses that had failed in the Depression, and the means by which they had limited liability by reorganizing the firm under so-called protective committees, which illegally placed the remaining assets of the industry into receivership.

Having worked in his short period of private practice on the largest reorganization of the bankrupt railroads in the nation's history, and conducted numerous studies into bankruptcies (including a law review piece that spring on protective committees), William O. Douglas was the logical choice to run the study.[66] So he got the job. In many ways, it was precisely the kind of study that he had been doing at Yale Law School in revising its corporate law curriculum. And since he would need a talented staff to conduct the investigations and hearings while he shuttled back and forth from teaching at Yale, who better to head that group than his exceedingly talented and knowledgeable protégé from Yale, Abe Fortas? As it happened, while together on the Yale faculty, he and Fortas had already been planning to undertake such a study on their own, and had put their own plans on hold during the summer while the SEC set up its program. So in accepting the assignment, Douglas was counting heavily on Fortas's collaboration.[67]

But by September, the exact nature of Douglas's work and staff had yet to be finalized. So, after another summer of drafting marketing agreements in the AAA, Fortas had to decide whether to pack up and return to New Haven to teach the fall term or remain in governmental service.[68] For a time, it seemed as if he did not know what to do next. While he kept blaming Douglas's uncertain plans for the lack of a decision, his colleagues at Yale felt that it was Fortas himself who could not make up his mind. Meanwhile, as Fortas continued to deliberate his fate just days before the opening of school, the rest of the faculty was thrown into a state of confusion, waiting to adjust the course schedule in accordance with his decision.

In the end, it was not the excitement that had originally brought Fortas to government that convinced him to remain in Washington, but simply the money. Fortas's annual salary in the AAA, after an early promotion from Jerome Frank, was now sixty-six hundred dollars. Even after Douglas's intervention with the dean, the most Yale would offer was thirty-five hundred dollars, fearing that the four thousand demanded by Fortas would cause a revolt by the other junior faculty at the same salary level. Moreover, the upper university administration was beginning to tire of lending its faculty to the New Deal on a part-time basis.[69] So Fortas decided simply to resign from Yale and take his chances in the more uncertain world of government employment. Any hesitancy in making this move was relieved by the knowledge that Douglas would surely find a place for him on the new staff.

For the time being, though, that left Fortas in the increasingly troubled AAA.[70] The vigorous efforts by the idealistic Jerome Frank to organize the farm industry had raised complaints of "socialism" and "radicalism" from the conservative head of the agency, George Peek. The two men continually fought over who had the right to make policy in the agency. Meanwhile, the farmers and the food processors fought over the fair rate of return for their products, farm owners and tenants fought over the acreage limits on their farming, and everyone was fighting the AAA in court. It did not take a psychic to see that the agency was a ship on the way down.[71]

Once more it was the patronage of William O. Douglas which ensured that Fortas was gone from the agency a few short months before trouble hit. Ignoring a directive from the president forbidding one of his agencies to raid the talent in another, in October 1934 Douglas launched a prolonged campaign to steal his star student from Jerome Frank's employ.

In offering Fortas the job as assistant director of the protective committee study, organizing and running the staff, Douglas was doing as much for himself as for his young protégé. By having Fortas run the staff in Washington, Douglas would be able to commute back and forth from New Haven for half of the school year and continue to collect his huge salary at Yale without wondering whether things were still running smoothly on the staff.[72]

Though the offer meant a loss of a thousand dollars in annual salary, the new Securities and Exchange Commission was now where Abe Fortas most wanted to be. Given his expertise in corporation finance, the chance to implement the new Securities and Exchange Act of 1934 seemed ideal. Moreover, the job of "chief of staff" represented a promotion in prestige over being just one of many members in the AAA's Legal Division. More important, though, there was now the obvious difference in the futures of the two agencies. While the AAA was encountering nothing but trouble, both internally and externally, the new SEC represented the heart of the New Deal, as the Roosevelt team sought to control the market abuses that had led to the initial financial crash. So the SEC seemed to be on the way up as fast as the AAA was on the way down.

But there was more. While Fortas's intellect and ability would take him so far, the speed and height of his rise in the government depended on the tragectory of his patron's career. A betting man could see that Douglas was a better choice now than Frank. He seemed to have the better contacts, the more important job, and a faster-rising agency. And there was one more factor that could not have escaped the attention of Fortas as he prepared to make the first major decision of his young career. Douglas was not Jewish, thus removing from his path one obstacle to rising into the inner circles of the New Deal administration. As it happened, simply from a strategic standpoint, Fortas's assessment could not have been better. In three months Jerome Frank would be out of a job, while Douglas was well on his way to becoming a favorite poker-playing buddy of the president. So, intellectually, Fortas very quickly decided that he *should* cast his lot with Douglas. But emotionally, he did not know whether he *could* make the switch.

No matter how compelling the reasons for joining Douglas, there were equally powerful reasons for remaining with Frank. It seemed a little callous to desert one patron for another. Fortas, for all of his own ambition and drive to succeed, was still very loyal to his friends. And it was Jerome Frank who had given him his first break in Washington at the risk of attack from the anti-Semites. Moreover, Frank had just singled him out for promotion among all of the other bright young stars. Now, with all of the personal conflicts inside the agency and pressures being placed on it from outside, Frank needed his good young staff people more than ever.

Accordingly, when Douglas asked for Fortas's release to hire him for the SEC, an angry Frank responded in "unequivocal terms" that he would not consider this request "under any circumstances." So Douglas left the matter in Fortas's hands, writing that there was a place for him on the study, but if he should decide not to leave the AAA Douglas would understand.[73]

With two suitors making him the object of their affections, Fortas fell into a pattern, begun with his uncertainty about returning to teach at Yale several weeks earlier, that would repeat itself throughout his career. At critical turning points in his life, his usual unshakable confidence and cockiness seemed to desert him. Normally charged with making hard decisions about the affairs of others, now he could not make critical decisions about his own career. This inability to decide what to do on these occasions resulted in the sort of hesitation and wavering that can be fatal in Washington once events get out of one's control. But this first time, Fortas had a protector looking out for him.

After another conversation with Frank, the normally cool young man sent an impassioned telegram to Douglas: HAVE DECIDED REMAIN HERE BECAUSE JEROME'S VERY STRONG FEELING. GOD KNOW[S] HOW MISERABLE I AM AT INCONVENIENCE TO YOU AND HOW DEEPLY I REGRET INABILITY TO WORK WITH YOU AND HOW SAD I AM THAT MINIMUM LOYALTY AND AFFECTION REQUIRE ME TO ACQUIESCE IN JEROME'S WISHES. . . . I REALIZE I AM SURRENDERING A CAREER WHICH YOU WERE WONDERFUL TO OFFER ME.[74] "I shall never forgive Jerome," Douglas responded, asking the young man for suggestions as to other possible nominees for the post.[75] It might have been Fortas's distraught state of mind that caused Frank to wire Douglas, saying that he had "reconsidered" and now "was willing that [Fortas] should do whatever he considered best."[76]

But what should have ended the discussion instead launched Fortas on a tortuous journey to have others make the decision to leave for him. He wrote Douglas that despite Frank's release, he did not mean it. So Douglas sent another letter to Frank indicating the young man's quandary. *"Abe is as free as the air,"*[77] Frank responded. Apparently two releases from his boss were not enough, as Fortas wrote Douglas that despite the obvious benefits of moving over to the SEC, he feared that "pulling out [of the AAA] might cause positive injury."[78]

Years later, Douglas would recognize Fortas's peculiar sense of paralysis at career turning points, but for now he believed completely that it was Frank's fault for continuing to put pressure on him to stay. So he wrote a *third* letter to Frank, trying to make him see the subtle, and perhaps not so subtle, pressures felt by the young man about leaving. But Frank no longer had any time for this nonsense, choosing to send word back through Thurman Arnold that Douglas was "all wet."[79] So Douglas tried a final appeal, this time using his colleague Wes Sturges, the man who had first brought Fortas to Frank's attention. Fortas would practically have to be *told* to leave the AAA, Sturges explained, before he would believe that Frank was blessing the release.[80]

Despite being angered by the pressure, Frank called Fortas in one more time to give him a release from the agency. For his part, Douglas was gracious in victory, writing Frank, "You are a swell 'old man'— none better."[81] By Douglas's account, now that Fortas's future was settled, he was "sitting on top of the world."[82] But ten years later Frank had not forgotten, or forgiven, the way that Fortas had acted. "Bill Douglas not only taught [Fortas] how to handle himself with the politicos," he wrote fellow New Dealer Rexford Tugwell, "but, when you met Abe, Bill was actively helping Abe with the boys on the Hill. Abe is more cynical than you, he is far less selfless, [and] far more interested in serving his personal career. When his career was threatened, he . . . had several able friends, including Bill, to turn to—as you did not. I don't mean that Abe is not a singularly able man, nor that he hasn't acquired an approach to administration which is more skillful than that of us older folk. But I think it's unwise, romantically, to overestimate the difference."[83]

The sentiment was echoed by Raoul Berger, who later watched Fortas from a distance while working in the General Counsel's Office of the SEC. "I concluded very quickly that Fortas was cold, ruthless, opportunistic, and he was overly interested in his own career," he explained.[84] And there was little doubt for anyone close enough to watch that it was William O. Douglas who deserved much of the credit for aiding Fortas's rise to the top.

The jump from the AAA to the SEC was the turning point in Fortas's early career. Had he remained in the AAA, within a matter of three months Fortas almost certainly would have been out of a job. After numerous conflicts between AAA Administrator Peek and General Counsel Frank over policy, in December 1934, George Peek was forced to resign. But then his replacement, a philosophical ally named Chester Davis, retaliated in early 1935 by convincing Secretary of Agriculture Wallace to purge Jerome Frank and most of his top legal team after a dispute over the crop acreage reduction program for cotton. As one of the top staff people under Frank, although not one philosophically committed to either side in the controversy, Fortas certainly would have been fired as well. None of that would have mattered much a year later, though, as the Supreme Court ruled that the entire law authorizing the AAA was unconstitutional.[85]

Much later, new problems would surround some of the members of Frank's legal team. Alger Hiss, Nathan Witt, Lee Pressman, and John Abt were accused of forming a Communist cell in the AAA during this period. Later in his life people would accuse Fortas from time to time of being a member of this group, but he vigorously denied any connection with the Communist movement during this period. "Once in a while, it's occurred to me to wonder why I was never aware of [the Communist affiliations of my colleagues], why there was never any attempt to recruit me, either directly or indirectly," he later told one interviewer. "If there was, I wasn't aware of it. Maybe it was because I was a southerner or too conservative."[86] The real reason he wasn't recruited, explains a close friend, was even simpler: "Abe wasn't a joiner."[87] Indeed, Fortas had never been by nature philosophically committed to any viewpoint other than getting ahead. And while he, like a number of other New Dealers at the time, joined one or two legal groups, such as the International Juridical Association, which were later accused of having members who were Communists, there is no evidence that he joined or even flirted with the Communist movement. But for his enemies it was enough that he once worked with others so accused for them to raise charges of guilt by association.

Thanks to William Douglas's lifeline, though, none of the immediate problems of the AAA affected him in 1935. Fortas was now working directly under one of the fastest-rising stars in the New Deal. With Douglas still spending much of his time teaching in New Haven, Fortas was given complete freedom to manage the staff in planning the upcoming hearings on corporate reorganization. Investigating the abusive and deceitful practices of businesses declaring bankruptcy required that Fortas and the staff conduct an extensive questionnaire survey of these enterprises and analyze the results for Douglas's questions in the hearings. As assistant director, Fortas supervised the staff's efforts in Washington on a day-to-day basis, taking time out only to send letters back to New Haven detailing the latest actions. He made recommendations about hiring and firing personnel, and fought a rearguard battle against the attempts by the talent-starved SEC to raid the protective committee staff that Fortas had assembled. Every day he searched for new angles to follow in the investigation of how investors were being bilked and, after suggesting them to Douglas, directed the actual research and helped to write the reports.[88]

No detail was too small for Fortas's attention. He was in charge of seeing that Douglas's mail was forwarded, scheduling conferences with various senators, preparing questions for the hearings, and timing various press releases.[89] It was his first experience in learning how to operate his own staff behind the scenes, and he had the confidence of knowing that the man back in New Haven unquestioningly supported all of his efforts.

Thanks in part to Fortas's efforts, the accomplishments of the protective committee study were impressive. The in-depth public hearings in which Douglas grilled various scions of the Wall Street financial world were thorough enough to produce an eight-volume report to Congress, covering two hundred thousand protective committees and over thirty-six billion dollars in investments.[90] After successfully documenting the abuses of Wall Street law firms, banks, and bond houses, Douglas and Fortas helped to revolutionize the bankruptcy laws in this country. Two major laws were passed, both of which had been drafted in part by the two men. Chapter X of the Bankruptcy Act of 1938 made the SEC the financial adviser for federal judges, who were charged with ruling on corporate reorganizations in bankruptcy cases but had previously been hampered by very little background in the field. Then there was the Trust Indenture Act of 1939, which raised the fiduciary standards of the corporate agencies established in the issuance of new securities.[91]

Despite these accomplishments, as the study was winding to a close in late 1935, Fortas was coming to another fork in his career. Since Douglas's efforts to lobby for his own appointment as a commissioner of the SEC had so far met with no success, Fortas would have to find a new appointment on his own. So in May 1935 he accepted an appointment to return to teach at Yale beginning in February of the following year. The plan was for him to teach administrative law and corporate management, and to assist Douglas in the corporate finance course. Then, in October, he was offered a full three-year contract at the law school with the rank of assistant professor. Once more, there was haggling over money with the dean. Since the job meant a considerable cut in salary from his government work, Fortas tried to minimize the damage. The original salary offer was thirty-five hundred dollars annually, but Fortas wired back that he would come only if he was offered five hundred more. In the end, Fortas accepted when the dean promised to raise the salary to four thousand dollars after his first semester on the job.[92]

The dean could not have known that Fortas had already taken action to ensure that the new career move would not be too financially burdensome. Since the protective committee study would not be completed before his return to Yale, Fortas arranged to work on it when he was not teaching. So, for more than a year, he continued on the government payroll while also being paid as a member of Yale's faculty.[93]

When Fortas returned to Yale, he brought with him his new wife. He had met a pretty, pert, and petite economist named Carolyn Eugenia Agger when they were both working in the Department of Agriculture. Standing a mere five feet one and a half inches without the high heels that she preferred to wear, Agger was considered by everyone to be a formidable woman with an intellect that was at least Fortas's equal. The daughter of Eugene E. Agger, an emeritus professor of money and banking at Rutgers University, she had graduated from Barnard College with a B.A. in economics and earned an M.A. from the University of Wisconsin. As one of the few women most people had ever met who smoked cigars, preferring the largest and fattest ones available, she made an unforgettable impression. The fact that she was not Jewish made little difference to the couple, and they were married on July 9, 1935.[94]

Since he had already decided to return to teach, Fortas convinced her to enter Yale Law School, making her one of only four women in the class.[95] When she enrolled in her husband's Business Units II course, there were no complaints registered from other class members. However, Fortas avoided any questions of propriety by sending her final exam to Washington for William O. Douglas to grade. He gave her a top-notch grade of 84.[96] When she graduated in February 1938, like her husband Agger was awarded a coveted *cum laude* degree, and earned the second-highest average in her class.

It was not long after Fortas arrived in New Haven in early 1936 that he remembered part of the reason why he had left in the first place. After his time in the hurly-burly political arena in Washington, the petty academic infighting in New Haven now seemed even less enchanting. And it was certainly less profitable. It is said that the fighting in academia is so vicious because the stakes are so small. And Fortas, a high-stakes player, certainly found that to be the case. So, just a few months after arriving in New Haven, a bored and financially strapped Fortas began arranging his schedule so that he could find remunerative work either with the SEC or somewhere else.[97] Not long thereafter, he began planning his final escape from New Haven.

Ironically, just as Fortas arrived in New Haven to teach, William O. Douglas was packing his bags to return to the capital, having just been named a commissioner on the Securities and Exchange Commission. Since this would mean his taking a leave of absence from the law school, it was left to his protégé, Fortas, to protect the empire of business law courses that had been developed.[98] And that was going to be a real challenge for the twenty-five-year-old assistant professor, who for the first time would be fighting his battles largely on his own.

As it happened, Douglas got out of town just in time to leave his head staffman with the big problem. When Fortas arrived in New Haven he very quickly discovered that morale among the junior faculty was already dangerously low due to the severe understaffing and depressed salaries.[99] In early 1936 Yale had hit a financial rock bottom, and the university president was looking for cost-cutting measures. Very quickly it became clear that the cooperative program between Yale's law school and the Harvard Business School was one being eyed for elimination.[100] So Fortas found himself serving as the point man in trying to save the combined program, as well as waging a series of battles to maintain the integrity of the corporate and financial law courses that he and Douglas had built up by hiring badly needed new faculty sympathetic to their outlook. But the young assistant professor soon realized that he was no match for the powerful alliance against him. He was facing not only an upper university administration ever concerned with the bottom-line financial status of the law school, but a movement within the school to drop experimental courses on functionalism in the law and to concentrate instead on more traditional courses aimed at ensuring that a higher percentage of graduating students passed the bar exam. Finally, there was the political problem caused by a split in the faculty between the commuting New Dealers, like Douglas and Fortas, who were teaching essentially on a part-time basis, and the full-time faculty, who for reasons of preference or a lack of opportunity remained in New Haven year-round, lamenting the impact of the carpetbaggers.

With every fight—over new hirings, honorary degrees, naming distinguished lecturers, choosing visiting professors—came the same split in the vote and another loss for Fortas's position. All he could do was console himself by sending long letters of complaint to Douglas in Washington. From a distance, Douglas tried to help out by writing to the law school's dean on such matters as the young man's teaching schedule and bolstering his positions on various issues, but the impact of these letters was minimal.[101] After ten months of this, Fortas had endured enough to know that he was only waiting now for his wife to graduate. "I am pretty well fed up," he wrote to Douglas. "When I was younger—that is, before the [protective committee study]—I could take it; but hyperacidity & reaction is too much. I'll try to stick it out and be sufficiently quiet not to be kicked out until February, 1938, but who knows?"[102] If he was going to fight, it would be for more money.

By his wife's graduation from Yale in early 1938, the time had come for him to return to the real battleground in Washington. Carol Agger had landed a job with the National Labor Relations Board, and soon thereafter moved to the Tax Division of the Department of Justice.[103] Fortas himself decided to resign from the law school, rather than take a leave, and once more it was William O. Douglas, now chairman of the Securities and Exchange Commission, who provided the new opportunity.[104]

He needed the young man as assistant director of the SEC's Public Utilities Division, created by Congress in the Public Utility Holding Company Act of 1935 to break up and then regulate the huge monopolies in the utilities industry. Fortas's specific duties were to take charge of all of the attorneys in the Legal Division who were empowered to implement the law. On the surface, the job seemed very similar to the one Douglas had entrusted to him in the protective committee study. And Fortas was duly appreciative. "I am very, very grateful to you," he wrote to Douglas. "The job is better than I could have hoped for."[105]

But as he was to discover very shortly, there was a very specific reason why Douglas had brought him into the agency. As always, there was something in this offer for Fortas's mentor as well. At the time, Douglas was locked in a battle with the other commissioners on the SEC over the director of the Public Utilities Division, C. R. Smith. Having gotten his job as part of a deal between Douglas and one of the other commissioners, George Mathews, Smith had become something of a nuisance to Douglas in his interpretation of the administration of the law. Realizing that it would be useful to have a hired gun to fight the proxy war directly with this staff man, Douglas could think of no one better qualified than his young protégé from Memphis. After all, hadn't he shielded the staff on the protective committee study from attack, and hadn't he preserved the courses at Yale from abolition? Now there was more that Fortas could do for Douglas by fighting Smith on his own level. The only problem was that Smith had the support of two of the commissioners, leaving Fortas, in his own words, in "a mighty uncomfortable job." In later reflecting on the task, he added, "I guess I would not have done it for anybody except Bill Douglas."[106]

While Douglas fought his battles with the giants of the utility industry, Fortas fought his battles with Smith. Philosophically, the issue was one of how strictly the Holding Company Act was to be enforced. Section 11 of the law, the so-called death sentence provision, empowered the SEC to reduce the number of holding companies in a utility industry until there was "a single integrated public-utility system."[107] Since this matter became an important issue for the attorneys within the agency, it led to a bureaucratic battle between the legal side under Fortas and the technical advisers under Smith as to who was in charge of interpreting and implementing the law.

Very quickly, the matter became one of turf and personnel control. Fortas soon became disenchanted with the procedures that required him to report to the director, Smith, and not to the commissioners directly. He complained that this prevented him from providing the SEC with "independent counsel." Smith charged Fortas and his legal pool with causing "friction" by their "aggressiveness" in legal advising. Interestingly, given the events of a few years earlier, it was newly appointed commissioner Jerome Frank who carried most of the fight on Fortas's behalf. Frank documented through lengthy memoranda a series of incidents that to him indicated Smith's "ineptness" as an administrator.[108] This spurred Smith and one of his patrons, Commissioner Robert Healy, to draft equally long memoranda denying the charges.[109]

The conflicts between Fortas and Smith heightened as each exercised his duties without consulting the other, leading to damaging administrative inefficiency in the enforcement of the Holding Company Act. An example of this lack of communication came in the so-called Victor Emanuel case. Emanuel, a banker, had been elected chairman of the board of Standard Gas and Electric, the second-largest utilities-industry holding company in the nation. Soon, though, reporters were charging that C. R. Smith had actually campaigned for Emanuel's election to the board. Knowing that the banker owned stock in the company contrary to SEC rules, Smith had relaxed those rules in allowing him to take the post. The understanding was that Emanuel in turn would voluntarily comply with the mandates of the Holding Company Act.[110]

What appeared to the reporters as a sellout of the New Deal principles caught the SEC commissioners, who had automatically approved the action, completely unaware.[111] With the entire commission under attack, the question was raised whether Smith's general counsel, Abe Fortas, had been consulted for legal advice on the relaxation of the normal commission rule. Smith claimed that Fortas had been consulted, and had given some bad advice leading to the decision. In fact, Fortas had warned Smith that the action was improper and emphatically advised against it, even going to the extent of having other bureaucrats lobby him against the elevation of this candidate. None of these doubts, though, had been transmitted by Smith to the full commission and, since Fortas was unable to communicate directly with the commissioners, the action had gone through.[112]

It was a tense situation, and soon the fight got even dirtier. Once more, Jerome Frank argued on Fortas's behalf, saying that Smith had placed the commission in a vulnerable position. Meanwhile, allies of Smith formed a "powerful cabal" against Fortas personally, and charges of his allegiance to Communism began flying around the office.[113] So Douglas, who had been maintaining a neutral posture after being promoted to the chairmanship, stepped in and decided to accept Smith's resignation even though it hadn't really been offered.[114]

Having survived this brutal scrape with a superior, Fortas found his position again becoming politically untenable when, on March

20, 1939, William O. Douglas was appointed to replace the retiring
Louis Brandeis on the United States Supreme Court. With his mentor
about to leave, the two remaining commissioners who had supported
Smith were now out to get Fortas. However, William O. Douglas was
once again hard at work planning the next move in his young protégé's
life.

II

ICKES'S
FIELD MARSHAL

With his protector William O. Douglas about to depart from the SEC for the Supreme Court, and Smith's friends out to get him, Fortas's career was clearly at stake. But after guiding Fortas's early career, the future justice was determined to see that his protégé was well placed. And Douglas knew just the sort of powerful people in Washington who would help to shepherd Fortas up the career ladder of success in Washington.

One such person was Secretary of the Interior Harold Ickes. In his six years of service in Roosevelt's cabinet, Ickes had developed a well-deserved reputation as an irascible, egotistical, temperamental, and scrupulously honest bureaucrat who, by means of a consummate infighting skill, was able to amass an extraordinary number of responsibilities under the rubric of his department. The combination of his first-name relationship with the president and his widespread contacts within high Washington circles made him one of the most important resources for those seeking employment in the bureaucracy. He quickly developed a reputation as a true conservationist, saving vast areas of land from development, and fearlessly took on causes that frightened others. While Ickes liked to think of himself as a liberal reformer, speaking on behalf of the nation's black population, he had unquestionable leanings toward anti-Semitism.[1]

But Ickes knew talent when he saw it. So, in April of 1939, when William O. Douglas's last official act before leaving the SEC was to recommend Abe Fortas to Ickes for employment, it did not take the "Old Curmudgeon," as he liked to be called, long to offer Fortas the job of general counsel to the Public Works Administration.[2] Though there is no evidence that the two men had met before this, the introduction from Douglas and Fortas's growing reputation in town were more than enough to convince Ickes to act. But what the secretary recalled after their first meeting as the reasons for the hiring were instructive as to the future of their relationship. "Fortas is one of the most brilliant lawyers in Washington," Ickes wrote in his diary, "and is highly recommended by those who know him. . . . While he is a Jew, he is of the quiet type and gives the impression of efficiency as well as legal ability."[3] This reserve on Ickes's part would eventually manifest itself as distrust.

Like it or not, though, the young man was on the way up. Having been rescued from the SEC by Ickes, Fortas now seemed to place his fate in his new mentor's hands. Knowing that the Public Works Administration was about to be liquidated, less than three months later he went to the secretary complaining of the agency's leadership and asked to be transferred. Fortas was so desperate to be moved that when Ickes offered him the job of general counsel to the Bituminous Coal Division at a lower salary, the young man snapped it up.

It was here that Fortas began to make a good impression on Ickes. Since the Bituminous Coal Division had been created to replace the disbanded Bituminous Coal Commission, Fortas became what journalists called the "spark plug" of the new outfit in overseeing the firing of a number of appointees sponsored by United Mine Workers President John L. Lewis. When he then went on to establish and successfully defend in federal court a pricing policy for coal, the labor leader became his sworn enemy.[4] It was not the last time that Lewis and the young bureaucrat were to cross swords.

Contrary to Ickes's initial impression of Fortas as a "quiet" Jew, it seemed that wherever the young New Dealer went he had the nasty habit of making as many devoted enemies as he did friends, if not more. Perhaps it was a jealousy about his quick success at an early age, or maybe the reaction of an anti-Semitic environment toward the success of any Jewish lawyer, that motivated some people. But there was no question that Fortas made many enemies on his own by adopting an overly aggressive style when confronted or attacked. In the Bituminous Coal Division the adversary was the acting comptroller general of the United States, R. N. Elliott, who reported to the Senate that the Coal Division had improperly used a legal intern. He also alleged that Fortas himself was a Communist because of his appearance on a membership list of Communist front organizations, and his participation in the International Juridical Association, which was alleged to have Communist members. For Fortas, the Communism charge was the same bugaboo that he had faced after the purge in the AAA and the C. R. Smith dispute in the SEC. In fact, it had become almost commonplace for liberal New Dealers who had joined a variety of liberal organizations, often to get useful professional journals and newsletters, to find later that the government had labeled these organizations "Communist front" movements.

Knowing that with each new charge of this nature more people began to take it as fact, Fortas did not treat the matter lightly. In a style that would become characteristically his own, he moved to destroy the report in a manner that reeked of overkill. "The discussion of the Tucker Dean matter in your Report contains untrue, misleading, impertinent and libelous statements," Fortas began in a five-page, single-spaced responding letter. As to the charge that he was a Communist, Fortas explained that his name had, in fact, *not* appeared on a list of members of alleged Communist front organizations, adding, "This error is due either to incredibly slipshod investigation, gross negligence, or willful fabrication." And, while he admitted being a member of the International Juridical Association, Fortas explained that this was merely a "technical, professional association," making the charge of his being a Communist "no more or less than a smear attempt which is unworthy of your high office."[5] Not surprisingly, after this letter was sent, the matter was dropped. But the charges were not forgotten, and years later Fortas's name was still being associated with the Communist movement.

This vehement and vicious response, which served only to antagonize his enemies further, was in a style that Fortas would repeat throughout his life. Perhaps because of his early days as a perceived "outsider"—being the young, brilliant, Jewish, poor southerner—these attacks triggered a fear that he might return to that status. Maybe there was an element of superb confidence that no one could best him in these spitting contests. Or maybe it was just that an attack on his work, which was consuming him at the moment, became an attack on him personally, and required that he respond in kind. Whatever the motivation, it soon became clear that one did not attack this young man lightly.

About a year after this attack, Ickes decided to set up a new power division in the Department of the Interior in hopes of taking control of the nation's hydroelectric power policy. Ickes hoped that the new division would develop a uniform planning and marketing policy for hydroelectric power nationwide, and thus become the focus of all governmental agencies dealing with this issue. With war imminent, the administrator of this new division would clearly be on a very fast track within the bureaucracy. The only problem was, Ickes told William O. Douglas at lunch, he did not know whom to appoint as the director.[6] Never at a loss to advance his former protégé's career, the justice mentioned Abe Fortas as a likely candidate.

While Fortas was not high enough in Ickes's pantheon to have occurred to him as a nominee, this new suggestion struck a responsive chord. Ickes had already recognized the young man's talents in this area by making him counselor for the Defense Power Policy Committee while its actual chairman, Benjamin Cohen, was away from Washington. Then, a short while earlier, Fortas had been in to tell Ickes that power matters were in a "critical condition," and to warn that the department's enemies throughout the government were trying to "sabotage" Interior's efforts in this area and were "gathering strength."[7] So in April 1941, the now thirty-year-old bureaucrat was offered the post of acting director of the Division of Power. Though "surprised" by the offer, the ambitious Fortas took the new job, much to the "relief and satisfaction" of Ickes. Soon, Fortas would be given full charge of the new agency.[8]

It took only minutes in this new job for Fortas to show his ability to skirt the minefields of the governmental bureaucracy. He was confronted with the "Burlew problem." Ebert K. Burlew, one of Ickes's most senior assistant secretaries, had been around long enough to know where all of the bodies were buried. And he did not want to be one of them. So when Ickes called in Fortas and Burlew to announce his plans for the new power division, Burlew said, "Fine, Mr. Secretary, as long as I retain my usual control over budget and personnel." But Fortas was equal to the challenge. "Mr. Secretary," he interjected, "let him take the policy and I'll take the budget." Ickes understood perfectly, and Fortas was given total control over the new agency.[9]

Now that Fortas was out of the shadows and for the first time in the political and bureaucratic limelight, he had begun to catch the eye of the president. FDR told his interior secretary that he was considering Fortas for appointment to the Securities and Exchange Commission. Quite understandably, Ickes expressed his reservations, only to find out that the young man's loyalties were strictly limited. Upon being told of the new opportunity, Fortas told his boss that it was his "ambition" to become a member of this board, despite the fact that he had been driven out of the SEC just two years before. So a disappointed Ickes went back and wrote the president that he "would not stand in [Fortas's] way."[10] But for reasons that remain unclear, the appointment was not made.

Since he was committed to Ickes's team for now, Fortas set out to fulfill the secretary's desire to consolidate authority in the department over the government's power policy. Whoever stood in his way in these bureaucratic turf battles was swept aside. Though Fortas was not ideologically committed to public power, he was once more the "technician," designing the solutions regardless of the ends being sought. For Fortas, one did not have to be a partisan to be an active participant.[11]

First, Undersecretary Alvin J. Wirtz of Texas, who had been appointed by Ickes just a year earlier with the express purpose of overseeing the issues of power, reclamation, and oil, resigned upon seeing that Fortas's operation would supersede his own. Then Fortas raided Wirtz's staff to take an old friend, power expert Arthur "Tex" Goldschmidt, and made him second-in-command in the new division. Since the division was charged with coordinating the construction of power units, the operation of those facilities, and the sale and distribution of the power from those units, the two men set out to capture power from those agencies within the department with similar functions.

But the other agencies refused to roll over so easily. The Bonneville Power Authority, charged with generating and selling power from dams along the Columbia River, refused to cooperate, claiming an exemption from the division's reporting requirements. And this was nothing compared to the hostility of the Bureau of Reclamation in the fight over control of the pricing policies for hydroelectric power. Since the bureau was charged with constructing the huge western dams, it was empowered to contract for the sale of their electricity. Fortas tried to capture sole authority to do this, arguing that the Bureau of Reclamation was an engineering group that was more concerned with water conservation than with pricing power as a means of gaining revenue. As a result, Fortas complained, the bureau was giving away contracts at prices that were not in the public's best interest. Indeed, the bureau refused to submit its contracts to the Division of Power for review and made deals with no regard for market forces or price potential. For now, Ickes was sympathetic to Fortas's aims, not only because they were in agreement that the market should be as wide as possible, but because the results of supporting the Division of Power were better for his internal coordination goals. It took a long and bitter reorganization battle, though, to end the practice of having the two agencies share the power to set prices.[12] As this conflict raged, moreover, Fortas's opponents began charging him with "socialized" thinking for advocating more centralized control of power matters.

Opposing forces came not only from within the department, but from without as well. For the first time, however, Fortas had the bureaucratic power to win such battles. The first man to be skewered by the lightning-fast intellect of the rising young bureaucrat was the powerful secretary of commerce and informal supervisor of the Reconstruction Finance Corporation (RFC), Jesse Jones. "Uncle Jesse," as he was called by some, was a former banker and businessman in Texas who was much more concerned with the welfare of big business than with the welfare of the government and the nation. And from his position, he was able to do much for the former while appearing to be at work for the latter.[13]

Tales illustrating Jones's real concerns abound. The story goes that one day in the middle of World War II, an aide raced into Jones's office, still out of breath from the dash down the hall, shouting, "There's terrible news, Mr. Jones—the rubber stockpile in Fall River, Massachusetts, just burned up!" Visions of jeeps without tires and planes unable to land were no doubt racing through the young man's mind as he transmitted the dire news. But Jones's concern was elsewhere: "It's insured, isn't it?"[14]

Young bureaucrats like Fortas were always willing to take on entrenched administrators such as Jones, knowing that he who controls the implementation of a policy controls the policy itself. The opportunity came with the attempted breakup of the Aluminum Corporation of America, or ALCOA as it had come to be known. As part of the buildup for World War II, Congress had authorized the Reconstruction Finance Corporation, through its subordinate Defense Plant Corporation, to make huge loans to critical defense industries for plant production. These loans were made to an entire industry, with plants being built by the government and leased to private industry for the defense effort. As the federal loan administrator, Jesse Jones was empowered to arrange these huge loans, which made his friends in business very happy.[15]

Since hundreds of tons of aluminum would be required for the airplane buildup, the subject of loans to the aluminum industry arose. The industry was then controlled by ALCOA, but a movement was under way in the lower divisions of the RFC to spread the wealth around, giving a number of new companies a chance to enter the industry. However, Arthur Davis, the chairman of the board of ALCOA, was a close personal friend of Jesse Jones. These loans provided a marvelous opportunity in his mind to solidify his company's monopoly in the field.[16] So, behind closed doors, Davis and Jones hammered out a loan deal that was sure to please the company's stockholders.

The original deal seemed relatively simple—ALCOA got everything and the government paid for it. Whereas the normal loan deal might have a company building a plant at cost, and turning over all of the production rights for the duration of the war to the government on a cost-plus-fee basis, ALCOA's projected deal was much sweeter. The government was assigned to build the plants, and ALCOA would lease all of the production rights in them for renewable five-year terms. However, if demand for aluminum was to fall below a certain level, ALCOA would have the right to cut back severely the production of, and perhaps eventually even shut down, the government-built plants first, in order to keep its own private plants in operation (while the government still had to pay maintenance costs on the others). Furthermore, the sale price of the newly produced aluminum was guaranteed to be the same as that set by ALCOA. In effect, then, the agreement ensured that there was no way ALCOA could lose in the deal.[17]

But neither man had counted on Abe Fortas and his friends. One of those friends was Clifford Durr, a Rhodes Scholar and corporate lawyer from Alabama who happened to be related by marriage and a philosophical ally of New Deal Supreme Court Justice Hugo Black. As chief of the legal section of the RFC handling the recapitalization of banks, Durr was placed in charge of ironing out the details of this new agreement between Jones and Davis. Shocked by what he saw, Durr tried first to undercut the contract on his own. After drafting the terms according to Jones's instructions, Durr then convinced his boss to run it by the Department of Justice, knowing that someone there would surely spot its grave antitrust problems.

The plan worked perfectly, as the agreement ended up on the desk of the head of the antitrust division, Thurman Arnold. "It's illegal as hell," Arnold kept screaming as he redrafted parts of the contract.[18] But this did not satisfy Durr, who wanted the entire agreement abrogated. So he decided it was time to invite his friends from Interior— Abe Fortas and his assistant Tex Goldschmidt—to his house for a chat. The three of them were so fearful that this conspiracy to oppose Jones might be overheard that all of their conversations were held in Durr's backyard, under his huge cherry tree.[19] Durr's wife, Virginia, later remembered that once he had heard what was going on, Abe Fortas was the one who seemed most anxious that Jones be stopped, and "he provided the motive power as well as brilliance to do this."[20]

The plan they concocted was simple. Fortas and Durr arranged to write each other nasty letters signed by their bosses, Harold Ickes and Jesse Jones, arguing about the contract. Early on, neither Ickes nor Jones was aware of how he was being used in this conspiracy, each thinking that the letters he received were being written by his adversary rather than by his assistant.[21] Since both Fortas and Durr knew what was coming long beforehand, it made planning a reply that much easier. Their goal was simply to convince the egocentric Ickes, in his capacity as a member of the advisory committee on metals, to take a personal interest in the terms of this contract. As the letters flying back and forth between Ickes and Jones got hotter and more insistent, the loan administrator began to see through the plan. "That damn guy Fortas" must be writing the letters, Jones told Durr. But the plan worked, and in the end the contract was redrafted in a manner that broke up ALCOA's monopoly by providing more loans for firms such as Reynolds, with its aluminum plants for wrapping cigarettes, and a number of other producers in the field.[22] The whole episode was a valuable lesson to Fortas in how to stop a seemingly more powerful opponent by working quietly through contacts in the shadows.

As Fortas's reputation spread, so did the rumors of his imminent departure from the Division of Power. But this was merely a ploy, aided by his old mentor William O. Douglas, to make him seem more attractive to Ickes. Late in December 1941, Justice Douglas came to lunch with Ickes bearing the distressing news that Fortas "might receive an attractive offer from some other place," specifically the SEC. Ickes could not have known that the antennae of the former SEC commissioner and poker-playing buddy of the president had probably already discovered that Fortas was no longer in the running for the commission post. Then Douglas reported that Interior Undersecretary John J. Dempsey was about to resign as well, which was news to both Ickes and Dempsey. It was left to Ickes to draw the obvious conclusion as to where the victor over the powerful Jesse Jones might like to go next.

When Ickes lamented that Fortas had already expressed his "ambition" to go to the SEC, Douglas was ready. Fortas was "very happy in Interior" and was "loyal" to Ickes, he told the vain secretary. Indeed, when Ickes returned to the office and raised these questions with Fortas, he found that the young man's "ambition" had now mysteriously become merely a "sentimental" feeling for his old agency. Of course, one reason for this changed attitude was the fact that the SEC position was being offered to someone else.[23]

The strategy worked. Douglas had played to both Ickes's weakness and his strength. The secretary could only have been pleased that despite all of these "pending" offers, Fortas was still "loyal" to him. On the other hand, Ickes was shrewd enough to know that his success depended in large part on attracting and retaining the best legal talent within his agency. So, after Dempsey resigned in May 1942 to pursue his political ambitions in New Mexico, Ickes suggested to the president that Fortas be named undersecretary. FDR had one reservation: Could he afford to appoint another "Hebrew" to a position of high authority? But Ickes, deliberately stretching the truth to get his way, assured the president that Fortas was "one of the quiet, unobtrusive types" and "one of the ablest lawyers in Washington." So the appointment was made.[24]

Even after Fortas's incredible rise to power to become, at thirty-one, one of the youngest undersecretaries in history, journalists were skeptical about his future. "How long Mr. Fortas will stay snuggled down was something for time, the terrible-tempered Mr. Ickes, and quiet, studious Mr. Fortas to decide," commented *Time* magazine. After all, this was just the "bat boy on the Corcoran-Cohen team," and the last two undersecretaries had only lasted a year apiece.[25]

For the young man from Yale, though, this was the perfect position, and he was determined to make it work. While Ickes craved the limelight, Fortas was content to remain in his shadows, performing all of his bureaucratic magic in the secretary's name. It was almost as if he did not want to be out in front—drawing flak in the form of untoward questions or criticisms. Perhaps it was a matter of history, Fortas having done the same thing for Douglas in the SEC. Or perhaps it was that, being Jewish, the young man believed staying out of the public eye was his only hope in an anti-Semitic world.

Whatever the motivation, after only forty-eight hours on the job, the new undersecretary wanted even more power. With an "overall jurisdiction," Fortas told Ickes, he could improve the administration. Ickes knew exactly what was at issue here, and approved. He promised to extend Fortas's domain, making the rival Burlew a direct subordinate to the new undersecretary and even more removed from Ickes.[26]

With this decision, Fortas was now free largely to run the entire department on his own, answerable only to the neurotic and image-conscious secretary.[27] The secretary set the tone, while Fortas operated the wheels of government. And when Ickes was gone, Fortas quickly grabbed for even greater power. With the secretary off on a trip to the Glacier National Park, Fortas began signing documents as the "Acting Secretary of the Interior."[28]

All of these new responsibilities came with the perquisites of power. Fortas's expansive desk sat at the end of a huge office that overlooked the Potomac and the presidential monuments. To many, it seemed like the trip from the office door to the desk took fifteen or twenty minutes. In addition, he had a large hideaway office with a private bathroom, a personal messenger, and a large secretarial staff.

The office had to be nice, though, because there was enough work to trap the young man there forever. The department was broken up into a wide variety of overlapping fiefdoms of power ruled by men whose loyalty ran more to the appointing president and supporting legislators than to the sitting secretary.[29] Since the undersecretary was supposed to extend control over this system of alleged subordinates, a wide variety of division chiefs—such as the heads of the Lands Division, the Bureau of Reclamation, the Bureau of Indian Affairs, the Division of Power, and the Division of Territories and Island Possessions—reported directly to him. It was not an easy task keeping everyone happy, given the tendency of Ickes to treat his assistants and division chiefs rather brutally.

On top of that, anything that was headed for Ickes had to pass first over Fortas's desk. The result was a never-ending mountain of paper delivered to his desk every day for disposition. Fortas would routinely draft many of Ickes's letters and memos for signature, exercise control over personnel, do budget and liaison work with Congress, and point out potential "trouble spots" for the department.[30] In time, moreover, his bureaucratic skill encouraged Ickes to saddle him with a wide variety of new tasks. With each week came a new series of items for

Fortas's agenda—the development of raw materials for the war effort, securing adequate electric power for the nation, conserving the forests and the West, developing land policy in California, and overseeing manpower and labor issues in defense plants. In addition, Ickes sought his help in writing speeches and negotiating power relationships with other executive officials.[31] Nor was it uncommon for the undersecretary to be given confidential chores, such as developing files of uncomplimentary information on individuals criticizing the secretary, for use in *ad hominem* attacks.[32]

As part of these widening responsibilities, Ickes allowed Fortas to attend the cabinet meetings in his absence.[33] It was there that Roosevelt, upon seeing the young substitute, passed a note to another official at the cabinet table asking his identity. "Fortas," came the reply from Attorney General Francis Biddle. "Not his last name, his *first* name," implored the president. Then he was able to call on the Interior Department's representative by saying, "Well, Abe, what's been going on at Interior?"[34] Soon, meetings between Fortas and White House officials—such as James Byrnes and Samuel Rosenman—became rather commonplace.[35]

The constantly varying nature of the job provided a wider circle of contacts and a long, revealing look at how the wheels of government really turned. Which office really held the power over an issue? Who could be called to accomplish a task in the quickest fashion? What corners could be cut? How many people could be cultivated by months of favors to become lifetime allies?

In all of his work, Fortas demonstrated a flair for identifying potential trouble spots and for defending his own position and that of the Interior Department. When the occasion demanded, he also displayed a brilliance at negotiating and drafting the perfect instrument for bringing about the resolution of a crisis. Fortas first made his mark publicly in the spring of 1943 during a dispute over a contract between the navy and the Standard Oil Company of California, for the rights to drill in the Elk Hills oil field. This land was owned by the oil company but contained a navy oil reserve. After spotting a number of problems in this contract, which gave too many advantages to the oil company, Fortas wrote a critical advisory memo for Ickes to forward to the secretary of the navy. On the basis of these allegations, the president instructed the Department of Justice to investigate the matter, and soon the contract was ruled illegal. Once the media got wind of the dispute, a scandal was brewing. So, both houses of Congress organized hearings on this "new Teapot Dome Scandal," and the Justice Department held a number of conferences to which Fortas was invited to review the deal. Eventually, the contract was restructured, and Fortas was credited as being "the first man in Washington to see through the Elk Hills oil deal."[36]

Fortas's reputation was also enhanced during the threatened coal miners' strike in 1943. The United Mine Workers were threatening to walk out on a monthly basis. Fortas, in his role as assistant to Harold Ickes, who had been named solid fuels administrator, was placed in charge of negotiating agreements between the mine workers and owners. It was grueling, sometimes around-the-clock work, in the no-win situation of toiling for a political party that favored the working class but needed the coal to win a war abroad. The president had put himself in a bad position by twice asking the miners to return to work, and twice being ignored, and by mid-June he was on the verge of doing it again. Trying to prevent that occurrence, Fortas worked with Ickes on redrafting a presidential message that "urged" the miners to return. On their insistence, the message now "ordered" and "directed" the miners to resume work. Then, at the same time, a private exchange of letters was arranged with United Mine Workers President John L. Lewis, ensuring that the strike would be ended before the Roosevelt message was even released, thus making it appear as though the president had accomplished the feat.[37]

Then there was Fortas's work for Puerto Rico. One of Fortas's most important contributions was to revitalize the Division of Territories, which had control over such areas as Alaska, Hawaii, and the Philippines. The issues raised by the war made these particular hot spots and served only to increase the young man's power. But his real interest and contribution here lay in the development of the commonwealth of Puerto Rico. In a relationship that would last throughout the rest of his life, Fortas became for the island a lifeline to the Washington government.

The war had put the small island in a very vulnerable position. Lacking industrial or even agricultural self-sufficiency, Puerto Rico relied on export of its sugarcane and rum to the United States in exchange for foodstuffs and industrial items. But the drain on the shipping industry after Pearl Harbor meant that there was never enough space for delivering supplies to the island.

Fortas oversaw the efforts to find scarce shipping space, given the military needs in wartime, in order to supply the island with much-needed foodstuffs and manufactured items and return with exported rum and sugar in payment. For the touchy and temperamental territorial governor, Rexford Tugwell, this kind of steadfast support was vital. It seemed that whenever Tugwell ran into a problem on the island—striking workers, incompetent subordinates, and even an investigating congressional committee sworn to "get Tugwell and clean up the Puerto Rican Reds"—it was Fortas who provided the flank support.[38] Then in Washington, he ran interference for Tugwell with the executive branch bureaucracy and Secretary Ickes himself, protected the yearly appropriations for the island, and surveyed possibly damaging press accounts about the American regime. A tough infighter himself, Tugwell could hardly contain his enthusiasm for Fortas: "Mr. Abe Fortas looked like a boy. A good many people had at various times presumed on this appearance and had had rude shocks. . . . His toughness, somewhat like Mr. Roosevelt's, did not show itself so much in the means used to gain ends, as in determination to gain the ends by some means—even unexpected ones."[39] Because of all of these efforts, including service on the president's committee to revise the governing Organic Act by which the island moved toward full independence when Puerto Rico achieved commonwealth status, Abe Fortas was viewed as one of the "founding fathers" of the island's new government.

By the middle of 1943, the doubting Thomases in the media had begun to see Fortas as something of a hero. He was now labeled "Ickes's Field Marshal" by *Newsweek,* "the man on whom Secretary of the Interior Harold L. Ickes relies for counsel, information and guidance . . . and his judgment carries weight."[40] And he was proclaimed to be "the first Undersecretary to get along with his boss and make his advice stick."[41]

When one looks at Fortas's expanding network of friends and allies in Washington during this period, the figure that keeps reappearing is a congressman from Texas named Lyndon Baines Johnson. In many ways Johnson was everything that Fortas was not. He set off Fortas's small, delicate features and quiet, refined taste with an awkward, gawky, six-foot five-inch frame, from which flailed long, constantly moving arms. He had the sort of boisterous, frequently profane nature that made him both the life of the party and sometimes an embarrassment to his friends. Fortas liked to listen and be consulted about problems; Johnson loved to talk, especially if it was about his problems, and then fell asleep when the conversation did not concern him. Fortas, with an inner confidence, could slip in and out of a party without anyone knowing that he had been there; Johnson would relieve his

personal insecurity by making himself the center of attention. But they
had one thing in common—their past. Like Fortas, Johnson had come
from humble origins—from the Hill Country of Texas—and through a
genius for people, sheer ambition, and a trace of luck, he had been
able to pull himself up by the bootstraps. Because of that experience,
like Fortas, he harbored a desire, more like a passion, for getting
something done, both for himself and for the people he now represented. He, too, was clearly a man on the way up, and now that he
was in Congress, Johnson would have his chance.[42]

Though many people either claimed, or were given, credit for introducing Fortas and Johnson, it was Tex Goldschmidt who performed in
1939 what would later be seen as a historic deed. By that time,
Johnson had certainly heard much about the rising legend of Abe Fortas. As the young bureaucrat from Yale went up the ladder of success
in Washington, Johnson couldn't help but notice.[43] And with Fortas in
the Public Works Administration, Johnson saw him as just the friend
he needed to help him build dams on the Lower Colorado River and
provide his district with electricity and flood control. So Johnson
looked for ways to make their friendship more intimate.

And getting close to people was just what Johnson did best—as
FDR and House Speaker Sam Rayburn could attest.[44] "LBJ had a way
of getting closer to someone he could learn from, lean on, or benefit
from. I think that's the way he felt about Abe Fortas," explained
Johnson's later aide Walter Jenkins, a man who saw this process firsthand.[45]

For all of his efforts, though, Johnson was on the periphery of Fortas's main crowd. It was an incredibly exciting time—with the nation's best and brightest answering FDR's call to help create a "New
Deal" and then to "win the War."[46] Like the others, for Fortas it
meant an unending string of fifteen-hour days, broken by an occasional
holiday to cure what seemed to be a continual string of bad colds and
bouts with the flu (though his colleagues suspected that there was a
touch of hypochondria at work here). Best of all for Fortas, who had
faced hostility toward his religion in Yale and Tennessee, people were
accepted no matter what their faith. All that concerned Washington
now was the quality of one's mind.

The socialization process of people working in such close proximity
over a period of several years was inexorable. Members of the New
Deal crowd originally lived in large rooming houses throughout
Georgetown, called "nunneries" by some of them, and then slowly
paired off, got married, and took up small residences in the same area.

They would hold large parties, filled with witty conversation and discussions of the topics of the day. These were not solely social occasions, though, because the guests were so caught up in their work that it became almost the sole topic of conversation. But there was some time for recreation—the kind of game playing one would expect with a crowd of animated intellectuals. "Let us consider," Jerome Frank said one day, "what would happen to the world if everyone turned blue after sex." After much eager discussion it was agreed that there would be money to be made in a whole new and very popular line of blue cosmetics.[47]

With the contacts came the cross-fertilization of ideas and the sort of networking that kept folks moving from job to job up the ladder in Washington. So the Fortases, the Tex Goldschmidts, the Clifford Durrs, the C. G. Davidsons, and the James H. Rowes all began gathering as a group.[48] After a while, the Yale crowd began gathering at Walton Hamilton's, with Hamilton and William O. Douglas as the stars of the usual group.[49] There were cocktail parties, an occasional softball game, and the Fortases became famous for their New Year's Eve parties and Easter egg parties (the latter of which always seemed confusing to some, given Abe Fortas's religious affiliation).[50] It was to some of these gatherings that Lyndon Johnson and his wife, Lady Bird, would occasionally be invited.

As a newly elected congressman in 1937, Johnson very much wanted to become a central member of this group. In many ways the insecure Texan from Southwest Texas State Teachers College in San Marcos was like the little kid on the block searching for ways to play in the games with the big boys. They were fun. They were already set in their careers. They were moving up fast. And, most important, they could do much to help him. So Johnson tried a little Texas hospitality. Fortas and the others were invited over for festive Texas cocktail parties at the Johnsons' on Sunday afternoons. The guest lists, drawn from the executive branch, Congress, and the Texas press, made for good fun and better politics.[51]

Even on these occasions, Congressman Johnson was never really at ease. "He was consumed with his work," remembers Mary Rather, who helped Lady Bird Johnson at most of these gatherings. "He couldn't talk about anything else. People like Abe could talk about other things so they would try to balance him off." In spite of his efforts, Johnson became the butt of jokes from the others. They saw him for what he was—a somewhat socially awkward interloper who wanted to be a member of the inner circle but did not have the govern-

mental experience to fit in. He was not well liked by many of them, as
he constantly probed to see what others could do for him or his constituents.

But Fortas seemed to like him, and Johnson did what he could to
solidify their relationship. Johnson began courting him with a shower
of gifts. They swapped crocks of pecans from their home states, accompanied by funny little notes attesting to the merits of the product.
Fortas claimed that his gift of Tennessee pecans marked "an epoch in
the civilization of my State." But to Johnson, these "Dixie pecans,"
coming from one "who is probably the world's most eminent bad
judge of nuts," looked "like samples." Later Johnson sent thirty-
pound Texas turkeys for Thanksgiving, grapefruits, pralines, tumblers,
and invitations to occasional stag dinners.[52]

Over time the two men came to realize the commonality of their
poor background, their skill at achieving their mutual aims, and, most
important, the things that they could do for each other. They each saw
themselves as "technicians"—problem solvers who acted from the
challenge of overcoming obstacles to a desired policy, rather than out
of strict adherence to a single ideological viewpoint. This indifference
to a single philosophy made Fortas much different from the devotedly
liberal New Dealers surrounding him, and thus much more palatable to
the "moderate" Democrat from Texas.

The first opportunity for Fortas to demonstrate his bureaucratic
problem-solving skills came when Johnson's financial backers, George
and Herman Brown of the Brown and Root construction firm, ran into
a snag while building the Marshall Ford Dam in Johnson's district as
part of the Lower Colorado River Project. The Browns had decided,
without any formal governmental authorization, to put a 78-foot extension on top of the 190-foot structure that was already built. Now the
question was how to get paid for it. Fortas was asked how to make the
construction contracts for the higher dam legal even though it was not
required for the production of power as mandated by the Lower Colorado River Authority. So he figured out how to redefine the project and
legalize the extension of the dam as a flood control project. But who
would pay for the extension? Neither the LCRA (charged with producing hydroelectric power) nor the Bureau of Reclamation (charged with
building flood control structures) could fund the full extension of the
dam. So Fortas drafted a complicated legal memo suggesting that a
third agency, the Public Works Administration, pay for the middle
portion of the dam. After arguing that this part of the dam would
sometimes be used for flood control and at other times to produce

power, Fortas concluded that such a "joint-use" structure, a term of his own invention, should be funded by an entirely different agency. Interior Secretary Harold Ickes bought the argument. As would happen many times in the two men's future careers, what for Johnson was a matter of intensely important politics became for Fortas a simple, technical question of legal analysis and writing. Johnson's "What?" soon became Fortas's "How?"[53]

With that successful entreaty to Fortas came even more requests from the Texas congressman. Could Fortas find a position for F. A. Reilly on the Federal Petroleum Board? Perhaps, was the response, but Reilly's chances were hampered by the fact that there were no vacancies available. Unpersuaded, Johnson pestered Fortas with two more letters on successive days concerning the same matter. "In answer to your letters of February 15 and 16," Fortas wrote, "I have rechecked and . . . it is still true that no vacancy on the Federal Petroleum Board is expected."[54]

Later, one of Johnson's friends, Bryan Spires, was having trouble with the Petroleum Administration for War on the regulation of hours for the distribution of motor fuel. So the congressman wrote to Fortas on June 19, 1943. Despite a promise of action, though, nothing seemed to happen in Interior.[55] Once more Johnson refused to take no for an answer, and pestered Fortas for help with repeated letters, drawing another rebuke from the administrator: "I have your letter of June 28 and am on the job." This time Fortas got the constituent an audience with the director of marketing for the petroleum administration, and a long explanatory letter from its deputy administrator, Ralph K. Davies. It turned out that the agency had already explained the new directive on two occasions to Johnson's constituent, who was now attempting an end run around the detouring bureaucrats. So the request for an exception to the rule, which would have increased the man's business, was once again denied.[56] But that was still not enough for the congressman from Texas. "I don't want to be persistent," Johnson wrote Fortas in yet another letter on the issue, "[but] I am fearful that Mr. Davies is in for a good deal of trouble unless something is done about Petroleum Administrative Order #4 right soon."[57]

In the end, the directive was changed. Fortas, though, could not help kidding Johnson about the tenacious manner of his lobbying: "Not having heard from you the past few days about our good friend," he began, Fortas assumed the new directive must have taken care of the situation. But Johnson did not back off for a minute. "Dear Abe, not having heard from our good friend, Mr. Spires, I assume that the directive as it finally came out is satisfactory to him. You can rest assured that if it is not, you will be hearing from me.''[58]

Indeed, the constituent was grateful, and his letter of thanks came within a week. ''Mr. Fortas, we are deeply appreciative of your untiring efforts in this connection . . . as Lyndon had told me on several occasions that you were putting up a stiff fight for us. . . . It is so unusual to find a government official in Washington open-minded now-a-days and we want to thank you again for what has been done for us.''[59] But Fortas, impervious to flattery, was still suspicious that this might be more of Johnson's lobbying—and it probably was. After thanking Spires for his letter, Fortas wrote to Johnson, ''Here is a copy of a letter from Bryan Spires. Whether or not you inspired it, I appreciate it, although it's not entirely deserved.''[60]

Over the next few years Congressman Johnson and the young New Dealers were able to help each other out quite a bit. Johnson was happy to comply with Fortas's request to enter his scorching response to the attack of the acting comptroller general on his Coal Division days in the *Congressional Record*. In 1941, when Johnson was making his abortive run for the Senate against Texas Governor W. Lee ''Pappy'' O'Daniel, the other New Dealers in Washington kept a close watch on the race to make sure it was conducted fairly.[61] But it did not help against the combined forces of the liquor industry and Governor O'Daniel's ability to steal the election with some ''new returns.'' O'Daniel's tampering with the ballot boxes was successful in spite of the fact that Johnson had actually started with a lead of over five thousand votes and held the lead for several days.[62] Later, in 1944, when Johnson and Wirtz were challenging in the Texas Supreme Court the selection process for a presidential elector in that state, Fortas and Tom Corcoran kept in close touch with the fight.[63] The list of lawyers involved in Texas on the suit represented a who's who of the state bar, and, combined with the two lawyers in Washington, indicated the powerful alliance of legal counsel now networked around Congressman Johnson.

After a while, Johnson began to see Fortas as something of a mentor, even though Johnson was two years older. Fortas had the longer and more varied experience in Washington governing circles, thus giving him the wider contacts. But there was something else about the young man. ''Fortas was old before his time,'' said one friend. He was ''born with the wisdom of years and experience,'' adds another.[64] So to a man as insecure as Johnson, who ''wanted everything done yesterday,'' this was a valuable ally to have.

Before long, the two men were, in the words of Walter Jenkins, "fast friends." "I never knew them to have a difference of opinion," he added from his many years of observation. Now people were beginning to see Johnson as part of the Corcoran and Fortas group of "extreme left-wingers," as they were labeled.[65] Men such as Vice President Henry Wallace were convinced that this group's opposition to his renomination in 1944, in favor of the nomination of William O. Douglas, had helped to unseat him.[66] Whether true or not, the mere charge indicates the sort of visibility and hence the sort of political capital that the young New Dealers had accrued. Johnson and Fortas were now part of a team.[67] Together they had learned how to operate the wheels of government and together they got on the treadmill to the top.

Fortas's friends and successes in government, though, were counterbalanced by a growing list of his enemies both inside and outside the office. His demeanor could quickly dissolve into fits of temper and biting, sarcastic, profane language if things did not go as expected. At first the enmity was something of an office joke. One day, Fortas came to work to find that the inner door connecting his office to Ickes's had been closed and blocked up with cardboard. When he protested, the undersecretary was told that his boss wanted more privacy. By the next day, the cardboard was gone—but so was the doorknob. Fortas quickly tired of having to circle around the outer office to gain entrance to Ickes's office through the main door and lodged another complaint. So, when he came to work the following day, the doorknob was back, only to disappear on alternate days. Finally, the door situation was straightened out, only to have people discover that Fortas's name had been removed from the letterhead of the official departmental stationery. It was an "economy" move, he was told. By now the newspapers were wondering whether the poor unnamed undersecretary would arrive at work one day to find his chair and desk cast out into the hallway.[68]

As Fortas repeatedly sought to have Ickes define the nature of his relationship vis-à-vis other bureaucrats, seeking to protect his lines of responsibility and his lines of direct communication to the secretary, the list of his office detractors grew.[69] Even his associates, troubled by his penchant for secrecy and playing things too close to the vest, started leaving the department for private business.[70]

By 1943 Fortas had made more than his share of enemies out of the office, too. One opponent was Oregonian Wayne Morse, the citizen member of the National War Labor Board (WLB). Morse had taken exception to Fortas's and the Interior Department's handling of the coal strike in 1943.[71] The main contractual sticking point was the so-called portal-to-portal pay for the time it took miners to walk from the pit of the mine to the coal seam they were working. But the real issue was whether the WLB or the Interior Department, which had seized the mines for the government, had the power to negotiate with John L. Lewis of the United Mine Workers of America.

When Ickes's negotiating power as coal mines administrator was questioned, Fortas claimed to have found a precedent backing the action from the time that the director of the Office of Defense Transportation had negotiated a contract with the Toledo, Peoria, and Western Railroad after a similar government takeover. But Morse, having been personally involved in that case, knew that Fortas was grossly misrepresenting the facts of that case as the director had, in fact, consulted with the WLB every step of the way.[72] So, in a confidential letter to the president, Morse accused Fortas of engaging in a "subterfuge" to enable the secretary of the interior to set the wages and working conditions in the coal mines.[73]

Once more, Fortas responded to this attack with particular vehemence. "I considered your erroneous statement . . . to be merely a lapse of memory," he wrote to Morse. Then, after "correcting" a number of the statements made in Morse's letter, Fortas added that his only motivation here was to restore order in the mines. "You might think about that a while," he suggested, closing with "I am not bothering the President with a copy of this comment upon your trivial letter, nor am I discussing it with the press."

But Morse wasn't done yet. First, he sent copies of the latest correspondence to the White House, saying, "After I am convinced that a person is not acting in good faith and I have told him so, further communications are useless."[74] Apparently, though, an exception could be made for Fortas. So Morse sent him another inflammatory letter, claiming that Fortas and Ickes had "written a disgraceful page of American industrial history" by resorting to "expediency" over "basic principles" and using "trickster" tactics.[75]

Fortas took the matter in the spirit in which it was intended. "Your letter is as intemperate as has been your entire conduct in the handling of the coal case," he responded. "After reading it, no one can doubt that you are completely unsuited for any position which requires the exercise of judgment and balance. . . . My only remaining hope for the War Labor Board is that your splendid colleagues will be able to restrain your unscrupulous, undignified, and irrational conduct."[76] In one of those ironies of politics, twenty-five years later Morse would be asked as a member of the United States Senate to exercise his "judgment and balance"—this time on the question of the future of Abe Fortas's career.

In time, Fortas's enemies tried to make his life miserable. With the war raging in Europe and the Pacific, the call went out for every available man to join the armed forces. Despite Fortas's preeminent position in the government, as a thirty-three-year-old male with no children, he was in the prime drafting pool. But the plain fact was that Fortas was a physical wreck. Among his many ailments was chorioretinitis, a tubercular condition of the retina, which had left him with a large blind spot in the peripheral vision of his left eye (a real disadvantage with projectiles coming at you from unpredictable directions). While the disease had been temporarily arrested, there was a possibility that the strain or adverse weather conditions encountered in combat might leave Fortas permanently blinded.[77]

All of which did not bother Fortas's enemies at all. A cry went up from certain members of Congress and the press asking why men like Fortas were not defending their country with their lives. Stung by the criticism, Fortas submitted his resignation in late April with the intention of joining the army. But FDR sent back a note saying, "You can best serve your country by continuing to do your job," and told his cabinet that the Fortas case was an example of the need for the Class II-B deferment for essential governmental employees.[78] There was, however, a limit to how far the president was willing to go to defend the young man. Seeking to duck the anti-Semitic forces, FDR decided not to single out the Fortas example in a public address on the need for such deferments. Fortas was quietly granted an extended deferment, but only until November, thereby inadvertently hanging him out as a target of attack.[79]

One of the reasons that Fortas was seen as so essential, besides the generally crucial nature of his work as undersecretary, was his involvement in the negotiations over Middle Eastern oil. The Interior Department was trying to arrange a deal between the Saudi Arabian government and two American oil companies—the Texas Company and Standard Oil of California—to pump and refine the newly discovered oil in the Arabian desert. A snag in the negotiations arose over how much of a controlling interest the United States government would retain in the company after fronting the money for the erection of a refinery in that region. So, after protracted and heated talks with the two oil companies, Fortas was placed in charge of a delegation of government and oil officials who were to travel to the Middle East for completion of the deal.[80]

By late August, though, the attacks on Fortas over his military deferment from the combined forces of the enemies of Fortas, FDR, and the Jewish community were more than he could bear.[81] So once more Fortas begged Ickes to let him resign and join the service. Ickes was by now concerned enough to grant the request, fearing that the young man would "break" under the "punishment that would be in store for him" otherwise.[82]

But yes did not seem to be the answer that Fortas wanted to hear. As in the crisis surrounding his departure from Jerome Frank's service for William O. Douglas's, all of the pressure once again seemed to unbalance Fortas. While he seemed bent on going on the Middle East mission, the young man who had seemed so confident and oblivious to criticism became a bundle of insecurities. His friends, of course, were able to see this pattern. It was the little things that tipped them off— the constant colds and physical ailments, combined with Fortas's hypochondria after periods of excessive work, and his uncertainty in choosing a course of action at career turning points.[83] Even Fortas could see this about himself, once writing William O. Douglas, "My case of the jitters merely substantiates my feeling that I am no damn good about my own affairs—I think I'm a swell hand holder for everybody except myself."[84] This insecurity, in turn, made Fortas vulnerable to attack, leading him to misstep.

It seems clear that in this case Fortas never really wanted to enter the service. Had he really wanted to do so, he could have followed the example of his friend James Rowe in the Department of Justice and used Congressman Johnson, then on the House Naval Affairs Committee, to force his acceptance into the service.[85] It would have been easy to arrange for a cushy desk job through various other executive branch contacts. But Fortas was much more content just to let the deferment expire, in hopes that he would then fail the physical.[86] In this regard, Ickes had arranged with his contacts in the military for a pre-induction examination of Fortas's file and received assurances that a medical deferment was inevitable.[87]

In spite of this, Fortas was accepted into the navy after a very cursory medical examination. Ickes immediately requested a delay in entry to allow time for completion of the Middle East operation. Then, mysteriously, he wrote a letter to the navy withdrawing the request, saying that the transportation delays in the mission now made Fortas's entry into the armed forces more feasible.[88] (Years later Fortas would jokingly tell a visitor that he had not gone on the Middle East mission because he did not have the right kind of long underwear for winter negotiating.)[89]

The true reasons for Ickes's quick reversal, though, were a lot less pleasant for Fortas. While Ickes was very supportive publicly, throwing him a farewell luncheon, privately he had run out of patience with Fortas's waffling over his departure.[90] Enemies in Congress were beginning to criticize Ickes directly for delaying his undersecretary's entrance into the military so he could take a trip to the Middle East.[91] Since the secretary was even more sensitive to criticism than his junior assistant, he wanted Fortas to enter the military immediately. Fortas, meanwhile, began to stonewall publicly, saying that he was going on the trip no matter who raised complaints.

When FDR heard about it, he told the assembled cabinet that Fortas was *not* going to the Middle East because his religion would make it impossible for him to negotiate effectively with King ibn-Saud. Since Fortas's religion had not changed in the months of preparation for the trip, it seemed curious that such a decision would be made so late in the process.[92]

So, after threatening to "get" whoever was responsible for scuttling the mission, a "terribly disappointed" Fortas left the government to enter the navy. Before leaving, though, he thanked his latest mentor in a long letter attesting to Ickes's "courage and integrity," which Fortas said had inspired him to offer "all the loyalty and devotion of which I am capable."[93] For his part, the normally hypercritical Ickes said, "You are the best Undersecretary who has ever worked in this Department . . . [and] I feel at a loss without you."[94] They sounded like two lovers never expecting to see one another again, and perhaps that would have been better for both of them.

Rather than enter with the other college graduates as an ensign, Fortas chose to join with the enlisted men. But he soon had cause to regret the decision. For the first time since Memphis, Fortas was back with the common man in the induction center at Camp Sampson in New York, and what he saw came as a real shock. Fortas found the men "illiterate and badly nourished." Since he was one of the few men in the barracks who could read and write properly, Fortas was put in charge of the gear locker to safeguard the brooms and towels. After proving that he could handle this executive chore, he was assigned to supervise the cleaning of the latrine, and then was made officer of the day, an amusing job for the young man who only a week before had

been running one of the government's largest bureaucracies. Since he
was in the "holdovers'" barracks awaiting review of his medical status, all of the usual drills and physical exercises for active trainees
were replaced by hours of simple marching and make-work cleanup
and office details. It was "a lazy, gold-bricking life," Fortas complained, and he regretted not going in as an officer. Despite the careful
handling, though, Fortas not only managed to resprain a bad knee and
lose weight, but also contracted a case of conjunctivitis in one eye.[95]

Once more, Fortas's uncertainty and underconfidence returned. His
wife had moved to New York City to practice tax law with Lord, Day
and Lord, and was finding it "pretty grim" living away from her
friends and husband.[96] And Fortas's own future was cloudy. What
would happen if he *was* discharged from the navy? he wrote to Ickes.
Would someone try to "railroad" him into the army? If not, would he
be welcomed back into the Interior Department? No amount of reassurance by Ickes helped here, though Fortas clearly craved those expressions of support. On the other hand, Fortas was not sure he wanted
to return to "Honest Harold," he wrote to Douglas, fearing that he
would be subjected to more assaults on his name and reputation.[97]

What seemed to be paranoia may not have been entirely unfounded.
Some people really did seem to be out to get him. Ickes had arranged
with Secretary of the Navy Frank Knox for a special medical reex-
amination, and after all of the tests, it was determined that he was to
be given a medical discharge. But for some reason the papers were
held up for weeks. Then word came down that he was to be released
from the hospital and report for active duty. Only after Ickes harassed
Knox was Fortas finally discharged. But the question remained as to
whether Fortas had been treated more harshly by the military bureaucracy because of his religion or his former governmental status.[98]
(Several months later, even after this well-publicized abuse of a clearly
physically disqualified candidate for service, the District of Columbia
draft board was still trying to capture Fortas. As a result, he had to
continue having examinations by prescribed oculists to see if his condition had improved.)[99]

All of this official persecution succeeded only in making Fortas even
more indecisive and he did not seem to have the least idea of what he
wanted to do next. While Ickes continued to make it clear that he was
welcome to return to his old job, Fortas debated his fate for nearly a
month, consulting with various friends for advice. For a time, he
thought about leaving government service entirely to practice law in
New York with his wife.[100] He seemed paralyzed in making the

choice, the pressure on him beginning to take a physical toll. Ickes found him to be "unsettled," with the appearance of "an anxious, ill man." Even William O. Douglas wondered whether Fortas was prepared to return and slug it out with his attackers.[101] The combination of an uncertain future and the damage done by previous assaults made him anything but the calm, confident operator who had gunned down John L. Lewis and faced off with Wayne Morse.

For now, though, men such as Ickes and Douglas were there to guide his way—although Ickes did not relish the role. By the end of December, after briefly considering getting out of government entirely and making some money in private law practice, Fortas had finally made up his mind, and prepared to go back to Interior.[102] But even as he did so, Fortas was looking for a way out. People kept telling him how much money could be made in the private sector, so he reserved the right to leave the undersecretaryship six months after his reappointment. Even with the passage of this period of vulnerability in his life, Fortas made it clear to his boss that he was no longer willing to fight battles just for the joy of winning. "Any punishment that I take during the next year will be taken in a fight that is more important to me than the pain which it may cause," he wrote.[103] Fortas honestly believed that he was returning to Interior more because Ickes needed his help than for the benefits to his own health and career.[104]

Once back in harness, however, the old confidence miraculously reappeared and Fortas began showing that he could deliver far more punishment than his adversaries. The Field Marshal was back in town. And it was not long before Ickes began to wonder whether having Fortas return to the department had been a good idea.

First, though, Fortas made a real contribution on the question of the internment of Japanese American citizens. In 1942 Franklin Roosevelt, reacting to claims of military danger on the west coast, had authorized the removal of 112,985 Japanese American to internment camps. The supervision of these camps was placed under the War Relocation Authority (WRA) and its strident director, Dillon Myer.[105] When the WRA was transferred to the Interior Department, it was left to Undersecretary Abe Fortas to deal with the matter. Fortas's views on the internment operation were harsh, calling it a "terrific mistake" and saying that he could hope only "to ameliorate the evils which resulted from it."[106] When New York Mayor Fiorello La Guardia feared a wave of released Japanese Americans flocking to his city, "creating a very dangerous situation," it was Fortas who discovered that only about twenty evacuees actually had such travel plans.[107] Meanwhile,

the young undersecretary worked with Ickes and John J. McCloy of
the State Department to secure full release of all of the detainees.[108]
While McCloy was impressed with Fortas, he found the undersecretary
to be "something of an operator" in the behind-the-scenes efforts. In
the months that followed, Fortas argued that the interned citizens
posed no real military threat, and that an improving war environment
made releasing them a means of eliminating a very thorny public relations problem for the president.[109] At the same time, he negotiated
between Secretary Ickes and WRA Director Myer to establish procedures for releasing as many of the detainees as quickly as possible.[110] Finally, in December 1944, the efforts of Fortas and others
paid off, as the president revoked the exclusion order.

Before this effort was completed, though, a major misstep by Fortas
permanently altered his relationship with Ickes. As part of the negotiation process over the construction of a refinery in Saudi Arabia, Fortas
had been named secretary of the government's Petroleum Reserves
Corporation (PRC). The move was designed to bolster Ickes, who, in
collecting government posts like trading stamps, had managed to become both the president of the PRC and the petroleum administrator
for war. Both of these jobs gave him considerable say over the progress of the negotiations, which by now contemplated the building of a
pipeline to the sea in addition to a refinery.

The preliminary negotiations seemed endless, with the governments
of three countries—the United States, Great Britain, and Saudi Arabia—and of course a number of oil companies now jockeying for position. The issue came to a head in early April 1944, when Secretary of
State Cordell Hull asked Ickes for three names to be added to a so-
called technical subcommittee of the PRC, which would be charged
with conducting the negotiations abroad.[111] Ickes chose three oil executives, one of whom, Ralph K. Davies, was both an officer and a
major stockholder in one of the firms involved in the negotiations, the
Standard Oil Company of California.

Fortas took exception to Davies's appointment, lecturing Ickes in a
four-page single-spaced memo about what seemed to him to be the
obvious conflict-of-interest problems here. "For the first time during
the years in which I have worked for you, I am compelled to advise
you that because of my convictions with respect to a fundamental issue, I can no longer be of service to you on certain matters within your
jurisdiction," he began. How could Ickes appoint oil executives who
stood to benefit from the negotiations to represent the interests of the
American government as well? he complained. But that was not all.

After virtually accusing his boss of selling out the public interest on the issue, Fortas objected to being "circumvented and ignored" in the making of this decision. It seemed to him that any person whose company stood to benefit by the course of these negotiations should be disqualified from participation in the talks. "I would not as a lawyer—and certainly I will not as a public official—permit myself to be associated with a situation in which a person having such a direct and immediate conflict of interest is your principal representative," he concluded.[112] With that Fortas resigned from the PRC, and offered his resignation as undersecretary of the interior, the latter of which was not accepted by Ickes.

It was a brash thing for the thirty-four-year-old subordinate to do—lecturing a man who had been in Roosevelt's cabinet longer than he had served in government on the subject of ethics. And it was absolutely the worst thing one could do with a man like Harold Ickes, who was so concerned with cleaning up graft and corruption in the previous administration's Department of the Interior that he had put a full-time detective on the department payroll to keep an eye on things. Biographers would later explain that the secretary, basically an honest man, "could never tolerate any questioning of his integrity" and "reacted vehemently to even the most muted suggestion of impropriety." And there was nothing muted about this suggestion.[113]

Not even a short accompanying memo from Fortas, reassuring the secretary that he had no intention to take this issue before the public, could soften the blow.[114] Instead, it made Ickes even madder, for he believed that by writing "the most extraordinary [memorandum] that I have ever received from anyone on my staff," Fortas was simply trying to "build a record" on his own behalf.[115] So he answered Fortas's four-page letter with an eight-page memo of his own.

Everything could be explained, he argued. Playing a shell game with his positions, he said that in appointing the oil executives he was acting in his capacity as petroleum administrator for war and not as secretary of the interior. Accordingly, there was no reason for Fortas to be apprised of these negotiations, which he argued had been going on much longer than had been charged.[116] In the end, Ickes made a fairly persuasive case that these particular oilmen were actually Hull's choices, and with their expertise could be trusted to represent the government's interests well. Should there be a conflict of interest in the future, Ickes said, he was willing to leave it to the appointees themselves to recognize it and disqualify themselves. In short, the whole matter was none of Fortas's business: "Recently the frequency of your memoranda and their tone have worried me. I would much have preferred to argue this out with you personally, even if we had not been able to come to the same point of view. Your memorandum left me no option except to meet it point by point at a cost to me in time and effort that it would seem to me you should have realized that I could ill afford."[117]

The two men did not discuss the issue again, but this was clearly the turning point in their relationship. Now Ickes, who liked to play favorites on his staff and ignore the rest, began to find fault with Fortas's work.

It was not long before he was given even more reason for criticism. After over a year of unproductive negotiations in the coal industry, John L. Lewis was back in the Interior Department demanding that the mine operators pay everyone forty dollars in back wages. By this time the labor leader seemed to have a good working relationship with Ickes, who had been running the mines since the government's seizure and was reasonably sympathetic to the plight of the miners. Moreover, Ickes prided himself that his penchant for straight and honest negotiations seemed acceptable to Lewis. After hundreds of wildcat strikes, Ickes decided to end the threat of more strikes with a personal meeting bringing all of the parties together to hammer out a compromise monetary settlement.

But Fortas had another idea. Charged with drafting the secretary's opening statement for the meeting, Fortas delivered his draft too close to the opening of the meeting for Ickes to make any alterations. So Ickes began reading the statement to the group as it was and, after running out of breath, handed it over to Fortas for completion.

The reason for all of the subterfuge soon became apparent. In what Ickes later called an "astonishing" final paragraph, John L. Lewis was referred to in such an "insulting" fashion that the union leader marched out of the meeting denouncing the entire process. This put Ickes in the untenable position of either publicly denouncing his undersecretary and losing the advantage to the coal miners, or supporting him and watching the entire negotiation break down. Normally, the statement would never have been published because of Ickes's rule that nothing went into the newspapers unless it had his approval. But Fortas had that covered as well, having already released it to the press. So Ickes had no choice but to apologize to Lewis, who was only partially placated. "I knew that you had not written it and I know who did write it," he told Ickes, demanding that the apology be repeated in front of all his men. "It was Fortas. Fortas hates the United Mine Workers."[118] Later, the union leader would tell reporters that Fortas was "evilly disposed toward coal miners and is our cold and calculating enemy."[119]

For his part, Fortas told his boss that it was not the United Mine Workers that he hated, but Lewis himself. Ickes seemed to have made up his mind in the dispute. Fortas's ruthless and privately manipulative style was not to his boss's liking. "The truth is that I am not sure that Fortas was not unwilling to use me, if he could, and by accident he was able to get away with it. This has shaken my confidence in Fortas considerably," Ickes confessed to his diary.[120]

After these incidents, the secretary started to look for things to criticize about his subordinate. It did not take long to find them. First, there was Fortas's lifestyle. With his wife still working in the New York law firm, the Fortases were involved in a commuting marriage. Every other weekend the undersecretary would travel to New York, leaving on Friday afternoon and not returning to work until the following Monday afternoon. Besides thinking that this was a "queer way for a man and his wife to be living," Ickes did not like the fact that Fortas was no longer constantly at his beck and call. So he complained to Fortas that he should not leave when both of them would be out of the office unless it was "a matter of imperative necessity." Fortas's explanation that he was using the time in New York to schedule working dinners, and to visit the New York offices of the War Relocation Authority, did not placate Ickes.[121]

Increasingly, Ickes became disenchanted with Fortas's work. A campaign speech he had drafted for Ickes in August was too sarcastic, referring to Thomas Dewey as "the little man who wasn't there," and had to be entirely redrafted.[122] There were too many calls on unimportant matters, and too many "memos for the record" when the two men disagreed on policy. And now the secretary was seeming to take the constant complaints from co-workers about Fortas's intrusive and ruthless operating style more seriously.[123]

All of this inevitably took its toll. Ickes now viewed Fortas as being too bright and too ambitious for his own good. Even issues that they had once handled together now became a source of criticism.[124] One such case was the relationship between the Division of Power and the Bureau of Reclamation. Since both groups reported to Fortas, he was able to tilt strongly toward the Division of Power during the inevitable disputes over water use. It was a slant that Ickes himself had fostered initially. But now, when the chief counsel for the bureau, J. Kennard Cheadle, gave up and resigned, after complaining that Fortas was "dictatorial, insolent and hard to get along with," he found a sympathetic ear in the secretary's office.[125] Fortas was "arrogant," another assistant, Michael Straus, confirmed, pointing out his practice of signing papers as "acting secretary" when the boss was out of the office.[126] Then, after hearing another of Fortas's usual complaints about a fellow reporting directly to Ickes and not going through the undersecretary, Ickes commented, "I have never had anyone talk to a fellow employee in my office the way Fortas did on one occasion."[127] Fortas's style and attitude had not changed at all, but Ickes was seeing it through different eyes after the PRC and Lewis incidents.

By December 1944, the break had become complete. "I have reluctantly come to the conclusion that Fortas is too much disposed to take from my shoulders the running of the Department, particularly, and that when it comes to selecting personnel he plays favorites," he wrote in his diary.[128] Then, three weeks later, Ickes added, "Fortas is always seeing the worst in things and he likes to think of himself as always saving a situation after 'working hard' on it. He does not let his light shine under a bushel and he is never reluctant to give himself credit. I don't mean to be too critical because Fortas is a very able man and has been and is useful. I think undoubtedly, however, that he has a disposition to enhance his own value and I haven't the slightest doubt any more that he is very ambitious."[129] Others, of course, were saying the same about the secretary, but only one of them could be the boss.

With the bloom definitely off their relationship, Ickes decided to turn the control of the Division of Power over to Assistant Secretary Straus, and turn a deaf ear when Fortas complained.[130] But the problems between them continued. In February 1945, Fortas made what Ickes considered the unforgivable mistake of attending a meeting at the White House in his place without first getting permission from the secretary. Since Ickes had, in fact, refused the invitation to attend the meeting, this drew a public rebuke from him. He added in his diary: "I do not know on what theory a man can project himself into a meeting as a substitute for me when I do not know anything about it."[131] When Ickes began to suspect Fortas of leaking items to columnist Leonard Lyons, and refused to authorize his memoranda on personnel and policy, it was clear that the young man's time in the department was drawing to a close.[132]

The death of Franklin Roosevelt on April 12, 1945, made this fact even clearer. With Harry Truman as president, the New Dealers were scrambling for cover, and Abe Fortas was no exception. Everyone's career was at a crossroads, as more and more cronies of the former senator from Missouri were inserted into the various agencies. For those New Dealers who remained in government, the questions were obvious. Would Truman replace them? Would others be removed first, offering the chance for advancement? Or should they leave now and make their best deal elsewhere?

The Interior Department was ripe for change as an assortment of people were being touted around Washington as possible replacements for Ickes. So in July, Fortas began fielding offers of new job possibilities. When he gave Ickes the impression that he would resign around the first of September, that was fine with the now thoroughly offended secretary.[133] The accumulation of small slights to the secretary's ego and the inevitable clash of two very strong personalities had taken their toll.

As usual, when faced with the stress of another career crisis point, Fortas now fell into his familiar pattern of anxiety and paralysis. Fortunately, his friends were still willing to try to help place him. Washington lawyer Tommy Corcoran tried in late August to put him on the United States Court of Appeals. When it turned out that the president had committed the seat elsewhere, Corcoran spoke to Fortas about going onto the U.S. District Court for the District of Columbia. But Corcoran quickly discovered that the young man's confusion should not be interpreted as a lack of ambition. Fortas said that he was willing to take the lower-court seat only if there was a prospect for later advancement up the judicial ladder. So "Tommy the Cork" was off and running again, talking up the new idea with Attorney General Tom Clark.[134]

Meanwhile, Fortas tried to discuss his new prospects with Ickes, but the secretary had little patience for such talk. Believing that the young man wanted to be told how much he was needed in the Interior Department, Ickes would only say that he should "look out for his own best interests and he alone could tell what they were."[135] In fact, the secretary had decided privately that maybe a resignation would not be a bad thing overall.

With the search for a judicial appointment stalled, Fortas began to look for other prospects. He had William O. Douglas writing letters of recommendation for law school teaching positions all over the country. When positions looked promising, though, Fortas would be unwilling to commit himself, in hopes of getting something better. For this reason, he rejected an offer from the University of California at

Berkeley.[136] Thinking that a return to Yale Law School might be possible, Fortas also let Dean Ashbel Gulliver know that he was "definitely interested and would accept an appointment at any time." So,
by the end of September, a recommendation went forward to the university president, Charles Seymour, for the appointment of three full
professors—Fortas, Thomas I. Emerson, and Harold Lasswell.[137] This
preliminary recommendation letter, though, had one interesting feature. The dean warned that of the three nominees, the Fortas appointment might be a "somewhat controversial case" with the conservative
elements in the legal profession. In fact, later in the letter he made it
clear that there were elements within the law school itself that did not
back Fortas. (Whatever opponents existed must have been in the administration, as the vote of the faculty was later reported to be unanimously in favor of the appointment.)[138]

The fact that Yale was now interested in hiring Fortas at all was an
indication of the great change that had occurred in the relationship
between the two. In 1940, the law faculty had passed over Fortas in
favor of several other men for new faculty openings.[139] But now, six
years later, at least the faculty members seemed to be very interested
in having Abe Fortas rejoin them. Yale's law school was in a crucial
period. Salaries had been held artificially low during the war years and
many faculty members were openly discussing the prospect of leaving.
Since Yale was seeking to make its curriculum more "progressive" by
updating its courses to modern standards, the Fortas appointment
seemed to make a great deal of sense.[140] But once more, Abe Fortas
had made too many enemies. Some of the more WASPish graduates
wondered whether the Jewish New Dealer could be a good "Yale
man," and in the end, he wasn't welcome there either.[141]

Fortunately for Fortas, his old luck reappeared. It seemed that whenever his career had been threatened, someone—whether it be Jerome
Frank, William O. Douglas, or Harold Ickes—always appeared on the
horizon to throw a lifeline. Just about the time it was becoming crucial
for Fortas to find a new position, his former law-school teacher Thurman Arnold appeared to offer him one.

Bored by the dullness of serving on the United States Court of Appeals, Arnold had resigned in July 1945 and gone into a private legal
partnership with Arne Wiprud, one of his associates in the Justice Department's Antitrust Division. He and Wiprud, an expert in transportation law, had taken on a major case involving the effort of Robert
Young, a prominent railroad man, and Cleveland financier Cyrus
Eaton to take over the operation of the Pullman company, which had a

monopoly over the operation of railroad sleeping cars. Naturally, this effort to gain control of the major share of passenger train traffic in America was soon opposed by the legal firms representing every major railroad company. Arnold and Wiprud valiantly characterized this opposition as a violation of antitrust laws—and promptly lost their case.[142]

With the loss of the case, the two men's legal partnership was on the rocks, which brought Arnold to the doorstep of his former associate at Yale. Arnold knew enough about Fortas from the Yale days, and had seen enough in his dealings with Interior from the Justice Department, to appreciate the brilliance of this young man. Since Fortas had lined up a five-hundred-dollar-a-month retainer to become the director and treasurer, as well as special counsel, for the American Molasses Company, the basis for a partnership was there. When negotations for a three-way partnership with Wiprud broke down, Fortas toyed with the idea of either renting an office from Arnold or entering into partnership with Assistant Solicitor General Hugh Cox and Fowler Hamilton of the Foreign Economic Administration. However, Fortas worried that his connection with Cox and Hamilton would not generate enough business.[143] At that point, Arnold's partnership with Wiprud dissolved and, in what he called "the smartest decision I ever made," Arnold decided to snare Fortas.[144]

While Arnold courted Fortas with an offer of a full partnership, the young man's alternatives were running out. When word came from Ickes's rumor mill that his undersecretary was being touted by his friends to take over the entire department, with several senators and Supreme Court justices already behind the move, he had endured enough. Perhaps hoping that it would get back to Fortas, the secretary told Tommy Corcoran that if a resignation was forthcoming, "the sooner the better."

Seeing Fortas's hesitation in accepting Arnold's offer, Corcoran theorized to Ickes that Fortas's wife, Carolyn Agger, was making it "difficult" for him to make a career decision. "She makes more money than he does," Ickes recorded in his diary, "and she may even be a better lawyer, although there is no doubt that Abe is an able lawyer."[145] To a man who believed that no women should be lawyers, as opposed to Corcoran's more liberal view that no *married* women should be lawyers, this seemed to be a likely explanation of Fortas's indecision. By the end of the year even close family friend William O. Douglas would be agreeing that the relative difference in the Fortases' incomes appeared to be a problem.[146] Indeed, Carolyn Agger was later described by reporters and people who knew her as someone who liked money and the things that it could buy. Reportedly, at one time in her life she owned 150 pairs of shoes, a priceless jewelry collection, a houseful of Victorian antiques and furniture, and a portable rink for ice skating in her backyard.[147]

By early November 1945, Fortas's hypochondria began to resurface. Though privately believing that Fortas was "a little soft," Ickes approved a ten-day vacation for him to recover and consider his fate.[148] Fortas had not completely lost his perspective, though, as he jokingly suggested to Douglas that perhaps he should join a law firm named "Iwanttoberichtoo."

It was not until the middle of December that Fortas finally appeared to have made up his mind. After telling Ickes on the fifteenth of December that he had finally decided to leave the Interior Department for a partnership with Thurman Arnold, Fortas promised to have the formal resignation letter on his desk in a week. But cutting this last tie seemed to be too much for him, and he delayed for several days after his self-imposed deadline before acting.[149]

While he seemed to be certain enough of his direction to notify the law school on the seventeenth that he would not be coming, no one told his detractors there.[150] Someone leaked the names of the three nominees for full professorships to broadcaster Fulton Lewis, who announced to the nation on December 18 that the men were so controversial that they had been held over for thirty days of additional consideration. If the leak was calculated to build opposing fires against the nominees, the strategy worked perfectly. Open season was declared on Abe Fortas. Over the next month, Fortas's detractors—many of them former government co-workers—appeared and loudly protested that he would surely taint the sacred reputation of the school.[151]

The law school was so upset by this leak of confidential information to the press that a protest was lodged with the university president. But it was too late to help the main target.[152] The telegrams and letters that landed on the doorstep of a sympathetic Yale President Seymour characterized Fortas as a "pinkish tinted" man determined to brainwash the flowers of the young legal community. Fortas was "an instrument for propaganda" to one, "opposed to the American principles" to another, and "unfit to teach young men in a truly American school of law" to a third. To some, though, he was just too Jewish and too much from the "extreme left wing" to be of Yale caliber.[153] It made no difference to these people that his religious affiliation was in name only, and that his commitment to New Deal philosophy was so loose that a Texas congressman was comfortable with his views. What mattered to them was his name and his reputation—and they didn't like either.

The attack had a definite impact. First, the president backed away from his commitment to Fortas. Then in mid-January 1946, when Fortas withdrew his own name, Seymour "confidentially" leaked the news to an offended alumnus, giving him the impression that the young man did not have a choice given the mounting negative reaction.[154]

Even after making his decision, Fortas seemed reluctant to reveal to his allies that he was going into private practice instead of Yale.[155] The whole departure process gave Ickes a sense of déjà vu: "It took a long time for Abe to produce his resignation. . . . Fortas has put me through a repetition of what he did when he was in the Navy one moment and out the next. In those days he seemed utterly incapable of making up his mind and taking a firm position. I always felt that he wanted me to throw my weight against his going into the Navy which would have left him with a clear conscience."[156] Now Ickes had the impression that the young man still wanted to be begged to return to Interior. For his part, Tommy Corcoran, having failed to put Fortas on a court, was still arguing that he should go to New Haven. Finally Fortas insisted that he had to go into private practice to make a place for William O. Douglas in case he wanted to leave the Supreme Court.[157] The idea that Douglas would leave the court for private practice was almost as preposterous as the idea that he would need anyone's help in doing so. If the justice was part of this reasoning process it was news to him, as he was asking Ickes about Fortas's plans even after the announcement of the undersecretary's resignation had hit the papers.[158] It seemed that his true reason for going into private practice—the opportunity to make a great deal more money—was one that Fortas did not care to discuss. His indecision, however, gave his enemies an ideal opportunity to vent their spleen toward him.

After months of vacillation, Fortas suddenly acted. Though Ickes had been told that the young man would stay on until the beginning of February, the secretary came in on Monday, January 21, 1946, to find Fortas's desk cleaned out. The firm of Arnold and Fortas opened for business that same day.[159] Later, Fortas would insist that he had left Interior with only his "hat and coat and debts."[160] But the Field Marshal had begun one final campaign before he left, and in so doing had already ensured his immediate financial future.

.   .   .

After aiding Abe Fortas's meteoric rise to the top of the bureaucratic
world, Harold Ickes had a right to expect that his favors would be
repaid. But when the time came, he was destined to learn what Jerome
Frank and others had learned before him—for some people Abe Fortas's loyalty seemed to begin and end with the term of his employment.

February 1946 had become a very bad month for the interior secretary. The problem began when Edwin Pauley, former treasurer of the
Democratic party and a close friend of President Truman, was nominated as undersecretary of the navy. The choice shocked Ickes, who
recalled that on September 6, 1944, with the presidential campaign
heating up, Pauley, Democratic party operative Robert Hannegan, and
party publicity director Paul Porter had come to visit him with plans
for a series of nationwide radio campaign broadcasts. After they had
discussed plans for the campaign, Hannegan and Porter left the room
so that Pauley could have a private chat with Ickes. Ickes understood
Pauley, who claimed to be speaking for the president, to say that if the
Interior Department did not assert legal title over offshore oil fields in
California, he would be able to raise $300,000 from the oilmen in
California who had a vested interest in the fields. While the secretary
gave no immediate response because the matter was still before the
courts, he privately found this to be "the rawest proposition that has
ever been made to me."[161]

When he was called to testify in the confirmation hearings for
Pauley, the secretary decided to tell the story as he recalled it even
though it was destined to provide election year fodder for the Republicans. The fact that this account was entered in his diary gave Ickes
small comfort, knowing that he would be locked in a credibility battle
with the president's man and a member of his own party. Fortunately
for the secretary, though, he had protected himself by bringing in a
witness to listen to the original conversation with Pauley—Undersecretary Abe Fortas.

Before testifying, Ickes wanted to make sure that Fortas would back
him up. So he anxiously called Fortas in San Juan, Puerto Rico. As
they talked on the phone, Ickes could not have been more reassured.
His former assistant did remember the conversation in every detail,
and was prepared to testify in that manner. Pauley had talked about the
offshore oil leases, he said, and also about the prospects for heavy
contributions from the oilmen. So Ickes delighted the Republicans by
confidently telling his story to the Senate Naval Affairs Committee

later that week. Since Pauley had denied this allegation under oath, the stage was set for Fortas to decide the issue for the Senate and the nation. Since both Ickes and Pauley seemed to have vested interests of their own to protect, it would be left to the presumably neutral witness—who was now entirely out of government—to decide the matter.

But while there was no doubt in Ickes's mind that Fortas knew the truth, he continued to worry about whether he would tell it. So the secretary was relieved when Fortas came in after returning from Puerto Rico to tell him how surprised he had been at the time at the nature of Pauley's conversation. In fact, he even had records that confirmed Ickes's account that they had been in the meeting together on September 6, 1944. Fortas said that even Paul Porter now knew that he was going to verify the secretary's account in testifying before the Senate committee. With a smile on his lips, Fortas concluded to Ickes, "Pauley talked in front of a witness for you after he had gotten rid of his own witnesses."[162]

But something had happened by the time "Ickes's witness" made his way to the Senate hearing. Ickes was now *former* secretary of the interior. The prospect of being a crippled member of the cabinet meetings that would probably now include Pauley was too much for him to bear. Ickes had offered his resignation to Roosevelt many times. Now there was a man in the White House who quickly accepted it. And just as quickly, Fortas's memory seemed to fade when he faced the Senate questioners. The prospect of testifying against the combined forces of the White House and the Democratic party no longer seemed palatable when it was on behalf of a *former* cabinet secretary.

When questioned by the senators about Ickes's account, Fortas said that while he did recall the conversation, the value of any testimony on his part was suspect since he had "kept no notes, [and] made no memoranda," and had not "specifically charge[d his memory] with the details of the conversation."[163] For some reason, the calendar pad that Ickes had been told verified the account now could not be found, and neither could the memories that went with it. So all Fortas would say definitely say for the record was "I have a recollection that at that time, when the three of us remained in the office, Mr. Pauley mentioned contributions to the Democratic campaign by oil interests: and that he also mentioned the tidelands suit."[164]

In short, Fortas was supporting neither side. They had talked—about two different subjects—and whether they were connected or not was up to the senators' imagination. This testimony was certainly much less than Ickes had been led to expect was coming. And it was certainly not what the senators were seeking. One by one, four senators repeatedly asked him versions of the same question: Were the two subjects connected? Each time Fortas answered, he moved further and further from Ickes's side and more toward Pauley's.

SENATOR TOBEY: Mr. Fortas, referring to that conversation which you listened to and were present at, could you say whether or not the clear sense of Mr. Pauley's remarks was that the filing of the court suit would be unwise politically?

FORTAS: I knew at the time, to the best of my recollection, and I knew subsequently, that Mr. Pauley was opposed to the filing of the suit. Now, Senator, perhaps one of the reasons why I did not make any attempt to charge my memory with the details of this conversation was that Secretary Ickes had made up his mind. He had made up his mind he would recommend that the suit be brought and that the suit be pressed.

TOBEY: Did you understand, to the best of your memory, that Mr. Pauley told him that the filing of the suit might be a deterrent or would deter California oil men from contributing to the campaign?

FORTAS: I don't know what Mr. Pauley had in his mind. And it is a little difficult, Senator, to separate recollection from reconstruction, in a situation of this sort. It seems to me perfectly obvious, though, that when you bring a suit against people, it acts as a deterrent upon campaign contributions.

TOBEY: Did you get the impression, listening to that conversation, that he did not think the suit should be filed?

FORTAS: Perhaps the most accurate way of saying this is that Mr. Pauley's opposition to the suit was well known to me.

One by one, the senators exhausted themselves trying to jog Fortas's memory. Finally, after all of this verbal fencing, he testified more unequivocally, "I do not remember that there was a contingent factor expressed by Mr. Pauley."[165]

By the end of this appearance, everyone was confused. Fortas had been so evasive that the newspapers split half and half over whether he had supported Ickes or Pauley. What he had said was neither the truth nor a lie. It was, however, misleading. And there was little doubt that in this dramatic moment he had failed to give the unequivocal support to Ickes that had been promised. The impression, Ickes was later to say, was much like that "of a man balancing himself carefully on the edge of a sharp razor." When the hearing appearance was over, Fortas called Ickes to explain that "the questioning was the most inept that he had ever seen." But in fact, that had nothing to do with it.[166] By this time, Fortas had his own agenda—building a law practice. If this meant deserting the man who had given him his big break, so be it.

Ickes did not see it this way, though. He had a different explanation: "In a way I am disappointed but really I did not expect too much from Abe. No one else did either. I have been the champion of the civil and human rights of the Jews all of my life but I have always known that they would not fight and that in a pinch they would either equivocate or run. Abe Fortas proved this to me all over again. . . . He could not slough off the racial habits of 2000 years."[167] But Ickes was wrong. Religion had nothing to do with it. This was an exercise of raw ambition, and Fortas was prepared to sacrifice Ickes's career for his own.

III

THE
LEGAL
GUNSLINGER

There were two camps of alumni from the Roosevelt era in 1946: those who labored further for a New Deal for the nation, and those who wanted a "new deal" for themselves. For the most part, though he wanted people to believe otherwise, Abe Fortas fell into the latter camp. The difference between the two worlds, and the obligations imposed by each, was apparent to all of the former Rooseveltians. One day Congressman Lyndon Johnson asked two of his closest former New Deal allies, now practicing law in the city, Abe Fortas and Tommy Corcoran, whether the rejuvenation of the National Youth Administration might not provide jobs for the returning veterans from World War II. Corcoran pooh-poohed the idea: "Lyndon m'boy, Roosevelt is dead, the New Deal is over, you've got to come into the real world." When Fortas readily agreed, Johnson stomped out of the room. Minutes later, he returned with eyes flashing. His friends were "traitors to Roosevelt," he shouted, they had "sold out" to the corporations to build their law firms. "Which will it be, God or Mammon?'' Johnson challenged. ''You have to choose: God or Mammon?'' This from a man who was claiming at that moment to have amassed mammon in the amount of one million dollars.[1] The hushed silence in the room was broken only when Corcoran left in a huff.

In Johnson's terms, Fortas still wanted God, but not at the expense of his mammon. He had already done some good; now it was time to do well. Having helped to fashion the rules, he found it so easy to switch sides and help to interpret and bend those rules for the very corporations that had been targets of his earlier governmental efforts. Later, Fortas would argue that he had not forgotten his past and had not deserted his old principles. He would describe the transition to private practice in almost religious terms: ''The purpose of the [Arnold and Fortas] firm was to provide a means for its two partners to make a living. Neither partner quite knew how this was to be done. At the outset, neither had a single client or any prospects; but both were dedicated to the great cause of economic survival which they had undertaken. Somehow, by the mysterious process of law and life, the venture went forward, and increasing numbers of partners and associates joined it.''[2]

While this made nice theater, in reality the location of clients was no mystery to either Fortas or Arnold. In fact, Fortas had already seen to it that food would be kept on the table for a long time to come. He simply stole his first lucrative client—the island of Puerto Rico—from the roster of the Interior Department.

The representation of the commonwealth of Puerto Rico's legal interests in Washington had long been a problem. Too many governmental offices, too much overlap, too many changing faces, resulting in too little coordination, and too little concern in Washington were just a few of the problems that the island had to face. In 1943, after Puerto Rico expressed dissatisfaction with its private legal assistance, the Department of Justice was given the responsibility for the island's legal representation, at no expense. But despite the fact that only one of the eighteen cases briefed and argued before the federal courts was lost, it was not a happy marriage. Dissatisfaction continued over the bureaucratic snarls, and more and more reliance was placed on Undersecretary of the Interior Fortas to serve as a lifeline for the island.

In 1946, there was a new call for change. Less than two weeks after Fortas had left the government, he was in Puerto Rico, at Governor Rexford Tugwell's request, to work on some litigation problems for the island's Agricultural Company. While care had been taken to secure the informal consent of the Interior Department for the visit in late January, Fortas and Tugwell had neglected to say what was really being planned. After his arrival in San Juan on January 30, the two men spoke with future governor Luis Muñoz-Marin over the course of Fortas's eight-day stay about much bigger plans. What if the newest Washington law firm, Arnold and Fortas, were to take on the island as a client?

Without discussing the matter with an Interior Department official then visiting Puerto Rico, the governor simply sent a letter to Thurman Arnold on February 5 saying that the Office of Puerto Rican Matters intended to retain the firm on an annual basis. Since Fortas was still working on the island at the time, it is entirely likely that he was consulted on the wording and timing of this letter, if not put to the task of actually writing it.[3]

By the sixteenth of February, though, everything looked like it might fall apart. With the wholesale defections and firings of New Dealers from the Truman administration, Fortas became concerned that the cantankerous Tugwell might leave, too. So Fortas argued in Washington for Tugwell's retention as governor, and wrote to him advising that he "sit tight and keep quiet."[4] Then, three days later, Fortas asked Tugwell if he couldn't "complete arrangements" for the retainer agreement as soon as possible, because the legal work ahead would take "a good deal of my own time."

Indeed, in a matter of weeks Tugwell was out—but not before Arnold and Fortas had a new lucrative account. To the surprise of the Interior Department, on February 26, the Office of Puerto Rican Matters simply issued a press release stating that Arnold and Fortas had been retained as counsel "in all future proceedings before the United States Supreme Court, the United States Circuit Court in Boston, and agencies of the Federal Government." So, for the next thirty-three months, the island of Puerto Rico was committed to paying Arnold and Fortas an annual retainer of twelve thousand dollars, plus any additional legal expenses over and above that amount.[5]

When the Interior Department was informed about this new legal arrangement, eyebrows were raised. From Puerto Rico's standpoint it made perfect sense. How could one put a value on the prospect of having the former number-two man in the Interior Department, with all of his knowledge of the problems facing the island and the key people in Washington who might help, as a paid advocate? However, the revolving-door aspects of hiring a government official just out of the very offices he would be lobbying raised questions. So the departmental solicitor, Warner Gardner, searched his files for precedents to argue against the arrangement, and found something written by an Interior Department official almost exactly a year before. The island had tried to hire private counsel in response to its many legal problems then too, but the request had been denied. The reasons were stated by the official in such unequivocal language that it was hard to imagine the matter ever being raised again: "I believe that continuing representation of a Government or a governmental agency by private attorneys is unsound and unwise. . . . Governments and governmental agencies should in my opinion be represented by lawyers who are public officials. In my opinion, it is neither seemly nor appropriate for governmental agencies to be represented by counsel who are not regularly constituted public officials. . . . [It] is apt to lead to embarrassment, regardless of the unimpeachable character of the private attorneys who might be concerned."[6]

The name of the official protesting the island's intentions so vigorously? Undersecretary of the Interior Abe Fortas. But, of course, that had been before Fortas went into private practice. When Solicitor Gardner raised the apparent change of principles with the former undersecretary, Fortas argued that he would be merely "supplementing" rather than "superseding" the legal services provided by the federal government. But Gardner had a better idea—he simply let the new Washington lawyers have the account all to themselves.[7]

Fortas was not the only one gathering clients. His new partner, Thurman Arnold, had friends of his own. The former snipe hunter from Yale and native of Wyoming was a remarkably versatile genius, with a wit that could have launched him on a new career as a comedian. During the course of his career he won a seat in the state legislature, where he delighted his colleagues by once nominating himself for Speaker, filibustering for three days on his own behalf, and then dramatically announcing that he would not accept the nomination. Then he served as mayor of Laramie after a nine-vote election victory. In 1927 Arnold became the dean of West Virginia University's College of Law, from which he moved three years later to the faculty of Yale Law School. After a sterling teaching career, Arnold was drafted by Franklin Roosevelt in 1938 to be assistant attorney general in charge of the Antitrust Division of the Justice Department. During the next five years, Arnold launched 230 antitrust suits—more than had been filed in the fifty-year history of the Sherman Act—against some of the most prominent corporations in America. In 1943 it was on to the United States Court of Appeals, where Arnold became bored quickly: "All I

do is sit here and write little essays to read at the end of the trials.''
Private legal practice appealed to him more, as evidenced by the chapter in his book *Fair Fights and Foul* on the topic titled, ''The Practice
of Law Is a Profession of Great Dignity, the Pursuit of Which Requires
Great Learning.'' So two years later he left the court for private practice.[8]

Judge Arnold, as he was called, was a character of the first order.
His remarkable intuitional genius ran so far ahead of his tongue that he
would ''degenerate into an almost incoherent succession of elliptical
sentences and phrases that mean a lot of Arnold, but very little to the
unpracticed listener.''[9] On top of that, he was so absentminded that he
once delivered a masterful summation in a case for the plaintiff, only
to be reminded that he was in fact representing the defendant. Whereupon Arnold simply gave a new speech refuting everything he had just
said, and won the case.[10]

Arnold began building his law practice with Arne Wiprud by turning
to his old New Deal contacts. James Farley, a former postmaster general for FDR who was now serving as president of Coca-Cola, was one
such example. After seventy-five years the patent on the formula to the
drink was running out, and soon new competitors would be springing
up everywhere at the company's expense. So Farley hired Arnold hoping that he might extend his practice of law to the practice of some
politics. Could he lobby old friends in Congress and get a renewal on
the patent? Of course he could, said Arnold, for the right fee. So, in a
pattern used by the firm in many of its later actions, litigation was
avoided in favor of lobbying in other arenas for the rules of the game
to be changed. When the effort succeeded, Coca-Cola became one of
the cornerstone clients of Arnold's new firm. Later, an old New Deal
buddy of Arnold's asked him, during a fancy lunch at the law firm's
expense, how he could reconcile his work for the monopolistic Coke
with his principles as a former Justice Department trustbuster. Chuck-
ling over his dinner, Arnold conceded that this was a good question,
explaining, ''But they are paying us so *much* money.''[11]

The story of the growth of Arnold's law firm after Fortas joined him
could fill a book in itself. Just the highlights, though, show how Fortas, a thirty-six-year-old ex–government bureaucrat, could in less than
two decades become one of the most powerful behind-the-scenes lawyers in America. With the money from Puerto Rico and Coca-Cola it
was possible for the two men to expand their firm very quickly. The
two of them began with a single associate, Milton V. Freeman, in a
townhouse once owned by Theodore Roosevelt on the corner of Nine-

teenth and N streets in Washington. Then in May 1947 they added a new name partner—Paul Porter.

Porter liked to call himself the Bobo Newsom of the bureaucrats, referring to the pitcher who had played for countless baseball teams, because over the years he had held so many different jobs in the Democratic administrations of Roosevelt and Truman. Most recently, as chief of the United States Economic Mission to Greece with the rank of ambassador, he had launched the new Truman Doctrine and helped to end the Soviet-inspired civil war there. Prior to that he had served in the Agricultural Adjustment Administration, twice in the Office of Price Administration, as FDR's personal troubleshooter in the War Food Administration, as publicity director for the Democratic National Committee during the 1944 Roosevelt presidential campaign, and as chairman of the Federal Communications Commission.[12]

Porter was brought into the firm more for his extensive government experience than for his legal ability. Not considered a high-powered legal intellect (one lawyer called Porter's efforts in one losing case "the most stupid argument I'd ever heard"), Porter's story-telling ability and smooth salesmanlike personality were ideal for building a law firm and keeping people laughing while doing it.[13] Porter liked the frills of the firm—the large black limousine in the driveway with the chauffeur waiting, the membership at Burning Tree Country Club, and the dinners at the fanciest restaurants in town. And his gift for quick wit was renowned. Once, when pressed as FCC chairman for praise of the networks on their memorial programming after the death of Franklin Roosevelt, he told a media executive that it would be "commending a man for refraining from farting in a cathedral."[14]

Another time, a fellow member of Burning Tree accosted him with the words "I understand your firm represents only Communists and homosexuals."

"That's right, Senator," he replied. "What can we do for you?"[15]

Despite his shortcomings, Porter was what the firm now needed. His skill at presenting entertaining arguments before the courts fit perfectly with Arnold's intuitive genius for plotting legal strategy and Fortas's brilliance at researching the necessary precedents. The differences in their skills were best explained by Thurman Arnold, when he commented once, "Well, I said I'd try that case carload by carload; Paul would probably try it bunch by bunch; but only Abe would try it banana by banana."[16]

They were now members of the army of "Washington lawyers," a special breed of attorneys whose work is one part from the lawbooks, one part lawyerlike counseling, and three parts whom they know in town. Of course, the partners violently disagreed with this assessment. "We are marketing what we know, not who we know," said Arnold once. "We are representing people who have a lot more influence in this town than any of us ever had."[17] Fortas later described his mission in almost biblical terms: "The Nation's business was struggling under the mass of rules, regulations and restrictions which World War II had spawned. . . . Lawyers who were veterans of the New Deal and government service were presumed to be qualified to find their way through the maze, to guide and assist companies which had unfamiliar problems."[18]

To others, though, this was just called "practicing influence mixed with law."[19] Indeed, the complementary bureaucratic contacts and experiences of the three men were clearly very useful to their efforts in many of their cases. For example, one case involved Keifer-Stewart, an Ohio liquor wholesaler challenging the right of the Seagram and Calvert distilleries to cut off shipments when it had refused to follow established minimum wholesale prices. Since this case touched on the wartime price control statutes that Porter had helped to draft, the antitrust laws that Arnold had helped to enforce in the Justice Department, and much of the knowledge gained by Fortas in governing the Puerto Rican rum industry in the Interior Department, it was not surprising when the firm won a $1.2 million judgment for the client.[20]

With each well-publicized success by the firm came additions to the list of prominent corporate clients. And, in the vernacular of the legal community, these were "deep-pocketed" clients indeed. Pan American Airways, Lever Brothers, Western Union, Otis Elevator, Sun Oil, and the American Broadcasting Company were on the rolls by 1951. When the Federal Trade Commission challenged Federated Department Stores' acquisition of Foley's Department Store in Houston, Federated president Fred Lazarus, Jr., was unhappy with the response of his company's attorney. Having heard about Fortas, Lazarus phoned for help, and the attorney drafted a new reply in thirty-six hours. Lazarus was so impressed with the product, and its level of comprehensibility to the lay reader, that the firm of Arnold, Fortas and Porter was hired to deal with Federated's national matters.[21] (Soon Fortas became a director of the company and a member of its executive committee.) Later, such clients as Braniff International, the National Retail Merchants Association, Cyrus Eaton, Unilever, Investors Diversified Services, and Philip Morris were added to the list.[22]

For many, this made Fortas no more than a legal gunslinger, toting his legal briefs and lawbooks into any battle where the pay was right. Support for business monopolies, protection of the cigarette industry, making life worse for consumers—the list of legal accomplishments seemed antithetical to the interests of the common man he had represented so well in the New Deal. But Fortas did not see it that way: "Lawyers are agents, not principals; and they should neither criticize nor tolerate criticisms based upon the character of the client whom they represent or the cause that they prosecute or defend. They cannot and should not accept responsibility for the client's practices. Rapists, murderers, child-abusers, General Motors, Dow Chemical—and even cigarette manufacturers and stream polluters—are entitled to a lawyer; and any lawyer who undertakes their representation must be immune from criticism for so doing."[23] Once more, he was simply the technician, now bending the laws that he had once helped to make.

Of course the size of the firm also increased to handle the growing caseload. From three partners and four associates in 1947, a decade later the roster had grown to nine partners and six associates. The firm took a huge jump in size in 1960 when Carolyn Agger took the Washington branch of Paul, Weiss, Rifkind, Wharton, and Garrison with her to her husband's firm after the death of partner Randolph Paul.

And of course, as the client list grew, the firm needed more space. It took over a covey of four other surrounding townhouses, and in time would move catty-corner across the street to incorporate an additional five townhouses. The main building on this legal campus reeked of success. Upon entering through the large jalousied doors, one passed under a huge chandelier and up a carpeted stairway to a receptionist. Fortas's own tastefully decorated office was dominated by a huge desk made from the top of a Victorian grand piano.[24]

With all of this came filled coffers. The size of Fortas's salary depends on whose version one believes. Estimates of his earnings range from $150,000 to $325,000 a year, with most hovering in the $200,000 area. When added to Carolyn Agger's salary, reported to have been in the $100,000 range, this provided the Fortases with more than enough money to support their rich lifestyle.[25] There was their classic 1953 Rolls-Royce, the fancy Georgetown house, the summer house in Westport, Connecticut, the collection of objets d'art, antiques, and Chinese art, the three French poodles, Agger's 150 pairs of shoes, and the housekeeper. Soon, it was rumored that Fortas played his violin while driving around Washington in the backseat of his

Rolls, and that he spent his free time carefully polishing the crystal in his chandelier.[26]

This ostentatious lifestyle "kind of worried" one old New Deal ally, Clifford Durr, while others now say more bluntly that they found it "unforgivable" and "traitorous to the cause."[27] "I could have gone downtown and made my fortune like Fortas and Tommy Corcoran," said one old New Dealer practicing law for the underdogs now, "but I didn't want to be like every punk in this town. Those guys were not good New Dealers, giving in to corporate interests which were so contrary to the New Deal and all we stood for."[28] And when one compares Fortas's way of life with the financial problems of Durr, it is not hard to understand why they felt this way.

Fortas himself was a brilliant attorney. "As a lawyer, Abe Fortas had it all," recalls one law partner. "He had a penetrating intelligence, an extraordinarily quick mind, and outstanding analytical ability. His oral arguments were a superb combination of the rational and the dramatic. A newspaperman who followed one of his more publicized corporate cases told me he would rather hear Abe Fortas argue a motion than see a Broadway musical."[29] His strength was in taking the most complex legal doctrines and making them understandable to all those listening, no matter what their age, experience, or level of education.

Since Fortas was the most organized of the three name partners, the job of managing the firm fell to him. This did not make the younger lawyers working for the firm very happy. "No one liked Abe Fortas— he was a son of a bitch to all those below him," said one attorney.[30] "You should hear what the junior lawyers who come back here say about Fortas," reported an administrator at Yale Law School. "They say he's cold, arrogant, a real son of a bitch, and worse."[31] On the other hand, Fortas was a perfectionist, a "meticulous legal craftsman." "Take it back and put some poetry into it," he ordered one subordinate upon being handed a brief.[32] Since his specialty was words, and the shaping of appellate briefs and arguments to persuade even the most recalcitrant judges, Fortas required that his young associates excel in these areas. "Oh he demands perfection," said one old friend. "He would rework the Lord's Prayer if it came in a brief."[33] But, despite the negative assessments of his work style, perhaps the best view of Fortas was offered by one lawyer who worked with him: "Of all the men I have met he most knows why he is doing what he does. I don't like the SOB, but if I were in trouble I'd want him on my side. He's the most resourceful, the boldest, the most thorough lawyer I know."[34]

But his friends saw a different side of Abe Fortas. Personally, he was a devoted friend and a delightful dinner companion with a dry wit. Once, upon being told that a close friend was to face a congressional committee in New York but could not bring a lawyer, Fortas gave the necessary advice and then said that he would be in the city that day anyway, advising another client, in case more discussion should be needed. Only later did the friend realize that Fortas had gone out of his way to be in New York solely for the purpose of remaining available for his friend's problem. (Ironically, what the congressmen really wanted to know was the nature of the friend's relationship to a man named Fortas.)[35]

Just as there was a dual nature to Fortas's personality, so there was another side of the firm's law practice to balance off its lucrative corporate work. This was the time when government officials such as Senator Joseph McCarthy, with his investigating committees, and Pat McCarran, chairman of the Senate Judiciary Committee, were using their positions to challenge the loyalty of others. As Thurman Arnold put it in his inimitable style, "Everyone here who can investigate is investigating. Everyone who can't investigate is being investigated. Our firm is trying to do its part in the conflict."[36]

When a man named Morton Friedman, a friend of the firm's associate Milton V. Freeman, was discharged in 1946 from the War Manpower Commission for alleged disloyalty, he went to Arnold, Fortas and Porter for help. In a brief on the case to the Supreme Court, Abe Fortas eloquently stated the nature of the problem here: "This assault on freedom of opinion will not stop with Government employees. Assaults upon freedom have a habit of growing beyond a stated objective. They quickly attack not merely a manifestation, but freedom itself. So this crusade, once under way, will not stop with its victims in the federal service. It will spread and is now spreading over this country, blighting our democracy and bringing fear and distrust to American homes throughout the nation."[37] However, the Supreme Court denied the petition for review, leaving the dismissal in effect. Though such an action is usually taken without further comment, giving the appearance of unanimity in the court's decision, Justices William O. Douglas and Hugo Black were so persuaded by Fortas's argument that they took the step, extraordinary at that time, of dissenting from the action.

Soon, it was apparent that Fortas's prediction had been accurate. In the spring of 1947, when ten members of President Truman's State Department were looking to restore their good names and jobs after being terminated without a hearing for security reasons, the firm stood ready to help, even if it meant not taking a fee. All three partners signed and sent a letter to Acting Secretary of State Robert A. Lovett asking about the department's justification for not even giving a hearing or a specification of the charges to the accused employees. Thurman Arnold persuaded the publisher of the *New York Herald Tribune,* Helen Reid, to feature the case. After a series of articles by her prize investigative reporter, Bert Andrews, over an eight-day period, the employees were allowed to resign without any black marks in their records.[38]

The reasons for doing this controversial work, much of it unpaid or *pro bono,* seemed obvious to the partners. "We have to take it on," said Fortas, "because if we don't nobody else will." To which Thurman Arnold later added, "Isn't it wonderful to work on something in which you really believe?"[39] In the same spirit was Paul Porter's motto for the firm: "When in doubt, do the right thing" (later changed by Fortas once on the Supreme Court to "'We are never in doubt. We always do the right thing.' Sometimes we have to do it 5–4").[40]

The firm showed its mettle here in the case involving Dorothy Bailey, who had been dismissed on charges of disloyalty from her job as a training officer for the United States Employment Service. It mattered little that her job had nothing to do with national security, or that the government had not one shred of evidence to counter a series of character witnesses who sprang to her defense. The unidentified accusers with their unspecified charges always got their way. The firm appealed the case all the way to the Supreme Court, where the dismissal was upheld by a 4–4 tie vote. But then, when Bailey was dismissed abruptly from her local university job after the final judgment, the partners hired her as their office manager.[41]

Perhaps the prototype of their *pro bono* work in defending people against charges of McCarthyism was the case of Owen Lattimore. An expert on China and the director of the Page School of International Relations at Johns Hopkins, Lattimore was accused by Joseph McCarthy in 1950, preposterously, of being the "top Russian espionage agent in the United States." Since the senator also claimed that the man, who was then serving as one of the five members of a United Nations technical assistance mission to Afghanistan, was in fact the "architect of the nation's Far Eastern policy" and the head of an espionage ring in the State Department, it seemed that his future was in severe jeopardy. Because Lattimore worked in Asia, he was unable to be present to defend himself. Mrs. Lattimore remembered meeting Abe Fortas at a dinner party and went to see him for help. Later she would write, "In the sea of unreality in which I had been floundering I knew at once that Abe Fortas was another solid rock. . . . I hadn't been there ten minutes before I knew that going to see him was the wisest thing I'd ever done."[42]

With "breath-taking" speed, Fortas moved to widen the scope of the conflict and capture the heart of the press, knowing that there could be no fair hearing before the Senate subcommittee. The move was typical of Fortas, who, it was said, liked to practice law "with one eye on the news media."[43] After Lattimore's writings were gathered and analyzed, McCarthy was challenged to prove his charges or withdraw them. Since it was the dramatic theater of the absurd that Fortas was fighting, he could be equally dramatic. He orchestrated all relations with the news media. A press conference was arranged in New York with three visiting Mongolians, all of whom were virulently anti-Communist and were then working with Lattimore's operation at Johns Hopkins, and one of whom was the Living Buddha from Outer Mongolia. Fortas then had Lattimore's students gather quotations from his works for use in the propaganda battle with McCarthy. He asked Mrs. Lattimore to write up a list of possible character witnesses for the inevitable Senate hearings. ("Good Lord," he said upon seeing the list, "don't you know *anybody* important?") All of the information on Lattimore was carefully fed to newsmen such as Drew Pearson, who in turn kept Fortas apprised of developing events.[44]

Never in all of this did Fortas ever mention the word *fee*. His only question on first being approached by Mrs. Lattimore was "Will he fight?" Later on, though, he was careful to ask one other question of the professor himself. Could he recall ever having been a member of the Communist party at any time?

Informing Lattimore of all of these moves as he was journeying back to the States, Fortas telegraphed, "This may sound somewhat insane to you, but I assure you that we are operating in a situation characterized by insanity, and a certain amount of drama is not only desirable, but also completely unavoidable." By the time Lattimore arrived in New York, Fortas, who was there to meet him, expressed his fears that there might be a "frame-up" under way. So "frantic" was the attorney to draft the statement for the press and for the Senate hearings that once more under the strain of the fight he had contracted a very heavy cold.[45]

So the fight was on. Fortas sat by Lattimore's side throughout the legislative hearings in the Senate caucus room, just fifteen feet away from Joseph McCarthy himself, a man who, the professor noted, "cannot look you straight in the eye." When Lattimore was confronted with a series of rehashed charges and innuendos from former Communists, Fortas used a combination of gathered affidavits from rebutting witnesses, questions fed to friendly senators, and staged press conferences in an attempt to control the agenda. On one occasion, when the senators would not allow one of Lattimore's defending affidavits into the record, the attorney simply went outside the hearing room and released it to the press so that the fight could be continued in full public view. In the end, all that McCarthy could prove was that Lattimore's scholarly views happened to coincide with those espoused in Communist Chinese doctrine.[46]

Two things were evident in this early legal work by Fortas. First, there was his fetish for meticulous preparation of a case. In addition to all of the research being done by the law firm into Lattimore's life and work, Fortas himself did a good amount of gumshoe work trying to discover the full nature and source of the charges that would be flung at his client in the hearings. Thanks to these efforts, Fortas answered McCarthy's original March 30, 1950, speech charging Lattimore with spying with an elaborate defense pointing out over one hundred errors in this statement alone.

Then there was Fortas's consummate skill at angling witnesses into a corner from which they could not escape. When one accusing witness was put on the stand, Fortas fed questions to the friendly senators which proved not only that her charges were groundless, but also that she had pro-Nazi leanings, and had made similarly groundless charges about others in the past.

Eventually, the witness became so flustered that observers were calling her Lattimore's "best witness." By the end, even McCarthy himself seemed to be looking over his shoulder for Fortas. When Senator Dennis Chavez of New Mexico spoke against McCarthy's main witness, ex-Communist Louis Budenz, the Wisconsin senator told reporters that the information had been produced by "an unnamed Communist lawyer," making it clear that it was Fortas he had in mind.[47]

Being cleared once was not the end of the story for the embattled Lattimore. In 1951, the professor was hauled before Senator McCarran's new investigating committee to face thirteen days of harassing questions, with Fortas by his side every minute. And when Lattimore was indicted for perjury for denying that he had ever been a "sympathizer or promoter of communism or communist interests," Thurman Arnold took over the case. Not until 1955, after the charge had been dismissed twice, was Lattimore completely vindicated.

In the end the *pro bono* work that Arnold, Fortas and Porter did for Lattimore cost the firm thirty thousand dollars in expenses and time. Lattimore himself would later write of Fortas, "The story would have been different, and more tragic, if it had not been for the law firm of Arnold, Fortas, and Porter; and particularly for Abe Fortas."[48] Years later, reporter Anthony Lewis would write that Fortas had shown "courage in hard times," while the law firm had seen to it that Lattimore, although "soiled by McCarthy's mud," was "clear in the eyes of history."[49]

But others were more skeptical of the reasons for this *pro bono* work. Were the partners doing it to soothe their consciences for all of their corporate "treason" against the old New Deal agencies in their law practice? Were they taking the most newsworthy cases as advertising for their corporate practice (despite the fact that the work appears to have cost them at least one prominent client)? Were they taking the cases because they filled the time while the partners built up their client list?[50]

While the courage and expense that it took for the firm to handle over one hundred loyalty cases in the 1940's and 1950's are undeniable, there is some justification for skepticism about the true motives here. One partner recalls that while in the earliest years of the firm the *pro bono* loyalty cases comprised 50 percent of the hours spent in practice, after they lost the Dorothy Bailey case in the Supreme Court, the partners cut back their "loyalty practice" to take only the most exceptional cases.[51] So, with the highly visible Supreme Court challenge finished, the time-consuming and expensive individual defenses were now left to others. This time, of course, could then be filled by a burgeoning corporate client load.

Moreover, there were very definite limits to the kind of loyalty cases that the firm was willing to handle. One day Clifford Durr, now practicing law in Washington after his stint in the government, got a call from Abe Fortas asking him to come over to the partners' offices. Fortas had been approached by a Princeton University scientist asking for representation for an appearance before the House Committee on Un-American Activities. But, he explained to Durr, the fellow had once briefly been a member of the Communist party, and the Arnold, Fortas and Porter firm had decided that it could not afford to represent anybody who had actually been a party member. And now Fortas wanted to know if Durr could take the case off his hands. As he heard this story, Durr noticed that Fortas, who he knew to be "a pretty cold-blooded guy," had become "so emotional" that he was "almost crying." So Durr did, only to find out later that old clients were not speaking to him on the street for fear of being tainted, and his law practice suffered markedly.[52]

Then there is some question as to whether some of these cases really were such a drain on the firm's resources. A fellow named Willard Van Dyke faced charges of Communism because of some film work he had done in Russia in 1935. So he consulted a lawyer in Washington who claimed that Van Dyke could be cleared, but only if he swore that he was not a member of the party and paid ten thousand dollars for the legal work. When asked how the job would be accomplished, the lawyer said only, "Through Abe Fortas." Since Van Dyke did not have the money, he went to his congressman for the required help.[53]

Despite these accounts, what can never be forgotten is that Arnold, Fortas, and Porter, for whatever reason, risked their own careers to help others in trouble. As to why, perhaps the truest version here was Fortas's own comment: "There are some things you have to do in order to live with yourself."[54]

Fortas's liberal efforts had even deeper ramifications. In other *pro bono* cases he was able to shape the law. In 1954, the United States Court of Appeals for the District of Columbia appointed Fortas as counsel for Monte Durham, who had been charged with housebreaking and grand larceny. Here the attorney was able to convince the court to abandon the old legal test determining psychiatric competency of a defendant—the so-called McNaghten rule, stating that a person is responsible for his actions if he knows the difference between right and wrong and is capable of adhering to the right path. Using his knowledge of psychiatry gained from serving as a trustee of the William Alanson White Psychiatric Foundation and as a frequent contributor to psychiatric journals, Fortas persuaded the court to use new scientific evidence in creating a broader competency test. Now the legal standard would be changed to one that judged whether the defendant was suffering from some mental disease at the time of the action, and whether the illegal action was a product of that disease. The so-called Durham rule is the one now used by American courts (though it did Durham no good at all, as he was convicted again in the retrial that Fortas's victory made possible).[55]

But the case that made Fortas a legal legend was his *pro bono* work on behalf of Clarence Earl Gideon in 1962 and 1963.[56] Gideon, an indigent man convicted of breaking and entering in Panama City, Florida, had hand-penciled on lined sheets of paper an appeal to the Supreme Court asking to be freed and retried because he had been denied counsel in his initial trial. At the time, though, the state of the law, as established by *Betts* v. *Brady* in 1942, was that a defendant had no right to court-appointed counsel unless the court could find "special circumstances"—such as mental problems, age, lack of experience in the court system, or the complicated nature of the charges.[57] Since Gideon fit into none of these categories, the trial judge ruled that he had no right to a court-appointed lawyer. However, in the previous thirteen years the Supreme Court had managed to find those "special circumstances" in nearly every such case granted appeal at that level. So the time for Gideon to appeal his case was propitious.

As it turned out, though, Gideon's timing was even better than he knew. A majority on the Warren Court was now ready to fashion a new rule, because of the inherent unfairness of having some defendants get legal help while others were left on their own. Moreover, many errors made in initial trials by unrepresented defendants, which could have been avoided had counsel been present, were later resulting in successful appeals. So the Supreme Court decided to review Gideon's case as a prototype of all of these cases, and stacked the deck in his favor by appointing one of the nation's finest appellate attorneys, Abe Fortas, as his lawyer.

There was little question that Fortas would win the case. His challenge was getting a powerfully persuasive unanimous court decision, which meant persuading sticklers for following precedent, such as John Marshall Harlan, to go along. Fortas personally prepared the final draft of the legal brief (considered a model for its clarity and brevity). Once more, Fortas meticulously prepared for trial. He not only studied the trial transcript and a twenty-two-page letter from Gideon, but after supervising the preparation of the early memoranda and drafts of the brief written by his younger colleagues in the law firm, Fortas then locked himself in a room at the Biltmore Hotel for two days and two nights to produce the final version.[58]

His oral argument to the court in this case won such high esteem that Justice Douglas, a man who was known to write letters to friends and draft his memoirs on such occasions, would later call it "the best single legal argument" he had heard.[59] Fortas made three basic points for the justices. First, historic changes in the laws of thirty-seven states now mandated appointment of counsel in felony cases there. Second, the Fourteenth Amendment to the Constitution, which governs state procedures, required the appointment of counsel in the remaining thirteen states. And finally, the "special circumstances" rule was cumbersome and time-consuming, in that cases where counsel was not appointed were being overturned one at a time. Changing the rule would streamline the dispensing of justice.

But what was most remembered about the presentation was Fortas's ability to fence with the justices in oral argument. The key to the case came in an exchange with the justice most opposed to Gideon's side, John Harlan. Clearly reluctant to overrule *Betts,* Harlan challenged the lawyer's interpretation of the earlier precedent. Fortas had argued that while the *Betts* decision showed an "understanding sensitivity of this Court to the pull of federalism," its outcome was the unfairness of a person conducting a defense without access to an attorney. "Really, Mr. Fortas," Harlan responded sharply, "'understanding sensitivity' seems to me a most unfortunate term to describe one of the fundamental principles of our constitutional system." But Fortas "replied without a flicker of emotion": "Mr. Justice Harlan, I believe in federalism. It is a fundamental principle for which I personally have the highest regard and concern, and which I feel must be reconciled with the result I advocate. But I believe that Betts against Brady does not incorporate a proper regard for federalism. It requires a case-by-case supervision by this Court of state criminal proceedings, and that cannot be wholesome. . . . Intervention should be in the least abrasive, the least corrosive way possible."[60]

Fortas based a later portion of his argument on the assumption that the Sixth Amendment right to counsel was not already applied to the states. This assumption drew a challenge from Hugo Black, who had been arguing since 1947 that the entire Bill of Rights had already been incorporated into the Fourteenth Amendment due process clause and made applicable at the state level. Here, Fortas responded, "Mr. Justice Black, I like that argument that you have made so eloquently. But I cannot as an advocate make that argument because this Court has rejected it so many times. I hope you never cease making it." The laughter, including Black's, filled the courtroom.[61]

After its deliberations, a unanimous Supreme Court found in favor of Gideon, ruling that the Constitution required that all persons accused of "serious crimes" be granted the right to counsel at trial, and provided with a lawyer at no cost should they be too poor to hire one on their own.[62] Much later Fortas would greatly minimize his work on the case: "Frankly, my role has been greatly exaggerated. There were a few minor strategy decisions that I had to make and, as it turned out, it worked out very well. For example, whether or not to continue on the line of *Betts* v. *Brady,* or to go for a complete reversal. But my role wasn't that great."[63] Others, though, would disagree. And the legal gunslinger had another notch for his gun.

Within a few years of entering private practice, Fortas had it all. He was rich. He was famous. And if he was not liked, he was certainly feared and respected. More than anything, when he picked up that telephone he was powerful. But there was one other "client" of the firm who would take him to even greater heights.

"See that car?" one of the lawyers in the firm, Walton Hamilton, asked his daughter-in-law, pointing to the huge black limousine occupying most of the circular drive outside with the uniformed driver standing by its side. "It belongs to a good friend of Abe's. Some think he has presidential ambitions. He's the senator from Texas—the junior senator from Texas."[64] And everyone knew had it not been for Fortas, the man using the limo might never have become senator at all. Now, it remained to be seen just how far the two of them would go.

IV

FAVORS

"Do you know where in hell I can put my hands on Abe Fortas?"

Department store magnate Stanley Marcus could tell from the unidentified voice that it was Lyndon Johnson on the other end of the phone line. "He's right here," Marcus responded, handing the lawyer the receiver.[1] Johnson needed a favor—right away—and his mentor and personal lawyer, former Texas state senator Alvin Wirtz, had insisted that Fortas was the man for the job. Could Fortas drop everything and come over to Fort Worth? The lawyer said he was busy taking depositions in Dallas in an antitrust case, and he had a bad case of the flu, but he was never too busy to help a friend. So, after he had finished the day's work, Abe Fortas was on his way to join Johnson's legal team that night.[2] And what a challenge they were facing!

You count your true friends by looking around you when things are at their worst. By that measure Abe Fortas became Lyndon Johnson's best friend in September 1948. For years, dark suspicions would be raised about how Fortas had won Johnson's everlasting gratitude by singlehandedly helping him to save his political career. Fortas himself would later argue that he had had less to do with the matter than anyone realized, and deserved very little of the credit.[3] But whatever he did, one point was undeniable—Johnson would never forget it. Regardless of the amount of work he did, Fortas had been there when it counted.[4]

On August 28, 1948, the Democratic runoff primary had been held between Johnson and former governor Coke Stevenson for the vacant Texas senatorial seat.[5] Everyone knew that a win here meant an automatic trip to Washington. As they sat in a diner that night over a late supper of chili and eggs, Johnson's good friends, attorneys Don Thomas and John B. Connally, thought back to the special election for senator in 1941. Remembering FDR's admonition in 1941 to "sit on the ballot box," Connally said, "We've got this won if they don't steal it. The only way to keep them from stealing it is never to let 'em know how many votes they've got." So Connally called Sarah Wade on the switchboard, and asked her to call all of the Democratic county coordinators with the same message. She went right down the list, calling headquarters to headquarters, asking the same three questions: "What's the vote? How did you report it? If not, can you hold it?"[6]

By delaying the release of vote tallies, thus preventing the opposition from knowing how many votes it had to "find," Johnson's team was able to remain in front—by a mere 87 votes. Allegations were later made that "Landslide Lyndon," as he would now forever be known, had stolen the election. The fact that 202 votes appeared at the last moment from a single ballot box in Precinct 13 in Jim Wells County, then ruled by George Parr, "the Duke of Duval County," and were all cast for Lyndon Johnson in the same handwriting and ink, seemed to give the charge some credence. (Things became even more suspect when the election commissioners who were finally convinced to open the suspected box found it empty.) But the question in Texas was not who actually *won* an election, but who was most adept at *stealing* an election. According to Thomas, Johnson knew less about the facts of that election than anyone. "Till the day he died he never *wanted* to know," explained Thomas. "He was really afraid someone did something wrong."[7]

That mattered little now, as each side began to position itself for the inevitable ballot challenge. After a tough battle over charges and countercharges of voter fraud, both the state Democratic party executive committee and the convention certified Johnson's nomination. But Ste-

venson's allies, who were also being charged with electoral irregularities, decided to play the game by different rules and took the
matter to court. However, rather than go to a nearby state judge, they
chose to drive hundreds of miles to see the vacationing federal district
court judge T. Whitfield "Tiddy Winks" Davidson. Even though a
federal judge seemingly had little jurisdiction over a state-run primary,
Stevenson's team felt that a visit to this old ally of the governor's
would be much more productive.

Davidson did not disappoint them. He signed an order temporarily
invalidating the election results and set a hearing date for September
21 to determine the outcome of the matter. This put Lyndon Johnson
in a nearly hopeless time bind. Under Texas law, the names of all the
certified party nominees had to be posted on the 254 county courthouse
doors around the state on October 3. In addition, there was the problem of having the names ready for the printing of absentee ballots.
With each hour lost toward the deadline for printing the ballots,
Johnson's chances for the Senate for the second, and perhaps last, time
were slipping away.[8]

At Davidson's hearing, Johnson's legal team put up a minimal defense to Stevenson's charges of fraud, arguing only that the case
should be heard in state court.[9] By making a more extensive argument,
it was felt, Johnson would be admitting that the matter was one for the
federal court. However, probably no strategy would have made a difference. After taking all the testimony, Davidson began to issue his
judgment: "If I were going to decide this case based on personal affection and friendship I would have to decide it in favor of Johnson because Mrs. Johnson's father was my close friend in East Texas, where
we grew up." Upon hearing that opening thought, Johnson and his
legal team got up and left the courtroom. They knew already how it
would come out—their man was off the ballot. Laughing in recalling
the moment years later, Johnson aide Walter Jenkins said, "The instructions were given before the [Davidson] decision was ever handed
down. Johnson said to find Abe Fortas."[10]

Johnson knew that the time had come to call in legal reinforcements.
His entire political career hung in the balance. And there seemed to be
too little time before the printing deadline to do much. More than at
any other time in his life, he needed help. And he needed it fast. So,
when Fortas told him that he was on his way from Dallas, no man in
the world could have been more grateful.

By the time Fortas arrived in the sitting room across the hall from
Johnson's suite of hotel rooms in Fort Worth, he saw "acres of law-

yers.''[11] There was a babble of conversation among the legal team about the next step to be taken. "If you get a dozen lawyers together," Paul Porter later recalled, "no work gets done, just argument."[12] Fortas decided quickly that his main role was to cut through the sense of panic and legal rigamarole, find the heart of the case, and set the proper strategy for the assembled legal talent to implement. It was a small but vital "legal command" type of counseling role. So Fortas very quickly redirected the focus of the conversation from the politics of the situation to the *legal* issues involved. "What's the *law* on this?" he asked the others.[13] But no answer from the group was forthcoming, as everyone continued to fight for his own direction. After listening to another hour of fruitless discussion, Fortas said, "We had better get it on up to the Supreme Court, [Hugo] Black will handle it expeditiously." With that he gathered up all of the papers lying around, took Johnson's secretary, Mary Rather, into another room, and ten minutes later had synthesized all of the discussion into the necessary legal instruments.[14]

Fortas realized the near impossibility of the task at hand. "Time was very short—just a relatively few days," he later recalled. "The important thing was to devise a strategy which would work on time."[15] The problem was that this dispute could not be brought directly from the district court to the Supreme Court. So, Fortas drafted a brief summary argument for Johnson's Texas attorneys to present to a single member of the United States Court of Appeals, the next step in the federal legal ladder, in the hopes of getting a quick hearing date. But, as Fortas had expected, Judge J. C. Hutcheson in New Orleans refused, on September 24, to take any action until he could meet with his colleagues in the fall. Knowing that the opening of the court of appeals would be too late, Fortas laid plans to present the case to Justice Black individually, in his capacity as the presiding justice of the United States Court of Appeals for the Fifth Circuit.

Once more, all of Johnson's legal friends—this time the Washington, D.C., crowd—were convened in the Arnold, Fortas and Porter offices, to plan the argument for the Supreme Court justice.[16] Stuffed in the room were thirty-five lawyers, effectively the former shadow government for FDR—Tommy Corcoran, Ben Cohen, James H. Rowe, Jr., Hugh Cox, Francis Biddle, and Joseph L. Rauh, Jr. It was the "damndest mess" Rowe had ever seen. "It is a little bit that [Johnson] didn't trust anybody completely," he explained, "and he knew every good lawyer in town."[17] After listening to a new round of legal argumentation—this time in Washingtonese—Fortas once more took the leadership position by saying, "Somebody had better begin drafting." With that he left for the library and each of the attorneys was given a portion of the necessary legal research to handle.[18]

By now, Fortas was more convinced than ever that his legal position was a strong one—a federal judge like Davidson should not be enjoining a state-run election. So his partners, Porter and Arnold, had decided to present their petition for a hearing personally to Justice Black, who was still in the city. However, when they brought the document to the Supreme Court building, the court's clerk, a man nicknamed "Mr. Justice" Cullidan, said that he could not accept their plea. It had no docket number, he argued. "Well, take any number from one to ten," responded the whimsical Thurman Arnold. "We don't care." But Cullidan insisted that all of the formalities must be observed. "Well, now, look, Mr. Cullidan," said Porter, "we will effectuate a lodgement." As severe as this sounded, Porter didn't have the slightest idea what a lodgement was, except that he remembered hearing about this obscure pleading in a law course he had taken years ago at the University of Kentucky. With that, the Johnson lawyers left the papers. All they could do was return to their office and hope that the papers somehow got into the hands of Justice Black.[19]

Cullidan decided that he didn't want to face a "lodgement." After an anxious night of waiting, a phone call from Black's personal law clerk the next day told them that the justice would hear their argument. With that, Fortas, former Texas governor James V. Allred, Alvin Wirtz, and Washington attorney Hugh Cox trooped over to the Supreme Court building early the next morning. Dan Moody, another former Texas governor (apparently former Texas governors well understood what Stevenson and Johnson had been up to), joined them in Black's walnut-paneled court office to make the opposing argument.[20] All of the attorneys gathered in a semicircle around Black's desk and, while the justice rocked in his swivel chair, presented their arguments.

A fellow New Deal liberal, Black could be expected to have more sympathy for Johnson's position than for the conservative Stevenson. Though Fortas was uneasy about the short time available to prepare his legal argument, it made no difference. During the four hours of argumentation, Justice Black demonstrated a complete mastery of all the obscure Reconstruction-era cases governing this subject.[21] In response to the justice's sharp questioning, both sides repeated essentially the same arguments they had been making throughout the dispute.[22] Stevenson's lawyers leveled their charges of voter fraud. In response, Fortas argued that the matter was "irrevocably and incontestably vested" in Texas state law and should not be supervised by the federal courts. Then he added that the physical problems of posting the nominee's name in some of the remote Texas counties could make any delay in judicial relief an effective bar to Johnson's candidacy. It seemed to him that Stevenson, knowing that his own bid for the nomination was dead, was simply trying to spoil Johnson's chances. Since the mere thought of a ballot with no Democratic nominee at all was "perfectly appalling" to Fortas, he called on Black to remove the courts from the controversy entirely. "This is a political controversy, neither more nor less," he concluded. With that, the whole group broke for lunch and waited for the justice to decide Johnson's future.[23]

"It would be a drastic break with the past," the justice began after they had reconvened in his office, "to permit Federal courts to go into elections. Believing, therefore, that I have jurisdiction, that it is a matter of supreme importance not only to Texas but beyond the borders of Texas, and that there is no statutory provision for a Federal court to enjoin a step in an election, until the full court shall have time to consider the matter, the restraining order heretofore issued by Judge Davidson is no longer in effect."[24] Johnson was saved. The candidate's attorneys were told to submit an order granting the stay—which they did with great dispatch, flying it down in an oilman's plane to a friendly judge for implementation.[25] And so, Lyndon Baines Johnson was quickly certified as the Democratic candidate for the United States Senate from the state of Texas.

Black's decision in Johnson's favor on September 28, 1948, had really decided two futures. First, he had ensured that Lyndon Johnson would be a United States senator rather than returning to likely obscurity in the House of Representatives. And in so doing, the justice had also ensured that Lyndon Johnson would be forever indebted to Abe Fortas. Searching for a way to express his gratitude, Johnson telegraphed Fortas as he prepared the argument for the full Supreme Court to uphold Black's order, "I know all of you will see it through. I wouldn't be in the running now except for you. Thanks."[26]

For now simple telegrams would have to be enough of a repayment. The basic relation between Fortas and Johnson appeared to be set for the foreseeable future. Fortas was at the pinnacle of his legal career, and Johnson had just squeaked his way into the position of junior senator from Texas. Just as in the Interior Department days, it seemed that Fortas would be the dominant one in the friendship. He would be the one in the position to do the favors for the other. The choices were in his hand. But no one had figured on the ambition, and the ability, of

Lyndon Baines Johnson. Soon, he would have more power than anyone could imagine. And then the hierarchy of their relationship would
be changed forever. Then it would be Johnson who was in a position
to do favors for Fortas. It would be Johnson who dictated the agenda.

And Johnson had a very specific agenda in mind. Being a man who
liked to carry other people's IOUs rather than worry about his own, he
began to think about his accumulated debt to Abe Fortas. And very
early on, the new senator began to talk to Walter Jenkins about some
of the long-range possibilities: "Abe would make a great Supreme
Court Justice."[27] It was a sentiment that Johnson would repeat frequently over the years.

Once the way was cleared by Fortas, Lyndon Johnson's rise to
power was meteoric, and the man responsible was the senior senator
from Georgia and the head of the informal group of conservative
southern Democratic senators known as the Dixiecrats, Richard Russell. His relationship with Johnson was once described by Russell as
"one of the most peculiar in American history" and by a mutual friend
as a "hate-love relationship between two old horny-handed profes-
sionals." But when all was said and done, the many favors done by
Russell for Johnson created an intimacy in their relationship that
seemed unbreakable.[28]

Their thirty-year friendship had been launched in the late 1930's
over the issue of rural electrification. Year after year the funds for this
program were cut by the House, and Congressman Johnson would go
to the chairman of the Senate Subcommittee for Agricultural Appropriations, Richard Brevard Russell, for help in getting them restored. And
they always were. "[Johnson] knew what he was talking about, and I
thought to myself, 'That boy's a good Congressman,' " Russell recalled later.[29]

With Johnson's election to the Senate in 1948 came the first opportunity for Russell to show what favors he could do in promoting a
friendly new junior colleague. Using the southern-stacked Democratic
Steering Committee as leverage, he placed Johnson on all of the right
committees, including the Armed Services Committee he so badly
wanted. Later, when Russell became chairman of Armed Services, he
gave the very junior senator from Texas important subcommittee assignments. Such was the case when he put Johnson in charge of the
Preparedness Investigating Subcommittee, a vital post with the new
"police action" in Korea heating up. Then, making the plum even
sweeter, Russell took the extremely unusual step of temporarily chang-

ing the mandate of Johnson's subcommittee from investigative to legislative, by putting him in charge of the Selective Service Act extension. In this position Johnson was able to propose a system of universal military training that, though it never passed, gave him high public visibility.[30]

Johnson, who was looking for mentors along the lines of the ones he had followed in the House—Speaker Sam Rayburn and Carl Vinson, chairman of the House Naval Affairs Committee—now placed himself fully under the tutelage of the powerful man from Georgia.[31] The two senators seemed cut from the same cloth. Both worked fourteen- to sixteen-hour days, six and sometimes even seven days a week. "There was no one that worked as long, as many hours in the course of a week, in the United States Senate as Senator Russell unless it was Lyndon Johnson," says Russell's longtime Senate aide William Jordan.[32] The personal friendship that grew seemed inevitable, spurred all the more by the young Johnson's well-known ability to curry favor with more powerful senior colleagues.

Their conversation continued everywhere they went, including scores of late dinners with Sam Rayburn at Hal's fish restaurant, and frequent attendance at night baseball games. There was no one more "thoughtful and attentive" to Richard Russell than Lyndon Johnson. Since Russell had no family, on Sundays Johnson made sure to invite him for some of Lady Bird's home cooking. Then he put Russell on the long list of people who got small gifts on every suitable occasion.[33]

It was a match made in political heaven for both of them. Russell would later say of Johnson, "He made more out of my efforts to help him than anyone else ever had. He's a born competitor. I encouraged that."[34] Later, the Georgian added, "He is the most totally and completely political animal I have ever known. There have been times when I thought he was mad, and I don't mean angry, but there has been a method in his madness." Johnson was just as effusive about his senior colleague: "He is the most effective member of the Senate. I never had a party question in the Senate that I did not consult with him."[35]

Slowly the relationship began to evolve from the early mentor-student status to a sort of older brother–younger brother interraction. Some even called it a father-son relationship, though there were only eleven years between them.[36]

It was only natural that at the first opportunity Russell would use his considerable resources in the Senate to promote his young friend to a position of formal authority. When an opening for the majority whip's post occurred in 1951, Russell turned to Johnson, then with only two years of tenure, and said, "Lyndon, you got to take that job."[37] Then in 1953 Russell spurned the minority leader's post and passed it to Lyndon Johnson with such an unusually eloquent speech that no one bothered to question the fact that the young man had been a senator for only four years. "He doesn't have the best mind on the Democratic side of the Senate," said Russell to his colleagues; "he isn't the best orator; he isn't the best parliamentarian. But he's the best combination of all of those qualities."[38] Johnson said he would take the job only if Russell moved from his inconspicuous seat in the far wing of the chamber to the center aisle seat behind him. "I'll do the work," Johnson promised, "and you'll be the boss."[39] In 1955, when Oregon's independent Wayne Morse left the Republicans and voted Democratic, Johnson became the majority leader of the Senate.

From his vantage point Russell advised, and Johnson listened. They made quite a pair: Johnson, who was given to cussing out a member when things did not go his way, and Russell, whose main weapon was "a kind of innocent rectitude" that left even his opponents saying, "I simply couldn't do that to Dick Russell."[40] And nothing got by the Georgian. One time in 1954, during a Senate filibuster, Minority Leader Johnson asked Russell how to break it. "You can beat it easily enough," he was told. "If you hold sessions around the clock for a couple of days the filibuster will fall apart." Indeed, after a few days of twenty-four-hour sessions, the talkers did give up the ship.[41]

Then there was the time late in the 1950's when the conservatives were attempting to restrict the power of the Supreme Court by limiting its authority to hear appellate cases. Johnson allowed debate on the measure, thinking that it would just allow the judicial opponents to blow off a little steam, before taking the formal vote supporting the court. But when the liberals lost one of the early test votes because of a lack of attendance by their members, Russell leaned over Johnson's shoulder and said, "Lyndon, you'd better adjourn this place or they're going to pass that goddamned bill." Whereupon Johnson jumped to his feet and ended the debate by moving for adjournment. Sure enough, the next day certain key members of the conservative group could not find their way to the Senate floor for the final vote, and the Supreme Court had been saved by a most unlikely ally.[42]

In time, Russell was to regret the power he had handed to Johnson. For years they had seen issues the same way. Late in the 1950's, though, Johnson got the bug for national office, which meant modifying some of his positions. So in 1960, for the first time, the two old friends opposed each other on a major piece of legislation, the civil rights bill of 1960. Russell led the inevitable southern filibuster, following a segregationist line. Johnson, on the other hand, now was advocating a more liberal, integrationist position. The two men, one trained by the other, were like generals marshaling their troops for a battle that would begin to change the face of America forever. Using his training from Russell, the majority leader countered the filibuster with round-the-clock sessions.

But the teacher still had a few tricks up his sleeve. Three teams of speakers were organized, with one group on the floor talking to itself while the rest of the filibusterers slept. It got comical after a while. Russell would come down and tell Johnson he was tired and would be leaving. So Johnson would drag himself up to his office for some rest. Then in the wee hours of the morning the Dixiecrats' leader would pop out and demand a "live" quorum, requiring Johnson to produce forty-nine colleagues, in whatever condition, to keep the bill alive.[43] In the end, when Johnson's liberals gave up to fight another day, he asked his teacher where the earlier lessons had gone wrong. Russell chided, "We didn't discuss who was running the filibuster. The liberals couldn't stand the heat. They had been denouncing the filibuster for so long the publicity got to them. We didn't mind it at all."[44]

With Johnson's rise to power in the Senate came vast changes in his relationship with Abe Fortas. When one looked at the two men in the 1950's, their very natures still seemed just too far apart for them ever to be truly close friends. They were as different as fire and ice, bluster and grace, petulance and poise. Johnson was loud, funny, and profane. Fortas was soft-spoken and genteel, serious with only an occasional streak of dry humor, and polite to the point of excess. For Johnson there was only politics.[45] Fortas, though, was a man of great breadth—playing his violin with prominent musicians, making furniture like his father, and writing pieces for psychiatry journals. Johnson collected people of use to him; Fortas collected antiques. Johnson gobbled down whatever was put in front of him as fast as possible as an excuse to talk to the others eating around him about politics, while Fortas liked gourmet food and fine wines.

In dealing with others, each now used his resources to the fullest. Johnson, using his height of well over six feet, simply overpowered people in what folks came to call The Treatment. He would lean into them, pawing them and grabbing their lapels, talking a mile a minute directly into their faces.[46] There was what some called the half Johnson, when he just grabbed your arm, and the full Johnson, when he put his arm around you and "breathed into your mouth."[47] If he was even more serious, he would do all of this and start kicking you in the shins for good measure. "When Johnson wanted to persuade you of something," explained Ben Bradlee of *The Washington Post,* "you felt as if a St. Bernard had licked your face for an hour, had pawed you all over. . . . It was like going to the zoo."[48]

Fortas, though, was a man of learning rather than a man of the people. He was accustomed to having others listen carefully to his views. He spoke in a barely audible tone—so low and smoothly modulated that even those sitting next to him found themselves leaning toward him, to hear every word. Unlike Johnson, he told no fanciful stories and spoke ever so slowly and deliberately, but the words were carefully chosen and created vivid mental images. In offering advice, he did it with such a casual "this is what I think, like it or not" attitude that one tended to believe him just by the force of the presentation, regardless of the merits of the ideas.[49] And on legal issues, there was no more learned counsel.

Whatever distance existed between the two men was bridged by their common love of power. Having both been involved in making rules in the New Deal, they saw no reason to follow them now. But even here, they had vastly different styles. Johnson loved the limelight but needed help, while Fortas seemed to love the role of outside adviser. So, in spite of the fact that there seemed to be nothing the senator could do for the powerful lawyer, Abe Fortas would always be available when Lyndon Johnson called. As Johnson rose in the Senate, though, the lead position in their relationship shifted to him. Fortas could not help but love the excitement of being close to the center of political action. Moreover, the potential was there for this rising political star to reach even greater heights, and Fortas wanted to be there when that potential was realized.

And what friends they were. Politically, the two men were much alike. Neither of them really had a philosophy.[50] Often Fortas would tell Johnson, "Do what you've got to do, and get as few people mad as you can." As the two rose to power, more and more occasions arose for Johnson to call on the man who had saved his political career for assistance in doing just that. And Fortas was always there. "Fortas did not give his loyalty lightly," remembers a friend, "but once it was done, it was done forever."[51]

Most of the time these were calls requiring Fortas's legal and political savvy. He was asked to help draft constituent letters that explained Johnson's positions to the general public. One letter extolled the virtues of military isolation, and another dealt with President Truman's firing of General MacArthur. The MacArthur letter, sent in response to the heaviest constituent mail that Johnson's office ever got and backing the president's position as commander in chief, was sent out "by the tubful."[52]

Along with these tasks, there was the related problem of overseeing what Johnson said to the public. Since Fortas was being consulted on most of the "crucial votes," he began to take a role in drafting the senator's speeches. Frequently, Johnson would ask him, "This is what I'm inclined to do, what do you think?" To be followed by the more crucial question: "If I do it, how do I explain it?" So Fortas began to join the senator's informal group of speechwriters for brainstorming sessions. After a speech had been written by members of Johnson's Senate staff such as George Reedy, or friends such as Texas politico Booth Mooney or news editor Herbert Henderson, the senator would hand the work to Fortas explaining, "Here's what I'd like to say," and ask for a reaction.[53]

Over time, it seemed to Johnson's advisers that he was calling Fortas in on more and more issues of all varieties. One key request came in 1949, during the fight over the confirmation of consumer advocate Leland Olds's reappointment as Federal Power Commission chairman. As chairman of the subcommittee of the Interstate and Foreign Commerce Committee that was conducting the hearings, Lyndon Johnson had the stage all to himself. But the issues here were complex, and the debate was made even more important to Johnson by the fact that this was his first senatorial chairmanship. Accordingly, he was on the phone daily with Fortas consulting about questions to ask in the day's hearings. His choice of adviser made sense. The questions about natural resources this dispute raised and the legal thickets it created were right up Fortas's alley. For his part, though, Fortas had an obvious stake in seeing that a commissioner contrary to the interests of the oil companies he was now representing in private practice not be confirmed. In the end, it was Johnson's vehement, red-baiting attack on Olds that, in smearing his name, turned the tide against him. People were puzzled that Johnson, so much in favor of public power as a congressman, was now so much against the public power advocate Olds. But the senator's aides knew why. "Johnson would not have gone as strong or as far out on this without a lot of consultation with Fortas," explained Walter Jenkins.[54]

The same teamwork ensued when Johnson's Preparedness Investigating Subcommittee began hearings on military waste and the
lack of preparedness in general. Here again, Fortas used both his governmental background and his legal training to point out to Johnson
areas for possible investigation, even to the point of drawing up questions for the freshman senator to ask witnesses.[55]

On October 27, 1951, a single event changed the nature of their
relationship forever. Johnson's Texas mentor, former undersecretary of
the interior and political lawyer Alvin Wirtz, dropped dead of a heart
attack in the stands of a football game between the Longhorns of the
University of Texas and Rice University. The loss of the man who
some say most profoundly influenced Johnson's early political life left
a void that quickly needed to be filled. Wirtz's death gave Abe Fortas
one of the greatest opportunities of his life.

Alvin Wirtz was the first of what became known as Johnson's "political daddies."[56] With each move up the political ladder, Johnson
added more names to this list of mentors. There were Franklin D.
Roosevelt and Sam Rayburn when Johnson was in the House, and later
Richard Russell in the Senate. But always there had been Wirtz.

Wirtz had certain skills that lent themselves nicely to Johnson's
needs. Everyone agreed with the assessment of one mutual friend that
Wirtz was "one of the smartest men I ever saw—legally and every
other way."[57] He was also the one person who "could tell Lyndon
something was silly. . . . He molded him."[58] Indeed, "the senator,"
as Wirtz was called throughout his life in respect for his earlier position as a Texas state senator, had overseen every move in the phenom-
enal rise of his young political protégé. He had tapped Johnson for
Congress, provided help on water projects as interior undersecretary,
and helped to supervise all of his campaigns for office.

In his homespun Texas manner, Wirtz quickly became the main
"people person" for Johnson. He could anticipate public reactions to
the congressman's moves, and advise on how to handle them. Moreover, even though he was an attorney, Wirtz could speak and write in
a way that was easily understood—reducing the legal complexities of a
situation to brief but comprehensible language. This was evident when
Johnson proudly reported to his mentor how he had voted for a motion
in a House civil rights debate, saying that he'd done so to represent his
constituents' long-term interests rather than momentary passions.
Hearing this, Wirtz warned simply, "Well, Lyndon, it'll be all very
well voting for your constituents' interests as against their opinions,
but suppose they don't recognize and appreciate what you've done and

don't re-elect you?"[59] It was a lesson Johnson never forgot, and repeatedly he would rebuke other New Dealers who said he was not liberal enough by pointing out that unless he could get reelected he could do nothing.[60] Consequently, when there was a gut decision to be made, Wirtz's was one of the last and most important voices heard.

By the time Wirtz died in 1951, another man, Abe Fortas, was ready to take his place. In fact, the Johnson crowd was beginning to see the two men as interchangeable for the senator. "In many ways, Abe Fortas now took Wirtz's place in Johnson's eyes," recalls Walter Jenkins. "Johnson would do the same things and discuss the same topics with Fortas. . . . Abe filled part of the void [after Wirtz's death]."[61]

And why not, for while the two men had very different temperaments and styles, the force and nature of their advice were very similar. Rather than grinding his own ax, Fortas seemed to be concerned only with how to make Johnson look good, and asked for nothing in return. But there was much more to Fortas, in the eyes of Johnson and his crowd. He was "innately wise," said one intimate.[62] He "would listen and understand and try to see things the way they were," added another.[63] "No one occupied the same standing as he did with Lyndon. [He was Johnson's] true friend, who would give him solid honest advice," explained a third.[64]

So Fortas became part of Johnson's "court of last resort," receiving the call from the senator after all of the other advisory returns were in. As one Johnson intimate explains, "LBJ could reach out and get all of the information [and then] use Fortas to synthesize, clarify, and rip away the chaff of the problem."[65] Johnson appreciated both Fortas's intellectual soundness and his common sense in the ability to find solutions to practical situations. Wirtz had done this as well. But now Wirtz was gone.[66]

On top of all this was that Fortas confidence. He'd been around long enough to believe in himself, and his coolness under fire later earned him the nickname of the "ultimate unflappable man."[67] For someone with the personal insecurities of Lyndon Johnson, such confidence and coolness at crucial moments was vital.

With Wirtz's death, then, it was not surprising that Fortas became the main "people person" for Johnson. Now he gave the politician a sense of how the public would react to various moves and suggested some public relations tactics (a curious task for a man who had not lived among the common folk since high school). Fortas became the man in a postion to say no on occasion to Lyndon Johnson. All of this was a measure of both the absolute confidence that Johnson had in the attorney, and also the persuasiveness of his advice. And for Fortas, who had filled the same outside advisory role for Douglas and Ickes already, it was a very comfortable position to occupy.

Fortas tried to be as helpful as he could to Johnson after he became the majority leader. From time to time, Fortas would send general advice on how Johnson should conduct himself, or just words of encouragement—all of which was gratefully acknowledged by the politician.[68] Johnson was always willing to tell his friend how much this support meant to him. "I am deeply grateful for your friendship and believe me there have been many times in the past months when I would have been helpless had I not had the privilege of tapping your rich store of wisdom," he wrote after receiving one fan letter mailed just before the 1956 Democratic convention.[69] Then Johnson added, "Your remarks about the present session of Congress touched a deep chord in my heart. . . . As you know, I tried to do my best—and the fact that you think my best was adequate for the task is one of the most soul-satisfying pieces of information I have had in a long time. Praise from others I take with a grain of salt but praise from a man of your judgment is heartwarming, indeed."[70]

In time, Fortas was seen as the senator's personal lawyer in Washington. Here was the man with both the legal ability and the loyalty to Johnson to handle the impossible, and not have it end up in the next day's *Washington Post*. Such was the case during the 1956 campaign. A question arose as to whether campaign money raised by the Texas Democratic party to meet the state's quota for the national committee's support needed to be reported under federal law. Fortas called Jenkins with his evaluation. "I have looked at the statute and the few cases there are," he began, explaining that he had also "brainwashed" one of the other parties involved with the dispute. Then Fortas explained how to work just inside the limits of the law—which was where he put all of his clients. "The statute is by no means clear on this thing, but I think you are all right in not filing these returns. I don't think you ought to break your necks to do this. If you have to file this return this means that every State Committee has got to file the return because statutory provisions are the same and all of the State Committees make contributions to the Democratic organization. . . . My legal reasoning is that that section of the statute was designed to exempt committees whose activities take place in one State. Everett [Looney], I am sure, is worried because the language is not clear, but I think that is the sense and the substance." With that Fortas agreed to send Johnson a memo for his personal files on this question and to make more calls to those involved.[71]

As time went on, Johnson entrusted more and more personal and professional matters to the lawyer. In the months to come, Fortas made a number of political suggestions to Johnson. He advised him on such subjects as the Harte-Hanks antitrust case, manpower in the armed services, and the problems of air transportation in 1958,[72] as well as the humane slaughter bill, an issue of concern to Fortas the animal lover. It was this kind of legal work that gave Johnson confidence in Fortas's reliability.

Because of the destruction of records by the Johnson staff during this period, and both men's preference for dealing with each other orally, no one will ever know the full extent of the issues they discussed and the nature of the advice offered. But enough has survived to indicate that there were, as Jenkins has suggested, very few issues that did not now come up in their conversation. Johnson had come to rely on Fortas, who in turn had no other political figures seeking his advice. It was the sort of monogamous relationship that each man, in his search for discretion, preferred.

Soon a problem came up requiring a *very* reliable lawyer. The last thing that Johnson needed in his rise to the top was to have the Duke of Duval, George Parr, talking about his role in the 1948 election. But Parr, in his quest for legal vindication on a variety of charges, including income tax evasion, had run out of money. In return for Parr's silence, Johnson asked Fortas if he would take the case *pro bono*.[73] Every step of the way, Fortas carefully kept Johnson apprised through phone messages relayed by Walter Jenkins, and letters.

Not surprisingly, the nature of the give and take between the lawyer and the majority leader changed. Now it was Johnson who, with his rise to power, was in a position to do some favors, and whose attention was being sought. Some of the senator's Texas friends needed legal work done in Washington and were directed to the doorstep of Arnold, Fortas and Porter.[74] Fortas also began to inform Johnson of the names of friends and acquaintances who he felt deserved confirmation to various federal posts.[75]

One of the first return favors Fortas requested from Johnson, though, was on behalf of his first major client, Puerto Rico. In mid-1955, Fortas sent a memo to Walter Jenkins on the problems presented to Puerto Rico by the passage of a minimum wage and hours bill that was intended mainly to increase the wages of workers by twenty-five cents, or 33⅓ percent. Also under consideration was a section that would amend the Fair Labor Standards Act of 1938, to have this measure applied for the first time to Puerto Rico. In a two-page memo, Fortas outlined how this procedure would mean a "death sentence" for many industries on the island, and would ruin its entire industrialization program. He wondered whether the new provision could either be struck or amended more satisfactorily, or, in the last resort, whether the entire measure could be withheld from the Senate floor for a time while other support was gathered. When one's friend is the Senate majority leader, such an appeal has weight. With the successful amendment of this bill came a letter from Fortas of "thanks for your interest and help."[76]

In 1958 a proposal was under consideration in the executive branch which would permit the governor of the island to appoint the local adjutant general of the National Guard. The Pentagon refused to support the submission of proposed legislation to Congress so that hearings could be held. When the independence and nationalist groups on the island began a revolt, alleging a lack of sincerity by the United States, Fortas went into action. First, he called Johnson's office, telling the secretary, "This is the first time I've asked for your help, but I'm at my wits' end and at the same time at the end of the telephone from Puerto Rico." Asked to send a supporting memo, Fortas wrote one titled "In Desperation," and closed his explanation of the problem with the plea "God bless you. We will be very grateful if a report can be blasted out of the Pentagon."[77] After Walter Jenkins made some phone calls, the proposal went to Congress. A month later, however, Fortas was back on the phone with Johnson's office. The bill by now had gone to the Senate Armed Services Committee—on which Johnson served and had many friends, including its chairman, Richard Russell of Georgia. So Jenkins alerted Johnson as to Fortas's interest and added, "I would certainly like for us to be able to assist Abe if we possibly can and thought you might say a word to Senator Russell on behalf of the bill."[78] With friends like this, how could Fortas lose? Indeed, later that year, a version of the same bill became law.

Not surprisingly, when Johnson was thinking of making a run for the presidency in 1960, Fortas was there to help. "My liberal friends were startled," he later explained, "but I told them that I knew the man—that if he were to do only one-tenth of what he actually did but spend more time telling people about what he'd done and what he believed in, people would be falling all over themselves to get behind him."[79] But they weren't "falling all over themselves" in 1960.

Fortas used his wide contacts, and his understanding of people and the press, to advise Johnson on how to position himself politically in the fight. Johnson had the dual problem of facing a popular president's record, and watching from the sidelines as John Kennedy began to rack up popular victories in the Democratic primaries. In late May, Fortas suggested some strategy to Johnson's administrative assistant, Walter Jenkins. Fortas drew his attention to the current breakdown of the summit conference in Paris after the U-2 crash of Francis Gary Powers. Since it was obvious that President Eisenhower had mishandled relations with the intransigent Nikita Krushchev, Fortas advised, "We have to back up the President but we still have got to get to the bottom and to make sure that blunders of this type do not happen again. . . . The trouble is at the top and I think Lyndon ought to take that line. I think we can reflect the country's sympathy for Eisenhower, but at the same time we ought to know what the hard facts are: that we blundered into this and we played right into Khrushchev's hands."

As for Kennedy's win in the Oregon primary, Fortas offered, "That is fine, but . . . it did not prove much—look who he beat—Humphrey and Morse. I don't think that would be too much help." But should Johnson announce as a candidate? Fortas was asked. "You know I am so eager for him to make an announcement, but this is no place to do it. He has got to repeat what he said before—there is nothing to say but that no he is not a candidate, but if the opportunity presents him with an opportunity to run, he would do it. He ought to say—'I feel very deeply the responsibility the people have given me. I think it would be wonderful if [I] could say yes. I wish I could say that I was a candidate—there is nothing I would like better, but my position as Majority Leader demands that I do this job well and my responsibility is to the people.'"[80]

Two weeks later, Fortas was back on the phone trying to tell Jenkins whom to trust and whom not to trust in this effort to have the Democratic party draft Johnson as its candidate. One fellow was "enthusiastic," while another "got everything twisted up" and it was "important to keep curbs on that guy." Fortas was also trying to get the symbolic support of the observing delegation from Puerto Rico to the Democratic party convention. Despite the fact that there were two delegations from the islands, elected by rival conventions (such is the way of politics there), Fortas thought he had them where he wanted them. "I think the Puerto Rican delegation will not support Kennedy," he told Walter Jenkins. "Until the matter is settled they are keeping very quiet. They are going to do that until we get over the first hurdle, but all I can say is I believe they will be influenced by my decision.''

When things fell through on Fortas's Puerto Rico operation, he complained to Jenkins that the head of one delegation had "made a deal with the Republicans four or five months ago and we will just have to do something about it." However, Fortas reassured Johnson's aide that he had "some close friends in the [rival] group that I know are for Johnson, but at this point I don't want any of them to declare themselves." So it was left to Jenkins and the Johnson group to figure out a way to get this rival group recognized at the convention.[81] While this effort was not crucial to Johnson's future, there was no question that Abe Fortas had done his best to contribute. As new campaign issues arose, such as a proposal for a platform plank on the creation of a commission on equal job opportunity under government contracts, Fortas telegraphed his suggestions for action. In this case, the informal adviser for the nonexistent campaign was recommending support for such a plank.[82]

After the Democratic presidential nod went to John Kennedy of Massachusetts in Los Angeles on July 13, the ticket was balanced by adding Texas's Lyndon Johnson the next morning (over the objections of the latter's mentors, Sam Rayburn and Richard Russell). Fortas had clearly earned the right to contact the new vice presidential nominee. But after all of their efforts together, he seemed reluctant to do so. Saying that he had started several letters to Johnson, Fortas wrote that he had given the problems of the campaign and the vice presidency much thought, but the ideas were "too complex to be written." Since there had apparently been no phone call from Johnson at this crucial crossroads, Fortas seemed to have some insecurity about whether he had been dropped from the roster of advisers. Still, Fortas offered to provide whatever help he could: "I know you don't need my thoughts and it may be presumptuous of me to offer them, but if you think that you might be interested, I hope you will give me a chance sometime soon to talk with you." Fortas made clear that he stood ready to help "for anything" and reassured Johnson that the acceptance of the vice presidency was a "noble act."[83] Not surprisingly, he needn't have worried. The letter was answered by telephone by Jenkins, and very shortly thereafter Fortas was back in the Johnson inner circle looking for more help on a Senate confirmation problem.[84]

With the campaign in the fall, Fortas slipped into the role he had occupied over the last decade—that of public relations consultant for the senator. When Johnson was contacted to appear on *Face the Na-*

tion, he called Fortas and several other prominent liberal advisers to work on some ideas for the show.[85]

After the narrow Democratic victory in November, Lyndon Johnson was working out of the White House. But for him, the job of vice president was a prison and, in the words of Texan John Nance Garner, "not worth a pitcher of warm spit."[86] Since there was little for Johnson to do politically, Abe Fortas's advisory role was similarly limited. On the policy front, the two men worked side by side in early 1961 when Johnson was made head of the newly established President's Committee on Equal Employment Opportunity. John Kennedy had created the committee on March 6, 1961, by combining existing committees dealing with discrimination against government employees, and discrimination against employees by government contractors. His purpose was "to ensure that Americans of all colors and beliefs will have equal access to employment within the government, and with those who do business with the government."[87] The charge here was to establish by executive order nondiscriminatory hiring practices for the twenty million workers within the government and employed by private contractors for various government projects. Seeking good legal counsel in this highly technical area of employment discrimination, Johnson turned to Fortas for help. He made him an informal executive director for the investigation and drafting of a rigorous executive order regulating such practices for John Kennedy's signature.[88]

Working with Johnson on civil rights had by now become second nature for Fortas, after their mutual efforts in 1957 and 1960. In fact, in 1963 Fortas would once again be giving technical legal advice to the vice president on that year's civil rights measure, telling Johnson's secretary by phone that "the bad part of the bill is the part that relates to public establishments. They adopted some of my ideas in the public establishments section, but there were some other thoughts about it. I think particularly and urgently they ought to do something about the WHEREAS clauses in the public establishments part of the bill." After adding that the proposed Conciliation Service should not be put in the Department of Justice, Fortas left word that he could be reached for further consultation that day at his house if needed.[89]

On the President's Committee on Equal Employment Opportunity, though, the problems were more direct, and Fortas had much more personal control over the enterprise. As one staffer put it, even though Fortas was a private citizen, "any problems we had we were told to 'check it with Abe.'"[90] After lecturing the committee during its first meeting on April 11, 1961, on the rules and regulations in the area,

Fortas drew up the original version of the executive order, and then he
and his junior law associates supervised the revisions of the draft.[91]
But as it turned out, not only were Fortas's skills as a legal draftsman
needed, but his negotiating skills as well. There were three power cen-
ters on the committee—Vice President Johnson, Secretary of Labor
Arthur Goldberg, and Attorney General Robert F. Kennedy. Since
Johnson and Robert Kennedy were fighting with each other, Fortas
"moved in at the Vice President's request and negotiated it with the
Attorney General where they had problems."[92] So while the Labor
and Justice Department people commented on the early Fortas draft,
the attorney not only worked out compromise language but also helped
to deflect Kennedy's criticism away from Johnson. Through all the
turmoil, Fortas made sure that the work got done.

One of the members of the committee recalls that "Abe was invalu-
able in all of this."[93] Another recalls Fortas's incredible ability to
think ahead and second-guess where a discussion was heading. One
day, Floyd Feeney, a member of the committee staff, got a call from
Fortas shortly before one of the meetings telling him to make a number
of changes in the documents. The instructions seemed to be meaningless to him at the time, but he did as he was told. To his amazement, as the meeting progressed and the battle between Bobby
Kennedy and Johnson flared up again, it turned out that the instructions from Fortas, who was not even in attendance, fit "hand in
glove" with the methods needed to overcome the difficulties.[94]

While the committee's original job was to ensure that private contractors on federal projects would not discriminate in their hiring policies, Fortas led the way toward a more expansive approach. The
committee was given the much broader power to cancel contracts with
project directors when violations of the antidiscrimination directive
could be proved. Here, too, there was a change. The burden of proof
on a charge of discrimination was now shifted from the offended party
to the contractor, who was now required to show that there had *not*
been a violation. Since this regulation provided just the sort of government leadership in the field that John Kennedy was seeking, he happily
signed the order.[95] (In fact, the president was so happy with Fortas's
work that the following year he asked the attorney to serve on the new
Committee on Equality of Opportunity in the Armed Forces.[96]) The
result of all this was an even more liberal reputation for the vice president and a broader-based appeal to a more national constituency.

On the cultural front, Fortas scored some points for the Johnson
crowd by arranging for the reclusive cellist Pablo Casals to perform at

a White House dinner on November 13, 1961. This occasion was the
first return of Casals to the United States since its recognition of the
Franco regime in Spain, and was taken as a symbol of the cultural
heights reached by the Camelot administration.[97] Director of the Festival Casals in Puerto Rico and a great lover of music, Fortas had
gotten to know Casals quite well. In fact, he was so close to the
legendary musician that he once had to fly Casals's precious cello to
New York from the island for repairs on a split seam. Fortas bought
first-class tickets on the plane for both himself and the instrument;
though a moderate drinker, he ordered martinis for the occupants of
both seats and drank them both. In explaining later why he had been so
nervous, Fortas said, "Carrying a man's cello is like carrying his
wife."[98]

Even here, though, it took all of Fortas's legendary negotiating skill
to arrange the memorable concert. After hearing Casals express his
admiration for the new president, Fortas called Pierre Salinger at the
White House to see if Kennedy would be interested in a concert. Upon
being told that the president was "enormously interested," Fortas began courting Casals through a long series of phone conversations and
letters, while also negotiating the arrangements with the White House
aides. (He even went to the extent of drafting the letter Casals would
use in responding to the presidential invitation.)[99] In the end, Fortas
was able to persuade Casals that honoring Kennedy by playing in the
president's house would not break his vow never to play in a country
that recognized the Franco regime.[100]

In the two years that followed, Fortas had little to do with the White
House.[101] In 1963, however, there was again something he could do
as Johnson's personal lawyer. In October of that year, Johnson's former Senate aide Bobby Baker became embroiled in big trouble that
threatened to bring down the vice president as well. By this time
Baker, nicknamed the 101st Senator for all the favors he had done for
members of that body, had amassed interests in twenty-two corporations, dealing with vending machines, motels, housing developments,
and insurance.[102] When Baker was sued by a man who alleged that he
was in violation of one of his vending contracts, Arnold, Fortas and
Porter was bought in to deal with what appeared to be routine litigation.[103] After allegations began that Baker had been using his influence
to place vending machines in defense plants around the country, he
resigned from his position as secretary of the Senate majority.

But the issue did not die down, and soon Lyndon Johnson was on
the hook as well. On November 22, 1963, a fellow named Don Reyn-

olds testified before Senate investigators that Baker had been the agent through which two $100,000 insurance policies had been written on the life of Johnson. In return for his services, Baker was supposed to have received a commission, and some advertising time was bought by the insurance company on the Johnson radio stations. As part of the deal, a gift of a stereo set was allegedly sent to the Johnsons personally.

Contrary to the advice of others to ignore the Reynolds story completely, Johnson followed Fortas's directions and held a press conference. Incredibly, in an apparent fit of panic, Johnson denied that Baker was his protégé and said that he did not even know him at all. According to Johnson aide Reedy, Abe Fortas "gave [him] very poor advice" in convincing him to take this line of attack. Fortas seemed to underestimate the public relations aspect of the problem.[104]

Fortas compounded the public relations faux pas two weeks later by dropping Baker as a client after Johnson became president, thus giving the appearance that there was indeed more to the connection with Johnson than was being revealed. The reasons for this dismissal of a client are a matter of dispute. Baker said that he happened to be in Fortas's law office when they had received word of the assassination,[105] and immediately told the attorney, "Mr. Fortas, I know Lyndon Johnson will be calling on you for many services and your advice. If you represent me it might be embarrassing to the new president, and it might put you in a conflict-of-interest situation. I release you as my attorney, and I'll have a confirming letter on your desk by tomorrow."[106] One account even has Johnson telling Fortas to drop "that litle sonofabitch Bobby Baker" as a client, upon first hearing of the Reynolds allegations.[107] For his part, though, Fortas simply told the press at the time that he was removing himself from the case because "in the crisis of transition, I have undertaken certain assignments" for the new president that necessitated this action.[108] Much later, Fortas told an interviewer that he "subsequently, with Bobby's consent, withdrew from the case. As I remember I withdrew from the case because it looked as if it was going to have some very wide ramifications that I didn't believe I could appropriately be involved in."[109] Whatever the truth here, the actual reason was probably as simple as the fact that in this circumstance Fortas had two incompatible clients—Bobby Baker and Lyndon Baines Johnson—and there was never any real question as to which one had priority status.

But the Baker incident, coming right around the transition of power following the Kennedy assassination, showed something else. Now that the man from Texas was president of the United States, the nature of his relationship to the attorney from Memphis changed again. Once more, despite the fact that Lyndon Johnson had all of the power of the government in his hands, it was Fortas who was providing the favors of advice, unquestioning loyalty, and protection. And once more it would seem that there was nothing that he wanted, nothing that could be given him, in return.

V

"PRESIDENTIAL ADVISER, WASHINGTON"

The Rolls-Royce quietly pulled into the parking lot of the Executive Office Building near the White House before noon on the morning of November 23, 1963. Abe Fortas was terribly upset, but had come obediently in response to a late-night phone call from his old friend. As he was ushered by an aide into the vice presidential suite, he immediately "had a feeling of great comfort." As upset as he was, as upset as everyone was, Fortas was put at ease by the "studied calm" of the great friend he had come to visit. To be sure, it was the calm in the eye of a huge firestorm. But it was calm nonetheless.[1]

"Mr. President, at your service," he said to Lyndon Johnson.

For the country there had been a tragic ending, but for each of them now this was a dramatic beginning. And Abe Fortas knew that the new president needed his help more than ever.[2] Those first few hectic days were going to be a time for reassessment. Where was Lyndon Johnson now headed? Which of his army of friends were going to help him get there? Which ones could be trusted in the inner circle to help select the nation's future course, and the people who would guide it?

Any elected official is the hub of a universe of aides and ideas, and the president of the United States is no different. But after President Kennedy's assassination on November 22, the White House became a universe without a hub. The center had been wrenched from Boston and dropped in Stonewall, Texas. It was bad for both the old aides and the new president, but the need for stability, and time pressures, compelled LBJ to convince as many of them as possible to stay on. There was, however, something that Johnson could do for his own well-being. He could at least consult *his* people outside of the formal governmental lines of command.

There was never any question that Abe Fortas would be at the top of that list. Intuitively, Fortas seemed to provide just what Johnson needed. "He's the wisest man I have ever known," the new president told those around him.[3] Fortas's genius, explained one admirer, "rested on an intuitive knowledge built from the ground up of how bureaucracies worked and thus, how they needed to be addressed."[4] This was precisely the kind of experience that would prove so valuable to Johnson.

Fortas was more than just a political insider; in the new president's mind he was "Lyndon Johnson's insider." "Check it with Abe" became the watchword of the Johnson team. Congressman James Jones, formerly a Johnson assistant, explained, "Fortas was very good at so-called bedside manner, and really, for someone like Johnson who was very strong yet, in many cases, very insecure, Fortas was a great source of comfort." The reasons for this insecurity, added Jones, were rooted in Johnson's background. "The thing he envied about the Kennedys most of all was that their old school ties go back so many years and so when Kennedy became President, he had people he could really trust because he'd gone to prep school with them, college with them and all that. . . . Johnson didn't have these old school ties and friendships, people he met were ones he met in politics coming up where various people have axes to grind. Consequently, I think, people like Abe Fortas and others . . . that had been with him for years were the ones that he really relied on."[5] But the irony here, of course, was that Fortas himself was an intellectual of the same caliber as or greater than Johnson's "enemies"—albeit one from the "New Haven crowd." As the new president's main outside adviser, Fortas could be trusted to give, as Johnson's Austin lawyer and personal friend Donald S.

Thomas described it, "solid, honest advice, which was largely political in nature."[6]

Nothing made that fact clearer than the first twenty-four hours of Lyndon Johnson's presidency. Having already spoken on the phone just hours after the Kennedy assassination, both Fortas and Johnson were aware of how many loose ends from the previous administration and Johnson's own life had to be tied up. So they spoke at great length that morning of the twenty-third in the Executive Office Building, and later that afternoon resumed the discussion at The Elms, the fashionable brick mansion in Northwest Washington where the new president would continue to live until Jacqueline Kennedy could move from the White House.

Understandably, one of the most important early decisions that had to be made was how to investigate the Kennedy assassination. There was an element of tension as everyone wondered whether this was an isolated act or part of a much larger plot against the government. Johnson was very much in favor of having a state board of inquiry staffed only by Texans. He argued that a state board would be more consistent with legal procedures, since at the time killing a president was not a federal offense.[7] On the other hand, Deputy Attorney General Nicholas deB. Katzenbach argued quite correctly that this would be seen as a whitewash, and what was needed was a federal commission staffed by prominent figures of high public visibility.[8] Troubled by the president's thinking, Katzenbach went to see Fortas, the man he knew to be closest to Johnson, for help, telling him that the state investigation idea was a "ghastly mistake."

Future chroniclers of these days would insist repeatedly that it was Abe Fortas who advised Johnson on the creation and staffing of the Warren Commission.[9] Actually, the opposite was true. Fortas did what he had always done in the past—he supported Johnson's wishes and found a way to protect Johnson's public image from harm. "My God," Fortas used to tell James H. Rowe, Jr., "I convinced Harold Ickes, who was just as thin-skinned . . . just not to read the papers and not to read magazines. If we could convince Johnson to do the same thing, it would be fine."[10] But soon people would be writing about this president's isolation, his penchant for having yes-men, his domineering nature, and his neurotic closed-mindedness.[11] Now Johnson was determined to seek out *all* the newspapers and all criticism of him. Knowing this, Fortas understood without having to be told that his role was to take Johnson's side and try to find a way out for him. Like the new president, then, Fortas actually *opposed* the creation of a national investigatory commission.

So he set out to get others to see things the president's way. He called former secretary of state Dean Acheson, an extremely influential voice in the Washington political network, and said "he had advised the President not to have a Presidential commission" for two reasons. First, "people would gather there was more to it than appeared on the surface and there was no reason to give them an opportunity to do so." Second, "the country is upset enough and if the President superseded the ordinary procedures, it would further shake people's trust and confidence." Those ordinary procedures, of course, would be an investigation by the government of the state in which the assassination had occurred—Texas.[12]

Fearing that Acheson was not convinced enough to pass the ideas along, Fortas phoned Russ Wiggins and Al Friendly, respectively the editor and managing editor of *The Washington Post,* to tell them what the former secretary of state now knew. But all of these efforts to float the president's trial balloon came to naught. As Fortas told Walter Jenkins, the president's right-hand man, later that day, "I am afraid [the commission advocates] think they have a great idea." By making these calls, though, Fortas had made every effort to convince others of the president's position before Johnson had to cave in and create the federal Warren Commission.[13]

Now, Fortas's role in the Johnson presidency was set. He would be an outsider who was a presidential friend first and an adviser second. He would be, in Congressman Jones's words, "a hand-holder" whom Johnson could "bounce ideas off or kind of let his troubles hang out a little bit" in front of, without fear of a negative reaction.[14]

Creating the Warren Commission was just the beginning of the list of decisions to be made by the new president. The situation in the government was "incredibly bad," Fortas wrote to attorney Adolf Berle.[15] "That was an unimaginably stressful, short period of time before [Johnson] had to declare himself and take some crucial positions with which he had to live for a long time thereafter," he later explained. "The Kennedy program was a shambles. . . . Great, inspiring, new ideals for our nation had been launched, but nothing had been accomplished, really, in terms of implementing legislation on the basic issues."[16] Now it was Johnson's agenda, and Fortas made it known by his presence at the Executive Office Building that he was indeed ready "to serve."

And serve he did. For the next several days Fortas was by Johnson's side at The Elms day and night, as they mapped out the future course of action and planned the president's maiden speech to Congress. There was no time for white papers by study groups, no time for leisurely discussions of how to make the transition to the presidency, no time to solicit ideas from various departments of the government and send back language for further checking, no time for anything other than finding the right words to comfort a nation and get the government moving again. So, as the president's friend and outside adviser, Fortas was asked to pass judgment upon various ideas for reorganizing the White House. There seemed to be no limit to the fields that Fortas felt confident enough to comment upon. Most of his memos were personal, handwritten suggestions drafted especially for the president. All of these memos were characteristic in that they were either unsigned or signed only with a cryptic "A.F." Unless someone recognized the handwriting or the initials, the adviser's anonymity would be preserved. And that was just the way Fortas and Johnson wanted it.

The key item on the agenda now was to draft the president's first speech to Congress, which would set the overall course of the new Johnson administration. Since this was a subject that required Fortas's insight, he was invited to The Elms on the evening of November 24 for dinner with the Johnsons and a number of other couples.[17] The new president had decided that he would address a joint session of Congress at 12:30 P.M. on Wednesday, November 27, and the matter of what he would say became the main topic of conversation at the table. It was a very dramatic scene, that Sunday evening. The conversation rolled around to a discussion of what could be done in the area of race relations in this country. Should the new president place his imprimatur on the civil rights act that was then under consideration? And if he did, how high should that be on his list of priorities? It was Lyndon Johnson's first chance to demonstrate to his closest friends how the rise to the pinnacle of his profession had affected his outlook. Someone at the table warned Johnson not to make the Civil Rights Act a priority, fearing an early defeat in Congress and a diminution of the president's persuasive power.[18] A silence fell over the group as they waited for Johnson's response. He said nothing for perhaps thirty seconds—to Fortas it seemed as if thirty minutes passed—then Johnson boomed, "Well, what the hell is the presidency for?"

Hopeless as the measure looked at the time, and sensible as the advice had been not to put a presidency on the line so early in the administration, Johnson stood ready to use the full powers at his disposal, especially on a subject to which he was committed.[19] Fortas later explained that by saying this, Johnson had made it clear that he was "in a large part, [going] to vindicate and implement the Kennedy program. He seemed to regard his role in major respects as that of surrogate for President Kennedy. This was facilitated, of course, by the fact that on the basic social issues he shared deeply Kennedy's commitments."[20] Indeed, the call for civil rights legislation would occupy a very prominent place in the upcoming speech. Years later the scene was still burned into Fortas's memory, and the man who had defended Lyndon Johnson to his liberal friends would comment that the incident "renewed my pride in him."[21]

The work on Johnson's first speech to Congress proceeded at a hectic pace out at The Elms. Johnson had solicited drafts from a number of people—Ted Sorensen, John Kenneth Galbraith, Adlai Stevenson, and former Senate aide Horace Busby—letting all of the men think that they were writing the only draft.[22]

In truth, though, the men who would write the final draft were Senator Hubert Humphrey of Minnesota and attorney Abe Fortas of Washington, D.C. On the evening before the speech, all the drafts had come in and Johnson had invited Humphrey and Fortas to dinner at The Elms. The evening's entertainment, as they soon found out, was speechwriting for the new president. Johnson pulled out his favorite drafts and, handing them to the two visitors, told them to work out a final compromise version of the speech. They worked until 2:30 that morning, with the president reading the suggestions and daughter Lynda sitting at the typewriter.[23]

This would be Johnson's "most critical hour," and Fortas labored to get the speech just right. Later, he would modestly say that he had· only "added some corn pone" as he, in the phrase of one writer, converted the drafts into "Johnsonese."[24] In truth, Fortas did a whole lot more than that. Working from a draft that Ted Sorensen had written the day before, Fortas did his best to change the entire thrust of the message. The result was that roughly 25 percent of the final version was taken almost verbatim from Fortas's handwritten draft.[25]

Understandably, Sorensen had written a short, powerful eulogy for his fallen leader, leaving the new president to fend for himself. But there was a limit to what Fortas, the Johnson man, was going to accept. "All I have ever possessed I would have gladly given *not* to be here today. For the greatest leader of our time has been struck down by the foulest deed of our time," the Sorensen speech began. This had the proper ring, given the difficult circumstances. But when Sorensen then had Johnson saying, "And I who cannot fill his shoes must occupy his desk," Fortas quickly squiggled his pencil through it.[26]

After Fortas got through making some minor stylistic changes to the Sorensen call for continuation of the vision of John Kennedy, he took out a yellow legal pad and began to pencil his own speech. It was a role that he would fill numerous times in the years to come. In situations such as this, Fortas saw his role in advising Johnson as being very specific. He tried to compensate for what he believed was his friend's major weakness—an inability or perhaps just an unwillingness to conceptualize all of his goals before seeking them. "Johnson was fervently result-oriented," Fortas explained later. "He hated to put ideas in broad conceptual terms. He was, if you like, an operator. . . . He liked to face specific issues and to do something about them. He did not feel comfortable with using the White House as a 'bully pulpit.'"[27]

With this role in mind, Fortas decided that it was up to him to write a speech laying out the Johnson vision and agenda. Regarding international policy, Fortas wrote for the president, "This nation has demonstrated that it has the courage to seek peace, and it has the fortitude to risk war." Let everyone know that the United States "can also be a formidable foe to those who reject the path of peace, and those who seek to impose upon us or our allies the yoke of tyranny." On domestic policy he wrote, "We will serve all the nation, not one section or one sector or one group—but all Americans. . . . We have differences, but now, as in the past, we can derive from those differences strength, not weakness; wisdom, not despair."

Since Fortas had heard Johnson's comments about going forward with the controversial civil rights program, he was determined to make that clear in his speech draft. Writing and then frequently squiggling out phrases and sentences that seemed to lead nowhere, Fortas helped to set the tone for the new administration: "In this critical moment, it is our duty, yours and mine, as the Government of the United States . . . to show that we are capable of decisive action—[and] that from the brutal loss of our leader, we will derive not weakness but strength—that we can and will act, and act now." And one direction for that action was made clear: "I urge you again, as I did in 1957 and again in 1960, to enact a civil rights law so that we can move forward to eliminate from this nation every trace of discrimination and oppression that is based upon race or color."[28]

Building on Sorensen's strategy of tugging at the heartstrings, Fortas's draft placed Johnson firmly on the fallen leader's coattails. The new president called on Congress to "*act,* and act greatly" on the Kennedy program. But Fortas felt that Johnson needed to reassure his former colleagues in Congress on one point: "As one who has long served in both houses of the Congress, I firmly believe in the independence and the integrity of the legislative branch. And I promise you that I shall always respect this. It is deep in the marrow of my bones."[29] Whether Johnson would keep this promise remained to be seen.

It was a great speech, and got rave reviews from nearly all quarters. "Let us continue," Johnson said throughout, recalling John Kennedy's "Let us begin" in his Inaugural, and it was clear that the work of the government would carry on. To those closest to the new president, it was also clear that the work would carry on with one of those men who observed the delivery of the speech from the front row of the executive gallery in the Capitol, Abe Fortas, at Lyndon Johnson's side. For his part, Fortas could take pride in the speech's review by Anthony Lewis in *The New York Times:* "In emotion, in style, in accent, this was a Lyndon Baines Johnson performance. . . . It was a Johnson speech, not anyone else's." Indeed, Lewis found the Fortas addition on civil rights (without, of course, knowing its true source) "the most notable aspect of the content."[30] There could be no higher praise for the work of the adviser in the shadows.

While this drafting process was under way, another of the key items on the Johnson agenda—in many ways one of the most important to the new president—was how to handle his considerable wealth and substantial business interests in radio, television, and elsewhere, now that he was in the White House. Since Presidents Eisenhower and Kennedy had both publicly claimed that their resources were put in a blind trust and administered by others to avoid compromising their official duties, Johnson felt compelled to do the same. But he wanted to do so in a way that would avoid any public controversy, while also safeguarding his own financial interests. It was a delicate political task of the utmost personal interest to the new president. Drawing up the important and complex legal document needed to do this was a perfect mission for Abe Fortas. Johnson saw him as a man capable of devising intricate solutions that would safeguard the president's interests first and foremost.

In those first few days of the presidency, Fortas arranged a meeting at The Elms with Johnson's attorneys Donald S. Thomas of Austin and J. Waddy Bullion of Dallas; A. W. Moursund, a Texas judge known by Johnson to be an expert rancher; Horace Busby, Johnson's old Sen-

ate aide; and, from time to time, Johnson himself. Since everyone had
agreed prior to this that a blind trust would be created rather than a
wholesale dispossession of all the Johnson properties, Fortas came to
the meeting with a draft that he had drawn up with the attorneys at
Arnold, Fortas and Porter. (They had searched everywhere for John
Kennedy's well-publicized blind trust agreement, but no one could
seem to find it.) It was a typical Johnson legal meeting—"legal opinions by consensus," as his Texas lawyers would call it—a group of
attorneys and advisers all contributing their opinions and expertise on a
single problem.[31]

Fortas's role, though, was different. He was there as the president's
friend. So his purpose was to lead the assembled advisers and interpret
their consensus. At this time Fortas actually knew very little about the
Johnsons' personal financial affairs. Don Thomas recalls today, "Fortas had no, none, zilch role in our business operation."[32] But Fortas
still had a key role to play—it was his job to make the whole operation
politically palatable to the press and the country. And on that score he
had a number of ideas. "The problem at hand," he announced in
setting the tone for the rest of the meeting and negotiations, "is how
the Johnson family can live at the White House on anything other than
animal crackers."[33] Then Fortas launched into a discussion of why
this blind trust was being established, the procedures for doing so, and
the broad context of the provisions that had been drafted by him and
the Arnold, Fortas and Porter law firm. Each of the participants at the
meeting was then given a chance to read the draft, and the matter was
settled.[34]

Later, when the press challenged the nature of the blind trust overseen by two close Johnson friends, Fortas defended it as "the tightest,
toughest trust arrangement ever drawn for a public official."[35] Perhaps
it was—on paper—but as one of the trustees, Waddy Bullion, admits
today, "The words were tight, [but] conduct is something outside the
written page. Administration can be different from the letter of the
trust."[36] Don Thomas adds when asked whether Fortas's claim was
correct, "You've got to be kidding—you can't hide a ranch. And after
all, Johnson loved to play with it."[37]

But that didn't matter to Fortas the political adviser; he had accomplished his goal by giving the blind trust *the appearance* of being tight.
As Waddy Bullion explains, Fortas's role in this meeting was a key
one despite his lack of knowledge at the time about the business end of
the Johnson empire: "Law was *de minimis* of Abe Fortas's advice to
the President. On legal matters LBJ would get advice from someone

else. His view on politics and government was what LBJ looked to in Fortas. Fortas's advice was primarily political—the president himself was an excellent businessman."[38]

The agenda for the rest of the meeting was a discussion led by Fortas on the handling of the other Johnson resources in the future. Fortas wanted the family's business as noncontroversial as possible, so he talked about the dispossession of all properties that might in some way be politically controversial. He advised Johnson to sell all the bank stock owned by his Texas Broadcasting Corporation. But then what was to be done with these funds and future profits of the corporation? Fortas's recommendation was to take all surplus funds and invest it in noncontroversial Texas Hill Country real estate.[39]

Even in the real estate area, though, Fortas saw one political problem. Something had to be done, he said, about the size of the president's ranch. It did not look good for him to *appear* to be a Texas land baron with a ranch of several hundred acres that had exploded in size during the vice presidency. "What I want you to have," Fortas told Johnson, "is forty acres and a mule." Since Johnson had long wanted to deed the ranch, after a life estate for his family, over to the Park Service, Fortas told Don Thomas and the others to survey a small plot of land around the ranch and arrange the conveying deed for the rest. Only in this manner, the president's outside adviser told the gathering, would the press be satisfied.

Hearing that, Horace Busby exclaimed, "You don't know the press very well!"[40] Busby's comment was one of those offhand, kidding remarks that have more truth than one likes to admit. Johnson was relying on his Washington attorney to keep the president's name out of the papers on such matters—to explain things in a manner that the press would understand. And Fortas was not up to the task. He was an attorney looking for the technical angle, the lines between which the true message could be read. The press, on the other hand, knowing the insatiable demand of its readers for information on public figures, looks not always for those subtleties, but instead for damaging appearances. And Fortas had misjudged appearances here. The press wouldn't care how much land had been deeded off, only that the president still owned a great deal and was buying more elsewhere.

With all of this time-consuming work for the new president, Fortas's law practice began to take a backseat to the needs of his friend and his country. This concerned the president's counselor a great deal. He telephoned Tex Goldschmidt complaining that his law practice was "going to pot" and he was unable to leave the president's side. Gold-

schmidt, however, convinced him that the country needed him and that
it was his patriotic duty to stand by Johnson during such a troubled
time.[41] So Fortas made a decision—from now on he would be on
constant call for his number one, and only, political client.[42]

After those first few days in the White House, the basic pattern of
the relationship between the two men had been set. Fortas was more
than just Lyndon Johnson's lawyer and adviser; he was also his friend.
But what does it mean to be a close friend of the president of the
United States?

The intimacy of Fortas's friendship with Johnson allowed him to see
a man very different from the figure visible to others—and dictated a
very different relationship with him. The others had it all wrong, Fortas would explain later, because they never saw the whole game.
Using his remarkable skill for painting images in language, he said that
the books and articles that had been written about Johnson missed the
point because the authors were "like the little boy who would look
through the knothole to see a baseball game, and it was a very small
knothole and all he could see was the left fielder. The little boy would
see that game and he would think that action happens only occasionally because only then does the left fielder move back and forth and do
all kinds of things. But in fact the game is very different from what the
little boy saw." Similarly, people who had been with Lyndon Johnson
for only a few minutes during the day, and with whom the president
never would have discussed all of the matters on his mind, saw only a
part of his personality.[43]

You have to understand, Fortas explained, that Johnson had a "pack
rat mind, it was a great instrument. He would collect all bits of facts
and information about any problem, and store it in his mind, and use it
when the time was right."[44] An old friend of both men, Tex Goldschmidt, reinforces this insight with a story of Johnson's prodigious
memory. In 1939 Goldschmidt told then Congressman Johnson a
funny story about growing up in Fredericksburg, Texas, occupied at
the time mainly by immigrant Germans. To appeal to these constituents during election time, one candidate for the local bench had made
up a campaign slogan that was a nursery rhyme for children, using a
curious mixture of German and English: "Alfred Conrad Pater Petsch,
mak ein guden county jedge." Twenty-four years later Johnson called
on Goldschmidt to speak to a German diplomat who knew no English,
and upon hearing the protests from his friend that he knew absolutely
no German, said, "But what about Alfred Conrad Pater Petsch, mak
ein guden county jedge?"[45]

Fortas was quick to deny the image of Johnson as a man of limited viewpoint. "Contrary to the way that he's portrayed," Fortas later explained to a visitor, "he wanted desperately to get all sides of the issue on every question. And so, on occasion, he would meet with his advisers and he would call up someone in whom he trusted—usually either me or Clark Clifford—and he would say, 'Everyone's telling me this. Give me the opposing argument.' Whether I believed it or not, I was to just lay out the opposing argument so he could see what the issues were."

The format of the discussions had a style all their own. "They were not a give and take discussion." Instead, Fortas explained, Johnson "would ask a question, he would listen intently, but there was not a dialogue. . . . He was not quick to make up his mind. He would make up his mind only after having solicited and obtained opposing points of view, more so than anybody I know."[46] It was a style that impressed political experts such as former Roosevelt assistant James H. Rowe, Jr., who called Johnson "the most cautious politician I ever ran into."[47]

By the time Johnson came to the White House it was an established practice that one of the last people to be consulted after all of the other returns were in was Abe Fortas. The running joke among the presidential staff members was that the moment for a crucial decision had arrived only when the door to the White House was opened and filling the portal were, as Press Secretary George Christian called them, the "Bobbsey Twins"—Fortas and Washington attorney Clark Clifford—summoned by the president for a little chat. They were the "court of last resort"—the advisers who were more equal than others.[48] Clifford himself would later explain, "Either President Johnson said it himself or he may have quoted Mr. Sam Rayburn that 'you should look to the young men for activity and industry and action; you should look to the older men for judgment and wisdom.'"[49]

In the first month of the new presidency, Johnson asked a great deal of Abe Fortas, and Fortas always delivered. In those first couple of weeks, long lists of "Items for Decision" were prepared for the new president suggesting how Lyndon Johnson might follow up on the planned Kennedy agenda. But nothing was done until Fortas had passed on each of the items.[50] While this process was under way, Fortas worked with James Rowe on a reorganization plan for the new White House staff, and perused former Johnson Senate aide George Reedy's ideas for an "early definition of goals" for the new administration.[51] When Fortas was also asked to review the mandate of the director of the Bureau of the Budget on the clearance procedure for legislative proposals, it became evident how much the outside adviser had to say about the establishment of the new administration.[52]

All of this gave considerable force to the handwritten memos drafted by Fortas on any number of topics. These early memoranda displayed clearly that his function was to be far more concerned with the *symbolic appearance* of an action than with its substance. In one, he argued that the new president should visit Congress personally, as suggested by Hubert Humphrey, only if he first reminded the press of the extraordinary nature of such an occasion and reasserted the separateness of the two governmental branches.[53] Then, in suggesting a new line of succession for the presidency, taking the Speaker of the House out of the third spot in line, Fortas suggested that the post of "acting president" be created should the succession occur before the midpoint in the term of office.[54]

There seemed to be no subject beyond Fortas's competence. He spoke about foreign policy with Ambassador W. Averell Harriman, disagreed with the Treasury Department over a plan to have banks pay interest on government deposits,[55] suggested a way to present a planned Defense Department cost-consciousness program to the press, and drafted a six-point memo filled with mathematical calculations on how to reduce the funds required for foreign aid appropriations by subsidizing loans from the Export-Import Bank.[56]

With the success of his initial speech to Congress after the Kennedy assassination, it was only natural that the president would once again press Fortas into service as a speechwriter for the upcoming State of the Union address.[57] To plan the speech, Johnson gathered around the cabinet table on December 23, 1963, the brightest idea men in his administration: Secretary of State Dean Rusk, Secretary of Agriculture Orville Freeman, Secretary of Labor W. Willard Wirtz, Secretary of the Interior Stewart Udall, Deputy Attorney General Nicholas deB. Katzenbach, National Security Adviser McGeorge Bundy, Chairman Walt Rostow of the State Department's Policy Planning Council, main speechwriter Ted Sorensen, former Senate aides George Reedy and Horace Busby, present aides Jack Valenti and Walter Jenkins, and outside advisers Abe Fortas, Clark Clifford, and James H. Rowe, Jr. After dominating the discussion for a good portion of the one-hour-and-twenty-minute meeting, outlining the topics and directions that he wished to take in the speech, Johnson turned the meeting over to Fortas and Clifford.

Fortas, having already attended an earlier meeting with a number of other idea men concerning the speech, used a proposal offered by Princeton historian Eric Goldman in arguing that the traditional laundry-list speech should be replaced by one that was "new on [the] domestic front." After outlining the need for a resurgence of leadership on the state and local levels, Fortas called for the creation of "regional governments." Such regional meetings of state governors could deal with overlapping problems such as transportation, education, and civil rights. The time had come, Fortas concluded, for the "reduction [of the] number of spectators in national life," which would in turn help make it possible for the younger generation to enter the work force. While no one around the table supported Fortas's ideas, in the months to come he would work with Goldman in putting together a "quiet brain trust" of intellectual leaders around the nation to accomplish much of what the two men had been advocating. In so doing, Fortas filled his role well as a lightning rod for new, broader ideas that the president might consider.

After the first weeks of the new administration, there was no doubt as to where Fortas stood in Lyndon Johnson's mind. A quick way to tell how high one's star happened to be in the president's firmament was to see how Johnson signed the White House pictures that were sent out. Among the many autographed pictures that Fortas received in those first months, one in particular seemed to say it all. "To Abe Fortas," the president wrote, "than whom there is no better, with love, Lyndon B. Johnson."[58]

Even with all of the excitement of being one of the president's top outside advisers, there was a dark side to the role. With Fortas's new visibility in the White House, the press began to inquire into the nature of his relationship with the new president. And what the reporters lacked in facts they more than made up for by imagination. Less than two weeks after Lyndon Johnson came to power, the press was reporting that one of the most powerful men in this administration was Abe Fortas. Fortas was reported to have "been in and out of the White House office on numerous occasions," while the man himself acknowledged only that he had received "certain assignments" from the new president.[59] Try as he might to keep his name out of the papers, as the "president's friend" Fortas was now considered "fair game" for the press.

One area of inquiry by the press was any possible connections between Fortas's clients and new administration policy. There was no question that Lyndon Johnson's ascension to the White House had improved things for the firm. "The day they put the bullet in [Kennedy's] head, the firm really took off," one of the partners was heard to say.[60] After growing by four to a total of thirty members after Kennedy's death, the firm increased to thirty-five by 1965, with seventeen partners and eighteen associates. Fortas was now acting as what was called a rainmaker, drumming up new clients for the firm. In fact, when he was appointed to the Supreme Court, one of the partners was heard to say to a prospective client, "Fortas is going to the Court, do you still want to go with us?"[61]

Questions were first raised when the president failed to mention the controversial issue of cigarette advertising in his State of the Union address. Could it be that Fortas, one of whose prize clients happened to be the Philip Morris Company, was responsible for the omission?

Indeed, when the Federal Trade Commission, faced with a report from the surgeon general on the dangers of smoking, was threatening to put health warnings on cigarette packages, Philip Morris retained Fortas's law firm for assistance. Members of that firm, together with members of other prominent Washington law firms and former senator Earle C. Clements, the head of the lobbying Tobacco Institute, planned the counterattack. First, the group got the issue into the congressional arena, thus more subject to lobbying pressure, by persuading Representative Oren Harris of Arkansas, then chairman of the House Interstate and Foreign Commerce Committee, to write the chairman of the FTC that no action should be taken until Congress could "consider legislation" on the matter. It was not long before the press was reporting that the group "wrote testimony, drafted bills and amendments, served as central casting for witnesses most likely to sell the industry's point of view, and fed to friendly congressmen statements and questions to be asked of witnesses."[62] Fortas, it was reported later, had even drafted the compromise weakly worded package warning and gone to the Justice Department and key members of Congress on behalf of a self-regulatory advertising code for the industry drafted by members of his firm.[63] While no one could prove that he had altered the president's State of the Union address on behalf of his client, for a man of Fortas's extreme sense of discretion, publicity of any sort on this issue was unwanted.[64]

Soon, more questions were raised in the press about Arnold, Fortas and Porter's legal work as it related to administration policy—this time on the island of Puerto Rico. It was alleged that Fortas had used his White House influence with Lyndon Johnson to influence Secretary of the Interior Udall to allow the construction of a huge petrochemical complex on the island by Phillips Petroleum. Since Fortas's firm represented both the oil company and the island, it seemed a reasonable deduction.[65] In fact, when later pressed by the White House for details of this action, Paul Porter claimed that the firm had indeed been asked by the Puerto Rican government to negotiate the contract for Phillips, but that Fortas "was not involved in the negotiations although he was aware of these activities."[66] (Later events, though, would indicate that Porter's respect for the truth was suspect.)

But these negative stories were not enough to keep Fortas from expanding his services for the man in the White House. The year 1964 would in some ways be the most nerve-racking of Lyndon Johnson's career. All of the promise of Kennedy's Camelot had been passed to him, and in less than a year he would have to stand for election on his own, largely on the basis of that incomplete record. Somehow he would have to create enough of a program to win the Democratic party's and then the general public's hearts. This would not be easy for a man who a few short months before had been rumored to be on the verge of being dropped from the ticket by the Kennedys.

The key was the image developed by the new president, so Fortas turned his attention to this issue. In a two-page memorandum he dealt with a subject that had now become an obsession with him, the relations of the president with Congress. Congress was, for Fortas, "the greatest foreseeable danger," since with the large Democratic majorities in both houses the public would expect great movement for the Johnson legislative agenda. A messy, divided Congress would only hurt the campaigning president. So Fortas set out to dictate the method by which the administration would improve the relations there.

There were a variety of weapons available to a president in influencing Congress, Fortas lectured the former Senate majority leader. Informal contacts with members (even beyond the leadership), White House photo opportunities, the reassertion of presidential leadership of the party machinery, and the development with the leadership of a timetable for the consideration of various bills represented just a few of those possibilities. So Fortas proposed the institution of a comprehensive public information program, the maintenance of adequate liaison between the various executive agencies and Congress, the delivery of a series of fireside chats to the American people, and the revitalization of a grass-roots Democratic party organization. Finally, he suggested that the president explore whether, as newly crowned party leader, he could participate in the selection of committee appointments in both houses of Congress. The inconsistency of this last suggestion with his previous pleas for a vigilant defense of the separation of powers between the two branches seemed not to trouble the presidential adviser at all.

Johnson's action on this matter shed light on the relationship between Fortas, the outside adviser, and those political insiders left over from the Kennedy regime. The president followed his "decision by consensus" practice and sent the memo on for comment to the administration's congressional liaison, Larry O'Brien. Understandably, O'Brien was less than impressed by the implied criticism of his work—and told Johnson so in a strongly worded and detailed memo. These proposals, he said, did "not contain suggestions not presently in effect to a greater degree than envisioned by the writer," or proposed new ideas that were either "unrealistic," a "net minus," or "wheel spinning."[67]

There was little question as to which view would receive favorable presidential attention. O'Brien was a Kennedy man, and Fortas was decidedly a Johnson man. So the O'Brien memo was sent back for comment to Fortas, who seemed offended that his views were being checked in such a manner. Using the advantage of his close relationship with the president, Fortas complained to Johnson's top aide, Walter Jenkins, that the only part of the O'Brien memo that was comprehensible to him seemed to call for a meeting to "arrive at a program—and quickly." So, Fortas concluded, "the boss" should call the meeting and name the participants, "who, I hope, will *not* include me."[68]

As the year 1964 wore on, the counsel of Abe Fortas would be in even more demand by the president. During the first eight months of the year, most of the communication between the two men would be by mail and through memos. Only twenty times during all of these months did the two men speak face to face or on the phone. However, in *each* of the remaining months of the year, the number of conversations between them would either equal or vastly exceed that number.

Not surprisingly, a major focus of Fortas's energy in the early part of the year was devoted to restaffing the new administration. Ralph Dungan, the adviser on staff appointments for Kennedy, was still in charge of the formal bureaucratic recruiting enterprise. However, President Johnson had begun to develop a "two-tiered" selection system with a second and more important informal level composed of inside and outside political advisers who passed on the "political" merits of various appointments suggested by the initial bureaucratic screening. One of the key members of this second, informal network was Abe Fortas. For the next seventeen months, Fortas would serve as a headhunter searching for expert and, more importantly, loyal talent to implement the Great Society, a "full-scale domestic program" of increased spending in domestic areas ranging from urban renewal, medical care, and poverty reduction to crime control and highway safety.

Fortas's role in this second tier differed according to the situation. Generally, though, his task was to use either his knowledge of the local bar or his longtime understanding of the various circles within the city of Washington itself to judge a candidate's legal excellence and political loyalty to Johnson. In this role, Fortas was sometimes able to anticipate problems with certain appointees and correct the record beforehand. Such was the case with economist Mary Dublin Keyserling, whom Fortas was touting for a high-level administration post on the basis of her qualifications and her role as president of the Women's National Democratic Club. Warning that in the 1950's loyalty charges had been made against Keyserling, "as against most good people of her generation," Fortas sent along a file on her for White House perusal. With this highly positive assessment on record, it was not long before she was named director of the Women's Bureau in the Department of Labor.[69]

On numerous other occasions, Fortas played a more general role, responding to direct requests from the president or his aides with whole lists of names for possible appointments. These lists were then kept in the administration's "ready file" for the selection of future recruits. The memos contained not only short biographical descriptions, including loyalty checks, suggested posts, and lists of references (generally just "A.F."), but also Fortas's own rating chart ranging from "aaa to d."[70] When old Interior Department friends such as Tex Goldschmidt and C. Girard Davidson failed to get appointed, Fortas simply repeated his endorsements for them on later lists.[71]

Given Fortas's expertise in the arts, it was only natural that he would be consulted on a wide variety of the so-called culture appointments throughout the administration as well.[72] Even with these appointments, Fortas tried to use his political intuition and his close access to "the boss" to protect the president. A question had arisen as to the appointment of a consultant on the arts. Pierre Salinger was pushing speechwriter Richard Goodwin for the post, over the objections of Fortas, and thought he was sending the matter to the Oval Office for an objective tie-breaking vote. In fact, Fortas went behind Salinger's back and reported to Walter Jenkins for Johnson's ear that the appointment "would be a mistake and one the President would regret."[73]

In this role Fortas was always looking for a way to bolster Johnson's image as an administrator. Once, in a memo to White House aide Valenti, he suggested ways to deal with the criticisms that some new appointments had not been business oriented enough. The president should consult with various business leaders, he argued. The benefits of such a procedure were that, though business would almost never produce names of the sort that would bind the president, the businessmen he consulted would feel a part of the process. Then, if the president really wanted some useful names he could consult with various executive recruiting agencies.[74] Once more, it was the symbolic *appearance* of an action that concerned Fortas more than any *real* change in policy.[75]

When Johnson finally changed the selection process, and John Macy, chairman of the Civil Service Commission, was empowered to do the initial screening on most appointments, the ever-helpful Fortas had another access point for his suggestions. Over the next eight months, sometimes repeatedly on the same day, he inundated Macy with a stack of recommendations for positions ranging from the Federal Communications Commission to a variety of ambassadorial and judicial posts.[76] Some of these were the same names that had failed to impress the earlier bureaucratic officials.

But it was Fortas's work on a controversial cabinet appointment that indicated the true nature of his role in this selection process. John Connor, the president of Merck and Company, was nominated as secretary of commerce to replace the resigning Luther Hodges. This selection was intended as a means of bringing the administration closer to business circles; however, shortly after the announcement of the nomination on December 20, 1964, Connor's future in the administration was in doubt.

When Johnson became aware of a lucrative Merck stock option exercised by Connor before accepting the nomination, he was determined to get the candidate to divest himself of the stock in order to avoid charges of conflict of interest. While Connor prepared to defend this financial arrangement before the Senate, Johnson applied the pressure, summoning him to the White House for a conference. When Connor opted not to go, sending his attorney instead, it only served to anger the president further.

The time had come to escalate the pressure. Connor was summoned in a very peremptory fashion by the president to attend a meeting on

January 8, 1965, with Abe Fortas. Rather than negotiate, or even consider Connor's other options, Fortas's message was simple: Sell the stock or lose the appointment. In this fashion, then, Fortas was saving Johnson from an unpleasant task, acting both as his friend and as his attorney. Connor, though, was determined to place his fate in the Senate's hands, or, if worst came to worst, simply withdraw his own name from consideration.

But Johnson was not beaten yet. The next day he sent their mutual friend Clark Clifford to meet with Connor and presumably get immediate results. However, less tied to Johnson, Clifford had a very different approach. He listened carefully to the candidate's desire for a negotiated compromise position. Then, after finding the middle ground, Clifford told Connor how to defend the matter before the Senate, and promised to sell the compromise to the president. In the end, the issue was never really a factor in the confirmation process. In years to come this scene of the contrasting postures of Lyndon Johnson's two most intimate outside advisers would be replayed, with Fortas taking the president's side come hell or high water, and Clifford independently searching for a different, and perhaps better, way.[77]

Over and above these appointment efforts, Fortas continued to function as the president's main adviser on legal questions facing the administration. Having proven in the early weeks of the administration to be equally facile on all topics, at least as far as Lyndon Johnson was concerned, Fortas was now consulted on most hot topics as they arose. And on the rare occasion when he was not consulted, the White House could now count on volunteered advice from the favorite partner at Arnold, Fortas and Porter.

The first such task was simply to oversee the entire legal process on the handling of executive clemency. When Johnson became concerned by the large number of requests for presidential pardons being presented to him for signature, Fortas was called in to review the process. The problem, Fortas argued in a lengthy memo, was that while 98 percent of these requests were routine, a few were "politically significant" and "involve debatable questions of principle." So he suggested an additional step in the bureaucratic procedure by which the special counsel in the White House would tag, using a draft form provided by Fortas, those cases that deserved special attention. Once more, Fortas's concern was to protect Lyndon Johnson rather than safeguard the possible interests of those in the legal system.[78]

When the Senate investigation of Bobby Baker heated up in early 1964, it was only natural that the president would call in Fortas to keep matters from getting out of hand. The question had become whether Walter Jenkins, a presidential aide who knew where most of the bodies were buried in the new administration but who certainly did not want to talk about any of it, could be compelled to testify. So Fortas had his law firm research whether a confidential administrative assistant to the president could decline to appear before an investigating congressional committee on the grounds of executive privilege. Not surprisingly, the law firm, in a confidential twenty-six-page legal brief, concluded that Jenkins could safely duck any subpoenas.[79] And in the end it was arranged that Jenkins could avoid testifying by simply signing an affidavit denying the charges of insurance man Donald Reynolds.

In the months to come, Fortas's advice was sought on a wide range of other legal issues. He argued that White House staff papers were privileged and should not be made available to Congress without the prior approval of the president. He passed along advice on the investments of the Government Employees Insurance Company, the balance-of-payments situation, and the national organization of the United Givers Fund. He helped to formulate the White House policy on the acceptance of gifts from foreign nationals by embassy officials acting in the name of the president.[80] He even wrote a "secret" memorandum suggesting a way for Johnson to remove a troublesome member of the Board of Governors of the Federal Reserve System, even though prevented by congressional power and Supreme Court rulings from doing so.[81]

Two issues of continuing concern to Fortas during this period were the arts and the island of Puerto Rico. Having arranged for the appearance of Pablo Casals at the Kennedy White House, Fortas was now recognized as one of the main links between the world of culture and the presidency. It was not uncommon to have the president's friend, who played the violin so well that on Sundays he hosted a gathering of professional musicians at his Georgetown home for a regular string quartet, introduce himself at a White House dinner by saying, "I'm Abe Fortas. I'm a violinist." Frequently he would arrange for White House appearances by other internationally known musicians, such as Isaac Stern, Alexander Schneider, and others. And on occasion, Fortas would borrow a violin and perform a duet with the visitor, once prompting Lyndon Johnson to ask one of his guests, president of the AFL-CIO George Meany, "Do you reckon Abe has a union card?"[82]

But it was not all parties for Fortas in the field of the arts and the White House. There was hard lobbying involved, and he was determined to leave his mark here, while also erasing the snobbish eastern notion that culture for the Johnson White House was a Texas two-step and a barbecue. Years later this charge still rankled Fortas, who lambasted one critical interviewer: "That's just plain, ridiculous slander. Johnson was very interested in the arts. His was the first Administration in history in which the federal government materially aided the arts. And *he* did it. And the reason he did it—although he was not interested in it particularly; he had the intellectual scope and was wise enough to recognize its importance to the development of the civilization of the nation—the development of civilized values."[83]

It was mainly Fortas who had ensured that Johnson would one day have this defense available to him. He moved the president toward an organized national effort to support the arts. In January 1964 he helped to formulate an overall cultural program for the administration, including the establishment by executive order of an advisory council for the arts. Then, when the matter was later taken up by Congress, Fortas advised the White House on which version of the bill to support, and what changes to make.[84] Of course, Fortas then freely suggested who might serve on the council's board of directors, and offered comments on a plan to fund the arts from an extension of the copyright provisions. Finally, it was Fortas who helped draft the legislation creating the Kennedy Center for the Performing Arts, followed by a very active involvement in the workings of that institution, even to the extent of planning the groundbreaking ceremonies in November 1964. All of these efforts, together with Fortas's constant suggestions for various culture-related appointments, prompted Bill Moyers to write him in March 1965, "If you only worked as hard for us as you do for culture, just think where we might be!"[85]

Fortas's other passion was the island of Puerto Rico.[86] Having helped to invent the commonwealth form of government there, become a central foreign adviser to its first governor under the commonwealth, Luis Muñoz-Marin, and served as a central participant in the economic development program known as Operation Bootstrap, Fortas's interest was long-standing. Whether spurred by his own love for the island or the money that it brought in as a prime client of his law firm, Fortas now took on the role of goodwill ambassador for Puerto Rico in the Johnson administration. He made sure that the president acknowledged by messages (sometimes drafted by Fortas) all of the important island holidays, and received all important governmental visitors to Washington such as Muñoz-Marin and his successor, Roberto Sanchez Vilella (even to the extent of drafting briefing papers for the president). Furthermore, Fortas kept Johnson fully informed about all of the political rumors then being circulated in the Puerto Rican government and ensured that government emissaries, sometimes even the adviser himself, were sent to all the important functions. By acting as the island's lobbyist and its symbolic supporter in the government, the president's friend made sure that his Caribbean client got high visibility in the administration. And for Fortas personally, his demonstrated ability to place the issues of the island before the highest officers in the land only served to enhance his prestige and personal power in Puerto Rico.[86]

Whether the other aides liked it or not, Johnson's trust in Fortas was set. By now there was no matter too complex or too small for the lawyer to be consulted on, even when the matter was not one of high politics or high finance, but simply high jinks. One day, it was simply that the president wanted to swim in his outdoor pool year round.

Winter in Stonewall can be pretty nippy, and Lyndon Johnson was not the kind of man patient enough to wait until spring for a dip in the pool. He knew that the Fortases had installed a plastic bubble over their outdoor pool behind their fashionable Georgetown home (no doubt to the delight of the other residents in the exclusive community) to permit year-round use. What was good enough for the adviser was good enough for the president, and one was installed at the Texas ranch as well. However, weather patterns being what they are in Texas, the humidity got so great inside the bubble that the president's glasses "got fogged up" and no one seemed to know how to dry the place out. "Call Abe Fortas," Johnson barked to his aides, "and find out how you take care of this durn thing." Fortas's answer to the plea for help from presidential assistant James R. Jones was simple: "Grow a lot of tropical plants." Johnson got "a kick out of" the advice and told his aide, "I sure hate to mess up this place with a bunch of damn plants, but I guess we'll have to."[87]

None of Fortas's efforts, though, were as vital as his continuing interest in Johnson's reelection in 1964. The tension, and even paranoia, of a presidential campaign requires that the candidate have cool heads around offering trusted judgments as each new crisis arises. Having served in this capacity already in the 1948 Senate campaign, Fortas was once more enlisted in this vital position.

Fortas's role here, together with Washington lawyers Rowe and Clifford, was to serve as part of what Theodore White called "a senior court of review." While the three men rarely met as a group, working independently one or more of them would pass "as presiding appellate judge for any major speech, any major appearance, any major television show, any major change of schedule, [and] any decision of policy."[88] Much of this work was done orally, but the surviving files do contain some evidence of it. It was Fortas and Clifford who nixed any presidential appearances on the popular news interview programs like *Meet the Press* as being "too commercial, not controllable," and "not dignified rostrums" for the president of the United States. Fortas also suggested that the president sew up the state of Tennessee by speaking in Fortas's hometown of Memphis on the TVA.[89] Finally, according to one account, it was Fortas who, with the other two senior advisers, devised the plan to dump Bobby Kennedy from a possible vice presidential slot by having Johnson tell the press that he was excluding all cabinet members from consideration for the position.[90]

Perhaps Fortas's most valuable service, though, occurred during what turned out to be the great unplanned transition in the White House staff on October 14, 1964. The White House went into what one insider called "an absolute panic" when a call came to Lady Bird Johnson's press secretary, Liz Carpenter, that Walter Jenkins had been arrested a week earlier for alleged homosexual activity in the men's room of the local YMCA.[91]

For many in the White House, Jenkins was the "selfless" and "indispensable man." He was the only aide authorized to sign Lyndon Johnson's name to letters and documents, and people calling the president were comfortable just to speak with Jenkins and leave a matter in his hands. Somehow, he kept the staff in harmony and kept Johnson open to new people and ideas.[92]

But when an anonymous tip about his arrest led the *Washington Evening Star* to begin an investigation, and this investigation led to the discovery of a similar arrest five years earlier, Jenkins knew he was in trouble. And, after years of watching Lyndon Johnson's actions at such times, he knew just where to turn for help. He immediately called Abe Fortas.

By the time Jenkins arrived at the attorney's home, Fortas could see that he was in such a state of shock that he "could not at that moment put one word consecutively after another."[93] The president's friend knew exactly how to control the damage. After he and Clark Clifford talked to Jenkins, they quickly had him hospitalized. Meanwhile, at 3:57 P.M. Fortas and Clifford reached the presidential candidate in Suite 35-A of New York's Waldorf-Astoria as he was preparing to give a speech. Fortas and Johnson were in nearly constant phone contact for the next fifteen hours.[94] Despite the swirling sense of fear in the White House over the implications of this incident for the campaign, one observer recalls that Fortas's reaction "was one of great compassion and calm'' throughout the incident.[95] Another observer adds, ''What was uppermost in Abe's mind was Jenkins's welfare.'' After much discussion between Fortas and Clifford at the White House and Johnson in New York, it was decided that Jenkins should resign as soon as possible.[96]

This enabled Fortas to travel to the offices of the *Star* later in the day to make a pitch to its editors that they should not break the news in their next edition. He told them of the hospitalization and the imminent resignation. Think of Jenkins's wife and six children, pleaded the attorney. In the end, the *Star* decided to follow its normal practice in such morals cases and not print the story. Later, Fortas would say, ''I shall always honor these men at the *Star*. I shall always as a human being feel grateful to them.''[97] As luck would have it, though, the story had also gotten to United Press International and the news was broken that evening. In the end, Jenkins forfeited the bond rather than face the charges in court, an action that was not considered an admission of guilt and did not lead to a conviction. Once more, Fortas's role in the blackest part of a rather spectacular campaign for Johnson was not lost on the president's staff. As Liz Carpenter recalls, ''That was the day that Abe Fortas rose so high in my estimation, and I thought how fortunate we were [to have him around].''[98]

But for Fortas, the task was not over. Yet another call came from the president saying, ''Mildred needs you.'' So Fortas went to the White House to show Jenkins's assistant how to handle the sensitive FBI files that were maintained on presidential appointees and visitors. From then on, Mildred Stegall later recalled, ''innumerable times'' she would be told by Johnson to bundle up some of the president's most sensitive confidential documents, dealing with either his personal affairs or some political problem, and take them over to Fortas for advice. ''You just knew that you were wrecking his appointment schedule,'' she said, ''but Mr. Fortas took all the time that was necessary and never gave you the appearance that he didn't have all the time in the world for you.'' His suggestions were then taken back to the president and unfailingly implemented.

Years later Stegall explained that while most of these personal documents had been destroyed because of their sensitive nature, she did recall that many of them concerned tax questions on the president's personal finances. So a number of times, Stegall would also bring the matters before Fortas's wife, Carol Agger, because of her renowned expertise in this area. Since the president was supposedly unaware of his personal business because it was in ''the tightest, toughest trust arrangement ever drawn for a public official,'' written by the man whom he now was frequently consulting, the sensitivity of these requests on financial matters was obvious.

The political problems placed before Fortas by this ultraprivate technique were also ones that, if they got in the hands of the press, could blow up in the president's face. For example, after the 1964 presidential election there was a vast amount of campaign money left over, money that by law could be spent only on political expenses and could not be converted to personal use. Since there were no such campaign expenses remaining, Johnson left word to ''send it all back to the people who sent it.'' But how did one determine which of the thousands of contributions had yet to be spent? And how would one decide whom to offend by returning the money, indicating that their expected access to the White House might be diminished? Stegall was told to carry the files over to Arnold, Fortas and Porter. Whereupon Fortas personally reviewed all of the lists, deciding who would get a refund, and since such an operation could not possibly come out of the White House, the checks were then issued from his law firm. The president ''just really admired Fortas's judgment,'' Stegall concluded in reflecting on their relationship, adding with reverence, *''and when the advice was given he listened.''*[99]

It was not long into the campaign before, as Horace Busby had predicted, the press began to ask questions about the Johnsons' rapidly expanding financial empire. So it was left to Fortas to ''handle'' the press, trying to keep reporters out of the president's personal affairs. But the adviser was as unsuited for this role as he had been in speculating about press relations in the first place. In May 1964, Tom Collins of *Newsday* called Fortas for confirmation of information he had acquired on the Johnson empire. Questions were raised about the Johnsons' use of supplies from the broadcasting company, their use of company cars, the rumor that advertising time on the station had been traded for land, the role of Johnson in the business operations, the size of other land holdings, and, showing that Busby and not Fortas had been correct about the press's continued interest, the size of the ranch itself.[100]

Fortas was not what one might call a friendly buffer to such inquiries from the press. A lifetime of having his name, and those of his clients, plastered over the pages of critical newspapers had colored his judgment about the fourth estate forever. And he treated the press accordingly. Fortas lost his temper at the end of his conversation with *Newsday* reporter Collins and said, ''Why in the hell don't you people leave them alone. . . . The President [is] trying to do his public job."[101] Having already recommended to the president that the accounting firm of Haskins and Sells draw up a statement of the entire Johnson holdings, and supervised the study personally, Fortas made that material available to the reporter.[102] From then on, Fortas was just not available when Collins called.

When the Johnson finances became even more controversial as the presidential campaign heated up, Fortas was in charge of "handling" the press once more. On July 29, 1964, at the president's request, an enterprising investigative reporter named William Lambert was sent by *Life* magazine in an effort to clear the problem up once and for all. Rather than dealing with Johnson, though, he was directed to the Arnold, Fortas and Porter office. There Lambert was met by Fortas himself, who announced while tapping the briefcase on his desk, "I've been the President's attorney for thirty years, all the material is right here." But rather than divulge any information, Fortas "tried like hell for two hours" to talk the reporting team out of pursuing the story. Finally, Lambert told his host, "Mr. Fortas you're wasting our time and we're wasting yours." At that, Fortas phoned the president, and the entire group was invited over to the White House for four more hours of hospitality, Texas style. After a dinner of White House leftovers and a 2 A.M. tour of the building, they finally sat down to talk. Over the objections of Fortas, who was seated at the president's side, Johnson proceeded to give them all the information they were seeking. It was not the last time that Abe Fortas would underestimate the relentless nature of the press in general, and Lambert in particular.[103]

Considering everything, there was ample reason for Fortas, with tongue firmly anchored in his cheek, to put in his entry in the 1965–1966 volume of *Who's Who in the South and Southwest* that his present position was "Presidential adviser, Washington." And his present office? Of course, "care The White House, 1600 Pennsylvania Avenue, Washington." Even jokes like this, though, have the potential to come back to haunt the president's friends—and this one would.[104]

VI

THE
DAVIDSON
OPERATION

Life can get pretty exciting when one is the president's friend. And after eighteen months in the role, not to mention the twenty-five years of close association prior to that time, Abe Fortas had come to expect the action—but nothing quite like this!

The problems began on April 24, 1965, when a coalition of military leaders and civilian groups started a coup in the Dominican Republic with the intention of returning to power former president Juan Bosch, who had been living in exile in Puerto Rico since his own ouster two years earlier.[1] Four days after the outbreak the president became convinced that American lives were at stake on the island and the marines, on Johnson's orders, invaded without warning. Within a short while the invading force had grown to twenty-three thousand men. This seemed to be more than sufficient for rooting out the fifty-three, or was it seventy-seven (the FBI could never be sure), known Communists allegedly spotted on the island.

Lyndon Johnson now had a king-sized problem. In a lesson that he was doomed to relearn, it was always easier to send troops into a foreign land than to get them out. Determined to avoid the collapse of another Caribbean nation in a Cuba-style revolution, he had sent forces in unilaterally without the sanction of the Organization of American States (OAS). The longer the fighting went on, with proof of the existence of the so-called Communist revolutionaries still lacking, the more likely an outcry from the Americans at home. So Johnson needed both to justify past actions and to search for the means to limit future involvement. In trying to accomplish both aims, the president short-cut normal diplomatic and foreign policy channels and became what one State Department official called "his own case officer," taking complete charge of every action in the region.[2]

Why not bring in Abe Fortas as well? reasoned Johnson. Surely part of the president's thinking was that Fortas, over the years he had taken an interest in Puerto Rico, had gathered many wide-ranging and high-level contacts there. These contacts might be helpful in locating Bosch, who was now holed up transmitting radio broadcasts to the forces fighting in his name in the Dominican Republic. Moreover, Johnson knew that his friend, like him, hated Communists, and hated the thought that they might take what FDR had called a grip hold, or even several grip holds, in the American hemisphere. Finally, Johnson knew that Fortas could help in the areas of legal advice (justifying what had been done), diplomatic efforts (trying to negotiate a solution and an American withdrawal), and political advice (explaining the problem domestically after the crisis had ceased).

Shortly after the invasion took place, then, Abe Fortas became one of Johnson's most important advisers on the entire crisis. Once more, Fortas was in practically constant contact with Johnson. Over the next three weeks, the two men spoke on the telephone sixty-nine times, which was more calls than Johnson made to his ambassador on the scene, his secretary of state, and his secretary of defense combined. Then, in addition to the ten formal meetings they attended together at locations ranging from the White House swimming pool to the so-called Situation Room, there was a time during the latter part of the crisis when Fortas virtually lived in the White House. This was a Lyndon Johnson operation from start to finish, with Abe Fortas destined to be by his side every step of the way.[3]

The crisis had begun on April 28 when Colonel Pedro Benoît, representing the Dominican Republic's ruling military junta, called on the United States for "unlimited and immediate military assistance" to put down the continuing rebellion, which he said was being directed by the

Communists with the intention "to convert the country into another Cuba." By 5:30 P.M. the same day President Johnson was handed a "critic" memo, reserved for messages that deal with the most urgent matters of national security, from the American ambassador, Tapley Bennett, saying that the landing of the marines was required to protect the Americans trying to evacuate the island.

So the invasion was ordered. By the time Fortas called the White House later that night, he had already performed a valuable service for the president. He had located and talked to the elusive Juan Bosch.

No one in the American government seemed to have much influence over or contact with the deposed leader, or much faith in him either. While he was not a Communist, members of the Johnson administration thought that his leadership skills left much to be desired. George Ball said of him, "I have rarely met a man so unrealistic, arrogant, and erratic. I thought him incapable of running even a small social club, much less a country in turmoil."[4] Tom Mann, then assistant secretary of state and the man in charge on the scene, added, "[Bosch] wasn't a very practical man. They said he was a good man, an honest man, an academician, but not really qualified to rule, and I think Bosch's administration showed that."[5] It was said that whenever Bosch was faced with a crisis he would take the knob off his door so that no one could get into his office, allowing him to contemplate his problems in peace.

Bosch had simply concluded without the benefit of an election that he was still the rightful constitutional leader of the Dominican Republic even after his overthrow—hence the name "Constitutionalists" for his military rebel followers—and he waited for the expected triumphant return to power. But now Bosch was hiding in Puerto Rico, fearing for his own safety, while the fighting raged in his behalf at home. Only Fortas seemed to have a line of contact to Bosch, or at least so Lyndon Johnson thought. While Fortas had never met the man, they had a mutual friend in Jaime Benitez, the chancellor of the University of Puerto Rico. So, using that contact, Fortas tried to get what information he could for the president.

After speaking with Bosch on the phone that day, Fortas's assessment of the man squared with the views of others. He seemed to be a "very poetic, very dramatic man . . . a Latin American hero type. He was not a practical or pragmatic man, but he was a man of intense idealism—but very, very emotional, very emotional."[6] For a man of Fortas's cold rationality, dealing with such a figure was going to be a problem. Nevertheless, until a line of communication could be set up

by the American troops in the Dominican Republic, with the installa-
tion of a provisional government, Fortas was Johnson's only alternative.

Meanwhile, Fortas sought only to convince the leader to return to
his country for free elections. But Bosch said he would do so only
after the fighting had ceased, and the elections had been held. So the
two men agreed that an immediate cease-fire had to be arranged. In
reporting all of this to Lyndon Johnson, Fortas said that he "would be
standing by to do anything [they] wanted him to do."[7] Though Fortas
had not really accomplished much, by opening a valuable line of communication to the deposed leader he had ensured that he would become
a major player in the crisis in the days to come. Accordingly, the
president notified Tom Mann that he had effectively drafted Abe Fortas
for service in the State Department and was "transferring" the attorney to Mann's operation.[8]

Two days later Fortas and Johnson were on the phone with each
other almost literally all day long, conversing a total of twelve times,
as the Washington lawyer continued to try to bring Bosch around. The
task now was to convince Bosch to ask the Latin American members
of the Organization of American States to take a more active role in
mediating the conflict toward a cease-fire. Of course the OAS's reluctance to move was in large part due to the fact that it had not been in
any way consulted before the unilateral American intervention two
days earlier.[9] By May 1, with bands of armed civilians roaming the
streets, it was pretty clear that the OAS was not going to do much
more than send down an investigatory commission made up of the
representatives of five member states in an attempt to reestablish peace
and order. The effort here was so paltry and unproductive that the
United States was forced to send its own diplomatic team, consisting
of National Security Adviser McGeorge Bundy, Thomas Mann, and
former ambassador to the Dominican Republic John Bartlow Martin,
in an effort to establish a dialogue between Bosch and the rebels.
However, the Americans expected little help now from Bosch, who
despite two attempts by Castro to overthrow him during his 1963 presidency was now welcoming Cuban support.

Anticipating that the diplomatic efforts would bog down, Fortas decided to solve the crisis himself. After all, this seemed to be simply a
matter of getting people to talk to one another and negotiate out a
compromise agreement. It was nothing more than what a good Washington lawyer does scores of times in the average work week. So Fortas sent a memorandum labeled "very secret" to the president, which

impressed Johnson so much that he in turn read it over the phone to Thomas Mann for a reaction. "If the OAS does not move," the memo began, "it seems to me you might consider the following: after careful checking with Bosch and everybody else, the designation of [Romulo] Betancourt [of Venezuela], [José] Figueras [of Costa Rica], and Luis Muñoz-Marin [of Puerto Rico] as an interim committee might be attempted. This is my own idea, not communicated or checked with anyone."[10] Fortas's idea was to name these three men to act as trustees or overseers of the effort to bring order to the Dominican Republic. The advantages were obvious. Not only would this ruling commission take the United States and the OAS off the hook, even more important from Fortas's standpoint they would remove the high level of risk to Lyndon Johnson's presidency.

In many ways the proposal represented the nature of Johnson and Fortas's work not only in foreign policy, but on domestic problems as well. They were trying to bend the rules and manipulate other players like pieces on the chessboard. Hadn't they done the same in the Interior Department days, building the Marshall Ford Dam? Wasn't it simply a matter of angling the 1948 Senate primary controversy so that the arguments could be made before Justice Black? Wherever the two men worked—the Senate, the Kennedy Committee on Equal Employment Opportunity, even the White House—wasn't the game the same, and the result inevitable? There was always someone to be called, an ally to be found, an enemy to be subverted, and a play to be made.

But in foreign policy the game was never that clear. The pieces on the board and the rules for their movement were always changing, if they ever existed at all. In fact, it was never clear what game was being played. Despite his unwavering confidence, Fortas's political judgment and level of expertise in this area was highly suspect. This was not a world of rationality and reasoned judgment like law, which could be mastered after a few hours' study of the relevant books. Here there were no rules, no predictability, and no judges. Indeed, the players were not even Americans, thus giving them a wholly different world view. Stripped of the tools of his trade, then, Fortas had to fall back on his own instincts. He was convinced that his knowledge and instincts were good because he knew the right people and had been working with these issues over a period of years. Lyndon Johnson believed this, too.

But the problem here was that Fortas, even if he truly understood the issues, never approached them with a truly open mind. Instead, his first instinct was to protect Lyndon Johnson. Like the premier lawyer that he was, Fortas worked first and foremost to defend his longtime client's interests. With so many forces poised to attack the president, Fortas adopted a "damage control" rather than a "problem-solving" mode. The client would act; the lawyer would justify. And Lyndon Johnson liked that attitude very much.

It was one thing to tell the emperor that he had no clothes, but who would have the courage to tell the emperor's tailor that he didn't know how to dress his employer? It took a diplomat of Tom Mann's stature and experience very little time to conclude that the new plan was totally naïve. He saw it as a rational, lawyerlike solution that was totally inappropriate for the situation. It wasn't in any way tailored to the Latin Americans' reactions, to their ambivalence toward different types of governmental systems. "The idea was never practical," he said later, "if you know inter-American law and inter-American relations, because of the non-intervention rule. . . . It's prohibited absolutely in the charter of the OAS. That's so firmly embedded in inter-American law that there was never any chance."[11] Not only that, how would it sound to the Communists on the island, if there were any, to say that three foreign leaders were being sent into the island to represent the United States? "It couldn't represent the OAS," concludes Mann, "and it couldn't represent us." Furthermore, why would three foreign leaders consent to put themselves in such a difficult spot, to say nothing of the reluctance of the individual governments to allow their leaders to do so even if they were so inclined? From the start, an idea with so many obvious flaws was, in Mann's estimation, "doomed."

But Lyndon Johnson liked it. And he did so because his friend and adviser, Abe Fortas, had proposed it. After all, Fortas's involvement meant that the president's own best interests were surely being safeguarded. So to Mann's amazement, it was not long before many in high Washington circles were investigating whether this commission idea couldn't be made to work.

For the next several days Fortas continued to negotiate with Bosch over the phone, hoping to secure some movement for his proposal. But movement was hard to find. He told Bosch "that the essential point now is that the rebels are still firing in a time of cease-fire and that no one could answer for the consequences if this firing did not stop." Try as he might, though, Fortas advised McGeorge Bundy that he expected little from this contact and suggested that John Bartlow Martin make a "desperate effort" to reestablish contact in the Dominican Republic in searching for a cease-fire.[12] Still, he seemed to be able to keep in touch with Bosch himself, no matter how unproductive the results.[13] Meanwhile, Mann, despite being "very skeptical" of Fortas's three-man trusteeship plan, was pitching the idea to his good friend, Venezuela's Betancourt.[14]

Fortas then tried a new approach. Through intermediaries, he communicated to Bosch that it "was in his own long-range political interests" to "withdraw from present political ambition and let an interim government be formed without him." As if this wasn't enough, Fortas wondered whether Bosch might also make a public statement acknowledging that this was a Cuban-led revolution, and calling for the help of both the United States and the OAS to share in the responsibility of driving them out. Then, perhaps he could call for the American forces to stay as long as they were needed, while also pledging that he would work for the restoration of peace and order, to be followed by steps toward "early free elections." So all Fortas was asking was for Bosch to give up the ship, ratify all that the United States had already done and intended to do in the future, and then probably ruin his chances for future election to the post that people were now fighting to give him. Not surprisingly, the Dominican exile refused. Nevertheless, Fortas, fully confident of his own persuasive abilities, promised to get back to McGeorge Bundy as soon as he got some results.[15]

By the fifth of May the American government had discovered that it was difficult to get any foreign leader to serve on anything. An OAS committee visiting the Dominican Republic had accomplished little, and no progress had been made by the Americans on Fortas's ruling-commission idea. Meanwhile, Fortas turned his attention to convincing Romulo Betancourt that the revolution in the Dominican Republic had been undertaken by Communist forces, and thus that the Venezuelans should make a public statement to this effect.[16] For its part, the White House was now fully occupied with an effort to explain the initial invasion to the press. Now that the initial excitement of the dramatic venture had worn off, an attempt was being made to justify the unilateral intervention by identifying the Communists on the island. So Fortas turned his attention to the public relations effort. The legal adviser to the Department of State had put together a document entitled "Legal Basis for United States Actions in the Dominican Republic," and it clearly required approval by the president's favorite attorney.

In a closely reasoned, six-page brief drafted at the request of a number of congressmen, Legal Adviser Len Meeker argued that the United States was well within its rights in protecting "American lives and property abroad" by intervening in the Dominican Republic.

Promising that this was just a preliminary step toward the united action
of the entire Organization of American States, Meeker cited a variety
of sections in the OAS charter and key events in the dispute (including
the call by island forces for foreign help) as evidence that the United
States had been compelled to invade.[17] The United States still supported popular sovereignty in this hemisphere, the memo concluded,
but not if it meant "falling prey to international conspiracy from any
quarter." So, as soon as order was restored by the OAS, the Americans would return home. All in all, it was a powerfully persuasive
legal document, and one that the State Department thought it could
stand upon.

But Abe Fortas didn't like it. He felt that the document did not serve
the political interests of Lyndon Johnson at all. In his opinion, the
effort to set out "a technical *legal* basis" for action, rather than the
"moral and pragmatic" position, would lead to "criticism and some
scorn." Knowing that Johnson abhorred both of these reactions, the
self-appointed foreign policy adviser set out the posture that would
best serve the president's interests. In so doing, he once more contradicted the experts in the field of international law.

Fortas's draft of an argument in response to this document was cast
in the sort of vivid political language designed to incite action. While
the American government greatly regretted having to act unilaterally,
he wrote, the blame should be placed on the inability of the OAS
machinery to respond to an emergency of such magnitude. The problem, Fortas was arguing, was not the exuberance of a rambunctious
president, but the ineptness of the international alliance. Furthermore,
the purpose of the invasion was to protect the lives of foreign nationals, making a withdrawal something "which no civilized nation
could contemplate." The chaos resulting from a withdrawal, he added,
would mean the loss of thousands of lives and the denial of freedom to
an entire country. This argument, of course, would only persuade
those who believed along with Fortas and Johnson that another Cuba
was imminent. All in all, one was left wondering after reading this
two-page argument why anyone would have the gall to question
Johnson's decision to intervene.[18]

While this debate was going on, Johnson was beginning to feel the
pressure of leading an undeclared war. "We just have to get something
moving pretty quick," he told Tom Mann on the phone on May 9. "It
has been going on over two weeks and [I am] afraid it [will] fall in on
us and we will have a real crash here at home." By the next day,
though, it was clear that the Fortas "wise man" ruling-commission

plan was bogging down. The OAS visiting committee was forced to adjourn its organizing meeting when Venezuela refused to contribute either troops or its leader to the cause. But Johnson had not lost hope. Though all of the steps to convince other leaders to serve on the ruling commission had failed, he instructed Tom Mann to talk to Fortas once more. "He keeps in close touch with these people," the president added.

But now, Mann could see that the president's confidence in Fortas was misplaced. No amount of effort on his part was going to bring the ruling-commission idea to life. Furthermore, Mann was unhappy that while the American embassy team placed its efforts in a more productive attempt to draft a rallying statement for Ambassador Bennett to read to a public meeting of foreign ambassadors, Fortas offered nothing more than criticism of the enterprise. "It would be better to go down with this wise man thing," Fortas argued, adding that the plan represented "a grand gesture and then the blame will be on" the commission members. Mann now had no choice but to express his growing doubts to the president about Fortas's involvement. They had already lost four days pushing the commission idea, he told Johnson, and the OAS would never "buy this." In fact, he added, literally everyone else opposed Fortas, indicating that "it would be inconceivable to stick on the wise men. This would get us nothing." Therefore he recommended ignoring Fortas's advice. It was clearly not what the president wanted to hear.[19]

So the State Department searched for another presidential initiative to rally the foreign leaders, and replace the ineffective Fortas proposal. By now it was apparent that everything hinged on finding some way to get both the OAS and Bosch to act in their own best interests. When Mann and the president spoke on the phone on May 11, they canvassed new avenues for lobbying the deposed Dominican leader. Was there someone they had missed? One by one they reviewed the State Department personnel available for duty, but no one seemed to offer anything new. The big problem, Mann told the president, was political. "If we went down [to Puerto Rico]," he explained, "we would have to assume that it would leak [to the press] and that it might look as if we were looking for someone." This assumption would put the pressure on the State Department to solve the crisis immediately, or appear impotent diplomatically.

Then Mann hit on an ingenious solution. How about sending Abe Fortas to Puerto Rico? Perhaps he could persuade Bosch to come out of hiding, arrange a broadly based provisional government in the Do-

minican Republic, and return to stand for free elections. Knowing the
confidence that the president had in the Washington lawyer, combined
with Fortas's contacts in Puerto Rico, Mann believed the elements
were there for a genuine conversation with Bosch. Then, too, over the
past two weeks Mann had been impressed, despite the problems with
Fortas's one big idea, with his tough negotiating ability as well as his
ability to remain discreetly behind the scenes. If the effort should fail,
there was no likelihood that others would know enough to have the
basis for criticism of the administration. It was just the type of solution
that appealed to Lyndon Johnson, who, in an extraordinary subversion
of normal diplomatic channels, quickly approved the drafting of Fortas
into the State Department.[20]

Though Mann did not express it, there was another equally good
reason for involving Fortas personally in the negotiations. Now the
pressure for results would be shifted away from the State Department
and onto the president's good friend. If the effort failed now, Fortas
would have no one to blame but himself.

But a man of Fortas's supreme self-confidence did not see it that
way at all. Even though none of his long-distance diplomatic efforts
had borne fruit so far, Fortas had every reason to anticipate a successful face-to-face negotiation with Bosch. After all, how many people in Washington over the years had ever successfully resisted his
entreaties in intensive negotiations? Not even a dreamer in the Caribbean could resist rational argumentation. Of course, Fortas's
"doomed" ideas had not improved any, but that did not seem to matter either to him or the president. So Fortas flew down to Puerto Rico
on May 12 to see what could be done.

Still, Fortas was not entirely unrealistic about the situation. Knowing the risks of failure here, with its attendant press criticism, he arranged a dramatic secret means of communicating with the president.
He took on the code name of "C. J. Davidson," no doubt harking
back to their mutual friend, C. Girard "Jebby" Davidson, who had
worked with them both in the Interior Department days and for whom
Fortas had been fruitlessly trying to land a job in the administration.[21]
The entire cover-up operation, though, was so clumsily managed that
it is difficult to figure out just whom the two men were trying to fool.
The first two times Fortas phoned back to the president from Puerto
Rico he was simply listed in the White House diary as "Fortas." Then
realizing the error, the secretarial listings of phone calls started to alternate between Fortas and "Mr. Davidson." By the time Fortas had
returned to Washington five days later, the secretaries no longer knew

how to list his calls, recording that "Mr. Davidson" was now placing local calls to the president.

But it wasn't just the White House secretaries who were having difficulty getting into the spirit of the world of supersecret diplomacy. Fortas, as superspy, was confused about the initials in his own code name. "C.G." would have made sense, being Davidson's real initials, and "J.B." would have been a clever reference to Davidson's nickname, Jebby. But "C.J." made no sense at all, unless Fortas fancied himself the chief justice.

McGeorge Bundy was even more baffled. In his explanatory memos to the president, he kept alternating between talking about the Fortas mission and the C. G. Davidson mission.[22] The conversations in White House meetings on the secret diplomatic effort routinely fudged the distinction as well, referring first to Fortas then to Davidson, and then to no one in particular.[23] By the end, everyone was so confused by the superspy routine that one administration figure thought Fortas's code name was "Mr. Jackson," while another thought it was "Mr. Arnold."[24]

Then Fortas himself began forgetting his cover. One handwritten note sent back to the White House by him carefully explained that some of the language of an accompanying statement was in "AF" handwriting. Realizing his egregious error, Fortas simply crossed out the "AF" and wrote "Davidson" above it. This baffled the secretaries, who had only just figured out how to handle the phone call listings. So they did their best to preserve the ruse by typing up what they labeled as the "Davidson" message, but then carefully attached it to the corrected handwritten document from Fortas showing where it had really come from. The important thing, though, was that the press did not uncover the operation until three years later (and then, like everyone else, the reporter got the code name wrong).[25]

For all of his efforts, the peripatetic superdiplomat was no more successful in persuading Bosch to do anything in person than he had been on the phone. The two men met in Jajome, a huge mansion which was the summer home of the governor of Puerto Rico, located in the hills overlooking San Juan. There was no more isolated a place on the island. And perhaps they would have been able to keep the meeting a bit more secret had it not been for Jaime Benitez, who "inadvertently" told folks that his good friend Abe Fortas was down there negotiating for the president.

Sitting on a chair across from Bosch, who was given the softer accommodations on the couch, Fortas and his friend Benitez worked on the leader. They made an interesting team, Fortas with his cool, quietly confident manner and Benitez, a hot-tempered man who was known to be able to apply considerable verbal pressure. While Benitez pressed Bosch to return to the Dominican Republic, Fortas, fully aware that this posture would not work, tried to restate all of the arguments for an interim government. Knowing that "the situation was pretty formless at the time," Fortas tried to convince Bosch to "cool off his own faction in the Dominican Republic."[26]

But Fortas had never met an adversary quite like this one. With each new onslaught of argumentation, Bosch, who was known to have a troubling heart flutter, would clutch his chest with his hand as if to indicate that he was about to keel over from the pressure at any moment. No one wanted to be responsible for the collapse of the man in whose name people were being shot on another island, and certainly not an emissary from the American president who was on a mission so secret that no one could seem to remember his name. So they backed off.

Fortas came away from the initial meetings with the same impression he had had all along—Bosch was going nowhere.[27] As the talks progressed, it seemed to Fortas that Bosch had a very tenuous link to his own forces, and that the events had simply gotten out of his control. So, armed with a continual supply of information and instructions from the White House, he tried a new approach. What if President Johnson issued another public statement regarding the search for peace and order in the Dominican Republic? Seeing the positive response, Fortas succeeded in having Benitez and Bosch draft the desired message.[28] Then "Mr. Davidson" dictated back to the White House their combined wish that the president say, "I hope that the OAS mission presently in the Dominican Republic will rapidly find a solution that will at the same time assure for the Dominican people the principles of a Democratic Constitution and a government of national unity able to maintain economic and political stability." To which Bosch then added at the bottom, "If the good offices of the OAS succeed in achieving this solution the U.S. Government will offer all necessary assistance towards rapid economic development."[29]

But getting Bosch to agree even halfheartedly with the combined American-OAS effort was only part of Fortas's charge. The other problem was deciding what to do with the "Communists" on the island. Fortas, or rather "Mr. Davidson," had arrived at his own solution on the scene. "Concerning active Communists and Trujillistas," he dictated to Washington for the president's use, "it is agreed that they present the problem for democratic government in the Dominican Republic and that effective measures must be taken by the constitutional government to protect the Dominican people from their subversive activities. These measures will involve their separation from the Dominican community. They may take the form of their internment in some isolated area under Dominican jurisdiction or their departure from the island, identification of such persons to be effective promptly by mutual consultation, and prompt action will follow as aforesaid.'' Strong and surprising stuff indeed from the man who had fought so vigorously in the 1940's against the internment of Japanese Americans in the United States. Moreover, given the fact that the government had yet to identify any ''active Communists'' on the island, it is interesting that the man once falsely accused of being a communist, and who as a lawyer was so concerned with individual rights in his own country, would offer such a solution. But such inconsistencies were unimportant when the problem was protecting the reputation of President Johnson.[30]

Meanwhile, back in Washington, the high command in the White House was beginning to consider contingencies should the Davidson mission fail. Meeting with all of his foreign policy advisers shortly before 6 P.M. on May 14, the president got total agreement from everyone on one issue—they could not allow Communism to flourish in the Dominican Republic.[31] Johnson was now worried that not much was happening with the Davidson initiative, and there was always the risk of a damaging discovery of the mission. Though the president was feeling some pressure to end the conflict, he told the gathering, ''You're not gettin' much shot at. You've got time.''

For several minutes the president continued to update the group on all of the mysterious Davidson moves. In the middle of this review, ''Davidson'' himself called in to report that he had gone about as far as possible and needed more diplomatic help from Washington. Someone officially representing the president had to come down to speak with all parties involved (including the ineffective OAS team). Fortas also reported that the current Dominican president, Antonio Guzmán, who had been Bosch's minister of agriculture, had agreed to head a new broadly based coalition government. So, Fortas said, someone needed to talk to Guzmán and bring a statement from President Johnson. But then it became clear from the tenor of Fortas's conversation that he was feeling uncomfortable with his mission, and wanted to consider whether he should keep up the negotiations. Perhaps it was the forty-eight hours of intensive negotiations that had burned him out, or maybe Fortas was discouraged to find the solution as evanescent and Bosch as intractable as when he first arrived. Whatever the cause, Fortas told the president that it would be better if the new visitor was "someone without a continuing role."

This message troubled Johnson greatly. This was *his* man on the spot, and the president trusted his abilities as well as his protective instincts. Johnson's response to Fortas was radically different from the upbeat optimism of the meeting until then. All of a sudden the president saw problems everywhere. People were not reacting as expected, he said. The "right wing [is] organized here" and, to make matters worse, "I've got my ambassador, and general, and CIA and admiral about to revolt. . . . We have plenty of troubles," Johnson concluded.

Fortas agreed. Perhaps depressed or just feeling stymied, he told Johnson that these were the same rebels they had seen before, and they were in a retaliatory mood. Every time a baby was killed in the rebel movement, the United States would lose a marine.

Johnson got the message—the time had come to move. When Fortas hung up, the president read the riot act to his subordinates. "I would button this whole damn thing in 36 hours. I would send anyone—no one is tougher than Abe Fortas. [Let's] try to do it through [the OAS] Committee." Finally, Johnson concluded in his most vivid Texas ranching imagery, the time had come for a "belly-to-belly deal. . . . Someone has to go belly-to-belly to Guzmán." In the desperate search for the right representative of American toughness, even J. Edgar Hoover was contemplated as a possible choice.[32]

As Fortas continued to call in throughout the evening, it was clear that the negotiations were deteriorating by the moment. By the time he phoned at 9:50 P.M., it had been decided that the critical negotiating role would fall to McGeorge Bundy, heading up a team of Assistant Secretary of State Mann, Deputy Assistant Secretary of Defense Cyrus Vance, and Assistant Secretary of State for Inter-American Affairs Jack Hood Vaughn. In addition, fulfilling Fortas's suggestion of getting another negotiator who was completely independent of the administration, former ambassador John Bartlow Martin was tapped to go on a separate mission approaching Guzmán and various other parties whom he knew. But Fortas was feeling even less confident, telling the president that he was "not going to take one ounce of responsibility for Guzmán."

Fifty minutes later, Fortas reported that Guzmán was already "lost," and he was now trying for the "subordination" of Colonel Francisco Caamaño Deñó, one of the rebel leaders fighting in Bosch's name, as a possible direction. But the roving secret diplomat was even more depressed now than before. The "debate ain't worth a damn," he complained. It was "too big a job," and "they are scared." With the mission going sour, it seemed now that Fortas wanted to bail out as soon as possible.[33]

So the Bundy negotiating team left for the Caribbean, relying on Fortas to arrange the initial meeting with Bosch in Puerto Rico.[34] For the next ten days, though, the matter was completely deadlocked. The Bundy team was in contact with everyone. Bosch had seemingly agreed to allow Guzmán to serve out the remainder of his own presidential term, but both men were proving intransigent in the rest of the negotiations. Meanwhile, the opposing military forces had consolidated their gains and divided the city, with the marines defending a line of communication separating the two forces. By the end of this period, though, the situation was stabilized enough for the OAS to step in and launch new reconciliation efforts by convening a meeting of foreign ministers on May 27.[35]

Even at this late date Fortas had not given up on his treasured ruling-commission idea. He sent a message to the president on the twenty-seventh asking, "Should we not consider what happens to our proposal and plan of getting rid of Communists when the three-man OAS committee takes over?" Fortas wanted the Dominican Republic to police the Communists, even to the extent of immediate deportation, to prevent the appearance that the Americans were exercising such police powers. Should the Dominicans fail to act, Fortas was considering the withholding of economic aid as "leverage" to accomplish the task.[36] After considering the various options, the president decided not to adopt the Fortas formula.

Fortas never did seem to get into sync with the diplomatic efforts. By mid-June, the American OAS ambassador, Ellsworth Bunker, was in the Dominican Republic as part of a three-man diplomatic mission. It was the beginning of an effort that would eventually stabilize the island to the point that, a year later, free elections could be held. For the time being, though, Bunker and Tom Mann drafted a cable favoring the establishment of a temporary "apolitical government of technicians" rather than holding elections that year. Surprisingly, for a man who considered himself to be an apolitical technician and was proud of it, Fortas told McGeorge Bundy that he thought "less than nothing" of the plan. This was, to his thinking, a euphemism for another "hardnosed right wing government" and the United States should be for progress "right from the start."[37]

Once more, Bundy and the entire foreign policy machinery had no choice but to unite against this outsider who seemed to have the best access to the man in charge. When Fortas registered a protest over the State Department's draft of the president's accepting response to the new proposal, Bundy, having approved both the draft and the new plan, counterattacked. "We [are] trying to get agreement and not disagreement among the President's advisers," he wrote Fortas. But the president's friend stood his ground and played his ultimate trump card in expressing his disapproval. "I am going to Texas with the President," he told the national security adviser, the unspoken message being that the argument would be continued at least on one side at the Johnson ranch. It was the same problem that Mann had faced earlier. Everyone with the formal responsibility and expertise was agreed that the correct move was to send *this* positive message. But the president's friend on the outside thought otherwise. This time, though, Fortas lost—the cable was sent out on June 11 in precisely the form that the State Department had written it. However, as a concession to the lawyer's objections, the message was unsigned, giving it the anonymous appearance of a general State Department directive that Bunker could *explore* with the Dominicans, rather than telling him outright that this was the preferred option, which *must* be implemented.[38]

Despite the fact that Fortas had failed the president in both his long-distance and his face-to-face negotiations, there was one more service to be rendered here. The lawyer would have to help cover his own tracks. The Senate Foreign Relations Committee, under Arkansas's William Fulbright, soon began to raise questions about the entire incident. Since word had trickled out in the islands about Fortas's role, the senators were sure to inquire about it. So Fortas was asked to help prepare the testimony of Tom Mann for the Senate investigation.

On July 12, two days before Mann was to appear before the Senate committee, Mann spoke with the president about how much should be revealed in response to Senate questions. Specifically, what if he was asked about Abe Fortas's "secret" mission? The president was quite emphatic in his orders here: "Stay away from [Fortas]. He was a presidential consultant, not one of yours. These people are located in Puerto Rico. [Fortas] is an authority on Puerto Rico and he would advise his government."[39]

Accordingly, the written "talking points" that had been drafted for Mann's testimony covered up the full extent of Fortas's role in the entire affair. "My contacts with Abe Fortas were limited to discus-

sions concerning the possibility of getting the OAS to enlist the services of Betancourt, Muñoz-Marin and Figueras in doing the mediation
job for the OAS in the Dominican Republic—either as a part of the
then existing five-man OAS committee or supplementary to its activities.'' No mention was made here that this had actually been Fortas's idea, or the incredible lengths he'd gone to in order to implement
it over the objections of the experts in the State Department. Then
Mann was supposed to add ''I have no personal knowledge of Fortas's
role vis-à-vis Bosch.''[40]

The following day, Abe Fortas joined McGeorge Bundy in reviewing Mann's upcoming testimony. After an hour and forty minutes of
conversation, all seemed to be in agreement with the answers being
contemplated, with one small exception. Mann was not planning on
giving an opening statement, arguing that he had been given ''very
clear and explicit instructions direct from'' the president not to do so.
Fortas, though, advised the use of such introductory remarks, which,
in his mind, left the witness in a stronger position to have a ''base-
point'' for use during cross-examination.[41]

Johnson was worried enough about Mann's testimony to quiz him
the day after his appearance. What had been said about Abe Fortas in
the Senate questioning the day before? Mann responded that ''somebody had mentioned him,'' but the question had had little to do with
Bosch, and more to do with his talks with Betancourt and Figueras.
Mann concluded that ''he did not think we were hurt at all.'' But
Johnson was not satisfied. Without explaining, he pressed for more
information about the questioning. Who had asked the question? Mann
could not remember the source, but reassured that ''he had fuzzed it
up.'' Only by the end of the month would Mann come to understand
why the president was so concerned with Fortas's image in the Senate.

By now this entire incident had become typical of Abe Fortas's role
as a friend of President Lyndon Baines Johnson. Eighteen months of
advisory involvement in the presidency had led to a pattern of behavior
that was now having an impact on a world scale. When Johnson had
become committed to an action in a foreign country and needed help in
both extracting himself and justifying his actions, he had called in Abe
Fortas to protect him from repercussions. After all, the attorney had
been doing the same thing for Johnson since the 1948 election. While
some would see Fortas as a Rasputin behind the White House throne,
in fact Fortas was merely acting once more as a lawyer for his presidential client. There was an excitement to this dual life of public

Washington lawyer and private presidential counselor. But it was an excitement made all the greater by the fact that nearly all of the actions were secret.

For all of Fortas's manipulations, suggestions, and efforts in the Dominican crisis, he had accomplished little more than spinning the government's wheels. But for Johnson, this was enough. After all, hadn't Fortas done all that was humanly possible to protect the president's reputation while preserving all of his options? More than that, hadn't Fortas been intensely loyal in all of his work? Hadn't the mission been so secret that no one would ever know about it? And, while Fortas's advice had been less than fruitful, hadn't the American action been so overwhelming and so successful in general that no one would care? Even in failing, Fortas had won the gratitude of the one man who fully believed that his best interests had been served—Lyndon Johnson. All of this guaranteed that in any future foreign policy crisis, Abe Fortas was destined to have considerable influence with the president.

For LBJ, though, there was one further problem remaining from this whole episode. In the middle of the crisis, Johnson had begun considering once more how to reward his faithful friend. Just a month earlier the FBI, at the request of the White House, had completed a "name check" investigation of Abe Fortas for what was listed as "Presidential Appointment."[42] But Fortas wanted no part of it, and Johnson knew that fact. Six months before, he had made it emphatically clear to the president that there was nothing in the administration that could lure him back to government service.

With Robert Kennedy's resignation as attorney general in August 1964 to run for the Senate, Johnson, according to an account by columnist Drew Pearson, "moved heaven and earth" to get Fortas to take the position.[43] "Carol is absolutely opposed," Fortas was reported to have told LBJ. "She won't think of my taking on any extra work." To which the great persuader was said to have responded, "Well, if Carol says no, I won't try to put myself ahead of her." However, Johnson might have been adding privately, "For now."[44]

When asked about his plans by inquiring reporters, Fortas said he was not interested in any government position. He explained, "I have made it clear to the President that I'm simply not interested in returning to government. I've been through all that. Now I'm fifty-four years old. I want to be able to give time to my music. I have a law firm with large interests. We've got a lot of fine young lawyers who marry fine young wives and have fine young babies. I have my responsibilities here."[45]

But it was more than just a matter of money and lifestyle for Fortas. Like Felix Frankfurter, who had refused a similar offer to enter the administration of Franklin D. Roosevelt as solicitor general, Fortas understood the value of being an outside adviser. As an outsider, Fortas owed nothing to the president or any other administration official, giving him the sort of independence and freedom of action that in itself can become a power base. Fortas well understood that with a man like Johnson, who enjoyed bullying those subordinate to him, it was better to remain the president's friend rather than becoming either his employee or his debtor.[46]

Even after witnessing this uncharacteristic lack of political ambition in Washington, some of the reporters speculated that perhaps Fortas could be pressed into public service. But, they said, it would take "something very special"—say a seat on the United States Supreme Court.[47]

VII

THE
AMBUSH

Life for President Johnson was a series of snapshots. The White House photographer, Yoichi Okamoto, was seemingly everywhere, taking thousands of formal and candid photographs. Johnson loved to pore over the piles of pictures, which were meant to establish a complete pictorial record of his administration, and select a number of them as gifts to friends and visitors. One such photo, with the president's inscription, vividly describes the turning point in the professional life of Abe Fortas.

The picture shows the two men standing in one of the White House hallways, the day *after* Fortas's appointment to the Supreme Court. Well, they weren't really just standing there—they were more leaning there. For the picture was of Johnson, both hands stuffed in his pants pockets, giving his friend "the treatment," towering over him, leaning into the smaller Fortas at about a 70-degree angle from the floor, nose to nose, dominating Fortas's space, mouth split into his widest "election eve" grin, breathing his air, and taking away his will to resist.

And Fortas, looking much like a slim reed in gale-force winds, was doubled back under Johnson until he resembled a reverse letter *C*. But the president's inscription said even more than this curious depiction of two people defying the laws of gravity on film. It was Johnson at his best—with a mixture of gloating and bold truth. "For Abe," he scrawled, "who's resisting me with all the horsepower that God gave him!"[1] But both men knew that it hadn't been enough—for God had given greater horsepower to Lyndon Johnson.

Nobody said no to Lyndon Baines Johnson. This was especially true when he was determined to give someone something. And it was even more true when the gift he had in mind was an appointment of some kind.

No less a force than James H. Rowe, Jr., had once tried to prove this axiom wrong. When Johnson was Senate majority leader in 1956, he tried to "give" the former Franklin D. Roosevelt assistant and prominent Washington lawyer a job as his assistant. But with a thriving law practice and contacts throughout the government, Rowe had no reason to look to Johnson for such help. There wasn't a single reason for him to accept the job—except for the fact that the majority leader wanted him.

"I can't leave my law practice," Rowe responded, explaining that financial considerations and the need to support his growing family, while keeping his current list of clients happy, were now paramount considerations. Still, despite these concerns, Rowe offered one day a week of help. That was Rowe's second mistake, his first having been listening to Johnson in the first place. For Johnson saw the opening, and liked to tell the story of the man who allowed his camel to warm its nose in his tent and soon found that the animal was wholly inside while the man was outside. Here, Johnson was the camel.

So the two men negotiated, and Rowe soon offered two days of help. Then he raised it to three days of help. But Johnson wanted *every* day of Rowe's attention, and nothing else would do. It was time for "the treatment." Johnson was charismatically persuasive, learning the weaknesses of his quarry and exploiting them, slowly weaving a web around him, backing him into a corner, until there was no resisting anymore. First Rowe's law partner came by to say, "You just can't do this to Lyndon Johnson." Then people Rowe saw on the street would come up and say, "Why aren't you helping Lyndon? How can you let him down?" Then his own wife made an appeal. No matter where

Rowe went, no matter what business he visited, a member of Lyndon Johnson's army was there prepared to do battle.

Rowe tried to call off the blitzkrieg, telling Johnson no once more. But the senator said, "Don't worry about the clients. I'll call them." And Rowe knew that was no idle threat. But still Rowe said no.

Finally, they had one last meeting on the subject. But even a negotiator as skilled as Rowe was no match for Lyndon Johnson. As soon as Rowe gave his final no, it brought tears to the powerful majority leader's eyes. "I am going to die," he whined, reminding his visitor of his recent massive heart attack. "You are an old friend . . . [and] you don't care. . . . It's typically selfish." Seeing the flood of tears, and no doubt thinking of having to face Lady Bird at the funeral, Rowe had no choice. "Oh, goddamn it, all right." With that, the waterworks stopped, Johnson quickly straightened up, and said smartly, "All right, just remember I make the decisions, you don't." It was, Rowe had to admit, "a great performance."[2]

It was ironic that the man who later found it impossible to persuade the American people when speaking to them on television had such a hypnotically convincing manner when speaking in person. Johnson was charismatic, and he knew it. He fully believed that given just a few moments, he could persuade anyone to do anything. It didn't matter whether that person really wanted to do it or not. Years after the Rowe incident, when Johnson used a similar technique to "convince" George Ball to leave his new partnership at Lehman Brothers to serve for six months as ambassador to the United Nations, the president's quarry said, "My negotiating posture was destroyed. . . . L.B.J. surrounded me."[3]

However, Abe Fortas had proven that he was one of the few people capable of resisting that irresistible force. And his refusal in 1964 to take the attorney generalship nettled the president.[4] After all of the things that Fortas had done for Johnson over the years, including his formative efforts in the reelection effort, it was inevitable that the president would try again to give him an important job in the government.

In fact, for years, Johnson had known the perfect governmental post for a man of Fortas's talents—a seat on the Supreme Court of the United States. Johnson had been thinking about this possibility nearly as long as he had aspired to become president. In the early 1950's, as Johnson's black limousine could be seen more and more frequently at the Arnold, Fortas and Porter office while he sought advice from Fortas, he began to think about where a lawyer of this caliber belonged.

Johnson frequently told Walter Jenkins, "Abe Fortas would make a great Supreme Court justice and I would put him there if I could." Jenkins remembered how frequently Johnson would express "his great wish" that he could accomplish this goal.[5] Johnson believed he knew no wiser man. And, more important, there was no one to whom he owed more. But realistically everyone knew that no southerner had a chance to win the presidency. Of course, no one ever expected that the office would be handed to one.

But now he was president, and when the news came to Johnson on July 14, 1965, that United Nations Ambassador Adlai Stevenson was dead, his course of action was inevitable. Soon two men who made their living negotiating out concessions would bend to Johnson's will. Both would eventually come to regret it. But in the end, both knew there was no way they could have avoided it.

When Johnson was informed that Ambassador Stevenson was dead it did not immediately occur to him that this was not just a loss for the administration, but also a chance to do something he had been waiting nearly fifteen years to do. At the time, all that he knew was that there still was a debt to be paid. Despite his millions, Johnson lacked the resources to repay one of the biggest favors of his life. For the man he owed wanted nothing, asked for nothing, and needed nothing that Johnson had to offer. Soon, though, Johnson would see a way to reward him. And, with the best of intentions, he would force Abe Fortas to take a seat on the Supreme Court.

The only problem for the moment was that such a seat was not available. But it was Harvard economist John Kenneth Galbraith who unwittingly first suggested the move that would make it possible for President Johnson to set his plan into motion. And all Galbraith was trying to do was avoid the same charismatic persuader that two others would soon face.

As Galbraith sat in a Washington Cathedral pew listening to the memorial service for Adlai Stevenson on July 16, he received a note from one of his friends:

> *Oh God, our help in ages past*
> *Our hope for years to come*
> *You are the first on Lyndon's list*
> *In our eternal home.*[6]

To his horror Galbraith quickly concluded that they might be right. In the two days since Stevenson had died of a heart attack in London, Johnson might well have concluded that Galbraith, his former ambassador to India, was the perfect man to take the United Nations job. Who could better understand the plight of the third-world nations than an economist concerned with the poor, who had lived and worked in a poor nation? Then, too, not only was Galbraith a genuine liberal, but he was a Kennedy liberal. Wouldn't it be nice, as LBJ removed many of the JFK old guard, to prove to them with this appointment that he still saw things their way? Finally, Galbraith was a *Harvard* professor, and everyone knew that impressed Johnson, even though he did not like to admit it. Confirming Galbraith's fears was the fact that there had been a phone call to his home in Cambridge from Lyndon Johnson the previous night, which he had missed.

But there was a hitch. Galbraith did not want the job. He had a book to write, and the United Nations ambassadorship was not a job for a person of independent viewpoints (a lesson that the man who eventually took the job would soon learn). So Galbraith, in order to resist the entreaties of the "Great Persuader," concocted a foolproof plan. He would suggest another target—Supreme Court Justice Arthur Goldberg.

Galbraith remembered a conversation he had had with Justice Goldberg a few weeks before in Cambridge. He understood that the justice was unhappy with the "more deliberative pace" of the work on the court. For a man like Goldberg, who was accustomed to the fast-paced excitement of labor law negotiations, this new position made him restless. In truth, this was probably the same gripe that all new members of the Supreme Court who come to the post from something other than the relative quiet of a law school teaching position feel as they adjust to their new lifestyle. Nearly all the justices make that transition sooner or later, though, as they realize that this is a lifetime appointment from which they can not only make the law, but make history. The truth of the matter here was that Goldberg was perfectly happy on the Supreme Court. Galbraith, however, decided to take the complaint "seriously."[7] He had to—it may have been his only effective way out of an appointment to the United Nations that he did not want, but that Johnson might force him to take.

This problem was on his mind when at 2:30 that afternoon, while meeting with McGeorge Bundy on a different subject, Galbraith and his wife were summoned by the president to the Oval Office for a chat.

The conversation lasted only fifteen minutes, but it was long enough for Galbraith to take himself off of the hook and put the Supreme Court justice on it. "That Stevenson," Johnson began. "Why did he have to die right now? He was always off in his timing. Who am I going to get to take his place?" So Galbraith immediately launched into his suggestion, saying that he had been told that Goldberg "was a little bored on the Court."[8]

While there is no evidence that LBJ had before this time considered this possibility, it did not take him long to grasp its many possibilities. Could Goldberg be persuaded to take the job? Then, after speaking on another topic, Johnson came back with "How would Arthur get along with the A-rabs?" Indeed, a Jewish ambassador to the United Nations might well have some problems. But Galbraith was not deterred and emphasized Goldberg's skills as a negotiator. It was clear from the way that Johnson kept returning to the subject that this new idea had found a home.

But who would give up a lifetime appointment to the Supreme Court, with its absolute freedom of movement and thought, for a spot in a cauldron of controversy circumscribed by the orders of the State Department and the administration? Certainly not a man of Arthur Goldberg's intelligence. Unless, that is, he met an irresistible force. And that force was Lyndon Johnson.

It would not be the first time that Johnson successfully manipulated what he called "my Supreme Court," and it would not be the last. As he considered the moves he was about to make, Johnson might well have thought back to 1963 when he had first persuaded a member of the Supreme Court, Earl Warren, to do something he did not want to do. But then it was a time of national crisis following John Kennedy's assassination that had prompted Johnson's efforts.

Johnson's candidate for chairman of the independent commission charged with investigating the tragedy was Chief Justice Warren. Not only was he a Republican, but he was, in the new president's mind, "the ultimate in this country from the standpoint of judiciousness and fairness and personification of justice."[9]

However, there was a snag to the plan. Warren sent word to the White House that he was "vigorously opposed" to the idea and so was the entire court.[10] This was not surprising, given the history of the Supreme Court and the man himself. For the court to have become involved in what would surely be one of the most controversial investigations in the nation's history was a risk to its prestige and independence. But even had Johnson asked the chief justice to perform a less controversial political task, he surely would have refused that as well. Paradoxical as it seemed, Warren, even though he had come to the court after a stint as a highly political governor of California, took the monklike nature of his judicial position *very* seriously. Justices were not supposed to become involved in politics. To him, it was a violation of the myth that people understood to be the separation of powers.[11]

But nobody said no to Lyndon Johnson. It was late afternoon on November 29, 1963, when the two men met at the White House. Johnson had settled on all of the other names for the commission and now he went to work on securing their head. "I know what you're going to tell me," the president began. "But there's one thing no one else has said to you. In World War I, when your country was threatened, you put that rifle butt on your shoulder. Now when your country is threatened with confusion and division and the President of the United States says you are the only man who can do the job, you're not going to say no, are you?" After telling Warren that "there was nothing you could do in that uniform comparable to what you can do for your country in this hour of trouble," Johnson continued with an argument that no one could resist, not even the reluctant chief justice. So grave was the situation, the president said, that the country might have to go to war, and that would mean a nuclear war, which would result in forty million deaths in this country.[12]

Not wanting to be responsible for all of those deaths, Warren's hand was forced. "Mr. President," the chief justice said, "if the situation is that serious, my personal views do not count. I will do it."[13] Once more, Lyndon Johnson had accomplished what no one thought possible.

Nearly two years later, on a sunny July afternoon in Washington, Johnson realized that by similarly persuading Goldberg he could finally accomplish one of his dreams. He could put his old friend Abe Fortas on the United States Supreme Court. It was a moment that Johnson had been anticipating for a long time—repaying all of his friend's kindnesses with the biggest gift within his power. But there were two problems. Goldberg did not want to leave the court, and Fortas did not want to join it.

So Lyndon Johnson began his quest to get Fortas onto the Supreme Court. It would have to be planned carefully. If Fortas sensed what was going on too early, he would back off and not even Lyndon Johnson would be able to move him. So the first step was subtle, and seemingly impromptu, while also being impossible to refuse (after all, every good salesman says the way to make a hard sale is to get your quarry to keep saying yes to everything). Who could resist a seemingly innocent spur-of-the-moment invitation to dinner at the White House alone with the Johnsons?

Not surprisingly, this was not the way that Johnson later recalled these events in his memoirs. Lest people conclude that the president had been "masterminding a great shift in the top echelons of government," Johnson recalled that he had not moved on the appointment until *after* Goldberg's decision to resign from the court on the twentieth of July, *after* "conferr[ing] with many friends and advisers," and *after* studying "the list these advisers had compiled." In fact, there was no list for Johnson, and by the time Goldberg had definitely decided to leave the court, Johnson had already offered the position to Fortas—twice.[14]

Late on the evening of July 16, Lady Bird Johnson was sitting on the Truman Balcony speaking on the phone with Abe Fortas when the president came on the line and invited the Fortases to the White House for a late dinner. As the four of them sat down at 9:45 to eat, the president casually turned the conversation to the hot topic of the day, whom he should appoint ambassador to the United Nations. Since the required skill there was one of negotiation, they discussed the best negotiators that they knew, and Johnson surprised everyone with a suggestion of the brilliant labor mediator Arthur Goldberg. When questioned as to whether Goldberg would leave his secure position on the Supreme Court for such a job, Johnson replied cagily, "He's the sort of man who would cry if he saw an old widow woman and some hungry children. He feels that quality would be useful in dealing with underdeveloped countries and poorer nations."[15]

Johnson was full of surprises for his guests that night. He then asked, just supposing that there was a vacancy on the Supreme Court, would Fortas take it? The president's friend was "moved, quiet, [and] grateful," but he declined. While Lady Bird Johnson wanted very much to see Fortas in this lofty position, she feared that such an appointment would leave the president and her as "the loneliest people . . . in time of trouble."[16]

In truth, little had changed since the attorney generalship offer in 1964 to convince Fortas to return to government service. If anything, there were now powerful disincentives to reconsidering that decision. The Fortases had just committed themselves to a very high mortgage to pay for their newly purchased $250,000 house in Washington's Dumbarton Oaks area. Moreover, replacing Fortas's present salary—estimated, by some, to be in the neighborhood of $200,000 annually—with the $39,500 then being paid to members of the court would not allow them to complete the planned redecoration of their house.[17]

But Fortas later claimed to a visitor that there were many other reasons for not wanting to change his life pattern at that point, and, he added forcefully, "none of them were financial."[18] As before, there was the challenge of continuing to build and manage one of the most powerful law firms in Washington at that moment. A dozen new attorneys had been added to the firm in the past eighteen months to handle the recent upsurge in business since the coming to power of the Johnson administration. With even more to be added shortly, the firm was suffering growing pains.[19] In addition, one of the founding partners, Thurman Arnold, was in poor health. So there was much truth to Fortas's claim to Lady Bird Johnson that he was responsible for "stabilizing" the law firm and that it would take a couple of years to do so.[20]

But there was more that Fortas was not telling Mrs. Johnson. And, while it would not become evident until later that summer, it may have been the most powerful reason why Fortas felt he had to refuse the prospect of an appointment to the Supreme Court. That reason had to do with the fourth participant in the dinner on the Truman Balcony on that balmy July 16 night—Carolyn Agger, his wife. While Agger stated on that occasion that "she felt that he would make a good Justice," indicating her agreement with, or at the very least her nonopposition to the selection, events later would prove that she felt very differently.[21]

For now, however, Johnson had a more immediate problem to work on. He knew whom he wanted for the job, but now he needed to create the position. All of his persuasive powers would be needed to charm Arthur Goldberg out of his court seat.

Unbeknownst to John Kenneth Galbraith, for President Johnson's purpose, he could not have suggested a better member of the court for the appointment to the United Nations than Arthur Goldberg. Of course there would be the loss of a liberal from the court, but most of the justices were liberal, and, in the eyes of the president, so was the prospective nominee, Abe Fortas. What made Goldberg especially attractive was that he occupied the one seat—the so-called Jewish seat—that everyone could agree should go to Fortas. He would be the latest in a line of great Jewish justices dating back to the 1916 appointment of Louis D. Brandeis by Woodrow Wilson. Brandeis, Benjamin Cardozo, Felix Frankfurter, and now Goldberg had all been seen as forces for liberalism and ethnic minorities. In fact, though, the four men had differed widely on the matter of the role that the court should play in shaping the nature of the law. But for now, the public saw at least one of the seats as reserved for a member of the Jewish legal community.

Of course, no one would begin to suggest that Abe Fortas was not absolutely qualified in every respect. But the fact that Fortas was Jewish would make things that much easier for the scheming president. So Johnson prepared to make his first move.

Unless Arthur Goldberg chooses to tell his side of the story, all of the precise details of his private conversations with President Johnson during this period will never be known. To one scholar inquiring about this matter, the former justice would only say, "Have you ever had your arm twisted by Lyndon Johnson?"[22] But one thing seems sure from an examination of the materials in the Confidential Office Files of the Johnson Library in Austin, Texas. It did not happen the way that the president recounted it in his memoirs.

According to Johnson, he told Goldberg that he "had heard that he might step down from the Court and therefore might be available for another assignment." The justice is supposed to have responded that "these reports had substance." Whereupon, when offered the post of secretary of health, education, and welfare, Goldberg allegedly told the president that "the job sounded fascinating but that he had become increasingly interested in foreign affairs." So, after a night's reflection, at the president's behest, Goldberg is supposed to have told White House aide Jack Valenti "that the job he would accept was the U.N. Ambassadorship."[23]

Lyndon Johnson was never one to let the truth stand in the way of a good story. While Goldberg had indeed talked to Valenti, in fact the president knew very well from the memos at the time that he had said just the opposite.

According to Valenti's account of their conversation, the justice was "happy on [the] Court," and was not inclined to leave.[24] But that did not stop a determined LBJ. Like Earl Warren before him, Goldberg had to be made to understand that it was in his and the nation's interests that he leave the court at that moment.

So, three days after the Fortas dinner at the White House, the president and Goldberg chatted as they winged their way on Air Force One on Monday morning, July 19, 1965, to the funeral of Adlai Stevenson in Illinois. The two men spoke of the importance of the position in the United Nations, especially in these troubled days of the growing Vietnam War. As Goldberg later recalled, the president used a version of the argument that had been so successful in convincing Earl Warren to put aside his judicial duties temporarily. He said that only Goldberg could help solve this problem and hinted at what might happen if he did not: "[LBJ called on him] to join in the greatest adventure of man's history—the effort to bring the rule of law to govern the relations between sovereign states. It is that or doom.''[25] At that point, Goldberg later explained how little there was that he could do. ''I correctly felt that our country was in very great trouble over the Vietnam issue, and that I could not put my personal predilection which was, of course, to stay on the Court—my highest ambition—before the country's interest.''[26]

Lyndon Johnson had had three days to consider his moves and he had refined his argument for the plane ride. In case Goldberg was interested in domestic affairs or in a position of greater governmental authority, the president also offered him the soon-to-be-vacated position of secretary of health, education, and welfare.[27] The cold truth was that he didn't really care where Goldberg ended up; the president just wanted him off of the Supreme Court. He wanted that seat vacated for Abe Fortas, whether Fortas thought he wanted it or not.

Johnson knew well that the jobs of UN ambassador and HEW secretary, while worthy positions, did not seem adequate trades for a seat on the Supreme Court. Why would anyone give up a cherished lifetime post for a short-term stint in a job of arguably limited policy impact? For this reason, one of the true mysteries from this period has always been why Arthur Goldberg even considered such a prospect, much less accepted it. Even within the administration, the speculation on this matter was interesting. Some believed that Johnson had offered Goldberg the prospect of being reappointed to the court, perhaps even to the chief justiceship, when the war was over. While this might well have been mentioned, the truth was that the president held out much, much more for Goldberg to consider. He offered him the chance to make history—how would Goldberg like one day to become the first Jewish vice president of the United States?[28]

This was Lyndon Johnson at his most persuasive. Huey Long used to talk about two kinds of owls in the woods—the hoot owl and the scrootch owl. The hoot owl, he said, looks for food by banging into the outside of the chicken coop wall, bursting in the window, and scooping up a hen for dinner in a flurry of feathers and noise. The scrootch owl, though, gently sidles up next to the hen, speaks softly into her ear, and simply charms her into falling into the owl's lap.[29] While Johnson could be both a hoot owl *and* a scrootch owl, with Goldberg on this occasion he was only the scrootch owl. Here he not only offered the reluctant justice something that already belonged to Hubert Humphrey, but he convinced him to take it. ''You never know what can happen, Arthur,'' the president began. Then he painted a

picture of a vacancy occurring some time in the future, and Goldberg
not being in a position to do anything about it. "You're over there on
that Court, isolated from the action," he said, "and you can't get to
the Vice Presidency from the Court." So, Johnson insisted, it would
be better for him to prepare by taking on a more political role.[30] To
Goldberg, the prospect seemed irresistible.

But the irony was even greater. Johnson managed to convince Goldberg that, once in the United Nations, he would be offered the chance
to take his place among the prominent presidential advisers on foreign
policy. This offer, too, was illusory. As Goldberg would soon discover
to his dismay, the man who actually had the most foreign policy influence with the president was also the same man who would get Goldberg's seat on the court (not to mention the offer of the chief
justiceship later on)—Abe Fortas.[31]

Having already made his pitch to Goldberg and fully confident of
the results, the president called Fortas from Air Force One while still
on his way back from the funeral. "I am arriving, and I am going to
announce your appointment to the Supreme Court," Johnson declared
proudly. Fortas was stunned; this was a whole lot more serious than
the hypothetical offer at dinner on the sixteenth. "God almighty, Mr.
President, you can't do that," he responded. "I have got to talk to you
about it." So Johnson demurred once again—but only for the time
being.[32] Did Fortas want to do this? asked Paul Porter when the conversation had ended. "I don't," Fortas responded immediately. And
the matter seemed closed. After all, there was no vacancy on the court
anyway.

All of that changed, though, shortly before ten the next morning.
President Johnson phoned Arthur Goldberg and made him an ex-justice
by formally offering him the appointment as UN ambassador.[33] Just
thirty-six minutes later he sealed the arrangement by announcing Goldberg's new appointment to the press in the Rose Garden. And, as
Johnson was never a man to waste time, one of his guests at the White
House an hour later was none other than attorney Abe Fortas.[34]

But there was one final twist to this tale of seduction. A memorandum in the Confidential Office Files of the Johnson Library indicates
just how reluctant Goldberg was to leave his seat on the court. It seems
that the departing justice did not even know for sure, at the time he
was giving his decision to the White House, what new position he
might be agreeing to take. After considering the president's offer of
either the HEW or the UN post, Goldberg spoke by phone with Jack
Valenti sometime that night or early the next morning.[35] According to

Valenti's notes on the conversation, the justice said that he had "understood [that the] President had focused on [the] U.N. job—and therefore [he] did not give further thought to H.E.W. . . . If [the] President wants him in [the] U.N., he will do it. If, on [the] other hand, [the] President wants to focus also on [the] H.E.W. job, he [Goldberg] would need to talk further with [the] President on this particular assignment.'' Valenti could not have been clearer in his recapitulation of the conversation: ''SUMMARY—No change of heart on [the] U.N. Ready to go. If Pres[ident] wants him on H.E.W., [he] needs to talk with [the] Pres[ident].''[36] Either way, Lyndon Johnson had his man.

But there was much work to be done before the president could pat himself on the back. Before this he had had a nominee, but no vacant court seat. Now he seemingly had a court seat, but no nominee. For now. In Lyndon Johnson's world, though, some folks just took a little longer to say yes.

After Johnson had phoned with his second appointment offer on July 19, Fortas had taken out a piece of his personal stationery and poured out his heart. So moved was the president by this penned rejection that he kept it in his coat pocket and read it aloud to his entire family at the dinner table. This was Fortas, the loyal friend, at his most eloquent. Having offered his thanks for the honor, Fortas explained:

> After painful searching, I've decided to decline—with a heart full of gratitude. Carol thinks I should accept this greatest honor that a lawyer could receive—this highest appointive post in the nation. But I want a few more years of activity. I want a few more years to try to be of service to you and the Johnson family. And I want—and feel that in justice I should take—a few more years to stabilize this law firm in the interests of the young men who have enlisted here.[37]

But while the president was moved by this passionate declination, he was not convinced. LBJ was determined that his old friend would go onto the Supreme Court. And so were others.

Quite understandably, the quick resignation of Arthur Goldberg from the court led to a great deal of speculation as to the name of his successor. Much of that speculation came from those men who were most affected by the move, the other sitting justices. It was Goldberg's replacement of the judicially self-restrained Felix Frankfurter in 1962 that had changed the overall philosophy of the court to a much more liberal viewpoint. Thus, that seat was still the crucial one in dictating whether the new direction would be maintained. Of course, one could expect Lyndon Johnson to *try* to appoint another liberal, but everyone knew that liberals come in all varieties and that presidents have been known to make mistakes in predicting the future actions of their nominees.

Perhaps it was that sense of uncertainty that bothered Justice John Harlan the most. For years he had fought with his brethren, seeking to make their decisions more restrained in several areas and forcing them to become more disciplined in their approach to legal questions. Since his ally on many occasions was Justice Hugo Black, the two of them were on the telephone on the evening of the twentieth discussing the disruptive events. It had been a hard day for Black, too. Goldberg had been reluctant to tell him about the move off the high court, fearing that Black, who was known to despise extrajudicial work, would disapprove.[38] As Black tried to reassure Harlan on the phone, they turned to a discussion of the possible replacements. Like everyone else, they arrived at the name of Abe Fortas. They also decided that United States Court of Appeals Judge Thurgood Marshall was another possibility should the president decide to appoint the first black to the court.

It seems, though, that Chief Justice Warren's sources of information were a little better than his colleagues'. By the next day he had been informed that the post had been offered to Fortas, and also that he had already refused it. Feeling comfortable with the selection, the chief decided to try to influence Fortas's decision about his future course of action. Knowing that Hugo Black was better acquainted with Fortas— after all, it was he who had heard the crucial 1948 suit by Johnson on his Senate race—Warren phoned to ask whether Black would speak with Fortas about the decision. Black was happy to do so and he immediately placed the call. But while Fortas was grateful for the news that both Warren and Black wanted him on the court, he was noncommittal as to his course of action. All he would say was that his office was meeting at that moment to discuss the matter.[39]

Meanwhile, the justices' avowedly liberal colleague, and a man who had always had great interest in Fortas's career, William O. Douglas, was out of the mainstream of things at his summer home in Goose Prairie, Washington State. But Douglas was never out of the action. That same day he wrote to President Johnson, recommending Fortas for the position, calling him a "superb choice." After expressing the wish that Fortas be "release[d]" for the job, Douglas used his own life experience to reassure Johnson that such a selection would hardly affect the adviser's ability to continue to "serve" the president.[40]

While the Supreme Court was getting involved in the machinations, Lady Bird Johnson used the occasion of an afternoon discussion over the future presidential library at the University of Texas to make her own appeal to Fortas about taking the court seat. Saying that her husband would have to make the appointment shortly, she wondered whether the decision not to accept the post was "irrevocable." Once more, Fortas explained his need to "stabilize" his growing law firm, and he made an even more persuasive argument to Johnson's most loyal supporter. "If the President was faced with any real troubles," he said, "I would want to be around to help him. And if I were on the Court, I could not. That was the difference between the possibility of a Court job and the Attorney General job."[41]

Plainly, the private practice of law offered Fortas the best of both worlds, a challenging and rewarding *independent* legal career, and the frequent chance to be in the center of political power when needed. While the attorney generalship would have reduced these opportunities, the seat on the court surely would have eliminated them completely. Fortas had grown too accustomed to being in the center of the action to give it up now for what appeared to be a sideline seat making law on the court while others implemented it. So he was not inclined to take up Mrs. Johnson's closing warning that he ought to get in touch with her husband soon if he had any "doubt" about his decision.

In spite of his insistence that the financial sacrifice involved in taking the position was not of paramount importance to him, this issue unquestionably weighed heavily on Fortas's mind. He made this clear to a client taken on by his firm early that June, millionaire industrialist Louis E. Wolfson. A man given to financially supporting friends and various charitable causes,[42] Wolfson had already twice attempted to offer financial assistance to outgoing justice Goldberg, once when Goldberg was on the court and then again when he was leaving for the United Nations post.[43] Both of these offers had been rejected summarily. Perhaps it was this experience that made it seem natural to Wolfson to be concerned with the financial problems of Fortas, a man whom he had known less than two months.[44] But of course there was also the reason that, as Wolfson later admitted, "Fortas was known to be close in administration circles."[45] It was always nice to have friends in high places.

When rumors of Fortas's pending court appointment began circulating, Wolfson phoned his new friend for confirmation. But the reluctant candidate denied "that he was even considering this appointment." Fortas added that not only could he "not personally afford the financial sacrifice," but "in addition, his senior partners in the law firm, along with him, had agreed to remain in the partnership for at least three years in order to build the firm up together." Wolfson tried to persuade him otherwise, speaking of the service that one can render to the nation from the court, and arguing that financial considerations should not be a factor here. Then he made, and reiterated in a letter dated July 22, 1965, an offer of "any financial assistance that he felt necessary" from Wolfson's personal and family resources. But for now, Fortas simply gratefully declined.[46]

While all of this was occurring, the Department of Justice was now hard at work in developing its own list of potential nominees in case Fortas really meant no. The resulting memorandum, which was delivered to the president on July 22, contained no surprises. Despite the fact that this comprehensive memorandum was offered by Attorney General Katzenbach after Fortas had already twice refused the job, it is apparent that Katzenbach had no knowledge of these events. In first examining whether the tradition of the "Jewish Seat" should be continued, the attorney general stated that "most Jews share with me the feeling" that religion should not be the main criterion for the position. After adding that at least one Jewish justice should be appointed before 1968, Katzenbach concluded by saying, "On balance, I think if you appoint a Jew he should be so outstanding as to be selected clearly on his own merits as an individual." Then he prefaced his recommendation of such noted legal scholars as Harvard law professor Paul Freund, University of Chicago law professor Edward Levi, court of appeals judge Henry Friendly, and eight other people, with this evaluation of his top candidate: "Before making these recommendations I think I should say that from a completely objective viewpoint Abe Fortas has every qualification for the Court. If you did not know him he would be my first recommendation—and still is."[47] It was the second time in two days that a prominent member of the administration had suggested to the president Paul Freund, the man who had so narrowly lost out to Byron White and Arthur Goldberg for the last two court vacancies, as a top candidate for the post.[48] But Freund was doomed to become the bridesmaid again.

Johnson decided that a more effective technique would be to have others attempt to persuade the reluctant prime candidate. Sometime during the next few days he contacted both Justice Douglas and former justice Goldberg to see if they could influence Fortas's decision. Douglas phoned Fortas from Yakima and received what he later described as "a firm refusal."[49] Goldberg, on the other hand, is said to have personally visited Fortas in his law office to convey his own hope that the offer would be accepted. While the response was no different from the one given by Fortas to all of the others,[50] Goldberg was in a most unique position to assess the future outcome of these efforts. As he told his newly appointed law clerks, "The president says he's going to appoint Abe and Abe says no. The president won't even consider other names. He's going to wear him down. He'll wait until the end of time." This Goldberg knew from experience.[51]

But Johnson's task wasn't getting any easier. During this period he had his appointments secretary, James Jones, place a call to the Fortas household one evening in order to make another effort to "wear him down." However, Carolyn Agger initially refused to put her husband on the line because, contrary to her statement at the White House dinner, she was now opposed to the court appointment. As Jones recalls the incident, "I relayed that to the president, and he talked to Abe."[52] While this call did not result in an immediate change of heart, Johnson was now warned that a significant obstacle lay in the path of his plans.

As of the night of the twenty-sixth, there was no doubt in Fortas's mind about his decision. So he phoned Hugo Black that night to tell him that he was definitely not going onto the court. Even Drew Pearson wrote in his column that day, "In one of the few such cases in history a lawyer turned down an appointment to the U.S. Supreme Court. He is Abe Fortas. . . ." But neither of these men had gotten the president's opinion.[53]

Tuesday, July 27, dawned bright and sunny. It had been a full week since Arthur Goldberg had decided to resign from the court. Because no definite announcement had been made as to his replacement, the White House correspondents continued to speculate on the names. Not surprisingly, given all of the backstage negotiations, Fortas's name surfaced frequently. Someone even asked Fortas about it, but his only response was that he was not interested in any government job "from President on down."[54] Then another member of the press quizzed Press Secretary Bill Moyers on the same matter. In confirming Fortas's account, Moyers went a bit further, reminding the reporters that he, too, had not wanted a government job, and yet "I'm here."[55]

Perhaps, thought the press corps, the president himself might be able to shed more light on this rumor. So after a 10:30 ceremony at the Rose Garden that morning announcing the appointment of John Gardner as secretary of HEW, the reporters asked Johnson whom he planned to appoint to the court. Was there any truth to these rumors about Abe Fortas? Looking straight into the eyes of the questioner, the president responded, "I have not even begun to consider that matter."[56]

Later that day, troubled by a difficult decision about whether to send more troops to Vietnam, Johnson met for two hours in the Oval Office with his noncandidate. More than just the decision itself, the problem of how to explain and justify it to the press and the American people troubled Johnson. During this meeting, the president made one more appeal to Fortas to take the appointment to the Supreme Court. By this time Fortas had been made to understand that more was at stake than just this appointment. Perhaps the opportunity would even come for Johnson to appoint him chief justice. For his part, Fortas was pushing his own nominee for the court, Chief Justice Walter Schaefer of the Illinois Supreme Court.[57] Schaefer was indeed very qualified, having been described in the Department of Justice memo as ranking "with the best of the State Supreme Court Justices."[58]

But the president was not persuaded. Instead, he used a new tactic. Johnson tried to invoke the wishes of one of Fortas's key advisers by showing him the letter from Justice Douglas recommending the appointment.[59] While this high praise from the man who had helped to guide most of the major moves in his career must have pleased Fortas, there is no evidence that it in any way affected his decision to remain in private practice. He simply wasn't going on the court, and President Johnson had to understand that fact. But Johnson, thinking that just as a politician aspires to the top job of president, so a lawyer must aspire to be on the Supreme Court, refused to take Fortas at his word. Someday, he surely believed, Abe would thank him for it.

For Johnson and his aides, July 28 was a fateful day. In a decision the country would later come to regret, Lyndon Johnson had already made the final decision to send fifty thousand more men to Vietnam. But the president knew that this would not sit well with a nation that did not fully understand the reasons for fighting in that small country in the first place. Knowing how the media worked, Johnson decided to hold a televised press conference at midday, when the viewing audience was small, and to make a move that would flood the news bureaus of the country, perhaps even deflecting a portion of the headlines away from this military decision. In so doing, he would solve the other problem that had been plaguing him for days.[60]

Early that morning Johnson turned to his assistants Joe Califano and Bill Moyers and said, "We've got to have some other news. I'll nominate a new justice and John Chancellor to be director of the Voice of America." The Chancellor appointment was no surprise to the two men, for Johnson had made the offer eleven days ago. Well, it had been more like a draft than an offer. The NBC reporter had been giving the White House fits with his dispatches, so LBJ decided to make him the head of the VOA, which had been leaderless since early March when Henry Loomis left the post to join the Office of Education. Despite some initial reluctance in taking the post, on July 28 John Chancellor no longer would be reporting *on* the White House, he would be reporting *for* the White House.[61]

But Johnson's orders regarding the judicial appointment came as a surprise to the aides, since they knew that Johnson had pursued only one man and he clearly wasn't interested. Moreover, after that declination the president had yet to confer fully with the Justice Department and the FBI about other potential nominees. So Califano, who had drawn the assignment of drafting the judicial nomination statement for the press conference while Moyers worked on the Chancellor announcement, had the challenge of writing about someone who did not himself know what was about to befall him. But the aides knew only too well that no one said no to Lyndon Johnson, especially when he had an appointment to make. Not only had Moyers been reluctant to serve in the government, but Califano's appointment as a presidential assistant had also been announced before he even knew what the job was going to be.[62]

So Califano wrote about the mystery appointee:

A President has few responsibilities of greater importance—or greater consequence to the country's future—than the Constitutional responsibility of nominating Justices for the Supreme Court of the United States.

I am happy today to announce that the distinguished American who was my first choice for the position now vacant on the Supreme Court has agreed to accept the call to this vital duty. I will shortly send to the Senate my nomination of _____ to be an Associate Justice of the Supreme Court.

For many years, I have regarded _____ as one of this nation's most able, most outstanding citizens—a scholar, a profound thinker, a lawyer of superior ability, and a man of humane and deeply compassionate feelings toward his fellow man. That opinion is shared by the legal profession, by members of Congress and by leaders of business, labor and other sectors of our national life.[63]

While some may argue that this description covered half the members of the bar, others may say that it covered none of them.

Meanwhile, as the White House aides labored, Abe Fortas was back at his office, seated at his desk and surrounded by piles of books, painstakingly drafting a brief for a case his firm was presenting before the Supreme Court. The last thing he needed now was to be interrupted. So of course the phone buzzed, but since it was the president the work could wait.[64] Even though the two men had spent all that time late the previous afternoon in the Oval Office, Johnson said he needed more help from Fortas. He was about to announce the increase in troops headed for Vietnam and needed Fortas's help in putting the final polish on the press statement. Could he spare the time to come over? Since it was twelve minutes before noon and the live, televised press conference was scheduled to begin in less than half an hour, there was little time to spare before the last-minute changes in the statement had to be made and placed onto the TelePrompTer. So, as he had done so many times before, Fortas dropped everything on Johnson's behalf.

But as Fortas got up from his desk preparing to leave, he smelled a rat. He turned to Paul Porter and mused, "Look, you don't suppose he is going to lean on me some more about this."

"Oh," replied Porter, "I think you are off the hook from what I have heard."[65] So Porter, enjoying one of the perquisites of working with a law partner who had an inside pipeline to the White House, turned on the television knowing that an important announcement was coming in a few minutes from the president's news conference.

One hopes that Fortas enjoyed some freedom and peace during his drive over to 1600 Pennsylvania Avenue that morning. It was the last that he would have of either for a long time to come.

As soon as Fortas arrived at the White House, he went to the living quarters to do what he had been doing so well now for nearly two years—look over what the president was about to say and give his approval. It was this scene—the two men, Fortas and Johnson, laboring over the script—that Joe Califano encountered at 12:15 when he entered the Oval Office with his mystery person's judicial nomination statement. The hidden identity had now been revealed. The time had finally come when Lyndon Johnson knew it was impossible for his friend and confidant to say no once and for all.[66]

Failing to show the other statement to Fortas, the president asked him to come down to the press conference and sit in the front row. After all, it was such an important event that Lady Bird and Lynda Bird Johnson would be there as well. As the two men walked to the elevator and began to descend, the president casually added, "I'm going to send your name to the Supreme Court.''[67] Not even Fortas's protests would be effective now. Johnson tried to minimize all of the previously stated objections by saying that he understood that it was "young lawyers at his firm who depended on him . . . and the mortgage payments on his house" that were bothering Fortas. Then the president of the United States added, "As to the rest of it, you better let me be the judge of where you can help me best."[68] Fortas *firmly* continued to decline. "Now look, Abe," Johnson continued, "they need you on the court. You may never have the opportunity again. *Take this job!*"[69]

But Fortas was still saying no, adding that the two men had been through all this before, when the elevator door opened. They were halfway down the hall to the East Room, where the throngs of anticipating newsmen were waiting, when Johnson bagged his man with one final, irrefutable argument: "Well you know, I'm sending all these boys to Vietnam, and they're giving their life for their country and you can do no less. If your president asks you to do something for your country, can you run out on him?"[70]

Fortas was beaten. "I'll accompany you," he said simply. Finally, his characteristic life pattern of hesitant uncertainty at critical career turning points had done him in. He had been overwhelmed by the persuasive magic of Lyndon Johnson. And so he marched in behind the president, sat in the front row, and waited with John Chancellor for the inevitable. Years later Fortas recalled, "To the best of my knowledge, and belief, I never said yes."[71]

There was a very solemn mood in the East Room that day as the observers sensed the grave decision that Johnson was about to announce. His opening remarks ran nine minutes longer than the expected quarter of an hour. It was Johnson at his most eloquent. In the middle of a very moving and effective explanation of his understanding of the need to be in Vietnam, Johnson indicated the toll that this decision was taking on him. "I don't find it easy," he began, "to send the flower of our youth, our finest young men, into battle. . . . I think I know, too, how their mothers weep and their families sorrow. This is the most agonizing and most painful duty of your President." Few would disagree with this assessment. The prepared text moved the Johnson women and even some hardened reporters to tears.

Then shortly before one o'clock, seeking to take the edge off of this tense moment and the harsh news, Johnson announced the appointments of John Chancellor and Abe Fortas. In deference to his old friend's reluctance to go onto the court, the president extemporaneously added another paragraph to Califano's prepared statement: "Mr. Fortas has, as you know, told me on numerous occasions in the last 20 months that he would not be an applicant or a candidate, or would not accept any appointment to any public office. This is, I guess, as it should be, for in this instance the job has sought the man." No one but Fortas and a handful of others knew how true that was.[72]

Despite the sad news early in the conference, Johnson was ebullient. He had finally accomplished one of his dreams. His old friend was finally going where he belonged—the Supreme Court of the United States. However, following the ceremony, all the normally cool and collected Fortas could tell reporters after being caught up in the Johnson cyclone was that he was "a little overwhelmed." Then he added in response to questions, "I had reminded the President that I was not seeking any government post, judicial or otherwise. The President was kind enough to say it was a place where I could perform superior service."[73]

That same day the White House tried to cover for the president's king-sized credibility problem on this incident by leaking an in-depth explanation of the events, which was attributed to "highly reliable sources." After all, not only had Johnson lied the day before, but throughout the courtship of Fortas, Press Secretary Moyers and other administration officials had been discouraging the press from discussing the possibility (though the aides probably believed their stories).

According to this new account, the president had first made the offer to Fortas on July 19, conditional upon Goldberg's resignation, thus knocking the underpinnings out of Johnson's statement that as of the day before he had not "begun to consider that matter." (Such self-contradictions were typical, though. White House reporter James Deakin recalls how Johnson himself let the cat out of the bag a week later. In seeking to demonstrate how brilliant he had been in persuading Fortas to go onto the court, he searched in his coat pocket—which was always full of memos, Senate head counts, and other relevant documents—and pulled out Fortas's handwritten rejection of the court appointment, which was also dated the nineteenth. Not even for Lyndon Johnson did 19 follow 27.)[74]

From then on the White House explanation contained more fiction than fact. "By noon yesterday [July 27]," it explained, "after long conversations with his wife and a few close friends, Mr. Fortas had all but decided to accept the offer. He called the President with his final decision this morning, several hours before Mr. Johnson's news conference."[75]

Maybe the White House thought it could fool the public, but there was no fooling Carolyn Agger or one of those "few close friends," Paul Porter. When they heard the news, they were very unhappy and upset indeed. But then Johnson probably knew they would be. No one seemed to notice at the time how curious it was that when Abe Fortas was being nominated to the highest judicial office in the land, his wife was neither present nor invited. As one observer noted, "It was no accident that LBJ approached Fortas at a time when Mrs. Fortas could not reassert her disapproval."[76] According to one account, when word reached her at the Internal Revenue Service offices where she was representing a client on a case, "she refused to believe it."[77] Later she would tell the press only, "All such drastic changes in one's life take considerable thought." When asked what she intended to do about her career, she responded, "I have been in the law all my life, and I don't expect to give it up now." Privately, however, she had no hesitation in complaining about the "dirty trick LBJ played" by putting her husband on the court.[78] "It's the goddamnest thing," a "livid" Agger told Johnson aide Douglass Cater and his wife a few days later after they had innocently offered congratulations at a White House reception. "We can't afford it. Now I'll have to make all the money in the family and support him."[79] And considering the drastic effect that this action would have on the plans they had been making both personally and professionally, who can blame her for feeling that way?[80]

Nevertheless, all that the president knew for sure was that two thirds of his strategy had worked. Johnson had finally persuaded Fortas to do what the president was certain was in his friend's and the country's best interests. And he had beaten the news media. They were not only kept totally in the dark on the court appointment, but also so overloaded with news that *The New York Times* was on its way toward writing an unusual front-page headline for the next day, split between the announcement about Vietnam on the right side and the announcement of the court appointment on the left.

Following the press conference, Johnson lunched with Fortas, then left the poor Supreme Court nominee to stagger back to his office in order to finish drafting his legal brief. With his shirt drenched with perspiration, Fortas went into Porter's office, "locked the door, and threw himself down on the couch." His puzzled law partner had witnessed the spectacle on the television and could only manage, "What happened?"[81] It was not the last time Fortas would hear that question that day, and like Goldberg before him, he probably didn't really know the answer.

Johnson, on the contrary, could not have been more pleased with himself. He phoned Justice Douglas and proudly reported all of the steps he had used in the effort to convince Fortas to take the court seat. "You bagged a good Justice, Mr. President," was Douglas's response.[82]

However, Johnson had yet to contend with Carol Agger. So the president set out to charm her, too. Another call went from the White House to Arnold, Fortas and Porter (soon to become just Arnold and Porter). This time Lyndon Johnson was looking for Fortas's wife. According to Paul Porter, though, by the time Agger returned to her office she was so "very upset" by the news that she refused to take the call.[83] By 8:20 that evening she was ready to talk to Johnson, and was so hard on him that years later he was still recalling the effects of the conversation in speaking with his friends.[84] "Oooh boy, Carol was furious with me!" he told assistant Mildred Stegall.[85] Even Abe Fortas said that "he never heard anybody talk to the president like Carol did." Fortas recounted for his law partner portions of the conversation.

"Carol, are you happy?" asked the president.

"No!" she responded.

"Are you mad at me?" he continued.

"What difference does that make?" she responded.[86] According to one account she also asked Johnson, "What are you trying to do, destroy Abe?"[87] This one was going to be difficult, but given all of his earlier successes, the president must have been confident that he could bring her around.

He was wrong. Unlike the two members of the court and countless other current or soon-to-be administration officials who had already fallen victim to what William O. Douglas described as Johnson's "hypnotic pressure," Fortas's wife proved to be not so easily convinced.[88] So the next day Johnson looked for more reinforcements. He phoned Paul Porter: "Paul, God Almighty, Carol won't speak to me, she is mad at me. You are my lawyer now, and you have got to straighten this out." In some ways it was curious that Johnson would believe that the other person whose professional life had been so disrupted by this move would help here. In fact, that same day, Porter had written to Johnson stating how unhappy he was from the standpoint of the nomination's impact on the firm. So, while Porter had once written that he was available should Johnson require help of any kind, this was one case he refused to take up.

Johnson explained, "Look, this was the only way I could do it, and I'll take complete responsibility for it."

"I know," replied Porter, and in a warning that only one of them believed he added, "You know, we are *both* going to miss him."[89]

Porter's refusal to act was the second time in a short period that someone had said no to Lyndon Johnson and made it stick. But it came too late to have any impact on the events to follow. After a perfunctory set of confirmation hearings in August, Fortas received the unanimous endorsement of the Senate Judiciary Committee and only three senators opposed him in the final vote. However, by late summer Agger was still not persuaded. And while the American people waited for the new justice to take his seat on the court, it soon became clear to some sitting members of the court that there was still doubt about whether it might ever happen. So other reinforcements were called in.

The man who had been in on every major career move in Fortas's life, William O. Douglas, got the troubling news at his summer home at Goose Prairie. Writing to Hugo Black he warned, "Abe Fortas's wife is very upset over Abe's appointment. It is apparently a very serious crisis." Could the Blacks, he wondered, who were still in the District of Columbia, do something to help resolve this matter?[90] The fact that the trouble had reached Douglas a full continent away, and in a place where he had to drive miles to Yakima just to get to a phone, told Black that the matter was serious. So he immediately phoned the Fortases to invite them to dinner. It was a mission of mixed emotions for Black. He had been very sorry to see Arthur Goldberg leave the court, but like Earl Warren he understood that the president had to be obeyed in this instance. On the other hand, Black was delighted with Johnson's selection of a replacement, expressing to Douglas his belief that Fortas could "render a great service on the Court."[91]

When the four of them joined for dinner at the Blacks' on Tuesday, August 10, it became clear how right Douglas had been in his letter. Carol Agger lamented to Elizabeth Black that the financial sacrifice caused by going on the court might force them to give up their new home and several other undertakings that had been started. Later, Justice Black delivered an eloquent speech about the importance of public service and the importance of a supportive wife in such endeavors. But Agger did not seem persuaded and asked "indignantly" whether Black was suggesting that she give up her law practice. "Certainly not," answered the justice. Then he explained how few cases Fortas would have to disqualify himself from as a result of such work. The dinner broke up at midnight.[92] The next day Fortas wrote to Black, thanking him for the dinner and adding, "I cannot adequately tell you how much the evening meant to me—and, I think, to Carol."[93]

But a new problem emerged in this letter. Just as he had the last time he'd made an important career change, the normally confident Fortas was now being plagued with doubts. He wrote Black about his fears of "inadequacies" and asked for help. No doubt the prospect of this very different lifestyle and work was weighing heavily on Fortas's mind—a concern that he would have much time to ponder before the court opened in October.[94]

Years later, the man who had ended up one "no" short in dealing with Lyndon Johnson tried to sum up all of these events. In speaking to the Senate Judiciary Committee during his confirmation hearings for the chief justiceship in 1968, Fortas stated, "I did not seek the post of Justice of the Supreme Court of the United States. That was not part of my life plan. . . . I dislike being in the position of rejecting a call by the President of the United States to public service. . . . He nevertheless, as is well known, insisted that I do this—that it was my duty to do it."

The deed was now done, and Fortas's life was changed forever, but not for the better.[95] For Lyndon Johnson had unwittingly set him on an inexorable course toward disaster. Many speculated on how the appointment could have happened. In his memoirs, William O. Douglas wrote, "Johnson used people's frailties for petty or perhaps venal causes or employed them, as in Abe Fortas' case, to ambush a man."[96] However, perhaps it was Fortas himself who provided the best and most candid assessment of it all: "He conferred on me the greatest honor in his power; the fact that I didn't want it was my tough luck."[97] But it was more than bad luck. For now, the rise of Abe Fortas's career had ended, and the ruin had begun.

VIII

DYING
ON THE COURT

For some, the imposing white marble edifice known as the Supreme Court building represents the nerve center of the nation's judiciary, but for Abe Fortas, entering it at age fifty-five on October 4, 1965, for his life-tenured term on the court, it was like walking into his own open tomb. And it was his good friend Lyndon Johnson who had interred him there against his will.

There is always an air of excitement accompanying the epochal change represented by the addition of a new member to the Supreme Court. The oath of office was administered by Chief Justice Warren in the Conference Room with only the other members of the court present. Then there was the formal public ceremony in the Courtroom. Fortas was escorted in front of a capacity audience, composed of his wife, family friends, the press, and the general public, to a chair at the clerk's desk to the right of the judicial bench. After the chief justice said a few words about departing justice Goldberg, and the announcement of the ceremony and Fortas's commission were read, Fortas solemnly raised his right hand to take his judicial oath. When it was all over, the most junior member of the court was escorted by the clerk to his seat at the extreme left of the bench. Fortas had a wry smile on his face as the man next to him, Justice Potter Stewart, stuck out his hand and said, "Welcome, Mr. Justice."[1]

Even though a trip to New York prevented him from attending the swearing-in ceremony, the president was still terribly proud of his accomplishment. He was now even with Fortas, after long years of being in the new justice's debt. As he did so often, the president signified his pleasure by sending Fortas a gift of White House pictures marking the occasion of the appointment for his scrapbook. But the photos he chose said more about Fortas than they did about the president. One was a shot of Johnson flanked by John Chancellor and Fortas at the fateful press conference on July 29. Perhaps it was the dazed expression on the new judicial appointee's face that inspired the president to inscribe it: "Don't look now, Abe, but they're announcing you!"[2]

It took only three days on the job for Fortas to begin to sense that he was going to be bored by his formal duties. This was not the bustling excitement of Washington law. There would be no stacked meetings, no urgent calls from wealthy clients seeking to extricate themselves from the latest emergency. There wouldn't even be the excitement of not knowing each day what the newest crisis would be. Here the meetings were ritualized and rigidly timed. The calls, if there were any calls that day, came from law clerks and secretaries. Now on the court Fortas would have the certainty of knowing days, weeks, and sometimes months in advance precisely what cases the brethren would be hearing, discussing, or writing about each day.

In the place of the buzzing telephones, the quick patter of scurrying junior partners' feet in the hall, and the frivolity of the gossip at the weekly Arnold, Fortas and Porter cocktail party, would be only long, quiet, mostly empty corridors. It was an intense, enveloping quiet. A reverential quiet. The sort of quiet Fortas had once rejected in the halls of legal academia at Yale in the 1930's when he deserted New Haven with Bill Douglas for the excitement of New Deal Washington. In place of the feeling that a single phone call from him could accomplish more than most people do in a lifetime, or several lifetimes, Fortas would be writing for a select audience, lacking the certainty that anything he could say would accomplish any more than spurring additional litigation. He was now a one-man law firm, married to eight other law firms, seeking to grapple with some of the most complex legal issues of the day. Even though these were frequently the issues that were too hot for the politicians to handle, there was no action here—only matters framed in the stylized combat of appeals lawyers, the stilted legal language known to only a few, and solitary reflection among tons of thick legal volumes.[3]

Making it an even crueler fate for an action seeker like Fortas was the fact that as he looked out the front of the building he could see across the street the center of most of the political roughhousing he now missed—the Capitol. But by the time the issues over there reached his desk, all the life would be wrung out of them.

Three days of this contrast was more than he could take. Fortas felt forgotten by his political friends—one in particular who had put him in this fix—and decided to do something about it. "I can only hope that you will continue to see me and to call upon me for anything that I can do to help," he had written the president the day after his court appointment was announced. To encourage this feeling, Fortas had a private direct phone line installed in his court office, and gave the new number to the White House operators and the president. Though Lyndon Johnson told his secretaries to "keep this number for me," the reaction was much less than Fortas had hoped.[4]

Johnson, who had other things on his mind at the time, did not get the hint. He did not recall all that the new appointee had done for the president between the time of his appointment in late July and the time he actually took his seat on the bench in early October. Then, as always, Fortas had been the man to be consulted on all the tough issues.

For example, in the first week of August, McGeorge Bundy had consulted Fortas and Clark Clifford for help in drafting a memorandum to set standards for public comments by former members of the administration who had resigned. Johnson was particularly concerned about some articles by historian and former Kennedy and Johnson administration official Arthur Schlesinger, Jr., making critical comments about Secretary of State Dean Rusk. After two long talks, the three men worked on a draft memorandum setting guidelines for behavior by former administration officials. However, rather than lay out a formal policy, which might make it appear that the administration was trying to "manage history," the three of them drafted a question and answer on the matter for planting at a future news conference. It was Fortas who wrote the final response, which made it appear that Lyndon Johnson was concerned not so much with how these writings portrayed him as how they painted "his associates," and thus influenced the "candid, cordial and informal relationships among officials [which] are essential to effective government." For his part, Fortas certainly didn't want departing officials revealing the close advisory connection that this Supreme Court justice was hoping to have in the near future with a sitting president.[5]

Once Fortas was actually ensconced in the Marble Palace, though, things seemed to be much different. He seemed to be no longer in demand, no longer in the center of the action, no longer on the president's "A" list of top advisers to be consulted on the most sensitive of issues. Life in the political arena was going on splendidly without him. He was out of the flow. He was, after all, a Supreme Court justice now, not a political figure.

Actually, the reasons for the president's silence were much different from what Fortas feared. Nothing on the White House agenda required the justice's attention. And the reason for that had less to do with Fortas than with Johnson. The president had been bothered since Labor Day with severe stomach pains, and four days after the opening of the court, he was in Bethesda Naval Hospital for several days to have his gallbladder and a kidney stone removed.[6] So debilitating was the operation that physicians said he could resume only "limited activities" until the end of the year and sent him to the Texas ranch for a lengthy recuperative stay (but not before he had lifted his shirt and shown the abdominal scar to the assembled reporters).[7] Concerns about a recurrence of his 1955 heart attack probably kept Johnson from thinking about the changed circumstances of his friend. And, after all, Fortas had visited him almost daily at the hospital, giving them plenty of time to talk.

But from Fortas's perspective that was not enough. He was now all alone. He was not being called upon for work. He was not being given assignments. He feared that he would not have enough to do. It mattered little that the fear was unfounded; Fortas was in such an insecure, vulnerable position that he saw it that way. After all, this was the same type of critical career turning point that had clouded his judgment in the AAA, and at various points in the Interior Department. It was the same insecurity on which Johnson had capitalized in putting him on the court. This was the time when, historically, Fortas was prone to making mistakes. And in a sense, he had already made one—by offering LBJ his assistance from the court.

Fortas's expectations hadn't changed with his job. That was why he had let the White House know in this not-so-subtle manner that he was still available for duty. Later he explained to a visitor why he had done it. He had "to keep alive" intellectually and psychologically somehow. Regarding extrajudicial actions, Fortas's rule was a simple one:

Engage in nothing that is "likely to pollute the clear stream of judicial consideration." By that he meant, nothing should be undertaken or discussed on issues that might later come back in some form to the court and compromise his ability to hear the case. So "anything not within the Court's scope" was fair game for Fortas.[8]

Loosely interpreted, this is a very permissive standard for a politically inclined individual. And Fortas was certainly that. There had to be some way to maintain a contact with the outside world, to get outside stimulation useful in decision making. "You can't possibly make such judicial decisions unless you're aware of what's going on in the world. It's unrealistic to expect otherwise," he later would explain.[9] For Fortas, the difference was between "talk" and "activities." All he had done was make himself available to speak to the president. It was not like he would be drafting legislation, working on a campaign, or appearing before Senate committees to testify. "There's a difference between actual activities and simply getting outside input. You have to have that outside input, but activities, on that basis, are not what I would allow."[10] The "tricky part," he added, was not to take up a "matter likely to involve you in undesirable relationships." But operationally defining an "undesirable relationship" with a sitting president for judgmental public opinion was always tricky.

And what if Lyndon Johnson ever asked him to move into this realm? That would be tough. The man who had already served, however briefly, three other presidents—Roosevelt, Truman, and Kennedy—would have a difficult time refusing the request of a sitting president who happened to be one of his closest personal friends. "These were times of great stress," Fortas would explain years later. "They were times of great trouble, [and the issues raised were] matters of national importance. I just didn't feel that I could refuse."[11] After all, as Fortas was making the transition to Supreme Court justice, Johnson, following the massive troop increases in Vietnam in July of that year, was making the transition to wartime president.

Of course, there was always the danger that an issue raised by the president might later come before the court. However, Fortas felt perfectly confident that he could separate his judicial and political lives. First, if Johnson did somehow tread over the bounds, the justice could silently recuse himself from sitting on future related cases. This could be done effortlessly and, according to court custom, without any explanation to the public as to why the action had been taken. Moreover, who would ever find out that they talked on the phone? That was

precisely why he used this instrument. It didn't leave tracks. Fortas
was on the court for life, after all. There was no judging him now.

But for the present, making such ethical determinations was not a
problem—the phone was silent. It was a time of "decompression" for
Fortas—no time demands and no excitement.[12] Only a few short
weeks before his court appointment, he had been secretly negotiating
for the president in the Caribbean. After a year of literally hundreds of
White House calls passing between the president and Fortas, frequently three a day, once even fourteen in one day,[13] the quiet was
deafening. In the month after Fortas's ascension to the bench, the
phone rang fewer than a handful of times, and if it had not been for the
president's loneliness in his hospital bed for several days, Fortas would
not have seen him at all.[14] Over the next year they would only talk
about one third as much on the phone as they had the previous year.[15]
Even this was a lot more than some people thought Supreme Court
justices were supposed to talk to presidents. But how would they ever
find out?

Piled on top of the fast-growing sense of isolation and boredom was
a real uncertainty in Fortas as to whether he could handle the job. It
was the same uncertainty he had shown in the many job switches during the war, combined with a doubt about whether the job suited his
nature. Given the nature of his reputation and his relationship with his
mentor, William O. Douglas, who was then sitting on the court, there
should have been no doubt at all. But the doubt was still there.

Watching Douglas had taught Fortas about the difficult nature of the
judicial role. "A man may live a long and active life—even in the
aquarium of public office—without revealing and, indeed, without discovering his essential convictions," he had written in a tribute to his
mentor on the court. "But for a Justice of this ultimate tribunal, the
opportunity for self-discovery and the occasion for self-revelation are
unusually great. Judging is a lonely job, 'in which a man is, as near as
may be, an island entire. The moment is likely to come when he real-
izes that he is, in essential fact, answerable only to himself.' "[16]

There was a large difference between this judicial role and the ritualized combat with other attorneys in private practice, where one can
even defend what one does *not* believe. It was a change Fortas was not
confident he could make.[17] Even after the passage of months on the
court, Fortas would confess to Hugo Black his doubt that he had "the
philosophical assurance" that was required for the job. "Perhaps it
will come with time," Fortas added, "[but] perhaps not."[18]

One thing that wasn't helping was the pedantic, uncomplicated nature of the first few cases that came to the court in Abe Fortas's early weeks. There was a case alleging libel in the criticism of the director of a ski recreation center.[19] Then came a question of whether the Small Business Administration could collect repayment on one of its disaster loans from a married woman in Texas.[20] What is the enforceability of unrecorded federal tax liens? the court was asked in a third case.[21] And finally, the most interesting case of the early lot raised the question of the constitutionality of the Alabama loitering law.[22] Faced with the apparently unchallenging nature of the work on the court, Fortas's sense of foreboding increased. "I was used to working seven days a week, 18 hours a day," he later explained to a reporter, "and knowing myself I was afraid I might go to seed on the Court. . . . I couldn't bear the idea of not being fully occupied."[23]

But Fortas was greatly disturbed by more than just the light workload. He did not like the way he was being treated in his old Washington haunts. Fortas loved this life of Washington high society so much that a new fear began to overtake him. "The greatest fear of Justices on the Supreme Court is of dying on the Court," he later explained to a visitor. "I would come into a room and there would be a roomful of people and there would be lively conversations. They would be talking about everything and it was very exciting. Then I would hit the threshold of that room and there would be utter silence. No one would talk. And that was it—there was no conversation." Still recalling the pain of this period in his life sixteen years later, Fortas said, "Even my own friends would not talk to me anymore. There were people I had been talking to throughout my life. People I had been doing things with for years. But now they didn't know what they could say to me. They didn't know how far they could go. So they wouldn't say a thing to me. You just cannot understand the isolation of being on the Court."[24]

The suffocating loneliness of being on the bench for even this short a period of time forced him to look for "a breath of fresh air." He began to look around for some issue, some form of "social involvement" that could occupy his restless attention. Escaping this feeling of isolation, the fear of being buried alive on the court, required that he find an issue "which concerned [him] deeply" and put his considerable intellect to work dealing with it.[25] There was, of course, one person in Washington who could continue to talk freely to Fortas. But the phone wasn't ringing from the White House just then. And there was no certainty to a man in such fear of isolation that it ever would again.

So Fortas began to think of other avenues. That's when he remembered Louis Wolfson's offer.

Louis Wolfson was a self-made millionaire. And his was the kind of story that could happen only in America. Then fifty-three years old, he still had, at six feet two inches and a muscular 190 pounds, the lean, tanned, deeply wavy-haired look of the athlete that he once had been. As "Kid Wolf," he had boxed professionally as a teen-ager in his hometown of Jacksonville, Florida, and had been named an all-southern high school end in football, while also lettering in basketball, baseball, and track. From there he went on to play football on scholarship at the University of Georgia, with intentions of continuing in an athletic career. Had it not been for a severely injured shoulder in his sophomore year, he might well have taken that road and never crossed paths with Abe Fortas. But he was forced to return to Jacksonville to help his father rebuild the Depression-crippled family scrap-metal business. From there the family invested in the Florida Pipe and Supply Company, a mill supplies firm, with $10,000 raised from a family friend and loans on the family's pooled life insurance policies. It was hard work, involving eighteen to twenty hours a day loading trucks, selling pipes, and running the business. But it all paid off. In the first year sales grew to $100,000, and eventually the company was bringing in $4.5 million a year.

But Wolfson had only just begun. From the $10,000 he had borrowed in 1932 at age twenty, he rose to a net worth of well over $8 million by 1949, and after acquiring controlling interest in Merritt-Chapman and Scott, a heavy construction, marine salvage, and derrick business, he joined its board of directors. By 1951 he became its board chairman, and two years later he was the company's president. Under his leadership the firm grew until by the middle 1960's it did an annual business of over $269 million and was listed 210th on the Fortune 500 list. Wolfson had guided the company's massive diversification into a broad range of industries, including steelmaking, metallurgical products, and all phases of heavy construction. One of the companies that Wolfson had acquired, the New York Shipbuilding Corporation, undertook massive projects such as the building of the *Savannah,* the world's first nuclear-powered passenger-cargo ship, and the massive aircraft carrier *Kitty Hawk.*[26]

There were always mixed opinions about Wolfson. Some recalled his ruthless business tactics. In the late 1940's and early 1950's, his management of the Washington, D.C., Capital Transit Company, supplying public transportation to the city, became such a matter of contention that Congress eventually investigated, removed its franchise, and thus forced Wolfson to sell the company. Then he made more enemies while acting as a "corporate raider" in attempting to take over Montgomery Ward and later American Motors. Both coups proved unsuccessful and the latter attempt ran him afoul of the Securities and Exchange Commission. The SEC accused Wolfson of attempting to rig the market price of the stock by selling short (selling borrowed stock in the hope that the market price would drop and replacement shares could then be purchased at a lower cost). Wolfson claimed that the overselling of the stock had been done by his aides without his knowledge. In the end, the case was settled by Wolfson's agreement to a consent decree not to make any fraudulent statements about the company's stock or his holdings.[27]

However, others saw the philanthropic side of Wolfson. He had financially backed various charitable causes, high schools, prominent politicians (including the governor of Florida), and scholars. One reporter wrote of his generosity in helping a waiter at the track where Wolfson's horses raced. Upon hearing that the fellow had a bad throat that some friends thought was going to kill him, Wolfson sent him to the finest doctors and paid all of the bills.[28] Because of this fine medical care, the waiter recovered fully. It was this other side of Wolfson that Fortas seemed to appreciate more.

Wolfson had retained Arnold, Fortas and Porter in June 1965 to deal with two legal problems then plaguing his firms. His New York Shipbuilding Corporation had a claim of between sixty-five and seventy million dollars against the Navy Department for the construction of the carrier *Kitty Hawk* and some Polaris submarines. Moreover, the parent company, Merritt-Chapman and Scott, was then under investigation by the SEC concerning alleged irregularities in the trading of the company's stock. No firm in Washington could offer greater expertise on this combination of problems than Fortas's.

Initially, the case was Paul Porter's to supervise. But as managing partner, in the early stages of this process, Fortas met Wolfson at the home of Senator Stuart Symington. Then there was an opportunity for further contact when Porter's schedule did not allow him to attend a board meeting of Merritt-Chapman and Scott in Jacksonville. So Fortas agreed to go as a representative of the firm's senior partners.

It was during this trip that Fortas became aware of the extensive philanthropic efforts of the Wolfson Family Foundation. When he returned to Washington, Fortas told Porter, "You know, this Lou Wolfson is really an unusual person. He has built a wing on the Baptist Hospital there in Jacksonville in the memory of his junk-dealer father, and there is a plaque there, that [says], 'This facility is for the healing of the sick and the afflicted,' or words to that effect, 'irrespective of race, color, or creed.'" It made a deep impression on the New Deal liberal side of Fortas to see that kind of compassion combined with such courage in the racially troubled city.

While other members of the firm worked on the cases, Fortas continued to speak to Wolfson about the work of his family's foundation. After a time, Fortas offered, "Look, I have got some ideas as to how, if you are going to put the kind of money in here you say you are, the foundation—we have got millions of them scattered around the country—can effectively do some work in student relations, race relations, etc. Well, there's enough money being spent on medicine and the applied sciences and on research, so I would hope that this foundation takes a bolder, imaginative course." Wolfson wanted to hear more about those ideas. Who wouldn't be intrigued, knowing of Fortas's wide contacts with foundation work all over the country, not to mention his close ties to the president of the United States?

It all seemed to come to an end, though, when Fortas was nominated for a seat on the Supreme Court in late July, and turned down Wolfson's offer of financial help. What happened after Fortas phoned a surprised Wolfson to explain why he had taken the court seat is a matter of conjecture. Fortas told Porter that he had responded negatively to Wolfson's renewed offer of financial help and association with the family foundation. According to Porter, Fortas said, "Lou, while this will terminate our professional association, I still have great interest and please feel free to discuss your program with me at our mutual convenience."[29] According to Wolfson, though, the conversation went a bit further, with Fortas asking him "how much time would be necessary in order to fulfill any intended duties." When informed that the foundation was thinking of inviting him to one meeting a year, Fortas was supposed to have suggested "that he could prepare pamphlets and brochures on matters in which he and the Foundation had mutual interests, such as civil rights, the religious ministerial program, and his interest in juvenile court justice."[30]

For the time being the matter was dropped, until Fortas insisted that Wolfson come to Washington to attend the court reception that the

Douglases were throwing in the new justice's honor at 5 P.M. at the
Supreme Court building on October 22, 1965.[31] The real reason for
the justice's invitation came up in his discussions with Wolfson the
next day. Panicked by the growing isolation he was feeling during his
initial three weeks on the court, Fortas for the first time was willing to
make a definite commitment to the Wolfson Foundation. So, on October 23, the justice said to Wolfson, "Lou, I would like to be a
consultant on the foundation. I think I can give it the time and I would
like to do it."[32]

But now there were some problems. Wolfson remembers telling
Fortas, "Abe, don't come with the Foundation now. I don't want you
to be embarrassed. I understand this [SEC probe] may be serious."[33]
Fortas, though, said that he was aware of the charges from his contacts
with his old law firm and reassured Wolfson that they could not be an
embarrassment to him as they were merely "technical violations," and
"that nothing of a serious nature would develop as a result of the
investigation."[34] So the deal was made. Fortas agreed to serve as a
consultant to the foundation on the issue of race relations among juveniles in Florida. In return, since the amount of foundation work would
vary from year to year, the two men agreed that Fortas should be
compensated at a rate of twenty thousand dollars a year, plus expenses, for the rest of his life.[35]

The project served the dual purpose of blunting Fortas's feelings of
isolation and getting him directly involved in an issue of great concern
to him. As he insisted later: "That's why I got involved with that
board. . . . It was social involvement and I was greatly concerned with
what happened to children in Florida, whether they be black or white
or polka dot, they need to be treated well. . . . [And] I got involved
with the children simply to prevent dying on the bench, to get away
from that isolation. . . . It wasn't anything financial."[36]

But there is no getting around the fact that if Fortas had really been
all that infused with social altruism, it would have been just as easy for
him to do his work for a dollar a year, or perhaps just his expense
money. Money *was* important to him and, as had been made man-
ifestly clear at the White House, to his wife as well. "He had this
absolute obsession for having enough money," said one acquaintance.
"He could never have enough. Perhaps it was due to his poor childhood, but even though he had no kids, owned a Rolls and lived in
Georgetown, he never felt secure. He still wanted more."[37] "It was a
mania," agrees another, "and not rational at all."[38]

In spite of Fortas's insistence that money had nothing to do with his decision, there was no denying the oddity of the events that followed his conversation with Wolfson. When the justice's draft of the contract for their arrangement was later sent to Wolfson, there was one small but very important change from their verbal agreement. According to the terms of this document, not only would Fortas be paid a flat twenty thousand dollars a year for the rest of his life, as had been negotiated, but upon his death his wife would receive the same yearly amount for the length of her life, should she survive him.[39] In seeking to provide for his wife by the latter clause (and perhaps to ease the monetary fears she had expressed earlier), Fortas failed to understand how much the change would make the entire arrangement look like a payoff without any real social purpose. Why continue payments, people would ask, for work no longer being done?

In all of these negotiations, Fortas failed to understand the implications for the general public of the real size as well as the source of the fee, should it ever be discovered. Instead, still thinking like a Washington lawyer, he undoubtedly saw this as just the normal fee for one good case with a deep-pocketed client. He well knew that a man of his knowledge and contacts was worth a great deal to such foundations, and that meant being compensated for that value. But to many others, a Supreme Court justice earning $39,500 a year should not be receiving half again his salary for consulting work. Moreover, he should not be taking any money from someone who had warned him that he was on the verge of trouble with the SEC. Then, too, there was the unsavory appearance of a foundation giving out fully one quarter of that year's annual monetary awards of $77,680 to that one justice.[40]

But Fortas did not see it that way. To him, his actions were not unlike those involved in many conflict-of-interest cases he had helped resolve as a Washington lawyer for countless others. One such beneficiary of this advice had been Fred Korth, the former secretary of the navy in the Kennedy administration. After coming to the Kennedy administration from his post as president of the Continental National Bank in Fort Worth, Texas, Korth was charged by Senate investigators with retaining some stock in the bank while also awarding the contract for building the TFX fighter aircraft to one of the bank's debtors, General Dynamics.

After studying all of the relevant documents, Fortas concluded that absolutely no connection, direct or indirect, could be found linking the bank, Korth's former association with the bank, and the awarding of the contract for the TFX. However, Fortas was more concerned by allegations that on some occasions Korth had continued, in letters to potential depositors and creditors written on Defense Department stationery and in gatherings held on the presidential yacht *Sequoia,* to be concerned with the welfare and increasing the client base of the bank. So, in a final paragraph, Fortas found it "regrettable" that Korth had "not anticipated the possibility of embarrassment" that might have resulted from the public appearance of "continued solicitude" for these bank-related activities. However, Fortas concluded, "the incidents do not reflect an abuse of trust or material—or even significant—misuse of his official position. They represent natural, human actions towards friends and former associates. They had no impact upon his official duties or his public trust."[41] The question, Fortas was properly arguing, was one of appearances versus a very literal and technical reality. And in Washington, mere appearances have a nasty habit of being turned into reality by the press, one's enemies, and hence the general public. But what the Washington lawyer could see so clearly in 1963 eluded his understanding when his life drastically changed in 1965.

In looking at his own prospects with the Wolfson Foundation now, there was no doubt in Fortas's mind that the two duties—to the nation and to the foundation—were entirely separate. Indeed, looking at the strictly technical, very literal nature of this arrangement, it was very easy to draw this conclusion. First, even if Wolfson's case should ever come before the Supreme Court, an unlikely event at that point, Fortas would not be sitting on it anyway. Not only was Wolfson a personal acquaintance of the justice, but he had also been a client of Arnold, Fortas, and Porter during Fortas's work there. He would now clearly recuse himself as a matter of course should a case involving Wolfson come before the Supreme Court. For Fortas, the chances of his consulting even being raised probably seemed quite low. Accustomed as he was to operating in the shadows for over twenty years of practicing law, the new justice no doubt thought it highly unlikely that anyone would ever find out about this arrangement. After all, no one had yet discovered that his close friend and colleague William O. Douglas had a similar financial connection to the Parvin Foundation (this represented another miscalculation on Fortas's part, as that secret would be exposed a year later).[42]

In reaching his determination on this matter, Fortas made a classic mistake. He simply had not made an adjustment in ethics to fit his new circumstances. The Supreme Court, where the justices are seen by the public as unworldly monks, living like Caesar's wife when it comes to politics and outside interests, is not the place for lawyers' briefs artic-

ulating the technical distinctions between conflict of interest and connections that in no way affect public duties and trust. This is the place
for excessive concern with appearance over reality, form over substance, and figurative over the literal. Fortas, though, was still at heart
a Washington lawyer who now happened to be sitting on the Supreme
Court, so he could not foresee the inevitable common perception of
this arrangement—a perception that by its very existence would become reality. By contracting to receive compensation for the rest of his
and his wife's lives, Fortas made it look like any actions that he took
on behalf of the *foundation* would in fact be done on behalf of
Wolfson. And any conversations held on the problems of juveniles
would automatically be assumed by the public to be conversations on
Wolfson's trouble with the SEC. Like Korth before him, Fortas had
made himself vulnerable. The results of this vulnerability were soon to
follow.

Once the decision was made, the consummation of the agreement
came very quickly. On December 28, 1965, Wolfson reported to a
meeting of the family foundation his discussions with Justice Fortas
and announced the formation of the consultancy. Not surprisingly, the
group unanimously adopted a resolution appointing Fortas as adviser to
the foundation and directing Wolfson "to make the necessary arrangements for defraying expenses and compensation."[43] Six days later
Wolfson sent a copy of the resolution and the first check of twenty
thousand dollars to cover the work for 1966 to Fortas. The only formal
duty, as explained in the letter, was to attend the year-end meeting of
the foundation, so as not to "inconvenience you in your present duties
and responsibilities." In return for keeping the justice posted on the
foundation's work, Wolfson said he would welcome any "ideas, suggestions, or recommendations" Fortas might have. A week later, writing on Supreme Court stationery, Fortas closed the deal while looking
"forward to the opportunity to be of assistance to the foundation in its
fine work."[44]

The formal contract letter detailing their relationship came from
Wolfson in early February 1966. It explained that in return for the
yearly salary, Fortas would be receiving "a good deal of" foundation
material seeking his "views and comments." In addition, the justice
was encouraged to volunteer his "own thoughts and ideas as to the
most effective use of our facilities and our resources." These idea
exchanges would occur at the annual foundation meetings as well as
planned "frequent discussions" among Fortas, Wolfson, and Wolfson's associates.[45]

For Wolfson's foundation, the deal with Fortas may have been an expensive one, but if Wolfson was looking for access to people in high places, in addition to broad expertise on liberal topics, he was not to be disappointed. Two weeks to the day after the first payment of twenty thousand dollars was made, Fortas was writing to the White House about Wolfson. The justice suggested that the president might "get some pleasure" from looking at an "excellent" resolution adopted by Merritt-Chapman and Scott over a decade earlier as a "policy of non-discrimination."[46]

Once Johnson returned to health in late 1966, the personal relationship between Johnson as president and Abe Fortas as Supreme Court justice began to return to its familiar pattern. Their friendship had known no bounds in the past, and there was no reason in LBJ's mind to erect fences now around the offices of the Supreme Court. "It was really amazing," James Jones commented later. "Lyndon Johnson didn't look at—when he called Abe Fortas—he didn't look at Abe Fortas as a justice. He looked at him as Abe Fortas, a guy he likes and trusts his judgment, and things like that. I don't think it ever crossed Lyndon Johnson's mind that there was even the slightest hint of constitutional problem in calling on Abe Fortas. There was nothing clandestine about it, anything like that. Johnson mentioned many times in the White House that you don't, as Kennedy had said before him, that you don't make new friends when you're President."[47] And Fortas himself was perfectly comfortable with this continuing advisory role, because "it never would have occurred to Lyndon Johnson to ask me these questions if he thought they would have compromised my time on the bench or my actions on the bench."[48]

It was not very long before something came up that was right up the new justice's alley. The president was concerned about the state of the arts in Washington, D.C. "The Boss," Fortas was told, had said to "get [the justice's] opinion on what to do" about a series of problems concerning the construction of the Kennedy Center. For the man who had temporarily felt out of the flow of the political action, even this minor request must have come as a great relief.

The triggering problem was the latest in a series of obstacles to the development of the Kennedy Center. Objections were being raised that a part of the facility called the Opera House, planned to contain twenty-two hundred seats, would be too small. But in investigating this, the White House found that there was much more. It seemed that Bobby Kennedy had been "a real pain in the neck," allegedly sabotaging money-raising efforts and diverting money to the Kennedy Library, fueling controversy about the site selection, which had previously been made by his brother John, and undercutting efforts to establish the facility in a series of meetings with the new trustees and the program committee. Then, too, there were allegations that Senator Kennedy had substituted his list of new trustees for the one made by Jacqueline Kennedy, leaving her with a feeling later that "none of her people were on the board."[49]

It was perfectly understandable that the president would go back to his new justice for help here. Fortas was not only Johnson's resident expert on the arts, but already seemed to be involved in the matter. After all, it was Fortas who had suggested that the administration move in this direction in the first place. Furthermore, the handling of this problem, involving President Kennedy's widow and other members of the former First Family, would require very delicate diplomacy—a Fortas trademark. No one raised the problem that this adviser was now on the court and might be unavailable for such duty. Certainly no ethical problems could be presented by an issue that was so far removed from the court's work.

There was no reason for Johnson to doubt that he would be pleased by the results of this request. In this initial political encounter, Fortas was exceedingly careful that his advice remain concealed from inquiring eyes and the inquisitive press. The three-page typed memorandum from the justice was headed "FOR THE PRESIDENT ONLY," and then in case anyone missed the point he added "Memorandum for the President" below that, indicating its source only as "AF."

Fortas made it clear that thanks to his friend producer Roger Stevens, he already knew even more than the president about the crises surrounding the establishment of the Kennedy Center. And, even before the president's request, the justice had already begun to safeguard Johnson's interests. Fortas knew that Kennedy's widow had recently objected to the design of the center, and in fact he had already met with Oliver Smith, a trustee who had Jacqueline Kennedy's ear on architectural matters. As a result of this timely effort, Fortas continued, Smith had become fully convinced of the need to continue with the present plans, on which over two million dollars had already been spent, and would surely speak to Mrs. Kennedy in a way that would bring her around.

It was a masterfully crafted memo, serving to reinforce Johnson's belief that his friend on the court was one of the best-connected and most effective people in Washington. Fortas already had the matter well under control. And as for any future problems, the justice told the president, let Stevens, who was described as totally dedicated to Johnson and the center, handle them. Stevens knew that the object was to build and begin operating the center without domination by "the K's" but with an eye toward avoiding a public battle with them. Fortas forcefully advised that Stevens be retained as head of the Kennedy Center and the National Council on the Arts, argued that it was important for Johnson to identify himself with a few of these artistic endeavors, and reassured the president that he would continue to follow the developments in this matter in the hope of "keep[ing] things quiet and peaceful" while also avoiding anything that might "present a problem or an annoyance" for Johnson.[50] In complying with this initial presidential request, Fortas made clear where his loyalties were, and how he would view such a role in the future. It would be business as usual—protect the president.

This initial request was like the first crack in a dam. From then on, Fortas was back at the top of a list of people to consult whenever a problem with the arts was raised. He spoke with lawyer Sol Linowitz about "culture" problems, and sent a memorandum marked "Secret" to the president suggesting a number of places in the government where such a valuable man's services might be helpful.[51] Then, two days later, Fortas spoke with one of Johnson's assistants and speechwriters, Harry McPherson, on the same topic. A week later, Fortas's opinion was polled on whether to appoint Samuel Goldwyn, Sr., to a place on the arts council.[52]

During the following year Fortas was always there to lend a hand. Could someone help to negotiate the legal agreement by which millionaire Joseph Hirshhorn donated his twenty-five-million-dollar modern art collection to the Smithsonian? Not only did Fortas help S. Dillon Ripley, a representative of the Smithsonian, to negotiate the terms of the final agreement with Hirshhorn's representatives, but he also attended the White House meeting at which the final arrangements were announced.[53] Should Leonard Bernstein be made the artistic director of the Kennedy Center? Fortas was asked and as usual provided the sort of answer that LBJ was looking for: "There is simply no one else besides Bernstein who could do the job that must be done. Furthermore, he is very well disposed toward the President."[54]

After these first forays into extrajudicial politics, any residual doubts by Fortas as to his place in the Johnson White House evaporated as he began to play an expanded role for the president in the first weeks of 1966. All in all, January would feel just like the good old days when

Fortas had been a key presidential adviser. There would be a total of twenty-four contacts with the president—sixteen phone calls, four private visits, and four more meetings with the president and others.

One of the reasons for this expanded contact was Fortas's input on a speech that the new ambassador, Arthur Goldberg, was to make to the United Nations in explaining the American bombing pause in Vietnam. On January 4, the justice trekked to the White House for a three-hour series of meetings and lunch with Goldberg, Dean Rusk, George Ball, the president, and others. Now aware of the sensitivity of Fortas's involvement in these matters, the secretaries carefully noted in the presidential diary that these were "VERY OFF RECORD" gatherings.[55] Since things were not settled in the president's mind when the justice left the White House in the afternoon to return to his own duties, Johnson asked for more help later in the day. So Fortas returned for a private forty-minute meeting with Johnson in his bedroom, and the two men spoke on the phone twice more that evening. Just as before his court appointment, when a crisis arose Fortas was on call for a daylong series of meetings and discussions. Whatever it took to get the job done, Fortas would do it.[56]

Several days later, he felt comfortable enough to volunteer to Johnson his views on the state of American politics, in a letter directed through White House aide Valenti. The justice was concerned, as "for the first time" he saw "signs of resentment and reaction" toward the administration's civil rights program, a feeling that he attributed to tensions over Vietnam and "a reaction to Watts and to excesses by a few of the Negro leaders."[57] It was the sort of backlash that Fortas was trying to prevent when later in the month he gave a speech in support of Johnson's State of the Union message (a copy of which was immediately sent over to the White House).[58]

By the middle of February, Abe Fortas was ready to step wholly back into his earlier role as a presidential adviser, even to the extent of volunteering legislative suggestions.[59] "Dear Boss," Fortas wrote on February 10, enclosing in the letter two pictures, one of which, he said to Johnson, was a shot of "your" Supreme Court. However, the real purpose of the letter was clear from the second picture, in which, the justice explained, were a number of beagles in the captivity of dognappers and on their way to sale to medical laboratories for experimentation. Johnson well knew that Fortas was very concerned about the treatment of animals.[60] In fact, several weeks before his nomination to the court, he had been working on a list of names for placement on any governmental committee dealing with animals. Now Fortas was bringing to the attention of the president a bill introduced in Congress requiring that such dealers and laboratories be licensed.[61]

Even though Johnson himself had come under criticism from animal advocates for lifting his own beagles by their ears, killing them for research purposes was something far more egregious. Johnson thanked Fortas for his "subtle propaganda" and prepared to get his people moving on the matter.[62] The problem is that administrations and presidents do not always move in the same direction. The reaction of the Bureau of the Budget and the Department of Health, Education, and Welfare to the problem a month later was to endorse the "encouragement of voluntary efforts to clean up the animal situation." A letter was drafted arguing that "voluntary accreditation and compliance . . . should be given a chance to show what it can do." Fortas believed this would do little to solve the problems of dognapping and inhumane treatment of animals, so he wrote "a very strong letter" indicating how distressed he was with this approach. But the bureaucrats would not back down. They conceded that Fortas's views were "entitled to great respect," but they were satisfied with their conclusions.[63] A phone call was made to Fortas in the hopes of persuading him of the merits of their position. However, two united government agencies proved to be no match for the president's close friend. Fortas had persuaded Johnson, and all he needed now was a bill to sign. By August, a measure introduced by Senators Joseph Clark and Warren Magnuson, the first ever from Congress dealing with laboratory animals, had been passed and was ready for the president's signature. When polled as to whether there should be a signing ceremony, Fortas said "there was a lot of political mileage in it and a ceremony would dramatize the bill."[64]

The delicate political nature of the bill ensured that Fortas was going to have to shepherd this through to the end. The opinion was unanimous among the president's advisers that this was a "highly controversial" bill. It pitted the antivivisectionists against the medical research community, a cleavage that cut sharply across normal political grouping lines. Presidential assistant Charles Maguire was sent around to various advisers for one last check on whether the president should endorse the bill into law. But the advisers were nearly unanimous—run and hide. Sam Hughes, the deputy budget director, called it "controversial and unpredictable in effect." He saw it as a weak bill, satisfying no one, and concluded, "Maybe the President should stay out of it entirely." Wilbur Cohen, assistant secretary of HEW, added that the bill could "cause tremendous trouble." Just by appearing to agree with the antivivisectionists, the president would be seen as endorsing their cause. White House staffer Henry Wilson worried that this was "a can of worms" and that the implied opposition to scientific research meant that "editorial writers will have a field day."

There was no earthly reason for Lyndon Johnson to become involved, they all said. And it made sense. In a period in which the White House needed every ounce of prestige and support to run either the Vietnam War or its Great Society programs, let alone both of them combined with the civil rights effort, why should the president even think of wasting any resources on animal rights? Why make enemies out of present friends? The answer was simple. It was not the sheer numbers of opinions that mattered in the Johnson White House, but the source of those opinions that carried the day.

Only one adviser was behind this. But his name happened to be Abe Fortas. He had been polled, too, and the report of his comments were placed at the end of the initial report.[65] By the time the report got to the president, though, there had been one important change. Fortas's comments were moved to the top of the list. After that, the aides knew, what followed would not matter very much. The justice agreed that it was "a very controversial bill." But it had been passed, he added, and it has "wide public support." Like all of the others, Fortas agreed that if the president was going to sign the bill he should do so with "a low-key, minimal statement . . . to take political advantage of the complex circumstances." Who could draft such a delicate political document? Abe Fortas, of course. The justice offered to create "a compassionate, simple, 'reverence for life' draft—and let the decision as to the ceremony rest on its acceptance."[66]

Whatever one might think of Supreme Court justices drafting presidential signing statements, this initial effort from the court made perfect sense for Fortas. It allowed him to retain control of the political agenda. There was no way that Lyndon Johnson, put in the position of grading his friend's writing assignment, would back down. Moreover, Fortas had confidence that he, one of the few full-fledged supporters of this bill, could find the perfect words to help the president.

Even before the justice had put pen to paper, presidential aide Robert Kintner saw this outcome clearly. He was now sure that there was going to be a presidential signing. So Kintner suggested that they use the Cabinet Room, "on the basis that the statement from Abe Fortas will be acceptable to the President, as I am sure it will be." This carefully drafted document would be released to the press after a few ad-libbed remarks by Johnson.[67] Indeed, Fortas's one-page draft of the remarks, which arrived the next day (citing Albert Schweitzer's words that "the quality of a culture is measured by its reverence for all life" and reassuring everyone that progress in science and medicine would not be impeded), did the trick. As unusual as it might be for a Supreme Court justice to be present at the signing of a piece of legislation, those in the White House well knew how deserving Abe Fortas was to be one of the thirty-four witnesses present that day. For some reason, the nine observing members of the press never seemed to question that presence.[68]

By mid-1966 Fortas was making no special effort to hide his continued close relationship with the president. In late May, when a number of people were lobbying for the administration to back an increase in funding for legal services for the poor from twenty-two million to fifty million dollars, they found their efforts stalled. To get the proposal moving again, someone hit on the bright idea of bringing it before one of the nation's most important lawyers—Supreme Court Justice Abe Fortas. Would he be interested in "sell[ing] LBJ" on the plan, they asked? Any discomfort about the propriety of making such a request was overridden by the observation of one of them that "this is really the way things get done in Washington." Nothing could be truer. Fortas not only spoke with the president, but sent some supportive language for a speech to presidential assistant Harry McPherson. As a result, late that summer Johnson announced in a speech in Syracuse, New York, that the funding was being increased.[69]

The court position no longer seemed to bar even ceremonial diplomatic junkets by Fortas on Johnson's behalf. In late July it was agreed that someone from the government should be sent to Puerto Rico for the observance of the fourteenth anniversary of the founding of the commonwealth. It was not surprising, given the justice's close connection to the island over the years and his close friendship with many in the Puerto Rican government, that his name would be suggested as the ideal representative to the observances. Since Fortas saw no problem in going, Johnson had no problem in sending him. So the justice flew down as the president's personal representative, carrying both his own greetings and those of Lyndon Baines Johnson.[70]

These first forays by Fortas into extrajudicial politics set the pattern for what was to come over the next three years. Both men now fully understood that when matters came up in the future on which Johnson felt the need for a trusted outside voice, Fortas would be just a phone call away. The reason was simple: Fortas once again displayed an understanding of the priorities involved. He would deal with problems, regardless of the issue or the circumstance, from the proper perspective—protecting first and foremost the image of Lyndon Johnson. Just as he had been all along, Fortas was the technician. Now, though, he would anticipate future problems and search for the most politically acceptable solution for his friend in the White House. In that way he was the damage control operator. For the political fighter from Texas, he became the cut man in the corner of the ring deciding whether a styptic pencil or a cold iron was necessary to close any cuts and reduce the swelling from any onslaughts. He was also the trainer shouting instructions from the corner to help his charge avoid future blows from the body politic. Fortas, however, could not make those moves for him. And there were no white towels to throw into the ring for the president of the United States when things went badly.

Fortas again became the ultimate lawyer, and the president the ultimate client. But Johnson was a very special client—he was also one of his lawyer's closest friends. As before, the normal professional distance from the client's problems evaporated, with Fortas becoming personally involved, taking on the problems and vulnerabilities of the presidency himself. And Lyndon Johnson, though he didn't realize it, became the weak link in the chain of Abe Fortas's career.

As Fortas's freshman term as a justice began to wind to a close, so did Louis Wolfson's ability to outrun the SEC. Since the spring of 1965, the SEC had been investigating what appeared to be irregularities in the sale of stock in two of Wolfson's companies: Merritt-Chapman and Scott, and Continental Enterprises.[71] Fortas was made aware of the proceeding investigation and Wolfson's deteriorating legal position both by accounts from Milton Freeman, a partner in his old law firm, and repeated letters from Louis Wolfson.[72] Fortas later admitted that "in some of the the letters that [he] wrote [to Wolfson] and in many of the letters [back,] there [were] long discussions or short discussions of the SEC problems and this and that and what goes on."[73] Fortas believed that this was not "legal advice," saying that "it did not amount to a damn thing." For his part, though, Wolfson was "comforted" by "the opinion of a friend" who happened to be serving on the United States Supreme Court.[74]

By March of 1966, the SEC had referred the Continental Enterprises case to the Justice Department, recommending criminal prosecution. However, according to practice, Wolfson's attorney's had not been notified. Word came to Fortas by mid-May that Wolfson was thinking of resigning as chairman of the board of Merritt-Chapman. As he had done so many times before in delicate situations with men such as Lyndon Johnson, Fortas handwrote Wolfson a letter on May 17 with the intention that it not be for the record or get into anyone's files. Speaking from the heart, Fortas's message was simple: "Lou, for God's sake, do not resign at this time."[75] Wolfson took the advice and remained at the helm.

At some point, Fortas, explaining to Wolfson that he had been responsible for the Johnson administration's appointment of SEC Chairman Manuel F. Cohen, said that he would speak with that government official about the case. But after "think[ing] it over, and inquir[ing]," Fortas did nothing. ("It would have been like lighting a fuse on our own dynamite," he later explained to Wolfson.)[76] Still, secure in the knowledge that his contact on the court would intercede on his behalf, Wolfson remained confident about the outcome.

On June 10, 1966, though, things turned from bad to worse for Wolfson when the Justice Department received from the SEC the second case, the one against Merritt-Chapman, with another recommendation for criminal prosecution. Wolfson's fate was now in the hands of one of the most fearless United States attorneys, Robert M. Morgenthau of the Southern District of New York.[77]

But Wolfson still had hope. Four days after this action, Abe Fortas flew down to Jacksonville for a meeting of the Wolfson Family Foundation trustees. According to the minutes of the meeting, during which a variety of requests for foundation contributions were considered, Fortas undertook a foundation study concerning the handling of juveniles within the American legal system. When the meeting concluded, he and Wolfson traveled to the industrialist's thoroughbred racehorse farm in Ocala, Florida.

Each man's account of their meeting the following day differs. While Fortas later recalled that they had not discussed the SEC problems, Wolfson remembered telling the justice, "I am very concerned about this." At which point, Fortas is supposed to have said, "Lou, I still think a technical matter [is involved here] and I have not changed my opinion and I have not heard anything different."[78] It was not the last time they would discuss Wolfson's legal troubles. After he was indicted, Wolfson discussed the action with Fortas once again. There seems little doubt that Louis Wolfson believed that he was getting important advice on his growing legal troubles from a sitting member of the United States Supreme Court.

But Abe Fortas had come to realize that it was necessary to sever the connection. Part of the credit goes to his law clerk, Dan Levitt, who had been called by the White House operators searching for Fortas at the behest of the president.[79] He told them that the justice was in Florida with Louis Wolfson. Levitt learned from Fortas's secretary the next day about the foundation payment received in January of that year. Knowing about the SEC troubles, he relayed through the secretary, Gloria Dalton, a warning that the relationship might mean trouble for the justice. Fortas, through the secretary, told Levitt to "mind your own business." Ironically, this is just what a much younger Fortas had heard from Harold Ickes when he had raised the same sort of ethical issue concerning the Petroleum Reserves Corporation.

But Levitt was right, and Fortas knew it. The justice had learned by now that the SEC cases had been referred to the Justice Department for consideration of criminal prosecution. So, in a letter dated June 21, citing "only the burden of the Court work," Fortas informed the foundation that he was canceling the agreement, and severing his association with the organization.[80]

One thing that Fortas did not do, though, was return the money. At least not right away. According to Paul Porter, the reason for this was humanitarian. It had not been a good year for Wolfson. The government legal establishment was closing in, he already had a cardiac condition, and his wife was dying of cancer. Fortas told Porter, "I can't kick this guy in the teeth under these circumstances when he comes to Washington." In December, though, the justice came across the record of the payment once again while preparing his tax information. "I'm going to send this damn money back," he told Porter. "I probably should not have accepted the check in the first place, but I didn't want to kick him in the teeth." Others, though, seeing the same chronology, might well say that it was the public announcement that fall of Wolfson's indictments that spurred the justice's new actions.[81]

In returning the money on December 15, 1966, Fortas expressed gratitude for the foundation's "kindness and generosity," adding his hope that "the repayment of these funds will enable the Foundation to proceed more vigorously with its fine work." While there is no evidence that the aborted relationship produced any tangible results, he told the foundation to treat his now unpaid efforts as a "contribution."[82]

It was strange for the justice, after a career of exploiting the vulnerabilities of others, to leave himself so vulnerable by writing in this fashion. After making the initial mistake of involving himself with Wolfson's foundation, he then compounded it by committing the entire matter to paper left in another person's files. Everyone knew his abhorrence for leaving a paper trail—no copies, no typed documents, no bulging file folders.[83] That was why Fortas preferred to do his most sensitive work on the telephone. And it made sense, given the nature of his work as a counselor for powerful political and corporate heads in the worst kind of trouble, to protect their confidentiality fiercely. But there was another reason for this devotion to secrecy. Continuing his life as a man of mystery, Fortas later vowed to journalists that he would "take with me to my grave" the secrets learned in the service of the president, and would "leave no papers as grist for historians after [I am] gone." Saying that "one of the gravest sins of officialdom is to kiss and tell," Fortas explained that "history has a claim on a Secretary of State, but not on his adviser. If the Secretary of State has a person to whom he pours out his heart, that man owes the same duty of silence as a lawyer, or a doctor or minister."[84] Years later Fortas would proudly tell an inquiring visitor, "I kept no copies of anything. I don't even have copies of the speeches I gave."[85] But other people kept copies, and Fortas's trail was more apparent than he realized.

Much later Fortas would tell a reporter, "My only regret is that I did not have or make an opportunity for terminating [the arrangement] as generously as I would like to have done. I didn't see [Wolfson] man to man to explain my admiration for the work he was doing and express my feeling of propriety which forced me to terminate the nature of the arrangement."[86] But it was not true. Fortas did arrange for a meeting with Wolfson in Miami in January 1967. No one had yet told the embattled financier that he no longer had a Supreme Court justice on his family foundation's team. When they met on January 8 in the Hotel Deauville in Miami, though, a very uncomfortable Fortas could not bring himself to explain what he had done. Instead he promised Wolfson to "give some thought to the program" they had discussed.[87] And, according to Wolfson's later account, they also discussed in some detail the SEC indictments then pending against him (although it may be that Wolfson did most of the talking with Fortas merely listening).[88]

As far as Wolfson was concerned then, their consulting relationship was still solid and nothing had changed. In a letter written three days later, Wolfson said that he expected to hear from Fortas further and would wait until the following month to "send [Fortas] some data that [he] wanted [him] to read at [his] convenience" in the hope of "getting [his] opinion." Whether this new material was foundation business or more on the SEC indictments is not known. Instead, some time later it fell to Wolfson's attorney to inform him that the relationship with Fortas had in fact been severed some six months before their Miami meeting, with the financial consideration long since returned.[89]

For now, Fortas felt safe. However, the typed, signed letter of contract sitting in a file in Jacksonville lay like an unlit fuse—harmless for now, but deadly should someone have a reason to strike a match in the vicinity.[90]

IX

MR. JUSTICE FORTAS

That first term on the bench, the man who had feared that he was "dying on the Court" very quickly realized that he had more work than he could handle. While Lyndon Johnson and Louis Wolfson kept him busy off the court, there was still the large task of fulfilling his formal duties as a Supreme Court justice.

Abe Fortas's appointment to the court had sparked nothing short of a celebration by the liberal community, which anticipated a continuation of the Warren Court legal revolution. "The appointment of Abe Fortas is an especially pronounced return to the reformist tradition," declared former New Dealer Raymond Moley.[1] Here was a man, columnist Anthony Lewis added, who had "received a high mark as a liberal."[2] As a result, it was being reported that "it's virtually certain that the shift from Goldberg to Fortas will not change the court's balance."[3] By all accounts, Fortas was expected to be a virtual clone of the activist, liberal Arthur Goldberg.

For Abe Fortas, the appointment to the Supreme Court represented both an opportunity and a challenge. He was now an integral part of Lyndon Johnson's legacy to American law. With Arthur Goldberg's shift in the direction of the court, Fortas now became the first liberal to be appointed to the court *as a liberal* since the New Deal days of Franklin Roosevelt. The liberal wing of the court included two senior New Dealers—Alabamian Hugo Black and Washingtonian William O. Douglas—each of whom had already served on the court for more than twenty-five years. Then there were two other members of the reformist wing—New Jersey's William Brennan and Californian Earl Warren— both of whom had been placed on the court by Dwight Eisenhower, who mistakenly believed them to be conservatives.[4]

On the other side of the perfectly balanced group of justices were four conservatives. Two of them were also Eisenhower appointees, New Yorker John Marshall Harlan and Ohioan Potter Stewart. Both were generally exponents of the "judicial restraint" school, urging deference to legislative and state judgments in resolving disputes. Then there was the last remaining legacy of the Truman era, Texan Tom Clark, an earnest and likable man who seemed out of his depth on the court. The conservatives were often led by one of John Kennedy's appointees, Byron White of Colorado. Contrary to what Kennedy had intended, rather than voting as a New Frontier liberal, White charted frontiers on the far right of the court's ideological spectrum. Over the years, this conservative bloc had attempted to stem the tide of social reforms created by their liberal colleagues, and to limit the government's legal powers over the corporate world.

The challenge for Abe Fortas was to put his mark on an otherwise balanced court. He knew that by voting cleverly, he could place himself in the catbird seat of the court, with his vote determining the court's direction in case after case. Mishandling that opportunity, however, would relegate Fortas to the position of public whipping boy for legal, academic, and journalistic supporters of both judicial camps—in addition to antagonizing his colleagues and factionalizing a court that was already well along the way toward changing the face of legal history.

Abe Fortas was ready to accept this challenge, and to turn it into his own personal opportunity. Perhaps no other lawyer in America was better prepared for the task by his past, and better knew the other members of the court upon his arrival. Years of residence in the Washington community, not to mention his many appearances before the court, had afforded Fortas more than ample opportunity to form personal and professional judgments as to the nature of his colleagues, and what would be required to deal with them. More than that, the senior sitting justices had been able to form an assessment of the intellectual capacity of the man who would be joining them.

A mutual admiration society was created almost immediately. In previous years, Earl Warren had thought highly enough of Fortas's work to appoint him to the committee rewriting the Federal Rules of Criminal Procedure and to suggest to his colleagues that he be assigned as *pro bono* counsel in the landmark case of *Gideon* v. *Wainwright*.[5] And Fortas had the same high opinion of the quality of Warren's mind: "What a rare and wonderful man, the Chief. And how I wish I could work the straight, uncluttered, unsubtle way he does. Me with my ins and outs and intricacies and everything covered, as I always say, right back to the invention of money. And still we mostly come out the same place—with the same answer."[6] Earl Warren was clearly a man with whom Abe Fortas was predisposed to work.

Then there was William O. Douglas. How fitting it was that the mentor and his longtime protégé would once again be working together. After all these years, Fortas had a clear understanding of his patron's strengths and weaknesses. When writing for the record, Fortas said of Douglas, "His mind is a cutting instrument of fabulous sharpness. His intellect is a well-ordered, highly organized machine. For this man of intense sentiment, sentiment which cannot be sharply and effectively deployed is slop. To himself, to friend and foe alike, Mr. Justice Douglas is a harsh critic who lies in wait for the slothful, the untidy, the drooling, the soft and sappy."[7] Fortas would tell friends that Douglas and Louis Brandeis were his two judicial heroes.[8] When speaking off the record, though, Fortas's view of the man was more realistic. While Douglas was "a genius on the court," Fortas told an interviewer, "unfortunately Bill just plain got bored, and so, in his later years, he got sloppy in writing his opinions."[9] As time went by, Fortas came to see his relationship with Douglas on the court as much like their interaction on the Securities and Exchange Commission, especially in business law cases. Douglas would be the idealist, using the broad brushstrokes of a house painter, while Fortas, who had been in the "real world" much longer, paid careful attention to details, much like an artist dabbing in colors with the tip of a small camel's hair brush.

Some of the others on the court, all of whom had been persuaded by Fortas's arguments in *Gideon,* were equally well known to the new justice. A bond soon developed with John Harlan, whom Fortas thought was "a man who knew judging."[10] While Harlan, one of the great judicial craftsmen in the court's history, followed a philosophy of judicial self-restraint that often put him on the opposite side of a case from Fortas, the two men got along very well personally. This view made for "exactly the right mix in the carburetor," Fortas explained, adding, "We need reminding now and then of that super-self-restraint view—so long as it doesn't too often prevail."[11] Over the years, the two men would visit each other's summer houses, which were located close together in Westport, Connecticut.

Fortas was not long on the court before he understood that the real power was wielded by the chief's close friend and philosophical ally William J. Brennan, Jr. By positioning himself in the center of the court ideologically, Brennan was often able to dictate not only the direction of the institution's decisions, but their tone as well. Soon Fortas would be working with Brennan in staking out that middle ground. For Fortas, most of the other justices—Byron White, Tom Clark, and Potter Stewart—were simply not important enough to bother with. The power lay elsewhere.

It was clear from the start that Fortas would not be just another freshman justice, expected to serve out his apprenticeship quietly while he learned the ropes. He knew the ropes well, and soon would be relied on by his more senior colleagues.

That was why it was inevitable that Hugo Black, the most senior man on the court, was destined to clash violently with his new junior colleague. In 1948, Black had been sufficiently persuaded by Fortas's talents to save Lyndon Johnson's career. Then, in the summer of 1965 Black had tried to convince Fortas and his wife that joining the court wasn't such a bad idea. But once Black saw his new colleague in action on the bench, his enthusiasm waned very rapidly. Not only was Fortas quickly gathering power, but in Black's mind he was using that power in all the wrong directions. It was the due process clause of the Fourteenth Amendment that brought their differences most clearly into focus. Created by the Reconstructionists in the late 1860's as part of an effort to guarantee the rights of the newly enfranchised black population, the due process clause immediately became a matter of controversy. Did it mean that judges should examine only the *procedural* guarantees and actions of governments dealing with citizens? Or did it also empower judges to examine the *substance* and *wisdom* of those actions, in effect making the court into a superlegislature?

Hugo Black dealt with these questions the same way he handled all other issues in constitutional law—by following the lodestars of his jurisprudential philosophy. Black was a lover of the Constitution to such an extent that he interpreted its words literally. "The Constitution is my legal bible," he wrote; "its plan of our government is my plan and its destiny my destiny. I cherish every word of it, from the first to the last, and I personally deplore even the slightest deviation from its least important commands."[12] Impelled by this view, he next argued that the guarantees of the Constitution must be interpreted absolutely, with no other interests overriding them.[13]

Those judges who believed otherwise were Black's enemies. To his way of thinking, only by following the commands of the Constitution literally could one be a truly objective decision-maker. Those judges who looked beyond the written words in an effort to interpret the "spirit" of the Constitution were, for Black, interested only in substituting their own personal preferences for the mandates of the Constitution's framers. Accordingly, he stated, "I strongly believe that the public welfare demands that constitutional cases must be decided according to the terms of our Constitution itself and not according to the judges' views of fairness, reasonableness, or justice."[14] For Black, the result of such judicial "rewriting of the Constitution under the guise of interpretation" was devastating. It permitted judges "to roam at will in the limitless area of their own beliefs as to reasonableness and actually select policies, a responsibility which the Constitution entrusts to the legislative representatives of the people."[15]

Abe Fortas was one of those judges. He was not afraid to interpret loosely the Fourteenth Amendment due process clause and the rest of the Constitution in order to safeguard the rights of others. As Fortas put it; in the area of defendants' rights, "The Constitution contains specific language relating to criminal justice, such as the guarantees of due process of law and the right to counsel . . . [and] the courts have a special obligation and special mandate to assure that rights of parties in the criminal process are realized in fact."[16] For Abe Fortas, the very job of a jurist was to expand the rights of the Constitution in order to protect minorities, the downtrodden, and the oppressed. So for him the due process guarantee represented a means of ensuring fairness for defendants in the system. Only by examining the clause's spirit, as opposed to limiting himself to a confined reading of its literal meaning, could the new justice accomplish this goal. Consequently, Fortas represented everything that Hugo Black feared in judges.

Despite holding these views, Black was willing to try to convert Fortas during his first months on the court to the "proper" mode of interpretation. But events very early on would make it clear that this effort was destined to fail. Soon, Warren's former law clerk Benno

Schmidt later recalled, Black came to "despise" Fortas, because "intellectually, he was a due process guy."[17]

Within a matter of months, Fortas began to stake out his position of leadership on the court. Like many of the more ambitious new justices, he began to develop areas of substantive judicial expertise where he might lead the thinking of his colleagues. His vast experience in Washington as a corporate counsel gave him the confidence to make business cases one such area. Then, using his background in criminal law and his understanding of psychiatry, Fortas strove to take a leadership role on the rights of juveniles in the court. Though he was destined to write only 106 opinions in his brief tenure on the court—40 for the majority, 45 dissents, and 21 concurrences—Fortas quickly established a reputation for being able to walk the tightrope between the two groups of justices at opposite ends the political spectrum. By one set of measures he seemed to vote with the liberals. In his first term on the court, Fortas agreed with Chief Justice Warren in 75 out of 84 cases and with Justice Brennan in 72 out of 86 cases (as opposed to voting with Justice Harlan in only 43 out of 86 cases). And in his first three terms on the court, Fortas agreed with Warren 86 percent of the time, with Brennan 82 percent of the time, but with Harlan and Stewart only 50 and 60 percent of the time, respectively. However, Fortas also managed to vote many times with the conservative bloc in the area of business. In time, his efforts became so persuasive that one study of leadership and acquiescence on the Warren Court concluded, "There is little doubt that Fortas was one of the most persuasive justices in the sixteen years of the Warren Court. Not only [did] his opinions for the Court elici[t] changes of votes; his dissenting opinions, more than those of any other member of the Warren Court, persuaded members of the majorities to join him in dissent. . . ."[18]

As he did this, Fortas also established a reputation as one of the most stylish writers ever to have served on the court. Concerned that his colleagues were constantly trying to tailor the issues in antitrust business cases so that the government always won, Fortas accused them in one case of creating a "strange, red-haired, bearded, one-eyed, man-with-a-limp classification," and in another case of conducting a search that was more than a "snipe hunt."[19] In the areas of civil liberties and civil rights, Fortas proved to be equally eloquent in his expression. Trying to safeguard the rights of the accused from certain discovery procedures employed by the state, Fortas argued, "A criminal trial is not a game in which the state's function is to outwit and entrap its quarry. The state's pursuit is justice, not a victim."[20]

Such eminently quotable sentences, combined with the scholarly nature of his heavily footnoted opinions, made them among the clearest, easiest to understand, and best-written opinions of that court. Fortas was particularly adept at the mental gymnastics required to take the reader from A to Z in his logical train of analysis. He also showed a desire to investigate to the minutest detail any relevant historical materials, social science data (especially that from psychology), and evidence from the practice of the real world.

Fortas also proved to be a very active and snappish participant in the oral arguments, often reminding people of the hyperactive Felix Frankfurter as he peppered the visiting attorneys with questions, treating the proceedings more like a law school class than an appellate court case. Frequently, he also displayed what one observing reporter called "a penchant for sarcasm."[21] One such vigorous exchange occurred in the area of police interrogations. "I suppose that prior to the Magna Carta and the Bill of Rights most people convicted were criminals. Nevertheless the wisdom of the ages has provided safeguards . . . designed to eliminate the unusual case of the unjustified conviction and lay out a standard for the relationship of the state to the individual," he lectured one of the state prosecutors. Then Fortas added that he supposed that Communist nations convicted the guilty efficiently, "but I equally suppose you join me in horror at convictions obtained without counsel or fair trial."[22] As the new justice hammered away at the government's position in the landmark case *Miranda* v. *Arizona*, considering the rights of the accused in police interrogations, one of the defendant's lawyers passed a note to a friend reading, "If God be Fortas, who can be against us?" Indeed, exhibiting the crucial nature of his new swing position on the court, Fortas would silently cast the deciding fifth vote in the case, which established that subjects of police interrogations must be warned of their constitutional rights and provided with the assistance of counsel if requested, for their statements to be admissible in court.[23]

In another instance, when the court was considering the gubernatorial election procedure in Georgia, whereby the legislature would pick the winner if no candidate achieved a majority of the popular vote, Fortas clearly wanted to institute a popular runoff election procedure. In the middle of oral argument, he shocked the state's attorney by glowering down at him as he waved a volume that, the justice said, contained the Georgia state constitution of 1771. How could the election by the legislature be defended now, he demanded, when in the state's original constitution the governors of Georgia had been elected by the people? The courtroom lapsed into an embarrassed silence after the stunned attorney admitted that he had never seen the early Georgia constitution and did not know its contents.[24]

Understanding Fortas's philosophy for deciding cases, however, is much more problematic. His law clerks believed that he did not have one. "Fortas's law clerks absolutely despised him," explained Benno Schmidt. "They said the most awful things about him, which really surprised me since most clerks tend to revere their justice. They said that he was not a man of principle on a principled court, what with the finished jurisprudential philosophies of men like Black, Douglas, and Harlan. Instead, they saw him as a politician who would listen to the clerks' principled arguments for a particular decision and say, 'Well, yes, in theory that is where we should come out. But we just can't do that in this case.'" Then Schmidt added, while making a chopping motion with his hand as though dividing a child, "Fortas seemed to them to be too Solomonic, too much the wheeler-dealer. In time, the clerks came to see Fortas as totally unprincipled, and intellectually dishonest."[25]

As harsh an assessment as this seems, any analysis of Fortas's opinions must conclude that he *did* lack an overarching judicial philosophy. Instead, it was as though he were back in his Interior Department days with Congressman Lyndon Johnson, playing the role of the ultraflexible technician. Moreover, while Fortas clearly possessed the requisite judicial intellect for the job, he often failed to demonstrate the necessary judicial temperament. Never one for the ethereal ivory-tower world of academic legal scholarship, he seemed to have trouble switching from his "secular" background to the cloistered legal analysis required on the court. And he had little respect for the occupants of the legal academic world. "Clark Clifford and I get more done in one day on the telephone than they do in 20 years of law-review writing," Fortas would later tell a reporter.[26] On the court, though, Fortas was in the same position as those sterile intellectuals. As a result, the same drive that was impelling him to flirt with the ethics of the court by continuing his close personal relationship with a sitting president also affected the way he approached his formal judicial duties.

While Fortas did not follow a single judicial philosophy in his case-by-case approach to decisions, he was guided by some general decision rules. First there was "the rule of law," the idea that society must be governed by binding statutes that are crafted by representatives of the people and interpreted by judges. "I am a man of the law," Fortas would say over and over. "To me the structure and theory of our law and its practice—what we call the 'rule of law'—represent the summit of human achievement, the peak of man's amazing progress."[27] For that reason, Fortas wrote, "I have dedicated myself to uphold the law."[28] The breakdown of the rule of law meant for Fortas that civilized society would be lost, and man would return to a life of anarchy and violence in the "trackless jungle."[29] Protection of the rule of law, then, required protection of the government.

Which led Fortas to his next rule—what his former Yale colleague Fred Rodell termed his "almost physical abhorrence of violence" of any kind. Rodell saw this impulse in Fortas as being "almost abnormally active and strong."[30] Expressing his concern with assaults on the body, Fortas wrote of the police extraction of a suspect's blood for an alcohol content test, "As a prosecutor, the state has no right to commit any kind of violence upon the person . . . and the extraction of blood, over protest, is an act of violence."[31] Fortas was also concerned with acts of violence perpetrated on the psyche. When speaking of the press's relentless hounding of its subjects, Fortas said that "when words were used as 'instruments of aggression and personal assault' they might lose their constitutional immunity."[32]

Fortas was just as concerned with violent and aggressive protests against the government, which ensured the existence of the rule of law. His liberal instincts seemed to disappear sometimes when words and actions were directed against the government in protest. "We are a government and a people under law. It is not merely government that must live under law. Each of us must live under law. Just as our form of life depends upon the Government's subordination of law under the Constitution, so it also depends upon the individual's subservience to the laws duly prescribed. Both of these are essential," he later wrote.[33] For this reason, Fortas argued that no person could violate the law to protest what were perceived as other evils in society. Those who did take such actions must accept responsibility for them, even it it meant punishment. "If the right to protest, to dissent, or to assemble peaceably is exercised so as to violate valid laws reasonably designed and administered to avoid interference with others, the Constitution's guarantees will not shield the protestor."[34] So Fortas argued that the protester's first efforts must be to make changes through legitimate processes such as through the ballot box rather than through disruptive behavior. Even in later protesting, though, there was one form of action that was totally unacceptable to Fortas—violence. "Violence is never defensible—and it has never succeeded in securing massive reform in an open society where there were *alternative methods of win-*

ning the minds of others to one's cause and securing changes in the government or its policies.''[35]

Perhaps because of this abhorrence of violence, Fortas seemed to cross over the line of being compromised by his extensive political work with President Johnson in deciding only one case. Most of the time, the only effect of the heavy extrajudicial load on Fortas was that he occasionally came to work somewhat unprepared and "bleary-eyed.'' But he did not miss any work.[36] The danger, however, was that a case would arise on an issue that touched on the White House or the discussions in which Fortas had taken part. This happened in the strange case of *Watts* v. *United States.*[37] During a political debate, Watts had said that if he were ever inducted into the army and made to carry a rifle, "the first man I want to get in my sights is L.B.J.'' The court in a *per curiam* summary decision held that this was simply crude political hyperbole and did not constitute a knowing and willful threat against the president. If ever there was a case from which Abe Fortas should have recused himself, this was it. But he saw no reason to step out from a case that involved some form of threat against his close friend. Instead, Fortas, along with Justice Harlan, argued that the court should not have decided the case without first having a full hearing on its merits.

A final set of rules for Abe Fortas concerned the workings of the free-market economy. Ever the practical justice, Fortas believed that government should remove itself as much as possible from the workings of the business community. With that in mind, the courts must do the same. In what came to be seen as a particularly eloquent statement of Fortas's judicial philosophy in the corporate law area, he argued, "The courts may be the principal guardians of the liberties of the people. They are not the chief administrators of its economic destiny.''[38] Having seen the actual workings of big business since 1946 in his corporate law practice, Fortas was confident in adopting his stances against government regulation and in favor of business.

Abe Fortas served notice in his first days on the high bench that he intended to take a leadership role when it came to business. Because of that, the usual custom of breaking in a justice gently, as his colleagues gave him their support after the assignment of some easy opinions, was not followed in Fortas's case. Instead, Hugo Black squared off immediately with the freshman justice on the issue of how Supreme Court justices should do their jobs. Fortas was assigned the opinion in what appeared to be a straightforward tax case, occurring when the IRS had tried to collect on a tax lien it had failed to record properly

against what became a bankrupt company. Fortas generously interpreted both the language and legislative history of the relevant statutes
to hold against the IRS.

In response, Hugo Black wrote a scathing solo dissent, lecturing
Fortas on his seeming willingness to stretch the language of the statutes and creatively interpret the intent of Congress. It mattered little to
Black that Fortas had correctly read the spirit, if not the actual letter,
of what Congress intended. Ever the literalist, Black accused Fortas of
giving the law "an entirely artificial, fictional meaning," on the basis
of "frail and inadequate support."[39]

Commentators missed the intensity of Black's comments, perhaps
thinking that it was simply an effort by a senior justice to instruct the
newcomer. They could not have known that the real reason for the
attack lay elsewhere. Behind the scenes, while this opinion was under
consideration, Fortas had already angered Black by stealing thunder in
another case.

In *United States* v. *Yazell,* Abe Fortas not only stole Hugo Black's
majority opinion, he also served notice that he was in the process of
stealing the leadership position on the Warren Court that Black had
wanted for himself.[40] The dispute before the court was a minor one. In
1957 the Small Business Administration (SBA) had made a disaster
loan to Delbert Yazell and his wife, Ethel Mae, after their shop in
Lampasas, Texas, had been damaged by a flood. When the Yazells
defaulted on the loan, the United States government tried to collect
from both of them. Mrs. Yazell, however, claimed that under the
Texas law of coverture, which was designed to protect presumably
dimwitted married women from unscrupulous men or the stupidity of
their husbands by requiring that contracts binding their property first be
approved by the court, she could not now be held responsible for the
debt to the SBA.

When five justices voted in conference in favor of the SBA's ability
to collect, the opinion was assigned to Justice Black. While he was
writing the opinion, however, Fortas circulated a draft dissent that was
so persuasive that two justices—Brennan and Warren—switched their
votes, turning Fortas's effort into the majority opinion of the court.[41]
In balancing the interests of the Yazells and deference for the state of
Texas's "peculiar and obsolete" institution of coverture against the
interests of the SBA, the new justice held against the SBA collecting
on the debt and began to establish his credentials as the court's expert
in the area of business practices.[42] Justices like Black had been out of
the mainstream of business since the late 1930's, whereas Fortas had

just come to the court from a corporate practice. So he argued to Justice Brennan in a private letter that his *Yazell* opinion was grounded in his years of private law practice, as well as a study he had just completed of the SBA procedure manual.[43]

Black was as puzzled as he was hurt by the nature of Fortas's dissent-turned-majority-opinion and its effect. He could not understand how Fortas could take such a position upholding the practice of coverture as it related to women. In defending the rights of women to make their own contracts without requiring the protection of the courts through a coverture decree, Black told his own wife that he "had Carol Fortas in mind, as cool and competent a lawyer as ever put foot in a courtroom. The idea of *her* having to be protected from the male world was laughable."[44] But the senior justice did not seem to have the same high view of the competence of Mrs. Fortas's husband. In an opinion accusing Fortas of distorting the facts of the case to reach an unjustifiable result, Black argued that Mrs. Yazell was liable to pay.[45]

What had seemed to be a small private dispute between the two men broke out into an open display of Black's temper a month later, when a decision was announced in the case of *Brown* v. *Louisiana*. Here five blacks had entered the "whites only" area of a segregated library and protested the inequality of treatment there by remaining in silence for ten or fifteen minutes after being requested to leave. Although the demonstration had been peaceful and silent, the men had been arrested and convicted of a breach of the peace.

Abe Fortas was assigned the opinion, and wrote that the defendants could not be constitutionally punished for their behavior.[46] Central to Fortas's reasoning were two factors. First, the men had been prosecuted under the law against breaches of the peace, and there was not "the slightest hint" that any of their actions had actually violated that law. Fortas conceded that states might regulate their libraries, but not in a discriminatory manner. As much as anything else, though, Fortas seemed disturbed that the blacks had been kept from a library, which to him was a place of beauty, contemplation, and self-improvement.

This opinion drove Hugo Black to distraction. In an extreme and intemperate draft dissent, Black accused Fortas of being prejudiced against the South.[47] When he saw it, the chief justice tried to apologize to Fortas: "I am somewhat saddened by Hugo's dissent. It does not reflect the better part of his nature."[48] While Black later tempered his dissent to secure the agreement of three colleagues, his final opinion still displayed to the world his growing displeasure with his new colleague. "I am deeply troubled," he wrote, "with the fear that powerful private groups throughout the Nation will read the Court's action, as I do—that is, as granting them a license to invade the tranquillity and beauty of our libraries whenever they have quarrel with some state policy which may or may not exist."[49] Black saw himself as one of the few remaining bulwarks against the lawlessness and changes that he feared were about to come in the South. By the end of the opinion he went even further: "I say once more that the crowd moved by noble ideals today can become the mob ruled by hate and passion and greed and violence tomorrow. If we ever doubted that, we know it now."[50]

It was not enough for Hugo Black to write this harsh appraisal of Fortas's judgment. When the decision was announced in open court, he took the opportunity to express his outrage by delivering a thirty-minute oral tirade on the case. According to one reporter who heard it, Black's speech "made his strongly phrased written dissent seem pale by comparison." Trembling with rage, and periodically shaking his finger at the courtroom audience as he spoke, Black scorched Fortas with charges that his decision would lead "misguided" civil rights demonstrators to think that they would be "automatically turned loose, so long as whatever they do has something to do with race." To Black, the "psalm-singing" demonstrators were not protected by the First Amendment because their actions constituted conduct, and not free speech.[51] It was only a matter of time before Black's hostility toward Fortas took on even broader ramifications.

For now, though, Abe Fortas spent the rest of his freshman term staking out what seemed like a schizophrenic decision-making system. Invariably, he could be counted with the liberals in cases involving individual rights, but was more often than not with the conservatives when it came to protecting the rights of business from the regulations of big government. This middle-of-the-road philosophy was different from that of the seat's previous occupant, Arthur Goldberg, who had tended to side with the liberals in both areas. For Fortas, this posture meant that he was often on the opposite side of the fence from his mentor, William O. Douglas, in the area of government regulation of business.

The differences between Fortas and Douglas came sharply into focus in two cases near the end of Fortas's first term on the court—*United States* v. *Grinnell Corporation* and *Federal Trade Commission* v. *Dean Foods Company*.[52] In both cases, Fortas opposed his liberal colleagues' rulings upholding the government's efforts to restrict mergers. The Grinnell Corporation of Providence, Rhode Island, made high-quality burglar and fire alarm systems. Through a complicated web of market agreements and price manipulation practices undertaken by related affiliate companies, the corporation had managed to acquire 87 percent of the country's insurance-company-accredited central-station protective service market. The Justice Department had filed suit alleging that the monopolistic practices of this company had resulted in an illegal restraint of trade under the Sherman Antitrust Act. Contrary to the Justice Department's claim that the "relevant market" here for judging the existence of a monopoly was a national one, Grinnell argued that it should be judged only by its actions in each local urban market, where its alarms were sold through its many affiliates in competition with an array of other kinds of protective devices.

In his majority opinion, Justice Douglas had little trouble in voting against what he saw as the illegal monopolistic practices of the Grinnell Corporation. For him, the monopoly could be inferred solely by the predominant share of the existing market controlled by the company and its affiliates. He also accepted the Justice Department's view of the "relevant market" as being national in nature.[53]

Abe Fortas saw it quite differently. In a dissenting opinion, he lectured Douglas's majority about the "reality" of the business world. The problem, claimed Fortas, was that the court was "gerrymandering" the "relevant market" applicable in this case to ensure a finding against the defendant.[54] Fortas understood the "government always wins" technique of the former head of the Securities and Exchange Commission and others in the business regulatory crowd: Find a way to define the scope of the economic market as being small enough so that it is nearly filled by the company being charged.

Here, Fortas charged, the court had simply redefined Grinnell's business. Since it actually sold alarm systems within several small local markets, one should ask whether each city was monopolized, not the entire national market. Instead, the Justice Department and the high court had created a new business for Grinnell—so-called central-station protective services—through which the company's affiliates made deals with more national insurance companies. By creating such a "Procrustean definition," Fortas said, the court ensured a finding against Grinnell.[55] Fortas would have preferred that the case be remanded to the lower court for a market-by-market inquiry as to monopolistic practices.

In invoking this metaphor of Procrustes, one that Fortas used frequently in subsequent cases, he seemed to be laying the foundation for his later views in the area of business law. In this Greek myth, a giant of Attica named Procrustes would seize unfortunate travelers and tie them to an iron bedstead, cutting off their limbs or stretching them until they fit properly.[56] Through this image, Fortas would frequently charge that the government or a judge was using drastic measures to torture the law or the facts of a case into conformity with the charges involved. Driven by his abhorrence of violence, Fortas frequently alluded to this myth and images of surgery in an apparent effort to invoke a fear of the destruction of the whole body of the business or the "rule of law."[57]

Later in this dissent, Fortas went on to display some distress over what he perceived as a lack of real-world understanding of business by his colleagues. Douglas's approach, he claimed, "has no justification in economics, reason or law."[58] After frequent references to the "unreality" of his majority view, Fortas charged that Douglas had made "an incorrect and unreal definition of the 'relevant market.'"[59]

Fortas's concern over the liberals' ignorance of the realities of the business world also came out in *Federal Trade Commission* v. *Dean Foods Company*. When Dean Foods attempted to merge with the Bowman Company, creating a potential milk monopoly in the Chicago area, the FTC had asked the court of appeals for a restraining order and a preliminary injunction to block the merger. The court had held that the FTC had no power to bring such a suit. Rather it had only the power to issue a cease-and-desist order against the merger.

In a narrow 5–4 majority, with Tom Clark speaking for the court, the position of the FTC was upheld. The agency indeed had the power to ask courts of appeal to exercise their authority in order to maintain the status quo, pending a full administrative review. In a dissent that was longer than the majority opinion itself, Abe Fortas assailed his colleagues for their support of the government's position. It seemed as though Fortas, displaying real conservative tendencies in this area, was pulling out all the stops in an effort to build a majority for the future. Fortas hoped for the establishment of a peaceful coexistence between business and government, which would give big business free rein in the marketplace. Allowing and encouraging the FTC to block a prospective merger in court first, and then use its administrative review power, would not accomplish that goal. So Fortas opposed it with all the power of his pen. Using uncharacteristically violent metaphors, he argued that the FTC was "not intended to be a gun."[60] "Not every merger deserves sudden death," he added, especially when faced with this sort of "machinegun" approach of taking the matter to court first.[61] Instead, Fortas feared that "the patient [the company] may die while the 'temporary' anesthesia [of court remedies] is in effect."[62]

For Fortas, then, the majority opinion represented nothing more than "radical surgery" upon the law, creating a new power in the FTC out of thin air in a clear attempt to enforce the majority's own policy preferences against business mergers. Fortas demonstrated that repeatedly over the years Congress had been asked to confer such a power on the agency and had expressly refused to do so. So he wanted his colleagues to "indulge the Congress in its desire that at least the Federal Trade Commission should move with caution and deliberation," and use its statutory administrative powers first.[63] It was not as if suspect mergers could not be undone once they were completed, he added. Should the courts eventually rule the new merger to be illegal, they had the power to restore the situation to the status quo. For Fortas, then, that decision should not be left to antibusiness government bureaucrats.

There seemed little doubt after these two cases that Abe Fortas could be counted as an almost certain conservative vote when it came to the practices of big business. And Fortas's views found a welcome audience in more than just the business community. Already, journalists were hailing Fortas's "blend of New Deal liberalism and practical business experience" as "the wave of future Supreme Court economic rulings."[64]

Liberals did not despair over these decisions, however, because Fortas simultaneously established his alliance with their cause on the issue of the rights of juvenile defendants. In the case of *Kent* v. *United States,* Fortas indicated both his concern for the fairness of the legal system toward the accused, and his willingness in some instances to go even further than his liberal colleagues. The *Kent* case also demonstrated Fortas's desire to stake out a leadership role on the court with respect to the rights of juvenile defendants.[65]

Morris Kent, a sixteen-year-old, had been arrested for housebreaking, robbery, and rape. After a "full investigation," the District of Columbia Juvenile Court chose to waive its jurisdiction and send the case to the district court, which handled adult cases. In so doing, the court ignored a motion by Kent's lawyer for a hearing on the question of the waiver, and for access to his client's full file. Subsequently, Kent was convicted on six counts of housebreaking and robbery. So the question confronted by the Supreme Court was whether the waiver of jurisdiction by the juvenile court without a hearing was valid.

When Abe Fortas was assigned to write the opinion for a five-man majority, he decided to lay the groundwork for a later, broader opinion on the rights of juvenile defendants in the legal system. Customarily, juvenile courts are allowed wide leeway in the handling of young defendants on the theory that they are acting as *parens patriae*—that is, in the position of surrogate parent to the juvenile. Thus, what is done in the court is designed to ease the trauma on, and promote the rehabilitation of, the defendant as much as to administer punishment. Consequently, certain legal procedures of adult courts do not apply to juvenile courts. For Fortas, however, the *parens patriae* philosophy of the juvenile court was not to be seen as "an invitation to procedural arbitrariness."[66] He ruled that due process required that a hearing be held when basic rights were at stake, and that counsel have access to all relevant documents on the defendant. So for him, the court had violated the Constitution when it failed to hold a full hearing on the question of whether Kent's trial should be waived to the district court.[67]

Fortas then looked at the larger question of the basic requirements of fairness under the due process provision as it applied to children. While conceding that juvenile courts had a substantial degree of discretion, Fortas insisted that henceforth the accused must at least be given a hearing. Then, after being given access to all relevant reports, and receiving a hearing, the defendant must also be given a full statement of reasons for the juvenile court's eventual decision as to the waiver. Only these procedures would permit a meaningful opportunity for appellate review of the case later on.

Plainly, Fortas was heading toward the eventual creation of a "Juvenile Bill of Rights." His concern for the fairness of the procedures, and the rule of law as it applied to juveniles, two views that were entirely consistent with the rest of Fortas's judicial decision-making rules, necessitated an eventual extension of more rights to children in court. For example, what if the child did not have access to competent counsel? Fortas showed how far he was willing to go after explaining the need for guaranteeing a full hearing: "These rights are meaningless—an illusion, a mockery—unless counsel is given an opportunity to function. The right to representation by counsel is not a formality. It is not a grudging gesture to a ritualistic requirement. It is . . . the essence of justice. Appointment of counsel without affording an opportunity for hearing on a 'critically important' decision is tantamount to denial of counsel."[68] For now, though, the rest of the court was not willing to go that far.

By the end of Fortas's first year on the court, the reviews of his work were glowing. *New York Times* reporter Fred Graham called the freshman justice "a promising member of 'the club'" and a man who was fast becoming "a power on the Supreme Court."[69] *Newsweek* hailed him as the "rookie of the year."[70] And *U.S. News & World Report* predicted that Fortas could be "counted among those who will set the tone and style of the Court in the future."[71]

One sitting justice, though, did not agree. And he was determined to teach this young pretender to the throne of leadership on the court a lesson he would not soon forget. That was why Hugo Black was so glad *Time* v. *Hill* had come along at the end of that first term.

This new case raised the sort of privacy interests in opposition to the rights of the press that separated Fortas from his liberal colleagues in the First Amendment area. The case concerned the family of James J. Hill, who as residents of a Philadelphia suburb had been held hostage for nineteen hours by three escaped convicts. In order to escape the publicity caused by this event, the Hills had moved to Connecticut. Gradually the incident was forgotten, until Joseph Hayes wrote a novel entitled *The Desperate Hours*. This novel, which Hayes said was based on the Hill incident and other similar hostage situations, was later adapted into a play and a motion picture. When the play went into pre-Broadway tryouts, *Life* magazine was persuaded by the play's promoters to do a story on it. So a photographer from the magazine went to the original Hill home and arranged for actors in the cast of the play to stage scenes for the camera in the house. While the early drafts of the magazine story indicated that this play was a "fictionalization" of the Hill encounter, the article was rewritten in the editorial process to make the connection between the two more direct. Now the Hill incident and the play were inextricably linked in the public's mind.

In fact, the play was very different from the actual incident. The real hostage takers had been "gentlemanly" and nonviolent, whereas in the play one convict was shown shaking one of the young sons, and another had his gun hand bitten by the daughter. The Hills, upset by the spotlight placed on an ordeal they had tried to put behind them, sued Time Inc., publisher of *Life*, to recover damages for the invasion of their privacy under New York's "right of privacy" statute, winning a judgment of thirty thousand dollars.

Fortas had what his friend Fred Rodell called a "tremendous respect" for the right of privacy.[72] "There are great and important values in our society," Fortas would write in *Time* v. *Hill*, "none of which is greater than those reflected in the First Amendment, but which are also fundamental and entitled to this Court's careful respect and protection. Among these is the right to privacy."[73]

More than that, Fortas had what can only be termed a hatred of the press. Over the years he had observed what he believed to be character assassinations by the press of his clients in the McCarthy witch-hunting days, of the unfortunate Walter Jenkins, of his friend Lyndon Johnson, and even of Fortas himself. To Fortas, members of the press were "mongers," who were both "dirty" and "crooked" and "misuse[d] the information" that they got in an effort to look out only for themselves.[74] For him, the press was "murderous" in its technique: "It's no different from the McCarthy thing. You destroy people by making these accusations. You destroy their self-esteem. The fracas can be brutal."[75] In fact, as a private attorney, Fortas had once been so angered by an article about one of his clients that he sent the reporter a letter containing only the salutation and his signature. Later he explained to the puzzled journalist that he had started to dictate a responding letter, "but then I thought about the laws of libel and just signed it and sent it on."[76] Clearly, this justice was going to be no friend of the free press.

Time v. *Hill* turned out to be the Supreme Court debut of failed presidential and California gubernatorial candidate Richard Nixon, who was now attempting one of his many comebacks. In what was described by one reporter as "one of the better oral arguments of the year," Nixon pleaded for the vitality of the right of privacy. "How is an individual to remain an individual in our mass communication society?" he asked. Nixon's opponent, Harold R. Medina, Jr., son of a prominent federal judge, argued that this story was a valid news account of the play, and thus came under the protection of the First Amendment.[77]

When the original vote was 6–3 in favor of the Hills' right to privacy, the chief justice assigned the opinion to Abe Fortas. Fortas's early draft was an assault on journalism: "The facts of this case are unavoidably distressing. Needless, heedless, wanton injury of the sort inflicted by *Life*'s picture story is not an essential instrument of responsible journalism. Magazine writers and editors are not, by reason of their high office, relieved of the common obligation to avoid inflicting wanton and unnecessary injury. The prerogatives of the press—essential to our liberty—do not preclude reasonable care and thoughtfulness. They do not confer a license for pointless assault."[78] Fortas did not buy the argument that the play was a "fictionalized version" of the Hill hostage incident, or that the *Life* piece was a newsworthy account of the new play. Instead, he saw the article as calculated to sell *Life* magazine and box office tickets at the expense of the Hills' peace of mind and right of privacy.[79]

No doubt remembering his stinging defeat in the *Yazell* case, Black was quick to recognize the opportunity presented to him by this draft. He told those around him that this "was the worst First Amendment opinion he had seen in a dozen years." And Black added that "it would take him all summer to write his dissent, [which] would be the greatest dissent of his life."[80] Of course, Black well knew that the effect of this action would be to put the case off until it was reargued the following term, thus giving him more time to steal the majority away from Fortas.

But how could he justify this delay to his new colleague? Black got his chance a week later, when Fortas circulated a somewhat more temperate draft in response to the comments of his colleagues. After staying up half the night to write comments all over the margins of Fortas's new draft, Black wrote a petulant note to his junior colleague complaining that this was now an entirely new opinion, which had reached him too near the end of the term to write a proper dissent.[81] So Fortas had no choice but to propose that the case be restored to the docket for reargument in the fall.[82]

True to his word, Black labored all summer to produce a memo that would sway his colleagues.[83] He made a very persuasive attack on the "weighing process" used by Fortas to hold against the press. As an absolutist, Black argued that the right of privacy should not be balanced against the right of free press so as to restrict the latter. After mocking Fortas's "rhapsodical descriptions of the great value of [the] 'right to privacy,'" Black added a verbal slap across the face of his junior colleague: "After mature reflection I am unable to recall any prior case in this Court that offers a greater threat to freedom of speech and press than this one does, either in the tone and temper of the Court's opinion or in its resulting holding and judgment. For even if I were to agree, which I do not, that First Amendment freedoms can be weighed by judges against a judge-made right of privacy, or some other judge-made right, at the very least this weighing should be done with a clear and complete understanding of what is being weighed against freedom of the press."[84]

Black could see that the sharp nature of this attack had left Fortas "hurt and angered."[85] It also left Fortas in the minority. When the other members of the court saw the memo early in the fall, all but the chief justice were quickly persuaded to side with Black. So the opinion against the Hills was given this time to William Brennan. Taking note of both the "fictionalization" of the play and the newsworthy nature of both the play and the Hills' hostage nightmare, Brennan argued that the Hills would be able to collect only if they could prove that the magazine piece had been published with "knowledge that it was false, or with reckless disregard for whether it was true or false."[86] So the case was sent back to lower New York courts for a resolution on this new standard.

Fortas simply could not stomach granting so much latitude to the press: "I, too, believe that freedom of the press, or speech, assembly, and religion, and the freedom of petition are of the essence of our liberty and our values. . . . But I do not believe that whatever is in words, however much of an aggression it may be upon individual rights, is beyond the reach of the law, no matter how heedless of others' rights—how remote from public purpose, how reckless, irresponsible, and untrue it may be."[87] Like it or not, though, Hugo Black had won this round.[88]

It was only a matter of weeks before the two men were squaring off again. A case came to the court in early December challenging the Georgia practice of choosing a governor in the state legislature from the two candidates who had won the most popular votes in the general election when none had received a majority. It was on this basis that Lester Maddox had been chosen governor. Initially, six justices indicated a willingness in conference to uphold the practice. When William Brennan changed his mind the next day, though, a scramble was on for control of the majority opinion.[89] Abe Fortas, feeling strongly about the public's right to vote directly for a governor, started to lobby for a fifth vote against Georgia's practice, which would give him the majority.[90] Black responded bluntly to this effort by saying that he could think of nothing that Fortas might write that would influence him to make any changes in his opinion.[91]

So Black got the majority opinion. After drafting a states' rights opinion, upholding the constitutionality of the election procedure, Black pressed for an immediate announcement of the result to inform the Georgia General Assembly as to what could be done.[92] The move was not totally magnanimous. Fearing that Tom Clark would desert the majority, Black wanted to hurry the announcement of the decision to avoid another *Yazell*. Meanwhile, William O. Douglas began pressing for a delay in the announcement, saying that he needed time to work on his opinion. Black wrote another memo tweaking his colleague for the uncharacteristic care that he was now willing to take on his opinion, and accusing him of delaying in hopes of changing the vote.[93]

Fortas liked neither the haste nor the fact that the opinion was now Hugo Black's. He wrote a dissent arguing that this selection scheme violated the equal protection clause of the Fourteenth Amendment. For him, the right to vote, and to have each vote counted equally with the votes of other citizens, was fundamental. Empowering the legislature to select a governor on occasion served to usurp the rights of the voters. "If the voting right is to mean anything, it certainly must be protected against the possibility that victory will go to the loser," argued Fortas.[94] Not only were voters for the candidate with the highest total having their votes devalued, but the legislature that eventually did the selecting had itself been put into office from malapportioned districts. So the legislature's vote for governor was not truly representative. Fortas could not finish without a swipe at Black's opinion, calling it "a startling reversal; a belittling, I say with all respect, of our Constitution's dynamic provisions with respect to the basic instrument of democracy—the vote."[95]

Still stinging from the loss of his majority in the *Time* v. *Hill* case and perhaps the harshness of Black's response to the lobbying effort in this case, Fortas started "sulking" about the course of the Georgia case. He told Black that if he "changed *one* word in his opinion, [Fortas would] refuse to let it come down" immediately.[96] Then, during the oral announcement of the decision, Fortas read his dissent "with more heat than usual," while noticeably "flushed with anger."[97]

But Hugo Black had won another round. "This Court, *this* Court, this *Court,* is not allowed to write laws," he had stated emphatically. "We are here to interpret only."[98] It was not the last time the two men would clash.

X

LYNDON'S FIRST STRING MAN

"Fortas is the true *éminence grise* of the Johnson Administration. *No one* outside knows accurately how many times Abe Fortas has come through the back door of the White House, but any figure would probably be too low," *Time* magazine would say in 1968.[1] And the periodical was correct.

By late 1966, Lyndon Johnson was fighting and losing battles on both the domestic and foreign fronts. The wave of legislative successes instituting the Great Society had led to unmanageable costs, which were overshadowed only by the ravages of the war in Vietnam. On top of that, rampant crime in the streets had led the public to prepare for a new domestic war in that area. By the end of the year, there would be nearly four hundred thousand American troops in Southeast Asia. By the end of 1967, one Gallup Poll would rate Johnson's personal popularity at a paltry 38 percent, while also revealing that he would lose a new presidential race to any of five Republican opponents.[2] At the same time, another poll would indicate that 46 percent of the American people now regarded the war as a "mistake."[3] Slowly, the wave created by the huge political mandate for Johnson in the presidential election of 1964 was dissolving into a series of whirlpools and eddies representing the plethora of crises that would soon sink his administration. For the president, friends were harder and harder to find.

But, of course, there was one notable exception. During this period, as the White House crises heated up and allies disappeared from sight, Abe Fortas became even more important to the president. After the lull of his first year on the court, Fortas worked his way into much the same advisory role he had enjoyed during the years before his judicial appointment. Depending on the occasion, Fortas served as political adviser, speechwriter, crisis manager, administration headhunter, legal expert, war counselor, or just plain cheerleader. While the norms for Supreme Court justices involved in political advising might have restricted the actions of others, it is doubtful that the two old friends even considered these issues except to avoid discussing matters currently before the court itself. The situation was the same as always—Johnson needed Fortas's help and Fortas was more than willing to provide it.

Only the White House aides knew the astonishing range and extent of the contacts between the justice and the president. While rumors that he "talked on the phone almost daily with Johnson" were much exaggerated, from October 1966 to October 1967 the two men had a total of 105 contacts that were recorded by the White House secretaries (some of which included group meetings with a number of other people).[4] Then in the fourteen months that followed, there were 149 more contacts between them. (This compared very closely with the 111 contacts during 1964.) The vast majority of these contacts came in the form of personal phone calls, with the two men speaking together on an average of once every four or five days, while their personal meetings averaged more than one per month.

These gross figures, however, are misleading. Many of these personal phone calls and meetings came in binges during the crises facing the president. So the two men might go for a period of days without any contact and then Fortas might be in constant contact with Johnson, even to the point of virtually living in the White House day and night until a particular crisis was resolved. And all of these statistics ignore the number of contacts between the two men through White House intermediaries. By now Fortas had learned that by using any of a number of conduits—Jack Valenti, Harry McPherson, Joe Califano—messages could be reliably exchanged without disturbing the president's usual routine. It had gotten to the point that after a short hiatus Fortas was back on the "regular mailing list" of people to be consulted for comments on a certain speech or action before it was taken.

The relationship between the president and the justice by now was one of such ease that Fortas's letters to Johnson were frequently addressed "Dear Boss." For his part, Johnson would respond to his many services in the only way he knew how—by offering gifts of White House photos containing the justice. To Johnson, these were more than snapshots of occasions, they were glimpses into what was contained in his heart as well. "You and I have shared many happy and important moments together," he wrote with one batch of photos early in 1967. "The click of a camera shutter cannot capture the warmth of our closeness, but these photographs do give evidence of the cause and value of friendship. I thought you might like to have them as a lasting expression of my gratitude and appreciation."[5]

By the end of 1966, then, the relationship between the president and the advising justice had been set for the rest of Johnson's time in office. There was nothing that could not be placed on the Fortas agenda. As a result, Fortas's importance as an outside assistant grew.

One area in which Fortas continued to be of considerable help was in speechwriting. Once the president's civil rights message had been drafted in early 1967, taking into account the suggestions made by the Bureau of the Budget and several other agencies, the new version was sent on to Fortas for final comments. In response to the justice's recommendation, the aides "put more emphasis on the fact that states and cities have fair housing laws and that such laws have not brought about the dire results predicted by their opponents."[6]

And of course there were the inevitable policy suggestions during periods of crisis. Sometimes these suggestions came even in the absence of any requests from the White House. When the Six-Day War broke out in the Middle East on June 5, 1967, Fortas waited a couple of days before deciding that Johnson could use his help. Indicating that he would appreciate a phone call but did not want to bother the president, Fortas passed suggestions along through Joe Califano. As the aide explained:

1. [The justice] thought you should refrain from getting into the "neutrality" issue any more, particularly through an argument on the Neutrality Act. He believes we have taken care of that issue with the American-Jewish community and he has deep reservations about the applicability of the Neutrality Act to this situation.

2. He believes that once there is a cease fire, the United States should not try and draw up blueprints for restructuring the Middle East. His view is that we should let the Israelis and Arabs negotiate this out, and save ourselves until the last half of the ninth inning in the negotiations. With respect to the second point, Abe believes the post–cease fire situation is going to be the trickiest from the viewpoint of domestic politics as well as international politics.[7]

Once more, much as in the Dominican Republic crisis, Fortas's advice was more concerned with how to protect Johnson's public image than with the specific military or political issues involved.

Times of crisis like these continued to cement the close relationship between the president and the justice. And even under great time pressures, each did what he could to keep the intimacy of their friendship alive. That year, when Carolyn Agger threw a dinner party in honor of her husband's birthday, Johnson made plans to be a surprise guest. Fortas himself returned the favor by exercising his celebrated eloquence in handwriting a three-page birthday note to Johnson. "My Dear Friend," it began, explaining that the president had been in his thoughts throughout the day. In talking about the "great debt" that millions of people owed Johnson, Fortas reassured the president that "greatness is not happiness." Since, to the justice's way of thinking, Johnson had the first of these, he could not expect the other unless he realized that the happiness was of a "different kind."[8]

But as their interaction grew, Fortas's confidence in his ability to maintain the secrecy of their relationship seemed to ebb. The turning point came with a meeting at the White House on the evening of November 3, 1967. Marvin Watson, James H. Rowe, Jr., Arthur Krim, and Fortas had been called to the second floor of the mansion for dinner and an evening of conversation on how to secure the president's reelection in 1968. For four hours they talked about the sort of advance preparation that one needs to launch a campaign of such magnitude. As the men were leaving, though, Fortas turned to Rowe, the savvy Washington insider, and said, "I shouldn't be at these meetings."

"No, you shouldn't" was Rowe's only response.[9]

Still, Fortas ignored his own instincts. He placed no restrictions on his personal chats with the president, though the White House secretaries were now even more careful about the recording of the contacts. So it was on November 30, when Fortas heeded the White House's call to attend what was listed in the diary as a "very off record" meeting with Johnson. While no record of that meeting exists, more than likely it centered on the announcement just two hours earlier by

Eugene McCarthy that he was formally challenging Johnson for the Democratic presidential nomination. Fortas also continued to attend group meetings at the White House about one issue, the Vietnam War, in spite of the fact that no one could keep his presence at *these* meetings quiet.

No issue better illustrated Justice Abe Fortas's position in the constellation of advisers and subordinates surrounding the president than the war in Vietnam. Some saw and now still see Abe Fortas as the ''architect'' of the Vietnam War. But rather than being an architect, Fortas could be likened to the draftsman who takes the ideas of others, carefully portrays them on paper, and perhaps makes a suggestion here and there. Like the draftsman, Fortas acted in a manner to make the plan look as good as possible to the public eye. Like the draftsman, he was also incredibly supportive of the original design. But also like the draftsman, he found the design with all its flaws already formed by the time he entered the process. Any change he made was either to spruce it up or for damage control—a difficult role to be sure if one does not support the architect, or is not initially predisposed toward the design.

However, Fortas supported Lyndon Johnson. Like the friend of any president facing enormous opposition from war critics, the justice thought it was the least he could do. But by now, Fortas was more than just Johnson's friend. The two men were close enough to be brothers. So the policy for Fortas here was going to be ''protect the president at all costs.''

The problem was that Fortas had never been included in any of the meetings that originally cast the policy miring the United States deeper in Vietnam. In 1964, Fortas's only effort was to recommend that it might be helpful for McGeorge Bundy to spend time with a doctor from Walter Reed Hospital who had been sent to South Vietnam to do some psychological surveys of the Americans there.[10] Even regarding the crucial July 28, 1965, decision to send fifty thousand more troops into battle, the main issue discussed by the president and Fortas was not Vietnam. Rather, Lyndon Johnson used this time to convince Abe Fortas to accept his gift of the Supreme Court appointment. The only role that Fortas seems to have played in that escalation was approving the wording of the press statement announcing it.[11]

Why would Lyndon Johnson fail to consult Fortas on such a crucial turn of events? Because he knew, as did all of Fortas's friends, that Fortas would support him. And it was good that Fortas played a small role in the process. For despite all of the many subjects of the justice's expertise, foreign policy was not one of them.

Fortas knew international leaders, but he knew no international theory. He operated in a different world from the international sphere. He was a lawyer in the world of diplomats, using briefs and words where often only guns are heard. He revered the rule of law, whereas internationally it is impossible at times to know who the players are, let alone the rules by which they play. He was the technician, whereas internationally only power brokers are respected. And he would search for the "logical" lawyerlike solution in an international sphere where there is no logic, only passions and emotions.

Fortas's swashbuckling efforts in Puerto Rico in May 1965, clandestinely trying to negotiate away the Dominican Republic crisis, clearly showed his weakness in foreign affairs. In trying logically to construct a government policy, he forgot that Juan Bosch was a man in fear of his life. As former diplomat Thomas Mann explains it, "The problem here was that Fortas was thinking like a lawyer rather than like a diplomat. That just won't work."[12]

Even Fortas's closest friends saw this weakness. Tex Goldschmidt remembers a time when he made the mistake of inviting both Fortas and the South Vietnamese observer at the United Nations to his summer home in upstate New York. After listening to arguments from the foreign guest about ending the bombing and searching for a peaceful solution to the war, Fortas spent the whole time belittling that approach and making a fool of himself with the naïve nature of his hardline hawkish arguments defending America's, and more specifically Johnson's, policies. Goldschmidt says, "In all my years as a friend of Abe Fortas, it was the only time that I've ever felt embarrassed about him. He just was talking when he shouldn't have." But policy advice failures in the Dominican Republic and a lack of faith by his friends could not deter the justice. "Fortas was so self-assured," Goldschmidt concludes, "that he felt he could take on any subject and master it given a reasonable period of time . . . and Vietnam did not lend itself to that intellectualized task."[13]

Why, then, would Lyndon Johnson include Fortas in later Vietnam discussions? To put it simply, Fortas may have known nothing about Vietnam, but he knew everything about Lyndon Johnson. And for that reason the president trusted Fortas's instincts. Zbigniew Brzezinski, national security adviser to Jimmy Carter, explains, "The President [Johnson] once said to me that the only people in whom he could really have confidence in terms of good solid judgments in international affairs were Fortas and Clifford, that these were the only people who gave him solid, sound advice, and these were the only people who were not taken in by circumstances or events or even other individuals. . . . [The president] recounted some story to the effect that the Soviet ambassador [Dobrynin] can influence people on the Hill, he can even influence McNamara, he can even influence Rusk, and the only people who aren't taken in are Clifford and Fortas. Then he made some remark to the effect that he knows and they know . . . that in politics, sometimes it's very important to grab your opponent by the balls, to squeeze hard and to twist, not to let go. And this I thought was very Johnsonian.''[14]

As time went on, and more and more presidential subordinates began to desert the presidential policies, Fortas's role became even more important. He felt that his job was to bolster the president of the United States. In many ways he had now become too close to the president to function as an adviser on Vietnam. Instead, he served as a reinforcer, backing whatever program the president had devised. With this role came another function, of devising means to justify those actions to the press and the American people. This public relations function—interpreting the desires of the American people and charting a strategy for presenting the war to them—became even more vital as the public's skepticism of the war increased.

Fortas understood his role. Years later, in one of the few times that he consented to discuss his work with Lyndon Johnson, Fortas explained his functions here. ''I freely admit that I discussed the Vietnam War with Lyndon Johnson,'' he began. ''You have to understand that there was a streak of paranoia here. Lyndon Johnson needed someone in whom he had absolute, utter, total confidence to discuss these matters, and I think I was one of those people. . . . These were times of great stress,'' Fortas continued. ''[They were] times of great trouble. This was a matter of national importance. And I just didn't feel that I could refuse. . . . What should also be understood, though, is that I never would have decided anything for him, or offered him a decision, because it's my nature that whenever I make a decision or advise any course of action, to immerse myself in all of the facts, to make clear to myself everything about that issue. There was no way—I didn't have access, to all of the information that Lyndon had about the Vietnam War—and there was no way that I could advise him about such matters. So I would just offer him my counsel on these occasions and serve mainly as a confidant, or even a sounding board.'' Fortas saw his job, then, as simply "to allow Lyndon Johnson to air his views and to come to his own conclusions hearing his arguments sounded out."[15] In performing this task, Fortas was once again functioning like a court of last resort. As he put it, "My function with the President was to listen and then tell him what I thought it added up to."[16] It didn't matter whether he believed the argument or not, only that he, as a skilled solicitor, presented it for decision.

With respect to the war, then, Fortas played a combined role of friend and lawyer. As a friend, he was essentially a supporter—never testing policies, but only allowing the president to hear his own views and arguments sounded out. And as a lawyer, he gave the appearance of competence on any issue while acting as an advocate. Once his "client," the president, set the policy, Fortas as "lawyer" told him how to do it. So Fortas's posture was more to protect and serve, rather than to question and critique.

What did Fortas personally get from this role (besides the seat on the Supreme Court, which he did not want)? Partly, there was the satisfaction that comes with helping a friend in need. Moreover, feeling confident of his own abilities here, Fortas could be pleased that he was making his own contribution toward shaping national policy. It is undeniable, however, that there was a third, baser motive at work. Now Fortas had developed a taste for being near the center of power and participating in its exercise. This desire could be satisfied only by serving the president of the United States. And, given Lyndon Johnson's insecurities, continuation in this role required that Fortas put aside his normally independent, critical judgment to support the president blindly on the issue of the war. To put it bluntly, Fortas had to become a yes-man on Vietnam.

This role had a consequence for Fortas. His views became almost indistinguishable from those of the president. This meant that he would be seen by others as being the same kind of unregenerate hawk as the president, who was already committed to the war. And it also meant that the vulnerabilities of that president in being responsible for the policy would one day be his adviser's as well.

But was Fortas really a hawk? To be sure, he wanted others to think so. David Halberstam tells how the justice, rather than being upset that a *New York Times* article had hinted at his close presidential advisory relationship on this issue while on the court, was more concerned that the word *not* had been dropped from the phrase "Justice Fortas, who is not a dove."[17] But for a "technician," a man committed throughout his life to no definable philosophy other than the solution of problems, such a slavish devotion to a hawkish stance seems surprising.

So then, rather than *whether* Fortas was a hawk, the more important question becomes *why* he would take such a stance. Was it his considered belief, or just a costume donned for other reasons? There are some good reasons why he may well have wanted the hawk label. This New Deal liberal may have wanted to appear hard-line in foreign policy. Or the man who had been accused more than once of being a Communist may have wanted to prove his patriotic mettle with a macho policy here. Almost certainly, though, the real reason for his posture was dictated by a very different concern. All that he needed to know was that Lyndon Johnson was committed to the war, and his presidency as well as his role in history depended on the outcome. So Fortas's main concern became not how to win the war, so much as how to win the propaganda battle of selling the war to the American people. Foremost in his mind was the idea of protecting the public image of this president. Therein lay the double irony. Fortas was offering his expertise in two areas in which he had none—foreign policy and public opinion.

Perhaps the most accurate indication of Fortas's true role in this controversy could be seen in the intuitive judgment of those staffers who were classifying his documents for the White House Central Files. It was not uncommon for his materials to be placed with the "public relations activities" materials of the so-called country file on Vietnam. The judgment was a fair one. Most of Fortas's concerns centered around how to make the president look good, and how to sell his program to "the public." Time and again, the justice would seem to say that only he knew what the American people really wanted, and how to tap those innermost desires. While protests raged in the streets and the press wrote about Johnson's "credibility gap," one by one the president's allies in Congress and the White House deserted him. But Fortas never wavered. Instead, he became even more devoted to the president's cause, with his aggressive policy mirroring Johnson's and his reassurances that "the people" were still behind that policy.

By the end of 1965 it became apparent to Secretary of Defense Robert McNamara, who had just returned from a fact-finding mission to the war zone, that the July infusion of fifty thousand American troops had not had the intended effect. In searching for alternatives to further troop increases, the defense secretary suggested to Lyndon Johnson the possibility of another bombing pause, this one much longer than the one tried in May of that year. The strategy here was that a stoppage in the bombing might persuade the enemy to negotiate a peaceful end to the conflict (whereas increased bombardment would serve only to harden the resistance).[18] Johnson decided that a meeting discussing such a crucial decision required the presence of his favorite outside advisers. This would be the first White House meeting to which Abe Fortas had been invited since going on the court. And it was his first opportunity with the war advisers to indicate whether he was truly with the president, or whether, at this first critical juncture since the troop escalation, he thought the earlier action had been a mistake.

Present in the Cabinet Room at 12:30 P.M. on December 18 were those administration officials most involved in the war-making process: President Johnson, Defense Secretary McNamara, Secretary of State Dean Rusk, National Security Adviser McGeorge Bundy, Undersecretary of State George Ball, White House aides Bill Moyers and Jack Valenti (there to keep notes), former deputy ambassador to Vietnam U. Alexis Johnson, Fortas, and the other outside adviser, Clark Clifford.

Johnson knew exactly what Fortas would say and do.[19] After all, they had enjoyed a three-hour intimate White House dinner the night before, which followed an hour-long meeting during the day. Johnson knew that the justice was prepared to support him to hell and back. And that was precisely why he was invited. No one questioned the invitation of a member of the Supreme Court to this meeting, least of all Fortas himself.

For the next four and a half hours, including lunch, the assembled advisers gathered around the large conference table in the Cabinet Room. They debated Johnson's fear of the "military risks" posed by the beefing up of enemy forces during a bombing pause, versus McNamara and Bundy's willingness to try this new tack of seeking a political solution knowing that "we can resume bombing at any time."[20] By lunchtime, it was pretty clear that Lyndon Johnson, hunched over in concentration with hands alternately clasping and unclasping, was a significant minority of one against the plan.[21] Dean Rusk had led off with the argument that the American people "are isolationists at heart" and would "do what has to be done in a war situation if they are convinced there is no alternative." To keep up the public's morale, he argued, "we must be able to say that *all* has been done." Even if there was "one chance in ten or twenty" of success by such peaceful means, he concluded, "I would take it." After three other members of the administration echoed this posture, it was left to McNamara to summarize the case for a pause before they broke to eat, saying that it was the "strong feeling of [the] American public that [the] Government peace efforts have been superficial and inadequate. [The] military solution is not certain—one out of three or one in two. Ultimately we must find alternative solutions, we must finally find a diplomatic solution."

Almost immediately after returning from the break for lunch, Johnson made certain that the discussion did not go too far afield and foreclose his options. "Let me hear your views, Abe," he said. By calling on his trusted outside adviser so early in the second half of the meeting, he would be able to control the agenda of the ensuing discussions. Rather than simply summing up the supportive arguments of all of the administration advisers lined up on one side, and of the military (and presumably the president) on the other, Fortas became the judge choosing between the two sides—and a heavily biased judge at that.

Beginning in his usual smooth, low, almost inaudible voice, his face lined in an earnest, serious, "counselor" demeanor, every now and again Fortas raised his hands in a crisp gesture to make his points. The sedate manner of his presentation belied Fortas's severe harshness toward the bombing pause plan under discussion.

The problem should be divided into two parts, he said, the psychopolitical aspects and the military effects of a pause. For him, the case for a pause had not been proven on the first score. "[I] think public reaction will be negative—showing uncertainty." The idea of trying a pause, he argued, was to "respond to manifestation[s] of public opinion [saying] 'you're not doing enough'" to find peace. Fortas believed that all the people really wanted was the "cessation of hostilities." Instead, this tactic would show a lack of resolve by the United States toward its war effort. Six months after the huge troop infusion, we would now be looking for a diplomatic way out. "Anytime there is evidence of [a] lack of certainty on the government's part, it leads to negative thinking in the public mind," Fortas explained. "It will cause people to worry about [the] depth of conviction in [the] government objective." So from a psychopolitical view, the "net balance" for Fortas here was negative.

The president's adviser then followed this rather baffling attempt to psychoanalyze the nation with an assessment of what he labeled the "real question": "Would this strategy lead to actual military results? . . . As I understand it, this action will not be done with prearrangement with [the] Russians. This is an action ambivalent and ambiguous. We use the Christmas season—and by that fact and presentation we are diluting the effort in its hoped-for psychological and

political results. [We are] also diluting [the] effect on [the] Russians—
and any bringing about of peace negotiations.'' Since the Russians
were maintaining a public posture of neutrality, while privately arming
North Vietnam, their role in this effort to secure peace was critical.
Fortas added that his main concern was what would happen if the plan
failed. Not only would the government get no "credit for it," but
"there will be renewed pressure for drastic action. We'll have obstacles to negotiations because of [the] failure of a major and spectacular
effort.'' On balance, Fortas concluded "that the arguments that have
been made are not sufficient to justify a pause.'' It was a remarkable
performance for the man who had once been paid thousands of dollars
to explain the law in clear English to his clients. Now in the service of
the president, Fortas seemed more intent on using political jargon and
obscure argumentation to cloud the issues for the other advisers more
than reveal them.

From this point on, the meeting took a very different turn. The other
outside adviser, Clark Clifford, added his lengthy and well-reasoned
support for Fortas's views. Though the two men were in the minority,
some advisers were more equal than others. Whereas before lunch it
was the president who countered the pause advocates' arguments, after
lunch he let Abe Fortas do it for him.

"Should we pursue [the] military estimate of [a] 50-50 chance of
victory,'' asked McNamara, "or what should we do?''

"In carrying the political battle,'' added Rusk, "I need something
more than we have at the present time. We need to make clear that the
United States is honorable and has been given no alternative. We
strengthen our position by proving we want peace.''

It "seems to me,'' countered Fortas, that "you have already made
your case for peace [with the May bombing pause]. Perhaps it looks
different on the inside than it does on the outside.''[22]

The truth of the matter was that accounts of what *might* happen if
the United States made the first overtures toward peace bothered the
lawyer in Fortas a great deal. Years later, he would tell author Merle
Miller, in language far less diplomatic than he had used that day in
December 1965, "I think I heard all of the proposals that were made
about how if we cease the bombing Chou would talk to Sam, and Sam
would talk to Ho Ho Ho and Ho Ho Ho would talk to so-and-so, and
something good would happen. Candidly, as I told Johnson and the
assembled group at the time—different words on many occasions—
they all sounded to me like horseshit. And they were. Horseshit!''[23]

On this occasion, further meetings convinced Johnson that the bombing pause was worth a try. But after thirty-seven days of empty skies, from December 25, 1965, to January 31, 1966, and whirlwind diplomatic efforts around the world by administration officials such as Averell Harriman and Hubert Humphrey, all that was accomplished was the renewal of the conflict with increased vigor.

There was one silent result, though. Now LBJ was more inclined than ever to listen to his outside advisers' "I told you so's" in the future whenever new ideas for such pauses surfaced. This effort had been, Fortas and Clifford reminded the president, his "worst mistake" in the conflict.[24] And Fortas became an even more valued adviser to the president. Over the next three years, he sat in on at least thirteen formal meetings on Vietnam. There is no way ever to know how frequently this matter was raised in Fortas's private face-to-face and phone conversations with the president, but it is hard to imagine that in a period during which they discussed nearly everything else, a topic of such magnitude was not at the top of their agenda.

By taking the president's position on these occasions, Fortas could not lose. It was a self-fulfilling prophecy. The more he supported Lyndon Johnson, the more the president wanted to hear what his friend on the court had to say. But the other executive officials viewed this behavior less favorably. After one such meeting Robert McNamara reportedly told Johnson, "I can't understand why you bother consulting your experts. For in a pinch you pick two guys off the street, bring them in, ask their views, which are opposed to the views of the rest of us, and follow their advice."[25] Later, Chester Cooper, assistant to Ambassador-at-large Averell Harriman, would write that "for some of us the Clifford-Fortas relationship with the President was a source of frustration and despair."[26] Another account of the period even argued that McGeorge Bundy had left the administration in 1966 because he did not like the way that the president "turn[ed], after all the normal players had made their case, to people like Fortas and Clifford for last-minute consultation."[27]

After the justice's intensive involvement in the bombing pause meeting, it was only natural that when the White House considered how the United Nations ambassador, Arthur Goldberg, should explain it to his diplomatic colleagues, the president felt a need for Abe Fortas's speechwriting talents. So, on January 4, 1966, the justice participated in another set of meetings. It was particularly ironic that Goldberg, who had left the court with the prospect of having more influence in foreign policy, was watching his judicial replacement exert at least as much influence as he, if not more, while sitting on the court.[28]

A week later, it was more of the same. Fortas was asked to examine a draft of the president's 1966 State of the Union address to Congress. Unhappy with the mundane, domestic-issue-centered nature of the early draft, the justice took pen in hand and drafted large portions of a new one. Fortas's major suggestions came in the section of the speech concerning Vietnam. While none of his language actually made it into the final speech as delivered, the hawkish nature of the words represent a mirror of the state of his mind on the subject, and most likely of the tenor of his private conversations with the president. Fortas wanted the president to say in the first minutes of the speech: "In the world, no matter how long it takes or what it may cost—we shall fulfill our mission—to resist aggression."

Later, he added, "So far as South Vietnam is concerned, every dollar, every ship, every plane, every gun, every ounce of food and material to support our forces and our allies and to rebuild that unfortunate country will be provided. We shall not stint. Let there be no doubt about this." And what would be the result? "Even though we have deliberately chosen to bring to bear only a tiny fraction of our force—carefully confined to restricted areas—the tide has begun to shift [and] time has begun to run out for the aggressor."[29]

But fewer and fewer others inside and outside the administration shared this view. So, with the war going badly and advisers turning against the current policy or simply leaving the administration, Fortas moved from a peripheral position as Johnson's outside adviser to a position of preeminence by October 1967. And the trend made a good deal of sense. After all, when things are going poorly for the client, the lawyer is called in more often. An indication of Fortas's rising importance comes in an analysis of his presence at White House advisory meetings on the war from the time of the July 1965 escalation until the end of Johnson's administration. Only three invitations came in the first twenty-six months after the initial escalation. However, from October 1967 until June of the following year, when things were at their bleakest for the president, Fortas was present at fully ten formal White House meetings. Based on the surviving notes of some of these meetings, as well as the few written documents sent by him to the White House, former Undersecretary of the Air Force Townsend Hoopes is right in charging that "Fortas continued to play the curious role . . . as spokesman for those private thoughts of Lyndon Johnson that the president did not wish to express directly."[30]

But despite all of his counseling wizardry, Fortas could not change the facts. Life for Johnson had become very difficult by the fall of

1967. By the end of the year over five hundred thousand American troops would be engaged in the conflict, with more than fifteen thousand being killed in a twenty-four-month period. Even with the torrential rain of bombs dropped from American planes, the war was still stalemated. Accustomed to winning such conflicts, and promised that such an event was imminent, the people at home began to lose faith in the entire effort.[31] Now only four out of ten people said they approved of the manner in which Johnson was handling his job.[32] Soon, his popularity would decline even further.

As things got worse, the president became even more isolated and the streak of paranoia that Fortas had noticed became more apparent. For Johnson, the problem was not one of policymaking, but a media-led conspiracy separating him from his supportive constituents. "No matter what anyone said," he later told biographer Doris Kearns, "I knew that the people out there loved me a great deal. . . . The problem is that I was sabotaged. . . . [The people] began to think that I might be wrong about the war. And gradually they stopped coming to my speeches."[33] It was an odd view for a man whose only safe havens for giving speeches were military bases, far away from the crowds yelling, "Hey, hey, LBJ! How many kids did you kill today?"

But it was a view that Abe Fortas shared. And if this was merely one giant public relations problem, then Fortas was certain he could help solve it. He had the utmost confidence in his own ability not only to master the intricacies of foreign policy, but also to know what "the people" wanted. Never did it occur to him that having spent nearly his entire adult life in Washington, he did not have the foggiest notion of who the common folk were, let alone what they wanted.

So, after one particularly depressing Saturday-night phone call from the president in the fall of 1967, Fortas sent to the White House an unsigned two-page memo that was really nothing more than a pep talk of solid support and confidence. In it, Fortas offered the president his advice on how to win what he saw as the real war—the "propaganda battle."[34] Arguing that the problem was not a lack of military might and skill, Fortas saw only a need for whipping up enthusiasm among the young men subject to the draft. They required a sort of "Uncle Lyndon Needs You!" effort.

The justice suggested that a new presidential speech be delivered shifting the justification for involvement away from the notion of helping the South Vietnamese to the idea that we were fighting to make the world safe for democracy. This was "new" Communist subversion, which had to be met before it was on the American doorstep. "We cannot and will not permit South Vietnam to be a monument to freedom's defeat—or a franchise to infiltration and subversion,'' the justice proclaimed. Since retreat was unthinkable—Americans had never lost a war and would not tolerate losing this one—the resolve to win would stir free peoples on every continent to resist Communism. The three-part Fortas program, then, was simple: first to make ''a commitment to success,'' then to go on the offensive in the ''propaganda war,'' and last to stir the enthusiasm of the young men subject to the draft. The whole memo seemed so preposterously unrealistic that the White House staff didn't seem to know what to do with it—file it or frame it. One wrote on the top, ''To Rostow for files I suppose.'' ''But keep handy,'' another added, perhaps thinking of the president's need for quick reinforcement on occasion.[35]

Such devotion to the president's views ensured that Fortas would be an honored participant in early November 1967, when the idea of a bombing pause was being broached again. With the enemy in the midst of a bloody offensive, Secretary of Defense McNamara had begun a total reassessment of the war.[36] In a meeting on Halloween Day with the regular war policy group known as Johnson's ''Tuesday Lunch,'' he had told the president that the ''continuation of our current course of action in Southeast Asia would be dangerous, costly, and unsatisfactory to our people.''[37] Then the next day he sent the president a draft memorandum on the ''major risks of widening the war,'' concluding that ''the alternative possibilities lie in the stabilization of our military operations in the South (possibly with fewer U.S. casualties) and of our air operations in the North, along with a demonstration that our air attacks on the North are not blocking negotiations leading to a peaceful settlement.'' Faced with so radical a set of recommendations from one of the men who had planned and wholeheartedly backed the war to this point, Johnson immediately went in search of more welcome advice.[38]

There was little doubt what the president wanted to hear. Of the four men he hand-picked for comments on the memo—Fortas; Clark Clifford; General Maxwell Taylor, former chairman of the Joint Chiefs of Staff and ambassador to Vietnam; and National Security Adviser Walt Rostow—all were self-avowed hawks at the time, and three were outside his formal administration entirely.[39] And to the extent that the president wanted to hear nothing but reassurance that he was still on the right road, these men would not disappoint him.

While the president waited for their responses, another enormous advisory meeting on the war was called in the White House. This time, though, the makeup of the group was very different. Dubbed the "wise men," a group of largely eastern establishment foreign-policy giants were convened and asked by the president to "consider things generally, not just a pause."[40] Translation: Did Lyndon Johnson still have *their* support?

The group that had been summoned could not have been more illustrious: Clark Clifford, Walt Rostow, Maxwell Taylor, Dean Rusk, Robert McNamara, Averell Harriman, George Ball, McGeorge Bundy, Director of Central Intelligence Richard Helms, former secretary of state Dean Acheson, Undersecretary of State Nicholas Katzenbach, former treasury secretary C. Douglas Dillon, five-star general Omar Bradley, twice former ambassador to Vietnam Henry Cabot Lodge, former ambassador Robert Murphy, chief Korean War negotiator Arthur Dean, and Assistant Secretary of State for Pacific and East Asian Affairs William Bundy. More important for the president, they could not have been more supportive.

After opening the meeting by launching into an angry blast toward the news media, the president then asked for comments around the table.[41] Having been exposed the night before to nothing but positive briefings from General Earle G. Wheeler and from CIA analyst George Carver (rather than the changing views of McNamara), the group's views were perhaps predictable.[42] One by one those seated around the table voiced their opinions. Dean Rusk noted that "steady progress [was] being made, [but] much still needs to be done." Then one of the great advocates of Communist containment, Dean Acheson, said, "I am encouraged by the ground fighting in the South and that we are taking the initiative. I got the impression [from the Carver briefing] this is a matter we can and will win." Then he added, "I would not talk about negotiations any more. You have made it clear where you stand. This isn't the Communist method. If they can't win they just quit after a while." After both McGeorge Bundy and Douglas Dillon generally agreed with Acheson's position, Henry Cabot Lodge took a new approach. He suggested the use of smaller fighting units rather than the present "seek out and destroy" effort: "Public opinion is more concerned with U.S. casualties than with our bombing program. If the casualties go down, nothing else matters so much." Finally, Omar Bradley added, "The more we talk about negotiations, this is a sign of weakness to them. . . . We are winning, but we must have patience."

Just before lunch, though, the president offered the floor to his former in-house critic, now out of the administration—George Ball. Not surprisingly, Ball became the only man all day to argue for a different course. He recommended that the bombing tactics be changed by shifting the targets away from the harbor and the dikes to the demilitarized zone, specifically in order to interdict men and supplies. "This would clearly show the other side that we are creating the conditions to let them stop the fighting."

As for the question about maintaining American support for the war, Ball's views were radically different from the others. He pointed out that, given the huge disparity in the size and strength of the two nations' military machines, "many students can't understand why we are using our air power against a primitive people that has no air power." Moreover, "very few Americans really see a political solution as another Munich. We don't talk about getting out." Given the Korean experience, he argued, the public did not believe the administration's predictions of American troop withdrawal in six months. All in all, Ball argued that "we are in a position now instead of arguing how we got there as to what we do about it now that we're there."

Since the Ball speech had represented a negative reading of the "American public," it was only natural that as they all sat down for lunch Johnson would repeat his strategy in the December 1965 bombing-pause meeting and turn to his own public relations adviser—Justice Abe Fortas—to reset the tone of the discussion. And once more, the justice concentrated on his own agenda—how to protect the president by selling the war to the people. Fortas began by saying that he found the presentation by George Carver to be "remarkable. . . . The nation is totally unaware of this side of the Vietnam conflict. . . . [Furthermore] these briefings would be contrary to the opinion of the country that there are no improvements." So he suggested that CIA analyst Carver be allowed to brief the cabinet, then the press (in a "low-key way"), and later members of Congress and "other opinion makers."

This initial suggestion clearly demonstrated how colored Fortas's judgment had become in the search for help for the president. Nothing could have been more futile, with the credibility gap widening between the administration and public, than issuing a new report of any kind on the progress of the war—let alone from one of the initial war-planning agencies.

Not surprisingly, the reaction of the group was immediately negative. "Neither George nor the CIA should brief the press," stressed Dean Acheson. Director of Central Intelligence Helms added his concerns, saying that he was willing to allow Carver to be used only on an off-the-record basis. Even hawkish McGeorge Bundy told the others that the administration should "let [the] good news speak for itself: don't strain publicly to convince people [that] progress is being made."[43]

Somewhat nonplussed, the justice then tried to counter Ball's analysis of public opinion. "I believe there is a good deal of over-reaction to what appears to be the public attitude of the United States. This opposition exists in only a small group of the community, primarily the intellectuals or so-called intellectuals and the press. The opposition is not as widespread as we think." It was the old half-empty or half-full question. While Ball and others outside the administration were looking at the six out of every ten Americans who opposed the president's war policy, Fortas chose to look at the four who still were in his corner.

Then Fortas closed this argument with his own analysis of what he knew "the people" really wanted. "Public opinion is a fickle thing and a changeable thing. The American people are committed to a few propositions that are contrary to the rash of opposition. The public would be outraged if we withdrew. We are not now prepared for a 'Fortress America,' nor are we for the foreseeable future. It is very important to separate the superficialities of expression from the fundamentals of American belief." No doubt it was just this sort of argument that Johnson found persuasive in their private meetings.

All of this led Fortas to offer recommendations that he would repeat in memos to the president with respect to Ball's discussion in favor of a "political solution" for the war. "Negotiations are symbolic rather than a real thing," he began. His fear now was that such a call could be "an ingenious trap" to corner Johnson into negotiations on the basis of terms that, or at a particular time when, they could be "corrosive" to the U.S. position. "We've been fortunate so far," he argued, "that North Vietnam has rejected our offer. When the time comes what will happen will be a cessation of hostilities, not negotiations. The American people are not interested in negotiations. That is merely a symbol. That is why the people don't understand when you say you're willing to negotiate, because the American people really don't believe in negotiations." Distinctly lacking in this argument was any evidence to support Fortas's reading of the "American public." In fact, negotiating acceptable terms for closure of the conflict instead of expanding the war seemed to be precisely what a majority of the "American public" was now demanding.

If there was any doubt that Fortas was among the most hawkish of those now at the table, he settled it by concluding, "It would serve no purpose to continue to emphasize our willingness to negotiate. You have already stated your position. Don't repudiate what you have done but tone down on it in the future. To continue to talk about negotiations only signals to the Communists that they are succeeding in winning over American public opinion."

Johnson had to be pleased that the course of the discussion was now back on track. Fortas had reestablished the nearly unanimous consensus at the table in favor of the president's war policy. As if to ensure that fact, the president then called on his other "outside insider," introducing Clark Clifford as "one of his most valued advisers who is most generous with his time." Saying that the president was well aware of his views, Clifford concentrated solely on the question of bolstering the attitude of the American people. "The thing to keep in mind however is that . . . this will not be a popular war. No wars have been popular," he began. Then, after a short history lesson on public support during the war, Clifford concluded with a ringing endorsement of the present Johnson policies. "This has been an enormous success but we won't be able to convince the American people of that as long as it is going on. So we should go right on doing what we're going to do. It is important that we do so. Any cessation in the South or the North will be interpreted as a sign of weakness in the American people. If we keep up the pressure on them, gradually the will of the Viet Cong and the North Vietnamese will wear down." For now, there was little to separate him from Fortas in the nature of his distinctly hawkish recommendations to the president.[44]

The president could not have asked for a more vigorous ratification of everything that had been done, and had been planned to be done, in Vietnam. And the same was true over the next few days as the responses came in from his advisers on the McNamara memo. Fortas's memo was the first to arrive, three days after the "wise men's" meeting. For the normally reserved and diplomatic Supreme Court justice, accustomed by his legal training to using words to mask rather than reveal his true feelings, the two-page memo was a model of hyperbole regarding McNamara's call for another bombing pause.

Saying that he was in *"total disagreement"* with the proposal, Fortas argued that it was an "invitation to slaughter."[45] Since in Fortas's mind McNamara's entire set of recommendations were based on his assessment of American public opinion, the justice then offered a six-point counterreading of the same facts. The president should not assume that the American public opposed a prolonged war, he began.

Such assumptions should not become operative, added the justice, until the public opinion polls and the Congress made it impossible for the president to follow the course he considered "to be right in the national interest."

Then, acting more as a cheerleader and supporter than as an adviser, Fortas added, *"Our duty is to do what we consider right*—not what we consider (on a highly dubious basis with which I do *not* agree) [what] the 'American people' want. (I repeat that I believe they do not want us to achieve less than *our objectives—namely, to prevent North Vietnamese domination of South Vietnam by military force or subversion; and to continue to exert such influence as we reasonably can in Asia to prevent an ultimate Communist take-over.*)"[46] More than any other paragraph, this one carried the entire Fortas philosophy on the war in a nutshell. Fortas argued steadfastly that the people be damned, Johnson must follow the course that had already been laid out. In addition, by persuasively arguing that *he* alone knew what was in the minds of the "American people," Fortas enabled the president to ignore the falling polls, critical press, and sniping congressmen, and focus instead on the justice's reading of whatever positive data could be found.

Given Fortas's reading of American politics, the strategic recommendations that followed in the memo were not surprising. Seeing this bombing pause recommendation as a "step in the process of withdrawal," Fortas invoked images of Neville Chamberlain, arguing that this would be a "profound retreat to the Asian dominoes." Instead, he counseled increasing the pressure on the North Vietnamese and widening the destruction of the enemy by ratcheting up and diversifying the American military effort. He argued that neither the hawks nor the doves wanted a negotiated withdrawal, but rather an initial achievement of objectives without more significant costs to American men and women. They would realize that the bombing was the only source of protection for the military, so the domestic effects of a halt here would be "illusory." Rather than halting the bombing, then, Fortas argued that negotiations should be kept alive only as a propaganda symbol.

The document is remarkable for both the virulence of its statement in favor of hard-line Johnsonian hawkishness, and the total lack of evidence or closely reasoned argumentation for any of its claims. Nothing more than a vituperative pep talk, it continued to ignore the realities of both the falling support at home and the fact that the man being skewered here—McNamara—was one of the architects of the early war who was now following a different path. Gone was any sense of objectivity. By now, Fortas was so closely identifying himself with the Johnson program that there seemed to be absolutely no discernible difference between them.

As the pressure mounted on Johnson to make some progress on the war front, Fortas frequently sent him messages to bolster his spirits. One of the more moving "fan letters" was sent on November 9, 1966. While sitting on the bench that day listening to oral arguments, Fortas had an inspiration: Perhaps by getting the president to look at some of his other achievements, his fears about current problems might be eased. So he wrote, "The Lord should feel good about this Nation's achievements exhibited last week. . . . One, two Negroes elected as mayors of two of our greatest cities; two, the first Negro Justice of the United States Supreme Court politely and wisely questioning the Assistant Attorney General of Alabama who was arguing a segregation case before the Court; three, just now the Negro Senator from the Commonwealth of Massachusetts moved the admission to the Bar of the Supreme Court of the United States of his friend, a white lawyer, and I know that when on October 21 standing on the stage of Constitution Hall Pablo Casals embraced a Negro girl who was a member of the fine Howard University Chorus the Lord must have smiled. Only a few years ago that stage was barred from Marian Anderson. I hope, Mr. President, you feel good deep down in your heart about helping to make all of this possible. I am sure history will recognize that part and that unique role in the great progress that mankind has made."[47] When the letter was handed to the president as he was flying on Air Force One to New York City to deliver a speech, he was so moved that he decided to close his remarks by quoting it in full. Later, in thanking Fortas for the sentiments, Johnson once more acknowledged the justice's own role in his successes on civil rights: "Best of all, I know you will be the partner of all who reach for new equality and opportunity."[48]

Fortas made it possible for Johnson to turn a deaf ear to his most potent dissenter, the newly converted dove Robert McNamara. And the justice also helped in Johnson's latest project, the plan to ease McNamara out of his job and into a new post as president of the World Bank. With the help of Clark Clifford, this plan would come to fruition in February of 1967.

Despite the harmony among Johnson's remaining advisers, the war did not go better, either abroad or at home. On January 31, 1968, violating their own self-proclaimed truce in observance of the lunar New Year, seventy thousand Communist soldiers launched an all-out

coordinated series of attacks throughout South Vietnam, commonly referred to as the Tet Offensive, catching the entire American military
machine off guard. The attacks not only caused enormous casualties,
but destroyed any illusions of impending victory for the Americans and
South Vietnamese. As part of this massive battle, the Americans had
been ordered to hold an outpost at Khesanh. Now, in the middle of
what would turn out to be a futile two-month engagement, the images
being beamed back nightly into American living rooms evoked memories of the 1953 battle for Dienbienphu, which had brought an end to
the French military involvement in Indochina. These events came on
the heels of the North Koreans' seizure of an American naval intelligence ship, the USS *Pueblo,* operating off their shore. America was
losing its self-image of strength, and the American people were turning
against the president by the millions. Polling data showed one of the
most precipitous drops in presidential support in history. Over the next
six weeks, Johnson's personal popularity would drop 12 points (to 36
percent support), accompanied by a 14-point drop in approval of his
handling of the war.[49]

On top of this, what would turn out to be a mass exodus of high-
level support for Johnson had already begun. McNamara was out, as
was HEW Secretary John W. Gardner. At the end of February, the
voice of the heart of American public opinion, Walter Cronkite, announced on the evening news after a trip to Saigon that he was "more
certain than ever that the bloody experience of Vietnam is to end in a
stalemate."[50] Then in mid-March, after being asked to undertake another study of the war, Dean Acheson reported to the president that the
country "was no longer behind the Administration, nor did Americans
any longer believe what the President was telling them."[51] It was not
what Lyndon Johnson wanted to hear.

But during this bleak period, Johnson still had one unswerving supporter—Abe Fortas. Now the counsel of Abe Fortas was nearly all that
Lyndon Johnson wanted to hear on Vietnam.[52] William O. Douglas
could see this growing dependence: "Though Lyndon was not at home
with the 'intellectuals,' over the years he became very dependent on
Abe Fortas for all his decisions. Not that he always followed Abe's
advice; he often did not. But he had such confidence in Abe that he
was crippled without him."[53] Former congresswoman Helen Gahagan
Douglas would recall how, at the end of the Johnson presidency, Lady
Bird Johnson "spoke of the president's torment and unhappiness over
the war . . . and of what solace the friendship of Abe and Carol Fortas
had been to him and to her."[54]

With the Supreme Court in its February recess, and the justice and his wife preparing to set off for Ste. Adèle, Quebec, Canada, for two weeks of skiing, Fortas still found a moment to send his friend a note of support. Fortas was troubled by an article in *The New York Times Magazine* by Max Frankel that described Johnson as being tired and subdued. Though he did not believe the charge, having seen Johnson personally just three days earlier at a dinner party, there was little question in Fortas's mind of the effect that the disintegrating war effort and public support were having on his friend.[55]

Fortas wrote to Johnson about his upcoming trip, trying to cheer him with a joke. They had originally been planning a trip to the French Alps, he said, but after the president's recent balance-of-payments statement they were going to Canada instead. Then the justice added, "If I can help, I am always available, as you know."[56] This offer came at precisely the moment when Johnson most needed it.

Even though Johnson knew the workaholic Fortas needed his vacation, he didn't hesitate to interrupt it after just a few days. Talk had sprung up in the White House meetings once more about stabilizing the war effort. So Johnson placed two calls to the justice during the week of February 11 to solicit his advice.[57] After a few days of thinking about the phone calls and the situation back in the White House, Fortas sat down and drafted a summary of his views on the war and this president. Like all of the other Fortas written and oral statements on the war, this seven-page, double-spaced typed letter was more a combination fealty oath and pep talk than a closely reasoned statement on the war. *"The only thing that matters is how it all comes out!"* the justice began.[58] Assuring Johnson that his policies were "sound," Fortas urged him to follow through on them. Once more he urged the president not to be drawn by his critics into negotiations. These talks would only stir doubt about this nation, weaken Johnson's posture, and encourage the enemy. Only by being tough, the justice believed, could anything be accomplished. The Vietnamese knew how to contact the president, he added, and they would do so if they were so inclined.

Having said that, Fortas delivered an ode to the domino theory of Communist containment he had been offering over the years of the war. Once the United States got involved in a shooting conflict, the justice believed, the country had to play to win. Since the justice saw America as the only deterrent force left opposing the Communists, he argued that a loss here would encourage aggression around the world.

For him, then, the choice facing the president was no choice at all. Failure to "win" here, Fortas argued, would mean the end of Amer-

ica's position in the world community. It would mean the change of
the total national personality. The loss would be followed by years of
national self-doubt and timidity, which would be evident in every aspect of American life.

By now, though, even Fortas realized that the war could not be
"won" in the classic sense without an incredible and unacceptable
toll. So like any good lawyer Fortas tried to redefine the term *to win* in
order to advance his argument. Begging for Johnson's forgiveness for
even uttering the view, the justice wondered if the government had
adequately considered the idea of reducing the military participation in
the South without changing the basic situation in the North. Then Fortas added the most amazing part of his new plan: "I doubt if it is
possible to conclude this war *without bringing it home to North Vietnam.*"

Thus, at a time when all others were deserting the president by suggesting some form of troop withdrawal, Fortas turned military strat-
egist and began to suggest ways to widen the conflict to the North.
First, he wanted to consider further "punishing" North Vietnam by
stepping up the air strikes there. His goal was to force the enemy to
end the conflict just for self-preservation. How far could the United
States widen the war, he asked as a starting point, without actually
launching an American invasion of the North?

He suggested the need for an "all-out air strike," short of using
nuclear weapons, against Hanoi and any other target in the North.
Such hostility would be intended to break the resolve of the enemy.
Discard the theory of attacking only the supply and infiltration routes,
he pressed. Just bomb the hell out of the North and say that it is a
continuation of the war. Since the enemy had answered American
overtures for peace with brutality, he explained, the United States
should retaliate in kind with particularly brutal escalations of the war.
With that in mind, Fortas argued that the brutality should be planned
now and held until it could be timed in response to some new atrocity
by the enemy. He expressed confidence that by planning for Khesanh's
aftermath or some future bloodbath by the enemy, and blaming the
U.S. response upon the Communists' plan to change the war into a
"massive-maximum destruction effort," the desired impact could be
reached. The alternative to carrying the fight home to the North, he
feared, was another fruitless long-term involvement like that in
Korea.[59]

It was an extraordinarily audacious move for a Supreme Court justice to be proposing military strategy. Moreover, the fact that the man

who had shown so much compassion on the bench for poor people, juvenile delinquents, and the criminally accused was now so incredibly bloodthirsty might seem shocking to some. But Abe Fortas knew that the only eyes he was writing for would appreciate every word of it.

For whatever reason, when he had finished this fervent appeal, Fortas chose not to send it on to the White House. Long after he had returned from Canada, though, the justice mentioned that he had written something for Johnson and the president asked for a copy. So, on March 12, a copy was stuffed into a manila envelope labeled "For the President Only: Abe Fortas." By 9:50 that evening, when Johnson had gotten around to it in the pile of his "night reading," he believed the document to be too important (and too supportive of his own views) not to share. So he ordered a secretary to type up several copies and send one over to Dean Rusk as well as another to newly appointed secretary of defense Clark Clifford, who was then heading a task force reviewing war policy. Like all of the other Fortas memos on Vietnam, it stuck in the president's mind, but was quickly lost in others' file cabinets. On the back of Clifford's copy was his simple comment indicating how unpersuasive these arguments had been: "War can change quickly."[60]

By offering such unwavering loyalty, Fortas had ensured that he would be called in on every new matter of importance. On March 14, 1968, a call came from the president asking if the justice, who was about to leave to hear the court's scheduled oral argument, could come immediately to the White House for a conference. In all the years of simultaneously serving on the court and as an informal presidential adviser, this would be the first, and only, time that his duties would conflict to the point that Fortas actually missed work on the court while it was in session. But this time the issue—involving the key matters of war and the president's political future—was vital enough to make an exception. Clark Clifford was about to meet with Senator Robert F. Kennedy, and Johnson wanted Fortas present when he and Clifford discussed how the matter should be handled. After the president's disastrous showing in the New Hampshire primary two days earlier, nearly losing to peace candidate Senator Eugene McCarthy, Kennedy was debating whether and when to enter the presidential race. For now, the senator wanted to discuss with Clifford a way to handle the war.[61]

Later that afternoon, Fortas returned to the White House for another discussion of the day's events in the Oval Office with Clifford, Johnson, and Hubert Humphrey. Kennedy had offered to stay out of the race if the president announced that he had made an error with his policy in Vietnam. Quickly agreeing with Clifford that Johnson could never do this, Kennedy said he would settle for an announcement that the president was reevaluating his war policy and was appointing a commission to help him do so (handpicked, of course, by Kennedy).[62] To no one's surprise, Johnson's "immediate and positive" reaction was negative. The following day, Kennedy announced that he was entering the presidential race.[63]

But this was only one part of a week that had begun with the debacle at New Hampshire, and the opening of the annual hearings of the Senate Foreign Relations Committee on the foreign aid appropriations bill. Chairman J. William Fulbright had used that opportunity to criticize the administration by grilling Secretary of State Rusk for two days.[64] Then the week ended on March 15 with Dean Acheson delivering a report summarizing the findings of his outside inquiry, which were that the war could not be won soon or easily. On top of that, an eight-page "EYES ONLY" memo arrived from United Nations Ambassador Goldberg. Now feeling that he had little access to the central decision-making circles on the war, Goldberg wanted to resign. However, with all of the planned resignations coming up, Johnson did not want it to appear like a wholesale desertion of subordinates, so the matter was shelved. Instead, the ambassador tried a direct approach to the president suggesting that a full bombing halt would have an impact on the war and might spur new negotiations. He could not have known that just three days earlier his replacement on the Supreme Court had sent the president his own memo on the war, arguing just the opposite position in no uncertain terms.[65]

Faced with a negative memo from a man within the foreign policy machine, and a positive memo from the outsider on the court, Johnson did the characteristic thing: He ignored Goldberg, and invited Fortas to the White House. It was a pattern that would be repeated on numerous occasions over the next two weeks as the White House chewed over this new proposal for deescalating the conflict.

On March 15, Fortas, who had already spent nearly two hours in the White House before court opened that morning (for the second day in a row), joined a two-hour late-afternoon meeting with the president, Clifford, Rusk, Generals Earle Wheeler and Maxwell Taylor, Walt Rostow, Deputy Secretary of Defense Paul Nitze, and others. Then the justice and the president spoke for a few minutes after the meeting in the Oval Office.[66] Though Dean Rusk had persuaded the president to circulate the new proposal for reaction,[67] by the next day Johnson's reaction seemed almost automatic. "Let's get one thing clear," he told the assembled advisers. "I am not going to stop the bombing. I have heard every argument on the subject, and I am not interested in further discussion. I have made up my mind." A "chilled silence" then fell over those in the Cabinet Room.[68]

But Johnson was not done yet. Having told his advisers privately, he decided it was time to tell the rest of the world. So Fortas and Rostow helped draft a speech for Johnson, responding to Bobby Kennedy and all those who held views similar to the ones privately expressed by Goldberg. Their efforts resulted in a new expression of recalcitrant hawkishness. On March 17, the president flew to the Midwest to speak to the National Alliance of Businessmen and to the National Farmers Union convention. Pounding the lectern in Minneapolis he shouted, "Your President has come here to ask you people, and all the other people of this nation, to join us in a total national effort to win the war, to win the peace, and to complete the job that must be done here at home. . . . Make no mistake about it—I don't want a man in here to go back thinking otherwise—we are going to win."[69] The language as well as the sentiments seemed to be drawn closely from the long memo sent to him recently by Fortas.[70]

The only problem was that few besides Fortas, Johnson, and Rostow could now swallow these sentiments. James H. Rowe, Jr., warned in a follow-up memo that even allies were saying that the speech "hurt us badly." The "doves" were now "infuriated," and Rowe was "shocked" by the number of calls he had received. "Everyone wants to get out," Rowe concluded, "and the only question is how."[71] Everyone, that is, except the two men who counted—President Johnson and his outside judicial adviser.

Even men who had been by the president's side in the early going, like Clark Clifford and McGeorge Bundy, had trouble with this approach. Bundy told the president in a later memorandum, "I'm afraid I agree with those who are worried about the line in Vietnam in your Minneapolis speech. If we get tapped as mindless hawks, we can lose both the election and the war. . . . We have skillful and ruthless opponents—and we have just got to do more than give them an easy target."[72]

Two times that week, Fortas was asked to attend meetings of the war advisers. With opposition growing and the bombing halt now the hot topic on the agenda, the president wanted the justice by his side. So Fortas attended the regular meeting of the Tuesday Lunch advisers on March 19. And, in a late-afternoon meeting the following day,

Fortas rejoined much the same group, this time including the author of the bombing halt memo, Goldberg. The topic was now more than just the bombing halt, but how the president should approach an upcoming speech to the nation on Vietnam.

Once more Fortas offered all of the familiar views. There was a "need to avoid empty peace gestures," he began.[73] So there should be a "limited objective for [the] speech," dealing with the need for "troops and economy." "Specific peace moves [such as a halt in the bombing] will be lost in this speech," he argued, and the "offer will be taken as [a] sign of weakness." Fortas's own reading of the doves in the nation continued to be both innovative and incorrect. "People's feeling of discontent is over whether the effort is being prosecuted intelligently and firmly. Our combination of war and peace is confusing." So the justice called for "troop reinforcement, strength and resoluteness" and an effort to "dramatize S[outh] V[ietnamese] involvement."[74] The idea of a bombing pause then, for the justice, was a "mistake" and "too one-sided in Hanoi's favor."[75]

But now, Fortas was losing even the other hawks. His oration was followed by a remarkable event—one of the very few times, if not the first, in all of these meetings attended by both himself and Clifford that the new secretary of defense had publicly offered a different view. "In World War II," Clifford responded, "'prevail we will' would work because conditions were right. Now they aren't." Having said earlier in the meeting that the "next 3 or 4 months could be a critical time in the war," Clifford now signaled his own change in views. Faced with Fortas's recalcitrant hawkishness, Clifford said "he was coming to the conclusion that the continued application of force did not promise ultimate success. [Furthermore] he thought most of the military plans he had heard discussed would widen the war. That was the reason he felt that we had to search for some approach toward peace that the President could advance now and build upon later."[76] He proposed a "gradual approach" of "stop[ping] all bombing north of" the 20th Parallel—"if in turn the enemy would stop their artillery, rockets and mortars from the DMZ area into South Vietnam." This deescalation might lead to a similar series of reduction offers from the other side, and would certainly be better than just rhetoric.

For the moment it was Fortas who won the president's head and heart. In a concluding statement Johnson virtually mirrored what the justice had said earlier. "We are mixing two things when we include peace initiatives. Let's make it troops and war. Later we can revise and extend our peace initiatives."[77]

Clifford was not the only adviser to desert the hawkish camp. Two days later, McGeorge Bundy sent a memo to the president, warning him that Fortas's advice was "dead wrong." But Fortas's message was still the only one Johnson wanted to hear.[78] So on March 22, Fortas was asked to spend the afternoon at the White House in a three-hour luncheon meeting with the war advisers. Neither man seemed concerned that this was now the fourth time in one week that Fortas had been involved in a formal White House meeting. With a war being fought, and the president's desire to have his closest ally nearby, Fortas's formal judicial duties seemed less important to him.

Now the sole topic was the upcoming presidential speech to the nation. Johnson opened the meeting by observing that, in his opinion, "there has been a dramatic shift in public opinion on the war, [and] that a lot of people are really ready to surrender without knowing they are following a party line."[79] With this in mind, the group began working on Harry McPherson's draft of the upcoming speech on the war, trying to incorporate suggestions from the Bundy brothers and Walt Rostow.

Even Clifford began sounding more and more pessimistic: "The major concern of the people," he told the group, "is that they do not see victory ahead. . . . The military has not come up with a plan for victory. . . . The people are discouraged as more men go in and are chewed up in a bottomless pit." So Clifford repeated his proposal from two days before to trade a bombing halt in the North for an end to shelling from the DMZ. Once more, he and Fortas clashed, as the justice protested that this "decision would be criticized as too little, too late and insincere."[80]

Fortas offered his suggestions for the speech, suggestions that were beginning to sound like a broken record. "The speech lacks an essential ingredient," he began, "in that it does not explain why we are in Vietnam. If we do not talk in terms of Communism, it is like a production of *Hamlet* without the prince." Fortas's version of the play, though, would have little place for the offering of the olive branch that was being considered by the others. Instead, the justice said "he would emphasize the invasion of Laos by the North Vietnamese and the brutal murders of the civilians during the Tet truce." Such a tack would accomplish that which concerned Fortas the most, protecting the president.[81]

Clifford tried to push the president in a different way.[82] At his suggestion a second meeting of the senior advisory group was convened on March 26, 1968. The "wise men" who assembled were virtually the same ones who had met and heartily endorsed the Johnson war policy in early November of the previous year. The only new participants were Johnson's diplomatic troubleshooter Cyrus Vance; John J. McCloy, former coordinator of United States disarmament activities under John Kennedy; former NATO commander Matthew Ridgway; and Arthur Goldberg.

Because of his court duties, Fortas was not able to join the group until just before their midafternoon lunch.[83] The issue was now the sort of thing that had been claimed by the justice as his turf—"the political situation in the United States."[84] By the time Fortas arrived, though, it was apparent to everyone that a large majority of the group had swung 180 degrees from their November posture of total support for the president.

It was left to McGeorge Bundy, who was asked by the president at lunch to sum up the group's present sentiment, to deliver the disturbing news. "There is a very significant shift in our position," he began.[85] "The picture as we remember it from our meeting in November was one of hope for reasonably steady—slow but sustained—progress especially in the countryside which was then emphasized to us as an area of particular importance. The picture which emerged from the discussion last night was not so hopeful, particularly again with respect to the countryside."[86] The group's answer, Bundy explained, was for the Americans to do whatever was necessary to bolster the South Vietnamese government.

The president was "visibly shocked" by the change in sentiment of these eminent men. "Change of sentiment in this country," he wrote diagonally down a scrap of White House stationery, adding that his advisers now wanted him to deliver a "clear cut statement."[87] Then Dean Acheson, seated at Johnson's right hand, added his forceful endorsement of Bundy's view: "Neither the effort of the government of Vietnam or the effort of the U.S. government can succeed in the time we have left. Time is limited by reactions in this country. We cannot build an independent South Vietnam; therefore, we should do something by no later than late summer to establish something different."[88] The clear message of the group, Johnson recorded, was to "adjust our course (and move to disengage)."

One by one, each of the other men around the table began to comment on the Bundy summary. The previous night's negative briefings from Philip Habib, an aide to William Bundy; George Carver of the CIA; and Major General William DePuy, a special assistant to the Joint Chiefs—not to mention the horror of the unexpected Tet Offensive—had clearly taken a toll on the group. "All of us got the impression that there is no military conclusion in sight. We felt time is running out," explained Arthur Dean.[89] The military should shift its strategy from "search and destroy" to shielding smaller areas of the South for greater development, offered Henry Cabot Lodge once more. "The briefing last night led me to conclude that we cannot achieve a military victory," added former secretary of the treasury Dillon.[90]

With that it was George Ball's turn to join the tidal wave of negative evaluations. "I share Acheson's view," he began. "I have felt that way since 1961—that our objectives are not attainable. In the U.S. there is a sharp division of opinion. In the world, we look very badly because of the bombing. That is the central defect in our position. The disadvantages of bombing outweigh the advantages. We need to stop the bombing in the next six weeks to test the will of the North Vietnamese. As long as we continue to bomb, we alienate ourselves from the civilized world. I would have the Pope or U Thant [secretary-general of the UN] suggest a bombing halt. It cannot come from the President. A bombing halt would quieten the situation here at home."[91]

The force of such a negative view was more than Fortas could bear. Looking to bolster the president, he broke in on one of Ball's speeches and, beginning "What George Ball is trying to say, Mr. President . . . ," proceeded to misstate the former State Department official's actual view completely. At this point, Ball turned to Fortas and snapped, "Well, you sure as hell aren't doing it."[92]

Cyrus Vance then offered his agreement with both Bundy and Ball, and added an even more ominous note. "Unless we do something quick, the mood in this country may lead us to withdrawal." Even more surprising, hard-liner Omar Bradley had changed his mind: "People in the country are dissatisfied. . . . We do need to stop the bombing if we can get the suggestion to come from the Pope or U Thant, but let's not show them that we are in any way weakening."

After this onslaught of negative opinion, it was left to Johnson's three remaining supporters at the table to try to help out. Robert Murphy was "shaken by the position of my associates. The interpretation given this action by Saigon would be bad." General Maxwell Taylor understandably echoed his sentiments: "I am dismayed. The picture I get is a very different one from that you have. Let's not concede the home front; let's do something about it." And finally, there was one man who *was* ready and willing to do something about it, even as a sitting justice on the United States Supreme Court.

Fortas's performance at this meeting was absolutely no different from his performance at the other four he had attended in the last two weeks. By the time he spoke, though, the vote against Johnson's position was overwhelming. So the justice, seeking to ease the pain for Johnson, tried one final time to use his legendary powers of reasoning and persuasiveness to do much more than just sum up. He appealed to the others to reconsider. But the logical reasoning was now gone, and Fortas had instead become Johnny One Note. "The United States has never had in mind winning a military victory out there; we always have wanted to reach an agreement or settle for the status quo between North Vietnam and South Vietnam. . . . This is not the time for an overture on our part. I do not think a cessation of the bombing would do any good at this time. I do not believe in drama for the sake of drama.''

But matters had gone too far for him to save the president's ego now. And the man who represented the main line of the rest of the group, Dean Acheson, let it be known that they had heard enough. No longer would the justice be allowed to have the final word. Abe Fortas was wrong, Acheson said, and so, by implication, was his client, the president of the United States of America. "The issue is not that stated by Fortas,'' Acheson stated bluntly. "The issue is can we do what we are trying to do in Vietnam. I do not think we can. Fortas said we are not trying to win a military victory. . . . The issue is can we by military means keep the North Vietnamese off the South Vietnamese. I do not think we can. They can slip around and endrun them and crack them up.'' All of this from the cold warrior who had been in on the first intervention in this quicksand conflict.[93]

Fortas had given it his best shot. In a memo sent to the White House the next day, even one of his adversaries at the meeting, McGeorge Bundy, had to concede to the president that his outside adviser had scored at least one debating point. "I think those who favor a bombing halt are unanimous in believing that Abe Fortas is quite right to warn against any empty dramatic gesture. This would have to be a cold and clear-cut decision, and it would need weeks of the most sensitive and sure-footed diplomatic preparation. It is emphatically not something which can have its intended effect if it is decided from one day to the next, or left as open-ended as our earlier pauses.''[94]

After this second advisory meeting, Johnson now knew the score. There would be no come-from-behind victory. Later he would write in his memoirs about the "wise men'': "I had always regarded the majority of them as very steady and balanced. If they had been so deeply influenced by the reports of the Tet offensive, what must the average citizen in the country be thinking?"[95] The time had come for a new approach, and not even Fortas would be able to talk the president out of it. For Johnson, the war was over.

Fortas had begun to sense from their conversations a new direction in his friend's thought. The pressures of the day, and the ripping of the fiber of American society in 1968, had begun to take its toll. Johnson told his friend that he was tired of the "crazies," as he called the protesters, tired of the riots in the streets, and beginning to have real doubts about his reelection chances. But more than that, he was worried about his health and well-being. "I won't survive another four years," he told Fortas on the phone, "and I think I'm entitled to a few years of peace at the ranch."[96] Fortas was "bowled over" by the notion, but after unsuccessfully trying to change Johnson's mind, he agreed.[97]

The final irrevocable announcement came on March 31, 1968. After announcing a unilateral halt of all American bombing above the 20th Parallel, an action that had seemed unthinkable when suggested in the Goldberg memo just two weeks earlier, Johnson announced that he would neither seek nor accept another nomination for president in the fall.[98] Fortas did what he could to ease the burden of his friend, who had given up the one thing he truly loved—power. "Give the president my love and love from Carol," he told a White House secretary on the phone that night. "I think he did a wonderful job on the speech."[99]

In the months that followed, there was more that Fortas could and would do to aid his friend's transition from the White House. Knowing that Johnson had to be occupied and would need something more to pour his energies into, Fortas encouraged his efforts not to retire, but simply "switch professions."[100] Johnson was telling people that he was "resuming [his] teaching career" and would supervise the building and staffing of his presidential Library and the Lyndon Baines Johnson School of Public Affairs. With important people to be tapped for the necessary funds, and plans to be drawn up, these projects were right up Fortas's alley.[101]

Then there were the usual odds and ends to clear up. The events of May 9 spoke volumes about Fortas's new role in the White House. In an "EYES ONLY" memo, Joe Califano asked Fortas to "give me your ideas, in whatever detail you believe appropriate, about how such an Institute [of public affairs] should be established and what its functions might be."[102] That same day, in another "EYES ONLY" memo from Califano, came a request that looked more like a final exam question: "The President has asked me to obtain a memorandum from you identifying what you believe to be the ten most significant problems facing this Nation at home and abroad."[103] As if that wasn't enough, that day brought yet a *third* "EYES ONLY" request from Califano on the president's instructions: "We are considering establishing a series of confidential task forces to deal with major problems of the Office of the Presidency. Since you have had a rare opportunity to see the problems of the Office of the Presidency, the President has asked me to obtain your views as to those areas which should be studied."[104] If Fortas was now "dying on the Court," it was from exhaustion.

So many favors, and so little that Johnson could do in return. But there was one way to at least say what was in his heart. Johnson picked up his black felt-tip pen and looked at the color picture from the White House dinner on April 10, 1968, when 180 people had been in attendance in honor of visiting Austrian chancellor Josef Klaus. The picture was of yet another of the justice's musical forays at the White House—this time participating in a small chamber group. For all of the apparent gaiety in the picture, there was little laughter in the president's heart. Thousands of boys were dying in a foreign jungle, and now the commander in chief had publicly acknowledged that his public career had died as well.

But with all of the dying going on in Johnson's life, one thing was still very much alive—his friendship with Justice Abe Fortas. Here was the one person in addition to Lady Bird who was still unshakably in the president's corner. So, in searching for a way to symbolize what Fortas had meant to him for thirty years, and what he meant to him now, the usually overly loquacious president became uncharacteristically succinct. "For Abe," he scrawled across the bottom white margin of the photo, "the Isaac Stern of the Supreme Court. My First String Man."[105] Nothing that Lyndon Johnson had ever said before or after could have been any truer for both men, or more dangerous.

XI

A Whale,
a Minnow, and a
Phone Booth

Washington can be a very strange town. Only here can a woman from Sapulpa, Oklahoma, named Beverly Updike get married and in so doing help in some small way to change the course of history. Though she had never met the president, chances are Lyndon Johnson would have preferred it if she had quietly eloped.[1] For while Beverly Updike planned to change the course of her life, in another part of town Earl Warren planned to change the course of the Supreme Court. He had decided to resign from his position as chief justice, thus marking the end of an era. For fourteen years he had served as steward of one of the most activist, liberal, and controversial Supreme Courts ever. He and his brethren had changed the face of the legal landscape, and in so doing they had made enemies, more than a few of whom were on Capitol Hill.

Warren waited until the last judicial conference of the term to tell his colleagues that he had decided to step down. It was his hope that there would be sufficient time to find a suitable replacement before the court opened again in October 1968. Then he sent word through Abe Fortas that he wanted to meet with the president.[2] The president had no prior knowledge of Warren's plans.[3] To be sure, like everyone else he had heard the rumors about a possible resignation, but no one took such stories seriously until they came from the horse's mouth.

Warren and the president enjoyed a very cordial fifteen-minute meeting on the morning of June 13, 1968, made even more so when Lyndon Johnson discovered the favor that was being done for him. The chief justice explained that at seventy-seven he felt that he had served long enough. His health was fine (indeed he would live for another six years, longer than LBJ), but he had "lost a step." It was time, he felt, to turn the reins over to another, younger individual.

But there was more. By resigning now, Warren wanted to make sure that it was Johnson appointing his successor. Both men knew that unless this happened, the chances were good—with the Vietnam War not going well, the cities literally in flames, and the economy in an inflationary spiral—that the Republicans would be making the selection.[4]

Perhaps Warren, a Republican, could have lived with the prospect of a Republican appointee if it had not been for one crucial fact. He now believed, with the death of Robert Kennedy by an assassin's hand the week before, that his longtime political enemy Richard Nixon had the inside track in the election. Having dueled with Nixon since their days as California politicians,[5] whenever Warren now spoke of him, it was in terms reserved for people who had committed serious violations of law or ethics. For him, the thought of Nixon getting his hands on any court seat, let alone *his* court seat, was unacceptable.[6]

Of course, Lyndon Johnson understood all of this, and he had his own agenda. Though later next month Johnson would tell reporters that he "did not have in mind any person to appoint as [Warren's] successor," the president knew immediately whom he would appoint.[7] And he had known for three years. For that matter, so did all of Washington.

"Well, have you got any candidates?" he asked the chief justice.

"No, Mr. President," replied Warren, "that's your problem."

Then Johnson thought for a moment and asked, "What do you think about Abe Fortas?"

And Warren gave the response that Johnson surely expected: "I think Abe would be a good Chief Justice."[8]

But the president failed to notice Warren's lack of effusiveness here. It was surely not the same as William O. Douglas's note to the president when he heard of the vacancy: "I hope you make Abe your new

Chief. He'd be superb."[9] In fact, while Warren and Fortas had been on the warmest terms, and were virtual voting twins on most every issue except business cases, Abe Fortas was not Earl Warren's first choice for a successor. In fact, he wasn't even his second choice. Warren later told Justice William Brennan that he should have been the successor and he also said the same to former justice Arthur Goldberg.[10] But Earl Warren was a fine politician and he understood that Fortas would certainly be the nominee.

At the end of this private meeting, then, each participant understood completely the foremost desires of the other. Johnson wanted Fortas, and Warren didn't want Nixon. But these were both very political moves and the court is, after all, according to myth, a nonpolitical institution. So each man understood that for a time the true motivations for their actions had to be hidden from the public. Duty required that prior to making the appointment the president should first consult with the attorney general, have the Department of Justice investigate all possible nominees, submit a short list of names to the American Bar Association for screening as to their qualifications, and finally hold extensive talks with many of the nation's leaders to consider the appointment.[11] And LBJ intended to do all of these things—in order to ratify a choice that had already been made. Thanks to Earl Warren, after all that had gone wrong in 1968—Vietnam, the *Pueblo,* two assassinations, inflation, balance-of-payments deficits, the fiery racial riots in Washington—Johnson now had one last chance to salvage something from his waning presidency. And by doing one final favor for his old friend, he could also leave his legacy on the Supreme Court.

For Johnson, secrecy now became the order of the day. If people were aware of the nature of his discussion with the chief justice, they would correctly suspect the political motives involved in making this change. And the "people" most concerning the president now were those serving in the United States Senate. For while Article II, Section 2, of the Constitution gives the president the power to nominate justices, it also gives the Senate a power of "advise and consent" by a majority vote in confirming those appointments. And the last thing that either Lyndon Johnson or Earl Warren wanted was for the Senate to make trouble over the next appointee to the court. So the president asked for, and the chief justice agreed to, the right to hold off any public announcements until he was ready. He figured on getting about thirteen days of secrecy, and by that calculation he came up about twelve days short.

It is at times like this that several axioms of life in Washington come into play. The nation's capital survives and operates in an atmosphere of mutual distrust. All of the politicians in the city understand that everyone else got there the same way they did—by making promises they could not, and did not, keep. Since no one in Washington can be trusted, the key to getting your way is to keep your actual motives and strategies secret until it is to your advantage to reveal them. So you end up with the central paradox of government in Washington: Success depends on secrecy, but secrecy here is almost impossible. Washington can be a very strange town.

Try as they might, Lyndon Johnson and Earl Warren were about to become the latest, but not the last, victims of this paradox. It really was not the fault of the chief justice. Later that day, as he sat at his desk to draft the actual retirement letter, Warren gave the matter considerable thought. Many of his colleagues on the federal bench before him had written such a letter stating, "I herewith tender my resignation to take effect upon the appointment and qualification of my successor." But Warren decided explicitly not to do that. Instead, he wrote out a one-line letter of resignation to the president: "Pursuant to the provisions of 28 U.S.C., Section 371(b), I hereby advise you of my intention to retire as Chief Justice of the United States, effective at your pleasure."[12] Perhaps hoping to lay to rest any speculation as to the possible political motives of this action, he also sent another letter explaining that the retirement was motivated "not because of reasons of health or on account of any personal or associational problems, *but solely because of age.*"[13] Everyone knew that he had often sermonized on the need for senior judges to step aside, so this seemed consistent with his philosophy.

Warren's love for the court moved him to take great care in the conditional wording of his letter. He wanted to maintain continuity in the operation of the institution.[14] Much of the administrative work of the court, including even an occasional emergency case, continues through the summer months, and a chief justice is needed for the institution to function smoothly. Knowing this, Warren sought to provide continuity in the leadership of the court by using the "retire . . . effective at your pleasure" language.

It would have been within the president's power simply to accept the retirement immediately and be done with it.[15] But this was not the way Lyndon Johnson did things, especially when it concerned "his" Supreme Court. Throughout his tenure in the White House he had continued to see the court as just another political institution that could be

manipulated as he saw fit, as Earl Warren, Arthur Goldberg, and Abe
Fortas could attest. So when faced now with the retirement of the chief
justice, Johnson did the natural thing for him and decided to do what
was politically most expedient. But that was not necessarily the best
thing for the court, or, as it turned out, for Abe Fortas.

With the options of accepting the retirement immediately or announcing the impending action to the public, Johnson decided to do
neither. Instead, in setting the strategy, he told Attorney General
Ramsey Clark he wanted to make the acceptance effective only upon
the qualification of the chief justice's successor. This was necessary,
the president explained, to enable Warren to withdraw the retirement if
something went wrong. So, relying on some wording sent over at
Johnson's request from Abe Fortas himself, a key sentence was added
to the White House's letter of reply to Warren: "With your agreement,
I will accept your decision to retire effective at such time as a successor is qualified."[16] By using exactly the language that Warren had
initially rejected, the letter took on the overtones of a political move.
That was why the White House then decided that it could not be released to the public for two weeks.[17]

The president needed time to build a political consensus for Fortas
as chief justice, and to find someone else to take his soon-to-be-
vacated seat. In deciding to sit on the retirement news for a while,
Lyndon Johnson was gambling that he could do what no one else in
town seemed to be able to do—keep the matter secret until everything
was in place. But there are some things even presidents cannot accomplish.

The morning after the Warren-Johnson meeting, the president called
Fortas from the Texas ranch, where he had gone to rest, and offered
him the chief justiceship. The post was not something Fortas had coveted, but since Johnson wanted him to have it, that was fine.[18] However, a one-paragraph item appeared on the front page of *The Wall
Street Journal* that morning that in effect destroyed the president's plan
for secrecy. The "Washington Wire" column rumored that Earl Warren had decided to retire from the Supreme Court in order to keep the
nomination from Richard Nixon, and that his successor would be Abe
Fortas.[19] There is nothing more damaging in Washington than a rumor
that happens to be true. While the latter part of the story was not
new—it had been surfacing in various news journals ever since Fortas's appointment to the court—the former, on Warren's retirement,
had a certain ring of plausibility given the timing of the end of the

court's term and the bubbling election-year politics. Still, people in Washington treated this rumor the same way they did the thousands of other rumors that they heard or saw each week. Everyone ignored it.

Everyone, that is, except the junior senator from Michigan, Robert Griffin. At forty-four, he looked like a short, dapper accountant or country preacher with thinning black hair. But his colleagues in the Senate knew better. Their views on Robert Griffin varied widely. To one set of friends he was "the mild-mannered man who changes into Super-Senator in a crisis, squelches the troublemakers despite greatly unfavorable odds and then returns to his sweet self quicker than you can say Clark Kent."[20] But to others, he was "a back stabber in the true Nixonian tradition."[21] Nearly all would agree, though, that he was a shrewd, ambitious, up-and-coming first-term Republican senator—just the kind of person capable of making a name for himself in Washington at others' expense.

There was something else traditionally American about Griffin: He loved to be an underdog fighting against overwhelming odds. And, even more American—he always seemed to win in those situations.

Born in Detroit on November 6, 1923, Griffin had worked hard for everything he achieved. In order to afford his college education at Central Michigan University, he had washed dishes, sold clothes, and even worked on an automobile assembly line. After stints as a sports editor and as a soldier during World War II, Griffin earned his undergraduate degree, then went on to take a law degree in 1950 at the University of Michigan. Upon graduation, he joined a private law firm and began thinking of the possibility of a career in public service.

His underdog pattern was set in 1956, when Griffin successfully ran for Congress against seemingly impossible odds. Once in the House, he quickly established a reputation for confronting the established party leadership, and each victory added to his growing reputation as a "giant killer." Few gave him a chance when in 1959, then only in his second term in Congress, he and a Georgia Democrat, Philip Landrum, successfully substituted their reform bill to protect the rights of union members for the one recommended by a majority of the Democratically controlled House Labor and Education Committee. Eventually the Landrum-Griffin bill became law.

Few gave Griffin a chance in his effort to unseat House Minority Leader Charles A. Halleck of Indiana. Halleck and Senate Minority Leader Everett Dirksen had become so successful in promoting the desires of the Republican party in Congress that they became known as the "Ev and Charlie Show." But Griffin and a number of other young

Republicans were not satisfied. So they led a coup in 1965 in which a young Michigan congressman, Gerald Ford, replaced Halleck.[22]

By now, it seemed that no odds were too great for Griffin. Seeking to bolster the state Republican ticket for his own reelection, Governor George Romney appointed Griffin in 1966 to fill the unexpired Senate term of Pat McNamara. After only four months in office, Griffin had to run in a special November election in order to win a full six-year term on his own. But even in this uphill fight against one of the most popular politicians in the state, former Democratic governor G. Mennen "Soapy" Williams, once again Griffin beat the odds, carrying seventy-five of Michigan's eighty-three counties, and amassing the largest plurality in a Senate race since 1946.

It was not long before Griffin had achieved the same reputation in the Senate as he had in the House. "Don't underestimate the power of this young man," Charlie Halleck had warned his counterpart in the Senate, Everett Dirksen.[23] After a number of tough fights, one senator said of his colleague, "I doubt if he has any scruples, politically or otherwise." And a Senate aide added, "He is very deceptive, loves to fight, and hits below the belt without a second thought."[24] All in all, Griffin was recognized as the sort of man who caused his enemies to contemplate hiring food tasters, and his friends to be sure to invite him to dinner as often as possible.

When the *Wall Street Journal* article on the manipulation of Warren's resignation came to Griffin's attention, he immediately recognized it for what it was—an opportunity. And Griffin was not a man to let such opportunities pass by.[25] Griffin knew he would be fighting an uphill battle. Opposing an appointment by a president, even a lame-duck president, in the Senate takes a powerful effort. This is especially true when the president's party controls that body. And there is generally little that a man who is in his first term of office in the Senate can do against such forces. But that just made Griffin even more interested.

What Griffin needed most to get started was a pair of things. First, he needed time. It would take careful planning to piece together even the rudiments of an opposing movement. While Griffin could not know that Lyndon Johnson had unwittingly decided to grant him this wish, he was certain that neither the president nor the other possible source in this area, Earl Warren, would provide him with the second resource that he urgently needed—information. People would demand hard proof of this political plot before they would be willing to believe

Griffin. And hard proof in this city of mutual distrust would be hard to
come by—especially since Earl Warren had decided to dodge the press
and no one in the Washington press corps seemed to be able to confirm
this rumor.

Still, Griffin decided to organize some of his Republican colleagues
into a rump group opposing what he believed to be Lyndon Johnson's
effort to pack the Supreme Court. Over the next several days he spoke
whenever he could to colleagues in the Senate, trying to muster up
some allies. Without a lucky break, though, he was doomed to fail.[26]

In Lyndon Johnson's scheme of things, Robert Griffin mattered little. For the president, there were two types of senators, whales and
minnows. The whales were the senators with power—the party leaders
and the committee heads. They were the ones who, in the words of
Harry McPherson, "had the negative power to stop legislation, either
because they opposed it or were indifferent to it." Johnson believed
that "the consent of only one or two [of the whales] was required to
give the rest of the Senate confidence that a bill—like a stock issue
backed by a respected underwriter—was all right to support."[27] Consequently, only the whales were fed in Johnson's presidential ocean, in
the belief that the senatorial fish of other sizes tended to follow in
schools behind these giants.

But one thing was very clear. In Johnson's eyes, Robert Griffin was
only a minnow, and a Republican one at that. The president never
would have dreamed he had anything to fear from him.

However, there was another Republican who was a fish of a different size. As the Republican minority leader, Ev Dirksen was still
the Republican whale, although an old and barnacled one. Even
though he led only thirty-six senators, there was always the threat of a
filibuster, which, by the Senate's ancient art of talking a bill to death,
could cause the administration to run out of either time or interest.
Knowing that it took a two-thirds vote of the Senate to vote cloture and
end such talkathons, Lyndon Johnson wanted at least seventy hard
votes in favor of his nominees. And, since the conservative southern
Democrats had their unpredictable members, the president knew that
there was only one way to get those votes. He needed Ev Dirksen.[28]

Everyone, it seemed, had a favorite nickname for Everett Dirksen—
not all of them flattering: the Wizard of Ooze, Oleaginous Ev, the
Chautauqua Hamlet, the Pagliaccio of American Politics, and Old
Doctor Snake Oil. But everyone knew that the nickname that best described him was the Master of the U-turn. "I am a man of principle,"
he would say frequently, "and one of my first principles is flex-

ibility." As a result, even in Democratic administrations the rule had become "clear it with Ev Dirksen."[29]

Now seventy-two years old, Dirksen had a long, sleek, jowled face topped by a shock of curly gray hair that looked as though it had never seen a comb. But his most impressive feature was that voice. Possessing a sonorous, melodious voice in the lower octaves, Dirksen maintained its resonance through the years by gargling each morning with Pond's cold cream and water, and then swallowing it, to "keep my pipes lubricated."

After three semesters of law school at the University of Minnesota (later he would get a "special dispensation" to take the bar exam without completing law school), Dirksen had served in World War I as a balloon observer for the field artillery units. After being elected to Congress in 1932, he served for eight terms. During that time, Dirksen showed just how "flexible" he could be. According to one study by the *Chicago Sun-Times,* in this tenure he changed his position thirty-one times on military preparedness, sixty-two times on isolationism, and fully seventy times on agricultural policy. But even with this promising career, in 1948 Dirksen resigned, hoping that the same eye ailment that had kept Fortas out of the navy, chorioretinitis, would be cured. When it was, Dirksen returned to Washington as a senator in 1951.

Dirksen was no more consistent in this setting than in the House. After once calling the notion of a nuclear test-ban treaty with Russia a "surrender," he delivered the speech that spearheaded the effort to ratify it in the Senate. On another occasion it was said that Dirksen had "delivered the best speech in favor of foreign aid and the best speech against foreign aid" that one editor had ever heard.[30] Perhaps his most memorable switch in this early period came in the 1952 Republican National Convention when Dirksen shook his finger at Thomas Dewey in a speech, booming, "We followed you before and you took us down the road to defeat." All of this despite the fact that Dirksen had been in favor of Dewey in both of the previous presidential elections.[31]

When he became the Senate minority whip, Dirksen continued to demonstrate his flexibility in working with the Democratic majority leader, Lyndon Baines Johnson. Dirksen later said that their partnership came from "a kind of code" in which each man believed that the Senate was "a two way street."[32] For his part, Johnson explained that he "based a great deal of [his] strategy on this understanding of Dirksen's deep-rooted patriotism."[33] Others, though, had a very different interpretation of Dirksen's compromising style. "He has a price for everything,'' said one observer.[34] ''He is the most venal man in American politics today, and perhaps the most venal since Daniel Webster,'' said another.[35] Dirksen was fond of sitting cross-legged on his desk, sharing considerable quantities of bourbon with his visitor, and swapping deals. Jack Valenti, the Johnson presidential aide who had been given the responsibility of handling the Dirksen ''account,'' remembered the process very well. ''The day would hardly pass without at least one phone call from Dirksen. . . . 'Jack, how's the boss today? . . . Well, tell him that I'm going to sort of cut him up a little bit on the floor tomorrow. I want him to know about it. I'm going to touch him up a little bit on this.'" Then after ranting and raving in his most eloquent language about the enemy in the White House, Dirksen would call later in the afternoon for an appointment with the president at which they could drink in private on the second floor of the mansion, swap tall tales, and cut a few deals.[36]

Dirksen and Johnson knew the rules of the Senate and how to bend them to forge a majority vote. Perhaps the best example of this came in 1964, when Johnson very much needed the help of his old Republican friend in the Senate to fulfill the legacy of John Kennedy in passing a comprehensive civil rights measure that would provide for equality in public accommodations, employment, voting rights, and education. With control over thirty-three Republican votes at that time, Dirksen possessed the power to dictate the extent of any filibuster. And early on, Dirksen, who felt that his black constituents had failed to recognize his efforts on both of Eisenhower's previous civil rights bills, let it be known that he was not so inclined to be helpful on civil rights. ''I trust I can disenthrall myself from all bias, from all prejudice, from all irrelevancies, from all immaterial matters, and see clearly and cleanly what the issue is and then render an independent judgment.''[37] In other words, he told Johnson, don't count on me. The result was that three platoons of southern senators, led by Georgia's Richard Russell, waged a sixty-seven-day ''extended debate,'' while Dirksen seemingly assisted them by offering dozens of amendments to the bill.

But the southerners did not know that behind the scenes, President Johnson had convinced the minority leader to fashion a new ''Dirksen'' bill. So, a mere ten weeks after his promise of opposition, Dirksen delivered twenty-seven filibuster-breaking votes and announced to the world that ''no army is stronger than an idea whose time has come. Today the challenge is here! It is inescapable. It is time to deal with it! No one on that floor is going to stop this. It is going to happen!'' And everyone was made to understand that he, Everett Dirksen, had made that possible.[38]

But the legend's time was coming to an end. When civil rights came up again in 1968, in the form of open housing, one half of his mostly younger, more moderate Republican colleagues—one of them his son-in-law, Tennessee's Howard Baker—opposed him, forcing Dirksen to switch sides and vote for the measure.[39] Then there was the matter of his declining health. He smoked and drank too much, and was a one-man pharmaceutical supply house for a variety of ailments that plagued him, including a bleeding duodenal ulcer, emphysema, coughing spells, and a variety of abdominal problems. More than that, the strain of too many Senate battles was beginning to tell on his heart.[40] But as long as there was still a breath left in him, he was a force to be reckoned with. And Lyndon Johnson was counting on that fact.

Judging what Dirksen's support would mean for Johnson in terms of actual votes was difficult at this point. As the leader of the Republican senators' conference, Dirksen could help to set the agenda for their consideration and thus prevent a hard opposing coalition from forming in that party. This might prove crucial in preventing a debilitating filibuster from developing. Besides his leadership duties, Dirksen's assistance could deliver somewhere between half a dozen and a dozen of his more liberal Republican colleagues. One of their names was Roman Hruska of Nebraska.

The White House believed that wherever the minority leader went, Hruska would be sure to follow. In fact, when Dirksen's name was put down in the "for" column on some White House head counts, it would automatically be followed by Hruska's name in parentheses. One of the truly unexceptional members of the Senate, Hruska would later defend one of Richard Nixon's nominees to the Supreme Court against charges that he was a "mediocrity" by saying, "Even if he is mediocre there are a lot of mediocre judges and people and lawyers. They are entitled to a little representation, aren't they, and a little chance? We can't have all Brandeises, Cardozos, and Frankfurters and stuff like that there."[41] When that nomination failed to be confirmed, Hruska got a chance to redeem himself with the replacement nomination, but became so flustered by a colleague's move on the floor of the Senate that he shouted, "The Nebraska from Senator objects."[42]

It was more than just hard votes, though, that made Dirksen a senatorial whale of the first order. As a key member of the Judiciary Committee, he could provide help there as well. Such help might range from asking

favorable questions of the nominee to leaking important information to
the White House, and even to helping the administration woo the votes of
other Republican colleagues. There was no question, then, that Johnson
needed Dirksen. And both men knew it.

But there was a trick to obtaining support from Everett Dirksen. It
was costly, and everyone understood that the support existed only as
long as Dirksen wanted it to. This was the risk that Johnson needed to
take. So, knowing that Dirksen liked to get the news first in Washington, a supremely confident Lyndon Johnson phoned him from Texas
late on the afternoon of June 19, ostensibly to discuss the anti-ballistic-
missile system and various ambassadorial positions. As an aside, he
happened to mention that Warren's resignation letter had just arrived
(neglecting to mention that it had been drafted nearly a week earlier, or
that the post had already been offered to Abe Fortas five days before).
So the two men played the "guess the new appointment" game. This
was an old ritual in which both men had their choices, but neither
wanted to tip his hand as to his favored choice for fear that it would
change the price of any impending deal.

It was an interesting chess match between the chief executive and
the opposing party's senatorial whale, neither of whom any longer
controlled either the pieces on the board or even the rules of the game.
Governing is a strange enterprise in the city of mutual distrust.

"Now, have you got any suggestions for a replacement?" opened
the president. But Dirksen was too cagey to give away his advantage
by asking for his own man. Two things were true in this circumstance,
and neither was favorable for Dirksen. Either the choices of the two
men differed, in which case Johnson would appoint whomever he
wanted anyway, or there was always the off chance that the two men
agreed on the choice from the outset, in which case the president
would make it sound as if he was doing the senator a favor by naming
him and the chance for a trade would be lost. "Well," replied Dirksen, "why don't you trot out some of yours."

But the president could be just as evasive. He tried the "reluctantly
rejected possibility" gambit. After suggesting the United States emissary to the Paris talks on Vietnam, Cyrus Vance, and securing Dirksen's agreement that Vance "would make a great Chief Justice,"
Johnson made clear that he had no intention of appointing Vance because "he's got a very substantial family, and . . . perhaps he would
feel that he couldn't maintain a position such as he ought to maintain
and get all those kids to college on the salary of a Chief Justice [then
forty thousand dollars]."[43]

So Dirksen countered with Secretary of the Treasury Henry Fowler. A respected Democratic member of the administration, with impeccable credentials and support on both sides of the Senate aisle, Fowler seemed like a fine suggestion. The only problem was Johnson didn't want him—so he too was "reluctantly rejected." "As a matter of fact," Johnson went on, "we owe Fowler because he moved out, moved into a very prominent law firm and I, along with another Senator, went down to the White House and we argued with him about coming back into government, and he did. Well, what would I do for a Secretary of the Treasury? We've got this gold imbalance and these problems abroad; Fowler knows the European bankers. If I got somebody who didn't know them, to start fresh and uninformed, that'd be quite a handicap, and I couldn't put my hands on somebody that quick."

Would the senator from Illinois be interested? Johnson considered. Of course the president knew that Dirksen would never say yes in an election year with at least the possibility of a Republican in the White House and maybe the chance of taking control of the Senate itself. Strangely, this might have been LBJ's best choice. No senator would dare oppose the confirmation of the beloved and venerable minority leader, a member of the senatorial club, to such a lofty position.

Thus far the game was about a draw, but Dirksen, after refusing the kind offer, almost put the president in check by proposing one of the names he really wanted. "What about William Campbell, the senior district judge in Chicago? He's been on the bench a long time, he's extremely popular, he's a good lawyer, [and] he has a fine judicial temperament." Of course, Dirksen also might have noted that he was from the senator's home state and thus would prove by his appointment that there was still fire in the old minority leader when it came to securing patronage plums from an "enemy" White House. Momentarily caught off balance, Johnson quickly recovered. "Great idea," he said, but pointed out, "Of course Bill's Catholic." Since William Brennan occupied the so-called Catholic seat on the court, and heaven forbid there might be *two* qualified Catholics, Johnson regretfully concluded, "I don't think I'd like to disturb the religious balance on the Court, and I'm afraid perhaps I couldn't take him." (Apparently adding another Catholic was more damaging to the court's so-called religious balance in Johnson's eyes than promoting the only Jewish member to the chief justiceship.)[44]

In ending Judge Campbell's best chance for such a promotion, Johnson eliminated another easily confirmable choice for the position—former justice Arthur Goldberg, the previous occupant of the court's only Jewish seat. He was certainly available for the post, having resigned from the United Nations in late April. And there may well have been the implied or stated promise in 1965 to return him there. But the White House understood that in resigning, Goldberg had been critical of his lack of influence on the making of foreign policy. As far as the thin-skinned Johnson was concerned, this criticism eliminated him from consideration.[45] (Regardless, the news media carried frequent rumors of Goldberg's imminent return to the bench, with one story even detailing how much he longed for the position.[46] Even Robert Griffin later admitted to the Michigan Press Association that he would not have opposed the nomination of Arthur Goldberg, because "in a sense he had been on a leave of absence." In this way, Griffin gave his actions the appearance of nonpartisanship.[47])

After trading more names with the minority leader, Johnson made his big move: "What do you think of Abe Fortas?"

"Well," replied Dirksen, "once upon a time he was on the Yale Law School faculty. He's a bright, brilliant lawyer, in fact, now he's been on the Court for three years. I know of nothing that has come to my attention to impeach his record or to denigrate him in any way." Since Johnson, who knew Fortas better than anyone, could not think of any such problem, agreement had been reached. Of course there was the matter of Dirksen's fee for his role in this action, but that could be settled later.

The last thing either man was concerned about as they spoke was a senatorial minnow named Robert Griffin. But as Griffin spoke to his colleagues in the Senate about the *Wall Street Journal* article, he continued to hear the rumors that Warren was indeed resigning and the succession deal had been arranged. All the "proof" he needed to launch his counterattack came in a radio report he heard on the way to work on the morning of June 21, repeating this allegation and attributing the rumor to the usual "authoritative sources."[48] That afternoon he went to the well of the Senate and delivered a blistering attack against any nomination of a chief justice by a lame-duck president, regardless of the nominee's party affiliation or political philosophy: "The Supreme Court has adjourned for the summer and the people are about to choose a new Government in November. For a lame duck President to designate the leadership of the Supreme Court for many years in the future would break faith with our system and it would be an affront to the American people."[49]

It was an aggressive but by no means foolish move. While Griffin had not yet fully put together his rump group, he knew that he could count on the immediate support of at least some of the ultraconservatives who would oppose anything this president did. And Texas's John Tower as well as South Carolina's Strom Thurmond did not disappoint him. If the proof could be found, Griffin had staked out his claim as the early leader of the opposition. But as June 21 closed, Griffin had nothing more to offer the press or his colleagues.

There was more than ample precedent for opposing a nomination by a lame-duck president. The White House would claim that there was a long history of successfully confirmed appointments to the Supreme Court by presidents in their final term of office, with two of them, William Brennan and Potter Stewart, then sitting on the court.[50] And it was true that throughout U.S. history there had been seven successful confirmations of Supreme Court nominees by presidents who were in their final *year* of office. Here, though, the White House conveniently overlooked the fact that another *ten* appointments in this category had been postponed, withdrawn, not acted upon, or outright rejected.[51]

But for all of this history, the most recent example of the Senate's treatment of a lame-duck appointment—the last time, in fact, that any presidential nomination had failed to receive confirmation—gave evidence of the strength of Griffin's argument. In 1959 Dwight Eisenhower had nominated Admiral Lewis L. Strauss as secretary of commerce. After months of bitter Senate debate and numerous public charges, confirmation failed by three votes. And who was the man leading the opposition, despite his promise not to make the fight a political matter? None other than Democratic Majority Leader Lyndon Baines Johnson.[52]

But nothing that the young Michigan senator did in any way worried Lyndon Johnson. There was no vacancy—at least none that anyone could prove existed.

So, on June 22, more than a week after Earl Warren had expressed his desire to leave the bench, Johnson found the time to call the man in charge of developing an appointment list—Attorney General Ramsey Clark.[53] Like most conversations with the president, it was one-way, with Johnson doing most of the talking. And, like most conversations with the president, it went a little differently than Johnson would later describe it to the press. The president would assure the public that he had consulted widely with the Department of Justice every step of the way, and lo and behold, after conducting its own extensive investigations, the department was in total agreement with him that a chief justice should be promoted from within the court. Moreover, according to Johnson, the department also agreed with him totally on the name of Fortas's replacement. But life was never quite as neat as Lyndon Johnson described. And it was up to the press, still chasing down the elusive Earl Warren, to figure out who was telling the truth.

In fact, this conference was the first word that the attorney general had gotten that there would be a court vacancy. But the game was over before the department could even offer an opinion, for the president made it clear that he intended to promote someone to the top spot from within the court. The attorney general was simply instructed to prepare a memorandum justifying the appointment of a chief justice at this point in the presidential term. Clark was not the only one slighted. LBJ did not bother to consult at all with Senate Majority Leader Mike Mansfield either.[54]

Actually, Ramsey Clark was happy not to be asked to investigate Fortas further. "You don't run a new F.B.I. investigation on a sitting judge," he explained later, for "there's a presumption because of the public exposure that he has, his conduct has been good." Additionally, Clark saw a genuine "danger" to the constitutional "separation of powers" in a member of the executive branch saying to a sitting, and presumably independent, judge, "Okay, now, are you an honorable man? Have you done anything dishonest? Have you taken bribes, or have you done things foolish?" So as far as the White House knew, everything was fine.[55]

Then the president turned his attention to the vacant *associate* justice's seat, and asked Clark for the names of some possible nominees. Two of the candidates suggested by the attorney general had already been mentioned by Senator Dirksen—Cyrus Vance and Henry Fowler—and two others were names that also would have found favor in the Senate: Edmund Muskie, senator from Maine, and Albert E. Jenner, Jr., chairman of the American Bar Association's Standing Committee on the Federal Judiciary, which makes informal inquiries as to the merits of proposed judicial appointments.

But the president made clear by his lack of enthusiasm that none of these names pleased him. Instead, he seemed only to want assurances about a new name that had risen to the top of his list—federal court of appeals judge Homer Thornberry.

He was a remarkable man—a true southern gentleman who was by all accounts fully qualified for the Supreme Court—and yet all people saw when they thought of this stocky, wavy gray-white-haired, blunt-spoken, fifty-nine-year-old judge was the image of his close friend Lyndon Baines Johnson.[56] Born in Austin, Texas, to deaf-mute parents (who slept in shifts so that a vigil could be maintained at his cribside, and communicated with him throughout their lives using sign language), Thornberry had been raised in poverty so dire that his folks had to save for two years to afford windowpanes in their house. Like Johnson, he had bettered himself through a political career. After working his way through the University of Texas Law School, Thornberry served as a deputy sheriff, state legislator, district attorney, and, after World War II, as city councilman and Austin's mayor pro tem.

It was after he succeeded Johnson in the United States Congress in 1948 that the two men were seen as inextricably intertwined. (This view was encouraged considerably by Johnson's practice of calling Thornberry "my congressman.") Senator Johnson introduced him to the powerful man who had helped his own career, Speaker of the House Sam Rayburn, thus ensuring that he got on the right committees. "It's just unbelievable how many things he and Mrs. Johnson did to help us when we went to Washington," said Thornberry later. "He knew more people in Washington that could be helpful to you than probably anybody, and he saw to it that I got to know them. He and Mrs. Johnson were helpful to us and our family. We were just young people then, at least we thought we were. Babes in the woods, and had children and my mother was with us. There were just many personal things they did for us; it's just almost impossible to enumerate them all. . . . I doubt that any other individual did as much as he did to see to it that a successor got started right."[57] And Thornberry was not a man to forget such favors, playing dominoes with the senator hour after hour to help Johnson recover from his massive heart attack in 1955.

Thornberry had Johnson's moderate-liberal political bent. Throughout his life Thornberry was concerned about protecting the civil rights of blacks and Jews, as well as the freedom of speech. After supporting John Kennedy 95 percent of the time as a member of the House Rules Committee, thus giving the president a one-vote margin of control, Thornberry was rewarded with a district court judgeship for the Western District of Texas in 1963. Two years later, Lyndon Johnson gave his friend's career a boost by swearing him in on the front porch of the LBJ Ranch as judge of the United States Court of Appeals for the Fifth Circuit. Thornberry hadn't sought the new appointment, in fact he had told Johnson he didn't want it; but nobody said no to the president, who simply called in the newsmen to announce the newest court elevation. It was here that Thornberry was able to further school integration, defend picketing as a form of speech, and strike down the restrictive Texas poll tax.

In late June 1968, though, Thornberry's name caught the attorney general entirely by surprise, and it is doubtful that Ramsey Clark could have been too enthusiastic about the prospect of making the appeals judge the second Supreme Court nominee. In a memo on the court vacancy the following Monday, Clark argued, "Non-political appointments to the Judiciary are the ideal. Politics should not enter in the deliberations of the Senate in exercising its power of confirmation. Only the qualifications of the appointee are appropriate for consideration."[58] This is not to say that Thornberry was unqualified for the post, but the politics of such an appointment would be obvious to everyone. Moreover, Johnson's appointment of a close friend to the Supreme Court, especially as a replacement for his other close adviser, who was being elevated to chief justice, would make it look like, in the words of one former White House official, "old crony week."[59]

While Clark could take solace that for now the president did not seem to be too set on the choice of a second nominee, for reasons quite beyond the president's control, Homer Thornberry was soon to become the only possible man to replace Fortas.

While all of this was happening, the news media raced to catch up with the story, which was now over a week old. There seems to be no rule as to how many times a rumor must be repeated in the press to make it a "fact," but United Press International did its part on Saturday, June 22, by reporting again on Earl Warren's imminent departure. Seeking a new angle to this nonstory, the dispatch speculated about the effective date of the resignation, saying "it could prove critical."[60] Meanwhile, the subject of the speculation—Warren—continued his successful effort to evade the press.

It was a dangerous game that the president and the chief justice had been playing, but time ran out on them that day. After all, Beverly Updike of Sapulpa, Oklahoma, had a promise to keep four blocks from Johnson's office, at the University Club. This would not have mattered except that it put her directly in the orbit of the elusive chief justice of the United States. Just as he commonly did, Earl Warren had also gone to the University Club for a swim and a rubdown. While there, the chief justice couldn't resist phoning a friend from the phone booth in the club's lobby to laugh about the flying rumors and his role in them. The rumors were true, he explained, adding that in a political sense the timing made all the sense in the world. It was not just Nixon's possible victory in November that worried Warren, but the prospect that Everett Dirksen, as the leader of the Republicans in the Senate, "would be given the appointment."[61] Remembering Dirksen's role in recent senatorial efforts to curb the powers of the Supreme Court, the chief justice lamented, "Dirksen has already tried to ruin the Court."[62] So the idea of his controlling the next appointment was unthinkable.

As he spoke, Warren was conscious of only one thing—the heat in the phone booth. There was so little air that he had to keep opening the door to get some relief. He was not aware of the two people outside the booth, but they were very much aware of him. In fact, as Warren spoke the people outside were also engaged in a deep discussion of legal theory in practice. The issue for the two people standing outside the door—Malvina Stephenson, the Washington correspondent for the Swanco Broadcasting Company, and retired colonel John Orr of Tulsa, an intelligence officer and lawyer, both of whom were waiting for Beverly Updike's wedding to begin—was whether it was legal to eavesdrop on a chief justice.

Chances are very good that it never occurred to Stephenson to ask for an opinion from the nation's top judicial officer. When the phone booth door was open, they decided, even the chief justice couldn't reasonably expect privacy. So Stephenson did what any good reporter with her own radio news program would do: She told her listeners about it.

Washington can be a very strange town. Earl Warren stepped into a phone booth and as a result Robert Griffin was transformed from a minnow into a whale—or, to put it more accurately, a shark. Now, with all the confirmation that was needed to convert the rumors into fact, Griffin searched in the senatorial ocean for allies. The fight was on.

Soon both Fortas and Johnson would come to understand what the president's good intentions had really caused. The White House staff had previously depleted its energy in ramming a tax surcharge and a new civil rights bill through Congress that year. Now that Johnson had to face the greatest Senate challenge of his presidency, he would find that after the March 31 announcement that he was not running for reelection, his influence there had been considerably reduced. Consequently, for one terrifying year Abe Fortas, the consummate insider and "operator," would see his life spin totally out of his control.

But the confirmation fight had even broader significance for the nation. It was like Pickett's Charge at the Civil War battle of Gettysburg. There Robert E. Lee, on the third day of the struggle, sent fifteen thousand crack troops, under Pickett's command, to their doom. Vastly outnumbered, and marching in a line a mile and a half wide over a mile of open field and up Cemetery Ridge, they ran into the teeth of the heavily reinforced Union troops. Today, as one walks the battleground, one wonders how such an order could have been given. "It was a glorious charge," says historian Allan Nevins, "but it was not war."[63] Now on top of this Pennsylvania ridge one finds a solemn granite monument, which is inscribed simply THE HIGH-WATER MARK OF THE REBELLION.

Paralleling Pickett's Charge, Johnson's Charge in 1968 represented the high-water mark of liberalism on the twentieth-century Supreme Court. In facing the superior firepower of the Senate, Lyndon Johnson used only his best friend, Abe Fortas. And, like the southern forces, by the time the White House troops knew they were going to lose, they were already finished. But unlike that earlier battle—where thousands upon thousands gave their lives—in 1968 only one man was mortally wounded, and he would not realize his true fate until months later. So, rather than a Fortas Court, there would be a Burger Court. Rather than a liberal, activist court, there would be a conservative, more restrained court. And the course of American history would be changed forever.

XII

LET'S
MAKE A DEAL

Power in Washington is very much
like the stock market—it rises and falls on a daily basis. And there
could be little doubt that Malvina Stephenson's broadcast had changed
the prices of several issues of senatorial stock. Take, for instance, the
price that Everett Dirksen was going to charge for his support. Both
the president and Dirksen knew that his support for the Supreme Court
plan was now even more vital. So early Monday morning, June 24,
1968, Dirksen readily agreed to the president's offer of a private chat
at the Oval Office later that day. It was important that they meet then,
both men knew, as the weekly meeting of the Senate Republicans
would be convened the next day—chaired of course by the minority
leader—and the court nominations were certain to be on the agenda.
And by now, Dirksen had settled on the price for his assistance in this
venture.

But Dirksen was not the only Senate whale to receive attention that
day. Stephenson's broadcast made it necessary for the president to

make moves in another direction—to the South. In considering carefully the senatorial whales to be fed, Johnson had to sail in two oceans—the full Senate and the Judiciary Committee, which would have immediate jurisdiction. The overall Senate was broken up into four groups. There were the conservative Republicans, consisting of new party member Strom Thurmond of South Carolina, John Tower of Texas, and more than a dozen others, who would be looking to oppose any action by Johnson in hopes of saving the appointment for a possible Republican president-elect in November. Then there were the moderate Republicans, such as Everett Dirksen of Illinois, Mark Hatfield of Oregon, Jacob Javits of New York, Edward Brooke of Massachusetts, and John Sherman Cooper of Kentucky, who could be persuaded to decide the matter on principle rather than partisan considerations if given the proper inducements.

On the other side of the aisle were the Democrats. But the fact that sixty-three members of the Senate were from Johnson's party did not make it a certainty that he could secure a Supreme Court confirmation.[1] To be sure, the vast majority of these Democratic members were ultraliberals who had been the backbone of the coalition that had passed the major elements of the Great Society program. But nineteen of the Democrats belonged to an ultraconservative coalition of southern senators known as the Dixiecrats, who frequently opposed Johnson's legislative proposals.[2] The more vigorous the president's efforts in the areas of integration and prosecuting the undeclared war in Vietnam, the more vocal their opposition had become. And the Dixiecrats' effective power exceeded their actual voting numbers because of the threat that they would unite with the Republicans, thus creating a new majority.

There was no clearer evidence of this fact anywhere than in the Judiciary Committee, which passed first on court nominations. Not only did the seniority-laden Dixiecrats have significant representation on the committee, they controlled the chairmanship. So the president went fishing for James O. Eastland of Mississippi.

After twenty-six years in the Senate, James Eastland had established the sort of reputation that made him an unlikely candidate for supporting the Fortas nomination. Marked by *Time* magazine as "the nation's most dangerous demagogue," and called by others "Mississippi McCarthy," Eastland was, according to one White House aide, "certainly a racist by today's standards."[3] A symbol of the notion of white supremacy, he would talk about the "mongrelization" of the races, and speak of blacks as "an inferior race."[4] To him, the civil rights movement had been infiltrated by Communists, thus leading him to use his chairmanship of the Internal Security Subcommittee to investigate this threat. Furthermore, he claimed that the Supreme Court was "the greatest single threat to our Constitution."[5] For him, this was especially true under the leadership of Earl Warren, who Eastland believed favored the Communist party.[6] So he invented a simple standard for decisions by the Supreme Court, labeling each of them as either "pro-Communist" or "anti-Communist."[7]

But he was the sort of man who had such power that during the Eisenhower years, even though a member of the opposing party, he had been given control over the patronage jobs in his home state of Mississippi. And over the years he had developed a close working relationship with Lyndon Johnson, who considered him to be "one of the best sources of intelligence in the Senate on what the Republicans were doing."[8] So effective was his work that since taking the chairmanship of the Judiciary Committee in 1956, Eastland was credited by one count with bottlenecking 127 separate pieces of civil rights legislation.[9]

And that was not to mention the scores of liberal nominees to the federal courts who had felt his wrath. Now he was particularly unhappy with President Johnson, after the appointment of a black justice, Thurgood Marshall, to the Supreme Court the previous year. According to one story, Marshall had gotten by Eastland's committee the first time, when he was seated on the United States Court of Appeals, only in a trade for the nomination of the chairman's candidate, William Harold Cox, for a Mississippi district court appointment. "Tell your brother that if he will give me Harold Cox I will give him the nigger," Eastland is said to have told Attorney General Bobby Kennedy on that occasion.[10] A man like this, Lyndon Johnson knew, was not about to give his support freely for the nomination of Abe Fortas to the Supreme Court. But without at least the neutrality of the chairman of the Judiciary Committee, the confirmation problems would only multiply.

Johnson had the White House operators track the senator down in Mississippi as he was about to board a plane to leave for a friend's daughter's wedding in Hattiesburg. But warmed-up planes and impending weddings were nothing when the president had some business to transact. So for fifty minutes the two men talked on the phone about the future of the Supreme Court. Even though Johnson claimed that he was "consulting" the senator for suggested names, like Ramsey Clark before him, Eastland could tell from his tone that the selection had already been made. So the senator would promise only to talk to

Johnson again after he had returned to Washington and had a chance to consult with his southern colleagues.[11] Seeing that Eastland was going to be a problem, the president knew he would need another champion among the southerners.

Given this impasse, it was logical for Johnson to think of his old mentor, and the informal leader of the southern Democrats, Richard Russell of Georgia. Through their mutual friend Edwin Weisl, Sr., a prominent New York attorney, Johnson had learned that Russell would vote for Fortas for chief justice, but he would "enthusiastically support" Homer Thornberry, his old duck-hunting buddy, for the second seat. "When you sit in a duck blind all day with a man, you really get to know him," the senator had said, "and [I know] Homer Thornberry. [I know] him to be a good man, an able man, and a fair man." This was powerful news to a president who already had "his congressman" at the top of his own selection list, and was beginning to fear the possibility of a Senate filibuster. Without "consulting" any further, he settled absolutely in his own mind on the Fortas-Thornberry ticket.[12]

The more Johnson thought about this ticket, the more he convinced himself that his judgment and strategy were sound. While the presence of the brilliant Fortas would help to carry the more political Thornberry through the confirmation process, it appeared that the Texas judge would more than carry his own weight on the judicial ticket. There seemed little doubt that, having already been twice confirmed by the Senate for the federal courts and, as a former member of Congress, deserving special courtesy from other members of the club, Thornberry would speed through the Senate once more. There was also the geographical balance of the court to consider. After the retirement of Texan Tom Clark, appointing a justice from the Southwest took on some importance. Finally, there was the matter of the philosophical balance on the court. The conservative Dixiecrats would be attracted to the trade of the moderate, self-restrained Thornberry for the departing liberal activist, Earl Warren. So while the liberals would get the top spot, in fact the overall philosophical outlook of the court would be shifted more toward the middle.

But even if *none* of these factors had been present, all that Johnson needed to know was that Richard Russell had expressed a desire for the Texas judge. And, given the political realities, whatever Russell wanted here, Russell would get.

Having settled on the ticket, Johnson really had nothing more to do until after he met with Everett Dirksen shortly before seven that night of June 24 to line up the Republican's support. Since the president would have to sell the new ticket having used none of Dirksen's earlier appointment suggestions, he was just going to have to meet the senator's price before announcing the nominations to the public. The two men met in the small presidential study just off the Oval Office. Barely big enough to hold the president's easy chair, a three-seat couch, the ever-present television, and a communications console, the room gave the meeting the sense of intimacy needed to conduct business between two old friends. Each man knew what to expect from the other. Dirksen would not be so bold as to set a price for his services on this issue, but there would be a few matters concerning him that he wanted to discuss with the president. And, of course, now Johnson had his own agenda. When the meeting was concluded there would be an understanding between them as to how things should be in the future.

They covered a lot of ground in fifty-two minutes, and Johnson used all of his persuasive powers in selling the idea of the Fortas-Thornberry ticket.[13] Even though he was not running for reelection, he told Dirksen, the Department of Justice research showed that he had a historical right to make such an appointment.

But Everett Dirksen fully understood the odds against the president.[14] Time was very much on the side of this lame duck's opponents. Every day brought the nation closer to the symbolic transfer of power signified by the party conventions in early August. There was the hard reality that there were only forty days left until the planned August 3 adjournment by the Senate, and even the Department of Justice was telling the president that the average time for securing confirmation of a Supreme Court appointment had grown to about fifty days.[15] Of course, it helped now that all but two of the sitting Judiciary Committee members had already voted to confirm Fortas's first nomination to the court in 1965, and the vote in the full Senate had been nearly unanimous. But support in the Senate, like the weather, changes frequently.

However, these facts were not important to Lyndon Johnson when he was trying to get someone to say yes. And neither was consistency. Now the man who several days earlier had told Dirksen that he did not want to disturb the religious balance of the court used a curious argument for appointing the first Jewish chief justice. Surely the Republican senators in an election year would not wish to antagonize Jewish voters and financial supporters, he said, so it made *political* sense for them to support this ticket.[16]

For his part, Everett Dirksen had a concern, and it, in turn, became

Lyndon Johnson's concern as well.[17] There was the matter of the SACB.[18] The Subversive Activities Control Board had been created by Congress in 1950 to root out Communist and Communist-front organizations in America by identifying and registering the names of their members through cases presented to the attorney general. Some now saw this as a bureaucratic dinosaur from the McCarthy era, rendered impotent by a series of Supreme Court decisions that had made the provisions of the original legislation virtually unenforceable.[19] But they had not convinced Ev Dirksen.

Support for the Subversive Activities Control Board represented Dirksen's symbol to the staunch conservatives that he was still with them. Of course, it was also true that it represented a convenient location for some of his friends seeking government positions.[20] And now, the SACB was under attack. Senator William Proxmire was understandably troubled by the fact that absolutely no cases had been brought before the five-person board for over thirty months (not to mention the fact that in the seventeen years of its existence, the board had yet to register a single Communist). And Lyndon Johnson had just appointed Simon F. McHugh, the twenty-nine-year-old husband of one of his White House secretaries, to the quasi-judicial board at a salary of twenty-six thousand dollars a year. Since the fellow lacked the requisite legal training, it seemed to fuel the charges that the board had no real function. Soon calls were heard for its complete abolition.

Despite these attacks, Dirksen had managed to secure another appropriation for the board for fiscal year 1968.[21] Following the lead of William Proxmire, though, the Senate got its pound of flesh, passing a "death sentence" for the agency, which, after considerable lobbying by Dirksen, would be lifted only if the attorney general referred at least one case to the board by June 30, 1968. Despite continual pleadings from the senator, here it was six days from the deadline, and no such case had been referred.

Attorney General Clark saw no reason to save the board. First, there were the obviously grave civil-liberties problems coming from it. Moreover, of the forty-three possible cases being considered by the Justice Department for referral to the board, all but seven appeared to be based on evidence gathered by electronic surveillance, evidence that under a Supreme Court decision in February 1968 might well have to be turned over to the defendants. While that issue was being litigated again by the court, for obvious reasons Ramsey Clark had no intention of proceeding. But maybe now, thought Everett Dirksen, there might be a way to change his mind.[22]

However, both Dirksen and Johnson knew how intransigent the attorney general could be on such matters. One gets an interesting reaction today when talking about the former attorney general with
members of the Johnson administration now living in and around Austin, Texas. Whenever one asks for an opinion about Ramsey Clark,
there is a long pause for reflection, and then each person responds with
the same line: "I loved his daddy." But Tom Clark had also created
and raised a remarkable son.

Ramsey Clark, then forty years old, may have been one of the few
men who could say no to Lyndon Johnson. But you would not believe
it either to look at him or to listen to him. The lean, jug-eared, six-foot
three-inch frame belied the unassuming nature of his demeanor. A gentle, low-key, candid man, he seemed to observers to be more like a
university professor than the highest-ranking lawyer in the government.

Because of the closeness of the families of Clark and Johnson, dating back to the latter's days in Congress, the president had watched
young Ramsey grow up. And how could one not admire Clark's progress through such a startlingly successful career? In a period spanning
only five and a half years, he had graduated from high school, served
in the Marines Corps and risen to the rank of corporal, received a B.A.
from the University of Texas, taken a master's in history from the
University of Chicago, earned a law degree from Chicago, and then
joined the family law firm in Dallas.[23]

But there was much more that Lyndon Johnson saw in this young
legal powerhouse. He loved his powerful and succinct speaking ability, and had great respect for Clark's moral character. So he moved
him up from the post he had held since 1961 as assistant attorney
general in charge of the Lands Division, to become the deputy attorney
general in 1965, and then to the very top position in the department in
1967. From a point of view based strictly on competence, Clark's appointment had never been a disappointment. Once, after listening to a
thirty-minute peroration by the attorney general reviewing the accomplishments of the Johnson administration in the field of law and order,
Johnson told speechwriter Harry McPherson that it was "the most brilliant, cogent, coherent, knowledgeable description of any problem that
he had heard from any Cabinet officer."[24]

Johnson also saw an advantage in Clark's profoundly liberal attitude. Here was a man who would ensure that the administration protected civil rights and liberties to the fullest. For that reason, to some
observers the president seemed to go almost too far in allowing Clark

to serve as the moral conscience of the White House, even to the point of obstructing policy. White House aide Larry Temple explained, "Most people . . . think well, Lyndon Johnson's the President. He's the boss. He can do whatever he wants to. I guess technically that may be true. But as a practical matter I never saw him order . . . Ramsey to do anything. He strongly expressed his views, and the independent guy that Ramsey was and is came to the fore. Ramsey ultimately did, in every instance I saw, just what Ramsey thought the right result was."[25]

Once there was a question of whether to appeal a case involving the Interstate Commerce Commission, and over the objections of both the president and Secretary of Transportation Alan Boyd, the attorney general was adamant in his desire to press it. After one of several meetings on the issue, the president ended by saying, "All right, Ramsey, I've told you what my view is. I recognize that you're the lawyer for this government and I'm not. I've told you what my position is. It's not really a very flexible position. . . . You do whatever you think the facts justify in merit. Whatever that is, I may disagree with it, but I won't disagree with your right to do whatever it is." And so, after saying he would "think it over in that light," Clark filed the appeal anyway the very next day.[26] Later the United States Court of Appeals upheld the ICC and thus the LBJ position.

In spite of Johnson's admiration for Clark, Johnson began to see that he had serious flaws as well. He was very young, was not politically astute in dealing with Congress, and had what one White House aide described as a "mustang independence."[27] Perhaps *New York Times* reporter Fred Graham best described the man when he concluded, "Those who know Ramsey Clark will say that his Achilles' heel, if any, is not complaisance to pressure from above but a tendency to stand on principle when practical men would compromise." For that reason, in time Johnson came to see him as a political liability, and by 1968 was "thinking about Ramsey maybe for some other job."[28]

For all of his stubbornness, though, on the issue of the continued existence of the SACB Clark was absolutely correct. It had no place in the America of the 1960's. And because of that, thus far the president had sided with his decision to delay movement.

But all of that changed on the evening of June 24. As soon as Everett Dirksen raised the issue of the SACB in the context of Abe Fortas's and Homer Thornberry's future appointments, the president quickly realized that it was not too high a price to pay for the confirmation of his two friends to the Supreme Court. So the president buzzed for Larry Temple. A brilliant and likable University of Texas Law School graduate, the young man had served as law clerk to Justice Tom Clark and administrative assistant to Governor John Connally. In mid-1967 he was brought to the White House to become, among other things, the White House liaison to the Department of Justice. Tonight was the christening for his most challenging assignment, coordinating the administration's efforts to secure confirmation of these appointments.[29]

"Larry," the president began, "I want you to get in touch with Ramsey Clark and tell him to refer some cases to the SACB." All Temple had to do was see the extremely pleased look on Dirksen's face to realize what was actually going on. After all, Johnson could have called Temple on the phone, sent him a memo, or just waited to give the order until the young assistant, who was one of the members of the so-called bedroom detail, joined Johnson in his bedroom early the next morning to set up the day's schedule of work. But it was clear to him that the president wanted the visiting senator to see this display of power in action.

When Temple conveyed the message, though, Attorney General Clark would say only, "Well, we'll see about what cases we have now." So the president himself contacted his attorney general and told him in no uncertain terms that this board, whatever Clark thought of it, was important to Everett Dirksen. And, since the administration desperately needed the senator's support on these court nominations, Johnson wanted those cases referred.

It was a tough spot for the attorney general. Temple could see clearly that Clark was very reluctant to make this move and was wrestling with his conscience over whether to do something he had no belief in for such political motives. But in the end Clark knew that the Fortas nomination was more important to the president than the demise of the SACB. So, just before the June 30 deadline, Clark referred the seven cases unrelated to the electronic surveillance problem to the board. As Larry Temple put it, "Ramsey did it knowingly, intentionally, reluctantly and unwillingly." And even though, as the attorney general expected, nothing ever came of these cases, the board members were happy. This in turn made Everett Dirksen happy, which meant that the president was happy as well. For a man of Clark's strong convictions and liberal conscience, though, this was a blow. There would be no more ordering around of Ramsey Clark, and the president knew it. But why should that matter? For the administration was coming to an end, and the Dirksen whale had been fed.[30]

*   *   *

Part of Clark's angst over his forced decision no doubt resulted from the public statements of the victorious Everett Dirksen. After the new announcement on July 2 that seven new cases had been referred to the SACB, the press asked Dirksen whether he had given anything to the president in return for this change in policy. The senator responded, "It had absolutely nothing to do with it, this is just a case where I mowed Clark down. . . . When you play for keeps, you play for keeps."[31] But when asked once more what had been "promised" for the nomination votes, Dirksen poked his finger into the reporter's stomach, and shouted, "That's, that's crass. This is a goddamned outrage to suggest that I would do this on the basis of a handout!"[32] As he left the Senate press gallery, Dirksen added sanctimoniously, "Why, my life would have been impoverished if I lived that way, only doing something in return for something. What makes me sore is a guy who can't take me straight. That is an insult." It no longer made any difference to the senator that the charge happened to be true.[33]

With the deal in place, Dirksen went to work for Lyndon Johnson, and quickly found out that it was tougher than he expected. Not even his own son-in-law, Senator Howard Baker of Tennessee, was interested in helping when told by Dirksen at dinner that night about the role that he had agreed to play in promoting the ticket. "Mr. D.," Baker responded, "I can't go along with you. I'll fight confirmation until we convene a new Congress and install a new administration."[34]

The news was no better for the White House on the other side of the aisle. As the rumors of the resignation and the names of the successors were quietly being confirmed the next day in the Senate offices and cloakroom, it became clear that there was substantial unhappiness regarding the move in the southern conservatives' quarters. James Eastland, having visited with his Dixiecrat colleagues after returning from Mississippi, passed along the warning to the attorney general that "a filibuster was already being organized against Fortas." Moreover, the senator concluded "that he had never seen so much feeling against a man as against Fortas."[35] It was not just his "liberal" Warren Court tendencies and Jewishness that bothered them, but a number of the southern senators, having butted heads with Fortas over the years, just did not like him personally.

And the reports coming in from the White House lobbyists seemed to confirm this impression. Robert Byrd of West Virginia promised to "do everything in [his] power" to oppose this "leftist" member of the court. Russell Long of Louisiana simply referred to Fortas as "one of the dirty five'' who sided with the "criminals against the victims of crime.''[36] Even Eastland himself was overheard at a cocktail party saying, "After [Thurgood] Marshall, I could not go back to Mississippi if a Jewish chief justice swore in the next president.''[37] And the second-ranking Democratic member of the Judiciary Committee, John L. McClellan of Arkansas, said that he was looking forward to having "that SOB formally submitted to the Senate" so that he could fight the nomination.[38] So, even before the formal announcement of Earl Warren's departure, the White House was in trouble. But the one ray of sunshine came when Eastland concluded that "a filibuster against Fortas would be a success," unless *both* Dirksen and Hruska supported him. And while Dirksen was "acting strangely," Eastland added that "it appeared that the President had won him over.''[39]

But the warnings were all forgotten shortly after noon the next day, as Dirksen himself called the White House to report his success in controlling the actions of that afternoon's meeting of the Republican Policy Committee. After stalling away nearly all of the time on other issues, in the few remaining moments he had raised the court appointment issue by saying only, "There's nothing about lame ducks in the Constitution.''[40]

In fact, though, Dirksen's performance had not been quite as successful as he believed. A number of the younger Republicans were so upset by the cursory handling of the matter that Robert Griffin began to look good to them. As the meeting adjourned in response to the bell for a Senate roll-call vote, California's George Murphy told Griffin, "To hell with waiting a week for the next Policy luncheon to decide on a position. Let's get up a statement declaring our opposition and get some of our colleagues to sign it.''[41] And within minutes after the close of the meeting, a hard core of opponents to the nominations— Senators Robert Griffin, George Murphy, Howard Baker, Hiram Fong of Hawaii, and Paul Fannin of Arizona—had begun to unite.

But even if Lyndon Johnson had been apprised of this nascent mutiny, he would not have cared. Feeling confident of Republican support by reason of the deal with Dirksen, Johnson prepared for his final effort to win over the Dixiecrats. The time had come to approach the other pillar of his lobbying strategy—Richard Russell. With such strong feeling by the conservative southerners against the proposed ticket, LBJ would need all the help that his old mentor could provide in bringing them into line.

And Johnson knew that his dinner with Russell on the evening of June 25 held the key to that alliance. If the information from Edwin

Weisl had been correct, the trick would be to make Russell think he had originated the Thornberry idea, and thus had a stake in the ticket. When the senator arrived, the two men repaired to the same small study off the Oval Office in which Everett Dirksen had agreed to the nominations. And once again, the news for Johnson was good. When the subject of the judicial appointments was raised, Russell reaffirmed, "I will support the nomination of Mr. Fortas for Chief Justice, but I will enthusiastically support Homer Thornberry." Of course, there was a big difference in the levels of support. Later, Russell would tell people, "If Johnson had nominated Thornberry as Chief Justice I would have spoken in favor of it on the floor of the Senate." [42]

But that mattered little to the president, who now moved to seal the deal. He had the White House operators track down Homer Thornberry at a party given by Robert Calvert, chief justice of the Supreme Court of Texas. "Homer," the president began as Thornberry tried to avoid the stares of the other guests, who knew that the call was coming from the White House, "I had always hoped that when I left this office we would be able to fish on the Pedernales River, but now I can't do that."

"And why is that, Mr. President?" asked the bewildered Thornberry.

"Because tomorrow I am sending your name to the Senate for the vacant seat on the United States Supreme Court." [43]

The news came as a complete surprise to Thornberry, and all he could manage to say was "It's an honor I never dreamed I could have—I'll do the best I can." [44]

Then Johnson added, "Wait, here's a friend of yours who wants to talk to you." Senator Russell got on the line and the two men talked for a few moments about the Senate confirmation hearing. And as Russell gave the phone back to the president, the senator mumbled something that Thornberry could not make out. "Did you hear that?" asked Johnson.

"No," answered the new nominee.

"He says, 'He's with you all the way.'" responded Johnson. Nothing could have been sweeter news to the president.

With this southern Senate whale safely on board, there was only one last move to make. Early the next morning, June 26, after being informed that Albert Jenner, Jr., of the American Bar Association had confidentially canvassed members of the Standing Committee on the Federal Judiciary and that both of the proposed nominees were found to be "highly acceptable from the viewpoint of professional qualifications," the president prepared for one final meeting with James O. Eastland. With Richard Russell's support, the president had some new ammunition. However, when Eastland came to the Oval Office shortly after 10:30 A.M. and heard about Russell's expression of support, he was not impressed. "Now Mr. President, I know Dick Russell told you he would support them, but he's not going to do it, he can't do it. I know what the Southern Senators are going to do."[45]

As the two men spoke, the president was handed a "red tag" memorandum, demanding immediate attention. The content of the memorandum was welcome news. In it, presidential aide Mike Manatos reported an important change of attitude in Senator Robert Byrd of West Virginia. Byrd had told him that "upon reflection he thought his comments were too harsh to Abe Fortas—that while he disagreed with most of the positions Fortas has taken as a member of the Supreme Court, he [Fortas] is a friend of the President—that he [Byrd] shouldn't have taken such a belligerent attitude." The West Virginia senator added that he still would not support Fortas's nomination, but he also promised that he would not organize or participate "in any way in any campaign aimed at bringing about the rejection of Fortas' nomination."[46]

The memo was just what the president needed at that moment, and he handed it to Eastland. But still Eastland was not interested. He told the president that Fortas represented to him the worst possible appointment. The senator particularly objected to an earlier speech by Fortas on civil rights, which he interpreted "as a conspiratorial call for Jews and Negroes to take over America."[47] Then Eastland warned, "Mr. President, this appointment is going to be terribly unpopular. He's not going to be confirmed by the Senate, and he's going to tear this country up. That is, it will generate a lot of ill feeling in the country." Realizing now that support here was impossible, the president asked only whether the chairman would let the nominations out of the Judiciary Committee. "Yes," Eastland answered, but then added, "At my own time."

Much later, the president would tell the Mississippi senator, "You were the only man who had kept his word 100 percent." But that is not hard when one promises very little.[48]

There was nothing more to be done. The president felt certain that he had, as he later told Homer Thornberry, "touched enough of the bases." Maybe so, but the ball had not been hit far enough. So the members of the press were called in for a "surprise press conference" at 11:38 A.M. Putting aside any doubts, Johnson read Warren's two retirement letters and the White House's conditional acceptance response. Then, after announcing the Fortas and Thornberry appointments, he was asked, "Do you anticipate having any trouble in having the Senate ratify these?" Disregarding all of the negative signs, the president said only, "I would suspect that they would review their records very carefully." He could count on that.[49]

In fact, the "review" process was already well under way. While LBJ and Russell had been dining the night before, across town their Senate opponents had already been plotting. Robert Griffin and George Murphy had drafted a petition that read: "The undersigned Republican Senators wish to indicate their strong view that the next Chief Justice of the Supreme Court should be designated by the next President of the United States; and that if such an appointment should be made in the waning months of this Administration while the people are in the process of choosing a new government, we would not vote to confirm it." As the president was announcing the new appointments on June 26, they already had gathered eight signatures. And by the end of that day, while Everett Dirksen was publicly supporting Fortas as "a very able lawyer" and Thornberry as a "very solid citizen," eighteen of his Republican charges had already jumped ship.[50]

Then, the evening news reports of the president's announcement sounded a new alarm. Thanks to David Brinkley, Walter Cronkite, and Frank Reynolds, the White House found out for the first time about the extensive and growing Republican opposition to the nominations. NBC and CBS quoted Richard Nixon as expecting "considerable opposition" and saying, "It would have been wise for the President to ask Chief Justice Warren to serve in the fall term, thereby leaving selection of new justices to the next President." But if they were unprepared for this attack, they were even less ready for the quick development of the next charge. All three networks expressed surprise at the appointments of two of Johnson's "close friends." The cronyism charge was already beginning. The opposition's development was much faster than expected.[51]

Later that day the president stared at the memorandum on his desk. The fun and exhilaration brought on several hours earlier by his phone call to Abe Fortas, congratulating himself for making these appointments possible, were forgotten now. According to a new report from Washington attorney Lloyd Cutler, not even Roman Hruska—the man Eastland said the White House needed and the man who was seen as being in Dirksen's hip pocket—was on board. Instead, he was expressing concern about this lame-duck president's powers to make any appointment. Apparently, the memo implied, Dirksen couldn't even guarantee one additional vote.[52]

The president took out a blank piece of White House stationery and, after doodling around the letterhead a bit, began to reflect on all that he had heard. He jotted down the names of the members of the Judiciary Committee. Down the right side was the list of lost votes. All of them were the conservatives, starting with the southern Democrats: James Eastland, who had never promised anything; John McClellan, who the president hoped might help in exchange for a deal on the pending crime bill; and Sam Ervin of North Carolina, who was sure to stick with the other two. Then there were the Republicans. Hruska now appeared lost, while Hiram Fong and the formidable Strom Thurmond had long ago declared their allegiance to the opposing Griffin forces.

Then down the left side of the page the president listed all of the liberals on both sides of the political aisle who could be counted on— Tom Dodd of Connecticut, Phil Hart of Michigan, Birch Bayh of Indiana, Quentin Burdick of North Dakota, Joseph Tydings of Maryland, George Smathers of Florida, Hugh Scott of Pennsylvania, and of course Everett Dirksen. Then, showing the state of the president's mind at the time, he put two names in the middle as being up for grabs. Not even liberal Democrats Edward Long of Missouri and Ted Kennedy of Massachusetts could be counted on yet. All in all, there were only eight certain votes for confirmation on the committee—not even a majority yet of the committee's seventeen members. There was potential here for a long and perhaps even an unsuccessful fight, and the nominations had just been made.[53]

Minutes later the news for the president seemed to go from bad to worse. John McClellan told Senate liaison Mike Manatos, "I'm only the second ranking man on the Committee, yet no one bothered to consult me. They talked to everyone else. So why should I now rush to make known my views. I wonder if we ought not have real long hearings." Furthermore, the word from Sam Ervin was that he would have to read all of Fortas's Supreme Court decisions before he could decide. Johnson knew what that meant, and left Ervin in the opposition column.[54]

Johnson now knew the score. The keys were the deals he had made—the SACB for Dirksen, and Homer Thornberry for Richard Russell. Nothing, absolutely nothing, could happen to disturb them. But over and over, he had to think about the alarm from James Eastland: *"Now Mr. President, I know Dick Russell told you he would*

*support them, but he's not going to do it, he can't do it. I know what
the Southern Senators are going to do."* And then, hadn't he added
that even Dirksen was "acting strangely"? The Senate whales might
swim the way he wanted them to; and if they didn't, might not the
young sharks sense their disorientation and act on it? With so much at
stake, Johnson resolved to crush the insurgency in the Senate immediately.

XIII

THE
EMPIRE
STRIKES BACK

"Mr. President, according to the Associated Press, President Johnson has announced the resignation of Chief Justice Warren and his selection of Associate Justice Abe Fortas to become Chief Justice. I wish to commend President Johnson for making this selection. I wish to commend to the Senate Justice Fortas, an eminent jurist, an able lawyer, and a patriot. He will write an indelible record as Chief Justice. It is with confidence that I make such a statement and it is with pride that I commend the selection."[1]

It didn't look like a formal declaration of war. But it was. By these words, the senior Democratic senator from Tennessee, Albert Gore, announced on the floor of the Senate on June 26, 1968, a war that had been raging in covert fashion for nearly two weeks. It was the last memorable thing that the senior senator from Tennessee would do in this battle, but like Isaac Davis, the first man killed in the battle at the Old North Bridge in Concord, Massachusetts, on April 19, 1775, Gore gets credit for being there at the beginning.

The leader of the first wave of rebels, Robert Griffin of Michigan, had to be pleased with the course of the battle to this point. The support of many of his allies was mainly symbolic, but Griffin truly believed that the fight could be won. True, the amount of effort required to defeat the wishes of a Democratic president with a Senate controlled by his party, on a matter involving two sitting and respected members of the federal judiciary, would have to be massive. But time was clearly on his side. The most important thing would be to get through the next few days with his coalition intact in order to give the rest of the opposition time to realize its true interests and get organized. The petition signed by eighteen senators was a significant accomplishment, but it was a long way from the 50 percent plus one member needed to win a straight confirmation vote, or even the thirty-four votes needed to filibuster the nomination successfully.

Griffin and his allies settled on an intelligent strategy, given their small numbers and the need for time. They launched a phony war using guerrilla hit-and-run-type tactics, hoping to pick up needed support from fellow Republicans or the southern Democrats. As the front man, Griffin's job was to convince the press that the rebellion was bigger and more cohesive than it actually was. Full of bluster and seeking to maximize the visibility he had already gained in the fight, Griffin promised to "talk at length" on the appointments, claiming to have the support of "22 or 23" Republican colleagues as well as a number of Democrats who "have told me they cannot vote with me, but have said, 'Keep going.'" Had the press investigated this claim fully, they would have discovered that, in fact, a vast majority of the remaining senators on both sides of the aisles were willing, some with more reluctance than others, to let the president have his way.[2]

However, in successfully masking the lack of strength of his movement, Griffin had already made a major miscalculation in his statements. By admitting that he would accept either Earl Warren's continuing in the post until November or the return of Arthur Goldberg from his leave of absence to take the position, Griffin had already separated himself from one potential group of allies—the southern Democrats.[3] For the Michigan Republican it was the politics of the issue and not the philosophy of the Supreme Court that had importance. Thus, he failed to appreciate the true issue for his Democratic colleagues—opposition to the liberal activism of the Warren Court— and ended whatever chance *he* might have had to lead them into battle. From now on, any actions that Griffin might take would serve as camouflage for the efforts of any southern Democrats willing to take up the fight behind the scenes.[4]

However, the rest of the Republican rebels' strategy was working beautifully. Their phony war consisted of raising whatever trivial issues they could find in order to buy time for the discovery and preparation of any real issues that could unite the opposition against the president. No one took seriously the issue raised in the initial petition of the right of the lame-duck president to make appointments. After all, it was difficult to convince senators who were then clamoring for the president to make all manner of appointments in the federal bureaucracy for their own friends to say then that he was a lame duck when it came to the Supreme Court. So, as Everett Dirksen had feared with the first mention of Homer Thornberry's appointment, the rebels turned to the dreaded cronyism issue.

But Robert Griffin's claim that these appointments were "cronyism at its worst, and everybody knows it,"[5] needed much more to make it effective. Everyone understood that nearly all Supreme Court appointees are "cronies." Hadn't Woodrow Wilson picked outside adviser Louis Brandeis? And hadn't Franklin D. Roosevelt picked his poker buddy William O. Douglas, and his personal legal adviser Felix Frankfurter? Then there was Harry Truman tapping his Senate colleagues Fred Vinson and Sherman Minton, and his attorney general, Tom Clark; and John Kennedy picking his staunch campaign supporter and deputy attorney general, Byron White. So LBJ's choices of Fortas and Thornberry were right in line with a long history of such selections.[6] That being the case, what the senators were really objecting to was not just the "friends," but the president who was doing the appointing. Any friend of Lyndon Johnson was not going to be a friend of theirs.

Not even Lyndon Johnson took this charge seriously. Upon hearing about the accusation he instructed his press secretary, George Christian, "Just tell the press I wouldn't know Homer Thornberry if I saw him on the street. And as for Fortas, tell them he *never* came to the White House. Well, maybe once or twice, but it was Lady Bird who invited Carol, and Abe just came along to light her cigar!"[7] (Fortunately, the White House aide knew enough not to try a strategy that had failed so miserably when first suggested by Fortas for dealing with the Bobby Baker controversy.)

To make this charge effective, Johnson's opponents would have to prove that these "friends" were unqualified for the job. And since both men were then serving on the federal courts, with one on the

Supreme Court itself, proving a "lack of competency" was impossible. So Griffin began to consider recasting this issue as a "separation of powers" question, saying that one or both of the men had worked with the president privately in a manner that compromised their integrity on the bench. Since proof of this charge would be helpful, the search began for corroborating evidence.

While none of these earliest moves represented any kind of real threat to the appointments, as everyone debated them, the clock kept ticking. By getting the jump, the rebels controlled the early action. But they would have to do much more to sustain their momentum.

The war may not have been public, but there was already a significant casualty—Everett Dirksen. This rebellion had caught him by surprise, and he had underestimated its strength. What had at first seemed to be just another skirmish for small gains—the SACB—had turned out, coming on the heels of the open-housing-law challenge, to be potentially a battle for his political life. So Dirksen was fighting mad. He had made promises to the president, and he was determined to keep them. To do otherwise would be to admit that his power might be slipping.

Dirksen decided on a very simple strategy. If he did not take the rebels seriously, maybe no one else would either. Publicly and privately, then, he spoke with the confidence of a man who had won too many battles not to believe that he could now crush this *very* junior senator from Michigan. Presenting himself to the press as the benevolent, forgiving leader, he offered warnings and second chances to his opponents. When queried about Griffin's list of rebel names, he told one reporter, "Several of the names on that list are not going to be there" after a few days.[8] At the same time, Dirksen sent private word to the White House that the opposition was "being chipped away. . . . Let it simmer a while," he added. "We'll take care of it."[9] To listen to Dirksen, it was as though the emperor of the Senate Republicans, together with the emperor in the White House, would crush this rebellion forthwith.

Johnson set out to organize his troops, as he had done so many times before, for one last Senate battle. This would be the usual all-out Johnson legislative effort, with battles being fought on several fronts. Larry Temple, the White House liaison to the Justice Department, was set up as the coordinator of the effort. Since the White House's ability to function depended on the accuracy of the information being fed into it, the president also ordered the production of several "hard counts" of Senate votes on this issue. Various members of the administration— in this case Senate liaison Mike Manatos; the Department of Justice liaison with the Senate, Harold Barefoot Sanders; and White House aide Joseph Califano—would contact the senators or their aides, to determine each member's present position on the issue. This would give the president a picture of the level and rigidity of support.[10] It was a time-consuming process, one that was repeated sometimes hundreds of times on a given issue—even on occasion on an hourly basis. But it was the only way that the White House could know whether it was winning or losing.

These counts were not a one-way street. Frequently the administration members could relay information from the White House to friendly senators about the course of the battle. And the president could determine what the price might be for a member's support. It wasn't as effective as when Johnson could buttonhole senators as majority leader, grab them by their lapels, put his nose in their faces while towering over them, and measure their true position and value to the cause himself—but it was all that he had. And the president's troops were fully seasoned from their previous battles.

There would be more to this than just surveys, the president knew. He would have to find a way to direct the course of the public discussion from the White House. Lobbying groups and outside activists had to be mobilized. The public debate had to be directed. So during one of the bedroom details, he instructed Larry Temple to have the White House speechwriters—Harry Middleton, Robert Hardesty, and the others—"knock out a few speeches in favor of the nomination for Senators to deliver on the floor."[11] And the president also designated the Justice Department as a sort of presidential research service, responsible for developing information that could be handed to the senators, converted into persuasive speeches, and used to answer questions anticipated from the opposition. Such material could also be leaked to favored members of the press for supportive articles and editorials.

People had to stop discussing cronyism, he thought, so one of the Justice Department's first assignments was to produce two memos on Fortas's opinions, one showing that he was a "liberal activist" and the other showing that he was a "restrained conservative."[12] No one was left out when Lyndon Johnson was lobbying.

While all of these early negotiations were taking place, Abe Fortas was chafing at the bit. Accustomed to being in total control of such fights, a position that was now denied to him as a "nonpolitical" sitting justice, he had turned to his former law partner Paul Porter for help. Porter had been anxious to do whatever he could to aid in the confirmation effort. So he took charge of some of the young Arnold and Porter lawyers in setting up an "outside" command post for the gathering and dissemination of information to the legal community in order to mobilize those forces into persuading the Senate. This operation made sense for a variety of reasons. It would increase the range of contacts and contact points in the Senate, while also disguising from the press the massive lobbying effort that came from the White House. Furthermore, the talented lawyers could research legal questions and even write speeches for friendly senators to deliver, free from criticism of presidential interference in the congressional function. Finally, this operation could conduct parallel head counts to ensure the accuracy of the White House information.

Most important, though, the operation would give Justice Fortas a convenient and covert way of having input in his own defense effort, free from press discovery. While Fortas occasionally went to meetings at the White House to plan the battle with all of the allies,[13] there was no way he could do that too frequently with all the charges of cronyism flying around. So Paul Porter became a conduit between the president and the justice.

The truth was that Fortas really didn't want to be in Washington that hot summer, accustomed as he was to spending those months in Westport, Connecticut. However, Porter had seen to it that he had to stay in town more than usual. One day the previous fall, Porter had been in Fortas's Supreme Court chambers and discovered that the justice had been traveling all over the country to lecture to universities and public groups. The fees from all of these speeches helped to replace a small portion of the income he had lost by leaving his lucrative private legal practice (and then severing the Wolfson Foundation relationship) for the $39,500 a year paid to Supreme Court justices. (And, since the chief justiceship only meant an additional $500 a year, things were not going to change very soon.)

Thinking this continual lecture tour to be a waste of Fortas's time and energy, Porter had gone to the dean of American University's Washington College of Law, B. J. Tennery, and said, "How would you like a summer seminar in which Abe Fortas, the Associate Justice of the Supreme Court, would get into this whole new area of poverty law, law and public policy, law and psychiatry, and teaching methods?" What law school dean in the country could turn down such an offer? But the dean lamented there was no money in the budget to fund such a class. "Oh forget about that," Porter had said. "If Abe will do this, he won't want any money. But whatever it takes, I will see if we can fund it."[14]

After a good deal of work by Porter, the seminar had come together and Fortas was now doing his first classroom teaching since his days at Yale Law School. In early June, he began meeting with his seventeen students every Tuesday afternoon, and was now involved in the preparation of the last of three reading lists for the seminar. Porter hoped that these materials would eventually be the basis of a law textbook and perhaps even a center for the study of "Law and the Social Environment."[15] Despite the extra work, and the forced time in the city, the justice very much enjoyed the course. But for reasons known only to Fortas, this was one of those things in his private life that should be kept *private*.

Which was why he was now writing to Porter. Word had reached Fortas that the Senate Judiciary Committee might extend to him an unprecedented invitation to appear before it as a sitting justice. No news could have been worse. From his vast experience with such proceedings, Fortas understood that there was a tremendous potential for disaster here. He could be questioned and held responsible not only for all of his own actions, or whatever he could be charged with, but also for all of the actions of the Warren Court *and* of this increasingly unpopular, liberal, wartime president. With enemies of all those actions on the committee, *there was no control in such a situation.* Bound by custom and common sense to refrain from answering questions for fear of compromising later actions from the bench, the justice knew that he would have to endure a Senate inquisition dominated by probing political lords and witness appearances by every quack in America, all intent on firing off whatever rumors they could about his life. And Fortas knew only too well that some of those rumors might even be true.

Seeking to avoid this trouble, Fortas jotted down a long list of instructions to Porter on a yellow legal pad.[16] The first item on the list was simple: *"Fortas should not be asked to appear."* Could Porter call George Smathers in the hopes of securing early Judiciary Committee hearings and ensuring his absence from them? he wondered. Fortas then offered Porter two arguments to make in taking this position, arguments that the administration later did use. No sitting justice had ever appeared before such a committee hearing, and it might not be legally necessary for an associate justice to be reconfirmed for the chief justiceship.[17]

But this first plea was for the one thing in the world that Paul Porter could never have accomplished. The Judiciary Committee was James O. Eastland's bailiwick. Those hearings were going to be held on his schedule, and Fortas would be "invited" to appear.

Then, on his yellow pad, the justice jotted down a long list of people to be contacted for their support in lobbying various senators, some of the instructions developing out of conversations he had held with President Johnson. Included in this list were several members of the Jewish community who the justice believed would be willing to help. Unfortunately, the justice did not take the dangers of this latter part of the strategy into consideration.

Back on Capitol Hill, the Senate was preparing to say no to the president just twenty-four hours after the appointments had been announced. Sam Ervin of North Carolina had given the matter some thought, and quickly decided that he had little use for a Supreme Court filled with activist liberals who, in his mind, wrote their own views into the Constitution. Later, Ervin would write "Abe Fortas was a brilliant person who possessed much personal charm. However, he and I didn't hit it off together because he concluded . . . with the other judicial activists that the Constitution is a 'plaything' for the Supreme Court Justices, while I believe that the Constitution is a permanent instrument for the government of the United States and cannot be changed except by an amendment conforming to the Fifth Article."[18] So, just as he had warned, Ervin asked the Library of Congress for copies of all of Fortas's opinions.[19]

But this master of the ways of the Senate knew better than to assault the administration frontally this early on limited information. So, when the Judiciary Committee met on the June 27 to discuss the upcoming hearings, Ervin raised the phony legalistic issue of whether there was even a vacancy on the court. "If a judge wants to retire, he should retire," he told the press. Ervin wanted a definite departure date inserted in Warren's letter so that such a retirement would occur.[20]

Ervin had accomplished his task. Trying to stall for time while the opposition movement mounted, the behind-the-scenes nomination opponent James Eastland called the attorney general to inform him that he would be the hearing's first witness on July 11 to discuss the vacancy question. Worse yet, the editorial board of *The Washington Post* seemed to agree with Ervin, calling in an article for "Another Letter, Please."[21] Then, Lyndon Johnson phoned Deputy Attorney General

Warren Christopher shortly before noon on the twenty-seventh and asked him to investigate whether the form of the letter should be changed, and if not, what material could be developed to defend it. So, while the administration was off on a snipe hunt, the North Carolina Democrat worked his colleagues in searching for allies.

Everyone missed the significance of this early move. For a time the leadership of the opposition had passed from Griffin to a genuine whale in the president's own party. But this was no cause for alarm, because the news coming back to the White House was still all good.

After a long day of setting up the lobbying effort, the president and his lieutenants—Postmaster General Marvin Watson, Ramsey Clark and his deputy Warren Christopher, Paul Porter, Larry Temple, Joe Califano, Mike Manatos, and Barefoot Sanders—met in the Cabinet Room at 5:30 P.M. on the twenty-seventh to review the day's progress. Things could not be going better, they were told. Sanders, Califano, and Manatos had all started their individual head counts of the Senate, and while they were not fully completed yet, it was plain to see that an overwhelming number of senators—well above the two thirds necessary to break any filibuster—were favoring the nominations.[22] By the next day one report would indicate a 69-to-30 vote, and Sanders would call it 67 to 28 in favor of the nominations.[23]

So a good deal of time was spent in the meeting reviewing each of the senators and assigning someone from the White House, from Porter's operation, or from the "outside" to keep in close touch with them. Perhaps United Auto Workers President Walter Reuther might be able to sway Griffin? Maybe Justice William O. Douglas could keep Mark Hatfield of Oregon on the team?

Still LBJ wanted more. He knew that it would be relatively easy to handle Senator Alan Bible of Nevada, who had said earlier in the day that he hadn't gotten enough presidential appointments and "wanted some help from Texas oil people in his re-election campaign." That should be easy enough for a president from Texas to arrange.[24] Another encouraging piece of news concerned Senator Milton Young of North Dakota, one of the Griffin rebels. In response, no doubt, to the efforts of Everett Dirksen, Young was saying that he was feeling "a little ashamed of himself" for signing the petition and indicated that he might well vote for the nominations.[25] Furthermore, the Dixiecrats seemed to be splitting, with Ervin's colleague from North Carolina, B. Everett Jordan, expressing unhappiness toward those who were "popping off" in the press, and giving every indication that he would support the administration.[26]

Abe Fortas was doing his part as well. He had called the White
House earlier in the day to report that "just about all bases are covered
or are being covered." Fortas and Paul Porter had mobilized an old
friend and client, Fred Lazarus of Federated Department Stores, to
work on one of Griffin's rebels, Wallace Bennett of Utah. And a
prominent Jewish industrialist from Detroit, who also was a Republican party fundraiser, Max Fisher, was working on Griffin directly.[27]
On the justice's instructions, Porter had also finished setting up what
was now known as "the central clearing house on information and
assignments" in the Arnold and Porter law offices.

In all of the glow of apparent victory in this initial meeting, no one
seemed to notice one oddity about the votes. Manatos had a question
mark next to the name of the Dixiecrat leader—Richard Russell of
Georgia—while Califano's count had him solidly in the negative column. Even Barefoot Sanders was informing the president, "I think
there should be some doubt about Russell."[28] The next day yet
another count would insist that Russell was in the "solidly against"
column. But Lyndon Johnson knew his old friend could be counted
on—he had Russell's word on that.

In the twenty-four hours since the nominations, the die appeared to
be cast. The battle lines were clearly drawn, and each side had developed its strategy. While both sides looked for converts, they played a
giant game of bluff poker claiming imminent victory. The next few
days would give one or the other side the momentum that might well
determine the eventual winner.

To the press, everything seemed to be proceeding routinely. The
journalists were impressed by the "volley of Democratic supporting
speeches" delivered on the floor of the Senate on the afternoon of
Friday, June 28. But the outpouring of affection was not as spontaneous as it appeared. White House speechwriters Robert Hardesty
and Larry Levinson had gone far beyond the president's expectations
and drafted "a four-part dialogue" of three- to four-minute coordinated speeches for delivery by friendly senators, led by John Pastore of
Rhode Island.[29] After receiving the draft from Mike Manatos that
morning, four senators—Pastore, Majority Leader Mansfield, Stuart
Symington of Missouri, and Stephen Young of Ohio—fulfilled the
mission, with Young faithfully sticking to the exact language of the
script. It was a remarkably successful opening salvo as the White
House was able to dominate the tone and direction of the early debate,
while reinforcing the image of the opponents as ambitious politicians

acting out of crass motives. The parade of senators expressed outrage at the phony arguments raised so far against the nominations—a "lame duck" appointing "cronies" to "no vacancy"—and implored their colleagues to act on the basis of "judicial merit" rather than "partisan politics."

The Griffin group responded by announcing the addition of John Tower of Texas to their cause. No number of claims, though, could hide the plain and simple fact that, as all the media noticed, no Democrats had announced their opposition. This robbed the rebels of the appearance of nonpartisanship.[30]

So Griffin turned to Richard Nixon. Well ensconced on the presidential campaign trail, Nixon had argued that the nominations were "unwise" and should be held for the next president to make. On the other hand, his opponent Nelson Rockefeller announced support for Fortas as "an outstanding appointment."[31] (As Johnson had suspected, one of the reasons for Rockefeller's position was his need to pick up votes in the Jewish community.) But Nixon proved to be a major disappointment to Griffin's group in the early going.[32] While the Republican front-runner had a keen interest in the outcome, for him to get involved with no certainty of winning seemed foolish.[33] So Nixon did no more than offer a simple positional statement, thus angering his fellow Republicans who were engaged in the lonely fire fight.

In fact, there may well have been reasons other than politics for Nixon's silence. While Nixon would never have picked Abe Fortas for the court, there was from his perspective a very important bond between them that could not be forgotten. Nixon vividly remembered two years before, when he had been struggling to recover from his disastrous defeat in the California gubernatorial race, and had taken the controversial *Time* v. *Hill* privacy case to the Supreme Court. Only one justice had written an opinion in this case upholding everything that Richard Nixon had argued about an individual's right of privacy when confronted by a probing press—Abe Fortas. In fact, in comments that probably traveled around the Washington cocktail party circuit, Fortas said that Nixon had made "one of the best arguments that he had heard since he had been on the Court," and that, with work, he could "be one of the great advocates of our times."[34]

While Nixon lost the case, Fortas's brilliant dissent made him proud enough to feel that he had actually won it.[35] That made Fortas a friend at a time when Nixon needed friends, and it was something that the candidate was not easily going to forget. So Griffin was out of luck— for now.

With the Republicans so obviously split, the White House moved to keep the pressure on them from the outside. Labor was mobilized and doing its part. Walter Reuther of the United Auto Workers followed up on a suggestion made by Abe Fortas and sent an endorsement telegram to every member of the Senate. Then George Meany, the president of the AFL-CIO, strongly endorsed the nominations, telling the press that he "trusted that cooler heads and more mature legislators" would see through the "political maneuvering" of the few and "speedily consent to these appointments."[36] Copies of the endorsement were duly mailed to all of the senators, while the union federation's chief lobbyist, Andy Biemiller, began his own efforts to sway doubtful Republicans, beginning with George Murphy of California.[37]

At the same time the White House began to tap whole new sources of potential lobbying pressure. Calls were placed to the presidents of all the major corporations with any contact with the administration, in search of support in swaying negative or doubtful senators. Heads of corporations, especially corporations dependent on federal contracts and immunity from government audits, had good reason to be interested when called by the White House in search of lobbying help. So the first wave of calls from the White House went to members of the National Alliance of Businessmen—the presidents of Textron, Ford Motor Company, Eastern Airlines, and Aloha Airlines, among others—and received very favorable responses. Henry Ford II even promised to "work on Griffin." When combined with Max Fisher's approach to the Michigan senator, this was bound to have an impact.[38]

As if all of this were not enough, in an effort to put the fight on higher ground, the White House drummed up lobbying support from members of the federal judiciary. Through federal appeals judge Irving Goldberg, the administration got a letter to the Senate circulated among Homer Thornberry's colleagues on the Fifth Circuit Court of Appeals, which endorsed his appointment. In addition, several court-of-appeals judges agreed to contact senators from their states personally.[39] Over the next ten days, a number of federal judges on the district and appeals levels took it upon themselves individually to send letters of endorsement for Thornberry to senators from all over the country.[40]

Finally, the war in the press was continued. In an effort to establish and maintain solid support in the newspapers, contacts were made with prominent editorial writers close to the administration. Always looking for the jugular, the president had even instructed his Senate liaison aides to see if the "right" senators would respond to a *Christian Sci-*

ence Monitor poll seeking their views on the nominations. However, his aides advised against doing so, fearing leaks of the propaganda effort to the press.[41]

The strategy of this multiphased lobbying attack by the White House was simple—blitz all of the senators with information, visits, and calls supporting the nominations. This relentless pressure was designed not only to convince reluctant and negative senators, but to give the appearance of invincibility in the fight.

In the face of such pressure, the Senate rebels cried foul. "Since I've been here," claimed Californian George Murphy, "I've never seen an arm-twisting effort as well-organized or as broad as this." His cohort Robert Griffin, adding that "the White House is pulling out all the stops," complained of receiving a call from an executive at Ford Motor Company.[42] Of course, Griffin's feeling that this call had come at the behest of the administration was correct.[43]

But if Griffin had cause for complaint, then Senator Tower of Texas had the basis for a formal protest to some higher body of political etiquette. Having just switched to the opposition, John Tower was seen by the administration as more "movable," so the White House did its best to ensure that every piece of mail that his staffers opened and every phone call they received reminded the senator of his obligation to the administration. An ambassador, a prominent department store magnate, and an Austin attorney named Ed Clark were all enlisted to help Tower have a change of heart.[44] Johnson gave Clark "the responsibility for John Tower" and told him he was to report on his progress in phone calls every evening at 7 P.M.

But this was not enough. On July 1 alone, ten more prominent members of the business community—including the presidents of the Hotel Corporation of America, Eastern Airlines, El Paso Natural Gas Company, and Ling-Temco-Vought, and the former chief executive officer of Wilson Corporation—were personally at work on Tower, while also mobilizing others in their own industries and throughout the business community to do likewise. These corporate contacts were made in addition to the loosely choreographed efforts of various visitors from the White House and the Department of Justice, as well as the Porter operation, conducting head counts and seeking to exert pressure of their own.[45] Then someone suggested that the Texas Jewish community might get to Tower. But the report to the president was not promising: "No Texas Jewish leaders with influence on Tower are available. All are Birchers and anti-Abe."[46] After a while it became sort of a perverse political chain letter with the senator at the receiving end. And the pressure on Tower was typical of the pressure being brought by legions of other industrialists on other senators.

But such pressure can backfire—especially if the senators see the organized nature of it. Such was the case after a number of the White House allies contacted one of the original rebels—Wallace Bennett of Utah, who also was seen as a "movable" vote. After a while the White House was told that Bennett was being called on by "too many people."[47]

Despite all of these efforts, another warning came from James Eastland that members on both sides of the aisle were "intending to attempt a filibuster."[48] But the other evidence did not support that view in the president's mind. A report came that John L. McClellan, the Judiciary Committee member from Arkansas, would "come around if someone begs him."[49] And another Dixiecrat, Allen Ellender of Louisiana, promised to "support that nominee unless something develops that shows him to be a real scoundrel," on the theory that any president has the right to make an appointment. If this was any indication of the thinking of the others, Johnson believed, Dixie was his once again.[50]

There was, however, one dark cloud for the silver lining. Some of the southerners, such as John Stennis of Mississippi, were not prepared to make a move until they knew where Richard Russell stood. And everyone had doubts now about where he stood. Two new Senate head counts late on the evening of the twenty-eighth, one of which gave the nomination opponents thirty votes and the other only twenty-nine, placed Richard Russell in the opponents' camp. Johnson had spoken with Russell on the telephone late that morning about the nominations and received no indication of any problems, but too much had come to the president's desk for him to be absolutely certain. So the president devised a strategy to keep his old friend on the team.[51]

Despite the fact that Russell had given his word, the president was a realist, and realized that sometimes promises have to be broken. So Johnson now decided that someone from the White House should pay a call on the senator from Georgia and present some new evidence to convince him that Fortas was his man. And sitting in the pile of nomination papers on the president's desk was just the ammunition for the job. In their massive research effort over the last couple of days, producing everything from detailed memoranda on Homer Thornberry's qualifications and judicial opinions to lists proving that this lame-duck president could still appoint judges, the Justice Department staffers had produced a real gem. In a memo entitled "Some Highlights of the

Judicial Career of Mr. Justice Fortas, 1965–1968,'' they had been able to summarize selectively and quote from various opinions to paint Fortas's judicial performance as "balanced and moderate." Justice Fortas himself had helped to select just the right examples of his latent conservatism.[52] The titles of the sections alone—"Respect for Law,'' "Respect for Congress,'' and "Respect for the States"—gave the appearance that the justice was really a conservative in liberal clothing.[53] It was just the sort of legal brief that could be passed on to reluctant senators and later converted by the White House speechwriters into a text for delivery by a friendly senator on the floor.

Deciding that this was exactly what Richard Russell needed to see, Johnson told Larry Temple to review the document and "see if [there was] anything offensive" in it. Then on Monday, when Russell returned from a weekend visit to his home in Winder, Georgia, Temple and another assistant, Harry McPherson, an old family friend of Russell's, were to visit the senator and bring a copy of the document.

As he thought about it, though, Johnson realized that there was more that the aides should bring with them. Several days before, Larry Temple had suggested that there might be more evidence of Fortas's "conservatism" in his new book on civil disobedience. Intrigued by this prospect, Johnson told the aide to get started on checking it immediately so that the president could use it in the morning to lobby some members of Congress at his weekly breakfast with the congressional leadership. Using a secretary from the all-night White House typing pool, Temple drafted a memo using the appropriate extracts. (One of the prices of being a presidential aide is that the work is never done until the president says so, and this president never said so.) Since the nine pages of quotes from the book also showed Fortas to be a "man of the law," Johnson ordered that it be taken to Russell as well. The meeting with Russell would be important—the aides had no idea how important—and with this new document they seemed to have all the ammunition necessary to keep the senator on their side.[54]

The news flowing into the White House continued to be upbeat. A summary of all of the head counts given to the president at noon on the June 29 noted that there were now 61 "solid right" votes and 9 "probably right" ones, compared to only 20 "solid wrong" votes and 9 in the "probably wrong" column. There were more than enough votes here to break even a filibuster.[55]

With everything going the White House's way, it was time to consolidate the advantage. Joseph Califano ordered a speech to be drafted showing that Griffin's lame-duck argument was specious.[56] Try as they might, however, the White House aides could not seem to get this speech—which labeled Griffin's revolt "a very amateurish performance" and "an outrageously irresponsible opposition that is obviously motivated by nothing more than political expediency"—or a redrafted version that went to Senator John Pastore, to be delivered on the floor of the Senate.

Unbeknownst to the White House, a major miscalculation had been made. On Fortas's instructions, Paul Porter had escalated the phony war by creating a new issue of his own—religion in politics. Since this was the first nomination of a Jew to be chief justice, why shouldn't all of the Jewish groups be mobilized to help? So the justice told Porter to get to the most prominent Jewish member of the Senate, Jacob Javits of New York, who had promised to "help in any way he can."[57] Then Fortas stressed the need for Jewish groups to contact members of the Judiciary Committee, even going to the extent of suggesting the names of possible allies. Like the president, he felt confident that no one would fool with a hot religious issue during an election year.

Porter then succeeded in whipping up the pressure from the nation's Jewish organizations.[58] All of the local units of the B'nai B'rith were alerted to the prospect of a Senate filibuster on the nominations and the existence of "support from bigots opposed to making a Jew Chief Justice." Moreover, the head of the American Israel Public Affairs Committee, I. L. Kenen, made this a matter for the special attention of the top 150 Zionist leaders in the country.[59]

The White House was doing its part on the religion front as well. The president was telling the members of the press corps off the record that he feared the intrusion of religion into the debate, thus alerting them to *look* for the pressure that his people were initially creating.[60] During the afternoon of June 28, seventy-five Jewish leaders were briefed by White House aides on the problem. By nightfall the report to the president indicated that this group had "gotten to" Jacob Javits, and that George Murphy of California—one of the original Griffin rebels—had "felt the heat" from the huge Jewish community in southern California, which was "going all out."[61] In response, Murphy was now promising not to participate in any filibuster. All in all, one report to the president concluded proudly, "We have gotten the Jews wound up."[62]

But neither Fortas nor LBJ understood that two could play the religion game, and the other side felt no obligation to fight fair. On such occasions, no one wins, and certainly not a controversial Supreme

Court justice who was in a position of not being able to fight back with his full arsenal of weapons.

By July 1, the administration was ready to mount its major offensive. For days the Porter operation had been working on researching and drafting the first major Senate speech designed to rebuild the image of the nominees and to destroy that of the opponents by depicting them as zealous partisans.[63] The speech had been worked over by members of the White House staff, and was intended to serve as a tool for introducing into *The Congressional Record* a number of the research memoranda that the Justice Department had generated over the previous week to combat the early charges made by the rebels.

After canvassing about for a mouthpiece for the speech, the administration decided that Florida Democrat George Smathers would be best. As he was a member of the Judiciary Committee, albeit not one of the true members of the Dixiecrat faith, Smathers's delivery of this would give the press at least the appearance that the South was indeed behind the nominations. Since Smathers was not running for reelection and there was no possibility of reprisals from his constituents, it was the sort of thing he could safely do. And, having worked with Lyndon Johnson on many projects over the years, the Florida senator knew this was the sort of favor that might pay dividends down the line.[64]

So Smathers was armed much like a college debater being sent off to a tournament. In addition to the thirty-one-page speech, he was given a short memo on the biographical qualifications of Homer Thornberry,[65] and Justice Department memos on the judicial decisions of both candidates.[66] In delivering the speech and reading the memos into the *Record,* Smathers gave the appearance that there was much indeed to contradict the apparently trivial legalistic arguments of the rebels.

While arguing that he "did not embrace or endorse all of the decisions or policies of the so-called Warren Court," Smathers portrayed Fortas as a model of judicial self-restraint. "Here is one Justice, at any rate, who recognizes that in our system of government, no one branch has a monopoly on virtue and power, and that there are matters as to which Congress—and not the courts—should have the ultimate say." After discussing some of Fortas's more vivid judicial-opinion passages on behalf of conservatism, Smathers reassured the Senate that Fortas had "joined no bloc on the Court." Further, the nominee was portrayed as the "finest writer to sit on the Court since Robert Jackson."

After going on to discuss the similar fine traits of Homer Thornberry, the speech closed with a stirring conclusion: "Only rarely, in
my judgment, do nations have available to them men of quality equal
to the challenge they face. Our Nation has been fortunate. Once again,
as we enter a period in which our institutions will perhaps be put to the
sternest challenges of history, we have an opportunity to place the
Chief Justiceship of the United States in the custody of one who is
extraordinarily qualified."

Smathers's arguments seemed on their face to be airtight. He answered the lame-duck argument by asking, "Must the work of the
Court grind to a halt and the process of filling vital jobs in other
branches of Government come to a standstill because a President has
entered a second term?"[67] Then, using the Justice Department research, the speech also seemed to accuse other senators of bad faith in
that eleven confirmations of presidential appointments to the judiciary
had occurred since the March 31 announcement by Johnson that he
would not seek reelection. In response to the no-vacancy argument, he
offered several examples from the lower federal courts where resignations had been offered subject to the qualification of successors.

Given a chance to respond, the only objections that the rebels could
mount were such metaphysical questions as whether it was conceivable
that two chief justices could end up sitting on the court at the same
time, and the "chicken or egg" question of which came first, the vacancy or the nomination? While Smathers betrayed some unfamiliarity
with the material by frequently referring questioning senators to his
previous remarks, and even on one occasion misquoting his own
speech, he seemed on safe footing.

But he was not—and Howard Baker knew it: "I have no desire to
engage in a smoke-shoveling contest. I have no desire to get engaged
in the matter of legalisms. But I do not find any precedent for a conditional *acceptance* of a resignation [by a president] of a Justice or a
Chief Justice of the Supreme Court of the United States. Can the distinguished Senator from Florida cite any such precedents?" Baker was
right. The examples that Smathers had offered from the history of the
Supreme Court simply did not apply.

By raising what seemed to be an abstruse legal issue, Baker was
conducting a guerrilla war with all of the skill that his experience in
the Senate had taught him. The burden was now back on the pon-
derously slow administration bureaucracy to prove that this "conditional acceptance" by Johnson of Earl Warren's resignation had a
precedent in history.

But while the administration might be faulted for failing to have the necessary evidence on this occasion, it was not for lack of trying. Late in June, Warren Christopher had phoned for help to one of his old professors at Stanford Law School, Charles Fairman, then considered one of the nation's foremost Supreme Court historians. In a seven-page double-spaced letter filled with research on the question of past Supreme Court resignations (in which he characterized the current no-vacancy argument as "so insubstantial and Ervinesque that, as Justice E. D. White once said, 'To state the proposition is to refute it'"),[68] Fairman concluded, "What Chief Justice Warren has just done—retiring at the end of a term with effect upon the qualification of his successor—is certainly the mode of succession most in the public interest."

But Fairman had found something even more important. According to a book of memorial proceedings for Justice Horace Gray, who had left the court after suffering a debilitating stroke in 1902 to be replaced by the legendary Oliver Wendell Holmes, he had resigned "to take effect on the appointment and qualifying of my successor." This language appeared to have great similarity to the Warren "resignation effective at your pleasure" letter.

After four days of frantic searching in the National Archives, the Justice Department found the full text of Gray's resignation letter, which seemed to be even more helpful to the administration's cause: "I should resign to take effect immediately, but for a doubt whether a resignation to take effect at a future day, or on the appointment of my successor, may be more agreeable to you."[69] But the presidential acceptance letter was missing.[70]

Meanwhile, the White House tried to buy time by encouraging George Smathers with a follow-up memorandum telling him that the administration "ha[d] learned" about the Gray resignation in favor of Holmes. The memo closed with "Was the nomination of Holmes a mistake? You may be able to get some mileage out of this one." But Smathers, who had learned his lesson, did not avail himself of the offer. So the president instructed Warren Christopher to take a copy of the Fairman letter and the historical material that they had gathered to that point to Everett Dirksen in the hope that he would offer this information on the Senate floor. Having seen what had happened to Smathers, Dirksen decided to wait several days before contacting Fairman personally to get more proof on these matters.[71]

It was not until a full ten days after Baker's challenge that the Justice Department finally located a copy of the response by President

Teddy Roosevelt, and it indeed proved to be strikingly similar to what President Johnson had written: "If agreeable to you, I will ask that the resignation take effect on the appointment of your successor."[72] Then it took another two days for the Justice Department to get the material into *The Congressional Record*.[73] By then, though, it was really too late. The rebel initiative here had stalled the debate until the day of the hearings, when new lines of inquiry could be opened and new momentum generated.

But the Smathers speech was only one half of the administration's line of attack. Members of the White House staff had worked on a sort of low-road twin to the Smathers speech. Even though presidential candidate Richard Nixon was not openly aiding the Griffin forces, he provided a convenient scapegoat for attacking the partisan implications of this battle. Entitled "Will the Real Richard Nixon Please Stand Up?" the speech argued that contrary to the campaign rhetoric that the candidate was a "new Nixon," he was acting true to past form. Nixon was described as "a Dixiecrat who speaks with a Yankee accent." It was even suggested that the Supreme Court seat might be held by the conservatives for a Republican luminary such as Ronald Reagan, Barry Goldwater, or Max Rafferty, who could be appointed by a newly elected Nixon.

It was an effective bit of political *ad hominem* attack. But the White House had to find someone willing to put his name on this piece. What was needed was a maverick who was not afraid to mix it up in the corners. It was perfect for the Democratic senator from Oregon, Wayne Morse.

After their memorable fight in the Interior Department in 1943, Wayne Morse had every reason in the world to refuse to help Abe Fortas in any way. Politics is funny, though. The rule is often not "forgive and forget," but "forgive and remember." Morse proved his mettle and delivered the White House statement (without attributing its authorship) in Portland, Oregon, at about the same time as the Smathers speech in Washington, repeating the performance in the Senate a week later. Thus there was a call for confirmation from coast to coast![74]

SMATHERS AND DIRKSEN BACK FORTAS, headlined *The Washington Post*.

With the Tuesday morning newspaper on July 2 came the announcement, and now all of Washington knew it. The rebellion was over. Even the title of the account made clear how total was the victory. A nonpartisan coalition was backing the administration. And, as the paper reported, this was "the first such affirmation of the President's court selections from the ranks of the mostly silent and uncommitted Southerners." There was no place, they said, for Griffin to go for new votes.

Of course, there was always the possibility of time being stalled away by a filibuster. But Dirksen, who smelled certain and quick victory, went as far as he could in backing the president here.[75] He announced to the press that he would vote to break any filibuster that developed.[76] Later in the day the minority leader continued the domination of the headlines by announcing after the weekly Republican policy luncheon that "at least two" of the Griffin petition signers had now switched sides. A week later he would claim that four of the senators had "vanished" from Griffin's list.[77] Thus the headline could read, MAJORITY OF GOP FAVORS COURT CHOICES, DIRKSEN SAYS.

But some reporters just have a streak of skepticism, and when one asked whether the Griffin rebellion represented a challenge to his leadership, Dirksen purpled and exploded, "Don't throw that kind of tripe at me. When you write that kind of tripe, the people back home say, 'Sonny Boy's leadership is being challenged'—now that's just billingsgate and you know it. . . . I'm their leader, not their dictator. No one challenges my leadership. Nothing happens around here without me."[78] This impression of invincibility was being fostered by Dirksen's aides as well: "Young guys just don't filibuster around here. If they are foolish enough to try it, they'll find that it doesn't work. And if, by some fluke, it should work, they'll pay for it."[79]

Even the rebels sensed that they were in deep trouble. Desperately searching for any evidence that might put a chink in the elusive Fortas's armor, one of the staff members stumbled on a five-paragraph squib in a late-March edition of *The Washington Post* announcing Fortas's upcoming summer course at American University. Since every lead was worth checking out, the information was fed to the newspaper reporters in hopes that their search for a story might turn up something useful.[80]

Meanwhile, back at the White House, as he surveyed the morning papers in early July, Lyndon Johnson had every reason to be happy and confident. He had one final task he wanted to accomplish before he stepped down as president, and in his coat pocket was the proof that he would succeed: a summary of two Senate head counts telling him that Abe Fortas would be confirmed as the next chief justice of the

United States. And sitting on the president's desk for the day's reading sat a letter from the office of his great friend from Georgia, Senator Richard Russell. No doubt it was more good news, as a result of the visit of the two White House emissaries the previous afternoon.

The contents of this letter, however, stunned Johnson to the point that, by the end of the day, he had given an order so extraordinary that even the White House secretaries were second-guessing it. Suddenly in a state of alarm over the chances for Fortas's confirmation, he decided that no one must ever know the true extent of the connection between the Supreme Court justice and this president over the years. And the only evidence that existed on this issue was in the White House files. So something had to be done—immediately and secretly. And it was. The normal office bureaucratic routine was bypassed so that an order could be sent on to Norma Arata, the secretary for Senate liaison Manatos. Because of the new events, she was instructed to gather up all of the letters in the White House Central Files involving Abe Fortas in any way—*and destroy them*.[81]

But there was no control here—not for Abe Fortas or even for the president of the United States. Long ago, as Senate majority leader, Johnson had ordered the destruction of huge quantities of documents from his earlier congressional career in order to make space in his files. It made sense to everyone, so the staff had done it. But no one could know that the southern majority leader would one day become president, and that those lost files would represent the only evidence of some of the most crucial early moves of a man who belonged now to history. So the staff vowed never to destroy any documents again, no matter what Johnson told them to do.

Johnson himself encouraged this attitude. After once being chastised by Johnson for having a full wastebasket of possibly valuable papers, the impish press secretary, Bill Moyers, delivered chicken bones to a secretary the following day telling her to file them as the remains of the president's lunch that day. So much was saved that it would fill thousands of boxes in the huge Johnson presidential library.

Another time, a memo on Johnson's relationship with Robert Kennedy so angered him that he told a secretary to "tear this up and flush it down the toilet." After dutifully typing up these instructions on a small piece of paper, the secretary then stapled it to the document and sent it to the White House Central Files—where it now sits in Austin.

Besides the fact that Johnson's aides felt it was their historical duty to preserve the Johnson-Fortas documents, they also realized the sheer impossibility of carrying out such a request. In this age of photocopying machines, paper leaves a trail, especially in the huge central files of the White House. Several copies of most documents are made and dispersed to any relevant file on that subject, according to elaborate cross-referencing schemes.

Still, an order had been given, and the staff had to do something to obey. So Arata spent the summer fishing out what materials she could.[82] But she also did something else that any good secretary in the West Wing of the White House would do in these delicate circumstances: She consulted with her supervisor, head secretary Juanita Roberts. Because of her years of service to Johnson dating back to the senatorial days, Roberts well remembered the tragic destruction of those earlier files. So she told Arata "absolutely not to destroy" the files. Instead, the search was to be conducted and "after this blows over" the files were to be sent to staff archivist Dorothy Territo, who in her capacity could make the decision as to whether another mass destruction should take place. The so-called Fortas file was developed for the rest of the year, and after a while the staff began the practice of sending new material concerning the justice directly to it rather than to the central files. Long after the November election the staff was still searching for relevant material, and it was all piled up in Territo's fireproof security file. There the documents sat, many loose items in a pile, some of them bound together with huge rubber bands, until all of the papers were transferred to Austin in January of 1969. And what they showed would surprise even the most cynical observer of the court.

XIV

THE
SCARLETT
LETTER

Phyllis Bonano couldn't stop laughing. Frankly, when she told the other White House secretaries what she had just seen, they had to admit it was pretty funny, too. Here it was, just after 10:30 in the morning in the place where something new and exciting was always happening, and once again here was something nobody could remember ever having seen before. But what the White House secretary saw that day wasn't funny. It wasn't funny at all. And there was no way she could have known how serious things had become.[1]

Even head secretary Roberts couldn't believe it when she heard about it. There they were—the most powerful political figure in the world and two of his most trusted assistants—sitting in the Oval Office and not one of them could dial the telephone. All that knowledge, all that education, all that power, and Lyndon Johnson, Larry Temple, and Tom Johnson seemed to be incapable of getting an outside phone line. Lyndon Johnson was cursing a lot, but even that didn't help. Of course, they all knew he could have asked for the secretaries to get the White House switchboard to place the call, but he chose not to. It was a funny scene—but only to those who didn't know what was really going on.

What made it even funnier was the legendary love that Johnson had for the telephone. He was on the phone for what seemed like the entire day. There were tales of him as a senator standing in front of a row of pay phones with all the receivers off the hooks. Whenever anyone approached with the intention of using one, Johnson warned the would-be caller off by saying, "Don't touch those, I have a call working on all of them." There were other tales of him as president roaring into someone else's office, grabbing the phone—Johnson always grabbed the phone, never just picked it up—right out of the hands of a poor secretary who was talking on it at the time. Then he would disconnect the other bewildered party and dial his own number.[2] Yes, Johnson loved the telephone, but not today. So Phyllis Bonano was called in to show these important men how to get an outside phone line.

The truth was that the president wanted to make a phone call without his office staff knowing where he was calling. And Johnson didn't have time to be embarrassed the morning of July 3, 1968. He was worried—very worried. Worried enough to give his staff the order to begin burying all the documents concerning Abe Fortas. And worried enough to do something else to frustrate the historians of the future. He was looking at the letter that had arrived on his desk early the previous day, the one that the White House had spent all of yesterday trying to deal with, and he wanted to make sure no one else saw it— ever again. More important, he wanted to tell his correspondent that everything would be all right. He hoped.

That was why he had such trouble with the phone. Of course he could have had the secretaries place the call, but then it would have been recorded in the president's diary. And this was a call he didn't want on the books. Disaster had struck the good ship Lyndon Johnson, and the president was going to try to plug the hole all by himself.

When Richard Russell got on the line, the senator knew he now held all of the cards.[3] "Dick," the president began, "I have your letter here in my hand. I don't think this letter reflects creditably upon you as a statesman. I don't think it reflects very well upon me as your President. I don't think it reflects very well on our long friendship. I just don't think that it is the kind of letter that I want to have in my file for historians to see. . . . I'm going to send it back to you. I'm not going to make a copy of it. . . . [And] I hope you'll destroy it. Whatever you do with it is your decision, because it's your letter. It's not mine. I don't want it, and I don't want to have it in my file."[4]

"Fine, send it to me" was all the response that Russell could manage, because the president had much more that he wanted to say. But as he listened, Russell knew that for this president, who spent so much of his time sorting through photographs and saving files to secure his place in history, to say that he did not want such a pivotal letter in his files meant that it must have hit its mark. So the senator decided that when his letter arrived back on Capitol Hill, he would destroy it.

When he finished with Russell on the phone, Johnson handed the letter back to his deputy special counsel, Larry Temple. The young assistant was troubled by the letter as well, but for quite a different reason. He had been in charge of Russell's bombshell since its arrival at the White House. As he waited now for the president's written response to Russell to be completed, Temple knew the senator's letter had historic importance. So Temple gave some brief thought to making a copy of it for the files. But he had his orders, and he had been hired to serve Lyndon Johnson, not history. If this was what the president wanted to do with the letter, then Larry Temple would do it.*

"Dick Russell nominated me for every honor and position I have ever attained," Johnson always told people. Of course it wasn't strictly true—little that the president said ever was unexaggerated—but it showed everyone how much Johnson valued this friendship. The senator from Winder, Georgia, was, he told everyone, "the dearest friend he had in the Senate."[5]

And what a friend to have. As the only man in history to serve in the Senate for more than half of his life, Russell was seen as the "senator's senator." There was no limit to his power, and no effort to reform the body to reduce the power of senior members could touch him. Others were limited to running only one major committee; Rus-

---

*But like his response to Russell's letter, Johnson's decision on the disposition of it came too late. Fourteen years later, after being told that all subsequent efforts to locate the letter both in the massive Johnson Library files and in those of the Richard Russell Library had failed, this researcher made one more effort to find it. Sometimes you just get lucky. A search through some seemingly unrelated boxes in the so-called Larry Temple files of the Johnson Library uncovered not one but four photocopies of what seemed to be a very hostile letter from the senator to Lyndon Johnson in July 1968. When Larry Temple, now practicing law in Austin, Texas, saw the letter, his face lit up and the years of self-doubt about this incident were over. "This is absolutely the letter. I can verify its authenticity! Well, I'll tell you, I'm delighted it's there. But I am curious as to how it got there. I can't tell you how much thought I gave to making a copy of the letter, and wanted to make a copy, and decided that it wasn't my prerogative to make a copy because the president told me not to do it."

sell by luck and design ran *two* of the most powerful: the Armed Services Committee, which he had headed for fifteen years already, and the Appropriations Committee, where, by reason of the infirmity of the even older Carl Hayden of Arizona, he was seen as the working "president" to Hayden's "chairman of the board." Others were limited to membership on only two major standing committees, but Russell served on three (the Committee on Aeronautical and Space Science being the third), not to mention his ranking membership on the Joint Committee on Atomic Energy. And others stood by and watched the action, while Russell controlled policy through his longtime membership on the Democratic Policy Committee and controlled committee assignments through his membership on the Democratic Steering Committee. Others complained about defense spending, while Russell, through his chairmanship of the Defense Appropriations Subcommittee, governed the military spending budget.

But it was not these roles that had compelled Lyndon Johnson and four other presidents to "go see Dick Russell." Everyone knew Russell could deliver with a simple nod of his bald head the votes of the conservative southern Democrats. Since in 1968 that meant the fourteen votes that could ensure the confirmation of Abe Fortas, in Lyndon Johnson's parlance that made Russell "the principal whale" in the Senate.[6]

Both men well knew that by all rights, it should have been Russell who made it to the White House. But Russell had little time or reason for lamenting his fate. He was the political wunderkind from Georgia, a man who had built his career by attempting the impossible and succeeding. By age thirty-three, when he ran for the Georgia governorship in 1930, Russell had already served ten years in the Georgia House of Representatives, four of them as its Speaker. After borrowing four thousand dollars to campaign, he traveled around the state in his beat-up Oldsmobile, and promised that if the voters sent him to the governor's mansion he would deliver them from the Depression. They did, and he did. Russell streamlined the state government from 102 agencies and departments into 18 (even throwing his own father off a state board). He also reformed the budget process, the education system, and the farming community. After only two years in the governor's mansion, he successfully ran for the Senate in 1932 to fill the unexpired term of the late W. J. Harris. Only death thirty-eight years later would return him permanently to Winder.

Russell set out to show the people in the nation's capital what the people of his state had already learned: He was accustomed to doing

the improbable. He prepared for his new senatorial role by memoriz-
ing the United States Constitution, the Declaration of Independence,
and the Senate's forty rules of procedure (as well as arranging for
special tutoring from the Senate parliamentarian). When, as the youngest man in the Senate, he was asked what committee assignments he
desired, Russell asked for Appropriations.[7] But that potent committee
was only for more senior members, he was told, and there was a long
list of people waiting for the next seat. So Russell said that if he
couldn't be on Appropriations, he didn't want to serve on any committee. The thought of another Huey Long, the reformist senator from
Louisiana who was then terrorizing the Senate club while not serving
on any committee, was too much for the others to bear. So Russell was
put on Appropriations, and in his first year chaired its Subcommittee
on Agriculture.

From there he continued to do the unexpected. When told that a
national school lunch program could not pass, Russell funded it for a
number of years by adding the appropriation to one of his agriculture
bills until he could sponsor the final legislation in 1936. Even though
he was only the junior senator from Georgia, he also was charged with
floor-managing key New Deal legislation, such as one bill creating the
Rural Electrification Administration and another establishing the Farmers Home Administration. Accused of being a flaming Rooseveltian
New Dealer, Russell said firmly, "I'm a reactionary when times are
good. In a depression, I'm a liberal."[8]

The southern bloc of Democratic senators agreed with that and by
1944 made him their leader. By the early 1950's this meant that he
could deliver as many as nineteen or twenty votes on any given bill.
But it was more than just votes that Russell could deliver. Through the
benefits of their long years of seniority the southerners, and thus Russell, now controlled nearly all of the committee chairmanships, and
most of the subcommittees of the powerful Appropriations Committee.

Russell had developed a quiet but effective compromising style. A
courtly, self-effacing man, he valued honor above all things. Only
when he was pushed too far would the terrible flashes of temper appear. After witnessing so many of Russell's legislative successes, one
colleague commented, "No major compromise can be concluded in
the Senate without submission to his professional hand. His role as
compromiser was once pithily characterized as that of the man who
says the blessing over the legislative wine."[9] He was just the sort of
man who should have been majority leader of the Senate, if not presi-

dent of the United States. But instead, he helped his protégé, Lyndon Johnson, to attain those posts.

By the time Johnson became president, the nature of his relationship with Russell depended somewhat on the time of year and the issue involved. "I think they reminded me at times, looking at it from one side . . . of maybe my six-year-old son and his playmates," said one aide who observed them at close range. "When they were thick, when they were friendly, they just couldn't be on better terms, but when they were at odds they virtually pouted in their relationship with each other."[10]

By 1965, Johnson needed Russell more than ever. He used him as a sounding board on all issues, most importantly on the problems of Vietnam. Every month or so Russell would stop off on his way to the Capitol for an off-the-record private breakfast in the second-floor dining room of the White House.[11] Just as often Johnson, who loathed eating alone, would invite Russell at the last minute for a late-night dinner. The meetings not only gave Johnson a chance to talk to someone he trusted, but served as a marvelous source of information on the Senate and its members.

Because of the battles over civil rights, the burgeoning federal bureaucracy, and the problems of Vietnam (which Russell was now calling "one of the great tragedies of our history") though, there was more to divide them than unite them.[12] Repeatedly, the old senator would tell his constituents, "Well, you know, I had a very close relationship with the President when he was in the Senate and when he was Vice President, but I don't have that same relationship now."[13]

Of course, the largest source of disagreement between them these days was the issue of civil rights.[14] But Russell knew he was fighting against the tides of time. "We're winning the battles," he would say, "but we're losing the war." He had opposed his former protégé on the historic Civil Rights Act of 1964, containing the revolutionary public accommodations provisions. This time, after an eighty-three-day filibuster—the longest continuous debate in Senate history—the southerners were broken by a cloture vote.[15] So disappointed was Russell by these events that when Johnson was nominated for a full presidential term, he arranged to be off inspecting foreign military bases in Western Europe during the entire campaign.

The first public indications of the strain between the two men came when Russell split from the administration on Vietnam. In 1965, after a lengthy hospital stay and recuperation from emphysema, Russell appeared on a live news interview program and said that he now believed that the North Vietnamese would probably win a fair election if one were held in that country. The protests from the White House came fast and furious.[16] Over the next three years, Russell continued to make clear in the press his personal distaste for the administration's Vietnam policy. "I don't buy this so-called domino theory," he told *New York Herald Tribune* White House correspondent Douglas Kiker in 1966. But since Johnson had inherited the fight, Richard Russell would follow a very different course of action. "I wouldn't fight this kind of one-handed war. The only thing to do is punish North Vietnam until they're willing to negotiate."[17]

Still the basic thirty-year friendship endured, as evidenced by Johnson's extraordinary and well-publicized attendance at the funeral of Russell's nephew, court-of-appeals judge Robert Russell, in 1965—a kindness that the senator never forgot.[18] And there is much that a president can do for a close friend in public life. Due to Russell's apparent political vulnerability after his long illness in 1965, the popular governor of Georgia, Carl Sanders, was ready to challenge for his Senate seat. Politically, Russell seemed to be in deep, deep trouble.

But in the face of "the toughest fight of his political life," Richard Russell always knew that he had one friend in Washington—Lyndon Baines Johnson. So, after a timely private dinner with the president, the embattled senator proudly announced to the press that a new $2.2 billion contract to build the C5A transport plane had just happened to land in the state of Georgia. Once more Russell ran unopposed, and was able to serve out the remainder of his years in glory in the Senate.[19]

By 1967, though, the split between Russell and Johnson on defense policy was a vast one. As a senator, Russell could afford to be more hawkish than the president. Generally, he tried to keep his disagreements with the White House behind closed doors. But the exceptions now came more frequently. After repeatedly urging Johnson in private to bring the battleship *New Jersey* out of mothballs and return it to active duty bombarding military targets in North Vietnam, Russell took his case to the Senate floor in April. He argued that this would be cheaper and more effective than the saturation bombing technique favored by the administration (not to mention safer for the American troops).[20] Soon thereafter, the battleship was reactivated by Defense Secretary McNamara (only to be decommissioned by the next administration in one of its first actions).

But Russell was not an unregenerate hawk, and on occasion he rebuked the administration for going too far. Just three months later, Russell again took to the floor to complain about the White House's foreign policy in the Belgian Congo. Cocking his head in what everyone knew to be his "no nonsense" pose, Russell angrily pounded his fist on his desk, denouncing the sending of three military planes to intervene in a rebellion there. Though he and the public had been told the planes were not for military use, Russell discovered that they were in fact shipping troops around the country to fight the rebels. Seeing this as the possible beginning of a new Vietnam, Russell gave a powerful speech against foreign incursions by American troops. Within minutes, as unlikely a group of allies as conservative John Stennis of Mississippi and maverick, dovish liberal J. William Fulbright of Arkansas rose to join in the protesting chorus of round-robin critical speeches. Then Russell drove the knife in even further by taking what was for him the extraordinary step of going up into the gallery to make a statement for the television and radio networks.[21]

The reaction to such a call was immediate. In the *Washington Star*, cartoonist Gib Crockett, in a frame titled "Doing the Cong," portrayed a dancing line with Johnson at the head and Senators Fulbright, Mansfield, and others, led by Russell, all lined up behind him and kicking him in the rear. Russell was so delighted by the portrait that he had an aide call up for the original, only to find out that the White House staff had already beaten him to it. When told that he could still get a copy, Russell demurred: "Well, I don't much like the idea of the White House knowing that I'm interested in getting a cartoon involving the President and myself with me and my foot in the rear end of the President."[22]

By 1968, though, the ravages of time had taken their toll on the physical and political powers of Russell. He was, as everyone could see, a dying man. His voice was a raspy whisper, and he was forever short of breath. So badly scarred were the linings of his lungs from his early days of heavy smoking that oxygen containers were kept in his office. The long working days had been reduced to three- to four-hour stretches, and soon he would be reduced to riding around the Senate halls in an electric cart.

Politically, he was waning as well. His once powerful group of eighteen or so senior conservatives was now down to a shaky group of fourteen.[23] No longer did these men hold a death grip on the leadership positions in the committees, as a result of all the recently enacted reforms.[24]

This lack of vitality seemed only to increase the distance between Russell and Johnson. The senator became increasingly pessimistic about the future of America. And it gave him the chance to nettle the president further. During the fiery riots in Washington after the assassination of Martin Luther King, Jr., in the spring of 1968, Russell returned to his office from a White House meeting only to discover that none of the soldiers ringing the Capitol building were armed.

So he picked up the phone and called Johnson: "Mr. President, I appeal to you as Commander in Chief to arm these soldiers who are supposed to be guarding the Capitol. We've got a lot of national treasures in there, and they can't do anything if the Capitol is stormed." An hour later, the soldiers on the Capitol steps received their supply of ammunition.[25]

As his legendary career was winding down, however, there was one more favor that this dying old friend was asking of the president. And it was such a small thing that he had every reason to expect to get it. Russell wanted to see his good friend Alexander Lawrence on the federal courts.

The matter began innocently enough in the spring of 1967 when Frank Scarlett, a judge on the federal district court in southern Georgia, wrote the president that due to his advancing age and poor health he wished to retire and be put on senior judge status, a sort of judicial semiretirement. Interestingly, Scarlett wrote that he wished to take this action "subject to the appointment and qualification of his successor."[26]

The selection process for federal district court judges proceeds very much like the one for the Supreme Court. Potential nominees are screened by the Justice Department, the Federal Bureau of Investigation, and the American Bar Association's Standing Committee on the Federal Judiciary. These reports are then transmitted to the attorney general, who prepares the nomination files and sends them to the White House. At the end of this process the president, or one of his assistants, reviews the files and the nomination is announced.[27]

However, there is one big difference between this process and that for the Supreme Court. Since the Senate has an "advise and consent" function to confirm the appointments, over the years the practice has developed that senators of the president's party, from the state with the vacancy, effectively make the selection of district court judges. On the rare occasion that a president ignores the practice, a senator is likely to invoke senatorial courtesy, saying that he or she finds an otherwise

suitable nominee to be "personally obnoxious" and worthy of rejection. In the clublike atmosphere of the Senate, this action spells doom
for a nomination.

Lyndon Johnson's White House knew these rules well, and was not
inclined to ignore the recommendation of a name for the federal district court by *any* Democratic senator, let alone the senior senator from
Georgia.

It was Richard Russell's right to make the nomination for Scarlett's
seat, and everyone knew it. He and the other Democratic senator from
Georgia, Herman Talmadge, had divided up the judicial patronage in a
way that gave Russell control over the Southern District, Talmadge
control over the Middle District, and both of them alternate control in
the Northern District.[28] Since Russell's first nominee for the position,
Mac Barnes of Waycross, Georgia, had withdrawn his candidacy after
developing a case of terminal cancer, he settled on a man from Savannah named Alexander Lawrence, Jr.

Some people might have called Lawrence a crony of Richard Russell's.[29] Russell had known Lawrence all of his life, having worked
with his father, a prominent member of the Democratic party in
Chatham County, Georgia. The two older men were so close that Russell named his son after Lawrence senior. Quite naturally, when the
younger Lawrence showed an interest in politics, he developed a real
appreciation for the legendary Russell. He was a "fervent supporter"
in Russell's races for the governorship in 1930 and for the Senate in
1932. When Russell made a brief run for the presidential nomination
in 1952, Lawrence traveled to Washington to offer his help. And in
1966, when Carl Sanders challenged Russell's Senate seat, Lawrence
offered advice on the political conditions in Chatham County.

So, when the district court seat unexpectedly became available
again, Russell was happy to be able to tell Lawrence in mid-February
1968 that his nomination had been forwarded to the president. Everyone in Georgia knew that was tantamount to taking the oath of office,
because the next steps were assured.

Lawrence's eminent qualifications seemed to guarantee that fact. A
Phi Beta Kappa graduate of the University of Georgia, he had served
as president of the Georgia Bar Association and just about every service organization in the state at one time or another. Moreover, he
served on both the steering and executive committees for the Georgia
Democratic party.

As if this were not enough, Lawrence was also a respected legal
historian, having written numerous articles and five books. Even here

his leadership traits were displayed, as he had served for years on the state historical commission and twice as president of the Georgia Historical Society. It was not surprising that Lawrence was frequently in demand around the state to give talks on matters of law, history, and politics to a variety of groups.[30]

When the nomination letter was sent to the White House on February 13, Russell was so confident of the outcome that he did two unusual things. First, to demonstrate his absolute commitment to Lawrence, he broke tradition and sent this single name rather than a "short list" of candidates to the White House. Then, forgetting his policy never to announce the name of a nominee publicly prior to the official appointment for fear that a breakdown in the appointment process might result in embarrassment for the candidate, Russell confirmed to the press that Lawrence was his man. This public announcement put the senior senator in the position of either securing that appointment and confirmation, or admitting that his days as a successful legislator were coming to a close.[31]

For the first month, everything went according to form. The informal ABA report indicated that Lawrence was "well-qualified" for the position. Then the FBI was launched on its personal character investigation. But no sooner did that start than the problems began.[32]

The president of a local council on human relations, the Reverend James Hooten, protested in a letter to the White House that while Lawrence described himself as a "moderate—in all things," he was in the council's opinion a "segregationist with extreme views."[33] While Russell's staff saw this as a "little objection by this crackpot . . . radical preacher" who headed up a splinter group, in fact Hooten represented a snowball that started to roll into an avalanche.[34]

After doing some research, Hooten and his group had found what they believed to be the "smoking gun" in proving their case against Lawrence. Speaking on November 12, 1958, before a "patriotic women's group" called the Magna Charta Dames, on "The Modern Garb of Tyranny," Lawrence had attacked the Warren Court. "Tyranny is always versatile," he said. "It has ridden with the sword; it has borne the scepter; we have seen it in cassock; it has carried the mace. Today it appears in new garb—black robes." It was desegregation efforts, such as the recent battle in Little Rock, Arkansas, that were most tyrannous to Lawrence. Then, referring to members of the Supreme Court as unrestrained "zealots" who now "rule[d] by uncontrollable will," Lawrence called for a search for the means to "impose some measure of restraint on the Supreme Court . . . [where] judicial independence has become judicial arrogance."[35]

Such virulence was right in line with national public opinion about the court's decisions in 1958. Indicative of this unhappiness was the so-called Brune Report, signed by thirty-six state chief justices, which vehemently criticized the Supreme Court for playing the "role of policy maker without proper judicial restraint." And as one would expect, this opposition was especially evident in the South. In fact, so taken was Senator Russell with the address that he had it reprinted in *The Congressional Record,* calling it "one of the ablest deliverances on the situation which prevails in the United States today."[36]

But to the civil rights groups in 1968, this made Lawrence an avowed segregationist, if not an outright racist. Very soon after their initial attacks, the press began to pick up the theme and develop new evidence against the man. An editorial in the *Atlanta Journal* called Lawrence "A Man Who Baited the Courts." Not only had reporters discovered that Lawrence had voted for open segregationists such as James Gray and Lester Maddox for governor, but they had confirmed that he still "stood by" the 1958 speech. The next day, the *Atlanta Constitution,* in an editorial entitled "LBJ Must Judge," picked up on this theme arguing, "It is not good enough just to be some senator's friend."[37] Shortly thereafter, the Georgia state chapter of the NAACP sent a telegram to the president "vehemently oppos[ing]" the nomination of Lawrence.[38] However, with Russell backing the selection, all that these groups could do was hope that someone on the Johnson team would listen.

That someone turned out to be Attorney General Ramsey Clark. The White House had dropped its questions after hearing from Senator Russell in early April that he considered the appointment "a must."[39] Russell had now made it his personal fight. After telling Lawrence to "stand his ground" in the face of the negative publicity as he "intended to do everything within [his] power to see that his nomination comes to the Senate and is confirmed," Russell had asked prominent attorneys in the state to use their connections to get an early reading on the ABA report. Using this advance information, the senator intended to go "over the head of the Attorney General to the President."[40]

But the attorney general had witnessed too much to let it go at that. As a member of the Justice Department in the Kennedy administration, Clark was fully aware of the disastrous failures in the early 1960's to staff the lower federal courts in the South with liberals. Time and again, the Kennedy administration had accepted nominations from key Senate Dixiecrats of outright racists for the courts, knowing that this was the price that would have to be paid to the powerful men who at the time held a death grip on all of the key committees in that body. Perhaps the worst case was the acceptance of Judiciary Committee Chairman James O. Eastland's nomination of his old college roommate, William Harold Cox, to the federal bench, where he turned out to be an obstructionist, bigoted conservative, once likening blacks to "chimpanzees."[41] Soon, prominent members of the ABA were moved to consider taking action against him.[42] Indeed, even the man whose vacancy was at issue, Frank Scarlett, had tried to reverse the *Brown* school desegregation decision from his position. The pain of these appointment failures was made even more acute by the fact that the Kennedy administration had adopted a strategy of solving the civil rights problem by litigation rather than legislation.[43]

But there was a way that the Kennedy liberals eased their consciences. They became staunch believers in the "Hugo Black legend," hoping that like the famous liberal Supreme Court Justice who had reversed his philosophical views since his days in the Ku Klux Klan, these new appointees would also change their stripes following their acceptance of life tenure on the courts. Time and time again, though, they were doomed to disappointment.

Ramsey Clark preferred not to leave such matters to chance. He had decided that whatever personal views Lawrence might now hold, professionally he could not be relied upon to enforce a policy of integration. So Clark would actively oppose him.

By mid-April, Senator Russell was beginning to wonder about his appointment, and decided to put his request to the attorney general in person. Clark agreed to consider the matter, and told Russell he would render a decision "in a few days."[44] In fact, the attorney general had already made his decision and was prepared to put it to the president in very blunt terms. "Mr. President," Clark began in a later Oval Office meeting on the subject, "I know that this is important to Senator Russell, and I know that he wants this man appointed, but we're receiving a lot of opposition from minority groups." After explaining the nature of the opposition, Clark reminded the president that appointing a segregationist to a southern court would surely impair the implementation of all the legislation that the administration had been passing in the area of civil rights. Moreover, while this might seem to be just a single appointment to a district court, it was really much more than that. Symbolically, it would cast doubt on the administration's entire court policy. Even worse than that, he added, the Court of Appeals for the Fifth Circuit, which covered southern Georgia, was at that time evenly balanced between segregationists and integrationists, meaning that the decisions of a segregationist district court judge might be upheld if Lawrence turned out to be what the NAACP feared.

But Clark had a plan. He argued that the final formal report from the ABA would probably not approve Lawrence because of his advanced age and potentially damning speech. So why not delay until then?[45]

This put Lyndon Johnson in a very tough position. Philosophically, Clark had persuaded him. Knowing that judicial appointments would affect the legal system long after the end of his tenure in the White House, the president felt a special responsibility to preserve his civil rights legacy to the South by promoting it in the courts. Moreover, it was not the president's practice either to force a cabinet officer to move against his will or to act alone contrary to recommendations—especially the recommendations of Ramsey Clark.[46]

On the other hand, politically speaking, the president desperately needed Richard Russell, and Richard Russell was demanding this appointment. In a situation like this, Johnson took the obvious route—he stalled. But his ambivalence at this time was not an indication of strict neutrality on the issue. He was leaning toward the senator at the moment. Telling Clark that Russell "was the dearest friend he had in the Senate," the president added that he "didn't want to do anything with the federal judiciary and the critical problems that they faced in the area of desegregation." Then, reversing his field, he explained that he did not want to offend the powerful senior senator from Georgia. "If we come to the final conclusion that we can't appoint him," the president said, "then we'll come to that conclusion. We'll cross that bridge. But if there's any way at all that we can posture this man in a way that he can be appointed without hampering the judiciary, without doing anything to undermine the judiciary, I want to do it. I want to appoint this man."[47]

Richard Russell, however, had waited long enough. When he did not hear from the attorney general by Saturday, May 4, as promised, the senator decided to take the issue directly to the man in charge. Calling the White House at noon, he asked for five minutes of the president's time, and immediately got a seventy-five-minute luncheon meeting in the Oval Office in which the two old friends had what the diplomats call "a frank exchange of views." The president asked aide James Jones to bring in the voluminous Lawrence file and listened to all of Russell's arguments. Then they discussed at length the contents of the White House's file and the nature of the opposition in Georgia. The president argued, "Well, I can't nominate him because if I do the Attorney General is going to resign." To which the Georgian visitor responded, "Well, Mr. President, that's the best thing that could happen to your Administration." Later Russell added, "Are you President or is Ramsey Clark?"[48]

Seeing his visitor's agitation, Johnson searched for a way to appease him. First, he told the senator to write him a letter incorporating all of his views that Johnson could use in speaking once again to Clark. Then Johnson told him to check back with Alexander Lawrence about the 1958 speech, since that seemed to be the most damaging evidence against what had been an otherwise exemplary legal career. Finally, the president promised that Ramsey Clark would be sent to talk with Russell in the hope that he might be persuaded.

The plan didn't work quite the way the president had in mind. Russell's legislative assistant forwarded a long letter to the White House answering all of the objections raised by the Justice Department to the Lawrence appointment. According to this brief, Lawrence had told the aide "that if he is appointed he will follow the Supreme Court decisions regarding segregation because those decisions are now the law of the land and a District judge is bound to follow those decisions." Of course, further word that Russell was "very anxious" for the appointment to go forward made the president even more inclined to give Lawrence the benefit of the doubt.[49]

But it was not enough for Ramsey Clark. When the White House relayed the new information to the attorney general, he promised only to check into the matter further. But his investigation yielded nothing to change his mind. Not only were the civil rights groups prepared to continue the fight, the army of opponents had now swelled to include a number of religious figures, young Georgian attorneys (who were less inclined to be protectors of the "old boy" legal network in Chatham County), several members of the national press, and a court-of-appeals judge.[50] To them, the speech indicated that Lawrence would retard progress on the civil rights issue.[51]

But now there was more. The Justice Department had heard that Lawrence, as a member of the exclusive thirteen-member intellectual discussion group known as the Madeira Club, had once said "that the only way to solve the race problem is to get rid of the Negroes."[52] It no longer mattered what the Russell staff dug up—Ramsey Clark decided that he was absolutely not going to let his Justice Department send this nomination to the White House.

Having made that determination, Clark was now prepared to give his formal answer to Richard Russell. At 11:15 A.M. on May 11, Clark told the senator that he would not recommend Lawrence's appointment because "to millions, it would mean that segregationist judges are still being appointed in 1968." This appointment would be a symbol of the Johnson administration's view on civil rights, and after the judicial appointment failures of the early Kennedy administration, "something better must be offered in 1968." Finally, it mattered little to him whether Lawrence had promised to follow the letter of the law, because Clark found such a claim to be "doubtful" and also maintained that "the general public would have no opportunity to know after the initial appointment how well the judge might do."

Philosophically, Clark was on absolutely solid ground, and had built a very convincing case against the appointment. This was the late 1960's, when race riots had spread from Watts to Detroit to within blocks of the White House lawn. But politically the attorney general was in trouble. No argument from the ultraliberal attorney general could convince Richard Russell that Alexander Lawrence should not be a federal judge. Telling Clark that he was "surprised, distressed and disappointed" at what he had heard, Russell said he was "somewhat confused" by it as well, and shortly before noon that day he prepared to wage war on the White House.

Now it was a matter of personal honor to Russell, and Clark's decision was a reflection on him as well as the candidate. After all, *he* had *personally* vouched for Lawrence to the president. And hadn't the president indicated in their meeting on May 4 that he had every intention of eventually making the appointment? Now he was apparently taking the word of Ramsey Clark over Richard Russell's.

So Russell issued a warning to the administration. He told Clark if the appointment was not made he would be "deeply hurt," and "would never feel the same about" the president.

It was time for Johnson to choose between the two positions. But Johnson was not ready to move just yet. Instead, he instructed Clark to launch another investigation and to inform the senator that he was doing so.[53]

Johnson needed time to find a way out. Typically, he began to seek the counsel of trusted advisers outside the administration. As if by reflex, he told his staff to "check it with Abe." Who better than his favorite Supreme Court justice to decide how to proceed on a lower federal court appointment? Characteristically, Fortas listened to all of the arguments and then developed the position best protecting the political interests of the president—side with the powerful Richard Russell. This might be "considered a bad appointment," he argued, "except for the fact that Senator Russell is involved." As a practicing "liberal," Fortas said that he "would not be outraged if the President went ahead with this appointment." While the attorney general's courage was to be commended, this was a "reasonable price to pay for the essential good will" of Russell. Finally, while the arguments against Lawrence's appointment were "distressing," Fortas did not think that enough of a case had been made "that the good relationship between Russell and the President should be destroyed."[54]

However, matters had already gotten out of control. An increasingly anxious Senator Russell had decided to make one last-ditch effort to turn Lyndon Johnson around. He sent a four-page single-spaced letter reviewing all of the phases of the controversy. After going over familiar ground, Russell matched the smoking gun of the 1958 speech with one of his own. Eight years earlier, he told the president, Lawrence had given a presidential address before the Georgia Bar Association that "vigorously attacked" the Ku Klux Klan, and in it he had said, "The open and organized existence of bands of men hooded or unhooded for the purpose of intimidation of the weak is an unspeakable thing under the government of laws in the mid-twentieth century." The challenge for Johnson, then, was to decide which Lawrence was the real one—the KKK opponent of 1950, or the segregationist of 1958.

In the final paragraph, Russell made clear that he was now putting their friendship on the line: "I have never made a personal appeal to you for a Presidential appointment since you have occupied the exalted position of President of the United States. In this instance, however, where only a local appointment is concerned and a man of great competence and high character has been suggested, I feel justified in insisting most respectfully that you send Mr. Lawrence's nomination to the Senate."[55] Johnson knew now that there was no alternative to making the appointment. He would just have to find a way to corner the attorney general into saying yes.

For Johnson, the problem's solution seemed to lie with the American Bar Association. A highly positive report from the ABA might convince Ramsey Clark, who had been arguing that the organization would not give one. So, in an extraordinary move, Johnson met in the Oval Office with the chairman of the association's Standing Committee on the Federal Judiciary, Albert Jenner of Chicago. Knowing that the ABA usually conducted its investigation through a local attorney,

Johnson told Jenner, "I don't want to do that in this case. This is of such importance that I'd like to ask you to go down to Georgia. I want you personally to conduct this investigation, and find out what the situation is, find out what all the facts are and make a recommendation to me. I'm not trying to get you to prejudge it here. I'm telling you I want to appoint this man, but by telling you that, I'm not trying to make the decision for you. But I want you to be fair, and I want you to be thorough." So Jenner agreed to undertake the investigation on his own. There could be little doubt what the president hoped he would find.[56]

Meanwhile, Russell's former aide Tom Johnson, who was now deputy press secretary to the president, tried to keep the lines of communication open to the senator. Russell agreed to send Johnson a list of one hundred names of Lawrence's associates that the FBI could use in its further investigations. Then after reasserting how "very strongly" he felt about the appointment, he complained, "We are fighting a shadow on this one. Those who accuse Lawrence of speaking out against Negroes do not exist. I cannot find anybody who has made any such statement. Lawrence denies it himself." Finally, he closed by saying that "Ramsey Clark is no great asset to the President."[57] When the names reached the president's desk, he ordered the FBI to interview all of them and write a report on each one.[58]

Still no action was forthcoming from the attorney general. *Three* supplemental FBI reports were completed, instead of the usual one, but Clark's excuse was that he was still waiting for the formal ABA report (even though an informal one had found Lawrence "well qualified").

At the same time, more and more information favorable to the appointment was now coming to the White House. Strong recommendations came from the president of the state bar of Georgia, and several prominent members of the black religious and legal community in Savannah.[59] Senator Russell sent along a recommendation signed by nineteen past presidents of the Georgia Bar Association, and once more "most respectfully urge[d]" that the nomination be made.[60] Then a most significant endorsement came from Ralph McGill, the publisher of the *Atlanta Constitution,* who had come to believe that although Lawrence used to be "an old time segregationist," he would now handle civil rights cases fairly. Seeing this reversal of the paper's position, the president had it sent to Justice Fortas, who commented, "This is persuasive to me. I think we should go ahead on this for sure."[61]

By the time that the president and Russell met on June 25 to solidify their deal on the Fortas-Thornberry ticket, everything seemed to have fallen into place on the Lawrence nomination. During the three hours that they talked before dinner, Johnson pulled out the bulging FBI file on the candidate and reviewed it with Russell. It was just a matter of time, he promised, and Lawrence could serve on either the court of appeals or the district court to which he had already been nominated. But the senator was not in a mood to be mollified, and told the president later in the week that the district court job would be just fine.[62]

The truth was, though, that Johnson still could not convince Ramsey Clark to expedite the matter. The attorney general seemed to be waiting for more persuasive damaging information to be developed against the Lawrence candidacy. So, after telling the president that he was still waiting for the ABA's formal report, he added that there was no way that the nomination should be made. "I told my friend Dick Russell that if there is a way to appoint that man, I want to do it," responded the president. "Now I know you don't want to appoint him. I know you're opposed to it, and I'm not telling you that I definitely am going to appoint him. I'm just telling you that I want to if there's any way that I can. . . . If there's a way to posture him where we can nominate him, I want to do that. Now go get after it, and see if there's a way to do that."[63]

It was as close as the president could come to giving Clark an order. The mandate was now clear: Process the nomination as fast as possible. The time had come, thought the president, for Richard Russell to get his way. But the senator had already had enough.

As the last weekend in June approached, Russell began having misgivings about his commitment to the judicial ticket of Fortas and Thornberry, and his southern Democratic colleagues knew it. In many ways Russell was faced with the same problems that Dirksen had been battling on the Republican side. His grip on the votes of the southern Democrats was clearly slipping. There was no question that he was still revered and respected, but it was unlikely that he could persuade the others to act contrary to their own best interests. And all that Russell had been hearing for days was outright hostility and talk of open filibuster.

The Dixiecrats were every bit as angry as Eastland had led the White House to believe. To them, this was the Supreme Court that protected Communists, freed criminals, removed God from the classroom and put atheism in, reduced the power of the Congress to conduct valuable investigations, supported the rebellious protesters, and integrated the nation. The line had to be drawn, and it had to be drawn here. They would stand together and fight, or it would be too late. There was no middle ground—and Richard Russell knew it.

Now on top of this was Russell's personal struggle over the Lawrence appointment. After considering all of his options, the senator knew what he had to do. He called in his secretary and told her they were going to Winder, Georgia, for the weekend to write a letter. This letter could not be trusted to his aides. Russell would dictate his message to the president of the United States by himself. When they had finished, the letter would say everything that Russell had been wanting to say for quite some time now.

After returning to his office from his weekend retreat, Russell wanted to make sure that his letter would have the proper effect before sending it on to the president. So, on July 1, he met for an 8:15 breakfast with Alexander Lawrence and his Georgian Democratic colleague, Senator Herman Talmadge, in order to tell them what he planned to do. After reading them the letter, Talmadge said, "That'll dislodge the appointment. Alex Lawrence will be sent to the Senate shortly after Lyndon Johnson gets that letter."[64] And so he would.

Meanwhile over at the White House, Johnson was more concerned with his Supreme Court nominations. The South had to be held, and Richard Russell was the only one who could do it. While the senator had given his promise of support, the president had to be sure. So he sent Larry Temple and Harry McPherson to Russell's office at 5:30 that afternoon.

There were very definite reasons for the president to want Temple to take Harry McPherson along with him. "Dick Russell loves Harry like a son," he explained, "and that'll help you get entree up there. Harry will pave the way."[65]

When the two men arrived, Temple was shocked at what he saw. Russell struggled to his feet to greet them from the couch where he had been napping, and his drawn, time-worn face evidenced his declining health. But there was still enough life left in the old senator to greet an old family friend, and Russell's reaction made it clear how correct Johnson had been in sending Harry McPherson. The senator hugged him, and in a wheezing voice asked about his family and his children, seeming to want to talk about anything other than the difficult business at hand. The truth was that he had a very important message for Lyndon Johnson, but it was not the kind of message that one sent through intermediaries.[66]

When they finally got to the reason for the visit, Russell was very polite and very courtly, but noncommittal as to his views. While he said that he understood Fortas's philosophy fairly well, he seemed glad to have the Justice Department's memos to help in his study of the specific opinions. Russell even admitted that he had read Fortas's book on civil disobedience and there was little in there with which he disagreed. After explaining that he had no personal problem with Fortas, the senator added that they differed widely on philosophy.[67]

Clearly, though, it was the Thornberry nomination that was holding Russell's loyalty. "You don't need to tell me about him," he said brusquely when the name was raised. "I am strong for him and would like for him to be Chief Justice."[68] Later, he added, "You tell Lyndon that what he should have done was make Homer Thornberry Chief Justice because I could have endorsed that with a lot of enthusiasm, because he is a wonderful man. That's probably what he should have done. But that's not what he did, and I'm going to be for him. But he should have done the other."[69]

Had the meeting ended there, all would have been well (although it was clear to the White House emissaries that their meeting had "served absolutely no useful purpose in helping" the confirmations).[70] But there was one final question that Russell wanted Temple to answer: "Do you know anything about my federal judgeship?"

Did he ever. Temple carefully considered his answer. While Ramsey Clark was continuing to be as intransigent as ever, the president was all but ordering him to act. Worse, after Clark had been forced to choke down Everett Dirksen's pet SACB the previous week, there was no reason to expect a quick change of heart by the attorney general on this matter as well. But it was not the White House aide's place to tell what he knew. So, Temple said the only thing he could: "Senator, as a matter of fact, I do know the President has had a conversation with the Attorney General just this week about it, and they're still working on it."

"Well," Russell responded, "you tell the President that I said that I'm still very, very interested. I hope he'll make that nomination, and I sure would like for it to be done pretty soon."

Minutes later when Temple was repeating this to the president at the White House, Johnson knew exactly what *he* had to do. He said to contact the attorney general one more time and tell him to "get that nomination over to [the White House]."

But Clark knew what *he* had to do. By now he had on his desk two informal ABA reports as well as four FBI reports on Lawrence, some of them completed months before, amounting to over six inches of material. But they were not quite enough to convince him. So the attorney general stalled for time, saying that he was waiting for the final ABA report, which for some reason was very, very slow in coming.*

Meanwhile, back on Capitol Hill, Richard Russell now knew what *he* had to do. The emissaries from the White House had reassured him that he was not being hasty in doing what he had planned. He picked up the letter, the one he had been thinking about for so long, sealed it, and sent it by messenger. It was a turning point in the life of Abe Fortas, and there was nothing anybody could do about it anymore. For Richard Russell had given his word.

The letter arrived on the president's desk early on July 2. When he saw it he couldn't quite believe his eyes. Initially, he was "genuinely saddened," but very quickly the president became enraged. With one letter Richard Russell was serving notice of the end of their personal friendship. Moreover, the Fortas-Thornberry nomination was a new ball game.

James O. Eastland was the only one who had been giving the president the proper mathematical equation on this battle after all. No Russell, no Dixiecrats, little chance. The president was angry, very angry—but not at Richard Russell. There was someone else he wanted to make sure got an earful.

Minutes later Ramsey Clark was told that the president was on the phone. Mixed among all of the profanities, Clark heard the outraged president say, "Ramsey, I'm very unhappy. I think your foot-dragging on [the Lawrence nomination] has destroyed one of the great friendships I've had with one of the great men that has ever served this country. I'm unhappy about it."[72] As the president read the letter aloud, the attorney general quickly realized how bad the situation had become.

Russell's letter started calmly enough, much like the one that the senator had sent in May on the matter. Russell began by reviewing the history of their four and a half months of exchanges on this issue, saying that he was "only insisting on that which every Democratic Senator has had a right to expect since the formation of our Party." However, despite the support, and Lawrence's obvious qualifications,

---

*To Larry Temple these were all "foot-dragging activities," but years later Ramsey Clark would deny it, saying, "I don't think I was filibustering—that's not good government. We just wanted to be careful, to be sure of everything, and we had good information on Lawrence's views showing that he would lean the wrong way. After six appointment failures in the sixties from the South, we just could not afford another one at that point in our history."[71]

"for some reason, a minister or former minister at Savannah, Georgia, decided to demonstrate the power which he later claimed to have over you or your Attorney General and set out, with surprising success, to block the naming of Mr. Lawrence as Judge. It is only incidental that he displayed the poor taste to boast of the successful use of this power in an address he made recently to a civic club in Savannah." Still, Russell added, he had taken Johnson at his word that the appointment would be made even over Clark's objections.

But then came the passage that proved how agitated Russell had become: "To be perfectly frank, even after so many years in the Senate, I was so naive I had not even suspected that this man's nomination was being withheld from the Senate due to the changes you expected on the Supreme Court of the United States until after you sent in the nominations of Fortas and Thornberry while still holding the recommendations for the nomination of Mr. Lawrence either in your office or in the Department of Justice. Whether it is intended or not, this places me in the position where, if I support your nominees for the Supreme Court, it will appear that I have done so out of my fears that you would not nominate Mr. Lawrence."

So whether there was an actual quid pro quo or not, Russell saw it as one. Then came the coup de grâce: "I still dislike being treated as a child or a patronage-seeking ward heeler. When I came to the United States Senate some thirty-odd years ago, I did not possess much except my self-respect. When I leave—either voluntarily, carried in a box, or at the request of a majority of the people of Georgia—I still intend to carry my self-respect back to Georgia."

One did not have to read much between the lines to see that Russell was comparing his situation with that of Johnson—whose own personal fortune had swollen during his period of public service. So for Russell, the game was now over. "This is, therefore, to advise you that, in view of the long delay in handling and the juggling of this nomination, I consider myself released from any statements that I may have made to you with respect to your nominations, and you are at liberty to deal with the recommendations as to Mr. Lawrence in any way you see fit." While the senator vowed "to deal objectively with the nominations you have made to the Supreme Court," he wanted it understood "that it is not done with the expectation that I am buying or insuring the nomination of Mr. Lawrence to either the District or the Circuit Court and that I do not propose to make any future endorsements to you for judicial appointments even in my own state." For him, Lawrence and his family had "already been humiliated beyond what decent and honorable people should be required to bear at the hand of a motley collection of fanatics, mystics and publicity seekers.'' (Of course, here Russell overlooked that the opposition came after he had leaked Lawrence's name to the press.)[73]

It was a hot letter. And Russell meant every word of it. And this was more than just a tactical effort by him to dislodge the Lawrence appointment. Russell, a man whose word was his bond, and to whom self-respect was everything, was now accusing Lyndon Johnson of the worst possible offense—acting in bad faith. For him, this was unacceptable. So his professional relationship and what remained of his friendship with Johnson had come to an end.

Together on the telephone, Johnson and his attorney general tried to figure out what had caused such a dramatic turnaround in Russell's views. There had been no indication during his meeting the previous night with Temple and McPherson that this was even being contemplated. But a letter of this magnitude surely does not get whipped off in a single evening. The senator had clearly put a lot of thought behind this one, Johnson began thinking out loud. To him, the charge that the nomination of Lawrence was being used as a hostage to get votes for the Supreme Court nominations was ''just a lie.'' And there was reason to believe the president. If nothing else, the dates themselves made that clear. It had been four and a half months since the initial letter suggesting the Lawrence appointment, and it had only been a little over two weeks since the president had begun thinking about who would become the next chief justice. But the Georgia senator had worked out a plausible explanation for the huge variation in dates. Russell was now convinced that Johnson had known for months that Warren was going to resign and this holdup of Lawrence was part of the judicial master plan.

Johnson could see that there was a logical reason why he would not have done this. Had the president known earlier of Warren's retirement, he would have acted before his March 31 announcement that he would not seek reelection, when his power with the Congress was still reasonably intact. But it made no difference that Russell was absolutely and totally wrong here from a logical standpoint; what mattered most was what he *believed* to be true. Johnson speculated that perhaps someone among the opposition had whispered in Russell's ear and he had been duped. It was dirty pool, but that was politics.

The most likely explanation was that while a healthy Russell would have seen through this argument, the senator was far from healthy. He was dying. And before he died this man of honor had one account to settle: Alexander Lawrence was going to know that Richard Russell had done everything humanly possible to fulfill his commitment.

But Lyndon Johnson was also a man of honor. Alexander Lawrence was going to become a federal judge whether Ramsey Clark liked it or not. And Johnson no longer gave a damn whether this man was guilty of *all* the charges that he had heard. He was *president,* and his word was final.

So Johnson decided to order his attorney general to move, whether it meant his resignation or not. (Some think that Johnson may have even wanted Clark to resign at this point, making it easier to explain things to Russell and bring him back into the fold.) "I don't think Dick Russell has any commitment to me on this," he told Clark on the telephone on July 2, "and if he really believes what he has put in that letter, and I know he does believe it, then I don't fault him for saying he has got no commitment to me. But I still think I've got a commitment to him because I told him I was going to appoint his man if there was any way I could. And I think there's a way I can. I think there's a way that he can be postured to where he can be appointed, and it won't undermine the judiciary, and it won't tear down everything I've done with the judiciary. Ramsey, I want to go ahead and nominate him."[74]

Ramsey Clark, however, did not resign when he heard this. There was no reason for him to do so. He, too, had acted in good faith, using his best political instincts. Nothing had altered his reservations about Lawrence. By holding up the nomination until now he had made sure that any negative publicity would be fully anticipated and perhaps defused. The public would know that the White House had gone to extraordinary lengths to check this nominee out. And now even better than that, if it all fell apart, the White House staffers would be able to leak to a friendly reporter that they just *had* to send the nomination up—Richard Russell had virtually ordered them to do so. And everyone knew how important Richard Russell was to this administration. So rather than resign, Ramsey Clark did precisely what Russell wanted him to do. He decided to okay the appointment of Alexander Lawrence.

Three men acting out of conscience, and in the process an innocent bystander would watch his life continue to spiral out of control.

But there was still the matter of explaining all of this to the irate senator. There was nothing to do now about the past. The only hope, everyone at the White House agreed, was to try to draft a letter to Russell that would convince him that he had been misled, but not by the president. Perhaps just the right words would do the trick. So, for the rest of the day teams of the president's assistants, his speechwriters, and members of the Justice Department took turns drafting various versions of a response.

Given Senator Russell's apparently confused state of mind on this question, and the sensitive nature of the issue, it was not an easy letter to write. The two men who had visited him the day before—Larry Temple and Harry McPherson—worked very closely with the president on the early drafts. Then two other White House aides—one of them Tom Johnson, who had worked with Russell—were called in for accounts of their earlier contacts with the senator on this issue.[75] And, of course, with another sensitive drafting mission came the inevitable call to the president's favorite member of the Supreme Court. Abe Fortas reviewed one of the early drafts and made a number of stylistic changes, but none of them were accepted. Having nothing else to offer, shortly before noon the justice decided that he didn't want to spoil his holiday weekend and left the Oval Office for Westport, Connecticut. Meanwhile the White House staff continued to generate one draft after another, until just before seven that evening, when the president had time to sit down and work with aide Jim Jones in extensively rewriting the letter.

By 7:40 they had what looked like a good working draft, but there were several problems that the president wanted to discuss with Fortas. One had to do with a sentence that read: "If, at that time [when the final ABA clearance was received], you favor sending the nomination of Mr. Lawrence to the Senate, that action will be taken by me immediately." But the aides could not reach Fortas, who was now on the road to Connecticut. So Harry McPherson called Attorney General Clark, who argued that after all Russell had done to secure this appointment, he would probably interpret this as "If you still want this bum at that time, I'll appoint him."[76] The sentence was dropped as a result. Since a letter of this importance simply was not going to be sent until Abe Fortas approved it, the White House placed two more calls to his summer house to see if he'd arrived yet.[77]

For all of the work of the White House in its crisis mode, however, the letter did not seem to contain the key to blunting Russell's charges. They could not risk the admission that the president and the attorney general had been struggling over this appointment for weeks, and the president had been effectively powerless to get the job done. But all in all, the letter the secretary typed the following day was pretty good:

Dear Senator:

I have your letter of July 1. I am distressed by the evidence it gives that you are deeply disturbed over the Administration's handling of the vacancy in the Southern District of Georgia.

As you and I have discussed this matter at some length, I shall not repeat the full history of our investigations into Mr. Lawrence's qualifications. Suffice it to say that questions were raised about the appointment. I asked that extensive interviews be conducted and a fresh investigation be made on the basis of those questions. I have now personally reviewed the entire file and thoroughly discussed the appointment with my advisors.

I told you last Thursday I intended to nominate Mr. Lawrence for either the District Judgeship or appointment to the Court of Appeals. You called last Friday to say you preferred the District Judgeship.

I therefore intend to submit Mr. Lawrence's name for appointment as District Judge, along with other judicial nominations I plan to submit, the Senate willing, before the present session has concluded.

My nomination of Mr. Lawrence is in no way related to the nominations I have submitted to fill vacancies on the Supreme Court. You are fully aware of the difficulties surrounding the Lawrence nomination and the need to take special care to refute or verify the objections against it.

The necessary time expended to satisfy this need took place when there was neither a vacancy on the Supreme Court nor any resignation tendered. So relating any delay on this nomination to a Supreme Court nomination is without foundation in reason or fact.

When I sought your counsel in Georgia, and here, you told me you "would vote for the confirmation of Mr. Justice Fortas and enthusiastically *support* the confirmation of Judge Thornberry." I consulted you as I did Senators Mansfield, Dirksen, Eastland, and other members of the Senate without regard to whom they might favor for any other post. No mention was made of Mr. Lawrence because there was no connection between the nominations. There is none now.

I am convinced that I have nominated for promotion two of the ablest judges in America for these positions. I believe you can support them on their merits. But I assure you that your action in this regard is entirely separate from the nomination I intend to submit of Mr. Lawrence. I have not the slightest doubt that you know this and have known it all along.

I am frankly surprised and deeply disappointed that a contrary inference would be suggested. Both my own standards of public administration, and my knowledge of your character, would deny such an inference.

Sincerely,
Lyndon B. Johnson

There would be no further correspondence between the two men on this matter. But that did not mean that Lyndon Johnson had ended his efforts to persuade Russell of his good intentions. In times like this, the president left little to chance.

As the letter was being finished on the morning of July 3, with White House secretary Bonano's help, Johnson placed his call to Russell to inform the senator that his own letter was being returned. After expressing the wish that it be destroyed, the president made his own plea. Guaranteeing that the Lawrence nomination was forthcoming, Johnson added, "I'm going to tell you that I don't look upon you as having any sort of commitment to me with regard to Justice Fortas or Homer Thornberry. I know that you will do as you've done ever since I've known you, and that is make the decision your conscience and judgment dictates at the time that is right for that decision. I'm not going to ask you what that decision is. I'm not going to send anybody to you. I'm not going to have anybody else ask you. I'll know what your decision is when I see the vote tallied. That's as soon as I want to know."[78]

Of course, having made the promise not to "send anybody" to Russell, the president proceeded to send everybody. First, Tom Johnson (whom Russell liked so much he referred to him in his appointment book as "Tommy" Johnson) was sent over shortly before noon to deliver the senator's original letter and the White House response. Johnson told Russell how "very hurt" the president had been by the charges in the letter, and reiterated that there had been no connection between the two nominations. Instead, argued Johnson, the president had only been trying to "build a very good case" to rebut expected opposition.[79]

Then six days later Mike Mansfield brought Russell into his office in order to meet with White House liaison Mike Manatos. The aide told Russell, "There must be some way we can assure you that Alexander Lawrence will be appointed to the Southern District Court of Georgia." But Russell was no longer willing to be convinced, saying that since this issue had been discussed only with the president, maybe it would be wisest to "keep the matter in that posture."[80]

Realizing that Russell was now going to be a problem, and a big one
at that, Manatos suggested that it might be time for another presidential chat with the Georgia senator. But Johnson was determined to
soften him up a bit more first. He sent over their mutual friend Edwin
Weisl, the man who had originally suggested the senator's interest in
Homer Thornberry's appointment. Once again, no movement by Russell.

Then on July 12 the president sent Tom Johnson back to get a reading from Russell's staff. But they told him that Russell "very strongly
and very firmly believed what he had put in the letter." Moreover, the
senator was even more upset that it had taken him so long to see the
obvious. It was clear that no matter how many emissaries came from
the president, they were not going to be able to convince Russell that
he was mistaken.[81] And it was equally clear that no more emissaries
would be welcome, since one of Russell's staff members had said,
"This matter is now between the President and the Senator."

Seeing that it was time for a summit meeting with Russell, the president was happy finally to have some good news for him. After four
and a half months of waiting, it took just a week after Russell's letter
for the final ABA report to reach the Justice Department. As the senator had expected, the report was excellent. Attaching little importance
to the 1958 speech, in the belief that this had been Lawrence's view as
a much younger, less mature man, the committee members were persuaded that as a judge he would now uphold the law of the land. So
they rated him "well qualified," the second-highest rung on the ladder. Members of the Justice Department were marveling that this was
the first time they could remember such a high rating being given to a
man over sixty years old, which ordinarily served by the committee's
own rules as an automatic negative factor regardless of the candidate's
qualifications.[82] With the ABA report in hand, the Justice Department
took only another four days to process the rest of the nomination and
send it on to the White House.

So, when they met in the Oval Office for two hours on July 13, the
president was able to tell Russell formally that the nomination would
be made. He did his best to win back Russell's confidence. But for all
of their conversation, the senator failed to come around. Johnson's
effort to satisfy him was now too late to make a difference.

Homer Thornberry remembers how much President Johnson lamented what had happened. While eating a late dinner on the White
House's Truman Balcony with the Johnsons the day after the Judiciary

Committee hearings on the nominations began, he was puzzled to hear the president say, "I never thought Richard Russell would go against his word." Thornberry knew then that this meant he should not start packing his bags for the move to Washington.[83]

For his part, Richard Russell could afford to be magnanimous about the insult done to him by the president. He had to be impressed at the immediacy of the response to his letter. After waiting nearly five months for the Lawrence nomination to come from the White House, his colleagues on the Senate Judiciary Committee took a perfunctory half day of hearings to approve what many would call a crony of Richard Russell's, nominated by a lame-duck president, in response to Scarlett's conditional resignation letter.[84] Then, despite the fears of the White House, absolutely no objections were raised either by the press or by the various civil rights groups, and the nomination was quickly approved by the full Senate without incident.[85]

When asked later about the appointment controversy, Russell said only, "Oh well, I didn't have any feeling toward the President on that. . . . The only thing I resented was having to give up so much valuable time fooling with something that was so clear and apparent to me and to all the members of the Georgia bench and Georgia Bar Association. [Lawrence] will make a fine judge."[86] But others knew differently. The thirty-year friendship had been shattered forever. Russell and Johnson were now "pouting" like six-year-olds and it was apparent to all around them. Former White House secretary George Christian recalls "how very cool" they were at a dinner after all of this had occurred.[87] When a longtime Russell aide, Bill Darden, was being offered an appointment on the Court of Military Appeals, the senator gave the appearance that he did not care one way or the other what Johnson chose to do, and Johnson indicated just a bit too clearly to Darden that the nomination was not being made in deference to the senator.[88]

Later there was even more evidence of the permanent break in the Johnson-Russell relationship. In the final days of the administration, plans were being made for the staffing and organization of the Johnson presidential library in Austin. One of the tasks was lining up all of the president's friends and allies for participation in an extensive oral history project. But unlike most everyone else, Richard Russell told an aide that it "looked like the President was trying to flood the record with his own version and that he didn't want to participate." He refused even the entreaties of Lady Bird Johnson.[89]

When the Senate organized a series of farewell round-robin speeches to eulogize Johnson's contributions to politics and the American way of life as he left Washington, someone discovered that there was no speech from Richard Russell. Upon receiving a request for one, Russell's immediate reaction was "Well, I just don't want to make a speech." So his aide Powell Moore was assigned to draft a speech knowing that Russell, who was a stickler for producing his own work, would rework it. This time, though, Russell simply approved Moore's draft verbatim and added only that he had very pleasant memories of his trips with Johnson to night baseball games.

For his part, Johnson could be just as petty. Somehow in his visits to Washington during his retirement, there seemed to be no time to visit his old mentor. In fact, in the last two years of Russell's life there was no communication between them at all—written or oral. The two men who had lived together in the Senate were now dying separately. And when Russell died in January 1971, Johnson just couldn't seem to make it to the funeral. Some claimed that a long-standing appointment to meet with the president of Mexico had detained the former president, while others said it was the bad weather that had kept any incoming planes from landing.[90] But those closest to them knew why Johnson could not find a way to make it to the final occasion in the life of Richard Brevard Russell.

It was a political and personal tragedy. For just as Ramsey Clark had warned, Judge Alexander Lawrence became one of the most unpopular district court judges in southern Georgia. But ironically it was Richard Russell who was destined to be the most disappointed, as Lawrence was roundly criticized in the South for courageously *integrating* the schools in his district. Donning what he had once called the "new garb" of tyranny, Lawrence had in fact become the liberal-cored Hugo Black prototype that the Johnson White House had been looking for all along.*

For all of his candor in his letter to the president, Russell had not told the whole truth. By saying that he would now "deal objectively with the nominations you have made to the Supreme Court," Russell deliberately gave the impression that he was now a free agent who could still be persuaded on the merits. The real truth, though, was that Ramsey Clark had given Russell the opportunity to do what he now

---

*Someone sent the editorials describing Lawrence's actions to Homer Thornberry, and he sent them along to Lyndon Johnson, then at his ranch near Johnson City. "I'll send these along to Ramsey Clark. I know he will find them interesting" was the response of the former president, who now blamed his former attorney general for the whole matter.[91]

realized he should have done all along. He asked Robert Griffin to join him in his office for a few minutes. There was no reason for Griffin to think that this request would have any significance. But it did—it changed *everything*.

When Griffin arrived, Russell asked him about the strength of the rebels. Were the eighteen other negative votes firm? Was he personally serious about carrying the fight? Would he stick to his guns no matter what? Griffin's immediate answer to all of these questions was yes. Then came the words that Griffin had been waiting to hear. In his heavy southern drawl, the dying patriarch of the South delivered his "followers": "We're with you; I'm with you, but as far as the group that I'm with is concerned, namely the Southern Democrats, we'd rather not get out front because we would hurt your chances more than we'd help." As soon as Griffin heard it, his face broke out in a big grin. It was exactly what an ambitious young senator needed to hear at this point. Not only did he have the votes, but these were *Democratic* votes, thus giving him the high road of "nonpartisanship." And there was even more. By getting the southerners' *silent* support, Griffin could continue to make his moves secure in the knowledge that he would have the advantage of surprise.[92]

When the secret rapprochement was finally discovered by Sam Shaffer, a reporter for *Newsweek,* and the president was informed that the nominations were doomed to failure, his response was predictable. He whipped the latest Senate head count out of his inside coat pocket and insisted, "Sam Shaffer is wrong. I have the votes for confirmation. Here they are."[93] But this boast meant little if the matter *never* came to a vote because of a filibuster. More than ever, Lyndon Johnson knew in his heart that both he and Abe Fortas were in trouble.

XV

THE
HOLY WAR

e will win this one."

So Ev Dirksen promised the two White House emissaries, Mike Manatos and Postmaster General Marvin Watson, who were in his office on July 2, 1968. His advice just to let the issue "simmer over the holiday weekend" was echoed by another Republican who said that the "Griffin effort is slowly dying."[1]

But it was not going well—not at all—and the White House knew only part of the story. The administration had launched a schizophrenic effort. On the public level the staffers did their best to promote an air of confidence and inevitability. Soon, the media were so convinced of the eventuality of the confirmation that the very few stories being written all took that point of view. The reporters were missing the real story in the early going, and their misinterpretation of events was providing a cover for the actions of both sides. In reality, the administration and the rebels were privately waging an all-out war for every angle and every vote they could get. And reinforcements were coming, but not the kind that the rebels particularly wanted.

The "holy war" was on. When the president got the bad news, he picked up the phone himself and dialed it. The recorded message that he heard was shocking indeed. A member of the National Socialist White People's party in its "national headquarters" in Arlington, Virginia, was calling for opposition to "this despicable Jew with a 'red' record that smells to high heaven." Fortas had been a Communist party member, it claimed, and had been instrumental in integrating the schools by sending "millions of helpless white children . . . into the hands of young Negro hoodlums and rapists and thousands of blackboard jungles across the nation, and freeing known criminals." It was a hateful, spiteful message, and seemed sure to lead to the kind of fight no one wins.[2]

Soon other right-wing fringe groups were involved in the conflict. The Liberty Lobby sent its "Emergency Liberty Letter Number 21" to 280,000 people, urging them to oppose the nomination of a man whose "record of affiliation with known revolutionaries and revolutionary groups" was well known. It was clear to this group that with the Supreme Court "under Fortas's control, it will be 'business as usual' for the communists and the underworld and the big contractors who are cleaning up on cost-plus at the taxpayers' expense." Attached was a list of twenty charges "proving" these claims.[3]

To a certain extent, it's predictable that one fringe group or another will oppose any judicial nomination, but the intensity and early entry of these attacks was breathtaking. And Johnson knew only too well that similar anti-Semitic views were held by prominent southern Democrats. Even the chairman of the Judiciary Committee, James O. Eastland, was heard to say to a Senate colleague, "You're not going to vote for that Jew to be Chief Justice, are you?"[4]

So the White House cast around for some way to limit the damage. The existence of the Nazi tape was leaked to Drew Pearson, who in turn aired it in his newspaper column, under the title "Telephone Hate Tactics." Pearson portrayed Griffin's rebellious senators as being allied with the "white power" advocates. But the rebels had nothing to do with this, and preferred that their message not get any more muddied. They were not against Jewish chief justices, they said, but against Johnson-appointed chief justices.[5]

Pearson's column only had the effect of moving the National Socialist White People's party to make another tape answering these charges and repeating its venom against the Fortas appointment. Periodically, these tapes were changed to give the appearance that new information had made an update possible. Soon similar broadsides appeared from groups such as the Supreme Court Amendment League, the National Reprint Service, and the John Birch Society. Of course, many of these suggested that their followers use portions of the material to write wavering senators—which they did by the hundreds.

The whole thing was making everyone nervous in an election year. Even some of the allied Jewish organizations began to back off. The White House did what it could to generate and publish countereditorials that would "warn the opponents that there *are* reactionary voices being raised over this nomination, and that those who have more acceptable purposes in opposing Fortas might find themselves in bed with anti-Semites."[6] However, the journalists were reluctant to raise the religion issue openly. It was clear that this front, which the White House had opened, was now quickly getting totally out of control.

In times like this, senators tend to rally around their besieged colleagues. When Griffin and some of the other Republicans complained at their weekly policy luncheon about the pressure from the religious community, the Jewish senator from New York, Jacob Javits, said that he would personally defend any of his colleagues against charges of anti-Semitism.[7] Then he privately sent a warning to the White House "not to stress 'anti-Semitism.'"[8]

But these were just some of the problems that Johnson was facing in the days before the crucial Judiciary Committee hearings. The White House's once overwhelming number of votes was slowly evaporating. The White House and the Porter operation had been busy trying to dominate the war of words. They had collected every favorable news article and editorial printed around the country. These pieces were divided up and transformed by the White House speechwriters into introductory speeches for friendly senators to insert into the Senate record.[9] Senate liaisons Mike Manatos and Barefoot Sanders then arranged for different supporters of the nomination to deliver these speeches nearly every day that the Senate was in session.

Then a series of major speeches was prepared in order to continue the Smathers assault on the superficiality of the issues raised by the rebels. Majority Leader Mansfield read a version of a speech originally written for the president which argued that the loss of the chief justice for even a short time would bureaucratically stymie the court.[10] Several days later, New Mexico's Joseph Montoya delivered a major speech that the Porter operation had drafted portraying Abe Fortas as a "friend of business." It was a clever speech, dealing with the one area where Fortas was not only an unqualified, self-restraint-oriented conservative, but where he had most frequently and vocally split from his liberal colleagues.[11]

By having these speeches delivered the White House gave every appearance of having the confirmation debate well under control. But in covering this torrent of verbiage the press was missing the real story, and the beleaguered White House staffers knew it. Unless they took successful steps soon, their legislative blitzkrieg would soon become a war of attrition. The balance of power in the Judiciary Committee and in the whole Senate lay with the Dixiecrats, and now—with Russell no longer helping the administration—they were up for grabs. So representatives of the White House fanned out, armed with the memoranda showing the "conservative" tendencies of the nominees, to poll their leanings. By now, all the reports indicated that most of the southerners were "absolutely opposed" to Fortas, although their final votes and willingness to filibuster were open to question. Two senators, though, Byrd of West Virginia and Ervin of North Carolina, had been vague enough in their statements to become the latest recipients of White House attention.

Senator Byrd was proving to be an enigma to the White House. After his initial apology for his inhospitable remarks toward the president's appointments, accompanied by his vow not to participate in any filibuster, the reports on Byrd's position had hardly been encouraging. While he had not taken a definite position, Byrd was seen as a loner capable of doing virtually anything.[12] The only card that the administration had to play was the senator's well-known dislike for the stewardship of Earl Warren. Perhaps he would listen to the argument that the new nominations would at least accomplish the removal of the present chief justice.

But Byrd wasn't biting. He told two visiting White House aides— Harry McPherson and Stephen Ailes—that they were "wasting their time." Byrd was holding to his promise not to filibuster, but that was all. The senator warned that he opposed "forced integration and leniency toward Communists, atheists, and other immoral people," all of which were represented in his mind by the nominees. "These are my views," Byrd concluded, "and it doesn't matter how many people the President sends up here to see me about them; they won't change." Translation—forget Byrd.[13]

Twice now the White House had failed with the "slanted memo" approach, and Sam Ervin was about to make it three for three. Ervin received his guests—White House assistants Larry Temple and Peyton Ford—"very, very, inhospitably," uncharacteristically so for someone from the aristocratic and genteel South. The senator told his visitors that he had made his reputation in the Senate by mastering the Constitution, and he was quite willing and able to do his own research, thank you.[14]

The differences between his philosophy and that of the court ensured his opposition to Fortas. "I am opposed," he told the visiting aides, after lecturing them in great detail on the fact that no vacancy yet existed on the Supreme Court, "to anyone whose philosophy would permit a re-writing of the Constitution." Moreover, Fortas had provided the crucial votes in defendant's rights and racial integration. Refusing even to accept the White House memoranda, Ervin told the aides that he was waiting for the Library of Congress to send him all of Fortas's opinions in their entirety for him to read. Worse still, Ervin warned the White House that he had no compunctions about participating in a filibuster if necessary. "I have never voted for cloture and I believe a man ought to be consistent in at least one area," he concluded.[15] Translation—scratch Ervin.

Another subject raised by Ervin convinced his visitors that he would never cast a vote on behalf of this court or any of its prospective members. In 1965 he had, in a most unusual move for a United States senator, argued a major textile industry case before the court and lost. Even now, three years later, it was clear to Larry Temple that "he was still mad about that outcome." So it was more than philosophy—it was also personal.[16]

With all this bad news, perhaps most people would have thought about retreat, but to Lyndon Johnson this just meant one thing—it was time to play politics. John McClellan of Arkansas had gotten over being miffed about not being consulted prior to the nominations, and now was reported to be only "vehemently opposed." But in politics nothing is forever, so the White House unleashed "the dairy people" on him. Farming is an important industry in Arkansas and Johnson's aides recalled that they had secured McClellan's vote on an earlier transportation bill by using an ingenious technique. First, the White House found out from the dairy lobbyists which of the administration's considerable resources might be most useful to them at the moment. Having agreed on the price, the dairy group was then told to have Senator McClellan visit the president on "one of their problems," thus giving Johnson the chance to talk to the senator about "one of his problems." The dairy people decided they wanted the president to keynote their annual convention in the fall. They were told "to insist that McClellan come over and extend this invitation to the President." Which they did.[17]

Then came word that Senator Lister Hill of Alabama wanted one more appointment on the federal court of appeals before he left office in November. Given the Senate's concern about confirmations for lame ducks, though, completion of the deal might be a little tricky.[18] Johnson would do his best, but securing Lister's appointment—and his vote—might prove difficult. However, there was a chance to do some business with Russell Long of Louisiana. Word came to the White House that Long was "disinterested" in the issue but was willing to "talk to" the White House.[19] A week later, Senator Long's aide phoned the offices of Postmaster General Watson with two requests. He was seeking the appointment of a postmaster in Lake Charles, Louisiana, and a definite agreement to build a postal center then under consideration for Shreveport. The president was only too willing to help his good friend on these matters.[20]

One of the steps taken at this time by a Johnson supporter turned out to be a miscalculation. Earl Warren, who had been sent all of the Justice Department's research on the vacancy question with a note suggesting that he make it public, gave an unprecedented press conference in order to demonstrate his support for the nominations.[21] In the course of explaining how his resignation had occurred, the chief justice became a "team player" arguing that his resignation letter and the interpretation of the White House as to the effective date were identical. However, he did reluctantly concede that there was a possibility he might be back as chief justice in October. This statement, exactly the opposite of what Warren had intended when he carefully crafted his resignation letter, quite naturally became the lead news item from the conference.[22] And Robert Byrd was reported now to be "disturbed by the Warren interview and [was] reconsidering his position in light of Warren being able to choose his successor."[23]

All in all, despite its best efforts, the administration was stumbling into the hearings expecting to face stiff opposition from the Dixiecrats. But still there was no threat of a filibuster. Most typical was the reported position of Eastland, who would "have some fun in opposition initially but ultimately will go along and vote for confirmation."[24]

The key was still Richard Russell. With him all of these reluctant Dixiecrats would fall into line, but without him they would be free to follow their own instincts.[25] Knowing Russell as he did, the president believed that there was still a chance to get him on board. First, another of the White House emissaries went to visit him on July 9, only to hear that he had not made up his mind, and had no intention either to filibuster or to "inject himself into the matter." In other words, at the moment he was distinctly neutral.[26]

Since in Lyndon Johnson's world persuasion came from simply finding the right offer, the president gave Senator Abraham Ribicoff of Connecticut, a man who was particularly influential with Richard Russell, some special attention. When Ribicoff asked for permission to release a feasibility study on the creation of the Connecticut River National Recreation Area to show how the legislation he had authored was working for his constituents in this election year, Johnson, who usually only checked the yes or no box without comment in such cases, wrote, "Help him in any way W.H. can. Thank him for [the] fine statement on [the] Fortas nomination."[27] Until Russell was publicly announced as opposing the nomination, the president was prepared to continue wooing him.

But the Dixiecrats and their friends were not the only senators to receive presidential attention. An attempt was made to split Colorado's Gordon Allott from the rebels. Allott had already questioned why so much pressure was being put on the senators in this fight, and he was soon to find out that this could work in his favor. When Allott asked about an appointment to the National Labor Relations Board that he had previously discussed with the president, the appointment was announced three days later.[28] After a while, when word of some of these deals spread on the rumor circuit, the senators started "playing hard to get" with the White House emissaries to see what their votes would be worth.[29]

As will happen in a lobbying effort of this scope, the heavy pressure was beginning to backfire. When a leader of the Jewish community in Washington phoned Senator Ernest "Fritz" Hollings of South Carolina for his support, and was turned down, he responded with "All right, Senator. The Hell with Fortas. He hasn't been a religious Jew anyway, and he even married outside the faith. But I would appreciate it if you would do what you could to see that Israel gets those fifty F-4 Phantom jets."[30] When the White House got word that promises of more arms to Israel served to deflect the pressure on other senators from prominent Jewish leaders, it caused some considerable concern. After scurrying around, a presidential aide located a picture of Fortas in a yarmulke and argued that it could be used to ease any "doubts" about the devoutness of the justice's faith.[31]

Regardless of the facts, the press still saw it as a White House land-slide. "GOP Attack on Fortas Appointment Crumbling Under LBJ's Pressure," wrote Rowland Evans and Robert Novak. In describing the effectiveness of the White House pressure "against only the flimsiest of partisan arguments," the column portrayed the administration as a juggernaut poised on the verge of an inevitable success. Indeed, as if to signify the end of the contest, Senator Frank Moss of Utah rushed to the floor of the Senate with the column and delivered a speech deriding the "lonely 20" who, because of their "habitual obstructionism and no saying," had launched this "instinctive partisan attack" against the president's nominations.[32]

However, like the funeral bell tolling, Senator Eastland had phoned again on the ninth of July to say that "the nominations would be defeated in his judgment unless conditions changed."[33] And LBJ sensed that he was right. Too much time was passing before the hearings were started. Eastland himself had already delayed them until July 11. With the clock ticking closer and closer to adjournment, the party conventions, and the semiformal transference of power to the next nominee, LBJ did what he did best—he badgered his staff. "We've got to hurry. We've got to hurry. We've got to hurry," he yelled at his staff.[34] "We're going to be in trouble on this. We're going to be in trouble on this." The sense of crisis rising in his voice, the president added, "We've got to get this thing through, and we've got to get it through early, because if it drags out we're going to get beat."[35] When the aides told the president one too many times that it was wrapped up, he scolded them. "We're a bunch of dupes down here. They've got all the wisdom. All the sagacity is reposed up there. They're just smarter than we are. We're a bunch of ignorant, immature kids who don't know anything about this. They're up there. They're whipsawing us to death because they're dragging their feet. We've got to do something." In spite of Johnson's accusations, the young, battle-tough staff was already fighting its hardest in the senators' arena and by their rules.[36]

Eventually, in one of these speeches designed to whip his staff into a frenzy, Johnson confessed the real reason for his concern. There was something he knew only too well, but which his staff could never have guessed. There was a reason to fear delays. "Dirksen will cut and run. Dirksen will cut and run," claimed the president.

"But he's publicly committed," Larry Temple would object.

"Just take my word for it," responded the president. "I know him. I know that Senate. If they get this thing drug out very long, we're going to get beat. Ev Dirksen will leave us if we get this thing strung out very long."[37]

But for now Abe Fortas had a chance to regain control of his own destiny. Or so he thought.

The young Fortas as a twenty-four-year-old New Deal whiz kid in 1934

Fortas being sworn in by Supreme Court Justice Hugo Black
as undersecretary of the interior on June 24, 1942, while
Secretary of the Interior Harold Ickes looks on

Fortas before the Senate Naval
Affairs Committee during the
confirmation hearings for
Edwin Pauley as
undersecretary of the navy,
February 20, 1946

Harold Ickes's "Field
Marshal" in 1942

William O. Douglas, forty-year-old chairman of the Securities and Exchange Commission, hears the news that President Roosevelt has nominated him for the Supreme Court on March 20, 1939.

Lyndon Baines Johnson campaigns for the Senate in 1948, the first to do so by helicopter.

"Don't look now Abe, but they're announcing you," Lyndon Johnson wrote on this picture of Fortas being presented as a Supreme Court nominee on July 28, 1965.
UPI/BETTMANN NEWSPHOTOS

Abe Fortas's wife, Carolyn Agger, helps him put on his judicial robes for the first time on October 4, 1965.
LIBRARY OF CONGRESS

The Supreme Court as Fortas entered it. *Left to right, seated:* Thomas Clark, Hugo Black, Earl Warren, William O. Douglas, John Harlan. *Standing:* Byron White, William Brennan, Potter Stewart, Abe Fortas
COLLECTION OF THE SUPREME COURT OF THE UNITED STATES

Clark Clifford *(left)*, Abe Fortas, and Lyndon Johnson drafting
the 1966 State of the Union address on January 12, 1966

The counselor and the decision-maker

The Fortases relaxing at their Westport, Connecticut,
summer house

The president, two hawks, a bulldog, and a general. Abe
Fortas, Robert McNamara, J. Edgar Hoover, and General
Harold Johnson with Lyndon Johnson during the Detroit riot
crisis meeting on July 24, 1967
LYNDON BAINES JOHNSON LIBRARY

Debating the Vietnam War. Abe Fortas *(center)* at the
president's second wise men's meeting, March 26, 1968
LYNDON BAINES JOHNSON LIBRARY

Later in the 1968 hearings, Fortas silently reacts to a senator's comment.
LIBRARY OF CONGRESS

Fortas and Tennessee Senator Albert Gore waiting to testify on July 16, 1968
WIDE WORLD PHOTOS

Facing the Senate Judiciary Committee during the 1968 Supreme Court confirmation hearings. Abe Fortas is on the right at the microphone.
LIBRARY OF CONGRESS

The last hurrah. Abe Fortas leaves the Supreme Court with
his wife, Carolyn Agger, after returning to argue a case on
March 22, 1982.
WIDE WORLD PHOTOS

XVI

THE
BATTLE OF
CAPITOL HILL

"I want to say that I am very happy to be here. And I am very happy to answer any and all questions that the committee may ask. I am not a novice in Washington. I am not a novice in Senate hearings."[1]

It was not the last time Abe Fortas would fail to tell the truth to the Senate. The truth was that he would rather have been anywhere other than where he was at that moment. He should have been at home preparing for that day's seminar at American University. Barring that, he would rather have been in Westport, Connecticut, carting manure for his wife's garden, playing the violin, and reading the bags full of *certiorari* petitions awaiting him. *"Fortas should not be asked to appear,"* he had written to Paul Porter about these hearings. And he meant it. But the Senate Judiciary Committee thought otherwise.

It was an odd sight. The justice on the Supreme Court, back in the Senate hearing room where he had made his reputation as a defender of the politically oppressed, but now sitting in the witness's rather than the more familiar counselor's chair. "A lawyer who represents himself has a fool for a client," the old maxim goes. But Fortas had won too many trials in the past not to have confidence that he could best the aging senatorial fossils facing him. There was no problem. Long ago he had learned how to deal with these situations. Inquisitive senators had missed him before, and unless they were prepared to ask him very, very specific questions, Fortas was certain that they would miss him again. He would give them nothing—*nothing at all*! In a way, then, despite his admonition to Porter, there was a sense of relief at finally having his destiny back where it belonged—in his own hands. After so many days of squirming in "torment" and "frustration" while others bungled one thing after another, he was *back in control*. Or so he thought.[2]

During the week prior to Fortas's appearance before the committee, the White House had done everything in its power to ease his burden. Thanks to leaks from the offices of allied senators, it already knew the plans of its opponents well in advance.[3] An informant on the Republican National Committee had relayed some of the questions that the justice would face before the committee.[4] A number of favorable questions had been planted with one of the administration's allies on the committee, George Smathers, for use when Fortas testified.[5]

The Justice Department continued its preparation. Research papers were compiled to brief Fortas on troublesome issues before his appearance.[6] Meetings were held with the justice to plot strategy for his testimony. And Fortas was armed with juicy little tidbits, such as Senator Ervin's vendetta against the Warren Court.[7] Meanwhile, the president continued to lobby members of the press and the bar on behalf of the appointments.[8]

Despite all of this preparatory work, some members of the White House staff were second-guessing Fortas's decision to appear before the committee. Ignoring the obvious risks inherent in testifying, the justice's mind was made up. After his initial reluctance to appear, he now seemed anxious to testify. It seemed almost like a proof of his manhood to him. The White House aides knew how little control one has in that setting, and how much they had to fear. And yet, when Fortas kept assuring them that he could handle the committee, they had to take him at his word.[9]

Abe Fortas had developed a certain style of advocacy before congressional investigating committees, but not everyone appreciated it.

For him, truth was secondary when there was a battle to be won. And fencing with investigating legislators was a battle. Fortas had faced the best—and no one had beaten him yet.

His technique had first appeared when, as part of his responsibilities in the Interior Department, he had to appear before Congress periodically for budget hearings or for a review of his actions. From the beginning it became clear that he could not deal in a straightforward manner with investigating committees. Fortas worked shrewdly and efficiently behind the scenes, but something seemed to happen to him when his actions were questioned in a public forum, such as in Congress or the press. On such occasions he would appear to be caught among a number of different drives. Confident enough in his analytical and speaking abilities, he never hesitated to duel with the politicians or reporters on their own turf, even under their rules, which permitted wider leeway to the questioner than to the respondent. But on the other hand, he seemed incapable of giving a clear answer to their questions. It seemed as if the lawyer in Fortas wanted to be only technically correct, leaving the interpretation of the spirit of his words to others. Then, too, the politician in him did not want to be pinned down to anything that might be used to confront contradictory actions in the future. In refusing to concede anything of substance, Fortas developed the practice of being circumspect to the point of evasion in answering such queries.

This practice had bothered Harold Ickes, a man who considered himself to be especially skilled in the art of congressional relations, from the start. In 1941, subcommittees on appropriations in both houses of Congress were looking into a shortfall of seventy-five thousand dollars in the funding for the Division of Power. Ickes watched Fortas's performance, as he was quizzed on the matter, and he was puzzled. Neither he nor the senators could figure out what Fortas was saying. Rather than giving direct information in response to direct questions, he seemed to be "circumlocuting" by going "into long explanations of the whys and wherefores." In the end, Ickes concluded that Fortas just "would not be held down" to a direct answer. Later, the secretary recorded in his diary, "I told him afterwards . . . that it was better to take a chance and give a clear answer than to confuse people's minds." The risk, Ickes well knew, was that the elected representatives would lose their patience, and their willingness to trust anything that was being said, whether it was truthful or not. It was a lesson that Fortas, who soon came to be seen as a man of mystery, never really learned.[10] But Ickes learned the penalties of this practice in 1946 as he watched Fortas destroy the secretary's reputation with these evasions.

Fortas's style before such committees involved testifying with his own form of double-talk. Later he would explain the strategy to a friend, Tex Goldschmidt, who was being questioned during the height of the red scare. (Ironically, one of the main questions was about the nature of his relationship to Fortas.) Answer definitely, either positively or negatively, Fortas said, and then explain what you really meant.[11] Of course, the more confusion and vagueness you foster in offering this "explanation," the better. The secret then is: Don't give up anything without a price, think about how the testimony will look in print, and make the senators continue to ask for the same information until they finally just give up out of exhaustion. Tell the story in your own way. So long as no one checks carefully on your tale, there is no limit to how far you can go.

Later Fortas perfected his testifying craft to an art in the McCarthy era, defending such luminaries as Lillian Hellman and Owen Lattimore.[12] In 1965, when Fortas was asked about his close relationship with Lyndon Johnson during his perfunctory confirmation hearings for the Supreme Court, the evasive technique was now routine. Two things were "vastly exaggerated" about himself, Fortas explained in response to a question: "One is the extent to which I am a presidential adviser, and the other is the extent to which I am a proficient violinist. I am a very poor violinist, but very enthusiastic, and my relationship with the President has been exaggerated out of all connection with reality."[13] Of course, both his musical and his political friends knew better. And, when accused by one witness of a connection with the Communist cell in the AAA, Fortas claimed to have been "a boy fresh out of Tennessee three years before" who had worked in that agency only during the summer of 1933 and the following Christmas holiday. In so testifying he conveniently overlooked both his half year of service in 1933–1934 and his own *Who's Who* listing, which stated correctly that he had been "assist. chief Legal Division, A.A.A., 1933–34."[14] After two decades of such practice, Fortas was confident that no senator was capable of besting him in these duels. Why not testify in his own defense? Who could harm him?

Round 1 of the hearings opened on July 11 with the appearance of Attorney General Clark to debate the no-vacancy question. This initial witness indicated that as hard as the White House worked, its operation was badly hemorrhaging. Its political lifeblood—seconds on the clock—was slipping away, and finding the right clotting agent was not proving to be easy. Time and again, the president was assured by various members of the Senate that there would be no filibuster of the nominations once they reached the full Senate.[15] But the prediction meant little to a man who understood that time was so short that the opponents needed to generate only a "minibuster" on the Judiciary Committee to run the nominations out of time before the August 3 adjournment for the national party conventions.[16]

And Sam Ervin seemed determined to do this all on his own. After announcing that he would oppose the nominations, he asked that Fortas's committee appearance be delayed until July 16 to give him time to "complete [his] study" of Fortas's judicial opinions.[17] This meant that even if Fortas appeared for a single day of questioning, with another being reserved for Homer Thornberry, as James Eastland had originally promised, the many procedural rules of the Senate made formal action by the committee unlikely until just ten days before the planned adjournment.

But while the war against the clock seemed to be going badly at the moment, thanks to the efforts of Ramsey Clark and Everett Dirksen two major skirmishes had already been won in the Judiciary Committee. In the first session of the hearings, the tag team of southern defenders of the Constitution—Ervin and Thurmond—asked the attorney general two basic questions: "Is there now a vacancy on the Court?" And "if not, is it possible that the Chief Justice might not leave after all?" Just to make certain that Clark fully understood these two questions, it took the senators nearly two hours to ask them in as many forms as they could dream up. But there was little to argue with in the attorney general's clever repartee.

Could Warren withdraw his resignation? Clark was asked. "On the terms of the retirement, Senator, there have been scores of different methods of retiring. There has not been a form book for the language. The men have proceeded with honor, and the purpose has been accomplished in every case, and it has not been questioned heretofore."

"Well, everything is questioned for the first time once, isn't it?" inquired Ervin.

"Everything that is questioned is questioned for the first time," responded Clark.

"Unless it goes unquestioned forever," added Ervin.[18]

They also dueled over all of the precedents that the attorney general had raised in his opening statement, designed to prove that a conditional resignation from the court was legally acceptable. Senator Ervin was justifiably unconvinced. In fact, it was apparent that this was essentially the same research that had been used for George Smathers's earlier speech, and even with the discovery of the example of Justice Gray, who in fact had died long before Oliver Wendell Holmes actually took office, the administration had still not discovered a resignation quite like Warren's at the Supreme Court level.

After expressing his unhappiness over the failure of the White House to uncover a precedent for this conditional resignation and acceptance (the Horace Gray example didn't convince him either), Ervin promised to "keep silent hereafter," a vow that he only broke nearly a dozen times. "I am not impressed by precedents," he stated. "Most of them are not applicable to this situation. In fact none of them as far as the Chief Justice of the Supreme Court is concerned. I do not think that precedents can alter the words of a statute. Murder has been committed in all generations, and so has larceny, but the commission of murder has not made murder meritorious or larceny legal. The same thing about precedents which are in conflict with the law."

"Sam," responded Senator Philip Hart of Michigan, who was rapidly becoming the main administration advocate on the committee, "I have listened to you recite precedents in the civil rights debate until I thought the world would never end."

But Ervin was not to be outdone. "They were all sound ones, though—all sound ones."[19]

When the podium was turned over to South Carolina's Strom Thurmond, he warned that "there may be a little duplication" in his questioning, and then spent the rest of the morning repeating all of Ervin's questions. Finally, Chairman Eastland canvassed the committee members and declared that there was general agreement that this had become a nonissue. So a decision was made that the vacancy issue would not be voted on until *after* the nominations themselves had been handled.[20] Despite this move, Albert Gore seconded George Smathers's advice to the White House that another retirement letter should be written, this time with a fixed date of departure, in order to bury the matter forever.[21] However, the warning went unheeded.

Strom Thurmond then ended the day's session by announcing that if the meeting continued, he would continue talking until the full Senate opened its afternoon session. Since, according to Senate rules, no committee can hold its meetings while the full body is in session, it was clear no one would be able to say any more on this committee that day. This created a minor crisis for an anxious Robert Griffin, who had been waiting all morning to testify. Instead of waiting until the next day, he decided to give his address to the full Senate. In so doing, he unwittingly delivered himself into the arms of an adversary who had been waiting a long time to deal with the junior senator from Michigan.[22]

Griffin's staff had been working for weeks on the eighteen-minute speech, and for the most part it was a workmanlike rehash of the familiar arguments. After meandering through an exposition on the political philosophy of the nation's founding as it bore on the issue in question, and another exposition on cronyism, Griffin lambasted the administration for the partisan nature of its lame-duck appointments: "Never before has there been such obvious political maneuvering to create a vacancy so that an outgoing President can fill it and thereby deny the opportunity to a new President about to be elected by the people. . . . Particularly at this point in our history, the Senate would be unwise to put its stamp of approval on a cynical effort to thwart the orderly processes of change."[23]

As lofty as this sounded, Everett Dirksen was not in any way persuaded. In fact, like a man waiting for a hard serve in tennis, Everett Dirksen was prepared to send Griffin's shot back over the net much harder than it had originally been hit. So "with obvious relish" he captured the lion's share of the next day's press attention by lecturing the young upstart from Michigan in his most sarcastic manner: "I find that term 'lame duck' as applied to the President of the United States as entirely improper and a very offensive term. . . . It has absolutely no application to one who voluntarily retired from office. There are nine Senators who will not be in the 91st Congress. . . . Now, are we going to offend them, and affront them by referring to them as 'lame duck' Senators?" Then, after delivering a sermon on "Great Cronies on the Supreme Court," including, naturally, a native son of Dirksen's hometown of Pekin, Illinois—David Davis, the former campaign manager of Abraham Lincoln—he went for Griffin's jugular with a characterization designed to capture the fancy of the observing press: "[The cronyism argument] is a frivolous, diaphanous—you know what that means, don't you—gossamer—you know what that means, don't you—argument that just does not hold water. And I have not seen an argument yet that will stand up, durably stand up, against the nomination and confirmation of the two men who are—whose names are before us at the present time."[24]

They were laughing at Griffin on Capitol Hill. When Dirksen spoke about his phone call to Charles Fairman on the no-vacancy argument (failing to mention the White House's involvement here), Senator

Smathers asked if this was a crony of his. "Yes, a crony; that is right," said Dirksen. "He was a second lieutenant in artillery in World War I. So was I. That makes us closer cronies."

"Terrible," responded the Florida senator over the cackles of his colleagues.

They were laughing at Griffin at the White House. In a memo from the Justice Department outlining numerous other examples of Supreme Court justices who had enjoyed close friendships with presidents, Deputy Attorney General Christopher asked the president, "Would Senator Griffin prefer that the nominee be a friend of a friend of the President? Or perhaps a friend of a tycoon? Or of a big contributor? Or of a shady lobbyist?"[25] Only later would Christopher realize the prescience of his speculation.

But Griffin wasn't laughing—and neither were his allies. Would the Michigan senator be a party to a filibuster on the issue? George Smathers asked in the next day's Judiciary Committee hearings. Griffin tried to dodge the question entirely for the moment, saying only that "the Senate should take a great deal of time in these matters."

Smathers pressed: "In other words, you say [the president] has got the power but you just do not want him to exercise it?"

"He has only half the power," responded Griffin, as he pounded the witness table, "and it is about time the Senate realized that, especially with regard to the Supreme Court of the United States. He has only half the power, and we have the other half, and we ought to assert ourselves."[26]

And the Michigan senator had made more headway than the White House realized in asserting that power. While it was clear that the old issues were dying, Griffin had opened up an entirely new argument in his committee testimony that would soon change the agenda of the opposition. He charged that Fortas had been "participat[ing] on a regular, undisclosed basis in decisions of the executive branch while serving on the Bench," and had thus violated the doctrine of "separation of powers."[27] However, in seeking to convince the committee "to reexamine very carefully and in great detail the matter of this relationship" between the justice and the president, Griffin's argument was long on rhetoric, but short on evidence. All he really had to offer were shots in the dark—several charges appearing in a handful of paragraphs in published articles on the mysterious justice. In a *New York Times Magazine* article entitled "The Many-Sided Justice Fortas," court reporter Fred Graham, citing anonymous sources, charged that Fortas had been consulted by the president on major policy questions such as Vietnam, steel price increases, transportation strikes, and certain executive and judicial appointments; he had even drafted Johnson's statement dealing with the Detroit riots in late 1967.[28] Then there were similar allegations in *Time* magazine from the previous week.[29] Griffin argued that the real principle here should be Harry Truman's: "Whenever you put a man on the Supreme Court, he ceases to be your friend" (ignoring that what Truman had really been saying was that persons serving on the court no longer vote on issues the way appointing presidents would like).

Phil Hart recognized the new issue for what it was—a potentially devastating turn of events—and warned the administration that this would be made "an important issue by the opposition."[30] Here was a way to embarrass *both* Fortas and the president, charging them with exotic "separation of powers" violations while also blaming the justice for many of the most controversial actions of the administration. Success here would at the very least further delay the proceedings and might well galvanize the opposition alliance. The Justice Department was immediately instructed to research a new list of "Supreme Court Justices as Presidential Advisers" and Lyndon Johnson had more reason to be grateful that the order had been given to destroy the only evidence that could irrefutably prove nearly all of the Griffin charges.[31]

The remainder of Friday's session had proved to be a colossal bore. Chairman Eastland, claiming he had to "catch a plane," only permitted Homer Thornberry to be sworn in, and then asked that he return the following Wednesday for questioning after Abe Fortas's appearance. "I get the sense that this won't go through," a worried Thornberry told Fortas on the phone. But the justice insisted that all would be well, because Everett Dirksen had given his assurance that it "would work out all right."[32]

Then, a series of outside witnesses were permitted to question Fortas's loyalty to God, the Republic, and a moral way of life. But while few took this testimony seriously, in fact one of the participants had scored a direct hit.[33] A retired civil servant, Benjamin Ginzburg, focused his attack on Fortas's recently published book, *Concerning Dissent and Civil Disobedience*. While the justice's argument that demonstrators should resort to peaceful, rather than violent, protests seemed to be a sensible one, Ginzburg reminded the senators of the controversial fact that a sitting member of the Supreme Court had dared to make an argument like that in the first place.

In fact, the timing of the publication had been coincidental with the nomination, with its release coming just weeks before Earl Warren's retirement letter. But even the justice's liberal allies in the Senate deeply regretted that he had allowed the publication to go forward. Supreme Court justices were supposed to limit their comments to judicial opinions, the critics would argue, not write a book that sold 750,000 copies and that the Book-of-the-Month Club deemed so important that it was distributed free of charge to members. Furthermore, it was not lost on the participants on either side of the battle that Fortas had felt comfortable in offering his views in books, and in an early July interview on the *Today* show, and now would be asked to do the same for inquiring senators on the Judiciary Committee.[34]

As everyone awaited Fortas's appearance, there was a good deal of posturing by each side in the senatorial battle. While Mike Mansfield and Everett Dirksen were threatening to call the Senate back after the party conventions to get a vote on the nominations, Robert Griffin now claimed that he had added "16 or 17 Democrats" to his group of opposition rebels. But the main show was yet to come.

When Abe Fortas sat in Room 2228 of the New Senate Office Building at 10:40 A.M. on July 16, it was just the sort of historic event that Washington observers had been anticipating with almost as much enthusiasm as a Redskins-Cowboys playoff football game. The full house in the audience, and the anxious readers of the nation's newspapers, expected to be treated to a political spectacle of epic proportions. Never before in the nation's history had a sitting member of the Supreme Court nominated for chief justice submitted himself for questioning by such a body. And this was no ordinary member of the highest court, but the legendary Abe Fortas. In putting his reputation on the line, both as a justice on Earl Warren's court *and* as an advocate in such hearings, Fortas knew that he would have to give the performance of his career.

No matter how one looked at it, this testimony by Abe Fortas, and his ability to defend himself successfully against the expected senatorial onslaughts, would represent the turning point in the confirmation battle. Moreover, it would represent the turning point in the history of the United States Supreme Court for the rest of the twentieth century.[35]

In the customary lengthy introduction to the committee of the nominee by his home state senator, in this case Albert Gore, the committee was warned "that there are severe limitations upon the kind of questioning that a legislative committee may wish or may properly submit to a sitting Justice of the Supreme Court and that he may himself answer." But Sam Ervin served notice that it would be no-holds-barred questioning, "in order to afford the Judiciary Committee an opportunity to explore and ascertain [the nominee's] constitutional philosophy." It made no difference to him that Fortas had said, "I would like to discuss all questions that anybody may have in mind about the work of the Court," but because of the "kind of person I am—I shall be and continue to be conscious of the constitutional limitations upon me." Ervin and his allies knew all too well that in this sport one did not need a partner to play—just a target.[36]

With Robert Griffin seated in the packed house, Fortas was sworn in and then squared off first against the feisty chairman, James O. Eastland. Everyone in the Senate understood that the Judiciary Committee hearings would become whatever James O. Eastland wanted them to be. Thus far, his rulings as chairman had been helpful to both sides. While he had helped the opposition by delaying Fortas's appearance and putting off Homer Thornberry's testimony until after that event, he had also helped the White House by defusing the no-vacancy issue, and allowing the "outside" witnesses to appear on Friday afternoon so as not to waste another meeting day. With the myriad of rules that existed to permit delays of one sort or another in the committee, though, Eastland's future decisions could easily create either impassable obstacles or safe passage for the nominees in the hearings.

Already Eastland had done another favor for the president regarding Fortas's testimony before the committee. Since Strom Thurmond had already indicated that he would invoke the rule that committees may not meet while the full Senate is in session, the White House had negotiated through Senators Mansfield and Dirksen to keep the full Senate from meeting on the afternoon of the Tuesday that Fortas appeared before the committee. With Eastland's agreement to keep the committee in session all day, the administration's hope was that this would permit one full hearing day to finish all of the questioning of the justice.[37] Of course, while granting this concession, he probably well knew that his southern colleagues would have other ideas.

The nature of his questions now reflected that ambivalence of allegiance. Eastland had decided to lead off with questions relating to the charges by Griffin and Fred Graham of potential separation-of-powers violations. Setting the early tone with a "ceremonious politeness," Eastland opened:

> Mr. Justice, a Senator testified last week against your nomination, and he quoted from the New York Times magazine, and other

sources, about your activities. Now, I think it is very proper to go into that. The testimony is: "Fortas is also thrown into nonjudicial matters by friends who want government jobs, and know he still carries weight at the White House. Periodically word leaks out about Fortas's involvement in such matters as the unsuccessful campaign to land Bill Moyers the job of Under Secretary of State, and his efforts to secure a federal judgeship for David G. Bress, United States Attorney for the District of Columbia." Now, what are the facts about that?

Fortas fixed his eyes on the thirteen senators facing him from the committee table and began in his soft, even voice with a trace of a southern accent. He knew that the nature of this answer would set the tone for the rest of his testimony. Like any good lawyer, he divided the senator's question into several parts and began to answer each of them, carefully considering his answers in relation to both the facts and what he knew the committee could prove:

> I do not believe, Mr. Chairman, and I am rather certain of this, that I have at any time had—at any time, since I have been Justice of the Supreme Court, recommended anybody for any public position. I want to make a precise and specific qualification of that statement. I have been asked, just as all Justices from time to time are asked, my opinion about various persons. Sometimes that has been done by the F.B.I. Sometimes it has been done by officials of the government, and I have, of course, responded to those inquiries. Let me add to that, that I have never, since I have been a Justice—and I do not remember having done it before I was a Justice—initiated any suggestions or any proposal to the President of the United States.[38]

But of course Fortas knew this was not true. "Forgive me for suggesting persons for appointment," he had written to Lyndon Johnson in recommending Saul Haas as a member of the board of directors of the Educational Television Corporation and John Reed for the Tax Court in October 1967.[39] Earlier he had written that former California governor "Pat" Brown "would be a good man to have somewhere in your Administration, or in the Democratic Party."[40]

And these were far from isolated occurrences. By the time Fortas came to the court, the appointment process was well settled. Most of the programs were in place; the old appointees were experienced; some of them were now leaving after their turn in office. The appointment pool was becoming a bit stale, and people were wondering if the Johnson years were coming to a close. Someone was needed to bring in new talent, and Fortas saw that as part of his service to the president.

And so, shortly after his court appointment, the justice began making suggestions to White House staffers Jack Valenti and Harry McPherson, as well as Civil Service Commission Chairman John Macy, regarding names for such positions as membership on the District of Columbia Public Service Commission and the chairmanship of the proposed Tariff Commission.[41] These recommendations were immediately ranked ahead of those from people within the administration.[42]

Fortas also offered in mid-May 1966 his own unsolicited long list of possible candidates for positions. After two days of thinking about names for ambassadorial assignments, the justice forwarded eighteen names with short supportive comments on each of them. Some of these people he had previously recommended, and even though one had certain questionable features, Fortas "personally underwr[ote]" him for the president.[43]

Later that month, Fortas did his best to make sure that the top names on that list received the proper attention. Since Robert Kintner, former president of NBC, had just joined the White House staff to help advise the president on administration appointments, Fortas handwrote him a memorandum lobbying for what he termed the "outstanding possibilities" for appointment from this list.[44]

But Fortas did much more than just volunteer and lobby for his suggestions for names and positions. Part of his influence as a talent scout stemmed simply from his availability as a resource to be consulted by members of the administration in their own screening efforts. Among the names requested from the justice in 1966 were candidates for commissioner of the Trust Territories and governor of American Samoa, membership on the Federal Reserve Board and the Federal Communications Commission, general counsel of the Democratic National Committee and chairman of the Equal Employment Opportunity Commission. More than once the justice would think of additional names for the positons after his discussion and contact the caller later.[45]

By 1967 there was no end to the type and number of suggestions made by the justice. He recommended Pat Brown's defeated lieutenant governor, Glenn Anderson, for the ambassadorship to Chile.[46] When one friend recommended S. Thomas Simon for the National Transportation Safety Board, Fortas passed the name along to John Macy for examination.[47] And the justice urged that John Mathis, who was retiring from his position as chairman of the board at the Lone Star Cement Corporation, be given a position on the Atomic Energy Commission.[48] But apparently, all of these efforts temporarily escaped the justice's memory in July 1968.

So Fortas continued his answer to Eastland with: "Now, with respect to the two specific matters that you mentioned in your question—Mr. Moyers—that is completely, absolutely, totally without foundation in fact. I not only did not make any recommendation for Mr. Moyers in connection with any position; I was never asked. That is No. 1. I do not know whether he was ever considered for that position."

Once more Fortas knew that the truth was otherwise.

The New York Times's James Reston had printed a column suggesting that Moyers replace the departing George Ball as undersecretary of state in September 1966. When Fortas saw it, he liked the idea and took the matter directly to Lyndon Johnson. Pretty soon an annoyed president started calling Moyers, who was then assisting Sargent Shriver in the Peace Corps, complaining that the justice had been in his office with the suggestion. "Now you leave it alone," Johnson warned. "Someone's priming the pump and I want you to stay where you are." So Fortas's effort failed.[49] And by July 1968 he had expunged it from his memory.

"No. 2, with respect to Mr. Bress. Mr. Bress is a practicing attorney in Washington—he was—he is now U.S. Attorney. I have known him in that way for many years. I remember seeing in a column this statement to which you have referred. I did not recommend Mr. Bress for a U.S. judgeship."

Well, there was some truth here—but only because Eastland's question had not been framed properly. After all, the question had been about Fortas's "efforts to secure" a judgeship, not about his "consultation" on it. And nothing had been mentioned about how Bress got the United States attorney's position in the first place.

Fortas's status as a fountain of information for the White House on legal appointments—even from the court—was never so evident as in David Bress's case. On such occasions, Fortas was seen as just another of the Washington attorneys who received a routine phone call and sometimes even did some legwork investigating. A Harvard graduate and Washington attorney since 1931, Bress had had a controversial career, and by the time he was being considered for a U.S. attorney's appointment in 1965 he had earned the wrath of columnist Drew Pearson. So the columnist phoned Justice Fortas and Bill Moyers protesting the nominee's qualifications, a fact that was passed on by both men to the president.[50]

With the rumor that Bress would be sent to the judiciary eighteen months later, Pearson, who thought he had a promise from the president that such an appointment would never be made, wrote a letter to Johnson wondering if this wasn't just a "slipup."[51] But the enmity of the acerbic Pearson meant little to the White House when members of its Washington circle of lawyers, such as Abe Fortas, were recommending Bress to the White House. In early August, Fortas reported that he had checked up on Bress "as well as he could" and "would have no hesitation in going ahead with the nomination." He told Marvin Watson that in his opinion "the Bar does assume Mr. Bress will be nominated and will support the nomination." While "this does not guarantee that some lawyer will not testify against Bress," the justice added, "it is reasonable to expect this nomination to go through."[52] Perhaps as a result of this controversy, however, Bress never received the judicial appointment. In July 1968, though, this became another matter that slipped Fortas's memory.

Feeling more confident as he developed his answer, Fortas decided to go on the offensive: "To the best of my knowledge and belief, I have never, since I have been a Justice, recommended anyone for a judgeship."

But of course Fortas knew that this was only true to the best of *the committee's* knowledge—as the staffers in the White House well understood.

Shortly after coming to the court, Fortas had agreed to review Ramsey Clark's suggested judicial appointees and aggressively pursued his recommendations here.[53] Six weeks later he sent John Macy an unsolicited recommendation for a Yale Law School classmate, Allan Hart, for a new vacancy on the United States District Court in Portland, Oregon. After offering what he admitted might be "effusive" praise for his candidate, the justice reassured Macy that the Oregon senators would endorse him.[54] But once again, Fortas crossed

Wayne Morse, and so began a three-year effort to secure the appointment over the senator's objections. In the end, the appointment was not made.

Allan Hart was not the only nomination offered by Fortas for the federal bench. In March 1966, he suggested to the White House that Simon Lazarus, Jr., should be given a federal judgeship in the Southern District of Ohio.[55] Then, Fortas volunteered the name of a friend, Joseph Ball, for a nomination to the Ninth Circuit of the United States Court of Appeals. Unfortunately, though, Ball was sixty-four years old, meaning that he would not get the blessing of the American Bar Association. So no appointment was forthcoming from the White House despite Fortas's unqualified endorsement.[56]

Finally, in 1968, Abe Fortas was one of those consulted by the White House for information on John Pratt and June Green, two prominent Washington attorneys being considered for the United States District Court for the District of Columbia.[57] Both eventually were appointed.[58] Another of Fortas's "strongly endorsed" nominees for this court, Sidney Sachs, was not so fortunate.[59]

Finally Fortas endorsed Phoenix attorney John Frank, a former law clerk to Hugo Black. But this idea failed to pass muster with the president because of what was called, by Warren Christopher, Frank's "exceedingly controversial" reputation among Arizona lawyers.[60]

Had he known all of this, Senator Eastland would have said that Fortas took a great interest in the Johnson administration's judicial appointment efforts.

Lacking proof of this fact, however, Eastland simply went on: "Now, the charge was made that you were adviser of the President in coping with steel price increases and helping to frame measures to head off transportation strikes—with the increasing intensity of the war in Vietnam Fortas is also consulted more and more on foreign policy."

Fortas replied, "All right, Senator. Let me say in the first place—and make this absolutely clear—that since I have been a Justice, the President of the United States has never, directly or indirectly, approximately or remotely, talked to me about anything before the Court or that might come before the Court. I want to make that absolutely clear." Later he added, "It is not true that I have ever helped to frame a measure since I have been a Justice of the Court."

Here not only did the Justice fail to recall his efforts to protect animal rights, but also to protect the First Amendment from the newly passed campaign-finance bill.

When a comprehensive campaign-finance reform measure was proposed, among the options being considered by the White House was whether to expand the disclosure requirements for congressmen to cover large campaign gifts and all assets and income, and whether to provide public funds for all campaign expenses, or perhaps just for television and radio expenses. Joe Califano was charged with discussing the matter with Fortas, Vice President Humphrey, and Clark Clifford on May 24, 1967. Like the others, the justice called for total disclosure of assets and income. On the matter of funding, though, the justice saw some legal problems. In opting for funding only the expenses of bringing a candidate's message to the public on the media, he warned that "you should start with some narrow purpose and . . . even here there will be serious problems of enforcement and free speech. (For example, how could you stop an attorney or group of attorneys that felt so strongly that you should be elected from taking an ad on their own in a newspaper to urge your election?)" Fortas's approach, which foresaw the creation of political action committees, was endorsed by both the vice president and Califano.[61]

Understandably, as the president's election advisers gathered in the Cabinet Room later in the afternoon to discuss these ideas, Fortas was included among them.[62] In the end Johnson did opt for the Fortas-recommended proposal calling for public financing for all campaign media use, combined with an elimination of all other contributions for this purpose. However, the time was not right for action here, and not until 1974 was the Federal Election Campaign Act passed.

"No. 2, the President of the United States, since I have been an Associate Justice, has done me the honor, on some occasions, of indicating that he thought that I could be of help to him and to the nation in a few critical matters, and I have, on occasion, been asked to come to the White House to participate in conferences on critical matters having nothing whatever to do with any legal situation or with anything before the Court or that might come before the Court."

Fortas must have shuddered as he considered what this admission in response to Eastland's question would look like in the morning's newspapers. It was a dramatic moment, coming so early in the hearings. Never before had a Supreme Court justice willingly admitted in such a forum that he had knowingly violated the sacred myth of separate governmental powers. But what could he do? Too many people thought they knew the truth, having seen Fortas in the twenty White House meetings he had attended since coming to the court. Even there, however, the truth about the full extent of his involvement, especially on the subject of Vietnam, with one of the most controversial presidents in American history was devastating. So Fortas decided that the best thing to do was to minimize the involvement to "a few critical matters," make it sound like a patriotic calling, and try to avoid talking about specifics.

"What about the steel price increases—and helping to frame measures to head off transportation strikes?" Eastland probed, looking for those specifics.

So much for strategy. Fortas considered the truth. Yes, he had spent a day in meetings and on the telephone in January 1966, trying to help roll back the steel prices to relieve the nation's inflationary pressures.[63] But the truth about his actions during the threatened railroad strike in April 1967 was even worse.

The year 1967 was a period of turbulence for the nation, and thus for the president. One of the big reasons was the threat of a rail strike. So Fortas was forced to don his hats as presidential troubleshooter and crisis manager. When the White House held a meeting on February 17 in Joe Califano's office on the creation of emergency strike legislation that would establish a seventeen-member National Commission on Collective Bargaining to study and recommend mediation in certain cases, the justice was included.[64]

And when many of the same issues were raised in another meeting in early April, as presidential action during the actual threat was being considered, it was only natural that Fortas was asked back. After some study, the president's men warned that the prospect of a nationwide rail strike was a frightening one. One memorandum warned that even if a strike was settled in thirty days, "the economic disruptions from such a catastrophe could generate either a recession, or a galloping inflation—or maybe even both. *The chances of resuming a stable expansion would be very slim.*"[65]

With the completion of the eleven months of prescribed negotiations for averting a crisis, six shopcraft unions representing 137,000 employees who maintained the trains announced a strike date of 12:01 A.M. on April 13.[66] With that action would come a nationwide trucking stoppage as well, affecting about 70 percent of that industry. Since the unions had refused to extend the time for negotiations voluntarily, Johnson returned from Camp David during the evening of April 9 to assess a course of action with his advisers. Gathered around the huge conference table in the Cabinet Room, overlooked by pictures of

Franklin Roosevelt and Thomas Jefferson as well as a bust of Abraham Lincoln, were the men he trusted most with this problem: Secretary of Labor Willard Wirtz, Secretary of Defense Robert McNamara, Secretary of Transportation Alan Boyd, Attorney General Ramsey Clark, Undersecretary of State Nicholas Katzenbach, Deputy Defense Secretary Cyrus Vance, Undersecretary of Labor James Reynolds, Assistant Attorney General Harold Barefoot Sanders, Chairman of the Council of Economic Advisers Gardner Ackley, Special Assistant Joe Califano, David Ginsburg (a Washington attorney who had served on Johnson's appointed "emergency board"), and of course the two outside-insiders, Clark Clifford and Abe Fortas.

For well over an hour, they hashed over the issues and recommended solutions. Joe Califano began the meeting by blocking out the options available to the president. There could be a joint congressional resolution extending the no-strike period under the Railway Labor Act for another twenty or thirty days, possibly accompanying that with a special mediation panel appointed by the president. If not these ideas, then compulsory arbitration or government seizure, or even the sheer imposition of a settlement by the Interstate Commerce Commission, was possible. It was a "fluid situation," added Secretary of Labor Wirtz, who recommended against using the Taft-Hartley strike procedures in that area and favored the no-strike resolution along with creating the presidential outside mediation panel. There would be no voluntary extension of the period by labor, he argued, because the AFL-CIO lobbyist Andrew Biemiller "wants to embarrass the President." The no-strike option would not remove the workers' right to strike, but only postpone it for "one more chance" at collective bargaining. And as the meeting wore on, it became apparent that all of the government advisers favored this immediate no-strike option.

But after all of this had been discussed, it was left to the "outsiders" to "sum up." As was usually the case, Clifford and Fortas disagreed with the others. But then they were looking at the issue from a different angle—while others perceived the effects on the nation, these two were concerned with the effects on the public relations position of the president. Accordingly, theirs was the view that appeared to carry the most weight with the man who counted.

"The unions have complied with the law," Clifford began. "Now, under the law they have the constitutional right to strike. The President must therefore exercise great care because to delay a strike for 20 days is to take a great right a working man has away from him—the right to strike. The case for action now is not convincing." As Clifford made clear, he wanted the onus for action on Congress. If what he had heard was true, then let all hell break loose and force the other guys to take the heat.

Given this sterling performance protecting the political prospects of Lyndon Johnson, it is not surprising that the other half of the outside duo, a justice on the Supreme Court, would agree.[67] With his gift for eloquence, Fortas provided the tactile image that would grab the fancy of Joe Califano when he worked on the issue the following day. Forgetting his position in the fight with John L. Lewis during the coal strike of 1943, Fortas knew that this time it was in his president's best interests to take a different course—allow a strike to begin. The "stove is too cold" for an immediate action, he told the others around the table. "The time to act is after a strike occurs." Then, thinking a bit further about the public relations aspects here, Fortas added, "The next course of action should be to issue a public statement on both the trucking and railroad situations to alert the nation and urge that the parties come into agreement." Such a statement would "also alert Congress to get ready to take action promptly in the national interest." Neither the justice nor anyone else around the table seemed troubled by his willingness to address, off the bench, an issue that might someday come before the Supreme Court.

After hearing all the views, Johnson kept his options open by ordering that each option be followed for the time being. He wanted prepared both a congressional message invoking the no-strike legislation request, and the sort of warning statement that Fortas had suggested if the strike was allowed to begin.[68]

The argument among the advisers raged through the evening, and by 2 A.M. the following morning, the message to Congress had been drafted, reciting the horrors of a nationwide rail strike and documenting the need for extending the no-strike period.[69] At the same time, Fortas, Clifford, and Califano had drafted the warning statement that the justice had been suggesting for the president's possible use. "It is my duty to advise the American people and the Congress of the serious situation that confronts the nation as a result of the threatened railroad strike, and the announced shutdown in the trucking industry," it began. Then, going on to describe the elaborate negotiation efforts that had been attempted, it placed blame on the unions for not voluntarily delaying the strike. The two-page document concluded by saying that it would be up to Congress to act in the event of the total breakdown of collective bargaining. In other words, blame the unions, the railroads, or Congress, but not your president.[70]

No matter how cleverly the statement was worded, the idea did not sit well with the secretary of labor. Willard Wirtz told Califano that he "strongly opposed" such an "out of channel" last-ditch effort as this statement, warning that the public would see this as a "gimmick." But Fortas did not back down in the evening's discussions, and searched for the public relations strategy that would give the appearance that the president was in total control. He told Califano that the president should go as planned to the Punta del Este, Uruguay, conference with Latin American leaders, send no message to Congress, and perhaps dramatically leave the conference early in order to return to Washington for "a final around-the-clock effort to settle the strike." As in other areas, it was not solving the problem but making the president look good that mattered the most to the justice.

Indicating the quandary created by the competing groups, Califano himself recommended the sending of a message to Congress while conceding that "Clifford and Fortas may have a good point about serving it up to a cold stove." So, the aide concluded, perhaps the Fortas statement could be used the next day, with the formal message to Congress to follow after that.[71]

In the end, the Wirtz faction won out. Johnson sent the message to Congress calling for a twenty-day extension of the no-strike period while a "special mediation panel" serving under retired federal judge Charles Fahy searched for a solution through collective bargaining.

When these recommendations were rejected by both sides, and the no-strike period was about to run out, Fortas was invited back to the White House for another round of meetings. With the president at the ranch, Califano called together Wirtz, McNamara, Boyd, Larry Levinson, the members of Fahy's panel, Reynolds, and of course Clifford and Fortas, for a late-night meeting on the twenty-fourth of April. After two hours of discussion of whether to adopt the final Fahy Report legislatively, impose compulsory arbitration, seize the railroads, or extend the no-strike period with further mediation, however, the men could reach no decision for presidential action.[72]

So, just over a week later, Fortas was called back to the White House for his third meeting on the issue. The day before, Johnson had asked Congress for a forty-five-day extension of the no-strike period. After the meeting was over, it was left for Fortas to "sum up" once more in a private six-minute meeting with the president in the Oval Office.[73] As a new message to Congress was being drafted to accompany the new formal joint resolution, Fortas was one of the many advisers reviewing it.[74] Here, the president proposed, in an ingenious combination of nearly all of the options his advisers had been considering over the last few weeks, the appointment for ninety days of a five-member special board composed solely of "public members," which would first mediate, and failing that would eventually be empowered to impose the Fahy panel's recommendations as it saw fit, until the two sides reached a final agreement. And as the president continued to send various messages to Congress as late as mid-July on the general economic situation, Fortas continued to be one of the men solicited for comments on the draft before it was finalized.[75] With the aid of this compromise, the crisis was eventually averted.[76] But the justice's labors had not gone unnoticed by the press.

The possible next day's newspaper headlines if he answered truthfully about his efforts during the rail strike, though, frightened Fortas. So another lie was needed: "Mr. Chairman, I confess I cannot—I do not know what that refers to. I just cannot place it; I cannot identify it." And, Fortas knew, neither could Eastland.

Fortas then looked for shelter by launching into a civics lesson:

I do not want to talk about specific matters on which I have been consulted. But I do, if I may, want to tell you of the nature of the consultation, if it can be called that. It is well known that the President and I have been associated mostly as lawyer and client, for a great many years. The President does me the honor of having confidence in my ability, apparently, to analyze a situation and to state the pros and cons. In every situation where I have been called to the White House for this purpose, so far as I can recall, my function— the President runs conferences, as I am sure all of you know—my function has been to listen to what is said. The President has called on me last. And it is my function, then, to sum up the arguments on the one side, the considerations on the other side.

Fortas knew that no one was going to buy the "sum up" admission as being a minor role either. ("You give me a chance to 'sum up' a case," Washington lawyer Joseph L. Rauh, Jr., later said, "and I'll win for your side every time.")[77] All Fortas could do was hope that the senators bought the idea of his duty here, and how "honored" he was at being asked his opinion in these "situations."

"Mr. Chairman," Fortas added quickly, "it would be very misleading to allow the impression to prevail that this is a matter of frequency. It occurs very seldom."

Seldom is a relative term, Fortas must have thought. But then the senators didn't have access to the White House phone logs and diaries, did they?

"If you were helping to frame measures," Eastland responded, "that is a matter that would come before the Court." The senator smelled blood.

"I do not believe that is so. I am sure that is not so, Mr. Chairman," Fortas said, forgetting that the railroad strike actions were easily reviewable (as would have been the campaign finance law, if passed), and that judicial challenges were being launched against the Vietnam War as well as the protests against it.

"Then you say it is not true," Eastland pressed, hoping to get at least something on the record that might be contradicted later. He was not disappointed.

"It is not true. And I say I could not recall any such incident. It is not true that I have ever helped to frame a measure since I have been a Justice of the Court. I have described to you as precisely as I can the exact nature of the function," Fortas concluded, knowing that Eastland's newspaper articles with their anonymous sources were not enough to prove him wrong.

But Eastland still had hope of landing a blow: "Now, the charge was made that 'Fortas wrote the President's message ordering Federal troops into the city of Detroit.'"

"Again, Mr. Chairman, I do not want to—I do not think it would be proper to go into specifics, but I can say to you that I did not write that message. I did see it before it was delivered," the justice confessed, "but I did not write it."

"Did you approve it?"

"No sir, the President does not ask my approval."

Eastland thought he had a damaging contradiction: "Why was it shown to you, if you had no authority in it?"

But the question had not been precise enough. Knowing that he could not answer the question safely, or for that matter honestly, Fortas opted for delivering another civics lecture on the obligations of a presidential adviser: "Mr. Chairman, again, I do not want to do anything, say anything, go into anything that is an act of violence on the office of the Presidency, or that, in any way, may operate now or in the future to hamper any President of the United States in the discharge of his terrible burdens in consulting anybody he wants to. But I may say to you in this specific instance that the President, in that critical and desperate situation, called together not only members of his Cabinet, but as is his custom, as is well known, people in whom he has trust, to make sure that when he reached a decision, it was reached on the basis of taking into account all possible factors. And I was one of those people, and I am proud if I was able then or at any other time to be of the slightest service to the President or to my country.''

Once more, the true story would have shocked even Abe Fortas's allies.

As soon as the justice heard that it was the president calling on the evening of July 23, 1967, he knew there was something seriously wrong. ''Lyndon Johnson knew never to call me on a Sunday night— never,'' Fortas explained later.[78] At least not for any ordinary emergency. Sundays were sacred to Fortas, the one time during the week when Fortas got his relaxation—not counting the interesting conversations at various dinner parties around town during the week—while he played his fiddle, as he called it, with whatever prominent friends from the musical world were in town. The group was jokingly called the 3025 N Street Strictly-No-Refunds String Quartet, and among the reported occasional participants were Isaac Stern, Van Cliburn, Pablo Casals, and Rudolf Serkin.[79]

But this one time Johnson felt justified in interrupting his outside adviser, for the city of Detroit was burning to the ground. There was wholesale rioting there, explained the president, and the National Guard had been mobilized by Michigan Governor George Romney. Could Fortas drop everything and come over first thing in the morning? Indeed he could.

At 8:35 the next morning, Fortas moved into the White House for the next sixteen hours and remained at the president's right hand for meetings throughout the day on the second floor of the mansion, in the Oval Office, in Joseph Califano's office, at the lunch table, at the dinner table, in the swimming pool, and wherever else the advisers and the president chose to stop that day. What ensued was nothing less than ''a day in the life'' of an outside judicial adviser to a president in crisis.

By the time Fortas arrived on the second floor of the White House, Detroit Mayor Jerome Cavanagh was reporting that there had been 483 fires, significant looting, and eighteen hundred people arrested, filling the detention facilities beyond capacity. There were even reports that the mobs were about to turn on the homes of middle-class blacks who, in turn, were arming themselves. Parts of Detroit itself now looked like the aftermath of a bombing run.[80]

It did not take long for the justice, listening to the ''four or five men'' surrounding the president, to realize that if Lyndon Johnson followed their counsel he was headed for disaster. The president's men had just about convinced him to send troops immediately into the riot-torn city. In fact, the army had already been authorized to plan for deploying troops, the Pentagon command post had been put on emergency status, and by 4:20 that morning "alert orders" had been given to the paratroopers in Fort Bragg and Fort Campbell. Everything seemed in the "go" position, but before acting the president had one more opinion that he very much wanted to hear.[81] And Fortas very clearly saw the problem. As he later explained, Governor Romney "was adamant against requesting for the federal troops; in fact, he wouldn't even call out his own militia. He didn't want the political fallout."[82] The effect on his bid for a presidential nomination in 1968 would be predictably bad.

There seemed no way to change the governor's mind. He had been on the phone with Ramsey Clark five times throughout the previous evening, and was very equivocal about asking for support from the federal government. Shortly before midnight he had called to say that "a very dangerous situation existed in the city." Then at 2:40 A.M. on July 24 the two men spoke again, with Romney saying that "he might need Army troops to quell the rioting." With that Clark alerted the army and phoned the president with an update. Finally, shortly before dawn, Romney called Clark once more at his Justice Department office to say that "rather than take any chance, he should get Federal help." In fact, the governor added, he had just told the press that federal troops had been requested.

But the attorney general informed him that the matter was a bit more complex than that. A written request would have to be sent, certifying not only that the state had exhausted its resources in dealing with the problem, but also that there was a "state of insurrection" or "domestic violence he was unable to suppress." At this point Romney had to think things over, saying that the situation was not yet that bad.[83] By the time Fortas arrived at the White House, no further action had been taken.

When the justice was informed of all this, he quickly came to his own assessment of the governor's strategy here. "He was trying to force Lyndon to send the troops in without invitation," explained Fortas.[84] So the justice could see that his job was first and foremost to protect the president in any way possible.

"What do you think of it?" Johnson asked his favorite outside adviser. There could be little doubt that this was a matter within the purview of the court's powers over federal-state relations, and the president was asking for nothing less than an advisory constitutional opinion. But Fortas had no hesitation in answering. Years later, Fortas would explain to a visitor, "It's one of the few times that I was very glad that I was at a particular event and was very, very glad that I was able to assist." (But as honest as this assessment was in 1982, Fortas had not been quite so forthcoming in response to a similar question by the Senate committee in 1968.)[85]

Since he was being asked for his legal judgment on the course to be followed, that was what Fortas offered early that morning. "You must absolutely not do it," he declared. "It's a basic, fundamental precept of the government; [the states] have to request troops."

The reason, Fortas reminded the president, was the republican state government clause of the Constitution. That provision, found in Article IV, Section 4, reads: "The United States shall guarantee to every State in this Union a Republican Form of Government, and shall protect each of them against Invasion; and *on Application of the Legislature, or of the Executive* (when the Legislature cannot be convened) against domestic Violence [italics added]."[86] As interpreted by the Supreme Court, the provision gives the president the power to dispatch troops to the states in order to maintain domestic tranquility by proclaiming martial law.

So Fortas told the president that the first move, according to constitutional precedent, *had* to be Romney's. In reality, contrary to this advice, the courts had maintained over the years that the president need not "await an invitation" before sending in troops under the powers in this provision. Indeed, in similar circumstances, Presidents Eisenhower and Kennedy had deployed troops to keep the peace during civil rights disturbances in Little Rock, Arkansas, in 1957 and Mississippi and Alabama in 1962 and 1963, demonstrating that the president's greater powers here came from an entirely different constitutional clause. Using the power to "take care that the laws be faithfully executed," all the president had to do before ordering an intervention of federal troops was to issue a proclamation commanding the insurgents to disperse.[87] All of these legalities and recent events were surely well known to the Supreme Court justice.

However, the issue here was more than legality, it was Johnson's political future as well. By advising in this manner, Fortas was also telling Johnson that unilateral movement here would be political suicide. The fact that the governor was from the other party, and a potential adversary in 1968, did not make the situation any simpler. So, by offering this advice packaged as a legal opinion, thus making it easier for the others to accept, Fortas was actually telling Johnson what he wanted to hear—how to protect *both* his legal and his political flanks. It was a role that Fortas would continue to fill for the rest of the day.

"Yes, exactly!" came the president's predictable response. A way would have to be found to force the governor's hand. So members of the White House staff were instructed to find precedents and federal laws bolstering the justice's view. Shortly before nine o'clock, though, the issue seemed to be moot when Governor Romney called the attorney general again to ask for help. But there was still a problem. Romney's prepared statement was only *recommending* the use of federal troops. The governor would have to *request* the troops, Clark explained, and certify that after everything possible had been done by the state of Michigan, the violence still could not be suppressed. Only then could federal help be sent. So now the lines were drawn in this game of political chicken.

An hour later, Romney seemed ready to concede, calling Clark yet another time to read the text of a new telegram he was now thinking of sending to the president. "As Governor of the State of Michigan, I do hereby officially request the immediate deployment of federal troops into Michigan to assist state and local authorities in reestablishing law and order in the city of Detroit. There is reasonable doubt that we can suppress the existing looting, arson and sniping without the assistance of federal troops. Time could be of the essence."[88] The language was not quite what Clark had been demanding, but this was as far as Romney was willing to consider going at the moment.

While "reasonable doubt" seemed to be good enough for Johnson to order the movement of troops from one military base to another, it was still not the certification required to deploy troops to a city or state.[89] But now Romney seemed to have the president penned in. Politically speaking, all that an unsophisticated public would understand was that the governor had asked for help. The technical details of whether he had asserted that there was "reasonable doubt" of an ability to handle the problem, as opposed to admitting the existence of a "state of insurrection," would be lost on the average person. Should Johnson fail to respond, it would be his problem and not Romney's. So now a way had to be found by the White House to place the burden of the request back on the governor's shoulders.

The formal telegram arrived at 10:58 A.M., while Johnson was in a meeting at the White House with Robert McNamara, Abe Fortas, and George Christian. Knowing that the request might be on the way, they had already agreed to send Cyrus Vance to Detroit for an on-the-spot assessment and were now discussing how to deploy the troops in response to Romney's plea.

Johnson read the wire and passed it to Fortas and McNamara for their perusal. While the president directed McNamara to ready the troops for movement, Fortas, realizing that there would have to be a White House response to the Romney telegram, drafted "a statement" for Johnson's review. Once he was free, the president reviewed Fortas's statement, suggested some changes in it, and then handed it to George Christian to read over. Then all of them went to the Cabinet Room for another meeting.[90] The White House notes do not make absolutely clear whether this statement was in fact the first draft of the president's responding telegram to Romney. There is, however, a very high probability, according to the records, that this was the case.[91]

For the benefit of the new participants at the 11:15 meeting, Johnson, McNamara, and Fortas reenacted their earlier discussion. Johnson told the others—Ramsey Clark, Warren Christopher, Assistant Attorney General John Doar, Larry Levinson, Cyrus Vance (who had been called by the secretary of defense with his new assignment fifteen minutes earlier), and Roger Wilkins, director of the Department of Justice Community Relations Service—that he wanted to play down the military's role, using it only as "support and assistance," and play up the civilian role in the crisis. With that in mind, the president was sending Cyrus Vance to the scene. This drew fire from Attorney General Clark, who said "there were indications that the situation had been substantially exaggerated." To him the negative aspects of Vance's role seemed apparent. Since Vance was no longer part of the Department of Defense, it would appear to the public that the handling of the crisis by the current executive personnel had been so bad that someone had to be drafted into service from the outside to handle it. Furthermore, the attorney general added, it would make it appear that Johnson was "trying to disassociate himself from the crisis."

If there was any support for the Clark position, it was quickly beaten down by the members of the "rump caucus" from the hour before, who quickly moved to support the president's position. Robert McNamara praised Vance's performance in earlier crises and reminded the others that the former deputy secretary of defense had been out of the department for less than a month. Then Fortas chimed in his agreement with the secretary of defense and added his judgment that Vance should be dispatched to the city. With that, the president's view carried the day without further comment.

Then the president turned to a reading of the telegram that had been drafted for his response to George Romney. Saying that it was important to respond to Romney as soon as possible, Johnson then "directed" Fortas and George Christian "to read and edit the telegram." This was written in a manner that fully satisfied Fortas's earlier concern that the president remain consistent with the dictates of the republican state government clause of the Constitution.[92]

Whatever failures the wording might have had on other points, the final draft was a model of clarity on one point—Romney was getting what *he* had asked for.

> In response to *your official request,* joined by Mayor Cavanagh, that federal troops be sent to assist local and state police and the 8000 Michigan National Guardsmen under your command, and *on the basis of your representation* that there is reasonable doubt that you can maintain law and order in Detroit, I have directed the troops *you requested* to proceed at once to Selfridge Air Force Base, Michigan. There they will be available for immediate deployment as required to support and assist police and the Michigan National Guard forces. These troops will arrive at Selfridge this afternoon. Immediately, I have instructed Cyrus Vance, Special Assistant to Secretary of Defense McNamara, to proceed to Detroit for conferences with you and to make specific plans for providing you with such support and assistance as may be necessary. [Italics added.][93]

In effect, all Johnson was saying was that he could move the troops nearer to Detroit (this he could freely do without an executive order or proclamation), but deployment was still up to the governor. Even here, though, saying three times in a single paragraph that Romney had made the request seemed to be an excessive effort to persuade the public that any political fallout should be directed toward Lansing rather than Washington.

But while the politicians waltzed, Detroit rocked and shook to its foundation. Once he arrived on the scene, Cyrus Vance kept the White House apprised of events. The performance of the former deputy defense secretary as the president's troubleshooter here was nothing short of heroic. He was in both psychological pain, having just returned from his mother's funeral, and physical pain, with a bad back so debilitating that he could not even tie his own shoelaces and had to bring his wife along to dress him. Johnson had agreed to Vance's selection because he had been involved in the Kennedy effort to quiet the racial situation in Oxford, Mississippi, in 1962 by sending in troops. Now, with five thousand paratroopers (ironically enough, some from the same "Screaming Eagles" unit whose members had been ordered into Oxford five years earlier) poised on Detroit's outskirts later in the day, Vance drove with the governor and Mayor Cavanagh to get a firsthand look at the riot zone in an unmarked four-car motorcade, and reported back to the White House on whatever public phone lines had been left standing.[94] What they saw were shells of burning buildings, wholesale destruction, broken glass in the street, and looting.[95]

As Vance met during the day with the various political figures and assessed the reports from the military, it became clear to him that the governor was going to hold out until the last minute before heeding the White House's requirement to admit that things were just too far out of his control to handle alone. Even though there were only 730 state police available in the city as of late afternoon, Romney still was reluctant to certify that there was a state of insurrection, fearing that the result would be a voiding of insurance policies. Not even Vance's renewed explanation of the significant legal hurdles involved in sending federal troops could sway him. As night fell, then, the two sides were still at a stalemate, with the city bracing for another night of violence.[96]

While the White House waited for events to unfold in Detroit, the regularly planned policy meetings continued throughout the day. After all, other business has to continue in the White House, even during a crisis period. So Fortas simply made himself at home as just another member of the White House staff, sandwiching attendance at whatever meetings happened to be hot around a late-afternoon lunch with the president and McNamara. When the ambassador to Israel, Walworth Barbour, paid a call at midday, the justice, who had taken a sudden interest in the problems of that country during June's Six-Day War, was included for a round of conversation and picture taking.[97] Then an eighty-three-minute meeting to discuss tax policy began in Joe Califano's office, involving all of the president's financial advisers, so Fortas was included there.[98] Fortas also found the time during a hectic day to read over and approve Harry McPherson's draft of the president's message to Puerto Rico for its Commonwealth Day celebration the next day.[99]

Fortas remained at the president's side throughout the day, with the notable exception of a 6:07 P.M. briefing of half a dozen congressional leaders at the White House. It's tough to explain why a Supreme Court justice is a house guest of the president's to people who have considerable familiarity with the separation of powers.[100]

As the evening meetings rolled around, Johnson still wanted his constitutional lawyer and public relations consultant by his side until the crisis period had passed. Over a five-hour period Fortas and Johnson met with McNamara, General Harold Johnson, Secretary of the Army Stanley Resor, Attorney General Clark, and FBI Director J. Edgar Hoover.[101] Interestingly enough, in later writing his memoirs on this day that was "forever etched in his memory," Johnson tried to protect Fortas from attack by leaving his name out of the list of participants of one of these meetings.[102] But by then the effort at concealment was too late.

As the discussion group moved rapidly from Joe Califano's office to the swimming pool, to the Oval Office, to dinner at the mansion, back to the Oval Office, and then to the White House theater, things heated up once again in Detroit. By 10 P.M. the time for decision was at hand, and the staff had done the necessary research to apprise the president of his options. They had found three sections of the United States Code supporting Fortas's view that the law on the use of federal troops in cases of civil disorder required that a formal request be made by the governor. According to them, "whenever there is an insurrection in any State against its government" the president may, "upon the request of its legislature or of its governor if the legislature cannot be convened," call in federal troops necessary to quell the insurrection. However, since there had still been no such request from Romney, even as the fires started to rage again and the national guardsmen were being wounded by snipers, other options were explored.

In searching for historical precedents, the White House aides had discovered fifteen prior instances of governors' "requesting" the assistant of federal troops. The situations ranged from racial problems in New Orleans and Ku Klux Klan riots, to railroad and mining riots, to the Bonus Army facing Herbert Hoover in 1932. The precedents seemed strongly in favor of sending in troops. In the last twelve such incidents, troops had been sent in eleven times. And in the twelfth incident, which involved the Colorado mining riots of 1903, Teddy Roosevelt had refused to send in troops only because the state neither demonstrated its inability to control the situation nor made the request "as contemplated by law."[103]

But they also discovered that responding to a state request was not the only way to send in troops legally. A later section of the U.S.

Code explained that the president may take such action if "the constituted authorities of that State are unable, fail, or refuse to protect [a]
right, privilege, or immunity, or to give that protection." This step
required that the president issue a proclamation ordering "the insurgents to disperse and retire peaceably to their abodes within a limited
time."[104] Franklin D. Roosevelt had done this in handling the race
riots in Detroit in 1943, simply relying on a presidential declaration of
martial law accompanied by a proclamation ordering the rioters to disperse before sending in the troops. Within hours after the troops had
been sent into the riot area, the situation was quiet enough to withdraw
the military.[105] For a man who envisioned himself as being in the
mold of FDR, as Johnson did, the chance to follow such a precedent
had much appeal indeed.[106]

By the time the advisory group convened in the Oval Office at 10
P.M., this precedent had become the focal point of the discussion. No
precedent, however, regardless of the similarity, is ever quite identical
to any other situation, and this was no exception. Roosevelt's proclamation of June 21, 1943, carefully observed in the lead paragraph that
"the Governor of the State of Michigan has represented that domestic
violence exists in said State which the authorities of said State are
unable to suppress." This was precisely what Romney had been avoiding for hours, relying instead on the "reasonable doubt" language.
Then, further down in the proclamation, Roosevelt was careful to note
that in his case the governor had indeed "made due application" for
military help—something that Johnson had yet to receive.[107] Still, the
White House conferees agreed that the precedent held promise for
breaking the impasse between Johnson's and Romney's positions.

Meanwhile, the city was once again ablaze. "The situation is worsening," stated George Christian as he came out of the Oval Office
with a copy of the Roosevelt proclamation in hand. Since it was becoming increasingly clear that Johnson was going to have to act on his
own authority, he had taken to reading aloud to the others in the room
excerpts of a *New York Times* article following Roosevelt's declaration, hoping to discover the political fallout from the earlier move.
While the president bounced back and forth between hunching over the
AP and UPI ticker machines, hoping for more wire copy on Detroit,
and his desk where he was handling some other business, a phone line
was kept open to Vance in Detroit. Meanwhile, Fortas, McNamara,
and Clark remained glued to the ticker machines for the latest updates.

By now the advisers were considering whether or not Johnson
should go ahead and sign the proclamation and executive order sending

in troops and federalizing the Michigan National Guard on his own. The news from Vance shortly after 11 P.M. was grim: twelve hundred arrests, heavy sniper fire, arson, and burglary. "The situation is continuing to deteriorate," reported Vance. "You should sign the Order and federalize the Michigan National Guard. I urge this. It would put the Guard under General Throckmorton."

Johnson asked whether there was doubt in the mind of anyone on the scene, including the governor, that federal action was required. "There is no doubt in the Governor's mind," answered Vance. The number of incidents per hour, which had been rising at an alarming rate, was just too high now for continued reliance on the local authorities, in Vance's opinion.

A few minutes later Johnson decided he had to sign the proclamation on his own constitutional authority, and so informed Vance. With that the military commander on the scene, General John Throckmorton, made plans to divide up the city, telling the White House that the federal troops would take the east side and the soon-to-be-federalized National Guard would take the west side. In this way the danger would be about the same to both groups. "Well, I guess it is just a matter of minutes before federal troops start shooting women and children," Johnson somberly responded. Soon, the increasingly paranoid president told his advisers, there would be "the charge that we cannot kill enough people in Vietnam, so we go out and shoot civilians in Detroit." So Johnson repeated his insistence to the military on the scene that unnecessary firepower be avoided.

Meanwhile, as the troops maneuvered into position and the presidential proclamation was prepared for signing, Johnson was still concerned about the political fallout. Since Romney had not made the necessary written request for aid, the precise Roosevelt precedent could not be followed.[108] All that could be said was that Johnson was acting in accordance with the United States Code and by virtue of his authority as president of the United States and commander in chief. Translation: He was the only man in a very leaky boat. Romney seemingly had succeeded in forcing unilateral action.[109]

But the president wasn't done trying to take on the governor as a passenger—willing or not. "Are they operating under martial law?" he asked Vance, hoping for more help from the 1943 precedent. Only a "state of emergency," came the response from Vance, explaining that it was now a fear of the effects on the city's court system that prevented the governor from going further. When Joe Califano reminded everyone of the declaration of martial law in 1943, it sent the president scurrying to his bound volume of *New York Times* articles, which was lying on the triple television cabinet. Now he was on the phone again, explaining to Vance the merits of such a declaration. To Vance it was "six of one, a half dozen of the other." But to Johnson it was more: "This would show he has taken all the steps which he can take."

While Johnson was instructing Vance that a last-minute appeal issued jointly by him, Romney, and Cavanagh to the people should precede the use of troops, the news tickers continued to chatter. "They have lost all control in Detroit. Harlem will break loose within thirty minutes. They plan to tear it to pieces," warned bulldog-faced J. Edgar Hoover, who had joined the White House group. With that in mind, Johnson signed the proclamation.

Still, there was the very important matter now of explaining the entire action to the American people. At this point, Fortas switched gears from constitutional lawyer to public relations expert, as he and the president slipped into the conference room adjoining the Oval Office to work on a television statement. Together, they searched for a way to protect Johnson's political position. Though Romney had refused to join the president throughout the day, Fortas and Johnson were determined by means of a "*very* tough speech" to put him there anyway. Soon they were joined by Press Secretary George Christian, and by Harry McPherson, who had been in an upstairs room writing his own statement. McPherson read the Fortas-Johnson version and could see that it was far harsher than the conciliatory address he had prepared. Since this was clearly what the president wanted, the speechwriter okayed it. "Really?" asked a puzzled president, who expected some resistance. "You're not just saying that, are you?" added Fortas. McPherson reassured them, and the Fortas-Johnson draft was approved.[110]

As Johnson delivered the address at 11:58 P.M., the nation was informed that it was Romney who had asked for help and not the president acting on his own authority. First, there had been the governor's morning telegram "requesting that Federal troops be dispatched to Michigan" (the technicalities as to why they could not then be deployed were left unexplained). Then, ignoring the fact that Romney had never actually joined the president by making the required formal declaration of a lack of local control, or even a helpful declaration of martial law, Johnson explained:

At approximately 10:30 this evening, Mr. Vance and General Throckmorton reported to me by telephone that it was the then unanimous opinion of all the State and Federal officials who were in consultation—including Governor Romney, Mr. Vance, General Throckmorton, the Mayor, and others—that the situation had developed in such a way in the few intervening hours as to make the use of Federal troops to augment the police and Michigan National Guard imperative. They described the situation in considerable detail, including the violence and deaths that had occurred in the past few hours, and submitted as the *unanimous judgment of all concerned* that the situation was totally beyond the control of the local authorities. *On the basis of this confirmation of need for participation by Federal troops, and pursuant to the official request made by the Governor of the State of Michigan, in which Mayor Cavanagh of Detroit joined,* I forthwith issued the necessary Proclamation and Executive Order as provided by the Constitution and the statutes. [Italics added.][111]

Once more, Johnson claimed there had been the magic threefold incantation of "unanimous judgment," "confirmation of need," and "pursuant to the official request" from the waffling governor.

All of this allowed the president to conclude reluctantly, "I am sure the American people will realize that I take this action with the greatest regret—and only because of the clear, unmistakable and undisputed evidence that Governor Romney of Michigan and the local officials in Detroit have been unable to bring the situation under control." The administration, it seemed, was only a reluctant invitee.

His job done, with the stroke of midnight presidential counselor Abe Fortas changed back into Supreme Court Justice Abe Fortas. While J. Edgar Hoover, Ramsey Clark, and Robert McNamara stood behind the president as he spoke to the nation, reassuring the public that they had played a prominent role in the decision making, the man from the court who had played at least as influential a role quietly left the White House out of sight of any inquisitive reporters. After the evening had ended, Joe Califano would tell Lyndon Johnson, "Mr. President, I think you handled everything real well tonight."[112] But as he left for home, after the grueling and yet exciting sixteen hours of tension, Fortas could be pleased that he too had done "real well"—doing everything in his power, beyond his formal governmental role, to protect the president from political harm. Fortas also knew that he had earned the quiet of his weekend retreat to Westport, Connecticut—a peace that would be interrupted only twice by phone conversations with Johnson.[113]

Later Johnson would be criticized for issuing a statement that was blatantly political and much too technical for the public to understand. But the president's defense was simple. "I had the best constitutional lawyer in the United States right here, and he wrote that."[114] And Johnson was right. But in the summer of 1968 both men would come to regret the president's candor here.

The early fireworks in the Judiciary Committee hearings were over, for now. It had been a match between two heavyweight contenders. And the footwork by the Supreme Court justice was dazzling. He had slipped past all of the damaging questions—some by evasion, others by outright lies. But he now knew something he had not before he began. The Judiciary Committee apparently didn't have the evidence to back up Griffin's charges. If they had had it, Eastland, using his prerogative as chairman to be the first questioner, would have tried to capture the headlines by using it himself. Fortas knew he was winning. No one was going to reject a nomination for the chief justiceship on the basis of unsubstantiated rumor.

Now it was up to the second-ranking Democrat, John L. McClellan of Arkansas, to see what damage he could do. Despite the best efforts of the White House, it was apparent that he would soon be joining his colleagues Ervin, Byrd, and Long in opposing the nomination. But McClellan had not heard all of the earlier testimony, and simply offered Fortas a chance to "clarify" his remarks on his advisory relationship with the president.

Fortas began, recognizing the chance to help the assembled media write their stories the way he wanted: "No. 1, there have been very few subjects. No. 2, they have been matters of critical importance. No. 3, they have not been matters on which I have or claim any expertise, and the President knows it. No. 4, my role has been solely that of one who sits in the meeting while other people express their views. The President always turns to me last, and he then expects me to summarize what has gone on. And that is about the way it is, Senator, and that is the way it works."[115]

"What are some of these matters of 'critical importance'—can you give us some illustrations?" McClellan pressed.

"Perhaps I can say there have been stages in the fantastically difficult decisions about the war in Vietnam where I have participated in meetings of the kind that I described. I say that because it has been published, and it is true. Now, I am not an expert on Vietnam or the

Far East, or anything like it. But the President seems to think that I can serve a function by setting forth the considerations that have been stated by others on various sides of the question. And that I have done.''

Only the gift of understatement saved Fortas from another lie here, as all of Johnson's White House and military advisers knew.

''Are there any other areas of consultation you would be willing to identify, or feel you can identify?'' McClellan asked in closing.

''Well, I have already referred to one,'' Fortas responded, ''so I guess I can cite that, and this is when the riots started.'' Then, feeling very confident, he added, ''And that is about it, as I recall. I guess I have made full disclosure now.''

With this Fortas had put the committee members on the defensive. Who among them would dare to question the needs of a wartime president? Still, McClellan's questions had successfully captured the next day's headlines. FORTAS TESTIFIES HE AIDED JOHNSON WHILE A JUSTICE; ASSERTS THAT AT MEETINGS ON RIOTS AND WAR HE AVOIDED ISSUES AFFECTING COURT; HIS ROLE IN SESSIONS WAS TO SUM UP THE ARGUMENTS BY OTHERS, HE DECLARES, *The New York Times* titled the account written by Fred Graham, the same man whose earlier account of extrajudicial activities Fortas was now publicly labeling as inaccurate. TELLS SENATORS AID TO JOHNSON IS LIMITED, said the *Washington Star*. FORTAS ''PROUD'' OF ROLE AS A JOHNSON ADVISOR, screamed the headline of *The Washington Post*.

But in his confidence, Fortas had gone a step too far. ''I guess I have made full disclosure now,'' he had added in his responses to McClellan. Not only was this misleading in the extreme, it was now part of a systematically evasive testimony—and the White House aides knew it. From his position as Senate liaison for the Justice Department, Barefoot Sanders was personally aware that Fortas was offering testimony that he knew to be untrue. And his friend Larry Temple was ''amused'' when he heard about Fortas's description of his limited contacts with the president. He thought about a photo album Lyndon Johnson had given him as a present. In it was a picture showing the scene at the second floor of the White House during the Washington riots just that April following the assassination of Martin Luther King, Jr., when the president had been signing into effect the declaration of martial law in the District of Columbia. Standing in the background of the photo was one of the men who had helped all day to guide Johnson's actions—Justice Abe Fortas.[116]

Now, by saying that he had made ''full disclosure,'' Abe Fortas had

done much more than simply issue a challenge to the committee members to prove that he was lying. Indeed, if for whatever reason they
proved to be successful in this quest, Fortas had painted himself into a
corner. All they needed to do to impeach his whole testimony was to
reveal a single instance of extrajudicial involvement that was unrelated
to those he had already admitted.

Since the evidence that was in the White House files had been ordered destroyed two weeks earlier, for now all the senators had to base
their evaluations upon was the surface impression of the justice's testimony. And on the surface, it was extremely impressive. "I thought he
looked awfully good. He conducted himself extremely well," offered
Everett Dirksen to the assembled media.[117]. "He is just superb. He
made me feel like a plumber listening to him," was the evaluation of
Philip Hart.[118] But the original leader of the opposition, Robert
Griffin, who in reality knew that for the moment his quarry had neu-
tralized this potentially explosive issue, decided instead to nettle Republican leader Dirksen by labeling the performance "a diaphanous,
gossamer explanation of a rather unusual relationship between the Supreme Court and the White House."[119]

When McClellan quickly passed on further questioning, it looked as
though the administration's hope to finish this inquisition in a single
day could be a reality. But Senator Sam Ervin had other ideas.

XVII

THE TRIAL OF EARL WARREN'S COURT

North Carolina's Sam Ervin calmly prepared to filibuster away the remainder of the first day's hearing. His strategy was to question Fortas as long as possible in order to make the full interrogation of the other nominee, Thornberry, impossible.[1] And everyone knew he was fully capable of accomplishing this feat. Ervin had been described once as a man who could "tie up a bill longer, inject more tedium into an important hearing and better tax the patience and time of executive branch officials than anyone in Congress."[2] Furthermore, as the acknowledged expert in the Senate on matters concerning the Constitution, he clearly had much to say in this area. But his captive audience from the Supreme Court had outdueled two of Ervin's respected colleagues already, and had done enough homework to have confidence that the outcome here would be the same.

"Now, Mr. Fortas," Ervin began, avoiding the use of the judicial title that might concede that there was a way to duck his questions, "I read this statement in the U.S. News and World Report for July 8, 1968. It says this in an article entitled 'Abe Fortas, What Kind of a Chief Justice Would He Be?' 'In his own words, Abe Fortas is a man of the law, and one who believes that the specific meaning of the words of the Constitution has not been fixed.' Now, I want to ask whether or not these words which are in quotations, and which say that you are one who believes that the 'specific meaning of the words of the Constitution has not been fixed'—is that a statement that you made?''

"Senator, I do not recall that statement. I recall saying that I am a man of the law. I have said that many times. I do not recall saying that the words of the Constitution are not fixed. Perhaps I did. But I do not recall that.'' (Of course Fortas was conveniently forgetting here his jurisprudential debate with colleague Hugo Black.)

After fencing a bit more about the alleged quotation, Ervin tried a new tack: ''Well, don't you agree with me that law would be destitute of social value if the law—if the Supreme Court is going to indulge habitually in overruling prior decisions?''

Fortas had anticipated the question, and rather than sparring on the senator's ground he sprang his first trap: ''Senator, we should not overrule prior decisions lightly, except in the clearest kind of case. I came across a statement that you made, when you were on the North Carolina Supreme Court, in a case called State against Ballance, in 1949.''

"I am glad you recall that," Ervin responded. "Now, you might give us that statement.''

"I would be delighted to, Senator. I am sure you have it in mind. That was a case, if I may recall it to you, which involved the constitutionality under the North Carolina due-process clause of a statute providing for the licensing of photographers. About 10 years before you handed down your opinion, your court had decided that the law was constitutional. That was the only decision to that effect. It came—''

"By a sharply divided court, four to three," interrupted the senator brusquely, realizing now where Fortas was heading.

"Yes, sir; that is right. That is the way we divide quite often. Except we do it five to four,'' countered Fortas, scoring even more points with the quick reminder that he was a *United States* Supreme Court justice who was now lecturing a former *state* supreme court justice. "But then, Senator, the case came before you in 1949, and in a very cogently, carefully reasoned opinion, if I may say so, you arrived at the opposite result. And here are some of the things you said about the problem of *stare decisis*. You said—after pointing out there had been just one decision affirming constitutionality, you said, and I quote: 'Besides, the doctrine of *stare decisis* will not be applied in any event to preserve and perpetuate error and grievous wrongs . . . as was said in Spitzer against Commissioners, supra—"there is no virtue in sinning against light or in persisting against palpable error, for nothing is settled until it is settled right."' Senator, I would not go that far myself. This is what you said in that very well-reasoned opinion. And Chief Justice Stacy, as you may recall, wrote a dissent which sounds to me like some of the dissents that I write on the Court and some of my brethren write when we are a bit carried away, in which he criticized the majority for bending the constitutional prohibitions."[3]

Try as the senator might, there was no use denying that the advantage had already flowed to Fortas. Hoping that the nominee would slip, Ervin later tried to rephrase the question. "So the Supreme Court, in applying it, can give one interpretation of the Constitution one time and another interpretation later on."

"Senator, there is no way to avoid error in human affairs. And men can make error in a case that is being overruled, or they can err in overruling the case. You know that, Senator," Fortas responded.

"Well, I would say that I happen to agree with Justice Brandeis, who said on one occasion that it was better for the law to be settled than it is for the law to be settled right."

"Senator, when I said that perhaps your statement from *State* v. *Ballance* is a little broader than I would make it, that is exactly what I had in mind. There are many areas of the law where it is much more important for the law to be settled than for it to be settled right." With that Fortas launched into an explanation of the effect of precedents in various fields of law.

Ervin just wouldn't quit, though: "What criteria do you believe a Supreme Court Justice should follow when it comes to the question of whether he should overrule a previous decision?"

After a lengthy peroration on the techniques of judging given "the fantastic variation and complexity in the facts of life, to which you apply these strict rules," Fortas nettled the senator a bit more. "And you know—your own opinions, which I have read with the greatest care, and I may say admiration, demonstrate your own awareness of that, Senator. Forgive me for personalizing this."

"I never voted to overrule but one case," barked the senator.

"Is that right?" Fortas asked innocently. "Well forgive me for personalizing this. I guess I got a little carried away."

With that, Fortas's second trap was set. In a matter of moments, the senator walked in. "Well, anyway," Ervin lectured the nominee, "from all practical intents and purposes, when the decisions of the Court hold one thing for 177 years, and then they adopt an absolutely new, inconsistent interpretation, for all practical intents and purposes you have the words of the Constitution being interpreted to mean one thing for 177 years and another thing thereafter."

"Well, Senator, you know how difficult this problem is," Fortas began. "I call your attention to *Flast* v. *Cohen.* That was a case that you argued before us eloquently, and very well indeed. And that case, as we decided it, and as you argued it, did not involve a constitutional principle. But it overturned in a very significant and fundamental way what had been considered to be the law since *Frothingham* v. *Mellon* way back in the ancient days."

Ervin interrupted, "1923 is the date," trying to demonstrate his command of history.

"You presented that case [*Flast* v. *Cohen*] to us," Fortas continued. "And we decided it. You will remember that I wrote a concurring opinion in which I tried to confine the scope of the decision precisely to the facts of the case."

"That case did not overrule *Frothingham* v. *Mellon,*" said Ervin.

"That is what we said. But your adversaries thought it did," Fortas concluded.[4] Once more, the nominee had convincingly demonstrated that he had been in favor of past precedent while Ervin had argued for changing the court's rule on accepting suits by federal taxpayers.

Knowing he was beaten on the issue, Ervin had no choice but to grudgingly and indirectly express his admiration for what Fortas had done to him by quickly changing the subject and tactics to an entirely different matter. Fortas had demonstrated in this early verbal skirmish that he could easily hide behind his judicial robes to avoid questions on some decisions and then come out and beat the senator over the head with the ones that presented him as a moderate, self-restrained jurist. So Ervin devoted the rest of the morning to remarks aimed more at the press, the public, and history than at the skillful adversary sitting at the witness table. The senator began to read vast amounts of material into the record, barely stopping to ask Fortas whether he agreed with the insights or even cared to comment on them.

However, no matter where Ervin turned for delaying material, Fortas beat him using a skillful game of one-upmanship. Had the justice made a statement attributed to him in *Time* magazine? No, responded Fortas, indicating that the article had, in fact, made that clear.[5] Then when Ervin tried to read into the record long passages describing the need for a fixed and unchanging Constitution from Supreme Court cases, and various legal treatises and encyclopedias, Fortas pointed out that one of the senator's selected passages was in fact cited in the footnotes of another of his favorite passages. Minutes later, even James Eastland could see that his southern ally was in trouble and moved for the lunch recess.

It had been an impressive display. The Dixiecrats had sent into battle some of their very best, but the visiting justice was more than equal to the task. Fortas seemed in control. But was he? The early politeness of the Dixiecrats was gone now, and the quietly combative justice had flushed out Ervin's main strategy—killing seconds on the clock.

While Fortas had every reason to be pleased with his early performance, his main ally on the Judiciary Committee, Philip Hart, sensed trouble. No matter how angry the Johnson White House was at Robert Griffin, it could not blame the state of Michigan, which had also given it Senator Hart. With other liberals either unable or unwilling to protect anyone but themselves, Hart became the selfless point man in the Senate for Abe Fortas's confirmation effort. Unfailingly soft-spoken and polite, throughout his life Hart was a man loved by both his friends and his opponents. His talents were well recognized by observers, and he was described by one reporter as "perhaps the most civilized, and certainly one of the most respected, men in Congress," and by another author as the Judiciary Committee's "gentlest and also most incisive cross-examiner."[6]

When Hubert Humphrey became vice president, Hart donned the mantle as the leader of the Democratic liberal bloc, calling himself "a sort of nerve center" for that group. And his credentials were in perfect order. In the years since his election to the Senate in 1959, he had worked as chairman of the Antitrust and Monopoly Subcommittee and had labored to break up business conglomerates. Then in 1965 he successfully floor-managed the Voting Rights Act, relying on his experience as an assistant floor leader in Humphrey's effort to pass the Civil Rights Act the previous year. But by the middle of 1968 Hart was exhausted. The president had tapped him as a member of the National Commission on the Causes and Prevention of Violence, established after Robert Kennedy's assassination. Moreover, he was credited with being the senator most responsible for passage of the 1968 civil rights bill, including the open housing provision that had stirred such a long and bruising battle.[7] Despite his fatigue, when no one volunteered to lead the charge for Fortas in the Senate, and the White House asked for help, Hart felt obligated to accept the task.[8]

Acting on new information, Hart warned the deputy attorney general that he was going to ask Fortas again about his involvement in the Detroit riots in order to preempt a floor speech on the issue by Robert Griffin. The information was forwarded by the White House to Fortas's contact man, Paul Porter, in order to allow the justice time to prepare a new response.[9]

Any hope that the justice would be subjected to only a single day of hearings dissipated when Ervin returned to the afternoon session carrying a large pile of manila envelopes containing more prominent Supreme Court decisions that were not to his liking. When Ervin tried to establish his right to ask Fortas about matters that had come before the court during his tenure, the justice tried to offer an "advisory opinion" in defense of his right to silence here: "There is a very real problem, because the Constitution does provide for a separation of the judicial and the legislative branches, and the Constitution expressly provides, as you know, a principle in which I firmly believe, in so many words, that members of the Congress shall not be called to answer in any other place for their votes or statements on the floor. And I think that probably it is true that the correlative of that applies to the Court. I say this to you, Senator Ervin, not because I like to be in that position—I do not—because I am an outspoken man, I think, ordinarily, and I like to discuss things freely. But that is the problem that confronts me as well as it does you."

But Ervin wasn't in the mood to play semantic games anymore. "The proof of the pudding is in the chewing," he noted. And, he need not add, the more one chewed, the *longer* the meal. Not even Philip Hart could deter the North Carolinian by reading a statement passed on to him by the White House in which Justice Felix Frankfurter had also declined to answer similar types of questions during his confirmation hearings for the Supreme Court.[10]

Then without warning Ervin switched to one issue where he perceived a weakness in Fortas's morning responses. The helpful Hart could only watch in silence as the hostile questioner put the exact query on the Detroit riots that he had hoped to phrase a bit more delicately.

"I was a little concerned by your statement this morning that the order sending the Federal troops in to Detroit was submitted to you for perusal before the order was promulgated by the President," Ervin said as his leading remark.

"I would not agree with that way of characterizing it Senator," Fortas objected, even though this was much closer to the truth than he

had led the committee to believe earlier that day. "I tried to describe
the scene. I was one of a number of people there during that critical
moment of national danger, and I do remember that at one point the
remarks that the President was about to make on television were circulated among us. And that is the way to state it, Senator. It was not that
the remarks were submitted to me for perusal."

The answer seemed to be superficially more candid, but it was no
more truthful. Yet a frustrated Ervin knew that he could prove nothing:
"You were just there as an innocent bystander, just out of courtesy, or
because your opinions were desired?"

"I did not say that, Senator."[11]

Ervin knew he had his man—either Fortas had been there or he
hadn't. And since he had, it had been as something more than just a
tourist. So, like a good trial lawyer who knows never to ask a question
of a witness to which he does not know the answer in advance, the
senator simply registered his gains by closing the discussion with a
patronizing sermon and leaving the real answer to the vivid imagination of the newspaper-reading public. "I will not insist upon your answer, because it is a prerogative of communications in the executive
branch of the Government. But to my mind, it is sort of odd for a
member of the judiciary to be involved in those deliberations of the
executive branch of the Government. I was brought up by a very
orthodox father who said that when a man became a judge, that he
ought to use as his criterion the words inscribed over the inferno according to Dante—that he would devote himself to his judicial labors."

"Senator," Fortas offered, refusing to let the matter drop at that,
"whatever it may be, whatever opportunity I had to aid my country in
these crises to which I have referred, that opportunity will be concluded on January 20 of next year."

Hoping to get a damaging admission from Fortas regarding his relationship with the president, Ervin feigned confusion: "I do not understand the significance of that remark."[12]

"All I am saying to you, Senator, is that I—as is well known—I
did work with the President for many years, many, many years, over a
quarter of a century. During those years he did me the honor of having
some trust in my discretion, some belief in my patriotism, and some
respect for my ability to analyze a problem." Then, somewhat exas-
perated at having to establish for the third time that this was a calling
from the nation's leader, Fortas seemed to lose his patience for a moment: "I did not seek the post of Justice of the Supreme Court of the

United States. That was not part of my life plan. I wrote the President by hand a letter, of which I have no copy, but I wrote it to him in longhand, after he first suggested that I accept the position. I wrote it to him in longhand, Senator, because I was not writing it for the record. I dislike being in the position of rejecting a call by the President of the United States to public service. I did not want to make it a part of the record. He nevertheless, as is well known, insisted that I do this—that it was my duty to do it. And I took on this responsibility. It is in the same vein, I assure you, in exactly the same vein and reluctance, but with a feeling of pride and honor, that I have responded to his calls to come and help in these few instances of national crisis."[13]

Ervin smelled blood for the first time in well over an hour of verbal sparring. "Do you know what transpired about the call to send troops to Detroit? In other words, would your presence at that occasion disable you in any way or make you feel that you would be disqualified to sit on any case that might reach the Supreme Court of the United States out of the riots in Detroit, or other cities?"

Even in retreat, though, Fortas laid another deadly trap for the senator with a masterful response: "As you know, Senator, from your own judicial experience, that would depend upon what the issue was and how it arose. It is a little difficult for me to conceive of an issue that might arise. But if an issue arose in which I felt—or if upon discussion with my colleagues, any of them felt—that I should be disqualified, I would of course disqualify myself. It is, however, hard to imagine that such a thing would arise."[14]

As Ervin considered his retort, the justice recalled Larry Temple's account of his visit to the senator's office two weeks before. Still smarting over his loss in representing the textile industry before the Supreme Court in the *Darlington* case, Ervin had convinced White House aide Temple that this was the reason for his hostility toward Fortas and the Warren Court. In reflecting on that conversation, however, Fortas now had some much more interesting questions. Wouldn't it be nice to ask Ervin in this open hearing whether he had taken a fee in that case? And, even if he hadn't, how is it that a United States senator can be an advocate for an industry before the courts and then supposedly be a neutral maker of laws governing the same business in Congress? Is such a senator any different from a Supreme Court justice who speaks with a friend who also happens to be president of the United States? Exploring *these* conflict-of-interest problems, Fortas knew, could prove interesting indeed.[15] It would take the proceedings right into the gutter, but the justice knew he had already lost Ervin's vote anyway, and sheer embarrassment might even compel him to wrap this whole thing up quickly.

But Ervin, perhaps smelling the trap, never gave Fortas the chance. Instead, the senator appeared not even to have heard Fortas's response and launched into an informative lecture on constitutional law—Ervin style. Joseph Tydings of Maryland tried to avoid what he sensed was coming by gently suggesting that Ervin merely enter his material into the record after the rest of the committee had had a chance to question the very busy sitting Supreme Court justice. But Ervin was too coy for that and tried to bait the witness: "If he prefers it that way. However, I thought there might be some erroneous interpretations placed by me on these cases."

"Unless Justice Fortas objects," Tydings again offered, "I might suggest we all have our chance of asking him questions."

"I would appreciate that very much, Senator," replied the man who was uncharacteristically eager to return to the cloistered walls of the Supreme Court building across the street.

But Ervin was not about to let him get off that easily, and insisted upon his right to continue his questioning.[16] For the next two hours and ten minutes, Ervin held Fortas and the assembled crowd hostage while he reviewed the facts and various opinions from more than a dozen Supreme Court cases that to him best evidenced the tendency of the Warren Court to change the meaning of the Constitution. It made little difference to Ervin that some of his examples were drawn from the period *before* Fortas had come to the court, for the real enemy as he saw it was the entire Warren Court, not just this single member.

The performance had a stultifying effect on the proceedings. Having refused Ervin's offer to leave early in the lecture, Fortas, who had been so animated and even humorous in the morning, now spent most of the time slowly shaking his head, sucking lozenges, and sipping water in order to be ready, should he ever be allowed to speak again. Rather than focus on the questioner, he blankly stared either at the witness table or at the ceiling, and drummed his fingers while also rocking his foot on the floor. Meanwhile, the packed audience "grew noticeably restless," having waited in a long line for their precious seats, and the members of the committee, having heard this same lecture repeatedly over the previous spring's debate on the Omnibus Crime Control Act, wandered in and out of the room hoping to get into the action sometime before their terms of office ended.[17]

When the chairman mercifully closed the proceedings for the day, Ervin promised that he only had "about an hour's worth of material left.'' But it seemed a hollow promise when Strom Thurmond added that he too would take "several hours" with his questions.[18] Fortas was in for a long stay.

The next morning, Ervin managed to stretch his material to last nearly the entire session. There was no reason for the audience to rouse itself from its near-comatose state as Ervin wandered seemingly aimlessly from a discussion of defendants' rights to the Fourteenth Amendment, and finally to some of his favorite articles criticizing the court. During the southerner's monologue, Fortas tried to keep himself amused by doodling and playing with the ice pitcher in front of him.[19] Finally, the nominee was permitted to respond to a question based on Fred Graham's *New York Times* article "The Many-Sided Justice Fortas,'' which had been the basis of the questioning on the extrajudicial advising of LBJ the previous day. Thanks to the overnight research efforts of the White House, as well as his own work, Fortas had been able to prepare himself much better on this question.[20] The justice began a lengthy lecture of his own on the most notable examples of earlier extrajudicial actions by ten of the most prominent members of the court in history—including John Jay, David Davis, Louis Brandeis, and Felix Frankfurter—seeking to show that his behavior was certainly not "unprecedented.''

It was an impressive performance. And Fortas was completely correct here. He had done nothing different from a half-dozen other members of the court who had been equally active in extrajudicial behavior. The only difference—and it was a crucial one—was that their behavior had not become the subject of senatorial inquiry, and much of it had been unknown at the time that it occurred. Still, the conservatives hoped that by quizzing Fortas repeatedly about this matter, they could convince the general public that this was a very damaging issue indeed. It put Fortas in the delicate position of trying to justify his actions without full knowledge of what his opponents could prove, and in the face of a normative proscriptive standard that nearly all members of the court ignored, but that the general public still revered.

In fencing with Ervin for these few moments on the subject of extrajudicial activities, the justice appeared to the press to be "cool and articulate,'' and had clearly maintained the upper hand in the dispute.[21] Ervin renewed his delaying strategy by telling a story about his tenure on the North Carolina court, returning to a brief summary of his several-hour constitutional law lecture, and expressing his admiration for a statement by Judge Learned Hand of the court of appeals.

All of this gave the appearance that things were finally winding to a close. Which is exactly the way Sam Ervin wanted it to appear, for his trap was now baited. With the spectators nearly asleep, unexpectedly the senator now brought them to the edge of their chairs.[22]

"Now, I will go back to Fred Graham's article, and he mentions that there had been a meeting of businessmen down in Hot Springs, Virginia. Now, Mr. Graham said he made a mistake in naming the man in Hot Springs. But I will ask you this. Did you call any businessman at a meeting in Hot Springs and remonstrate with him concerning a statement he had made about the increased cost of the Vietnam War, and tell him that the President was very much dissatisfied with this statement about some $5 billion figure, about increasing costs of the Vietnam war?"

It was the worst thing that Ervin could have done to Fortas. After losing round after round in this battle, the senator now had thrown a potential knockout punch. Here was a specifically worded question about extrajudicial conduct to the man who had claimed the previous day to have made "full disclosure" on such matters. Worse still, it was a charge that he had actually lobbied from the court on behalf of the president's war effort. And worst of all, it happened to be true. Fortas knew he was trapped, and so did Fred Graham, the reporter who had written this account and was then sitting in the press section, having already heard his own accuracy being questioned by the evasive witness on several occasions the previous day. The justice had no choice but to admit the veracity of the statement.

"I called a friend who was at Hot Springs at a businessmen's meeting," he admitted, "a man with whom I had served on the Board of Directors of one of the largest companies in the country. I told him at that time, as a citizen, that I was very distressed about a statement attributed to him that I considered to be wrong and which had as its purport—as its possible purport and possible effect the presentation of an incorrect view to the American people of the consequences, financial consequences, of this Nation's participation in the Vietnam war."

But when Ervin pressed for details Fortas would say only, "I am a Justice of the Supreme Court, but I am still a citizen."[23] But the damage was done.

Now the press had the next day's headlines. FORTAS CONCEDES MOVE TO CORRECT WAR-COST CRITIC, blared *The Washington Post.* FORTAS TESTIFIES HE REBUKED CRITIC OF WAR SPENDING, said *The New York Times.* FORTAS SAYS HE CRITICIZED WAR REMARKS, added the *Baltimore Sun.* And now that Ervin had shown that "full disclosure" had not been made, it was open season on Abe Fortas. While the justice had tried to protect the identity of his friend, it did not take the press long to confirm that Fortas had indeed phoned his friend and former client Ralph Lazarus, the chief executive officer of the Federated Department Stores. In his role as a member of the Business Council and chairman of its Committee on the Domestic Economy, Lazarus had reported to the press that the administration was planning a five-billion-dollar increase in the cost of the war over the next year, and Fortas's phone call persuaded him to back away from the remark. The question that was left unanswered, of course, was whether, as the original newspaper account clearly implied, Fortas had undertaken this task at the behest of the president.[24]

At first glance, it seemed that since the Judiciary Committee did not have the necessary evidence to prove any more on this issue, the lasting effects of this damaging admission proved to be minimal. But an important question had been raised: Was there more to be discovered about Abe Fortas's private life?[25]

For now, Ervin had accomplished his goal—time and the psychological advantage were now his. So, after delaying the proceedings for nearly seven full hours with his questioning, Ervin finally turned the reins over to Philip Hart, who gave the embattled justice a chance to catch his breath and, with the help of several set-up questions, to repair the damage that had been done to his image. A carefully choreographed colloquy between the two men on the issue of extrajudicial relationships enabled Hart to conclude that Fortas had been "a very restrained Justice in the light of history."[26] When the senator failed to ask a question provided him by the Justice Department about the Warren Court's decisions, Fortas took the opportunity to answer it anyway by delivering a long lecture on *Warden* v. *Hayden,*[27] a case in which the court had ruled *in favor* of the interests of the police. (Even here, Fortas neglected to point out that *he* had written a separate opinion arguing for defendants' rights.)

Now that Fortas's credentials had been reestablished, the timing was perfect for Hart to answer Ervin's assault by introducing, without revealing its source, the memorandum he had received from the Justice Department portraying the nominee as a disciple of "self-restraint."[28] "In fact, if I did not realize I was not in your league as a lawyer," he told Fortas, "I might quarrel with you" about a few of the more conservative decisions.

But the announcement by Hart that he and two other liberal senators—Burdick of North Dakota and Tydings of Maryland—supported the nomination did not deter Sam Ervin from trying to capture the hearts of the press and public one last time. He wanted Fortas to discuss those defendants' rights cases that reversed known precedents. This request, however, played right into Fortas's hands. After claiming that he was "inhibited" from discussing current cases, he spoke at great length about the "grandaddy of these cases," a 1932 decision known as *Powell* v. *Alabama*.[29] Ervin couldn't bear the thought of being one-upped again: "If *Miranda, Wade,* and *Gilbert* and those cases are descendants of that dictum, they are illegitimate descendants. They were not born in holy wedlock."

"The same thing was said about Alexander Hamilton," quipped Fortas. Realizing that Fortas had regained the upper hand, committee chairman Eastland did his part for the opposition cause by quickly declaring a lunch recess, and announcing that the contest would not resume until the following morning. Another day older, and Fortas was deeper in debt; but his losses were measured in time and not money.[30]

As he observed the first two days of questioning, South Carolina's Strom Thurmond had become more and more uncomfortable about the nominee's ability to sidestep the issues. Unless something significant was done, the man before them might well become the next chief justice of the United States. So the King of the Senate Filibusterers warmed up for his performance. And those who knew the pride that Strom Thurmond took in his filibustering skill knew that he would not be satisfied until he had surpassed his colleagues' delaying performance.

"He has been a hero to his friends, a devil to his enemies, and a puzzle to almost everyone in Washington," said *The New York Times* about Thurmond in 1968.[31] There was no predicting *what* Strom Thurmond would do, only *where* he would do it. He was sure to be in the middle of the hottest fight, and be the most visible of the combatants.[32] For a while it seemed as though he was on the conventional road for a politician from South Carolina. The son of a judge and local Democratic leader, and grandson of a Confederate corporal in the Civil War, Thurmond began his career as a high school teacher. He became a licensed attorney by reading for the law in his father's law office at night, and later became a state circuit judge. Then after a stint in the state senate, he enlisted during World War II in the crack 82nd Airborne Division and rose to the rank of lieutenant colonel. After the war he ran for governor of South Carolina and, though nominated for office through an all-white statewide primary, Thurmond established a record as a moderate progressive by supporting increased educational spending and establishing personal and political rights for the state's black population.[33]

But then Thurmond's career took a sharp right turn. In 1948, after President Truman announced a civil rights program, Thurmond served notice that he would lead the southern white opposition. In August, he led a walkout of his Dixiecrats at the Democratic National Convention in Philadelphia to protest the strong civil rights plank in the party platform. Then, running for president under the banner of the States Rights Party and claiming that Truman's civil rights program was a return to Reconstruction and would establish a "federal Gestapo," he garnered over one million popular votes and thirty-nine votes in the Electoral College.

With the new views came a new lifestyle. A bachelor until age forty-four, Thurmond married his twenty-one-year-old secretary, Jean Crouch. *Life* magazine took the wedding photo—a shot of Thurmond in his tennis shorts standing on his head. (When his wife died of a brain tumor in 1960, it meant a great deal to Thurmond that at the end of the long line of mourners, coming without warning, was Senate Majority Leader Lyndon Johnson. From that point on, the Texan, who had previously been called by the South Carolinian "a traitor to the nation as well as to the South," had a friend, if not an ally, for life.[34])

In 1954 it was on to the Senate to become the only candidate in history to be voted into that body on a write-in campaign. Once in the Senate, Thurmond became the defender of both the South and the Constitution. And everyone knew that he would use any means at his disposal to accomplish this task. "Look at old Strom out there," said a colleague in amazement once; "he really believes that ----."[35] About the Constitution, Thurmond once said, "The Constitution means today exactly what it meant in 1787 or it means nothing at all." Once, he handed a twenty-four-page cartoon book explaining the document to Attorney General Robert Kennedy and said with a straight face, "Study it . . . anyone can understand this."[36] As a defender of the South, Thurmond lobbied endlessly against the civil rights movement, even to the extent of drafting and circulating for signature a "Declaration of Constitutional Principle," a manifesto against the *Brown* v. *Board of Education* school desegregation ruling. Then in 1957 he delayed passage of Lyndon Johnson's voting rights bill by filibustering on his own for twenty-four hours and eighteen minutes, a Senate record that still stands today. (Two hours after he sat down, the bill was passed overwhelmingly.)

While these actions convinced people of the lengths to which Thurmond would go to get his way, it was another incident in 1964 that drove the point home. After taking exception to a presidential appointment under consideration by the Senate Commerce Committee, Thurmond personally tried to keep the group from achieving the quorum necessary to proceed. In front of some astonished reporters, he grabbed Texas Senator Ralph Yarborough's hand as if to shake it and then wrestled him to the floor, pinning him there for ten minutes to keep him from entering the meeting. Only when the chairman of the committee came out in a search party for the wayward Yarborough did Thurmond release him.[37] Now Thurmond was going to try to wrestle Abe Fortas to the floor, verbally of course, and make certain no one came to rescue the man who seemed to him to be an enemy to both the conservative South and the lovers of the literal Constitution.

In anticipation of larger crowds, the proceedings were moved on Thursday to the huge marble-columned Senate Caucus Room in the Old Senate Office Building, where Fortas had first made his reputation as an advocate. Before being treated to the main event, though, the audience viewed a comic short feature. Nebraska's Roman Hruska, now claiming to be firmly in the administration's camp, was allowed to put the questions most on his mind to the nominee. Why had Fortas sat in the case of *American Federation of Musicians* v. *Joseph Carol*[38] when everyone knew he was compromised in that he was a "violinist"? This was one set of questions about a recent case that the justice was happy to answer. Since he was not a union member, he responded—unlike Chief Justice Warren, who as a clarinet player in his school band had been an honorary member—and had never been so even when he played professionally in Memphis to put himself through school, there had been no need to step down.[39] It was, as *The Washington Post* reported, one of the session's "few light moments."

Then Hruska quizzed Fortas about the circumstances surrounding his addition of the government of Puerto Rico to his new law firm's client list in 1946. While this did not concern actions taken as a justice during the Johnson administration, Fortas knew that the issue was a delicate one for his own credibility as a witness. The allegations appearing in senatorial newspaper clipping files that he had reversed his field on the matter of whether there should be private legal representation for the territory in order to line his own pockets had to be answered with precision. So Fortas's memory, which had been foggy only minutes earlier as to the list of members of his own law firm in 1964, now was crystal clear on events occurring eighteen years prior to that time.

After admitting that as undersecretary he had written a letter opposing the use of private legal counsel instead of Interior Department lawyers for the island, Fortas explained:

When I resigned, Governor Tugwell and Don Luis Muñoz-Marin,
the majority leader of the senate of Puerto Rico, who subsequently
became its first elected Governor, asked me to come down there.
They paid my expenses. There was no fee in the first instance. I
went down there, and consulted with them—I do not remember the
subjects. I have a vague recollection that it may initially have been a
question of land policy and of their land law. Then I went down
several other times and told them I would not take the fee, but I
would continue to consult with them. Whether those were legal consultations or policy consultations or a mixture of both would be hard
to say. I rather think it was a mixture of both.

At that time, my legal work was just starting. Their demands
became greater and greater on me for this specialized type of work.
And I remember quite distinctly that they talked to me about the
unfairness of it, of my going down there for no compensation whatever. And what we finally did—and I do not remember when—it
was quite a while—what we finally did was to agree to what was
essentially a nominal retainer of $12,000 a year for the services of
Judge Arnold, my partner, myself, and my firm, on these specialized problems. That is the story, Senator.

Well, at least it was *a* story, Fortas knew, but it was not the truthful
one. He knew that there was no question that he had launched his law
firm by simply stealing one of his first lucrative clients from the rolls
of the Interior Department. Not even the particulars of his account had
been accurate. In fact, he *had* taken a fee for the first visit, there had
been *only one* and not several visits, and it was during this one time
that the retainer arrangement had initially been discussed. Furthermore, the demands on his law firm came as much at his suggestion as
that of the Puerto Ricans, and the retainer arrangement was first discussed less than three weeks after the president had accepted his letter
of resignation from the Interior Department (with final consummation
of the arrangement coming about three weeks after that). Lest anyone
think it was all a flight of fancy, however, the retainer *was* twelve
thousand dollars a year. But Roman Hruska had no reason to doubt
any part of this story, and Fortas's opponents had not thought to call
political scientist Rexford Tugwell, the one man who knew the incident's details well enough to testify. So, rather than dealing a crippling

blow to the nominee's general credibility, Hruska thanked the witness for his "candor" and the show went on.

With that, at last, it was time for the next turning point of the hearings—the *mano a mano* duel between Fortas and Strom Thurmond. The senator had decided to be even more aggressive in his questioning than the others, and just as time-consuming. He knew that every minute that he railed against the hated Warren Court was a minute lost to the administration before the Senate adjournment. But as excited as he was to have this platform, it pained him somewhat to have to use Fortas, whom he privately admired, for his target. "If only Abe was on our side," he would say later. In politics, though, there is no room for emotion, and Abe Fortas would receive no quarter.[40]

So the southerner came to the hearing with "a long list of prepared questions and a large sheaf of quotations, observations and citations," intent on exploring the court's decisions as well as Fortas's role in them.[41] He was determined not to be bested in this verbal boxing match. There was only one problem—Abe Fortas was no longer willing to play. Correctly determining that he was far ahead on points, and winning new converts to his position with each minute of patient willingness to subject himself to such unseemly abuse, the justice responded to Thurmond's first question on the issue of federal-state relations by saying, "Senator, with all deference, I must ask you to understand and to excuse me from addressing myself to that question. I do so only because of my conception of the constitutional limitations upon me. As a person, as a lawyer, as a judge, I should enjoy the opportunity—I always do—of discussing a problem of this sort. But as a Justice of the Supreme Court, I am under the constitutional limitation that has been referred to during these past 2 days, and must respectfully ask to be excused from answering."

To the press, it now looked like Fortas was doing his version of "taking the Fifth Amendment," much as he had advised his clients facing such Senate committees.[42] Over the course of the next two hours, Fortas would refuse to respond to some fifty-nine questions, using variations of this response ranging from "I have nothing to say to that" to "With the greatest, greatest regret, I must make the same response." Unlike the earlier questioners, though, who had accepted this posture, Thurmond decided to solemnly badger the justice.

It was an odd scene for many of the observing press and public. And it was not fun for the combative and game nominee either. Worn down by Thurmond's tactics, by the end of the day Fortas was answering as

many questions as he was ducking.[43] But as frustrating as it was for
Fortas, it was that much and more for the stalking Thurmond, whose
moment in the spotlight as part of an expected *pas de deux* had turned
into a monotonous solo performance.

So the senator tried to goad Fortas into responding. "Your views are
expressed in your decision. Why would you object to being asked
some questions about your views that you had expressed?"

"I cannot add to what I have said. I believe the Constitution of the
United States, which I am sworn to uphold, says to me that I must not
do it—that it is incompatible with a sitting Justice's obligation, and
incompatible with the theory of the separation of powers that our Constitution embodies."

A moment later Thurmond tried: "Every American today who is
going to read the paper tomorrow is going to see that you refused
today, that you failed today, to answer questions of vital importance to
them, and they are going to get an impression and maybe rightly so,
that you are using this as a screen or an excuse not to go into these
matters. The public wants these matters gone into. And a great many
people feel that you are withholding your real true views, if you do not
enter into the discussion of these matters as members of the Senate
committee prefer to do."

"Senator, all I can say is that I hope and trust that the American
people will realize that I am acting out of a sense of constitutional duty
and responsibility."

"Well, I am disappointed, even more so, in you, Mr. Justice Fortas."

"I am sorry to hear that, Senator," responded Fortas with the scattered applause rolling from the audience telling him that he had won
that round handily.[44]

But after several more unanswered queries, the senator tried a different tack. How was it that the justice could set out his views in a
published book and in speeches on college campuses across the nation,
yet was incapable of elaborating on those matters before the Judiciary
Committee? he asked. From that point on, Thurmond answered each
of Fortas's respectful declinations to speak with a solemn "So you
refuse to answer that question?"

After eight such pronouncements, the justice could take it no longer.
By this time, Thurmond's rambling line of questioning had turned to
the case of *Fortson* v. *Morris*,[45] dealing with Georgia's gubernatorial
selection procedures.[46] "In my judgment, it is preferable for a Governor to be chosen by popular election. Yet I am unable to find a require-

ment to this effect in the Constitution. Would you consider your dissent in *Fortson* v. *Morris* to be an example of translating a personal preference into a constitutional requirement?''

''I most certainly would not,'' insisted the justice. Then, realizing what he had done, he added, ''But I should not say that. I must stand on the constitutional position. I cannot respond to that, Senator.''

''I thought you did respond,'' pressed Thurmond.

''I am sorry. It was an inadvertence.''

''Well, maybe we need more inadvertent answers here this morning.''

''It is pretty hard not to make them, Senator, as I am sure you will understand. I just repeat—this is not a pleasant role for me.'' And with that Fortas returned to his self-imposed vow of silence.[47]

But this did not deter Thurmond from moving on to his questions about other decisions by the court. What was the basis for the court's decision striking down the poll tax in *Harper* v. *Board of Elections*?[48] No response. Did the Constitution's framers intend for the poll tax to be prohibited? No response. Isn't a poll tax within the state's power to regulate the exercise of the vote? No response. What was the basis for the court's decision in the apportionment cases—*Baker* v. *Carr* and *Reynolds* v. *Sims*?[49] No response. What was the basis for the court's jurisdiction in the poll tax case? No response. With each refusal to cooperate, the senator's sense of indignation grew until he was looking for an opportunity to lash out.

Such an opportunity presented itself when Thurmond turned the subject to the area of defendants' rights: ''Mr. Justice Fortas, I am concerned about the increased crime rate, as are many people in the United States today. I find it an inescapable conclusion that the numerous decisions of the Supreme Court which have resulted in an expansion of the rights of those accused of committing crimes, and which have made convictions more difficult, have been a significant factor in this increase in crime. I am interested to know whether you believe these [criminal justice] decisions in *Mallory, Escobedo, Miranda, Berger,* and other similar cases, have had the effect of increasing the crime rate. I am not asking you now about the decision. I am asking you if you feel they have had the effect of increasing the crime rates, and if so, what weight should this consideration have on the courts?''[50]

Fortas couldn't resist this one, lecturing at great length about the ''various studies made and articles written as to whether or not decisions, or particular decisions, made by the Courts have affected the crime rate.'' But the justice assured everyone that ''if judges are wise and Congress is wise, as it is generally in interpreting the Constitution—that faithful adherence to the Constitution will produce a result that is in the public interest. . . . [However] we can do nothing but decide the cases, and to the extent that God gives us guidance, decide them on the basis of the Constitution. And that is what I try to do, Senator,'' he concluded emphatically.

But Thurmond was not fazed in the slightest by this sanctimonious sermon. ''The first case I refer to was the Mallory case—*Mallory* v. *United States,* handed down in 1957, before you went on the Supreme Court. This was a case in which the defendant voluntarily confessed to a serious crime, a serious assault, in fact rape. He was convicted by the trial court, 12 men who heard his testimony, and the trial judge who heard it. They concluded the confession was voluntary. They concluded that all the details he had set out in that confession—he set out himself were true and correct. There is no question, no issue about the confession being voluntary. There was really no question that he committed the crime. But when it went to the Supreme Court, they reversed the case and the man went free. Why did he go free?'' Thurmond thundered in a demanding tone. ''A criminal, a convict, a guilty man, who committed a serious rape on a lady in this city. Simply because the Court said they held him a little too long before arraignment. Do you believe in that kind of justice? Don't you think the main purpose of the courthouses, of the judges, of the jury is to go to the heart of a case and render justice, to convict them when they are guilty, and turn them loose when they are free, and not let technicalities control the outcome? And isn't that what happened in that case?''[51]

Fortas chose to respond to this machine-gun attack with the by-now-familiar incantation: ''With the greatest regret, I cannot respond to that, because of the constitutional limitation.''

That was all that the emotional Thurmond needed to hear. ''Mallory, Mallory, I want that word to ring in your ears—Mallory,'' he boomed solemnly in his raspy southern accent, then continued to read slowly from his notes: ''A man who raped a woman, admitted his guilt, and the Supreme Court turned him loose on a technicality. And who I was told later went to Philadelphia and committed another crime, and somewhere else another crime, because the court turned him loose on technicalities.

''Is not that type of decision calculated to bring the courts and the law and the administration in disrepute? Is not that type of decision calculated to encourage more people to commit rapes and serious crimes? Can you as a Justice of the Supreme Court condone such a decision as that? I ask you to answer that question."[52]

It was the low point of a war that had been raging between the southerners and the court for years, and in this latest battle for better than four weeks.[53] The attack was not planned and appears to have been an expression of Thurmond's emotions. There was much more than just the drama of a senator seemingly out of control here, and a justice playing the part of a human punching bag as he was accused of events that had occurred eight years before his ascension to the court. The outburst by Thurmond displayed in all of its ugliness the very core of the emotions fueling this holy war between the conservatives and the liberals over the course of the nation and, in particular, the Supreme Court. To the liberals these decisions were based on "rights" for "defendants," to the conservatives on "mere technicalities" protecting "criminals." To the liberals these decisions expressed "the forces of history," to the conservatives "a lack of respect for precedent." To the liberals these decisions were "justice," to the conservatives "unrestrained rewriting of clear constitutional mandates." And to Abe Fortas, who was neither fully liberal nor fully conservative, this had suddenly become a battle for his professional life. Thurmond signaled now a willingness to use *every* means at his disposal to crush allies of the Warren Court, whoever they might be.

Not even the three days of verbal barbs and thirty-five years in the legal profession had prepared the unflappable Fortas for this personal harangue. He flushed visibly and sat perfectly still in the now shocked and silent Senate chamber for several moments, a look of disbelief on his face. Turning to the committee chairman for relief, he saw James O. Eastland, seemingly oblivious to the assault, slouched in his chair and calmly continuing to read the document before him. So Fortas leaned forward toward the microphone and, pausing for a moment to fix his eyes squarely on Thurmond, said in a firm, controlled voice, "Senator, because of my respect for you and my respect for this body, and because of my respect for the Constitution of the United States, and my position as an Associate Justice of the Supreme Court of the United States, I will adhere to the limitation that I believe the Constitution of the United States places upon me and will not reply to your question as you phrased it."[54]

"Can you suggest any other way in which I can phrase that question?" the frustrated and unrepentant Thurmond asked, now almost shouting at his quarry as the suddenly alert committee chairman attempted to bring the stirring crowd to order.

"That would be presumptuous. I would not attempt to do so."

"Would you care to make any comment at all on this question?"

"Not as phrased, no, sir."

"Well, as phrased differently, would you care to make any comment?"

"No. No, Senator."[55]

With that, as quickly as the storm had come it subsided, as Strom Thurmond moved on without warning to other cases where he felt the nominee's education needed completion. Time and time again, Thurmond made the same charge against the Warren Court that his southern colleague Sam Ervin had made—that the justices, contrary to the historical precedents, took it upon themselves to legislate new rules rather than interpret the existing Constitution. Since Fortas was determined not to respond, the senator acted as though he were a prosecutor working over a reluctant witness at trial. Repeatedly he made the same charge of judicial legislating, in the form of reworded questions concerning one court decision after another. At the same time, the audience was subjected to Thurmond's lectures on the police's use of confessions, electronic surveillance, and lineups, on the rights to counsel and trial by jury, and on government regulation of subversives.

By the end of the morning session, the badgering had worn Fortas down to the point that he chose to answer about a third of the senator's questions, but even these attempts to be responsive had little impact on the relentless questioning. For Thurmond the goal was no longer to get Fortas to answer him, but to make the questioning last as long as possible. And time was his for the moment.

Although Thurmond didn't realize it at the time, his discussion of one of the cases, *Witherspoon* v. *Illinois*,[56] lit a very long fuse. It seemed like a harmless reference to a recent decision by the Supreme Court barring the imposition of the death penalty in a case in which jurors had been excluded from service solely due to their opposition to capital punishment. And except for admitting that he had voted with the majority on the case, Fortas responded to none of the thirteen questions fired in his direction. But without revealing it to anyone, another senator at the committee table, the senior senator from Illinois, had listened to this exchange carefully and was most taken by the possibilities that this *Witherspoon* case held for him.

Finally, just before one o'clock, Chairman Eastland called for a recess—again until the next day, because the full Senate would be in session that afternoon. But for all of the hundreds of words that were ringing in people's ears as they left the room, the only ones that they would remember were "Mallory, Mallory . . ." And with that incantation, silently, swiftly, and surely, the worst thing that could have possibly happened to Abe Fortas had occurred that Thursday morning. Strom Thurmond had emerged as the real leader of the opponents in the confirmation battle. And Senator Thurmond was not accustomed to losing.

By day four, the Judiciary Committee's witch-hunt had indeed become the political spectacle of the year. As an acknowledgment of this new status, seated in the front row of the audience was one of Washington's most prominent hostesses, Mrs. Perle Mesta. James Eastland, still keeping a foot in each camp, had arranged with the committee that this would be the final day of questioning for Fortas, to be followed by an extraordinary Saturday session in which Thornberry would get his turn at bat.[57] As part of this arrangement to speed things up, though, the two nominations were separated, because some of the members of the committee refused to admit that there was a vacancy on the court until Fortas was, in fact, elevated to the chief justiceship.[58] So Thornberry's nomination was put into a kind of political limbo from which he might never return.

Strom Thurmond still had the floor, and the attention of the newspaper-reading public. Now that he had run out of constitutional law cases to cover, the senator had a few of his favorite articles that he wanted to bring to everyone's attention. Not surprisingly, these pieces were critical of the direction of the Warren Court. First, Thurmond read long passages from an article containing excerpts from Justice Hugo Black's recent Columbia University lectures criticizing the activism of the court, pausing only long enough for the nominee periodically to refuse to comment. But it didn't take long for Fortas's impatience to become apparent.

"Do you feel today that the Supreme Court is doing just what Mr. Justice Black said he feared?" Thurmond goaded.

"Senator, yesterday and the day before, and the day before that, in response to a question, I stated that I do not believe that the Supreme Court or the United States should or can appropriately make policy or seek to bring about social, political or economic change in this country. I repeat that."[59]

After fencing some more on the question of the court's role in the absence of congressional action, the senator abruptly changed subjects to the legislative apportionment cases and attempted a rerun of the previous day's combat. "Ever since this country was founded, it was concluded that the States had the power to structure their own State governments. But under the apportionment decisions now it is held that a county in a State would not have the right to have a Senator even though the legislature and the people of that State may desire such. Under what authority of the Constitution did the Supreme Court act on that case?"[60]

Visibly irritated by the question, Fortas decided the time had come to drop his teeth-gritted restraint and lecture his adversary:[61] "Senator, with the greatest regret I must say that we are back where we were yesterday. I tell myself every morning before I come here: 'You are not participating in this hearing as Abe Fortas, you are participating in this hearing as an Associate Justice of the Supreme Court of the United States, with responsibility solely to the Constitution of the United States.' It is on that basis, and with the utmost respect, with the utmost respect, that I have said to you that I cannot respond to questions of that sort, because I cannot and I will not be an instrument by which the separation of powers specified in our Constitution is called into question. And I will not and cannot discuss in this forum opinions of the Court of which I am a member. That is my constitutional duty, Senator, just as it would be the constitutional duty of a Senator if he were called before a court, no matter how much he might want to explain his vote or his opinion—it would be his constitutional duty, respectfully as I am trying to do here, to decline to answer questions that were put to him about his work in the Congress. That is the mandate of our Constitution, and that is what I am trying to fulfill here. Forgive me for—"[62]

"Mr. Justice Fortas," Thurmond interrupted.

"Forgive me for the emotion there, Mr. Chairman, if there was some. Sorry," Fortas concluded.

Ignoring the appeal, the senator moved on to the next series of questions and readings from the Black lectures. A few moments later, he quoted Black's version of Lord Acton's legendary axiom on power: "Power corrupts and unrestricted power will tempt Supreme Court Justices." Here Fortas could not resist commenting, "Senator, I not only agree with the proposition, but that maxim of Lord Acton which was paraphrased and which you have just quoted, is something that all public officials must keep in mind always, because power is in fact a dangerous thing."[63] But the senator acted as if he had not heard the comment.

A short time later Thurmond turned his attention to an address delivered that month by Chief Justice John C. Bell, Jr., of the Supreme Court of Pennsylvania. For the next fifteen minutes the senator read from the inflammatory speech, which made the criticism by Alexander Lawrence ten years earlier look like glowing praise. Then Thurmond read twice the hyperbolic conclusion of this section of the piece: "The recent decisions of a majority of the Supreme Court of the United States, which shackle the police and the courts and make it terrifically difficult, as you well know, to protect society from crime and criminals, are, I repeat, among the principal reasons for the turmoil and the near revolutionary conditions which prevail in our country, and especially in Washington."

"Now, Mr. Justice Fortas," challenged Thurmond, "the question is—do you agree with that statement by the chief justice of the Supreme Court of Pennsylvania, that the recent decisions of a majority of the Supreme Court of the United States which shackle the police and courts and make it terribly difficult to protect society from crime and criminals are among the principal reasons for the turmoil and near-revolutionary conditions which prevail in our country and especially in Washington?"

Like the *Mallory* bludgeoning the day before, it was almost more than Fortas could endure. Clearly angered, he paused for several moments to compose himself and answered simply and clearly, "No."[64]

This contentious exchange was just what the members of the crowd seated in the new location of the spacious Appropriations Committee Room had come to see. They laughed heartily at Fortas's simple response to such a convoluted and obviously inflammatory question, and a number of those seated in the back corner of the room began to applaud.[65]

"Let us have order," barked the chairman, knowing that this group spoke for much of the nation. "Another demonstration and the police will clear the room."

"Ah understood," intoned Thurmond in his best offended southern drawl, "there had been recruiting actions to bring people here today which would try to cause such a demonstration, Mr. Chairman, but I did not believe it until I now see what is happening in the back of the room."

"Now, Mr. Chairman," objected Phil Hart, "all that happened was that some people were pleased that the Justice did not agree that, whatever the crime rate is, it is a consequence of Supreme Court decisions. As I look over the room, everybody looks nice and clean and fine and fresh."

"I do not wish to comment on that," responded Eastland. "But we are not going to have demonstrations at this committee hearing."

"The demonstration consisted of mild scattered applause for a statement that I would have applauded myself," insisted Hart.

"But you did not, Senator."

Hart continued, "Happily, I can speak for the record. My impression of the Bill of Rights is that it was intended to handcuff government. That is the whole purpose of the Bill of Rights. It might mean one thing—if you cannot hit somebody over the head or hold him as long as you want—for a policeman but we are all better because you cannot."

But when a determined Thurmond reminded Hart that he had the floor and asked if he had more to say, the Michigan senator responded simply, "Yes. But I will resist the temptation, just the way Justice Fortas has." And Thurmond, undeterred, was off and walking with more public readings from his pile of literature.[66]

But the reaction of the assembled crowd seemed to rejuvenate the embattled nominee, and when given the opportunity he dueled Thurmond to a draw.

After a while, looking for some help in quizzing the nominee, Thurmond decided to yield some time to an ally—John L. McClellan, who wanted to take one last shot at pinning Fortas down on the issue of his extrajudicial activities. First he pressed Fortas on the phone call to Ralph Lazarus, which had rocked the proceedings two days before: "Did you, by direct statement or by inference, or by language from which there could be inferred, imply to him or state to him that you were transmitting Lyndon Johnson's ire to the Business Council over the statement he made?"

"No sir. I suppose if the President wants to transmit his ire, he will do it directly."

"The reason I bring this up," McClellan added a few minutes later, "is because it has come out in testimony here. And I would ask you if, in all candor, you think this is the sort of practice that members of the Supreme Court should engage in? Just taking the facts as you state and represent them to be, and what actually occurred—do you think this is a practice that should be followed by members of the Court?"

Again Fortas made a plea for public understanding: "Senator, I beg your pardon, but I do have to emphasize the fact that Mr. Lazarus was a very close friend, and still is a very close friend. He was an intimate business associate for over 15 years, and I suppose we have discussed everything in our association. I don't know how anybody can be a person and not discuss with his friends these days questions about the budget and about the Vietnam war. I'm a person too. I am a Supreme Court Justice, but I talk to people, and people talk to me. I don't see how you can avoid discussing questions like that. And with friends, particularly those with whom I have had a long business association, I do discuss economic problems, just as I am sure everybody else does. That is all there is to this, Senator, in my view. I may be wrong, but that is all I see to it."[67]

However, no matter how much Fortas protested that this was simply a call in the nature of a "parlor discussion" to "a very close friend," the nation's editorial boards concluded that Fortas had been wrong. *The New York Times* commented that the justice "had overreached himself."[68] Even the highly supportive *Jewish Week,* in a piece arguing that there was "circumstantial evidence" that the Judiciary Committee's proceedings were motivated by anti-Semitism, admitted that the phone call to Lazarus "was not an act of good judgment."[69] But after four days of grilling, this was certainly not enough to prevent Fortas's confirmation.

So McClellan tried to furrow new ground with his questions. Using information that was admittedly "not conclusive," the senator tried to explode the "full disclosure" statement.

"I would like to ask you whether you were consulted by the President or the Department of Justice about the President's safe streets and crime bill before it was drafted."

"No, sir; and I have not even read that bill."

"Were you consulted about his message that was issued at the time of signing it?"

"No, sir. As I say, I have not read the bill, and I didn't even read the newspaper accounts carefully because I was sure it was coming before us."

No matter how sanctimonious his replies, Fortas knew that he had failed to tell "the truth, the whole truth, and nothing but the truth" once more. Lacking the necessary proof, though, McClellan would never know how close he had come to breaking open the hearings. For the truth was that Abe Fortas had become one of the president's main men on crime control.

When Congress enacted in the fall of 1966 the first version of the so-called D.C. Crime Bill, its provisions seemed to be drawn from the Marquis de Sade school of crime fighting. Representing the philosophy that crimes committed in the detection of other crimes were no crimes

at all, the more heinous provisions included the changing of the so-
called Mallory rule, by which a suspect must be brought before an
arraigning magistrate "without unnecessary delay," to allow police
between four and ten hours of unrestricted interrogation time. In addition, police would be empowered to detain a material witness and even
a victim of crime for up to six hours, if there was a "reasonable probability that he will not be available to testify at the trial." Then, the
witness would have to post bond as security in order to be released. All
in all, the bill was the sort of exam question one might give in a
constitutional law final to keep the students writing for the next three
hours by simply asking, "What are the problems with this proposal?"
And all that stood between it and full legal status was President Lyndon Johnson's pen.[70]

So the White House turned to the president's favorite outside adviser. "Do you know anything about the D.C. Crime Bill?" Harry
McPherson asked Abe Fortas at a dinner party.

"Yes," responded Fortas.

"Have you been able to form an opinion of it?"

"Yes."

"What do you think about it?" McPherson pressed.

"It's an obscenity."[71]

Everyone in the administration agreed that while crime had to be
controlled, the problems of this bill were self-evident. But was it politically wise for the president to appear to be procrime by vetoing the
measure? As an alternative, Attorney General Nicholas Katzenbach
suggested that the president's signature be accompanied by a statement
declaring that he intended never to use the full range of powers offered
in the bill.[72] After much discussion, the president's men concluded
that a meeting of the Justice Department officials and the White House
speechwriters should be convened to discuss alternatives. And, sensitive to the judicial proprieties involved, they suggested to Johnson
that Abe Fortas be consulted separately.[73] However, even when difficult questions of a bill's constitutionality were involved, Johnson did
not give a damn about the ethical niceties here. And apparently neither
did Fortas, for the justice was included in just such a White House
meeting.

During the afternoon and evening of November 12, 1966, Fortas,
Clark Clifford, McPherson, and Ramsey Clark met and informed the
president that all of the participants recommended not approving the
bill. Since the second part of the group's mandate was to revise
Johnson's "statement of disapproval," should he opt for signing the

bill anyway, McPherson provided their version. The statement, as drafted by Fortas and the others, was nothing more than a constitutional judgment of the merits of the bill. In the portion dealing with Congress's direct assault on the Supreme Court's Mallory Rule it argued, "No one doubts the necessity of the police questioning persons on the street with respect to criminal activities. The law has always permitted this. The law properly provides, however, that after a person is deprived of his freedom—after he is arrested—the police must take him before a magistrate who will determine whether his arrest is arbitrary or based on probable cause. This must be done without unnecessary delay. I am advised that the periods of questioning provided in this bill go far beyond the necessities of interrogation in practically all cases." In the end, Johnson was persuaded to veto the bill.[74]

In working on the crime bill, even to the extent of attending a meeting in which the constitutionality of the measure was being analyzed, and continuing to offer substantive advice on the whole war against crime to the president, Fortas had to know that he had crossed the line into advising on an issue that was sure to come before his court. Nor would this be the last time he did so.

Over the next year, Fortas did his part to build the president's reputation in his fight against crime after the politically sensitive veto of the first D.C. Crime Bill. In mid-January, knowing that the president had agreed to present a new crime control program to the nation for the first time, Fortas turned speechwriter and called head secretary Juanita Roberts to dictate some suggested wording.[75] Later Joe Califano sent five copies of the finished crime message to the justice and, after reading the speech immediately, Fortas called the White House with a message for the president saying, "I think your Crime Message is excellent."[76]

Then, in February the justice was again involved in the speechwriting enterprise on the rejected D.C. Crime Bill. The issue remaining under dispute was whether the president should back a new provision authorizing police to question suspects freely for three hours after arrest and use any statements so derived at trial. In reviewing a speech draft, Fortas freely offered another advisory constitutional opinion that he "would not include such a bill on the ground that the question whether the length of time was coercive involves a case by case determination." Additionally, Fortas felt that the bill would put Johnson "in the middle of a fight that is nationwide and will not be resolved for some time."[77]

By the end of 1967, when the president was thinking of proposing a

"National Council on Crime," Fortas put together a five-point memorandum dealing with the presentation of the idea to the nation. "The
emphasis," explained his memorandum, should be on "action"—"that
is, to try to bring state, local and federal law enforcement facilities to
bear immediately and forcefully on crime—now—and to do it in the
most effective and powerful fashion." In this way, he argued, Congress could be asked to delay its calls for gun control and other anti-
crime measures (thus also relieving some of the legislative pressure on
the president). Not surprisingly, when the vastly revised D.C. Crime
Bill was sent to the White House for signature in late 1967, the helpful
Supreme Court justice was consulted once more about the nature of the
president's signing statement. Working with Clark Clifford and Harry
McPherson, Fortas made a number of suggestions in the wording of
the speech explaining why Johnson now found this new crime bill
acceptable.[78]

By early February of the following year, when the issue was the
nature of the president's message to Congress on "Insuring the Public
Safety," Fortas was once again enlisted as a speechwriter for the announcement of the new twenty-point program. After substantially rewriting pages of the draft he received, the justice penned a four-page
handwritten memo (its author identified at the end only by a huge
"A.") to the president containing his thoughts on the crime message.
He informed Johnson that in his opinion there were two fundamental
problems with the entire address. First, he argued that the speech did
not satisfy the public's needs by dealing with the problem of safe
streets in simple and direct language. Second, Fortas explained, the
president would have to do a better job of explaining the jurisdictional
problems of handling crime with three levels of government. To Fortas, the measures called for in the speech were all "indirect," and
represented only a starting point. What was needed, the justice added,
was a strong call for direct measures such as a federal gun registration
act. Interestingly enough, Fortas acknowledged that such a bill was
both "drastic and constitutionally dubious," and could not be enacted
in Congress. Fortas did not seem to care much what was passed in this
area, so long as it made it *appear* to the public as though Johnson was
doing something positive.[79]

In the typical way bureaucracies operate, though, when this memo
by the justice reached the record keepers, some of the contingencies
that should have been raised all along now came to the forefront. "Mr.
Califano," one of his assistants wrote, "these are Justice Fortas' comments on Crime Message. Shall we file here? . . . Shall we destroy

after reasonable time? . . . Shall we send to archives?'' It was indeed a harbinger of things to come.[80] For by the time the memo reached the central files in mid-August, another set of aides quickly removed it for destruction.

But neither McClellan nor any of the enterprising reporters covering the proceedings would find this out.

Seemingly trying to be hospitable, McClellan explained the source for part of his questioning: ''Mr. Justice, there was one Justice on the court who occasionally rendered some decision and made some side remarks, that gave me some concern at the time we were considering the crime bill. The Justice on the particular occasion, at that particular time, had taken the opportunity to make some statements to buttress one of the Court's decisions which the crime bill modified. But I wanted this cleared up for the record. I am accepting your word for it that it didn't happen.''

If anyone in the hearing room understood what McClellan was really talking about, it was no fault of the senator's. So mild-mannered and oblique was his statement that it obscured the fact that he had Fortas on the ropes once again, if he chose to make his move. He was accusing the justice of lying, and this time he had the proof to back up his charge.

In fact, Fortas had done exactly what the senator was now charging. Late in May 1968, coincident with the publication of his civil disobedience book, the justice had spoken with a reporter from *The New York Times*. During the interview, Fortas had indeed criticized indirectly the Senate's inclusion of a provision in the Omnibus Crime Control Act that week reversing three of the Supreme Court's criminal justice decisions.[81] Such extrajudicial commentary, which was duly printed in the column, would have made Fortas look too political once again. Rather than press this issue further, though, McClellan accepted the justice's ''word for it'' and let the matter drop.

But the senator from Arkansas, despite his passive, almost docile performance in this questioning, had once again renewed the suspicion in the public's mind as to what else the justice *might* have done in the service of President Johnson. And McClellan still had one more chip to play.

Strom Thurmond got the floor back, and killed the last hour of the day's hearings with a public reading of a ten-year-old *Georgia Bar Journal* article. Every few minutes, the senator would stop to see whether the nominee was still awake and ask whether he now wanted to comment on that portion of the text. After one particularly long passage, even Thurmond seemed to lose his place, asking a question of "Mr. Chief Justice—Mr. Justice Fortas."

A smiling Fortas promptly responded, "I thank you, Senator."

Even Thurmond had to crack a smile for the first time: "We all make mistakes."

"Well, yours is highly retrievable," offered the nominee. And so it was.

Finally, it was over. Grudgingly the senators had to admire the gentle professional who had outdueled some of them and withstood the fury of a riled-up South Carolinian for four full days, and only twice displayed even a trace of emotion.

As he looked back over his twelve hours and thirty minutes before the Judiciary Committee's inquisition, Abe Fortas had every reason for confidence. His cool and collected demeanor in response to the senatorial badgering and heckling of the conservatives had won the hearts of the editorial boards across the nation. "Nothing has emerged that tarnishes his reputation as a vigorous attorney, a highly qualified judge, and as a dedicated American," said *The New York Times*. The *Washington Star* concluded, "We see nothing in the Fortas testimony which is of sufficient gravity to justify a refusal to confirm him as Chief Justice." But perhaps the *Salt Lake Tribune* put it best: "The ordeal of Supreme Court Justice Abe Fortas during his appearances before the Senate Judiciary Committee is not the sort of price anyone nominated for high office should have to pay."[82]

What had started out to be a boxing match between the representative of the liberal Warren Court and the liberal president, and the conservative southern senators, had turned out to be a political minefield of explosive questions through which Fortas had been able to navigate. In many ways, the mines had been put there by the forces of history. The conservatives on the committee and in the Senate had done their best to reverse the liberal trend of over thirty years. Stopping the liberal effort to control the leadership of the court for the next fifteen years was only one phase of a larger plan, including perhaps a victory in the fall's presidential election. But there was now little question that one set of mines had been placed on the field by Fortas himself.

Using very little evidence, the senators had succeeded in portraying the justice as a man with little regard for the publicly worshiped myth of separation of governmental powers. In spite of their overall sympathy for Fortas, the newspapers had reacted negatively to his close relationship with the president. This relationship was labeled "injudicious" by *The New York Times,* "questionable" by the *Washington Star,* a "pitfall" by *The Washington Post,*[83] and "somewhat imprudent" by the *Salt Lake Tribune.*

Given the intense reaction to the few extrajudicial actions that he had admitted, Fortas knew he had done the right thing by responding as he had. He had approached these questions like a skillful legal operator—the Washington lawyer dodging, evading, and on several occasions even outright lying. No one would understand his desire to avoid "dying on the Court." Nor would they ever understand the duty he felt to serve any president, let alone his close friend for over thirty years. Nor would they ever have to understand, for the evidence that proved him wrong was locked away in the White House files, and in the process of being gathered for destruction.

"I guess I have made full disclosure now," he had said. And there was a technical kind of truth here—for indeed it was all the "disclosure" he was willing to make.

But the probing senators suspected that there was more. As the hearings ended, the Senate cloakroom was filled with comments that reflected the doubts that had been raised by the opponents. Several senators now expressed a general belief that LBJ had received more than a summary of views from Fortas at the White House meetings. Then more questions were asked. How could the Judiciary Committee act on Homer Thornberry until the Fortas post opened up? Could Chief Justice Warren withdraw his resignation, and if so, under what circumstances? When the GOP had a presidential nominee, would he and other Republican senators join Griffin's movement? Even Senator Dirksen was now speaking of the negative reaction toward the "intemperate" nominee for chief justice that he was hearing from judges and lawyers. Some observers took this comment as reflecting Dirksen's "worry and uncertainty" with his position on the confirmation. Whether all of this represented a perceptible shift away from the judicial nominees, however, was too soon to tell.[84]

Trying to encourage that movement, both of Fortas's main adversaries—Strom Thurmond and Robert Griffin—were in the market for a new issue. Somehow they needed to show that there was more to this man than met the public eye. The charge didn't even have to be true, it just had to be believable. Fortas had shown by his evasive tactics that he would play into their hands by answering in such a way that his denials would not be accepted.

That was why the phone call that came into Robert Griffin's office at the end of the hearings from a man identifying himself only as "a top official at American University" was so welcome. Vowing that his facts were accurate, but explaining that his career depended on the fact that he not identify himself, the disembodied voice charged that his employer had established a tax-exempt foundation to pay Justice Fortas for teaching a seminar at the law school. Moreover, he claimed that the donations for the fund came from several local businessmen. With all of the tips coming into the Griffin office on this issue, it was hard to know which ones were worth the time needed to follow up. But the senator agreed that this one had promise, and his staff went to work. With a little luck, they might just be back in business.[85]

For his part, Thurmond had a much more effective plan. He simply convinced James Eastland to allow James J. Clancy to testify. Thurmond was anxious for others to *see* what Mr. Clancy wanted to talk about. A new front was about to be opened in the "Battle of Capitol Hill," and once again, Fortas's life would spin out of his control.[86]

XVIII

PORN WARS

It happens in Washington every day. Twenty-one people were huddled in a darkened room around a coin-operated movie projector, watching a cinematic fantasy. This one was called *0-7*. The plot wasn't very much. An attractive young girl was doing a striptease down to her garter belt and transparent panties. For fourteen minutes the actress undressed and writhed erotically, with the camera repeatedly focusing on various parts of her anatomy, ensuring that no viewer missed the point. It was what they call a stag film.

But wait. There was something very wrong here. Rather than moaning and sighing, the audience was laughing—out loud. And it wasn't a problem with the film, but the viewing conditions. Since there was no screen in the room, the projection of the film on the wooden panels of the wall made it look as though the actress were "molting." Moreover, the people shouting out the rude jokes during the screening were not the usual trenchcoat-clad crowd at such exhibitions, but members of Washington's elite press corps. Even more incredibly, the gentleman feeding the coin-operated projector with silver was a United States senator. This was not a peep show in the penny arcades of Washington's red-light district, but Room 2228 of the New Senate Office Building. And the host was none other than the senior senator from South Carolina, Strom Thurmond.

While he may not have been laughing with the rest, claiming he had "shocked Washington's hardened press corps," Thurmond was satisfied. For the response from the audience told him that he had breathed new life into a dying nomination battle.[1] However questionable the tactics, it was an indication of how little control the White House now had over the course of this fight.

This "startling" new piece of "evidence" had been brought to Thurmond's attention by James J. Clancy, an attorney representing the Citizens for Decent Literature, Inc. Dedicated to "pressing for enforcement of the obscenity laws—laws which the history of our Government has proven essential to the development of good family living," the CDL was allowed, through the efforts of Strom Thurmond, to voice its concern about the nominee for chief justice to the Judiciary Committee. Clancy's testimony provided more than levity for the emotionally drained combatants and observers; it ensured that the remainder of the Senate judiciary hearings following Fortas's dramatic performance was not going to be anticlimactic. Thurmond was now going to try to pin the justice with the responsibility for corrupting the morals of the nation or, at the very least, spend the next two days attempting to do so. This meant more talk; and for Thurmond, talk meant time, and time meant victory.[2]

The movement of the committee from high drama to low farce, and from the great constitutional debate over the matters of separation of powers and judicial ethics to the gutter of stag films and pornographic materials, was a sign of how far Strom Thurmond was willing to go to win this fight. *Life* magazine would later say that the South Carolina senator had combined a "left to the groin with a right to the more general Southern and conservative hatred of the whole Warren Court."[3] Reporters later joked that the committee had simply moved from its "witch hunt" to a "bitch hunt."[4] But what started out as a joke in most observers' minds soon took on a life of its own and became a serious threat to the nomination.

For a time it had looked like the hearings would go out not with a bang but with a whimper. After spending ten days in a hotel waiting for his turn before the committee, Homer Thornberry was finally given his opportunity to testify on a Saturday morning, July 20, 1968. But even before he opened his mouth, the judge knew that he had wasted his time. Only four senators had bothered to show up for the questioning, and the chairman took this opportunity to announce that Thornberry had been placed in a sort of political limbo. The committee, Eastland now stated, would not formally deal with his nomination until *after* the vote on Fortas. Since some of the members still did not believe that a vacancy existed on the court, now for all intents and purposes this nomination did not even exist.

Of course, that did not prevent Sam Ervin from killing the next day and a half of the committee's time by asking constantly rephrased versions of two questions about Thornberry's opinion in a case opposing the poll tax in Texas and another supporting a Vietnam protest demonstration. This resulted in a sense of déjà vu as Thornberry justifiably followed Fortas's example and refused to comment on issues that might once again come before the court. Only Strom Thurmond's refusal even to question Thornberry until after the Fortas nomination had been voted upon kept the pointless questioning from going even further.

When it was over, Homer Thornberry called on the president before leaving for Austin and told his old friend that, based on his experience as a former member of Congress, he did not expect to be returning to Washington permanently. Thornberry could see from the manner in which the committee was treating him that some of the members were just trying to delay the proceedings. The look on the president's face told the Texas judge that his old friend already knew this to be true. But Johnson insisted that all was not lost. A quick vote by the committee, a short supporting Judiciary Committee report written by the White House, the Justice Department, and Phil Hart, and they could have this up for a vote by the full Senate before the adjournment, the president argued. Johnson knew how the Senate worked. But so did the former congressman from Austin, and before he left for home he told Ramsey Clark simply, "It's over!"[5]

But even before Thornberry could get back on Air Force One for the return trip home, James J. Clancy was doing his best to fulfill that prophecy. He testified to the committee that his group had analyzed fifty-two obscenity cases over the previous two Supreme Court terms and determined that in all but three of them Fortas had provided the "deciding" fifth vote for reversing the lower court's finding that the material was obscene. What he did not say was that in only *one* of these cases had Fortas gone beyond voting to write an opinion actually explaining his views. To hear Clancy tell it, Fortas was responsible for book racks filled with such classics as *Lust School, Lust Web, Lust Pool, Lust Job,* and *Lust Hungry* (could *Lust Horizons* have been far behind?), and movie theaters showing films ranging from such non–Academy Award nominees as *Erotic Touch of Hot Skin* and *Rent a Girl,* to ones that only letters and numbers could describe—*0-7, 0-12,* and *D-15.*

Seeking to galvanize the committee behind this attack, Clancy had brought with him a thirty-minute film documentary displaying some of these materials, and a print of the film *0-7,* which had been shown in the coin-operated arcades in Los Angeles and Beverly Hills, giving rise to the case of *Schackman v. California.*[6] The *Schackman* case was the major example of the court's permissiveness that the CDL was laying at Fortas's feet. Here, rulings by the California state courts and the lower federal district court that three striptease films were obscene had been overturned by the United States Supreme Court in June of 1967. And Fortas had provided the "deciding" fifth vote here, joining an action that had been taken by the court with absolutely no explanatory opinion—only the single-sentence announcement of the decision.

It was not difficult to discern the rather large hole in Clancy's attack. The variety of possible issues raised by such a case—the possible obscene nature of the material itself, the vagueness of the governing statute, the nature of the jury's instructions, the state of mind of the purveyor of the items, or even the nature of the search warrant or police conduct during the search—had split the justices' votes in too many directions for them to unite on a single opinion. But none of these subtleties mattered to Strom Thurmond, who suggested that perhaps the court's silence was due to the fact that it was "ashamed" of the decision.[7] Clancy argued that Fortas's actions in cases like *Schackman* had caused "a release of the greatest deluge of hard-core pornography ever witnessed by any nation—and this at a time when statistics indicate a pronounced breakdown in public morals and general movement toward sexual degeneracy throughout our Nation."[8] Thurmond had not seen the film, but Clancy's description was enough for him to determine that it was "obscene and filthy and obnoxious to any right-thinking person."[9] So it became his solemn obligation to see that it be viewed by the committee as evidence against the nominee.

In July 1968, Fortas's real position on the issue mattered little to certain members of the Senate. This was not the legal arena, where he had been grappling with how best to shape the law in a manner that did not do damage to the First Amendment. Instead it was the political arena, where Clancy and Thurmond, professing that "a community has a right to protect its young people," could simply portray the issue in black and white—you were either for smut or against it. And for them, the truth about Abe Fortas was clear. Once again, by being thrust into the home court of the politicians, Abe Fortas became the lightning rod for hostility to the Warren Court in general.

In trying to deflect some of this criticism, Senator Hart learned the price for trying to be helpful to the White House. As he had done once before, Hart introduced into the committee records another of the Justice Department's memoranda. This one dealt with Fortas's judicial philosophy, and was one intended to be a case-by-case rebuttal to the Ervin-Thurmond questioning. For some reason, though, Hart decided this time to acknowledge the department's assistance.[10] This enabled Sam Ervin to protest sanctimoniously that the administration was "propagandiz[ing] the committee" and demand an additional day of hearings to question someone from the Justice Department about this transgression. Thus, Ervin completed his major contribution to the opposition, having through his various arguments, and his nearly four days of pointless questioning, almost singlehandedly extended what had been promised to be three days of hearings into a committee filibuster lasting thirteen days.

The next day, Deputy Attorney General Christopher was called before the committee to explain the gaffe and was grilled by Sam Ervin on the many Fortas decisions that the justice himself had refused to comment upon. While Warren Christopher wisely chose to duck all of these questions, Ervin felt free to give a repeat performance as to *his* understanding of the cases. Having heard this lecture before, Strom Thurmond busied himself at the committee bench prominently reading the copy of *Nudie-Fax* magazine that had been placed before the committee the day before. To ensure that everyone in the room understood the point, whenever the magazine began to droop, one of the senator's assistants would race over and prop it up again for all to see.[11]

When Ervin ran out of either questions or interest, the rest of the day was devoted to Thurmond's bullets relating to the court's rulings on obscenity. But no matter how hard Christopher tried to impress upon the senator that it did not matter what his or the Justice Department's opinions or interpretations of these cases were, all that mattered was whether they demonstrated a competence by the nominee to serve on the court, Thurmond was not to be deterred. Sending a copy of the *Weekend Jaybird,* which one of his assistants had gathered the day before in a tour of the capital's red-light district, down to Christopher's table, the senator wondered if he agreed that it "is obscene, it is foul, it is putrid, it is filthy, it is repulsive, it is objectionable, it is obnoxious, and it should cause a flush of shame to the cheeks of the members of the Supreme Court who affirmed decisions that allow such material as this to go through the mails." [12] When Christopher politely refused to discuss material that had nothing directly to do with the cases decided by the Supreme Court, it was time for the now familiar Thurmond tirade:

> Mr. Christopher, how much longer are the parents, the Christian people, the wholesome people, the right-thinking people, going to put up with this kind of thing? How much longer should they do it? And you are up here defending Justice Fortas on his decisions. He has reversed the decisions, I repeat, in 23 out of 26 cases where the local courts held the material was obscene. He has thrown it out and said it was not obscene. This is the kind of material that they said was obscene, and yet Justice Fortas, and a majority of the Court, many decisions five to four, have allowed this material to be available and sold on the streets of this Nation. Cannot the States have something to do to protect themselves? Cannot the communities follow some course? Can you suggest something? [13]

But of course Thurmond knew that Christopher would not be willing to offer anything.

It was a cheap shot by the senior senator from South Carolina, but as the day's press deadline approached, he knew that it was effective. Now those senators on the fence had an issue that could be used as a public relations explanation for a negative vote against Fortas. Constituents who could not comprehend the subtleties of the separation of powers or condone a vote based on anti-Semitism, or political philosophy, nevertheless had an opinion on the proliferation of smut in their neighborhoods. And senators who did not dare admit their true biases in opposing Fortas could now freely seek refuge in the drive to "clean up America." It was, then, the perfect smokescreen issue—buying time and maybe even a few votes.

When the hearings mercifully ended, any hope by the White House for quick action on the part of the Judiciary Committee depended on the course of the committee's executive session on the morning of July 24. The great fear was that someone would invoke the unwritten rule allowing a week-long delay before taking a formal vote on a nomination. And, despite the efforts to avoid such an occurrence, someone did. This time, though, it was not the obstructionism of Thurmond or Ervin.

Still angry at the president for his signing statement on the Omnibus Crime Control Act ordering the attorney general and the FBI not to take advantage of the liberalized questioning guidelines in the new law, John McClellan wanted to show that despite his quiescent performance in quizzing Fortas he was still a genuine Dixiecrat.[14] So, after Phil Hart followed White House instructions and made a motion for immediate consideration of the Fortas and Thornberry nominations, McClellan said that he "wanted to know a good deal more about the obscenity film before a decision was made on Fortas." Having already viewed the Clancy film, he now "was convinced that any Senator who saw it would vote against the nomination."[15] So he insisted that the committee needed additional time to view this cinematic blight on America. Strom Thurmond immediately supported this motion for the mandatory one-week delay—and the clock was running again.

The move spelled more trouble for the White House than just the loss of time. It also meant that McClellan, who told White House aides the next day conflicting stories as to why, "much to his surprise," the committee had granted the extension, was now clearly no friend of the White House on this matter. But then, neither were the rest of the Dixiecrats. Only Russell could have prevented this, and Russell was gone.[16]

A stunned White House tactical team met late on the evening of July 24, and the men who had fought so long—Larry Temple, Barefoot Sanders, Joe Califano, Ramsey Clark, Warren Christopher, Mike Manatos, Marvin Watson, and Paul Porter—now surveyed the damage. The latest Senate head counts still showed that the numbers on the floor were there, if only they could get the nominations reported out of committee. Counting the probable votes, sixty-five senators were still willing to vote for cloture. That would be more than enough to stop a filibuster, since some of the nomination opponents, such as Milton Young of North Dakota, had assured the White House team that they would "take a walk" for the crucial cloture vote.[17] And on the actual confirmation vote, some talliers were now counting on between seventy-three and seventy-six positive responses.[18]

But the problem was how to get the darned thing out of the committee. There were only about ten days until adjournment, and seven of them were gone thanks to John McClellan. The secret, they all agreed, would be to have the majority report ready to go when the next Judiciary Committee meeting on the nomination occurred. So it was decided that Phil Hart would circulate among his colleagues a report drafted by him, Paul Porter, and Ramsey Clark.[19] Then, the only trick would be to make sure that a quorum of senators showed up for the next meeting and that the vote was taken. The timing was tight, but it seemed possible.[20]

Until then, it was movie time for the senators on Capitol Hill. The thought of septuagenarians huddled around the coin-operated projector in a small basement studio viewing pornographic films tickled the nation's political cartoonists.[21] Herblock portrayed the senator from South Carolina in his pin-up-filled film office with the sign STROM THURMOND, U.S. OBSCENATOR.[22] But the truth was even funnier than fiction. Another film, *Flaming Creatures,* was flown to the committee straight from Ann Arbor, where it had been seized in a police raid the previous year on the University of Michigan campus. This film, which had given rise to a case before the Supreme Court in which only Fortas had been willing to reverse the New York conviction, was described by one viewer as dealing "unblushingly with transvestism."[23] Then, to allow some senators to reach a judgment on "the evidence" while also denying to their constituents that they had been sullied by actually viewing the films, Thurmond had thoughtfully provided assistance. His aides made up over one hundred black-and-white glossy photographs from various frames of the seized films, which were then passed around among interested senators.

Having taken it upon himself to arrange some of the movie showings, Strom Thurmond once arrived late and had to bang on the locked doors to get in. While only six to twelve senators viewed each show, the reaction was all that he hoped for. One senator told a reporter that *Flaming Creatures* "was so sick, I couldn't even get aroused."[24] For a member of the Senate, this was strong stuff indeed. "I am not going back," announced Louisiana's Russell Long. "I have seen one Fortas film—I have seen enough."[25] And Jack Miller of Iowa, one of Griffin's original rebels and a member of the national advisory board of the Citizens for Decent Literature (thus labeled by Phil Hart the "committee's favorite film critic"),[26] voiced his concerns about the matter in a long speech on the Senate floor.[27] The fire of Miller's speech was somewhat blunted, though, when he candidly admitted, "We do not have Fortas's judicial philosophy on this subject."[28] There was even some serious talk of showing the films on the floor of the Senate and adding copies of them to the kits of committee hearing extracts being sent to women's groups and civic clubs around the nation.[29] No matter how shoddy the attack, there was clear indication now that some of the senators were taking this issue very seriously.

Sensing the turning tide, Everett Dirksen asked Warren Christopher for a memorandum answering Miller's charges on the question of obscenity. The next day he had the carefully drafted response, entitled "Memorandum Re the Views of Justice Fortas on Obscenity." Using Fortas's public voting record, it very effectively managed to portray him as taking "a moderate position in the center of the Court, with at least three and perhaps four Justices going substantially beyond" his holdings in protecting materials under the First Amendment.[30] But a curious thing happened. Dirksen never delivered a speech using the memorandum, or even entered it into the Senate record. So, once more, the only thing that stood was the unanswered attack.[31]

Soon there were some real storm signals that this whole issue was snowballing. Richard Russell warned the administration that while his constituents were not sophisticated enough to understand the nuances of the lame-duck issue, they did know smut and they could understand the private political work Fortas had done with the president. Worse than that, a man that all the Senate head counts had been placing in the "for" column, Frank Lausche of Ohio, told Phil Hart that he would "never vote for a man who would approve the films involved in the *Schackman* case."[32] "If the nominee were my brother," he would later tell the rest of the Senate in an impassioned speech, "I would not vote for him."[33] This was not good news, coming on the heels of another prominent desertion from the cause, by Norris Cotton of New Hampshire. Recorded on many of the administration's head counts as being in the "probably for" column, Cotton announced to his constituents at the close of the hearings that "on broad grounds of principle" against the entire Warren Court, "rather than specific objections raised against Fortas," he intended to vote against the nomination.[34] Clearly, the delaying tactics by Thurmond and Ervin in the Judiciary Committee had reminded many in the Senate of their hostility to the Warren Court while also making it possible for them finally to do something about it.

Fortas's main concern now was making sure that the erosion of support in the Senate had not expanded to his colleagues on the court. To John Marshall Harlan, he wrote that he had "not been a governmental 'busybody' . . . [and] never 'volunteered' suggestions or participation in the affairs of the State. On the other hand, I felt that I had no alternative to complying with the President's request for participation in the matters where he sought my help—or more precisely, sought the comfort of hearing my summation before his decision—that's about what it amounted to in the case of President Johnson–Justice Fortas." Fortas insisted that nothing he had done off the bench had, in his opinion, "injured the court as an institution."[35] Then the next day Fortas wrote to the chief justice that "the opposition in the Senate is a combination of Nixon-Republican partisanship, and non-partisan reaction on both sides of the aisle. The common element is bitter, corrosive opposition to all that has been happening in the court and the country: the racial progress, and the insistence upon increased regard for human rights and dignity in the field of criminal law. Other elements contribute to the mix, but it's my guess that they are minor."[36] While Fortas expressed innocence regarding these "weird events," in time others would see it quite differently.[37]

With all of the eroding support, and the furor surrounding the obscenity issue, the White House knew that it could not afford any more mistakes. Any new "revelations" would serve to fuel the opposition by destroying the "full disclosure" myth. Since Fortas was particularly vulnerable on the question of his relationship with Lyndon Johnson, while all of his papers were being gathered up from the White House Central Files, the contacts between the justice and the president were reduced to virtually nothing. Over the course of the two-and-a-half-month confirmation battle, there were fewer than a dozen phone calls between them and two face-to-face meetings. For two men who had been in constant contact for years to now have a long-distance relationship, even though both lived in the same city, seemed strange indeed. But it was necessary.[38]

So conscious was Fortas of the delicate nature of his public relations problem here that even when his help was needed by the White House, he was reluctant to give it. As the hearings ended, Fortas asked Joseph Califano whether it was wise for him to attend a luncheon concerning the creation of the Johnson Library. Worried about the possibility of a leak even from an off-the-record occasion, both men agreed that the necessary lobbying could be done by the justice at a luncheon given at his own home.[39] It was ironic, in a way, that Fortas was now shut off from access to the one man who had shut off his access to the rest of the world.

Sometimes, it took a little bit of luck to keep things hidden. After all of the efforts to conceal the Fortas advisory relationship, in late July a copy of a newly printed White House brochure entitled "I Want to Speak to You Tonight of Peace," on the president's March 31, 1968, speech, happened to cross Joe Califano's desk. The last in a series of thirty such glossy brochures put together by the White House as a historical chronicle of the Johnson years, it was to be sent out within days as a memento to prominent supporters of the administration. But as he flipped through the photograph-filled pages, Califano noticed something in one of the candid pictures of the administration hard at work that troubled him.[40] It showed the president at a long conference table in the White House listening intently to ten of his wartime advisers discuss the Vietnam problem, and there at the end of the table, comfortably taking in the scene with his hands casually clasped in front of him, was Supreme Court Justice Abe Fortas. It was just the sort of picture some of the opposition senators would have killed to be able to release to the press. When the matter was brought to the president's attention, he knew that there was no choice. He ordered the boxes impounded, saying that the picture's "caption [was] wrong." And so, today, the seventy thousand booklets now sit in the bowels of the Johnson Library, still wrapped and sealed in their boxes and awaiting distribution.[41]

But the administration's luck could not possibly hold out forever. What the White House staff said and did could be controlled, but what others said and did could not. Which was why an article by Daniel Yergin portraying speechwriter Richard Goodwin in the July 22, 1968, issue of *New York* magazine represented a potential land mine. In an anecdote designed to show what it was like to work as a slave on the president's plantation, the piece described the drafting process for the 1966 State of the Union address: "Johnson called [Goodwin] back to the White House to help prepare the [message]. He was up two days working on it and then a doctor came in and gave him an injection, as though he were a machine, so that he could stay up even longer. Then Johnson handed the speech over to Abe Fortas and Clifford, the old New Dealers and Fair Dealers, who began chopping it up. Goodwin retired to his hotel room, exhausted."[42] True, it was only an unsubstantiated rumor of a single speechwriting episode. Hardly the stuff of scandal. But then, it might well show that full disclosure had not been made by Fortas after all. As soon as this came to the attention of the opposition, it was leaked to the rest of the press to prepare for the next stage in the battle.[43]

Then, too, Robert Griffin's staff was hard at work tracking down possible leads on the anonymous phone call that had come into the office about the American University law school course. Since the tip had been about a tax-exempt foundation supporting the class, someone in the office was checking with the Securities and Exchange Commission and the Internal Revenue Service. At this point, though, nothing else had turned up.[44]

Unaware of all of this, the White House aides were hard at work to ensure that the Judiciary Committee vote on the Supreme Court nominations would follow quickly. Despite their best efforts, when McClellan's requested delay period expired, a quorum of senators could not find their way to the committee meeting on July 31, and Chairman Eastland was disinclined to do anything more to make his colleagues attend. In accordance with his promise to the president to move "at [his] own time," though, Eastland did schedule another meeting for September 4, but said it would be held only if everyone "cooperated."[45] Somehow that news did not cheer the troops at 1600 Pennsylvania Avenue.

Suddenly all of the news for the president turned bad. No one cared much that Robert Griffin, feeling the glow of victory growing, had predicted defeat for the nominations the previous night in a speech to the National Press Club. "Perhaps this debate can ultimately serve a higher and a nobler purpose. For it *can* serve to lift the Supreme Court, once again, *above* and *out* of politics. . . . In this battle, we are right. Because we are right, time is on our side."[46] Or at least time could be made to be on their side, Griffin knew, as he now claimed to the press that he had six more than the number of senators required to prevent a cloture vote (even though he still opposed the use of a filibuster and was looking for a way to defeat the nomination on a straight vote).[47] Once again, the best efforts of the White House to counter the one-sided opposition charges by having an ally debate Griffin at this meeting—either Phil Hart or Wayne Morse—failed, and all of the press ink went to the rebels.[48]

But the White House aides became more concerned when the public gloating by Griffin was mirrored by some of the private Senate head counts. Even though the White House head counts of the Senate continued to claim sixty-five supporters, Sam Shaffer of *Newsweek* was using different mathematics. He reported to the White House that the head counts coming from Majority Leader Mansfield were "totally unrealistic," and there were forty-three hard votes against cloture. Moreover, because of the "devastating" effect of the pornography attack, the mail in some Senate offices was now running twenty-five to one against Fortas. Finally, the rumor began floating that when the Senate returned, Strom Thurmond planned to filibuster solely on the issue of obscenity.[49]

As if this were not bad enough, Everett Dirksen, who had been confidently predicting victory all along, was now admitting to the press that a Senate vote on cloture would be "very close," and Mansfield was now saying that he had "always been doubtful" that it could be achieved.[50] And worst of all, James Eastland, the man who had correctly predicted the desertion of Richard Russell so many weeks ago, now added to these woes by predicting to the Justice Department that Everett Dirksen would eventually do the same.[51]

An optimistic Lyndon Johnson, however, chose to heed only the rosy Senate head counts stuffed in his coat pocket, and canvassed his staff for ideas on how to redirect the battle. From his position as Senate liaison for the Justice Department, Barefoot Sanders understood the problem, and told the president to "(1) Develop a theme; (2) Rally our supporters; and (3) Plan now for the filibuster in September." The goal was to blitz the senators with letters from prominent constituents, making them feel the heat of harsh letters to their home newspapers' editors. Sanders estimated that such a strategy might be very effective on the estimated twenty-five to thirty swing senators who might eventually support the confirmations. But Sanders also warned, "*Our Senate supporters are pretty discouraged*. They need to be pepped up. *The best—and perhaps the only—way that can be done is by the President*." So he recommended that Johnson hold a press conference in which he should come "down hard on his continuing interest in these two nominations being confirmed."[52]

This Johnson did on July 31. Answering a very convenient question at the end of his press conference just hours after the Judiciary Committee had failed to hold its vote, Johnson went to excessive length about the nominations. He had already resorted to threats, having told Democratic legislators at a White House breakfast, "I want Abe Fortas confirmed, even if I keep Congress in session until Christmas."[53] But no one really cared anymore. The only issue now was who controlled the clock—and the advantage now lay with the rebels.[54]

On Capitol Hill the first step of Sanders's strategy—a rash of strongly supportive speeches delivered on the floor of the Senate—never materialized. In fact, outside of Mike Mansfield's request for a suspension of the rules to allow the nominations to carry over the recess into September, there was no comment by the White House's allies at all.[55] Instead, it was Sam Ervin who once again monopolized the proceedings by delivering a seemingly endless address on Fortas's role in the history of constitutional law. Then he captured the next day's press by saying, "No man is fit to be a Supreme Court Justice if he lacks a sense of self-restraint or is unwilling to exercise it. The presence of such Justices on the Supreme Court imperils our most precious right—the right to be governed by the Constitution.''[56]

The thought of his reputation being continually besmirched without effective challenge proved to be too much for Abe Fortas to bear. He finally took out a sheet of legal-sized paper and began jotting down a new shopping list of instructions to Paul Porter on how to mount a counterattack. Like Sanders, the justice knew that what was needed was ''tough speeches, and statements, and 'publicity.''' So the justice listed the names of more prominent lawyers, union lobbyists, Jewish leaders, and newspapermen who might be contacted for help.

But try as the allies might, their plans now seemed to be constantly backfiring. Seeking to compensate for the silence of his supporters in the Senate, Fortas had Paul Porter arrange a supportive press conference at the American Bar Association meeting on August 2.[57] This was to coincide with Porter's efforts—in what seemed to some White House aides to be a pointless exercise, given the lateness of the hour—to establish an *ad hoc* committee of prominent attorneys around the nation to work in support of the nominations.[58]

But the press conference on August 2 did not go as expected. This ''spontaneous'' display of legal support for the nominations was ruined when Leon Jaworski, a Houston attorney known to be a close friend to both Lyndon Johnson and Homer Thornberry, admitted that *he* had conducted the ABA investigation of Thornberry. This revelation did not seem to square with the president's depiction in his press conference two days earlier of an ABA investigation so intensive that it had involved ''representatives of the 12 regions all over the country.'' To the press there seemed to be more credence to the opponents' claims of politicking on the nominations.[59]

Seeing this, Fortas decided that the time had come to stand up for himself. He had suffered the slings and arrows of his opponents for too long, saying in a speech to the National Postal Forum only that his ''anger and outraged silence'' might cause ulcers.[60] But if his reputation and future were going to hang over the fire for another month, Fortas decided that there were a few things that he had been dying to say to Strom Thurmond, Sam Ervin, and a host of other people. So he accepted an invitation to speak to the American College of Trial Lawyers in Philadelphia.

The original version of Fortas's speech was much more pointed in its tone, but after consulting with Paul Porter and other friends the justice decided to tone it down in the interest of caution. Still, the final product—which Porter had sent out in advance to newspaper people around the country, trying to muster support—was Fortas at his most eloquent.[61] If he was going to go down, it was going to be in flames, with the mantle of the flag and the robe of a Supreme Court justice wrapped around him.

After drawing laughter by saying, "I'm most grateful to you for confirming my nomination—that is, my nomination as an Honorary Member of this distinguished organization," the embattled justice made clear to his audience why he was now risking more criticism for giving yet another extrajudicial speech: "Until recently in this country, we had little reason for worry about the completeness of the Nation's dedication to our system of law. . . . We also assumed that all responsible people respected the law and the courts; that the principle of an absolutely independent judiciary was so firmly embedded and accepted that it was beyond attack. We properly encouraged criticism of the actions of courts and judges by the press, by people generally and by members of the Congress. We assumed that there was no danger that courts or judges might be subjected to pressures in connection with individual cases and specific issues, including constitutional issues, in accordance with the views of non-judicial office holders. . . . Now we know that we can no longer merely assume these things. We can no longer merely take it for granted that there is common understanding and common agreement upon this, the basic scheme of our Constitution—upon our system of freedom within peace and order which is the foundation of our form of government."

Then Fortas gave the answer he had been prevented from providing earlier in response to Strom Thurmond's *Mallory* tirade: "Insistence upon procedural standards, commanded by our Constitution, is *not* a technicality. To set aside the conviction of a man who has been tried in violation of the standards of our Constitution is *not* to set it aside on a mere technicality. Observance of the rights which secure freedom is not a technicality. Certainly it is not to us—as it is to the unfortunate people in totalitarian states—a mere technicality which may be disregarded in order to sustain a conviction. Constitutionalism is not a technicality. Constitutional rights are not technicalities. *This* is the phrase that should ring in the Nation's ear."[62]

It was a stirring address, with the responsive audience giving Fortas a tumultuous standing ovation. But coming as it did over two weeks after Thurmond's initial attack, the impact was somewhat muted. The denial never receives as much publicity as the initial charges, anyway. Fortas's friends, however, rallied once more to his cause. Although ailing, Fortas's savvy old law partner Thurman Arnold wrote him that the speech was "almost as important as your confirmation." In the end, Arnold insisted, history alone would be the judge of these days, in which a justice found himself in the vortex of the dramatic confrontation between a retiring president and an insurgent Senate. And history would realize that the "ideal of an independent judiciary" dwarfed the individuals involved in this particular dispute. In closing, Arnold added, "From now on, your recognition as a great Justice is secure. The only comparable achievement that I can think of at the moment is that of Rudolph the Red-Nosed Reindeer who, as you may remember, rose in a single night from an obscure member of the team to a permanent place in history."[63]

The usually perceptive Arnold was right once again. Fortas's place in history would be "permanent," but not for the reasons that he thought. He could not have known that in fact significant errors had already been made that one day would lead Arnold himself to revise his thinking on Fortas's career substantially.[64]

The satisfaction derived from this public response made the combative justice more and more uncomfortable with his passive role in the rest of the fight. Should he accept the Judiciary Committee's offer at the close of the hearings to return for additional questioning on James Clancy's charges? he wondered. But in the final analysis, Fortas knew that he could never return to the committee hearings. It would be another circus for his southern opponents, and he would never be able to develop his position safely. Paul Porter could see the psychological trauma wearing on his friend, and warned the White House about its impact. Fortas was a fighter, accustomed to waging his own battles. Now, however, he was forced to lead a completely cloistered existence and watch in anguish while others did the fighting for him. He was not in control of his own destiny, and he did not like it one bit.[65]

Had it not been for columnist James J. Kilpatrick, the justice probably would have remained on the sidelines for the rest of the fight. But after viewing one of the films involved in the *Schackman* case, *0-12,* Kilpatrick argued in his column that the Senate should save itself the time of arguing about the confirmations and simply show the film on the Senate floor. "The majority's brusque order of June 12, 1967, is part of a pattern that runs through the fabric of constitutional law as tailored by Mr. Justice Fortas. This was his idea of protected speech. Does the Senate agree? That's the size of the parliamentary proposition: Boil the issue down to this lip-licking slut, writhing carnally on a sofa, while a close-up camera dwells lasciviously on her genitals. Free speech? Free press? Is this what the Constitution means? The Constitution is, we may remember, what five judges say it is, no less, no more. So remembering, will the Senate advise and consent?''[66]

The attack was more than Fortas could bear. Having accepted silently the assaults of Strom Thurmond, and the delays of Sam Ervin, he decided the time had come for some lobbying. He thought back over the past three years as he picked up his pen and searched for a pad of legal paper.

These self-appointed protectors of the nation's morals had it all wrong, he believed. But why should they understand his position? They were not members of the court. And the nature of the court's work was such that the mechanics of its decision making were hidden from view.

Over the years in obscenity cases the justices had aligned themselves on what might be called a smut spectrum, based on the amount of allegedly pornographic literature or movies each would allow to be sold. The most permissive were Justices William O. Douglas and Hugo Black, who upheld the absolute right to print or film anything by using a literal reading of the First Amendment, which says in part, ''Congress shall make no law . . . abridging the freedom of speech, or of the press. . . .'' At the other end of the spectrum was Justice John Marshall Harlan, who, in arguing for near-total control of the problem, believed that this was a matter reserved for the state's powers to protect the health, safety, welfare, and morality of its citizens. Somewhere in the middle was Justice William Brennan, who became the court's expert at devising and interpreting compromise standards for determining whether an item was obscene and should be banned.[67]

The published decision record of Abe Fortas reflected the equivocal nature of his personal philosophy in this area. Fortas's only signed opinion on the subject, in the case of *Ginsberg* v. *New York,* dealt with the case of Samuel Ginsberg, the owner of a stationery store and luncheonette, who had been convicted in the state of New York for selling two girlie magazines to a sixteen-year-old boy, acting on the careful instructions of his mother. Ruling on the question of whether the state could rightfully convict Ginsberg for selling such materials to a minor under the age of seventeen, the court affirmed the conviction, saying that what had been ruled as permissible for sale to adults was in this case impermissible for sale to minors in accordance with the state law.[68]

In dissenting on the case, Fortas wrote an equivocal opinion in Ginsberg's defense.[69] ''I agree,'' he argued, ''that the State in the exercise of its police power—even in the First Amendment domain—may make proper and careful differentiation between adults and children.''[70] But Fortas's standard would focus more on the conduct of the salesman than on the items themselves. ''The state's police power may, within very broad limits, protect the parents and their children from public aggression of panderers and pushers. This is defensible on the theory that they cannot protect themselves from such assaults.''[71] Since Ginsberg had not ''pandered,'' he got Fortas's vote because the state had failed to show his criminal intent. However, the remainder of the opinion made it clear that Fortas's *real* fear here was the state would be used by parents to ban other books as a substitute for their own child-rearing responsibilities. All in all, the dissent was far from a ringing endorsement either for Ginsberg or for state control of obscenity even as it related to minors.[72]

The maddening problem for Fortas, as he considered Kilpatrick's column in the summer of 1968, was that he knew the key to his real philosophy on the issue of pornography lay in the unpublished working papers on the court's decisions. Privately, Fortas had argued to his colleagues that for him, obscenity was a ''cess-pool problem.'' But Fortas feared that the nation was about to turn to another wave of ''book burning.''[73] So, when fellow liberal William Brennan appeared to be ready to ban the sale of John Cleland's *Memoirs of a Woman of Pleasure,* more commonly known as *Fanny Hill,*[74] Fortas succeeded in convincing his colleague that the court in the coming *Ginzburg* v. *U.S.* case should look at the conduct of the book salesman rather than the material itself. Thus the ''pandering'' formula came into being, enabling the authorities to convict people for aggressively selling otherwise legal materials by exploiting their prurient nature. So, contrary to the CDL's claims, it was Abe Fortas who, in shocking his liberal friends by his vote upholding the prosecution, had actually *helped* to launch the standards that made convictions in this area even easier.[75]

In reality, though, Fortas was not as much in favor of state control as this lobbying action indicated. A few weeks after the court's announcement of the *Ginzburg* decision, Fortas began to reconsider his vote affirming the conviction. ''I think I was wrong,'' Fortas privately confessed in a note to William O. Douglas. But ''subconsciously,'' Fortas admitted, he had been ''affected by [Ralph] G[inzburg]'s slimy qualities.'' And if he ''had it to do over again,'' Fortas explained, he would have reversed almost all of the obscenity convictions. ''Well, live and learn,'' he closed.[76]

A year later, Fortas got the chance to explain his new thoughts on the matter to his brethren on the court in a private memorandum. He had concluded that the exceptions to the First Amendment, those actions that would not be protected, should be narrowed to include only certain types of *conduct* that were objectionable.[77] For him, then, the only state action allowable would be against the "persons responsible" for "conscious and purposeful pandering" of the material, and not against either the material itself or those who innocently sold it.

Fortas's emphasis on the conduct of selling made it difficult to place him on the court's smut spectrum. Depending on the facts of the sale, he could be seen as an ally of either the Douglas-Black "absolutist" camp as a protector of all materials, or of Harlan's role as a judicial censor. In truth, Fortas himself did not know where he came out on this issue, later telling Justice Harlan that it depended on how the reader of his opinion felt.[78] Unfortunately for him, though, the case that gave rise to this memo, *Redrup* v. *New York,* resulted in such a split vote on the court that only a short *per curiam* judgment could be issued. And, because of the vagaries of the timing of cases coming before the court, there had been no other opportunities to explain his new pornography principles to the public. So there was no public evidence for Fortas to use in counteracting the claims of Kilpatrick and the CDL.

Since all of this was private court debate, Fortas needed to find other means to defend himself. It was a question of finding a strong advocate to make his case. And even then, the problem would be how to explain his real position to the public without appearing as though he sanctioned pornography. The White House had proven unable to divert these specious attacks, and Paul Porter had done even less. Fortas thus decided that there were some things one *had* to do for oneself, even if they did violate several of the norms of sitting on the United States Supreme Court. Of course, he would not be able to defend himself openly. So it simply required that he become again a Washington lawyer, casting the argument in his own defense in the right light, and working in the shadows to place it in the hands of the person who could do him the most good without letting him be discovered.

With all of this in mind, Fortas pulled out his famous yellow legal pad and began to draft a defense in a hurried scrawl, frequently stopping to cross out excessive or inaccurate language. The Kilpatrick column was an "unjust, unfair and intemperate assault" upon the Supreme Court, he wrote. Then he did something that a member of the court is never supposed to do in public: He discussed the true reasons for the court's decision in the *Schackman* case. Overturning the conviction had had nothing to do with the films at all, he explained, but a technical violation of police procedure. The police had seized the film without first getting a proper search warrant, so they violated California law. All of this Kilpatrick might have understood, Fortas added, if he had taken the time to read the record of the Judiciary Committee, which contained a memorandum by Senator Hart explaining this fact.

Then the troubled justice went on to try to characterize his own views on the court's spectrum concerning obscenity. He was, he argued, "definitely . . . middle of the road." After all, conservatives such as Justices Byron White and Potter Stewart had voted with him to reverse in *Schackman,* and there were times when these two voted to reverse convictions while he voted to affirm. (Of course, this didn't happen very often, but Fortas knew that the newspaper readers were not going to check this claim out.) Consider his vote to convict in the "controversial" *Ginzburg* case, he argued, forgetting the confession of error he had made to Douglas. Then, selectively recalling the real reasons for his written opinion in the sale-to-minors case, Fortas pointed out his defense of states' enacting differential laws to protect minors in this area. In his best trial advocacy style, Fortas added that unlike the "venerable and distinguished" Black and Douglas, who allowed no censorship no matter how obscene some might consider the material to be, "this is *not* the view of Justice Fortas."[79]

The danger of this claim was that by placing himself in a no-man's-land in which no side fully accepted him as an ally, Fortas ensured that no one would take the responsibility for defending him.[80] But this was not the way the justice saw it, as he continued to draft his response to Kilpatrick. "I have the utmost . . ." Fortas wrote, and then caught himself, changing it to "Lawyers generally have the utmost confidence in Justice Fortas as a lawyer, judge and constitutionalist." The recent display of support at the two legal conventions attested to that fact. So there was no reason to be "subjected to such violent attack, based on a lack of understanding."

It was an impressive document, perhaps the strongest defense that could be offered for his position on this issue. And it had the potential to drain some of the image of respectability from the "public morality" brigade. But of course the problem was that Fortas could not send this on his own to the editors of the *Washington Star* for publication. So he did the next best thing. He sent it to his friend Edward Bennett Williams, the noted Washington trial attorney.[81]

The linchpin of the argument was the inside information that Williams would be able to reveal as to the *real* reason for the court's decision in the hotly debated *Schackman* case. This alone would reveal the true motives and lack of understanding of Fortas's opponents.

Williams, of course, would ordinarily have no knowledge of this inside court information or, if he did, would not announce it to the world in a newspaper letter. So that was why Fortas had referred to the obscenity memorandum introduced into the Judiciary Committee record by Senator Hart explaining all of this, which Kilpatrick had "missed." But the memo, Fortas discovered to his horror shortly after sending the letter over to Williams's law office, had never actually been introduced into the Senate committee's record. The reason was that the Justice Department had sent it not to Hart, who had already introduced two of the department's other memos and paid a price for it, but to Everett Dirksen.[82] And *Dirksen* had failed to enter it in the record. So Fortas had no choice but to call the Williams office and have the heart of his letter struck out.[83] Thus, the letter that was printed over Edward Bennett Williams's name could respond directly to Kilpatrick's main charge only by saying that "no inference can properly be drawn" from the one-sentence reversal of Schackman's conviction "that all the members of that majority are 'soft' on obscenity."[84] Though the rest of the letter was drawn largely verbatim from Fortas's original draft, it did not have the same bite.[85]

In failing to have the obscenity memo inserted into the Senate record in a timely fashion, the White House had failed Fortas again. From the time of Clancy's first attack, the Fortas-Williams letter had been the *only* response by the confirmation allies to the obscenity controversy, and its strength had been sapped through no fault of the justice's. And the next shot in this public war of words came not from the White House, but from another conservative supporter of Kilpatrick's views, William F. Buckley.[86] Try as he might, Fortas could not seem to regain control of events.

So some of his allies tried to help the justice regain that control, at least over the obscenity issue. Early in the fight Fortas had included in one of his shopping lists of suggestions to Paul Porter: "I think Dean O'Meara of Notre Dame Law School will help."[87] When nothing was done, Fortas repeated the suggestion.[88] It was time to play that card. Using the research produced by the Justice Department, the Porter operation produced a letter dealing with the obscenity issue that could be printed over the names of Dean Emeritus Joseph O'Meara of Notre Dame Law School and four other eminent law school deans. In effect, the argument was virtually identical to the one Fortas himself had forwarded to the office of Edward Bennett Williams—one could not determine the views of a justice solely on the basis of votes, but to the extent that it could be done, Fortas appeared to be a moderate on obscenity. Once the letter was finished, a copy was sent to each member of the Judiciary Committee by the dean, but it was not printed in *The Washington Post* until over two weeks later.[89]

Even with these efforts, too much damage had been done already on this issue to be able to counteract it effectively. Still, there was one man who could help Fortas regain control of his life—Lyndon Johnson. And now he showed a curious reluctance to do so. As he had been relaxing at his Texas ranch several days earlier, a call had come from James Eastland, then in San Antonio, asking whether he and some constituents could come and pay their respects. As they drove around the ranch later that day, the Mississippian told Johnson frankly that the Fortas nomination was dead. So far, the president knew, all of Eastland's predictions on this fight had come true. Indeed, some senators were now telling reporters that "when the debate gets under way it won't do Abe Fortas any good, it won't do the Supreme Court any good and it won't do the country any good."[90] This August meeting, then, told Johnson that he "probably could not muster the votes to put the Fortas nomination through." So why go through with what now appeared to be a hopeless battle?[91] Because no one said no to Lyndon Johnson, certainly not the United States Senate.

Johnson's decision was a key turning point in the battle. The trial would continue. But now it was no longer the president or the Warren Court that was the defendant. The formal trial of Abe Fortas himself had begun. Someone had already seen to that in Miami.

XIX

A
POLICY
OF SILENCE

Once the Senate recessed in early August for the presidential conventions, the only man who could save justice Abe Fortas from his fate was Richard Milhous Nixon. But even if it is true that politics makes strange bedfellows, the mere contemplation of such an affair between Nixon and the Johnson White House seemed too strange to be believed. Here was the man who had been responsible for Earl Warren's decision to leave the chief justiceship in the first place. Here was the man who had already launched his scathing indictment of the Johnson administration in early campaigning—calling for more "law and order." Here was the man who needed the support of the nomination opponents for his own presidential nomination and election. And here was the man who stood to gain the most—a seat on the Supreme Court through which to have an immediate impact on judicial policymaking—if this confirmation should fail and his election should succeed.

But contrary to appearances, there were some reasons why Nixon might be willing to play ball. There was now more than the *Time* v. *Hill* connection. It was now a question of Nixon's own political fate.

The position that he took on the Supreme Court, a sacred issue to many voters, would indicate whether his campaign was a moderate, middle-of-the-road one, or allied with the extreme right-wing efforts of independent George Wallace. Moreover, as Johnson had suspected, Nixon found that it was not politic to oppose openly a prominent Jewish justice in an election year. In fact, there were indications that, like Robert Griffin, the presidential candidate had become very uncomfortable about the allegations of anti-Semitism being attached to the opposition movement.[1] So Nixon had carefully walked a fine line, expressing his respect for the Supreme Court and praising Fortas as "an able Justice" while also supporting the right of the Senate to exercise its "responsibility" to advise and consent without any interference from him. And for him, this policy of nonintervention meant that he would make no "overt effort" to stop the threatened filibuster.[2] But would he make a covert effort either way?

The White House believed that Richard Nixon was privately more on its side than he had been leading the press to believe. One Fortas supporter, a prominent Republican Washington attorney named Eugene Bogan, had warned the Nixon camp of the hazards of this Senate fight for Nixon's nomination and election chances. Whether Nixon had supported Griffin from the start or not, he warned, the presidential candidate was now being seen as the man behind the opposition. This meant that Nixon was being stained by the allegations of anti-Semitism, and his ambivalent public statements on the fight did nothing to correct this notion. So Bogan warned Nixon's campaign manager, John Mitchell, that his people should either disavow the Griffin effort quickly in a public statement, or if they supported it, they should do so quietly while telling the senator to lay off. Failure to do this would risk the loss of political support in the Jewish community.[3]

For a while it seemed as if this lobbying effort had paid off. Nixon agreed with Bogan's analysis, saying that, contrary to the view of him as part of the Griffin movement, he actually supported Fortas, but the press had not printed it. So there was agreement in the Nixon camp that a clarifying statement should be issued to the press. But while this report gave the White House cause for hope, it was dashed the next day when Nixon resumed his public waffling on the candidate and supported the "responsibility" of the Senate.[4]

There was good reason to expect, however, that the Republican convention in Miami would change all of that. Here the harsh realities of securing the nomination would help to draw the lines on this issue in such a manner that there would be no middle ground for the candidate. Whoever won the nomination would have to take a position, thus sending a clear signal to all parties in the Senate fight.

Robert Griffin had started this fight in Washington, D.C., and he was determined to finish it in Miami. Knowing that the key would be the wording of the Republican platform, he had announced in his speech at the National Press Club that as a member of the Platform Committee he would seek the adoption of a plank supporting his position.[5] But while he was talking, the head of that committee, Everett Dirksen, was acting. And by reason of the continued existence of the Subversive Activities Control Board, he was dedicated to achieving victory.

Since Dirksen was now defending his rightful place as the party's chief senator, he was a tower of strength for the White House in this fight. Griffin had planned to appear before the Platform Committee and recommend the adoption of a plank prohibiting judicial appointments in a president's final year of office (while also seeking a strongly worded resolution against appointing Lyndon Johnson's "cronies" to the bench, before the Republican Credentials Committee). But after a "sharp backstage clash,"[6] he decided not to appear before the committee. Instead, he was allowed by the Dirksen and the Nelson Rockefeller allies to introduce only a watered-down compromise plank on the court, which gave no support to the insurgents, or anyone else: "Public confidence in an independent judiciary is absolutely essential to the maintenance of law and order. We advocate application of the highest standards in making appointments to the courts, and we pledge a determined effort to rebuild and enhance public respect for the Supreme Court and all other courts in the United States."[7]

When the White House asked why there had been this switch in plans, their Senate ally from Illinois could not resist crowing, "It might . . . indicate the strong battering he has been getting on the issue."[8] But that was not what Robert Griffin claimed. Pointing out that the plank *did* endorse his movement because he had been allowed to propose it, he told the press that because of his efforts two attempts to water it down further had been defeated.[9] Everyone could see, though, that the plank was far from the ringing endorsement that Griffin and the other opponents had been seeking.

While the battle of committees was over, the war in Miami had just begun. After all, the wording of the platform matters little when compared with the wording of the candidates. And since Richard Nixon needed the South to ensure his nomination, he turned to one of the region's favorite sons, Strom Thurmond, for help in finding those words. Following the advice of the South Carolina senator, Nixon prepared to argue before the southern delegates that he was "right" on the major legal issues of civil rights enforcement and crime in America.[10] But since he still wanted to present a moderate image, the candidate settled on a "policy of silence" with respect to the Fortas nomination itself.[11] So, in both his private and public statements whenever the question was raised, Nixon would criticize the courts, judges, and the Supreme Court in general, while saying that the Fortas question was still a matter for the Senate. But the answer to where he really stood on the confirmation issue could easily be implied from the other statements.

The first indication of this strategy came in his private meetings with a number of southern delegations. Speaking in a carefully choreographed question-and-answer format, Nixon drew applause when he said in response to a question on his position on court-ordered busing, "I think it is the job of the courts to interpret the law, and not make the law."[12] Later in the same meeting, a question from the floor gave Nixon the chance once again to give a clear signal on the court fight. "Do you have any disinclinations on appointing a new Chief Justice of the U.S. if you have an opportunity?" he was asked. Nixon's response seemed on its face to be unequivocal: "As you all know, before this appointment was made, I issued a strong statement urging that Johnson not make that appointment. The reason I did that was this: because of the courts—and whoever is going to be Chief Justice is going to be Chief Justice of the Court which is going to be making decisions that will affect this country for the next 20 years. I think that Chief Justice should represent the mandate of the future and not the Johnson mandate of the past. That is what I think." The spontaneous applause that followed was predictable. But then Nixon seemed to mix his signals a bit, adding, "I don't know what the Senate is going to do. But if I have the chance to appoint Justices to the Supreme Court, they will be the kind of men I want—and I want men who are strict constitutionalists, men that interpret the law and don't try to make the law. I want men, for example, who are for civil rights, but who recognize that the first civil right of every American is to be free from domestic violence. That is the kind of men we are going to have, and I think we need that kind of balance in the courts."[13] While some of the southern delegates took the comments as "an endorsement" of Strom Thurmond's tactics, Nixon was by no means fully in the senator's, or their, camp.[14]

Even in the speech accepting the convention's nomination for president, Nixon continued to be noncommittal: "Tonight it's time for some honest talk about the problem of order in the United States. Let us always respect, as I do, our courts and those who serve on them, but let us also recognize that some of our courts in their dissents have gone too far in weakening the police forces against the criminal forces of this country. Let those who have the responsibility to enforce our laws and our judges who have the responsibility to interpret them be dedicated to the great principles of civil rights, but let them also recognize that the first civil right of every American is to be free from domestic violence—and that right must be guaranteed in this country. . . . Our goal is justice, justice for every American. If we are to have respect for law and order in America we must have laws that deserve respect. Just as we cannot have progress without order, we cannot have order without progress."[15]

It was not long before some Republicans were interpreting this statement as more than just an endorsement of the Fortas confirmation fight, but an attack on the nominee himself.[16] But was the "real" Nixon the one who said that the courts had "gone too far," or the one who really believed that Fortas himself was "an able Justice" on a misguided court? In the end, Nixon's carefully ambivalent phrases were nothing more than mirrors revealing the true beliefs of the audience.

Each side took comfort in Nixon's inaction. The Griffin allies realized that Nixon could have easily deflated their effort by signaling that a continuation of the fight would impair his ability to be elected. They took his silence as a sign that he not only tacitly approved of the fight, but also approved the use of any weapon necessary to achieve victory. On the other hand, the Johnson White House was interpreting Nixon's silence as a sign that he might be willing to help out down the road. The task for them was to find the right incentive to convince the candidate either to undercut the opposition movement openly, or at the very least to make a statement opposing the use of the Senate filibuster.

The battle now turned on which side would control the political agenda in the fight. It was painfully obvious to everyone that the alliance of the Republicans and the conservative southerners opposing the nomination was a "shaky" marriage of convenience.[17] The question was whether a sufficient number of powerful issues could be found in this battle to cement the unity of the two groups.[18] Obscenity was clearly one of these safe issues, but this was not enough of a reason for rejection of a chief justice, especially since no one knew how much responsibility Fortas really bore for the court's actions in this area.

Eventually, both opposition groups realized that the main uniting issue could be a vicious personal attack on the candidate himself. This attack would need to go further than just his relationship with the president. Perhaps they could dig up some dirt on his personal finances or his previous legal activities that would prove him unfit for the office. So the Fortas opponents began leaking to the press some of the arsenal of weapons they were developing for what they called their "last ditch drive" to win the fight.[19]

Some of these new "sensational" charges, which the public was told had been discovered "during and since the judiciary committee's hearings," seemed laughable. Since the Fortases were rich, some of the opponents were determined to find out why. Their investigative technique was to leak tantalizing questions to the press. Were there problems with Carolyn Agger's serving as a senior partner in the Arnold and Porter law firm? Was it a "serious conflict of interest" for her to represent tax law clients who might benefit from rulings by her husband's Supreme Court on questions involving the Internal Revenue Service? Even the casual reader could see that these "charges" were pointless and would have no impact at all on the confirmation proceedings. If it had not bothered the Judiciary Committee in 1965 when Fortas went on the court that Agger maintained her legal practice, why should it make any difference now? But for the opponents, there was no harm, and possibly some benefit, in asking.

However, another allegation might have given the White House some pause for thought had someone noticed it. "Fortas has been giving a course in constitutional law at American University in Washington," one piece reported. "It is claimed he is paid for this teaching by a foundation established by him and one of his former law partners."[20] Of course this was nothing more than an account of the anonymous tip that had come into Griffin's office. It was a bomb without the fuse. No one had been able to confirm through government sources either the existence of the fund or whether, in fact, Fortas was teaching the course at all. But the significance of the article in general was clear. All the opponents needed was one break, and they were prepared to work like hell to get it. By leaking this tip to the press—long considered a senator's "extended staff"—they put the first step toward expanding the search into motion.

Meanwhile, in his own intuitive manner, Abe Fortas had already suggested to Paul Porter that the most effective road to advancing the nomination cause involved breaking the "identification of Republicans with Thurmond and Ervin."[21] Somehow the administration had to find a means of driving a wedge between the vastly different groups of senators. Since it was apparent that the different groups in the opposition were not comfortable with one another, the key lay in creating a political environment that reminded the opponents of their differences rather than their similarities. For Fortas and his allies this meant refloating the anti-Semitism charge.

On its face, the problem with the strategy was that anti-Semitism was next to impossible to prove. But that was also the brilliance of using this issue—it did not *have* to be proved, just mentioned. It was the same low-road tactic that Strom Thurmond had used. Now the issue would be bigotry versus smut. And if the voters *believed* that the Fortas fight was fueled by latent religious hatred, it would become unacceptable for liberal Republicans to lend their support. So Fortas instructed Porter that "tough speeches and statements" and "publicity" were needed by individuals and organizations such as "Jewish groups" during the Senate recess in August.[22]

For a while no one seemed to be willing to take the lead. Then the Democratic challenger for Jacob Javits's New York Senate seat, Paul O'Dwyer, made his move. Seeking to position himself favorably with that state's substantial Jewish community, O'Dwyer charged that anti-Semitism was "lurking behind all the mumbo-jumbo" of the prolonged Judiciary Committee hearings. Furthermore, he could not understand why "Mr. Javits, in his anxiety to curry favor with ultra-conservatives, has joined and thereby provided the Southern racists with an appearance of respectability for their reactionary stand."[23] No proof accompanied either of these charges, or the one that Javits had "grown insensitive with the passing years" to anti-Semitism, but from the sidelines Abe Fortas very much approved: "See Paul O'Dwyer's statement," he wrote to Porter. "This [fight] is anti-Negro, anti-liberal, anti-civil rights, [and] anti-Semitic."[24]

Even without supporting evidence, O'Dwyer's statement seemed to hold promise of accomplishing what the White House had thus far failed to do—convincing Jacob Javits to be more of a team player on the nomination. The long-term success of this low-road strategy required that a senator of unimpeachable credentials openly voice the charges, thus convincing the public that this was more than merely another partisan charge by a desperate Johnson team. And Javits, as both a Republican and a Jewish senator, had always been the most obvious candidate. Not only could he speak directly to the Jewish community, and the nation at large, but as a member of the other party he would diffuse the partisan nature of the charge. More than that, there was also the hope that Javits might pressure Richard Nixon to change his "neutral" policy of silence. But the first step on this road was up to Jacob Javits himself.

He was one of a rare breed—the liberal Republicans. The son of a janitor who had passed out favors for New York's Democratic Tammany Hall, Javits had worked his way out of the city's Lower East Side ghetto by selling lithographic supplies by day and attending Columbia University at night. After taking his law degree from New York University and a stint in the military in World War II, he turned to politics, serving in Congress for eight years. Since coming to the Senate in 1957 he had established a perfect set of liberal credentials. After building seniority he became a powerful force in the foreign affairs field, but his most important efforts in the 1950's and 1960's were in the battles for the various civil rights measures. Here, his inexhaustible supply of energy, and the persuasive skills he had learned from selling clothing from his mother's horse cart at the age of ten, proved to be most effective. "His talent was to get to the heart of the matter as well and as quickly as anyone I knew," a Senate colleague would later say. Many would also add that his status as the Senate's most visible Jewish member in 1968 made him the bellwether of the nature of the fight over Abe Fortas's confirmation. If Javits said it was a fair fight, then who among them could disagree?[25]

And no one knew this better than the Jewish justice under attack. So, shortly after the nomination first went to the Senate, Fortas had talked to Judge David Bazelon of the U.S. Court of Appeals for the District of Columbia, asking for help in getting Javits to support Lyndon Johnson's right as president to appoint a new justice. This effort, he told Paul Porter, was to be paired with the move to "get telegrams to the *Committee and individual members* of the Committee and the Senate, from Jews & Jewish groups particularly."[26] But Javits was proving to be a disappointment. The most he had done by early August was announce his support for Fortas, and his reservations about Thornberry.[27]

Javits's position all along was simple and sensible. Perhaps the opposition was not using proper tactics, but unless hard evidence could be found of anti-Semitism here, he would not raise the charge. "A mere 'gut' reaction is not enough," he told the administration. On the other hand, if the evidence could be produced, Javits said, he was "prepared to attack." Thus far, no such evidence had been produced.[28]

For a time, the White House respected Javits's desire to remain apart. Now, though, the New York senator had assumed a much more prominent place in the strategy than before. None of the other ideas for bringing the fight to closure were succeeding, and the anti-Semitism tactic might do the trick.

The O'Dwyer charge held promise for the White House, as it seemed to squeeze the senator between loyalty to his Senate colleagues and loyalty to his religion. Initially, Javits would say only that he was "on the record" as favoring the nominations. Then, trying to handle the charge indirectly, he publicly called on Nixon to oppose openly a Senate filibuster on the confirmation issue.[29] But it was not enough for him to claim that he was "militantly" in favor of Fortas, especially when the press pointed out that he had actually defended Robert Griffin against the anti-Semitism charge by placing phone calls to "a number of influential Jews around the country." So the next day Javits felt obliged to make a much stronger denial: "I yield to no one in my vigilance in fighting anti-Semitism at home and abroad, but I will not use it as a crutch or a weapon." Such a charge would not be made by him "without solid evidence."[30]

While Jacob Javits was occupied with publicly defending himself against O'Dwyer's charges, Fortas and his allies tried from behind the scenes to find a way to press the senator further. Seeking a means of encouraging Javits to take a "more aggressive position," Paul Porter began to mobilize the leaders of the New York Jewish community into putting pressure on the senator once again.[31] Then Fortas himself took one of the most vicious examples of the bigoted literature from the religious extremists and sent it to Porter, noting that a copy of it should go to "our friend Javits who purports to think that there's nothing naughty here." The justice had heard that one congressman's mail was 80 percent anti-Semitic. But then, showing his true motives, the justice added for his lieutenant's eyes only, "Of course, I don't believe it exists either, except some." For the eternally pragmatic Fortas, the whole issue of anti-Semitism was nothing more than a means of political warfare, rather than an ideological commitment.[32]

After a while, the pressure seemed to have an impact on Javits. He was now willing to go further in his efforts to bring Richard Nixon into the fold. With Paul O'Dwyer still hammering away, the senator announced to the press he would personally ask Nixon for help in securing Fortas's confirmation. In a meeting on August 21, Javits told Nixon that unless he used his influence to "at least help bring the Fortas nomination to a vote," he would be risking the loss of the Jewish vote. Javits also complained to Nixon about the dilemma that O'Dwyer's charges were putting him in, and asked him to "cool" Griffin and Thurmond in the fight.[33]

But Nixon had no desire to be caught in the same squeeze play that was now facing Javits. He was noncommittal on the question, telling the liberal New Yorker only that he now had "a lot to think about."[34]

Javits was not the only one who spoke to Nixon. Liberal senators such as Edward Brooke of Massachusetts were now trying to convince Nixon to make a public antifilibuster statement. Nixon opposed the filibuster, the White House was told, but the press was not reporting that fact.[35] The White House did not know, though, that the candidate's so-called Key Issues Committee, a strategy group of prominent Republicans, still repeatedly advised Nixon to remain silent on the issue.[36]

As more of these reports filtered into the Oval Office, Lyndon Johnson's worst fears seemed to be confirmed. Eastland's prediction was right; the matter was too much out of his control. Richard Nixon appeared to hold the key. And yet, why would a man who privately professed to believe something be unwilling to say it publicly when it was in the interest of his campaign to do so? To a man who saw the world only in terms of politics, there was only one explanation. So a sobered president dined with Homer Thornberry and his wife on August 27 and told them that something had happened to change his earlier optimistic predictions of confirmation. Nixon had made a deal, the president said sadly. He had contacted enough conservative Democrats and Republicans opposing the confirmation, and told them that if the nomination was held up, they would have a voice in his selection of the next chief justice. (It would be the last time that Lyndon Johnson—even after leaving the White House—could ever bring himself to discuss the nominations with his old friend from Austin. As intimate as they were, it just hurt him too much ever to discuss it again.)[37]

But had the candidate really made a deal? Like so many other rumors in this battle, this one could not be proved by the White House.[38] Whether it was true or not, what mattered was that the president now *believed* that it was true. In truth there probably was no need here for a spoken deal. Nixon did not have to tell the Fortas opponents that if this nomination was stopped the next appointment might be his. He did not have to tell them that given the opportunity he would appoint a conservative "strict constitutionalist." He did not have to tell them that those who had given him this opportunity would have a legitimate reason for claiming a voice in the next selection. They knew it. Everyone knew it. And Nixon's policy of silence told them that nothing had changed.[39]

However, Paul Porter still saw the Nixon card as the best option for ensuring his friend's confirmation. So he was determined to use every available means to bring the candidate around.[40] He had been hard at work developing the necessary materials for what he called the "Fortas Do-It-Yourself Kit." It consisted of a three-ring binder filled with various supporting memoranda and speeches, well over six hundred supporting editorials and new articles, a ringing endorsement letter signed by over five hundred ABA lawyers,[41] a commissioned survey of the positive national editorial opinion on the nomination, supporting correspondence, and a Lou Harris poll conducted on August 12 showing that the American people approved of the nomination by a two-to-one margin.[42] Throughout the month of August, while he continued to organize the committee of supporting lawyers and law school teachers, Porter had been sending copies of this kit to everyone who had ever crossed his path (and many who had not).[43]

Since no one else had moved Nixon, Porter decided to send this material to William P. Rogers, a close personal adviser of the Republican candidate, in an effort to get him to press the case with Nixon. Though he was now telling allies that anti-Semitism was a "fake issue," Porter warned Rogers that if the confirmation was not secured, there would be "possible ugly undertones of bigotry" resulting. All of this could be avoided, he promised, if Nixon would simply "blow the whistle" on the expected filibuster.[44]

Still there was no help from Nixon. Speaking on a television panel show in riot-torn Chicago on September 4 as the Republican nominee for president, Nixon continued to offer mixed signals on the nomination, saying that while he publicly urged Johnson not to make an appointment, if Fortas "is confirmed, I will work with him."[45] A generous offer indeed from a man who, even if he was elected president, would never work *with* any chief justice due to the separation of powers.

But Porter wasn't done yet. He tried the same approach with Thruston Morton, the liberal Republican senator from Kentucky who had originally joined the Griffin rebellion and now represented a key vote *for* the White House. A word from Nixon, he told the senator, was all that a lot of people believed would be necessary to spring the nominations. Then, following the script that Fortas had given him, Porter cited the O'Dwyer attack as proof that Nixon's continued silence would be linked to anti-Semitism and bigotry.[46] "I am for Fortas," Morton responded, "and I am working on Nixon in this regard."[47]

Since liberal senators such as Javits, Brooke, and Morton could not budge the new Republican presidential candidate, the White House thought that perhaps movie producer and Democratic party fundraiser Arthur Krim could. But after he had spoken "forcefully" and "pointedly" to the candidate, Nixon was still content to admit privately that while he "regretted his early statement on Fortas," he "felt obliged not to repudiate his statement."[48] So various Nelson Rockefeller allies were contacted by the White House in the hope that the defeated presidential aspirant from New York would pressure Nixon into publicly supporting the nominations.[49]

Finally, some hopeful news came to the president. Max Fisher, the prominent industrialist from Detroit who had tried earlier to convince Robert Griffin to break off his attack, had called a meeting between Nixon and twelve Jewish Republicans on September 9. Once again Nixon tried his waffling routine, explaining that while he "liked" Fortas, "some Senators were very jealous of their prerogatives—especially southern Senators." But for the first time he faced directly the charge that his policy of silence was fueling anti-Semitism. So, like a good politician, Nixon agreed to change his policy. He told the Jewish leaders that if the nomination became entangled in a Senate debate he would personally "let it be known that he does not favor filibuster on the nomination." All those in the room seemed pleased that they now had an understanding. But the White House, which realized that this statement would be far too late for its purposes (in many ways it was too late already), pressed on.[50]

After all of these futile efforts to sway the Republican candidate toward supporting the Fortas nomination, it was plain old election-year politics that finally did the trick. All of the frustrations of a badly botched Democratic convention in Chicago and an artfully dodging Republican opponent came out when the newly nominated Democratic presidential candidate, Hubert Humphrey, began a leisurely barefoot jog on the beach in Seaside Park, New Jersey, in mid-September.

Turning the opportunity into a moving press conference, the Democratic candidate lashed out at Nixon. This was not the much-heralded "new Nixon," he complained, but "the same Nixon, the real Nixon that we knew before." What better evidence of the now-latent extremism of his opponent, Humphrey charged, than the fact that he was "paying a political debt" to Strom Thurmond by attacking the courts and thus supporting the Fortas fight?[51]

It made little difference that the charge could not be proved—truth has very little place in a presidential campaign. Nixon knew that any identification with Strom Thurmond was just the sort of campaign rhetoric that could kill his efforts to capture the political center.[52] So when reporters asked him about Humphrey's charge, Nixon finally gave the White House what it had been seeking all along.[53] "The nomination is in the hands of the Senate," he told the press. "I don't oppose Fortas. I don't support him. I oppose a filibuster. I oppose any filibuster."[54]

Privately, Robert Griffin was "livid" about the candidate's new stance, even though he too was opposed to this tactic.[55] But publicly he could afford to be more charitable. Knowing that the statement had come much too late to have any impact on the fight,[56] a grinning Griffin told the press, "At the outset, Mr. Nixon said he'd stay out of this controversy and, frankly, I wish he would."[57] But Nixon's campaign allies were not going to stay out of the matter. And had Robert Griffin known what they had already set into motion, he would have been very pleased indeed.

In all of the joy over Nixon's statement, no one at the White House noted the curious behavior of the Jewish senator from New York. No matter how hard Paul O'Dwyer lashed out at Jacob Javits, the senator now was maintaining an even more oddly ambivalent posture toward Fortas himself. He continued to say only that there was "no hard evidence" to support the anti-Semitism charge.[58] Meanwhile, on the floor of the Senate he repeated his earlier argument that "to use charges of prejudice as a crutch—or a weapon—is the greatest disservice to the spirit of fellowship between the faiths and the way to create prejudice or more of it."[59] But there was no great public defense of the nomination from Javits; in fact there was no defense of the nomination at all. Far from being the point man for the White House on the nomination, Javits's new posture was that he no longer chose to be drawn by O'Dwyer into any discussion of the possible motivations behind the confirmation fight.

It was strange, as the fight wound down to a conclusion, that the senator who had commented in late July that he was "militantly" in favor of Fortas should now be so silent at such a crucial time. The White House team was too busy to notice Javits's own "policy of silence." They could not have known that this reluctance to speak now was no accident. Javits had been warned. And thanks to Richard Nixon's people, he was one of the privileged few who now knew just how much trouble Abe Fortas was in.

XX

THE
ICEBERG
BELOW

"It is a relief to return to the relative tranquility of the Nation's capital. And it is a pleasure to be here with you tonight. We have been in recess just over a month. I hope this pause may have allowed the passions to cool and the muddied waters to clear."[1]

After the disastrous Democratic National Convention in Chicago, even the ever turbulent Washington, D.C., looked tranquil to Phil Hart as he addressed the National Press Club. But the "hope" of the Michigan senator, as he kicked off on September 4, 1968, the final drive to deal with the Fortas and Thornberry nominations, would only partially be realized. The "muddied waters" were about to clear. Unfortunately for Hart and everyone else on the White House team, though, what would be revealed below would be more, but by no means all, of a hidden iceberg. And the men who had obscured this view for so long were Abe Fortas and Paul Porter.

The first sighting of the iceberg came in the office of Robert Griffin.

While Strom Thurmond planned his September smut filibuster, Griffin, thanks to a press leak, now had the charge that could become the "September surprise" finishing the nominations' chances.[2] Fred Graham of *The New York Times*, the same man who had written the original article about Fortas's extrajudicial activities that caused the stir in the July hearings of the Judiciary Committee, had discovered that Fortas had been paid fifteen thousand dollars to teach the law school course.[3]

As startling as the size of the payment was on its face, there were some significant questions left to be resolved. And no one at American University was providing any answers. Two questions were especially crucial in dealing with the ethics of this alleged transaction: Where had the money originally come from? And did the justice know the true source of the money? The answers here would change the issue from whether a justice should receive such extra compensation to whether Fortas had knowingly compromised himself in future cases before the court. Without provable knowledge of all the facts, though, Griffin knew that Fortas would be able to wriggle off the hook as he had in his July appearance. So his office's investigation continued.[4]

Unfortunately for the White House, and its ally Phil Hart, it had absolutely no knowledge of any of this. Fortas had never mentioned the matter. Unaware of the catastrophe coming in September, the White House was proceeding with the original plan. Of course the first major hurdle was getting the nominations out of the Judiciary Committee. And that effort depended on Phil Hart.

There was little question now that the senator from Michigan deserved the major credit for carrying the fight for Fortas in the Senate, although he had accomplished little. As hard as he tried, Hart was in possession of neither the information nor the power to make things happen. First there had been the unfortunate admission about the true source of his memorandum on Fortas's judicial philosophy for the Judiciary Committee report. Then the signals had gotten crossed in late July, preventing Hart's appearance with Robert Griffin before the National Press Club, and his entering the obscenity memo into the Senate record.[5] Finally there was the fiasco over the draft Judiciary Committee record. As planned, Hart had carried around the Justice Department's draft, hoping to get the signatures of a majority of the committee members before the Senate returned to Washington. However, only six of his colleagues were willing to sign the document.[6]

So, when the invitation came to appear before the National Press Club in September, Hart seemed determined that nothing would go wrong this time. It was bad enough that the response to Griffin was coming over a month late. The problem was that the whole campaign was taking more time than Hart had bargained for. And the battering that Hart had taken in the hearings had made him, like the White House, justifiably paranoid. As a result, before working on the speech he had written to Warren Christopher, "It's bad enough to put memoranda in the Record from the Department of Justice. Still worse would be giving a speech written by the Department!" Nevertheless, Hart wondered whether the "press artists" in the department could prepare a "memorandum" that he "might convert into a 'speech.' . . . Please!"[7] Presidential assistant Fred Drogula was then assigned to write a twenty-minute draft extolling the virtues of the two candidates and the importance of the Senate's being allowed to vote on them. And for the next several weeks Hart's office was blitzed with more useful information than it could handle, including, finally, the obscenity memorandum that he was supposed to have gotten in late July.[8]

By weaving all of this information together into his speech, Hart was able to very skillfully advance the themes suggested in Paul Porter's correspondence during August.[9] Here were two highly qualified candidates, the senator argued, who despite overwhelming support from the legal community were being held up in the Senate by "delaying tactics" and "various collateral objections."[10] This was nothing more, he demonstrated (using the newspaper clipping file forwarded to him by Paul Porter's office), than an attack on the Supreme Court as a whole, fueled in part by a "most dangerous campaign . . . by right-wing pressure groups" engaged in "frenetic attacks [that] come from a fanatical fringe."[11] As proof of these bold assertions, Hart tried, using the argument suggested by Fortas, to resurrect the charges of anti-Semitism by claiming that the opposition to the nominations represented "substantially four elements—critics of Supreme Court decisions, opponents of civil rights, political partisans and right-wing pressure groups."

After this stirring attack, Hart condemned the tactics of his opponents. Using one of the new memoranda from the Justice Department that had come to his office, but carefully not citing the source this time, he claimed, "Never before in our history has a nomination to the United States Supreme Court failed of confirmation because of a filibuster."[12] Chiding his Senate colleagues, he added that since some of them "hold 'precedent' in high esteem," here was a precedent that should be preserved. Why not just allow the full Senate to vote on this question directly? To do otherwise, Hart concluded, "would be a grave injustice" and "an assault upon our constitutional system."[13]

Unfortunately for him, earlier that day James O. Eastland had struck again. As promised, Eastland scheduled a Judiciary Committee meeting on September 4. But he never promised that anyone would come. When the southerners could not fit the meeting into their busy schedules it was canceled for lack of a quorum. Word then came that the next day was also inconvenient. Unless something drastic was done, the southerners seemed willing to keep this tactic going indefinitely. And the White House knew that should a quorum ever be assembled, all that was necessary to filibuster was for a single senator to use an unwritten rule allowing him to talk through the Senate's "morning hour," at which point the ongoing session of the full Senate would once again bar the holding of committee meetings. So long as Eastland was willing to recognize the intransigent delayers, and he clearly was willing to do so, the delay would continue.[14]

LBJ searched for a way to pressure Eastland. He devoted a good portion of his congressional leadership breakfast on September 5 to the problem, arguing that Strom Thurmond's "Fortas Film Festival," which had resumed in full swing for interested senators, made the Senate look ridiculous.[15] But the response from the breakfasting senators was not encouraging at all. Majority Leader Mansfield predicted that there would be a filibuster on the nominations and warned the president that he did not have the votes for cloture. Later in the day Everett Dirksen echoed these pessimistic sentiments, saying that the confirmation prospects were "not roseate." But the word from the White House, despite these reports, was that the president "would do all he could to push for confirmation."[16]

The new fall offensive began at 10:15 A.M. on Friday, September 6, when the president met in the Cabinet Room with Mansfield and Dirksen. After running through all of Paul Porter's favorite arguments about the existing support for the nominations and the Justice Department's research on the lack of precedent for killing a nomination by a filibuster, Johnson asked for help in getting the Judiciary Committee to act. The president's persuasive powers prevailed. Within hours the two senators had secured agreement from Chairman Eastland to hold a meeting the following Tuesday, while the day's session of the full Senate would be canceled to give the members time to resolve the problem.[17] Two days later Mansfield would tell reporters that he was prepared to seek a discharge petition to get the nominations out of the Judiciary Committee if they failed to act, and would even keep the Senate in session until January 3, 1969, if necessary, to win full confirmation.[18]

But this time Johnson was not going to rely on his sometimes uncertain allies in the Senate. He decided to use the full powers of the presidency by going over the heads of the senators directly to the people. Immediately after the meeting with the two Senate leaders, Johnson held a surprise press conference and lambasted the Judiciary Committee for its lack of action. The problem, he told the press, was that "a small sectional group" of senators was frustrating the will of the majority in support of the nomination. Since "between 60 and 70 percent of the people favored the nomination," the president added, "we should not allow a small group to be able, by parliamentary tricks, to filibuster and prevent the majority from expressing its viewpoint."

But Johnson did not stop there. He decided to play what he thought was his trump card in escalating the fight. Remembering the Porter operation's efforts, Johnson added, "In the case of Justice Brandeis, where we had a somewhat similar situation, several months passed in committee and there was a great deal of protest and controversy in the country. But after it was brought to the Senate floor, it took a relatively short time to be confirmed."[19] The implication here was unmistakable. For the first and only time, Johnson was willing to charge, however obliquely, that it was anti-Semitism that was fueling his former southern colleagues' efforts.

It was a risky move, and Johnson quickly discovered that he was quite mistaken if he thought that his new charge would intimidate the formidable southern senators who had been leading the opposition. Strom Thurmond told the press, "If President Johnson would take the necessary time to review four films—'Flaming Creatures,' '0-7,' '0-12,' and '0-14'—or any of them, it would be interesting to know if he still favors Mr. Fortas's appointment to the second most important public office in the United States."[20] Sam Ervin, on the other hand, merely commented, "If the President is making a new effort, all I can say is there will probably be a counter-effort."[21]

But Johnson genuinely thought he was dealing from a position of voting strength in the full Senate. According to the new set of head counts completed that day, there were still only thirty-one hard votes against the nomination. Even counting the half-dozen senators who were now counted in the "leaning against" column, it still seemed possible to twist some arms and secure a two-thirds cloture vote if necessary.

The complexities involved in charting the individual voting decisions of all the members of the Senate were staggering. One recent change, the president was informed, involved the Democrat from Alaska, Ernest Gruening, who had always been counted in the "hard for" column. For reasons that were unclear to the president, he had now been moved to the "leaning against" column. One vote could make a difference in a fight that was this close. So Johnson, remembering that this former governor of the Alaskan Territory had been involved with Fortas in the old Interior Department days, instructed Larry Temple to have the justice "see what he can do about Gruening."[22]

Had Johnson recalled the true history between the two men back in the early 1940's, he never would have done this, and instead would have placed Gruening in the column that he belonged in all along—"hard against." Unlike Wayne Morse, who had overlooked those earlier battles, Gruening had not forgiven anything. As governor general of the Alaskan Territory, Gruening had had more than his share of run-ins with Fortas and Harold Ickes, especially as a result of the governor's efforts to lobby members of the government for aid without first consulting the Department of the Interior. Finally, in 1944 Fortas started accusing Gruening of leaking unflattering stories about Ickes to the press, leading to an uncomfortable meeting in the secretary's office. When Ickes got confirmation that the governor had in fact spoken to a reporter, he said that Gruening "talked too damn much." The embarrassment of that conflict was one that Gruening never forgot, even twenty-five years later when Fortas's team came to him hat in hand.[23]

One of the wild cards in the whole counting enterprise was how many Republicans could be convinced to "take a walk" rather than vote against the candidates. In the early part of September, encouraging this looked like a viable strategy. Johnson anticipated that Margaret Chase Smith of Maine would leave. But the best news was that two senators who had been part of Griffin's original rebellion—Milton Young of North Dakota and Gordon Allott of Colorado, both of whom had always been counted in the "hard against" column—might also make themselves scarce on a close vote.[24]

Sorting out the truth from so many reports of "reliable sources" filtering into the White House, however, proved to be impossible. Gordon Allott, unimportant to the White House so far, soon proved this point. On August 24, after giving a speech to a Denver Young Republicans group on the virtues of public service and the state of American politics, Allott was asked in a press conference to defend his opposition to the Fortas nomination. The senator indicated that his "principal objection'' to Fortas stemmed from the justice's relationship with Lyndon Johnson. Allott then charged that on May 27 Fortas had been involved with the creation of an appropriations bill amendment that provided for Secret Service protection of presidential candidates. ''As a member of the Court,'' Allott concluded, ''he should not be dealing or even talking about legislative matters.''[25]

It was a bombshell, but for two weeks no one in Washington heard it hit. Since this was a completely new charge, it had the potential for proving that the justice had not made ''full disclosure.'' But even more important, if the charge was true, here was the evidence that he had actually *drafted* a piece of legislation that might later be reviewed by the Supreme Court. Thus, it might indicate that the justice had willingly placed himself in a very compromising position. But as luck would have it, despite the fact that Allott had already told several of his Senate colleagues this story,[26] neither the wire services nor the White House had picked it up. For a while, then, Fortas's allies were completely in the dark.

All of that changed on September 7. With impeccable timing, the story was finally broken by the United Press International. But as in the perverse parlor game of ''rumors,'' the story had changed somewhat in transmission. ''Allott contends,'' it was now reported, ''that as associate justice, Fortas took part in the drafting of an amendment to an appropriations bill providing Secret Service protection for all presidential candidates. Congress approved it the day after Sen. Robert F. Kennedy died of an assassin's bullet wounds in Los Angeles June 5.''[27] (In truth, Allott never told the reporter that Fortas had ''drafted'' the amendment, only that the Justice had ''cleared'' its wording.[28]) Moreover, now Fortas was alleged to have been involved around June 5, not on May 27 as Allott had actually charged. Since this was the first time that the White House was confronted by the new charge, these errors would have a great impact on its damage control operation. It helps in putting out fires to know where they are actually located.

The identity of the person responsible for this perfectly timed and deadly leak is one of those mysteries lost in the mists of time. But the results were predictable. As soon as the charge reached the White House on the night of September 7 on the UPI ticker, the White House went into its now-familiar crisis mode. There was understandable confusion as to why Allott had not launched these charges in the earlier Judiciary Committee hearings. The press had not been able to reach Fortas for comment, and at the White House all a surprised George

Christian was able to offer was "This is the first I have heard about it. I don't know anything about it."

The charge should not have shocked the White House. The time of Bobby Kennedy's assassination had been a crisis period, and Fortas had been there during all crisis periods. On that day the issue was criminal justice, an issue now so identified by the president with the justice that he had once told his aides to find Fortas "wherever he was" for a chat on the matter.[29] But the charge did surprise them all. So a frantic search was made in the comprehensive presidential diaries for evidence of the contacts between Fortas and the White House around the time of the assassination. Both Lyndon Johnson and Abe Fortas knew there was much to be found—though not what Allott expected.

Surely one of the least attractive aspects of the presidency is the certain knowledge that one will get more middle-of-the-night "bad news" phone calls in one year than a roomful of people do in a lifetime. The early hours of June 5, 1968, were no exception for Lyndon Johnson. When the voice on the other end of the phone told him at 3:31 A.M. that Robert F. Kennedy had been shot in California, there was little doubt about who was going to be receiving another wakeup call. Johnson waited for four hours before trying Fortas's Georgetown home. It was going to be another day of crisis at the White House.

By the time Larry Temple arrived at the president's side for the "bedroom detail" to plan the day, the scene was bedlam. W. DeVier Pierson, who served as associate special counsel to the president, huddled with Johnson, discussing how to convince Congress to enact authority for providing Secret Service protection to other presidential candidates. Once they had decided on attaching the measure to an appropriations bill that day, Pierson was dispatched to Capitol Hill to keep track of the language, with instructions to keep the president informed. Meanwhile, Johnson kept speaking with legislators on the phone about this measure (one of the calls was to Senator Gordon Allott). He had a crush of other duties to deal with as well: a new pile of memoranda requiring attention, a deal with Vermont Senator George Aiken regarding the limitation of milk exports in return for support of the president's call for a grain agreement, as well as decisions about aiding the Kennedy family in their time of grief. During all of this, Johnson finally reached Fortas by phone and asked him simply "to put down on paper and send to him his recommendations on what the President should do regarding a message on law and order to be sent to the Congress.''[30]

Despite the fact that the court was in the home stretch of its work for the year, a time when the pace of opinion writing is at its heaviest, Fortas devoted a good portion of his work day to writing an initial draft of Johnson's speech to the nation that night on the assassination. It was the sort of assignment to which the justice had grown accustomed, involving all of his roles as troubleshooter, legal adviser, speechwriter, crisis manager, and friend. Having served in the same role nearly five years earlier following the assassination of another Kennedy, he was perhaps one of the most experienced men in the president's camp for such a situation. But this time the result of Fortas's work showed just how compromised the justice had become in doing the president's bidding.

By 4:30 P.M., after unsuccessfully trying to see the president that afternoon, Fortas delivered the results of his labors to the White House. Having decided that there should be another "Warren-type" investigative commission, an interesting posture for the man who originally opposed this effort and had been urging for the last year that there should be more state and local work on crime and less federal intervention, Fortas suggested a possible list of seven names. In the end, though, the president settled on a different type of commission, this one to look into the causes and prevention of violence and assassination generally.[31] Also attached was a 1,725-word speech he had drafted for Johnson to deliver that night. After the expected expressions of national grief over the tragedy, the introduction of the investigatory commission, and a call for the nation to do its part in ending the wave of lawlessness, the justice wanted Johnson to respond to congressional attempts to use the 1968 Omnibus Crime Control Act to attack the Supreme Court itself. This bill, the president was to say, "includes some provisions which I did not recommend directed at curtailing the jurisdiction of the Supreme Court of the United States and overruling some of its decisions. I advise that some of these extraneous provisions are clearly unconstitutional." Then, looking for the "tools necessary to arrive at law and order," Fortas wanted the president to renew his call for a gun control bill, and his own version of the crime control.

Even Johnson recognized that Fortas had gone too far here in asking him to deliver the surreptitious advisory constitutional opinion. He left word with Jim Jones late that afternoon questioning "the wisdom about saying [the act] will be unconstitutional if [I] may have to sign it.'' But, since the president liked the speech with the exception of this part, he asked the speechwriters to use it as the basis for their own work and have a draft ready for the early evening.[32]

By the time the redrafted speech was ready, Fortas was back in the White House to help out. For nearly two hours he worked in the lounge off the Oval Office with the president, Senators Dirksen and Mansfield, Joe Califano, Harry McPherson, Ramsey Clark, and Clark Clifford, preparing the speech for delivery to the nation live at 10:00 P.M. No one seemed to question the presence of a Supreme Court justice.[33] For Fortas, it was just another day at his office, an event that would be repeated the next day when he returned to the Oval Office, after working at the court, for another long drafting session. This time the White House speechwriters had worked late into the evening drafting a presidential letter to the Speaker on the gun control bill, and Johnson told his aides to call Fortas to see if he could ''improve'' the draft.[34]

In all of these efforts by the justice, though, there was no evidence that he had discussed with the president a law providing Secret Service protection for presidential candidates.

Regardless of the provable facts, in the fall of 1968 the White House quickly realized that fashioning a denial of Allott's charges was going to be difficult. The presidential diary search revealed all of these contacts. Any doubt as to the accuracy of the entries was removed by the pictures in the White House files from that day showing the justice and a very weary, very concerned president talking privately in the Oval Office. Here was precisely the sort of evidence that now needed to be kept from the opposing senators.

On the other hand, placing Fortas in the Oval Office on that day said nothing about what had actually been discussed. And Allott's charge was *only* that the justice had helped to draft this one piece of legislation. However, saying that ''Fortas was in the White House during that period, but he was too busy working on other things to bother with the Secret Service legislation'' was probably not the best defense. So the aides looked for help.

Once the diary search was completed, head secretary Juanita Roberts phoned Fortas at his summer retreat in Westport, Connecticut. ''It's all nonsense,'' the justice said, adding that he had ''no memory of [the president's] discussing the S[ecret] S[ervice] issue with him at all."[35] But that was not enough to lift the burden of denying the charge for the White House.

The first step, Johnson's aides decided, was to find out in advance the precise nature of Allott's charge, in order to prepare a defense. So all those involved in the drafting of the Secret Service amendment were ordered to draft an explanatory memorandum of the events during that period, including their recollection of any involvement by Abe Fortas.

But the damage had already been done. The account of Allott's charges in the next morning's *Washington Star* had at least two very interested senatorial readers—Strom Thurmond and Robert Griffin. This was exactly the sort of information that they had desperately needed to break open the July hearings. And now it would be even more useful. They could use it as an argument that Chairman Eastland should reopen the Judiciary Committee hearings for another round of "investigations."

So Griffin wrote a memo to the committee citing the "matters [that] have come to light on the pending Supreme Court nominations which should be explored and carefully considered by the Committee." But all that Griffin included in this new bill of indictment against Fortas were Allott's charges and the article by journalist Daniel Yergin alleging that Fortas had helped speechwriter Richard Goodwin to draft the 1966 State of the Union address. There still was not enough hard evidence to launch the American University seminar missile. And there might never be. Still, the memo was effective, citing each of these reports while contrasting them with Fortas's "I guess I have made full disclosure now" statement (with careful underlining of the verb *guess*).[36]

When a copy of the Griffin document found its way to the White House, it caused a new wave of concern. For the second time in three days, the administration was surprised. Though the Yergin piece had been published on July 22, and had been commented upon in at least one other newspaper piece, this was the first time that the White House had seen it.[37] The staff knew that Fortas had been incredibly involved in the drafting of presidential speeches, but no one was certain whether he had helped on *this* one.

So the marching orders were handed down and duly noted in the margin of the White House's copy of the Griffin memorandum. Rather than go into a crisis mode again, the president had a much simpler solution—a fast cover-up. Ramsey Clark was to "get Yergin and say we don't know about it." Then the staff was ordered to "check our files and see what they reflect." It was the Johnson style—never mind whether it was true or not, deny it first, and search later.[38]

The search did not have to go too far before the White House realized how much trouble this new charge really presented. The proof for Yergin's report was incontrovertible. The White House diary indicated that on the afternoon of January 12, 1966, Goodwin had indeed been in the Oval Office starting at 1:46 for ten minutes. Then at three o'clock Fortas and Clifford entered the president's office, and the secretaries dutifully reported that they "went over with the President—word by word, page by page, the President's speech tonight."[39]

As devastating as this entry appeared, the White House files showed that, in fact, it vastly understated Fortas's true role in the creation of this speech. Contrary to the few hours of effort portrayed by Yergin, the justice had been involved in this process over the course of weeks. In fact, Fortas had taken one early version of the address, a standard State of the Union speech listing the past accomplishments and future dreams of Lyndon Johnson's administration, and entirely rewritten it, cutting whole sections and drafting new ones to give it an entirely different flavor. The justice rewrote and vastly expanded the section on Vietnam to justify the bombing pause effort then under way and portray the president in his "search for peace." This new foreign-policy emphasis to the speech was retained by later draftsmen, and of course Fortas felt comfortable offering substantial stylistic suggestions for one of these later drafts.[40]

As if the evidence in the White House diary and central files were not enough, once again Lyndon Johnson's mania for having such scenes photographically recorded for the historical record betrayed him. Sitting in the picture file was a shot from behind the president at his desk in the Oval Office as he looked at a sheaf of papers on January 12, with Clark Clifford on one side reaching for something across the desk, while Fortas, directly in front of Johnson, was pointing to one of the pages with a pencil in his hand, looking very scholarly, with his reading glasses on. Pretty tough evidence to deny. But then, so was the entire file of pictures, which showed similar scenes of Fortas discussing matters with Johnson and advisory groups of various sizes in every possible location in the White House. This file made it clear that these scenes were the rule rather than the exception.[41]

If the Judiciary Committee decided to press the investigation here, some hard choices would have to be made about whether the only witnesses to the incident, Fortas and now secretary of defense Clifford, should appear before the committee to testify.

By the time thirteen of the sixteen members of the Judiciary Committee responded affirmatively to Mike Mansfield's telegraphed appeal for a meeting on the morning of September 10, 1968, thus ensuring the necessary quorum for action, Robert Griffin had already supplied Strom Thurmond with all that was needed to secure agreement to reopen the hearings. Sympathetic to the opposition cause, James Eastland dispatched a telegram to Abe Fortas asking him to reappear before the committee for "interrogation on certain films and cases involving the issue of obscenity, matters raised by Senators Allott and Griffin and on other matters relative to your confirmation."[42] When Eastland met later that day with Deputy Attorney General Warren Christopher, he neglected to make clear how dangerous that "other matters" phrase might be. This was not a filibustering strategy, Eastland insisted. In fact, there "would soon be an agreement to vote in Committee to the nomination," but "a number of the members" had "expressed the desire" to have Fortas return for further testimony.[43]

The reason for this was explained by Everett Dirksen to the press in an impromptu conference after the Judiciary Committee's meeting. A relatively simple deal was developing: additional hearings as a prelude to the final committee vote. But the rest of Dirksen's comments to the press were even more troubling to the White House. The Illinois senator now was "not sure he would open a discharge petition [forcing the nomination out of the committee to the Senate floor] since that is a very drastic step." And he added that "he might have to reassess some of his thinking if the charges recently leveled were accurate."[44] Just as Lyndon Johnson had been predicting for so long, Ev Dirksen was readying the lifeboats in case he decided to jump ship.

Following the unproductive committee meeting, Phil Hart began a wide-ranging discussion with the White House team on whether Fortas should reappear before the Senate. Had they known the full extent of the charges, the chat would have been very short indeed. But for now the thinking was that the Yergin and Allott charges, whatever their nature, could be handled. Lyndon Johnson's first reaction was "that Justice Fortas should go back to testify and that it would be fatal if he would not do so." Ramsey Clark disagreed, though, saying that the only purpose here was "to try to embarrass" the court and Fortas further. Since Fortas would be out of town and unreachable until early the next morning, the discussion was adjourned.[45]

The final deal in the Judiciary Committee was consummated the next day. As much as the White House did not want further hearings, they were going to take place, with or without Fortas's testimony. It was also decided that the final vote in the committee would take place at 11 A.M. the following Tuesday and, surprisingly, both sides in the dispute agreed that they would be given only three days to prepare their confirmation reports. This meant that final debate by the full Senate could take place as early as Monday, September 23.[46] In return for this arrangement, though, the nomination opponents insisted that the chairman be given full power to subpoena *any* witnesses in addition to Fortas, unsupervised by the rest of the committee.[47] At the time, this concession seemed unimportant to the White House allies—but they should have known better.

Unwilling to concede anything, and perhaps smelling trouble, the hardworking Phil Hart tried one final maneuver to avoid the new hearings. He prepared a letter to James Eastland arguing that it would be "a disservice for Mr. Justice Fortas as a sitting Justice of the Supreme Court to return for further interrogation by certain members of the Judiciary Committee." The twelve hundred pages of record already in existence ought to "contain ample basis for action by the Committee."[48] By the end of the afternoon, Hart needed only one more signature to get a large enough majority in the committee to make reopening the hearings impossible. However, Democrat Thomas Dodd of Connecticut refused to provide that crucial vote. He told Hart only that "he strongly support[ed] Fortas, however, he [thought that] the Judiciary Committee [was] entitled to interrogate nominees." So he refused to sign.[49]

It was a devastating blow. After the circus in July, the White House simply could not afford to have Fortas testify again. On the other hand, refusing the "invitation" was equally bad, making it look like he might have something to hide and so *this time* he did not dare to face the committee. Since the opposition had cleverly agreed to the voluntary cloture of the committee proceedings by the Senate voting deadline early the following week, the White House could not even use the excuse that requesting Fortas's appearance was just a subterfuge for delaying the proceedings further. The only option was to have that request withdrawn, and the Dodd signature was all that stood in the administration's way.

So over the next twenty-four hours a parade of emissaries from the White House visited Dodd. Mike Manatos had a lengthy meeting with the Connecticut senator. Then the White House made plans to send the attorney general to his office. Early the next morning, Washington lawyer James Rowe was dispatched by the president to see what he could do. While Rowe spent over an hour with Dodd, the senator's position seemed to be hardening. Dodd said that it was a matter of principle for him. His position was "that the Senate and the Judiciary Committee have an obligation to fulfill the responsibility of 'to advise and consent' to a nomination. Therefore, if any Senator has any question to ask a nominee, they have a right to have that nominee appear." Then came later visits by Phil Hart and a number of labor union lobbyists and officials, including George Meany himself. But Dodd would not budge.[50] It was not the last time that he would disappoint the White House.

Meanwhile Abe Fortas had returned to Washington and had drafted a very strong letter refusing to respond to the committee's invitation.[51] Since the hearings were to start the next day, he wanted to send the letter as soon as possible. But the White House asked him to hold it up, hoping that a Dodd signature on the Hart letter could be used as an excuse for Fortas's refusal.[52]

In all of the excitement, none of the White House staffers noticed that their ally Everett Dirksen had also refused to sign the letter, saying only that he had a "little difficulty" with it.[53] Fellow Republican Hugh Scott noticed, though, and when Roman Hruska and Hiram Fong went with the minority leader, it left Scott as the only Republican signer. Not for long. Seeing the partisan consequences of his action, Scott withdrew his support and the opportunity was lost forever. When later efforts by Hart and Philadelphia lawyer Bernard Segal to get Scott back on board failed, Hart had no choice but to withdraw the letter.[54]

Abe Fortas was now in a no-win situation. He was going to have to deal with this new "invitation" on his own.

Still, the news was not all bad in the Oval Office. The internal review spurred by the Allott charges had been completed, and while it showed that Fortas had been involved in just about everything else during that period surrounding the Bobby Kennedy assassination, he did not appear to have dealt with the Secret Service protection amendment. Also, W. DeVier Pierson, one of the men involved in the drafting of this legislation, was finally able to pin down through his Senate sources the nature of Gordon Allott's planned testimony before the committee.

It turned out that, much to the White House's delight, the charges would be much different than what had been originally anticipated.

Allott's story now was that on the morning of May 27, not June 5, 1968, after the adjournment of hearings on a Senate appropriations bill, he had been approached by Undersecretary of the Treasury Joseph Barr. Barr had been on the telephone in the room speaking with someone in the White House. According to the senator, he was asked to include in the bill the language providing for the protection of presidential candidates by the Secret Service. Then Barr was alleged to have said that "the White House and Justice Fortas will have to approve this language."[55] Since this conversation took place out of earshot of everyone else, it was eventually going to come down to Allott's word against Barr's.

By all accounts, the president was assured that the senator's charges had no credence. Pierson's recollection, which was confirmed by a complete chronology of the development of the legislation, was that while Barr had received a phone call in the Appropriations Committee room that day from the president, in fact Johnson's instructions had been to *delete* the Secret Service language from the appropriations bill.[56] According to this account, the decision had been made to seek separate legislative authority for the measure, and the White House was in the process of doing that when the Kennedy assassination occurred. No one in the White House or the Treasury Department could understand why Abe Fortas would have had cause to be involved in such a routine piece of legislation.

Reports from the other three administration officials involved in this process echoed Pierson's recollection, and confirmed the absence of the Supreme Court justice.[57] "I don't remember making any statement like that to Allott," claimed Joseph Barr in one of those accounts. "In fact, I don't remember even talking to him after the meeting. I suppose it is possible that I made some wisecrack about everybody including the Supreme Court needing to see the language. We had just changed signals after spending several weeks getting committee support for including the candidate protection authorization in the Appropriations bill. But, if I said anything like that, it made no impression on me, and the other departmental people with me have no recollection of it."[58]

Even allowing for the fact that these men had a vested interest in protecting the justice and themselves, other independent evidence supported their account. The presidential diary showed that there had been absolutely no contact between anyone at the White House and Fortas on May 27. In fact, during the four-week period from May 8 until the day that Senator Kennedy was shot, Fortas had been in contact with the president only as a participant in four luncheon or breakfast meetings with groups of people dealing with such topics as Vietnam and the creation of the Johnson School of Public Affairs.[59] Furthermore, the memoranda written in late May and early June on the drafting process for the Secret Service protection legislation made absolutely no mention of Abe Fortas.[60] Because of the importance of his advice to the president, it was standard practice for such memos to detail carefully any such contacts and advice at the top.

It was the height of irony. In the first set of hearings Fortas had gotten off the hook because the senators had had no hard evidence to prove the accuracy of their charges. Now he was about to be hanged for something that by all accounts had not involved him at all.

As encouraging as it was to know that Allott's charges could be beaten in a straight fight, Johnson knew that this was not a straight fight. Whatever the facts, Allott was making clear to his Senate colleagues that he "had no doubts that the statement [by Barr] was made."[61] Few in the clublike Senate would doubt his word. Moreover, no one would care whether the charge was true, for too many were prepared to believe now that it *could* have been true.

Then there was the real question of whether there could be any defenders at all. For the administration it was the same "damned if you do, damned if you don't" dilemma that it had faced before. Subpoenas were going to be issued to several members, and former members, of the administration. Joseph Barr and W. DeVier Pierson had already been announced by the committee as witnesses on the Allott charges. And the press was told that Daniel Yergin's charges would be explored with former Johnson speechwriter Richard Goodwin and Clark Clifford. An appearance under oath by any of these people would allow administration opponents to hold them accountable for five years of "objectionable policies." Then if the White House chose to cite "executive privilege," the constitutional prohibition against congressional questioning of members of the executive branch about their official actions, it would be taken as evidence of the charges' veracity. In the end, the White House decided that Barr, Pierson, and Clifford should refuse to appear. Since Fortas was also declining his invitation, *no one* would be left to defend the justice.

One final time, the White House searched for a way out. Perhaps its allies in the Senate leadership could somehow persuade the Judiciary Committee not to "invite" these witnesses. But now even the Senate whales were balking. Both Mansfield and Dirksen gave a "sympathetic understanding of the administration's problem but nothing else." Dirksen even claimed not to know that he had given up the right of subpoena power to the committee chairman without a supervisory committee vote.

For the first time the White House realized the brilliance of the southerners' deal. Gordon Allott was going to have his day before the committee. Abe Fortas was going back on trial. And the White House was totally in the dark as to the full bill of indictment.

Worse still, Barefoot Sanders warned in a memo to the president, neither Dirksen nor Mansfield was "approaching this fight with any enthusiasm, confidence, or sense of outrage at what [the] Senate Judiciary is doing."[62] At the same time, Joe Califano warned the president that even the White House allies now harbored "an underlying, though hard-to-pin-down, concern about Fortas' veracity."[63]

And they had good reason for doing so. For while the White House in its damage control mode girded for another newsmaking circus, the Senate magicians—Griffin and Thurmond—prepared the main attraction. It was their finest trick. They were going to make the rest of the Fortas iceberg appear.

XXI

THE
TRIAL OF
ABE FORTAS

The time had come in the confusion of September 1968 for the former "Master of the Senate" to pull a rabbit out of his hat.[1] Lyndon Johnson looked at the sheaf of paper containing the latest Senate head count and searched for a way to simplify all of the numbers. The master strategy for securing the confirmation had to be here, he reasoned. Finally, as the president flipped through the pages of Senate members listed in columns according to party affiliation and level of support on the issue, it struck him. He wrote down on one of the inner sheets the simple mathematics of the whole enterprise: "39 & 18 = 57."

Fifty-seven was the magic number of supporters Lyndon Johnson believed he could expect on the cloture vote now. It was a workable number. Even if all of the members of the Senate were present for the final vote, an unlikely occurrence given the controversial nature of the issue and its timing during an election year, the amount of support was close enough to victory that arms could be twisted to achieve a favorable result.

But it was more than just the aggregate number that struck Johnson. It was the composition. The sheets that broke down the head count by political party showed that Johnson could rely on about thirty-nine liberal Democrats no matter what happened. The eighteen in his mathematical equation represented those Republican senators that the president could reasonably expect in his search for votes. On a separate sheet of yellow legal-sized paper he jotted down a list of eighteen names: "Aiken, Boggs, Brooke, Case, Cooper, Cotton, Dirksen, Dominick, Hatfield, Hruska, Javits, Kuchel, Morton, Prouty, Percy, Scott, Pearson, and Goodell." They were the names of the crucial swing votes that required his attention. Eighteen Republican senators who held in their hands the verdict on this issue. These were the votes he absolutely had to have in order to have any chance for success.

Perhaps trying to make it true just by the repetition of the exercise, "39 & 18 = 57" the president wrote again at the bottom of the page. But what he had written at the top of the page, and the check marks he placed alongside some of the names, told him the real story. By his own count, Johnson considered only "6 or 7" names from this swing list as now being firmly in his corner. Each of the members on this list was a precious vote—Oregon's Mark Hatfield, New York's Jacob Javits, California's Tom Kuchel, Kentucky's Thruston Morton, Illinois's Charles Percy, and Pennsylvania's Hugh Scott. And, of course, one of those names he checked off belonged to the biggest Republican of them all—Everett Dirksen. As long as the minority leader was on the team it was still possible to get the remainder of his party colleagues.[2]

Already though, events elsewhere in the city were dooming Johnson's last-ditch effort to defeat. Robert Griffin and Strom Thurmond had seen to that.

On September 12, Strom Thurmond engineered one more effort to stack the deck against the nominee. The appointment of New York Republican Charles Goodell to the Senate seat of the assassinated Robert F. Kennedy had changed the ratio of the two political parties in that body. As a result, the Republicans were awarded another seat on the Judiciary Committee. Senator Edward Brooke was all set to take the seat, which by reason of his support for the nominations would have lent more bipartisan backing to the White House. However, at the last minute Thurmond had Howard Baker, who was slightly more senior, and greatly more negative toward the nominations, installed instead.

By the next Senate term, Baker would be off the committee. While all parties later insisted that the addition of Baker was dictated purely by seniority, close observers of the scene found the moves too coincidental to be unplanned.

Finally, just hours before the new hearings opened, symbolically enough, on Friday the thirteenth, Fortas's opponents on the Judiciary Committee had developed more than just a "concern about [his] veracity." They knew he was lying. And now they could prove it.

Now there was more than just Gordon Allott's hearsay testimony. They had Dean B. J. Tennery of the Washington College of Law at American University. And he had just the sort of information that Fortas and Porter had tried for so long to keep from everyone, including the White House.

When all of the summer's efforts by Robert Griffin and his staff to confirm the rumors about Fortas's law seminar at American University had failed, the senator knew that he still had one card left to play. On this one was a picture of Strom Thurmond. Griffin's political instincts would not allow him to press the Fortas teaching-fund charge, but he knew that his colleague would be less scrupulous about employing the necessary tactics to make the charge stick.[3] So one of Griffin's aides carried the information to Thurmond's aides, who then phoned Dean Tennery with the request for his appearance at the hearing. Not surprisingly, Tennery refused to appear. When Thurmond heard about this, he called the dean personally and indicated that he knew all about the seminar fund. Tennery could not have known that this was a bluff, and that the senator had only heard a rumor as to its size. But the dean had little choice when Thurmond explained to him that he had two options: He could either appear voluntarily or be subpoenaed by the Judiciary Committee. Which option did Tennery think was better for the reputation of American University? Thurmond pressed. The dean said that he would appear voluntarily.[4]

The new set of hearings was now Strom Thurmond's show. It was Thurmond who had been responsible for securing the right to subpoena more witnesses in exchange for the agreement bringing the Judiciary Committee proceedings to a close.[5] It was Thurmond who had invited Allott to testify. It was Thurmond who had been exploiting the pornography issue, soon to be capped by the testimony of Sergeant Donald Shaidell of the Obscenity Division of the Los Angeles Police

Department, the arresting officer in the *Schackman* case. And it was Thurmond who had "persuaded" Dean Tennery to appear.

Now it was Thurmond who would become Abe Fortas's prosecutor. And destroying the nomination to him meant destroying the man himself.

(Ironically, had the White House sources been better they could have beaten Thurmond at his own game. His main issue was now whether a government official should receive a fee from a college. Nearly a week after the new hearings were opened, it was revealed by the *Hatchet,* the campus newspaper at George Washington University, that Abe Fortas had also agreed to appear at that school's orientation to lead a discussion of the *Gideon* case.[7] While the appearance had been canceled because of the confirmation controversy, the students were interested in the fact that he had agreed to appear free of charge. In fact, the same piece reported, only one public figure had ever requested a fee for speaking in the Alpha Phi Omega Distinguished Speakers Series at George Washington University—Senator Strom Thurmond of South Carolina.)[8]

But that matter was not questioned. Strom Thurmond wasn't on trial here—Abe Fortas was. And Thurmond wasn't answering questions—he was asking them.

It would be a curious trial. The defendant and over half of the invited witnesses had decided not to appear. So all of the negative testimony would go unchallenged and be taken at face value despite the fact that the White House had amassed more than ample evidence to dispute it. In short, the new hearings would become a trial *in absentia.* Fortas would be no more than a sitting duck in a circus penny arcade, with the senators shooting as many rounds as they could muster to try to knock him over for good. Thanks to Strom Thurmond, they would all be well armed.

Only Dean Tennery had been put in the awkward position of trying to protect the justice from being hit too badly. And as the law school administrator prepared his devastating testimony early on the morning of the thirteenth, he could not have known that his answers would be the first independent confirmation of the existence of the seminar fund.

In drafting his testimony, Tennery played the good soldier. He had already consulted Paul Porter, who advised that there was no option but to tell the story "fully and accurately."[9] However, to the extent that his conscience would allow, Tennery was going to minimize the true role of Fortas's former law partner Paul Porter in the establishment and funding of the seminar. Not surprisingly, before Tennery appeared to testify, his statement was reviewed and corrected by one other interested party—Justice Abe Fortas.[10]

The truth was that Porter had organized the creation and funding of the seminar from start to finish. In early November 1967, Porter began reworking the initial proposal written by Tennery's office. The initial budget called for programmatic costs of twenty-five thousand dollars, with half of that earmarked for "instructional expense."[11] Then the drafting process was passed on to one of the lawyers in Porter's firm, Abe Krash, to rework.[12] Even at this early date Porter made Fortas fully aware of the budget being considered, while also promising that he already had commitments to fund it.[13]

The final Porter proposal envisioned the seminar as part of an "Institute on Law and the Social Environment," which would serve as a center for teaching and research patterned on the Yale multidisciplinary approach to the study of law. Topics such as land planning and use, population control, juvenile delinquency, and the entire criminal justice system would be explored using what was called a task force approach, linking legal analysis to various social and economic forces. Porter envisioned Fortas as a consultant during the institute's formation process, "an obvious choice" for its advising board, and perhaps even, "if appropriate," the chairman. In addition, the initial proposal portrayed the justice as becoming an adjunct member of the law faculty, and editor of, as well as a possible contributor to, any materials published by the center. Fortas would be provided with an office and research assistants to accomplish these tasks. This kind of operation is never cheap, so a budget of $60,000 to $100,000 was anticipated for the first eighteen months of operation.[14]

Once Porter had Fortas's approval, he wrote to six prominent businessmen, all his personal friends and three of them clients of Arnold and Porter: Gustave L. Levy of New York, an investment banker with Goldman, Sachs and Company and the board chairman of the New York Stock Exchange; Troy V. Post, the president of Greatamerica Corporation; Paul D. Smith, a New York attorney serving as vice president and general counsel with Philip Morris; Maurice Lazarus, the vice chairman of Federated Department Stores; John Loeb, a Wall Street banker with Carl M. Loeb, Rhoades and Company; and Benjamin Sonnenberg of New York City.[15] Within two weeks, Porter had raised thirty thousand dollars for the project from five of the men.[16] It mattered little to him that the money had come from men who (it would later be revealed) held forty seats as officers, directors, or part-

ners in various business corporations that might one day have cases
before the Supreme Court of the United States.[17]

In soliciting the money, Porter promised to make a full "detailed"
report as to how the money was used. Dean Tennery's Senate testimony on September 13 was clearly not the kind of report he had in
mind. But then, it could have been so much worse. For Tennery's
written and oral testimony revealed a rearranging of the "facts" in an
effort to protect Fortas. After a rather lengthy discussion of his view of
the need for an "interdisciplinary approach to the study of law," Tennery gave the impression that *he,* rather than Porter, had initially conceived the idea for the Fortas course, and approached the justice as to
his availability. Moreover, Tennery told the committee that *he* was the
one who had raised the money, even going so far as to name the donors. After conceding that he had "had the complete and enthusiastic
cooperation" of Paul Porter in developing the project and raising the
funds, Tennery explained that only after "the financial ability to get
the program [was] underway" had he approached Justice Fortas as to
his interest in teaching the seminar. What had in fact been coincident
events—the fundraising and Fortas course development efforts—now
became a series of logical steps that appeared to be much less compromising.[18]

Having portrayed the seminar as something other than the brainchild
of Paul Porter, and knowing that no one could blame an enterprising
dean for enlisting such an illustrious teacher for his faculty, Tennery
then tried to dance around the next two major admissions—the size of
the fee and how much the justice had done for it. The dean planned in
his statement to say only: "Turning to the specific arrangements for
compensation, I did not ever discuss with the Justice what compensation he should receive. I was fully aware of the generous honorariums
that are paid to lecturers of his standing and caliber, and I told him that
I thought he should be paid. However, he left this entirely to my discretion. As a matter of fact, he was paid $15,000 for this teaching
effort which hopefully will become helpful to us in producing a prototype for this type of law school program." But Fortas was not satisfied with this account and added in his own handwriting to Tennery's
draft that the money was for the teaching effort "including the preparation of a syllabus and teaching materials for future use." And this
was how Tennery delivered the statement to the committee.[19]

It would have shocked most people to discover how little effort Fortas actually had put into the preparation and teaching of this course.[20]
His role in each of the sessions was limited to offering some introduc-

tory remarks, engaging in conversations with the students, and then providing a summary of the meeting.[21] After the conclusion of the seminar, the justice's course materials were in such an incomplete and disorganized state that one of his students had to arrange them into a basic course "syllabus" from his seminar notes. All Fortas had really produced were three lists containing some general discussion questions and the assigned reference material for class consideration. ("Justice Fortas, as an experienced teacher," law clerk Walter Slocom later told the Justice Department as an alibi, "would naturally have arranged the materials informally in the first year, and would put them together in a more formal manner after teaching from them."[22]) Had the justice's opponents known how little work had actually been done, the honorarium would have appeared even more exorbitant.

Unaware of the loose nature of these materials, Tennery had asked Fortas whether he might be willing to gather them for publication. When the justice responded only that they were "not in shape for publication," the dean visited Paul Porter. "Look," he told Fortas's former partner, "we have got some money left up here. I think I can wrap this up if I send Justice Fortas this check." Since Porter agreed, the justice may well have received even more than the fifteen thousand dollars agreed upon for his teaching effort.[23]

(In the end, no publication emerged from this effort under Fortas's name. Still, time and again Fortas's defenders would resurrect Tennery's testimony as evidence that he was only a short step away from publishing the materials. This meant, the Justice Department explained in one such memo to Senator Hart, "that the value to American University of the rights to the syllabus and other materials prepared and organized by Justice Fortas will eventually repay many times over the original investment made by the University in the seminar."[24])

But it wasn't going to make one bit of difference to the opposing senators whether Fortas had gotten the money for teaching, writing syllabi, heading an experimental "Institute on Law and the Social Environment," or walking old ladies across the street. All they cared about was that he got the money—and more of it than any of them had ever received for consulting. There was no clearer evidence of this fact than Strom Thurmond's reaction when Tennery, in reading his oral statement before the Judiciary Committee, reached that portion of it detailing the fee for the service. Because the dean had only finished writing his testimony early that morning, there were no copies for the committee members. The senators were being exposed to this testimony for the first time.[25] After listening politely to six pages of the statement, Thurmond suddenly became hard of hearing when Tennery mentioned the fifteen-thousand-dollar payment. So he forced the dean to repeat it in case anyone in the audience, especially in the press box, had had similar trouble.[26]

But there was something else that the opponents pounced on. Why was Paul Porter involved here and what was the nature of his activity? To them, it looked much like a setup to funnel money to Fortas. Sam Ervin tried to put the dean on the spot: "At whose initiative was this arrangement made with Justice Fortas?" Tennery had no choice but to take the credit, cleverly using the fact that his first *contact* with Fortas had actually been to ask him to deliver the prestigious Mooers lecture at the school as the beginning point of the negotiation process.[27]

Ervin was not ready to let the connection to Porter go just yet. After securing an admission that it was Porter who had raised the supporting contributions, Ervin asked for more details about the lawyer's role in the development process. However, Tennery stuck to the basic testimony that *he* had approached Porter for help, rather than the other way around.

Thurmond began questioning in a manner indicating that his short-term memory might be failing again. "Now, I believe you said Mr. Paul Porter, a former law partner of Justice Fortas, raised the funds; is that correct? Did you first approach him and ask him to raise these funds, or did someone suggest that you approach him to do that; or did he voluntarily come to you; or just how was that connection formed?"

"Well, it is all kind of mixed up in the last few months," the dean protested. "I can't remember specific things. But after I learned about the Justice's interest—and I met Mr. Porter, and I had known him before, and I knew that he was a former partner of the Justice—and that he might be interested in helping in this kind of program, and he was. I think I suggested to him, 'Could you be of assistance to us in raising the funds.'"

"Now, did you go to him about this," pressed Thurmond, "and if so, why did you go to him, or did some of his friends suggest him to you to go to? How did his name occur to you to approach him, or did he approach you?"

"No; he didn't approach me. I approached him."

"You approached him first."

"Yes."

Thurmond knew he was on to something, but he could not quite get the admission he wanted. Repeatedly, he pressed the dean on why Porter's name had come to mind for raising the money, and Fortas's name had come to mind for the seminar. Had it been a coincidence? Or, more likely, had the idea been suggested to him?[28] Still, Tennery stuck to his story. As skillfully and honorably as the dean played his part, though, even he did not know the full truth.

Any psychological advantage that Thurmond had in the questioning was lost when he started badgering the dean to reveal his own salary at American University as a point of reference for the size of the fee. This was too much even for Sam Ervin to stomach as he came to the poor dean's rescue: "Mr. Chairman, if I may interject myself at this point—I am sort of on the dean's side on this. I would like my creditors to think I make more than I do." As the laughter died down, Senator Hugh Scott echoed his protest over this "invasion of privacy," and Thurmond was forced to back down.

Strom Thurmond may have been caught unaware by the full nature of Tennery's testimony, but he was never unprepared. When the afternoon session opened, Thurmond was able to "reveal" from *Who's Who* the extensive business contacts of the five men financing the course, and raise the specter of a justice compromising himself in future cases. But there was more—the biographies showed that none of the men had even the slightest connection with American University. "Yet all of them," the senator editorialized, "when approached by Mr. Paul Porter, suddenly opened their purse strings to American University, with which they had no connection recorded in 'Who's Who,' and which is not even in the city where any of them live or work. This appears to be an extraordinary burst of spontaneous generosity."[29] Indeed it was.

It was one of the turning points of the entire fight. Fortas and Porter had both known about this skeleton in the closet all along. In fact, given the long history of court members involved in law school teaching, including Fortas's own colleague William Brennan, who was then teaching part-time in the summer at New York University, this involvement could have been explained (though the *source* of the money would still have posed problems). By remaining totally silent, however, Fortas and Porter allowed their enemies to raise it at exactly the wrong time with the worst possible interpretations. Worse still, there was no one left who was in a position to answer the charges. Or who had the desire now to do so.

Even the most avid supporters of the nomination were taken by surprise—and they felt betrayed by both the existence and the size of the funding. The suspicions of the opposition that Fortas had been holding out on information had been justified. Now they were trumpeting that by their calculations Fortas had been paid nearly a thousand dollars an hour for his efforts.[30] Albert Gore was said to be "fuming" over the source of the funding, and Phil Hart was said to share his aides' view that this was "a straight hold-up."[31] Word came to the White House that three Republican senators—Delaware's J. Caleb Boggs, Nebraska's Roman Hruska, and Kansas's James Pearson—all prominent members of the list of eighteen that the president felt he absolutely needed to win, were now being counted in the opposition camp as a result of this new revelation.[32]

But there was more. Gone now was the entire Republican Kentucky delegation—both of whose members were on the magic list of eighteen needed votes, and one, Thruston Morton, on the short list of six or seven positive votes. Morton—until this point considered a rock-solid affirmative vote—said later, "Abe Fortas didn't need the money, and this was rather shocking to a good many people." While Fortas was to him a "brilliant man," Morton also felt "the President used very bad judgment in the way he used Mr. Fortas." So, for him the fifteen-thousand-dollar fee coupled with Allott's new charges "just blew it right out of the park." Having switched sides in the fight once already, Morton decided merely to "take a walk" during the cloture vote and later announce his opposition.[33]

Then there was the other Kentuckian, John Sherman Cooper. Universally considered to be one of the fairest, most objective, and most respected senators in Washington, Cooper told White House emissaries that the American University disclosure "troubled him, and . . . it has troubled others more than any previous charge against Justice Fortas." Then he added, "My fourth cousin, Paul Porter, should have used better judgment."[34] Only later would Cooper explain, "I expected to support Abe Fortas for Chief Justice, but then the facts that were brought out changed my mind."[35] For him, the American University revelation had also been too much.[36] And since he had not yet announced a position publicly, Cooper planned to cast his vote for cloture, as promised to the White House, but announce at that time that he would oppose Fortas's confirmation in the final vote.[37]

And then there was Richard Russell. Though the White House would not get formal notification for nearly two weeks, this issue was all that he needed to justify finally deserting the ship. It was not just the size of the fund, he argued in a letter to the president, it was the propriety of the source of the funds that bothered him. In truth, his opinion had probably been formed two months earlier on the Lawrence issue. For whatever reason, though, one of the twin pillars in the president's strategy was now gone.[38]

The initial press reaction to the new bombshell in the hearings seemed rather curious. The top story was Fortas's refusal to testify again, and Tennery's appearance was given billing equal to or even lesser than the continuation of the smut accusations by Senator Thurmond. However, once the reporters, who were starved for new angles to the prolonged struggle, began to investigate Tennery's testimony, things worsened for Fortas. It was revealed that one of the five funding sources, Maurice Lazarus, was the brother of Federated Department Stores President Ralph Lazarus, the same man whose receipt of a phone call from Fortas defending Lyndon Johnson's Vietnam policy had caused such a stir when it was uncovered by Sam Ervin in the July hearings.[39]

Then doubts surfaced in the news accounts as to Tennery's initiating role in the seminar as well as his part in securing the initial funding. A more accurate picture of the true role of Paul Porter was beginning to leak out.[40] As more journalistic investigation was done into the nature of the "lectures" delivered by Fortas, it was argued that the justice had done much less work on his teaching than had been portrayed.

For Paul Porter now the problem was a simple one—damage control, and fast! Sure, the American University revelation was a sensation. But time and time again Fortas had survived similar "revelations." Like the revelations about advising the president on Vietnam and the Detroit riots, the Ralph Lazarus incident, the reaction to the civil disobedience book, the brutal attacks of Sam Ervin and Strom Thurmond in the hearings, and the smut film festival, this was just one more piece of news that could be minimized, if not proven to be untrue.

So Porter's staff, which had become quite skilled in this sort of thing, went to work. Research was done into the history of other justices who had been funded for lectures, showing that it was not uncommon for members of the federal judiciary to serve simultaneously as occasional law school lecturers.[41]

But of course this did not address the major objection to Fortas's situation—the *source* of the money. Porter's group began investigating all of the times that the justice had refused to hear cases involving people known to him, in an effort to show that he could not have been compromised by the seminar. The list showed clearly that Fortas would have taken himself out of any case involving any of the donors, since all the men were either his personal acquaintances or clients of Arnold and Porter.

All of this evidence was carefully framed into speeches that could be delivered by friendly senators on the floor, and letters that could be sent to others. But all the words in the world could not gloss over the most central remaining question. Had Fortas known the identity of the donors in advance?

What remained of Fortas's credibility as an ethical justice depended on this answer. Fortas's prior knowledge of the donors would give the distinct impression that the entire seminar had been, not an academic exercise, but simply an effort by Paul Porter to funnel money to him. Furthermore, it would give the distinct *appearance* that Fortas had knowingly compromised himself with regard to potential future litigants before his court.

So Porter devoted the rest of the month to writing and telling others that the justice was an innocent victim of a misunderstanding over the funding. Here was just an academic in a judicial gown who was trying to avoid being chained to the bench by getting back into the classroom. There was a teacher inside the justice bursting to be free. It was ironic that Fortas, who had been faulted during his days at Yale Law School when he occasionally left his academic duties for governmental work, was now being criticized for leaving his governmental duties to do academic work.

There was nothing sinister in the funding, Porter insisted. It wasn't as if Fortas had been aware that the donors were former clients, whose business interests might well bring them before his court. It wasn't as if those individuals felt obligated by Fortas's past services to them, or pressured by their own knowledge that the justice would know just who had helped and who had not. The rumor mill had it all wrong.

One statement from Porter never changed—*Fortas had had no knowledge of the identity of the donors prior to their exposure in the Judiciary Committee hearings.* Clark Clifford was told this by letter from Porter in a heavily underlined passage, and also assured that Porter had never discussed the issue of compensation with Fortas. The point was also made in a draft letter to *The New York Times* intended for Tennery's signature, but never used.[42]

To get the point across to the world at large, Porter made the same point three times in a speech he hoped a senator would read into the record.[43] Then, using a set of materials on the seminar provided by Fortas's law clerks, the Justice Department prepared its own defensive memorandum for use by Philip Hart. Drafted along the lines of Tennery's claim of near-total responsibility for the project, it also alleged that there had been "no further discussion of the compensation" after the original conversation establishing that Fortas would be paid.[44]

Over and over Porter repeated the same story: "Fortas did not know the identity of the donors in advance." The only problem was that it was not true—and Porter knew it. Fortas had known where the money was coming from all along. As the "donations" came in, Porter had made it his business to tell his old friend just who thought enough of him to support his excursion into academia. And, Porter informed those donors that the justice was grateful and touched by the support.[45] Now in the fall of 1968, Porter tried to see to it that the world did not find out what he knew to be true. But no matter what he said, others were not going to believe him. They assumed the worst. And this time they were right.

Even now, Fortas did not acknowledge that he had done anything wrong. He sent Porter the collected materials from the seminar with a note saying how much *he* had benefited from the "stimulus of the discussions" and from "the work (a lot of it!)."[46] Moreover, not a single bit of evidence had emerged showing that he had been, or would be, in any way influenced in his judicial duties by his connection to the financial donors for the seminar.

But the technicalities here no longer mattered. Fortas's support was eroding too fast for Porter to stop a landslide. The appearance was one of impropriety. As Fortas had done so many times before, he had left himself wide open to attack. He could have done the teaching for free, or at least for a much more modest sum. He could have canceled the class once he was nominated for the chief justiceship. Failing that, he could have made the issue public much earlier in the controversy, allowing the negative public reaction to dissipate. The very least he could have done was to tell the White House and its Senate allies what was going on, to prepare them for the worst. But instead he had acted like a Washington lawyer—working in secret in the shadows and stonewalling—confident that he would never be discovered. And this time he had been wrong.

But the Tennery appearance was only the first of a Thurmond double feature on September 13. Everyone could sense from the loaded film projector in the middle of the hearing room that afternoon that it was show time again in the United States Senate. This time, the star witness was Sergeant Donald Shaidell, a Los Angeles policeman who had been the arresting officer in the *Schackman* obscenity case. He had

been invited to testify on Abe Fortas's contribution to the proliferation
of smut in America.

Thurmond announced that Shaidell had brought with him, all the
way from Los Angeles, more evidence of cinematic and journalistic
blight for viewing by the committee. And part of it was *an entirely
new film*. So the committee took another trip into the seamy underworld of the red-light districts of the nation's cities, complete with
visual displays of books, magazines, and pictures brought by Sergeant
Shaidell. As Shaidell went through his descriptions, Strom Thurmond
seemed obsessed with asking about their retail prices and comparing
those figures to the actual costs of production. It made little difference
that none of these materials had anything to do with the Supreme
Court, for Shaidell's contention was that *Schackman* and other decisions were making it impossible for the authorities to prevent these
films from coming onto the market.

By the time this circus was finished, Phil Hart had had enough and
was willing to risk the wrath of his colleagues by coming to Fortas's
defense. He read into the committee record the entire speech that had
been prepared by the Justice Department in late July for Everett Dirksen on the views of Justice Fortas regarding obscenity.[47] Then he entered into the record the full supportive editorial letter signed by Dean
Emeritus O'Meara of Notre Dame and the other law school deans (but
of course produced by the Porter operation).[48] Not surprisingly, in
neither of these cases did Hart reveal the true source of these materials.

Hart was plainly sickened by Thurmond's enterprise. "The whole
setting makes you wonder where we lost our senses. It makes as much
sense to sit around here and look at this movie and conclude that we
know what persuaded the Court to act as it would if we looked at the
blackjack that Mallory or the spear or whatever Miranda used, and
concluded we know what was before the Court in those cases. This is
not a judicial proceeding. If it was, this would not be the whole content of it. I regret very much the day has arrived when we are here,"
he lectured his colleagues. Later Hart would issue a statement that the
efforts to brand Fortas as a smut peddler were as "obscene and dis-
tasteful as the movies themselves."[49] But the defense came too late to
have any real effect.

With a new round of the senatorial peep show under way, more
people abandoned the Fortas camp. Pornography gave people a reason
for voting against the nominee with a clear conscience. Milton Young,
who was being counted on by the president to be purposefully absent
during the crucial vote, was the first to desert.[50] Even though he had

announced as recently as September 9 that he still supported the nomination, Young told his constituents that after viewing the films, he had such a "feeling of deep shock and revulsion" that he could no longer support the man who had made a "grievous mistake" in voting for them on the court.[51] (For all of the mental anguish apparent in this reversal, there were those who later suspected that the true motivation for such a fortuitously timed announcement may have been a promise of campaign support for the upcoming election.)[52]

Meanwhile, Ohio Democrat Frank Lausche, long considered by the White House to be a "gettable" vote, announced on the Senate floor that even against the interests of his own party, he was coming to a similar conclusion. "I have begun to wonder," he argued, "how can a father or mother, under their parental responsibility, hope to build up the moral fabric of their children, when pictures of the type that I have described are being publicly shown under the alleged protection of the Constitution of the United States."[53] The incident quickly took a bizarre and unexpected twist. Without warning anyone, Everett Dirksen, who was still voicing support for the nominations, offered an amendment to strip the federal courts of all power to review obscenity convictions from the state courts. However, Dirksen's claim that this was intended to "blunt" the "misdirected criticism of Justice Fortas because of his votes in obscenity cases" had a certain hollow ring to it.[54] It was a little like defending the virtue of your daughter to others by announcing that you are locking her in a closet. While no one realized it at the time, the minority leader in fact was indicating that he had now walked to the edge of Lyndon Johnson's ship and was beginning to judge the distance to the water.

All that Dirksen had accomplished by this grandstand play was to focus enough attention on this issue to make the situation intolerable for other shaky senators. One of these men, Democrat B. Everett Jordan of North Carolina, soon decided that it was indeed time to leave. Considered another of the obtainable "leaning against" votes, Jordan confessed to the White House that because of Fortas's position on obscenity and the strong stance of his fellow North Carolinian Sam Ervin, "he just could not stand the pressure anymore." Told by the conservative state Democratic leaders that he would not be able to participate in the local party rallies unless he was prepared to say that he would oppose Fortas, Jordan knew that he now had no choice but to desert the White House.[55]

But winning new converts did not keep the opponents' train from making one more stop. There was still the matter of Fortas's reverence, or the lack thereof, for the myth of the separation of governmental powers. The hearings reopened on the morning of September 16 to hear the long-awaited testimony of Senator Gordon Allott. His story was substantially the one discovered by the White House. On May 27 (not June 5 as UPI had reported), at a meeting of the subcommittee on Treasury and post office appropriations, Undersecretary of the Treasury Joseph W. Barr, after spending about a half an hour on the phone, had allegedly told Allott, "I have been on the phone with the White House. . . . This is the amendment they want at the White House. It has been gone over by DeVier Pierson and Abe Fortas; they have cleared it, and they can live with it."[56]

No one seemed troubled by the fact that this account was pure thirdhand hearsay and there was no direct evidence that Fortas had in fact been involved in any way with this legislation. Likewise, no one seemed bothered by the fact that nothing had in fact been done on that measure until after the assassination of Robert F. Kennedy, and there was no indication that this was even the same bill. The committee members didn't even ask why Allott's memory had suddenly improved after total silence about this incident in the July hearings. But then, why should they? Since the White House had chosen to withhold its evidence and witnesses, it was left to Strom Thurmond to claim that this silence proved the veracity of Allott's charges.[57]

This new indication of Fortas's lack of respect for the "cherished" separation-of-powers doctrine was all that Senator William B. Spong of Virginia needed to justify coming out against his nomination. Now there was a clear-cut constitutional issue to add to the conflict-of-interest and promotion-of-pornography charges. The sheer weight of all of the new testimony, combined with Fortas's unwillingness to appear again in his own defense, had now claimed another opposition vote.[58]

And there were further storm warnings for the White House about Everett Dirksen. John Sherman Cooper told White House emissary Harry McPherson that while the minority leader was "throwing a lot of sand in everybody's eyes, no doubt he would like to come out as the savior of the nomination after a while."[59] Cooper seemed to be saying that the White House was going to have to prove once again that it could almost win the fight on its own before it got Dirksen's promised help.

The only good news for the White House came from Pennsylvania's Hugh Scott, another of Johnson's eighteen "must get" Republicans, who called on the twentieth to say that he still supported the Fortas nomination. However, Scott warned that "he was very concerned about the outcome," and "that he thought that the $15,000 fee for the American University lectures had struck a damaging blow to the Fortas case." Furthermore, his mail was running "very heavily" against the nomination, a sure indication of what was happening in other offices.[60]

With the completion of Allott's testimony, Thurmond and Griffin rushed to claim credit for leading the opposition by inserting into the record memoranda containing their long-familiar arguments against Fortas.[61] But Sam Ervin made the most damaging observation on the nature of the defense effort's response to the subpoenas: "The invitation of the committee to appear reminds me of the statement in the Scriptures about the man who gave the marriage feast and invited a lot of people to come to the marriage feast and the Bible records in substance that he began to make excuses. So we have the excuses rather than witnesses."[62]

The trial was over and the nation waited for the verdict. But it was not the upcoming Judiciary Committee vote that was at issue, for the working majority of liberals on that committee ensured that the nomination would be reported out. The key would be the vote of the whole Senate—if in fact the opposition was willing to allow that vote to occur at all. And no matter how many people jumped ship, the White House still had Everett Dirksen. As long as that was true, Lyndon Johnson believed that there was still a chance.

XXII

THE
VERDICT

Just before seven o'clock on the evening of September 16, 1968, the white-haired, bespectacled, rumple-faced gentleman from Illinois was ushered into the Oval Office at the White House. With the new Judiciary Committee hearings ended, Lyndon Johnson had invited him over hoping to hear the good news from the Senate. But Everett Dirksen had another mission in mind. He was there, he said, to "lay it on the line again" with the president. In fact, Dirksen was there to tell him that a death sentence was about to be pronounced on a nomination to the chief justiceship of the United States Supreme Court.

Together the two men stepped into the same little lounge off the Oval Office that had witnessed the rebirth of the Subversive Activities Control Board and the inauguration of Ev Dirksen's support on the nomination. For the next forty-five minutes, Dirksen told the president the new facts of life in the Senate. While there was a two-to-one favorable majority in the committee, by his reckoning twenty-six of the

Senate's thirty-seven Republicans now opposed the nomination on the final cloture vote. The president's strategy to line up the magical eighteen "must get" Republicans was in a shambles, and without them, the nomination was dead. Surprisingly, it was the "dirty movies" that had taken their toll, reported Dirksen. The American University matter was a "secondary issue," but the fact that Paul Porter had raised the money was "hurtful." Strom Thurmond had "taste[d] blood now" and the floor debate was bound to be "dirty." Overall, while no one would challenge Fortas's qualifications, the smut issue was "what the opposition needed to make their positions jell."

But there was another, even worse message, that was being left unspoken. Each man knew that being opposed by two thirds of his "followers" was an intolerable situation for the Republican minority "leader." So Dirksen tried to cast his dilemma in broader terms. He philosophized about the long-run implications of a loss on this issue. There were dangers to the separation of powers in the event of a defeat. This might well become the beginning of the Congress running the judicial branch. A defeat would prove to the legislators that they could challenge any nomination on the basis of the court's past decisions rather than the professional qualifications of the individual. Then there were dangers to Fortas himself. "Win or lose, the stain of this terrible ordeal will remain with Fortas on or off the Bench," said the senator.[1] How right he was!

It was a sobering warning. Just five weeks before, James Eastland had come all the way to Johnson's Texas ranch to say much the same thing. It wasn't just the Fortas nomination that was at stake. It wasn't just the president's pride. It was Fortas personally. Not only could he not survive a loss, now one had to wonder whether he could even survive a win. Because of the Senate attack, the skeletons were coming out of Abe Fortas's closet, and no one, not even Lyndon Johnson, could put them back.

Johnson could end this attack forever, argued Dirksen, by simply withdrawing the nomination, expressing his indignation, and giving his judicial friend some peace. But this was not Lyndon Johnson's style. He could not admit defeat in the rice paddies of Southeast Asia. He could not risk defeat in the Democratic primaries around the nation. And he certainly would not accept defeat in his town of Washington, D.C. This was his legacy to the country, and his present to Abe Fortas. The fight would go on. So it was left to Everett Dirksen to decide whether to sue for a separate peace.

*   *   *

Just as Dirksen warned, the newspapers and Senator Robert Griffin saw to it that the "stain" on Abe Fortas continued. Too much had been left unanswered in the American University seminar story for it to be dropped. A reporter had already discovered that Fortas's per-hour compensation was actually much higher than previously suspected, in that he had missed one of the seminar meetings to testify before the Senate Judiciary Committee in July. His replacement, juvenile court judge Orm W. Ketcham, had received no compensation for his efforts and commented only that he was "rather flattered to be asked."[2] Then it was discovered that the son of one of the funding donors, Troy V. Post, Jr., was appealing his conviction for conspiracy and fraud in the federal courts, raising the prospect that he might one day come before the Supreme Court.[3] The incident served as a living example of the dangers raised by the justice's involvement in the seminar.

Then Griffin began hammering away on the Senate floor regarding the crucial unresolved part of the American University money issue— the nature of its source and the state of Fortas's knowledge about it. By examining listings of Fortas's corporate board memberships before ascending to the court, the senator had discovered that he had served on several boards with three of the donors.[4] How could one believe that Fortas had not known the origins of such contributions from former business acquaintances? he argued.

By now, Fortas's Senate allies were too stunned to mount any sort of counterattack. Each time they had done so in the past, some new disclosure had pulled the rug out from under them. So it was left for Senator George Murphy of California to say that Richard Nixon should be allowed to make the appointment, because "I am sure that the people know he will respect the principle of separation of powers."[5] (Later others would have reason to question the Californian senator's psychic ability.)

The clock stopped for the Dixiecrats on Tuesday, September 17. James Eastland had promised the president that he would allow the Fortas nomination to come up for a vote before his Judiciary Committee "at [his] own time." And so he did, after sixty-eight days, or about two months longer than the White House wanted. But even as this final vote occurred, everyone now understood that it was Fortas whose clock had really run down.

Just as Dirksen had predicted for the White House, when the committee took its vote that day in executive session, the final count was

11 to 6 in favor of the nomination. Dirksen did his part by taking Republicans Roman Hruska and Hugh Scott to join their eight Democratic colleagues in supporting the nomination.[6] On the other side, it was a combination of the three Dixiecrats, James Eastland, John McClellan, and Sam Ervin, and the three early rebels, Strom Thurmond, Hiram Fong, and Howard Baker. But the important thing was that the nomination was out of committee. Now it was simply a matter of whether the Fortas allies could get enough votes on the Senate floor to impose cloture on the expected filibuster.

Even in victory, however, the White House could not avoid making more mistakes. On the face of it, the majority report of the committee, which by agreement was produced three days later, was very predictable. Having already been written by members of the Judiciary Committee and Phil Hart's office, it spoke of how "extraordinarily well qualified [Fortas was] for the post." After arguing that a vacancy did indeed exist on the court, and that the Warren retirement procedure was justified, it examined historical precedents to prove that there was nothing wrong with either Fortas's relationship with the president or his seminar at American University.[7] (Needless to say, the individual views filed by Eastland, McClellan, and Ervin took issue with each of these claims.)

The confusion continued in the Fortas camp. Senate rules require that a committee report be delivered personally to the floor, but Phil Hart was out of town. So Maryland's Joseph Tydings was asked to do the honors. The only problem was that Senator Tydings was facing a tough reelection battle in two years and had already gone to the wall in the defense of the White House's controversial gun control efforts. So Tydings agreed to take the report to the floor so long as Hart's name was put on it. And when his name was mistakenly affixed to the report, he was understandably "livid."[8] But he delivered the report anyway.

In assessing everything, former press secretary George Reedy echoed the warnings of Eastland and Dirksen in writing to the president that there were "real perils" to "an inconclusive debate resulting in anything other than confirmation." Regardless of the Fortas nomination's merits, Reedy warned, its debate would "lower the prestige of the Supreme Court, . . . denigrate the prestige of Abe Fortas [and] contribute to the very deep divisions within the country." All of these dangers led him to conclude that unless the confirmation vote could be won, it would be wise to withdraw the nomination on the "grounds that the debate is dividing the country." In doing so, he argued,

Johnson would be able to blast the Griffin-Thurmond opposition for "jeopardiz[ing] the nation's confidence in its political institutions for partisan political purposes."[9] The memo was like a "last gas" sign on a long, lonely highway. But Johnson was ready to drive on, whether his passenger, Abe Fortas, wanted to go or not.

While everyone waited for the full Senate debate, the White House, in a desperation move, tried one last time to launch a "holy war." Still lacking definite proof in mid-September of anti-Semitism in the fight, the Justice Department had drafted another historical essay depicting the similarities to the Brandeis confirmation battle in 1916 (neglecting the fact that in the Brandeis fight the Republican opposition had collapsed when the nomination got to the Senate floor).[10] Hoping in vain to get the piece published, the staff circulated it among friendly reporters.[11]

The basis of the White House's anti-Semitism charge stemmed partly from the current efforts of the American Nazi party. When one dialed for the latest "Let Freedom Ring" message, one would find that the attacks on Fortas had become much more polished and even less convincing!

We have no way of knowing if Abe Fortas actually is, or ever was, a member of the Communist Party, or if he is, or ever was, a Soviet agent. However, he has been in close association with proven Communist espionage agents, such as Harry Dexter White, Owen Lattimore, and Alger Hiss, for most of his career. Before the Senate Committee on the Judiciary, the Chairman asked Fortas about his connections with a Communist front organization called the International Juridical Association. Fortas replied, "To the best of my knowledge and belief, I never had any connection with it whatsoever. My mind is blank about that." Fortas' mind may be blank, but the records of the House Committee on Un-American Activities are not. Fortas is not only listed as a member of this Communist front, but served as an officer and national committeeman. Fortas worked with Soviet agents Alger Hiss and Harry Dexter White in drafting the U.N. Charter which, as one might suspect from such handmaidens, is patterned after the Russian concept of government. Abe Fortas is an ardent believer in so-called civil disobedience, and has declared his solidarity with such Communist front operators and racial agitators as Ralph Abernathy. He has even gone so far as to equate whites who believe in segregation with the genocide policies of the Nazis. To put it bluntly, Abe Fortas has proven through his

own words and actions that he is a left wing revolutionary, a protec-
tor of Communist agents, and is unfit to serve on any court. Abe
Fortas should not be confirmed by the U.S. Senate as Chief Justice.
He should be impeached.[12]

The White House was anxious to get this tape and some other similarly slanted attacks against Fortas before the Judiciary Committee.
Barefoot Sanders sent a copy of one of the "poison" phone message
transcripts to Andy Biemiller, chief congressional lobbyist for the
AFL-CIO, asking, "What do you think about getting some of these
put into the Senate Committee record—to show in effect the kind of
outrageous and extreme vilification to which Fortas has been subjected." Despite such suggestions, nothing appeared in the committee
hearings.[13]

The White House efforts did produce one positive action, however.
By September 18, the American Jewish Committee had decided to
counterattack, hoping to get some publicity as to the unseemly nature
of the opposition. The committee's Trends Analysis Division had
amassed a bill of indictment of twelve different actions by extremist,
conservative individuals and groups against the Fortas nomination. The
committee concluded, "To what extent the ultra right has been responsible for the flood of Senatorial mail in opposition to Mr. Fortas is a
matter of conjecture. . . . We do not view the Fortas case as being
rooted in anti-Semitism, but it seems clear that anti-Semites and extremists are exploiting and aggravating it. While Mr. Fortas's faith has
not figured in the statements of either right-wing or moderate opponents of his appointment, this has not been the case with organizations
in the nation's overtly anti-Semitic movement."[14] Once again,
though, the ripple effect of these charges was minimal, as only the
New York Law Journal saw fit to publish just a portion of the material.[15]

In spite of all these efforts, Robert Griffin was once again able to
secure the high ground. On September 20 he told reporters, "There's
been an effort to fan up this anti-Semitic thing, and I think it has
backfired. I think it is emanating right from the White House; that's all
they have got left now."[16] And Griffin was right. Without Jacob Javits, the White House had nothing. And Javits was still silent.

In fact, there were good reasons for the Jewish senator's posture.
When the American University scandal broke, Phil Hart had been so
stunned that he asked Paul Porter whether he could expect any more

embarrassing surprises. But Porter assured him that there "were no more skeletons in Fortas's closet."[17] However, by now Porter seemed constitutionally incapable of either remembering or telling the truth. What he probably meant by this new statement was that he was confident no more of the skeletons would appear in such an untimely fashion. And therein lay the reason for Jacob Javits's strange silence.

Shortly after the September hearings closed, a mimeographed letter arrived at the Senate Judiciary Committee.

Gentlemen:

Wasn't Fortas, in effect, involved in a criminal way with Louis Wolfson, a known and acknowledged operator outside the law in Florida and in the District of Columbia long years before he finally got into his recent trouble in New York?

How can Senator Dirksen favor such a character when he cannot help knowing that Secretary of the Interior Ickes never would have tolerated him if President Franklin D. Roosevelt had not been obligated to his "crowd" of fixers?

The Supreme Court cannot compromise with mischief, and that is what Fortas has done habitually again and again and would continue to do if he were Chief Justice.

Why does not your Committee, free to act in protection of the Court, be faithful to your responsibility?

A.W.

September 22, 1968[18]

It was a bombshell. In fact, it was *the* bombshell. But for now this was merely one clue among thousands, and the letter was ignored as the ravings of another anonymous crank.[19]

However, anonymous letters are not the only way to plant dynamite. And September had now become open season on the public life of Justice Abe Fortas. So it was inevitable that the rumors of his connection to Louis Wolfson would reach close associates of Republican presidential candidate Richard M. Nixon. Once that happened, one of their number made sure that a warning was sent to the one senator most sought by the White House at that time—Jacob Javits. The senator was warned not to "get too far out in front in defending Fortas," because "Griffin might prove something."[20]

So, no matter how hard Paul O'Dwyer hit on the anti-Semitism theme, and no matter how actively the White House complained about the extremist groups against the Fortas nomination, Javits had become persuaded not to respond.[21]

While neither Robert Griffin nor anyone else among the justice's Senate opponents knew of these charges, the seeds of Fortas's public destruction had now been sown.[22] Now that the story was in certain rumor mills within the Justice Department machinery, it was only a matter of time before it reached the ears of an enterprising reporter named William Lambert.

Fortas's fate was now in the hands of the full Senate, and quite a few of the senators still had a great deal to say. The debate opened on Wednesday, September 25, with the White House still counting noses on the cloture issue. The problem with such a vote is that many senators will vote against cloture as a matter of principle, in the interests of supporting the historical right and function of the Senate as a body to preserve democracy by slowing it to a crawl. Like the pornography and separation-of-powers issues, then, forcing a vote on the right to talk a bill to death was the opponents' means of giving the fence sitters yet another convenient reason for opposing the confirmation.

The White House head counts seemed to be holding very steady. As of September 25, Johnson personally had a count of 57 to 41 on the issue of cloture.[23] This represented a loss of only two affirmative votes from the count two weeks before.[24] But the dire warnings continued to flow in. "If Ev Dirksen is really trying to help us as he pretends to be," Mike Manatos wrote to the president, "he ought to be in a position to get Hruska and Winston Prouty of Vermont on cloture. Prouty has told Labor that he might vote for cloture if [George] Aiken [of Vermont also] does. He has always supported us on cloture in the past." But there was no evidence that Dirksen was being helpful to anyone but himself.[25] Why?

The same could not be said of Mike Mansfield, who used an intriguing strategy to try to get the debate off on the right foot. Knowing that a filibuster was coming and realizing that votes for Fortas could be lost simply on the cloture issue, the majority leader placed the White House's allies on their strongest possible footing by calling for a vote on a different procedural question—the right of the Senate to have an issue raised for debate. Mansfield created the procedural issue by calling the body into executive session on September 24, moving that the nominations be considered, requesting that a roll call vote be taken after debate on the motion, and then recessing the Senate. The filibuster was now on. But the issue was no longer the merits of the appointments, it was now whether a few members of the body had the right to block the rest of the group from even *raising* an issue. "It is not a complex issue," he explained to his colleagues. "It does not even deal with the merits of the nominees. I would think that it could be disposed of expeditiously."[26] So confident was he that this could be done that Mansfield estimated anything a member had to say on the issue could be condensed into a period of twenty to thirty minutes.

While the senators had a hearty laugh over that, they had to realize the shrewdness of the move. In a sense, Mansfield's motion simply to commence the debate had taken the high ground of "freedom of speech" for senators away from the administration's opponents, and given it to the allies. "We may evade the obligation, but we cannot deny it," Mansfield had said.[27] So delighted was Phil Hart by the move, having had so little to celebrate thus far, that he called it "the first encouraging thing that's happened in three months."[28] It was, indeed, the best chance that the allies had to secure a victory on the question of invoking cloture. (Of course the risk was that another filibuster would ensue on the actual question of the nominations' merits, but chances were good that a single positive vote on cloture could then be duplicated.)

Mansfield's true devotion to Abe Fortas's cause was questionable, however. Rather than deciding to keep the Senate in session around the clock to exhaust the filibusterers, as Lyndon Johnson had done in the civil rights debate, or even ruling that the debate must be kept strictly on this one issue, the majority leader devised what might be called a loose-rules filibuster. The Senate debate, he said, would continue only while the body observed its normally scheduled working hours, and the discussion would be interrupted to take up unrelated issues. In the absence of a restricting cloture vote, these rules would allow the obstructing senators to talk forever without breaking a sweat.[29]

Mansfield had at least two reasons for throwing this advantage to the administration's opponents. First, he had come to believe, after the revelations about Fortas in the second set of hearings, that the confirmation cause was lost. Moreover, he was now angry at Lyndon Johnson for failing to keep his part of a bargain. You get the northern Democrats, the president had told Mansfield, and I'll get you the southern ones. When it became clear that the votes of Richard Russell and James Eastland were not being delivered as promised, Mansfield saw no further reason to play ball with the White House. So he saw to it that the clock would continue to run toward the time when Earl Warren would have to return to the bench for the court's opening, on the first Monday in October, thus eliminating the appearance of a vacancy at all.[30]

As the senators began their talkathon the following day, the opposing camps more and more took on the appearance of two exhausted heavyweights in the fifteenth round, simply waiting for the bell to ring and knowing full well what the outcome would be. The White House's opponents evaded Mansfield's strategy by simply ignoring the stated issue and rephrasing the question under debate to be the merits of the Abe Fortas and Homer Thornberry nominations. For the next two days it seemed that all of the talking was done by the confirmation opponents. Only the new senator from New York, Charles Goodell, and the old regulars among the allies—Joseph Tydings and Phil Hart among them—could find the time to offer their support. And as the debate wore on, the White House realized that the "prospects for the two-thirds majority necessary to impose cloture grew increasingly dim."[31]

Then the administration's ship ran aground. And it did so because, as Johnson had long feared, Ev Dirksen decided to jump off of it.

Meeting with the press on the morning of Friday, September 27, the "master of the U-turn" reversed his position once more, repositioning himself in front of his "followers." Dirksen announced that he was now "neutral" in the fight. But far be it from the man from Pekin to admit that the upstart Robert Griffin's challenge to his authority had been the reason for his change of heart. No, there were new issues being raised here. First, the question was not the merits of the nominees, for whom his positive vote had long been promised and delivered already in committee. The question here was a matter of imposing cloture on the time-honored privilege of the Senate to exercise its deliberative powers. On this issue, Dirksen assured everyone, his vote had never been promised (except to the White House and *The New York Times*). Pointing over to his Democratic colleagues, he told the assembled reporters that it was "essentially their problem."[32]

To keep people from thinking that he would make such a change on a simple procedural matter, Dirksen announced that a "new issue" had arisen to change his thinking on the case: Abe Fortas's vote in the *Witherspoon* v. *Illinois* case.[33] Here the court had ruled in 1968 that the creation of a so-called hanging jury in capital cases—allowing the removal of potential jurors from the panel simply because they opposed capital punishment—was unconstitutional. As a result, Dirksen told the press, twenty-four convicted murderers would have to be retried in his state alone, one of whom was Richard Speck, who had been convicted of murdering eight student nurses. This whole matter, announced Dirksen, deserved "far better scrutiny than I have been able to devote to it."[34] Apparently, the time since July 18, when the case had first been raised in Dirksen's presence during the Fortas-Thurmond debate in the Judiciary Committee hearings, had been insufficient for the senator's "scrutiny." It was a phony issue, but it was all that the senator needed. Like Richard Russell before him, this other twin pillar in the president's strategy had been forced to accept the fact that his power was waning.

When Lyndon Johnson got the news, he was neither surprised nor angry; after all, he had predicted it all along.[35] He, too, realized that with the dying power of his two friends in the Senate came the admission that his presidency was in its dying days. And with these deaths came the termination of Abe Fortas's judicial elevation.

The evening before the first cloture vote, Ramsey Clark provided Fortas with a full rundown on his prospects for winning the vote. After a great deal of discussion, the justice said that "he fully agreed that [the White House] should stick it out and press for a vote."[36] Then, the next morning, providing help "too little" and "too late," Paul Porter called Joe Califano around 10 A.M. to say that he wanted to come over to the White House that afternoon for a meeting with the president and all of his lieutenants. Perhaps there were images in Porter's mind of being at the head of the cavalry, high on his fast-galloping horse, with the flags flying. He promised to supply a new way to handle the problem that would "save face" for everyone. The idea was to have the Senate pass a resolution declaring that there was "no vacancy," ending the need for a vote on the merits of Fortas's nomination. In fact, Everett Dirksen had already unsuccessfully proposed this idea to Griffin four days earlier (leading Dirksen then to change his overall vote). But the president had already begun to distance himself from the losing fight, and responded to Porter's message with a simple "See A[ttorney] G[eneral] & *NOT HERE* [at the White House]."[37]

Finally, on October 1, after twenty-five hours of debate on the cloture motion, all that remained was for each side to sum up its position. That task fell to the two opposing senators from Michigan, Hart and Griffin. "Never in our history has a matter of the nomination of a Justice to the Supreme Court been resolved by a filibuster," said Phil Hart after a stirring speech summarizing all of the arguments for the confirmation. To which Robert Griffin responded in a self-congratulatory fashion, "I took my stand, and I have worked so hard to build support for my position, precisely because I am concerned about the Supreme Court as an institution—because I believe the American people should respect the Court and hold it in high esteem."[38]

As the vote began in the Senate chamber on the afternoon of October 1, the White House could see from the very beginning that things were not going to be easy. Only eighty-eight members could find their way to the chamber, and nine of those absent were Democrats. Then came the announcement from Robert Byrd that Democrat Allen Ellender from Louisiana was "absent on official business"; however, if the senator had been "present and voting, [he] would vote 'nay.'" The same would have been case with Nevada's Alan Bible, who, true to his promise to the White House, now was "necessarily absent."[39] In a curious irony, Fortas's old adversaries from the Interior Department days—Wayne Morse and Ernest Gruening—canceled each other's votes with a "live pair," allowing one of the senators to be absent and still record his vote.[40] Morse took Fortas's side in the matter. Another curiosity was the absence of George Smathers, the Florida Democrat who had made the stirring early support speech written by Porter and the White House, showing that perhaps the pressure of his Dixiecrat colleagues had finally taken its toll.

But things went from bad to worse with the very first senator on the voting list. George Aiken, the independent thinker from Vermont, who as one of Johnson's eighteen "must get" Republicans had told the White House that he would get on board after a "reasonable debate," could not be found, but indicated that he would have voted nay. So the White House now knew it would lose his Vermont colleague Winston Prouty, another of the key eighteen. Then everything went true to form for a while: Allott, nay; Anderson of New Mexico, aye; Howard Baker, nay. Then came Alaska Democrat Edward Bartlett, another of the men who had told the White House he would be on the team after "reasonable debate."[41] But he was in the hospital recovering from a heart attack, and could be of no help now. Two votes gone from the fifty-seven the administration had been counting on, and the Senate had just started the *B*'s.

The only chance for the White House now was to lose no more from the "solid yes" block and hope for some surprise late switches further down on the alphabetic list. Everything went as expected, with even John Sherman Cooper doing the service for the White House of voting aye on cloture, while indicating later that he would oppose the final confirmation vote. The cause had lost Delaware's James Boggs and New Hampshire's Norris Cotton, two more names from Johnson's list of "must get" Republicans. Then came Dirksen's vote. Nay. Everyone knew wherever he went, Hruska was sure to follow, taking yet two more of the magic eighteen.[42]

Then came Democrat Tom Dodd. Here was a man who had helped the White House with support and information and a crucial vote during the Judiciary Committee ordeal. While he had hurt the nominations on Hart's withdrawal letter, Dodd was a man who was so solidly in the White House's corner that he was listed as a "solid yes" on every head count coming to the president's desk. But now, in the limelight, Dodd stunned colleagues, Senate aides, and the White House alike by voting nay. Later he explained that his vote was a defense of the right of those senators who still had things to say in this "discussion." But knowledgeable sources within the Senate later speculated about other possible explanations for the surprise move. Could it be that this was a retaliation against the Democrats for their censure of him on allegations of unethical conduct, especially in this case where there had been further charges of ethical violations? Or could this have been part of a deal with John McClellan in return for the southerner's support of a gun control measure?[43] No one knew for sure. Or at least no one who knew was saying. But whatever the reason, Dodd's vote indicated that barring unforeseen circumstances, the rout was now on. Fortas and more particularly President Johnson were on the verge of losing.

Unless a miracle happened. So the White House waited for the *H*'s in the Senate voting list, praying that a miracle was there. The one final hope was to split the southern Democrats and get someone to oppose the dying Richard Russell. Of those names, the Johnson aides had always thought that their best chance was Alabama Democrat Lister Hill.

While Hill was indeed one of Russell's Dixiecrats, almost to the end the White House thought that he was "gettable." In the early weeks of the fight, all of the White House lobbyists had been listing Hill as a "questionable" vote, sometimes indicating that he was leaning for, and other times against, the nominations.[44] By late July one contact to the White House was reporting that Hill was "okay."[45] Apparently, as the Johnson team had discovered, Hill was indeed willing to deal his Fortas-Thornberry votes for the right to name someone to the Fifth Circuit Court of Appeals.

However, by the middle of August something had gone wrong. Inexplicably, Hill was now being reported as leaning "hard against" Fortas. So in early September the White House designed a strategy to "do it up big" for the Alabama senator and "try to turn [him] around on Fortas" by playing up the extension of the Hill-Burton Act, which provided federal funds for the construction of hospitals in rural areas. Despite this effort, Hill did not waver from the solidly opposed group.

And those on Pennsylvania Avenue were left to wonder what it was that had changed his mind.[46]

The White House could not have known Hill's decision had been fixed forever by some lobbying from a very powerful and extremely knowledgeable constituent. This constituent was a man who not only knew Fortas well, but also knew well the role of the Supreme Court and the job requirements of the chief justiceship. And there was no way that he wanted Abe Fortas in that seat. So he convinced Hill to come out solidly against the nomination. It would be months before Fortas discovered the name of his adversary, but when he did he would be stunned and hurt.

With the loss of Hill and Dodd, the White House knew that, for all its efforts, the battle was over. The final tally showed that the administration had lost a full 25 votes from its original count of 70 supporters, and could muster only a bare majority vote of 45 to 43, far short of the 59 that would have been needed that day to invoke cloture.

Realizing that his nomination would never get to a vote on the Senate floor, Fortas asked Johnson to withdraw it. But even in total defeat, Fortas and Johnson remained true to form. After the incredible ordeal that had just been endured, Fortas still consented when he was asked to draft the president's explanatory message on the withdrawal. "I deeply regret that the Senate filibuster prevented the Senate from voting on the nomination of Justice Fortas," he wrote. "Had the Senate been permitted to vote, I am confident that both Justice Fortas and Judge Thornberry would have been confirmed. Their qualifications are indisputable." It seemed as though the two men had either learned nothing from the experience of the dangers in their extrajudicial relationship, or perhaps they no longer cared.[47]

When word came to Strom Thurmond of the justice's withdrawal, he couldn't resist gloating: "In my judgment, this is the wisest decision Justice Fortas has made since he became a member of the Supreme Court. I suggest Mr. Fortas now go a step further and resign from the Court for the sake of good government."[48]

Where had it all gone wrong? Much later, Johnson would explain to aide Doris Kearns how he had mastered the Congress. "A measure must be sent to the Hill at exactly the right moment and that moment depends on three things: first, on momentum; second, on the availability of sponsors in the right place at the right time; and third, on the opportunities for neutralizing the opposition. Timing is essential. Momentum is *not* a mysterious mistress. It is a controllable fact of political life that depends on nothing more exotic than preparation."[49] The president should have taken his own advice. After March 31, Lyndon Johnson should have known that he controlled none of these things. He had no momentum, too few reliable sponsors, and no means as a lame duck of "neutralizing the opposition."

But perhaps it was the sensitive and intuitive Lady Bird Johnson who offered in her diary the proper epitaph for it all. "It is a sad season. Troubles are crowding in on all sides," she wrote the day after Everett Dirksen's desertion announcement.

> Lyndon asked Carol and Abe to come over for dinner. I was glad. I had been hungry to see them for days and weeks. But I hadn't asked them, for a curious reason. I wondered if they could stand to see us, the unwitting architects of all the agony they have been going through. Lyndon's only thought—months ago when he had nominated Abe to be Chief Justice—had been to find the best Chief Justice the country could provide and to accord Abe an honor he so magnificently deserves. Well, it hasn't turned out that way. So often through the years I have seen this drama played out but with a different set of characters. Somebody was being maligned, torn apart, his character and life questioned by the Congress and press, and finally, you suppose, by people in general. But there was always a wise, able, and compassionate guide for them to turn to—and that was Abe Fortas. Now when Abe is the man who is being pilloried, where is there an Abe Fortas for him to turn to? There isn't anybody. And so the sorry story is nearly played out.[50]

Like a bad horror movie, though, the tragedy wasn't over yet.

XXIII

THE "FORTAS UNDER THE FORTAS"?

I f it was a more conservative court that Abe Fortas's confirmation opponents were seeking, Chief Justice Warren soon made clear that they were destined to be disappointed. "I can assure you," he told the Montana Supreme Court justices during the Senate battle, "that the delay [in Senate action on the Fortas nomination] is not because they want to retain *me*. If it's a choice of taking Abe Fortas or keeping me, they'll take Abe. But it looks like I'll be back to open the Supreme Court in October."[1] And, because of the conditional nature of the chief's retirement, so he was.

But that was not what Lyndon Johnson wanted either. He spent the last days of his presidency considering ways to ensure the continuation of a liberal in Warren's seat. After canvassing the opinions of a number of his top aides, the president considered the idea of sending another nominee to the Senate—one that it could not refuse. Names such as those of former justices Arthur Goldberg and Tom Clark, current justices William Brennan and Potter Stewart, Senator Phil Hart, and Vietnam peace negotiator Cyrus Vance were bandied about. Of these, Arthur Goldberg seemed to have the inside track. But all of them were liberals, and the conservative Senate coalition had already proven its ability to stop or at least delay any such appointment. Johnson had no real choice other than to cite the disruption to the court of submitting a new appointment and ask Earl Warren to recall his conditional resignation in favor of returning for more service at his post.[2]

This, in turn, put Richard Nixon in something of a bind. Forced to concede that the replacement of a chief justice in midterm was unthinkable, after the 1968 presidential election the Nixon forces privately arranged with Warren that he would stay on until the end of that court term.[3] A change of one seat in June 1969, however, would not allow the Nixonians to fulfill their promises of changing law through the Supreme Court, as many of the key liberal decisions were still supported by at least five justices: Fortas, Douglas, Black, Brennan, and Marshall. So immediate fulfillment of Nixon's promises for the court seemed out of his reach for the time being.

And Abe Fortas did not want to help Nixon's cause by resigning after the Senate debacle. However, the embarrassment of being turned down as well as the stain to his reputation led some to think for a time that he might just resign anyway. "He [had been] looking for an excuse" to get off the court prior to 1968, explained Paul Porter. "He talked about it many times."[4] In the middle of the Senate fight, former Yale law school colleague Fred Rodell worried that Fortas had become "deeply discouraged" and was "talking vaguely at times of resigning."[5] But on the frequent occasions when he expressed this sentiment, his friends would talk him out of it through a combination of kidding and appeals to his patriotic duty.[6]

Signs that the justice had returned to his former combative self came just one day after the Senate's refusal to vote on his nomination. The occasion was a celebration of the one hundredth anniversary of the Fourteenth Amendment at the New York University Law School. Ironically, the man introducing Fortas was his predecessor on the Supreme Court, Arthur Goldberg. After expressing his "profound regret at the wrongful action of the United States Senate," Goldberg explained that following the nonvote, his wife had called Fortas and reminded him of Benjamin Franklin's dictum "Do not in public life expect immediate approbation of one's services. One must persevere through insult and injury." It sounded much like the "greatness is not happiness" message that Fortas had sent to Lyndon Johnson during the depths of the

Vietnam War. And it required a response. So, halfway through his own speech, Fortas brought the audience to its feet for a three-minute ovation by departing from his text to look back at Goldberg and say, "Tell Dorothy that so far as I am concerned I shall persevere."[7]

By now, Fortas made it clear that even if he had been inclined to resign before the 1968 fiasco, the outcome of the debate had stiffened the justice's resolve to remain on the court at least for the time being. "I did not have my heart set on the post—far from it; and I've survived," Fortas wrote to attorney Adolf Berle.[8] His allies were heartened by the justice's new outlook. "Abe seems to have survived the ordeal very well. It was sad and disgraceful," close judicial ally William O. Douglas wrote to their mutual friend Fred Rodell.[9] Even Paul Porter commented to others about how well Fortas was taking the defeat.[10]

It would not be long, though, before Abe Fortas regretted his decision to remain on the Supreme Court. In short order it became apparent that the confirmation fight had strained his friendship with his court mentor, had sharpened the antagonism with his court adversary, and would eventually result in the ruination of his reputation forever. By remaining on the court, Fortas changed a "what might have been" debate into a series of unpleasant answers that soon became all too clear.

The first indications of damage from the confirmation fight came in Abe Fortas's relationship with William O. Douglas. A vain and egocentric but brilliant man, Douglas fancied himself the leader of the liberals on the revolutionary Warren Court, even though he most often wrote legal opinions only for himself. Now here he was, sitting on the Supreme Court with his protégé, Abe Fortas, and that protégé had deeply disappointed him in the confirmation fight. Douglas complained to Fred Rodell about the way Fortas "threw off" on him in the hearings, in an effort to separate the two men in the senators' minds. How could Fortas portray his own mentor as a "leftist" who was moved only by what he thought should be the result in the case, while portraying himself as a moderate relying on "reason and history" to decide cases? Douglas asked. In the time to come, Fortas might have to pay "a price" for this posture that "he may find excessive," Douglas added.[11]

Whether this was a prediction, a hope, or a promise was not clear. But it scared Rodell, who wrote back that he knew of nothing to indicate that Fortas had been denying the influence Douglas had had upon him in order to get confirmed. To prove this, Rodell included with his letter a copy of his article defending Fortas in *The New York Times Magazine*.[12] But as Douglas read the piece, he could not help but notice that Fortas was quoted as saying, "You must have noticed that I by no means vote regularly with Bill on antitrust and other regulatory matters."[13] Indeed, by this term Douglas was fifth among the justices in agreeing with Fortas on cases, with conservatives Harlan and Stewart close behind. No matter what Rodell said, Douglas had made up his mind about Fortas's attitude toward him.[14] (And he was correct in that determination, as evidenced by Fortas's effort to separate himself from Douglas on obscenity cases in the letter to the editor of the *Washington Star* bearing Edward Bennett Williams's name.)

By the 1968 court term, Fortas had been on the high bench long enough to provide the skeleton of his judicial philosophy, but much of the fleshing out remained to be done. It was now apparent how much Fortas envisioned himself in the tradition of his judicial hero, Louis Brandeis, in creating his own form of "sociological jurisprudence."[15] Rather than philosophizing about the legal precedents of the issues before the court, Fortas preferred to examine the practical, real-world consequences of his decisions, based on his analysis of the "progression of history," social science, current business practices, and of course his own view of the spirit and "fairness" of the Constitution. This led him at times to take very different approaches from the rest of the court in the areas of press rights, criminal justice, voting representation, and business law. What resulted, then, was a series of refinements on the basic "conservative on business, liberal on most individual rights" stance that Fortas had adopted in his first term on the court.

In one freedom-of-the-press case, Fortas continued to indicate his displeasure with the press and his preference for upholding the rights of the aggrieved subjects of published stories. In a case involving published libelous charges of criminal behavior, made by a candidate against a public official in the middle of a campaign, Fortas argued, "The First Amendment is not a shelter for the character assassinator, whether his action is heedless and reckless or deliberate. . . . The public official should be subject to severe scrutiny and to free and open criticism. But if he is needlessly, heedlessly, and falsely accused of crime, he should have a remedy in law."[16]

It was in the area of criminal justice, though, that Fortas's form of sociological jurisprudence seemed to propel him into interesting divergences from his colleagues' views. Fortas seemed to be crosscut by his love of the rule of law, leading him to want to provide all possible protections for the defendant, and his understanding of the real-world consequences of providing those protections, leading him to want to cut back on some of the court's rulings. So at times, most especially in the area of providing counsel for the accused, which would guarantee the rule of law for everyone, Fortas seemed to be way out in front of his colleagues. At other times, though, he seemed to be warning that certain decisions must not be taken to their logical extremes.

Unquestionably, Fortas was a bona fide liberal in defending the rights of the accused. He was particularly interested in ensuring that the fight between the accused and the state be a fair one, through his expansive reading of the due process clause of the Fourteenth Amendment. When the police extracted blood from a protesting defendant to determine its alcohol content, Fortas dissented from his colleagues' decision affirming the practice. "Under the due process clause, the state, in its role as prosecutor, has no right to extract blood from an accused or anyone else, over his protest."[17] Then, when the state failed to report information favorable to the defendant during the progress of a rape trial, Fortas found that to be a violation of due process as well.[18] And in a case involving an alcoholic who had been convicted of public drunkenness, Fortas displayed great compassion for those who could not help themselves. Relying on an impressive array of citations of psychological and sociological studies, he argued against the majority's upholding of the conviction. For him it was a "cornerstone of the relations between a civilized state and its citizens [that] criminal penalties may not be inflicted upon a person for being in a condition he is powerless to change."[19]

Fortas also read a liberal interpretation into the Fourth Amendment's search and seizure protection and the Fifth Amendment's self-incrimination provision. In a case where the majority upheld the right of police to search for "mere evidence" of a crime, as well as the instrumentalities and fruits of that crime, Fortas argued, "Such searches, pursuant to 'writs of assistance,' were one of the matters over which the American Revolution was fought. The very purpose of the Fourth Amendment was to outlaw such searches, which the Court today sanctions."[20] And in analyzing the breadth of the self-incrimination protection of the Fifth Amendment, Fortas explained his faith in the clause: "It prevents the debasement of the citizen which would result from compelling him to 'accuse' himself before the power of the state. The roots of the privilege are deeper than the rack and the screw used to extort confessions. They go to the nature of a free man and to his relationship to the state."[21] Fortas was horrified by the court's

willingness to allow the police to compel suspects in a lineup to repeat
the words used while committing a crime in order to aid an identification process. The result of this "compulsion of the will of a man is to
deny and defy a precious part of our historical faith and to discard one
of the most profoundly cherished instruments by which we have established the freedom and dignity of the individual. We should not so
alter the balance between the rights of the individual and of the state,
achieved over centuries of conflict."[22]

For Fortas, the rule of law could be ensured only by providing the
accused with the counsel of an attorney whenever the accused and the
state interacted—a much more generous approach than that of his liberal brethren. In discussing whether a defendant should have counsel
present when compelled to provide investigating police with a handwriting sample, Fortas wrote that only a lawyer could safeguard the
rights of the accused. "An accused whose handwriting exemplar is
sought needs counsel: Is he to write 'Your money or your life?' Is he
to emulate the holdup note by using red ink, brown paper, large letters, etc.? Is the demanded handwriting exemplar, in effect, an in-
culpation—a confession?"[23]

It was the attempt to provide protections for those who could not
protect themselves that led Fortas to establish his leadership role on the
court in matters involving the rights of juvenile defendants. Seeking to
extend the effort he had launched in the *Kent* v. *United States* case, Fortas
used his opportunity to write the majority opinion on *In re Gault* to create
a "Bill of Rights" for juvenile defendants. Fifteen-year-old Gerald Gault
had been taken into custody on charges of making lewd telephone calls.
When Gault was committed to the state industrial school after a hearing, a
suit was filed alleging that he had been denied various due process
guarantees. In examining the record, Fortas discovered a variety of
failings in the Arizona juvenile court procedures. From then on, he ruled,
juveniles would have to be given "adequate written notice" of the
charges that had been filed, and be afforded guarantees against self-
incrimination in any subsequent proceedings. Fortas also insisted that
counsel also be present at all times, that the juvenile be warned about the
existence of this right, and that counsel be provided at state expense if the
defendant could not pay. Finally, a juvenile would be given the rights of
confronting the opposing witnesses and of seeing any sworn testimony
taken from other witnesses for the purposes of cross-examination. All of
this made for a particularly broad set of protections for juvenile defendants.

Even more important than this new set of guarantees was Fortas's flowing language in the opinion and his vast body of citations of supporting psychological, historical, and sociological data. It was clear that given time he would be willing to write into law a still greater set of protections for juvenile defendants. As Fortas argued, "It would be extraordinary if our Constitution did not require the procedural regularity and the exercise of care implied in the phrase 'due process.' Under our Constitution, the condition of being a boy does not justify a kangaroo court."[24] So, while the court did not rule on the guarantee of an appeal from juvenile court hearings, or the free provision of a transcript of the proceedings for that purpose, it was clear that given time Fortas would provide those as well. Based on his performance in *Gault*, the rest of the court seemed sure to follow.

Occasionally there were limits to the protections for defendants that Fortas would enforce. In cases involving the application of the Sixth Amendment's jury trial rights to states, Fortas seemed to be warning his liberal colleagues about going too far in their decisions. The question was whether the "incorporation" of a guarantee in the Bill of Rights into the due process clause of the Fourteenth Amendment, thus making it applicable to the states, should be done "jot for jot," forcing the states and the federal government to observe precisely the same strictures. When the Warren Court seemed willing to achieve this sort of uniformity, John Harlan brilliantly warned his colleagues of the dangers of this approach. Uniformity, he said, could be achieved only by raising all the various rules of individual states to the same level as the federal government's, or by watering down the federal standard to the lowest common denominator of the most lax state standard. Fortas placed himself in Harlan's camp. Like his hero Brandeis, Fortas was willing to look at states as laboratories for innovation in their criminal procedure: "We should be ready to welcome state variations which do not impair—indeed, which may advance—the theory and purpose of trial by jury."[25] In another case, Fortas later summarized his stop sign for his colleagues in this area when he wrote simply, "Our Constitution sets up a federal union, not a monolith."[26]

The area of voting representation under the Fourteenth Amendment was another area where Fortas wanted to call a halt to the Warren Court's revolution. The rest of the court was in a rush to extend the "one man, one vote" equal representation rule outlined in *Reynolds* v. *Sims* to every conceivable type of election. Instead of insisting on rigid mathematical adherence to this catchy but impossible-to-implement slogan, Fortas preferred to look at the actual operation of the election at issue, and the consequences of a judicial decision for securing truly

equal representation.[27] "Constitutional commandments are not sur-
gical instruments," Fortas wrote. "They have a tendency to hack
deeply—to amputate. And while I have no doubt that, with the growth
of suburbia and exurbia, the problems of allocating local government
functions and benefits urgently requires attention, I am persuaded that
it does not call for the hatchet of one man, one vote. It is our duty to
insist upon due regard for the value of the individual vote but not to
ignore realities or to bypass the alternatives that legislative alteration
might provide."[28]

While he was elaborating on these liberal themes in the individual
rights area, Fortas continued over the years to be as conservative in the
business area as ever. For him, the notion of a restrained judiciary in
the area of business, combined with his understanding of how the real
world of business actually operated, led to a simple rule: "Bigness is
not necessarily badness." This, of course, was just the opposite of
what liberals William O. Douglas and William Brennan were holding.

No case better illustrated Fortas's probusiness stance than *Baltimore
and Ohio Railroad* v. *United States*.[29] This was a challenge, launched
by three minor rail carriers, to a decision by the Interstate Commerce
Commission (ICC) to allow the merger of the Pennsylvania and the
New York Central railroads. Writing for the majority, Tom Clark ruled
that the commission had erred in allowing the immediate consummation of the merger before the full challenge of the smaller railroads
could be heard and considered. Fortas was outraged by this decision.
For him, the question as to the legality of the merger should be left
with the ICC and not the courts. "The ICC has found that the merger
here will result in economies and efficiencies aggregating $80,000,000
annually by the eighth year, which it asserts will enable the roads to
effect the badly needed modernization of their facilities. This may be a
step in the wrong direction, as my Brother Douglas argues; but we
have neither the franchise to say so nor the power to do better."[30] By
ruling against the ICC, he charged, Clark had changed settled law and
usurped the powers of the statutorily empowered governing agency.
Fortas argued that the judicial role in such merger cases should be
different: "I think, with all respect, that the Court's decision in this
case is wrong in principle and unfortunate in consequence. It is a re-
version to the days of judicial negation of governmental action in the
economic sphere. We should be conservative and restrained, I think,
where all we can say is *no*."[31] But the liberals—opting for activism
on behalf of government controls over businesses and in favor of
smaller businesses—were not with Fortas on this one.

* * *

The evolution of Fortas's judicial philosophy exacerbated his problems with Hugo Black. During the 1968–1969 term, the agreement scores on cases would reflect that Black agreed with every other member of the court more often than with Fortas.[32] It seemed, too, that Black was taking on his junior colleague in an even sharper way than he had before.

The scene of the battle shifted once more to the South, as the court examined the teaching of evolution in public schools.[33] Bringing to mind the 1925 "Scopes monkey trial," many states in the so-called Bible Belt had passed laws prohibiting the teaching of evolution in public schools. In this case, a public-school teacher named Susan Epperson was challenging Arkansas's "anti-evolution" statute. The Supreme Court unanimously agreed to overturn the law. When Abe Fortas was assigned the majority opinion, however, Hugo Black decided once more to make an issue of how to write the ruling.

Fortas decided to overturn the Arkansas law on the narrowest possible constitutional grounds, saying that enacting this fundamentalist Christian view opposing the teaching of evolution constituted a violation of the First Amendment's establishment-of-religion clause.[34] "The overriding fact," Fortas wrote, "is that Arkansas' law selects from the body of knowledge a particular segment which it proscribes for the sole reason that it is deemed to conflict with a particular religious doctrine; that is, with a particular interpretation of the Book of Genesis by a particular religious group."[35] This lack of religious neutrality by the state negated the policy.

Hugo Black did not see the *Epperson* case the same way. For him, it was not an establishment-of-religion case, but one touching on the right of southern states to control their own public school curricula. So, in a concurrence that read more like a dissent, Black accused his junior colleague of arrogating too much power to himself and the court: "The Court, it seems to me, makes a serious mistake in bypassing the plain, unconstitutional vagueness of this statute in order to reach out and decide this troublesome, to me, First Amendment question. However wise this Court may be or may become hereafter, it is doubtful that, sitting in Washington, it can successfully supervise and censor the curriculum of every public school in every hamlet and city in the United States. I doubt that our wisdom is so nearly infallible."[36]

Black launched another attack against Fortas's intellectual integrity in the case of *Tinker* v. *Des Moines School District*. In cases such as this one in the 1968 term, Fortas had the chance to begin carving out his niche as a liberal in the free-speech area. He even seemed willing to consider a form of Hugo Black's absolutism here. So long as the speech was nonviolent, and did not touch on the interests of others, Fortas seemed willing to go to near-incredible lengths to protect it. No other governmental interest, unless demonstrated by overwhelming evidence, would override the free-speech right.

The *Tinker* case involved the efforts of public school students John and Mary Beth Tinker and Christopher Eckhardt to protest the Vietnam War by wearing black armbands to school during the holiday season. In response, the school administration had instituted a new regulation banning the wearing of such armbands, and expelled the students after they refused to remove the circlets.

The case came down to a conflict between the right of students to engage in a peaceful symbolic protest and the right of the schools to control the learning environment. Fortas was assigned the opinion for a 7–2 majority, and established that students and teachers are protected by the First Amendment even in the school environment. For Fortas, this "symbolic protest" was as close to "pure speech" as one could get. Since no words had been uttered, for him the wearing of the bands served as a silent, symbolic reminder of the war that was being fought. Thus the test used by Fortas put the judicial thumb on the free-speech side of the scale: "In order for the State in the person of school officials to justify prohibition of a particular expression of opinion it must be able to show that its action was caused by something more than a mere desire to avoid the discomfort and unpleasantness that always accompany an unpopular viewpoint."[37] With this test, the holding in this case seemed straightforward. There was no "evidence that the school authorities had reason to anticipate the wearing of the armbands would substantially interfere with the work of the school or impinge upon the rights of other students."[38] All in all, liberals could not have asked for a more stalwart defense of free-speech interests. It was clear that Fortas was prepared to defend any form of nonviolent protest with the full power of his mind and pen.

As one might expect by now, Hugo Black saw this very differently: "The Court's holding in this case ushers in what I deem to be an entirely new era in which the power to control pupils by the elected 'officials of state supported public schools . . .' in the United States is in ultimate effect transferred to the Supreme Court." For him this was not a silent protest, but a vicious, calculated attack by students against the American way of life. The result of this judgment was plain to Black: "School discipline, like parental discipline, is an integral and important part of training our children to be good citizens—to be better citizens. Here a very small number of students have crisply and summarily refused to obey a school order designed to give pupils who want to learn the opportunity to do so. . . . This is the more unfortunate for the schools since groups of students all over the land are already running loose, conducting break-ins, sit-ins, lie-ins, and smash-ins. . . . I, for one, am not fully persuaded that school pupils are wise enough, even with this Court's expert help from Washington, to run the 23,390 public school systems in our 50 States. I wish, therefore, wholly to disclaim any purpose on my part to hold that the Federal Constitution compels the teachers, parents, and elected school officials to surrender control of the American public school system to public school students."[39]

To all of this Fortas had an answer—one of us is reading the Constitution literally, and it appears to be me. "The Constitution says that Congress (and the States) may not abridge the right to free speech. This provision means what it says. We properly read it to permit reasonable regulation of speech-connected activities in carefully restricted circumstances. But we do not confine the permissible exercise of First Amendment rights to a telephone booth or the four corners of a pamphlet, or to supervised and ordained discussion in a school classroom."[40] By now, it seemed clear that neither justice would agree with the other, no matter what was said. But things were destined to get even worse.

Open warfare finally broke out between Black and Fortas in the case of *Gregory* v. *Chicago*. During the discussion of this case, Abe Fortas found out where he really stood with his senior colleague from Alabama. In Earl Warren's own words, Dick Gregory's battle with Mayor Richard Daley's city of Chicago was a "simple case." Gregory, accompanied by the Chicago police, had led a group of protesters in a peaceful march from city hall to Daley's residence in order to press for the desegregation of the city's schools. When the onlookers became unruly, the police demanded that the protesters disperse. After they refused, Gregory's group was arrested.

The unanimous court had no trouble in concluding that the protesters had been well within the exercise of their First Amendment rights. They had been peaceful and orderly; no evidence existed in the record to indicate otherwise.[41]

The problems came not from the actual decision, but from the way it was reached. Initially, Hugo Black was assigned the opinion. Going in a direction different from his colleagues', he struck down the disorderly conduct statute as overbroad. Now openly hostile toward civil rights demonstrations, though, he was strongly critical of those convicted under that law. When Black circulated his opinion, none of his colleagues were willing to sign it. Trying to be the mediator between Black and the liberals, William O. Douglas spoke with Fortas and Brennan, and then convinced Black to make a number of changes in the early draft. While the result was not wholly to Douglas's satisfaction, he agreed to join the Black opinion, expecting that the others would follow after further tempering changes were made.

As it turned out, Douglas had guessed incorrectly. Brennan was not satisfied, and Fortas, who had written his own short opinion in the case, became "more and more incensed" with Black as time went on.[42] Writing to Douglas that he could not sign Black's opinion, Fortas mockingly complained about its language on "boisterous and threatening conduct that disturbs *tranquility*." "What the hell doesn't?" Fortas asked.[43]

While the relationship between Fortas and Black had never been good, it seemed to Douglas that it was now worsening rapidly. The two men became "very cool" toward each other. Then Fortas began complaining that Black's early draft in the *Gregory* case had been nothing more than a direct attack against his own opinion.[44] And he was right.

Fortas had written a concurrence that, amplifying on his *Brown* opinion dealing with demonstrators in a public library, once again outlined his philosophy protecting nonviolent demonstrations. For Fortas, acceptable governmental regulation did not include the right to ban such behavior, only to circumscribe it in a manner consistent with the ability of the rest of the populace to enjoy access to the same spaces. So, Fortas said he was agreeing with all of the decisional parts of Black's opinion, but none of his reasoning. While this concurrence was never published, and from its form was probably never intended to be published, it did indicate to the rest of the court Fortas's horror over the language of the Black draft opinion.[45]

If it was the *Brown* case that Fortas wanted to resurrect, though, then Hugo Black was all too willing to refight that battle. Toward the end of his published opinion, Black argued, "Were the authority of government so trifling as to permit anyone with a complaint to have the vast power to do anything he pleased, wherever he pleased, and whenever he pleased, our customs and our habits of conduct, social, political, economic, ethical, and religious, would all be wiped out, and become no more than relics of a gone but not forgotten past. Churches would be compelled to welcome into their buildings invaders who came but to scoff and jeer; streets and highways and public buildings would cease to be available for the purposes for which they were constructed and dedicated whenever demonstrators and picketers wanted to use them for their own purposes. And perhaps worse than all other changes, homes, the sacred retreat to which families repair for their privacy and their daily way of living, would have to have their doors thrown open to all who desired to convert the occupants to new views, new morals, and a new way of life. Men and women who hold public office would be compelled, simply because they did hold public office, to lose the comforts and privacy of an unpicketed home." Then, in case anybody missed the point, Black concluded this paranoid vision of peaceful demonstrators as storm troopers with "Picketing and demonstrating can be regulated like other conduct of men. I believe that the homes of men, sometimes the last citadel of the tired, the weary, and the sick, can be protected by government from noisy, marching, tramping, threatening picketers and demonstrators bent on filling the minds of men, women and children with fears of the unknown."[46]

As it turned out, there was more working here than just the obvious gulf between the judicial philosophies of the two justices. There was now a very real personality clash between them. The question for Abe Fortas was why his old mentor, Douglas, was siding with the enemy, Hugo Black, rather than with him. For Fortas there was no middle ground. At this point, Chief Justice Warren had no choice but to take over and write a short opinion that the rest of the majority could quickly sign.

Warren created a problem for Douglas, who wanted to sign the new majority opinion but had also given his word that he would sign Black's revised opinion. So Douglas diplomatically avoided a controversy by joining both opinions.[47] This outraged Fortas, who "complained bitterly" to his mentor over the decision to remain associated with Black's opinion in any way. While Douglas was not too happy over the result either, he felt that he had no choice.

From that point on, Douglas observed, the relationship between Fortas and Black "grew worse and worse." Only then did he find out the cause. Fortas had discovered the incredible truth about one of the remaining mysteries from the previous year's confirmation fight. He learned that it was Hugo Black who had persuaded Alabama Senator Lister Hill to "come out against" his nomination.[48]

Once Fortas learned that fact, his relations with Black were beyond repair. The result was an almost unprofessional version of judicial warfare that did nobody any good. Hugo Black continued his attacks on Fortas, while the junior justice began to lob some mortar shells back. Black chose to make his most withering attack against Fortas to date in a closely contested case involving police lineup practices. A man named Foster had been subjected to what is commonly called a showup lineup, without benefit of representation by counsel. The defendant, who had been arrested for armed robbery of a Western Union office, was put in a lineup with two other men who were nearly six inches shorter than he, and only Foster was told to wear a leather jacket similar to that worn by the robber. When the manager of the Western Union office could not positively identify the suspect, Foster was brought in to face the witness alone, and then several days later placed in another four-man lineup. Finally, the manager became "convinced" that Foster was the culprit.

In writing the opinion for a five-man majority, Fortas continued his argument from previous cases that the lineup procedure was a "critical stage" in the judicial process, which mandated that the protection of counsel be provided for the accused. Here, the repeated confrontations between the suspect and the witness, and the conduct of those confrontations, presented to Fortas "a compelling example of unfair lineup procedures."[49] He concluded that, in effect, the police had repeatedly said to the witness, "*This* is the man," resulting in a procedure that "so undermined the reliability of the eyewitness identification as to violate due process."[50]

In a dissent that was more than twice as long as Fortas's majority opinion, Hugo Black disagreed violently with every aspect of this analysis. After supporting the police conduct of the lineup, he concluded that the majority was using its own personal view of "unfair" lineup practices, rather than relying on the Constitution, which "does not anywhere prohibit conduct deemed unfair by the courts."[51]

Then, in a second section of his opinion, Black used the occasion to comment on the entire body of Fortas's judicial work in the area of the Fourteenth Amendment due process clause. Black argued that his colleague's views would do nothing more than "encourage judges to hold laws unconstitutional on the basis of their own conceptions of fairness and justice. This formula imposes no 'restraint' on judges beyond requiring them to follow their own best judgment as to what is wise, just, and best under the circumstances of a particular case." And of course, this view was very different from Black's own restrained, literal reading of the Constitution, which "plainly tells judges they have no power to hold laws unconstitutional unless such laws are believed to violate the *written* Constitution."[52]

Fortas had endured all these attacks in uncharacteristic silence. In fact, his only response had been the private anger vented to William O. Douglas. Perhaps it was his sense of etiquette, or his view of the role of a judge, that kept him from responding publicly to Black's attacks. But the revelation about the Lister Hill vote, and this last extraordinary personal attack in the *Foster* case, seemed to be more than even Fortas could endure. So, for the first time, he began to fire back.

While Fortas was justified in lowering his cannons, he chose only to fire shots across Black's bow in two minor cases. In a case involving a complaint against the U.S. Steel Corporation's use of a subsidiary credit company to arrange financing for land on which that company's prefabricated houses were to be built, Black wrote a majority opinion declaring this to be a "tying" arrangement, which was therefore a per se violation of the Sherman Antitrust Act. Fortas attacked the ruling as unrealistic, its effects as actually restricting competition, and its author as a shoddy scholar. "The effect of this *novel extension*—this *distortion,* as I view it*—*of the tying doctrine may be vast and destructive," Fortas concluded.[53] Three weeks later, in a jurisdiction case involving the interpretation of an amendment to the Federal Rules of Civil Procedure, Fortas attacked another of Black's majority opinions: "Now the Court, for reasons which in my opinion will not stand analysis, defeats the purpose of the amendment as applied to cases like those before us here and insists upon a perpetuation of distinctions which the profession had hoped would become only curiosities of the past."[54] There seemed little doubt that Fortas had come to see his colleague Black as another of those "curiosities of the past." And, given the difference in their ages, Fortas was confident that he would dominate the future.

Late in the court's term, Fortas got a chance to begin adding more flesh to his judicial philosophy of the First Amendment. The case involved a man named Street who, upon hearing that civil rights leader James Meredith had been shot, had taken an American flag to a nearby street corner and burned it. What might have been simply symbolic speech became speech itself when Street also said at the time, "We don't need no damn flag. If they let that happen to Meredith, we don't need an American flag." Writing for the court, John Harlan reversed the conviction for mutilation of the flag, largely because of the possibility that the conviction might have resulted from the words that had been uttered, rather than for the flag burning itself.

Fortas indicated the limits to his free-speech protection by drawing the line at flag burning. This did not fit under the nonviolent form of protest that Fortas was willing to protect. Instead, he viewed it as "an act of desecration," which was to be tested by the standard governing "conduct" rather than speech. This meant that, in order to be upheld, the regulation or prohibition must be "reasonable, due account being taken of the paramountcy of First Amendment values."[55] For Fortas the flag was a special form of personal property that itself was the symbol of a nation, and thus subject to protective laws. The fact that the flag had been burned as a form of protest did not for Fortas immunize the demonstrator against prosecution: "One may not justify burning a house, even if it is his own, on the ground, however sincere, that he does so as a protest. One may not justify breaking the windows of a government building on that basis. Protest does not exonerate lawlessness. And the prohibition against flag burning on the public thoroughfare being valid, the misdemeanor is not excused merely because it is an act of flamboyant protest."[56]

While liberals worried about whether this meant that Fortas was backsliding in his defense of free-speech interests, he was already working on two majority opinions destined to thrill them. In the first one, the University Committee to End the War in Vietnam, operating at the University of Texas at Austin, had run afoul of the law in protesting Lyndon Johnson's war policy. When the group members traveled to nearby Central Texas College to protest a speech by Johnson, they were accosted by soldiers from nearby Fort Hood, arrested, and charged with disturbing the peace.

Why Lyndon Johnson's main adviser on this war did not feel that he should step down from hearing this case, called *Gunn* v. *Committee to End the War,* is open to serious question. Not only was this group protesting against the war he had supported, but it was groups like this that had convinced his best friend in the White House not to run for reelection. Nevertheless, Fortas decided to sit in the case, and drafted an opinion for the six-man majority. Proving his ability to segment his personal and his professional views, Fortas held for the protesters. He argued, consistently with his strongly written views in favor of peaceful protest, that the Texas "disturbing the peace" statute, banning "loud and vociferous" language, was much too vague to override the free-speech interests involved. For him it did not matter whether the protesters had been "loud and vociferous," because much political debate could fall in this category. Furthermore, the determination of the decibel level of such debates was much too subjective to use as a basis for limiting First Amendment rights.[57]

While that draft was being circulated among the justices, the court was just waiting to announce Fortas's other major First Amendment decision that term, in the case of *Brandenburg* v. *Ohio*. Clarence Brandenburg, a leader of the Ohio Ku Klux Klan, had been convicted of violating the Ohio criminal syndicalism law. This statute prohibited advocating terrorism as a means of achieving political reform, and assembling to teach or advocate the doctrines of criminal syndicalism. Here a reporter at a KKK "rally" had filmed the burning of a wooden cross by twelve members of the group, one of whom was Brandenburg. This case was identical to a series of earlier cases in which the legendary team of Louis Brandeis and Oliver Wendell Holmes had announced and explained the doctrine of "clear and present danger." While ostensibly a test for balancing the right of free speech against the right of a government to regulate speech in order to protect itself, in fact the test went a long way toward protecting nearly all kinds of speech. Only when the connection between the speech and untoward conduct could be shown to be "immediate" would the words be controllable.[58]

Unfortunately for Fortas, though, this "clear and present danger" doctrine had been substantially altered by the court in a later case, and was not viewed as a workable test.[59] So in *Brandenburg,* he seemed to wipe the slate clean by saying that only speech that incited "imminent lawless action" could be punished by the state. When one examined the new doctrine closely, however, it was plain that this was just the old "clear and present danger" test in new packaging. Using this generous new test, Fortas had little difficulty in striking down the vaguely worded Ohio act, which could be used to punish "mere advocacy" of ideas as opposed to action, and even peaceable assemblies for such discussions.[60]

Like the *Gunn* draft, this new *Brandenburg* opinion persuasively reasserted Fortas's desire to bend over backward to protect free speech. Even Hugo Black was impressed with this opinion, and after failing to convince Fortas to strike any reference to the "clear and present danger" test, with which he did not agree, he decided to concur in the result.[61] Together with Fortas's *Tinker* opinion, issued earlier in the term, these new cases would establish and solidify his reputation on the court as a leader of the liberal defenders of free speech. Given his analytical and writing ability, it seemed likely that in time Fortas would be able to write doctrines, similar to the "imminent lawless action" standard that he had just crafted, which would protect free speech for decades to come. Maybe one day his First Amendment opinions would be remembered with those of Holmes and Brandeis.

But such was not to be the case. After agreeing to the *Brandenburg* draft, Justice Harlan suggested that Fortas wait to announce the final decision until after Black had finished his work on two related opinions.[62] Since the court's term was coming to an end in a few weeks, Fortas readily agreed. Perhaps instead he should have been warned by the other events then transpiring in his personal life that it would have been wiser to issue the opinion as fast as possible.

Because of those events, Fortas's name was destined never to be attached to his *Brandenburg* opinion. Instead, that decision was issued by the court as an unusually long, unsigned *per curiam* opinion, after being only slightly altered by William Brennan from the final Fortas draft.[63] Moreover, the *Gunn* case, which was not as far along in the drafting process, would be set for reargument the following term, and Fortas's opinion remained unpublished.

In many ways, this was Abe Fortas's most turbulent term on the court, but also his most productive. With Lyndon Johnson gone from the White House, Fortas was now able to concentrate all his considerable energies on the judicial tasks at hand. He showed a willingness, despite the severe clashes with Black, to strike out in some bold new directions, especially in the free-speech area. But what remained to be accomplished soon became only a source of speculation for historians. Perhaps Abe Fortas himself put it best: "Maybe if I stayed on the Court long enough I'd have discovered a Fortas under the Fortas under the Fortas. But it didn't happen."[64]

There wasn't time. The venomous forces that had been unleashed against Fortas in the bitter confirmation battle could not be turned off like water from a spigot. More than that, the new president in whose name some had fought this battle, Richard Nixon, was now in a position to make things happen. Only later did Fortas come to realize the bind he was in. "They had [my seat] promised," he told an acquaintance. "They had it promised—Nixon had it promised to Thurmond."[65]

XXIV

DEATH ON THE SUPREME COURT

Richard Nixon had promises to keep. He had promised in the 1968 presidential campaign to produce his "secret plan to end the war," to end the eight uninterrupted years of financial profligacy by the Democrats, to change the government's civil rights policy, and to "walk softly and carry a big stick" in foreign policy—especially with the big Russian bear. But more than all of this, he had promised to bring back "law and order"—even if it was done over the bodies of a few judges here and there. Finally, correctly or not, Abe Fortas believed that the president had made a promise to Strom Thurmond. However, presidents quickly find out that promises made on the campaign trail in September and October are difficult to keep once in office. And the promises that are most difficult to keep are those concerning the judicial system, where the judges you have lambasted on the campaign trail now must help you out by either retiring on the spot or dying. Not even President Nixon had power over the departure of sitting members of the federal court system. Or so everyone thought.

They did not know, however, that on one more issue Fortas was vulnerable, terribly vulnerable. And by October 1968, a good many people in Washington—ranging from the Justice Department staff to Jacob Javits and even to anonymous tipsters—seemed to have a sense of that fact. But not enough had been known by this time about the connection between Fortas and Louis Wolfson to make the information public. That is, until William Lambert of *Life* magazine, the same reporter whom Fortas had so brusquely handled in the 1964 investigation of Lyndon Johnson's personal finances, came along.

"Why don't you look into the relationship between Fortas and Wolfson?" a "low-level" bureaucrat asked Lambert while he was working what he called his "vacuum cleaner" operation on October 28 around different government offices.[1] So the stocky bookish-looking reporter with horned-rimmed glasses began to explore the tip. By all accounts a "relentless" investigator, he needed only "about four" calls to discover that "money had been exchanged" between Wolfson and Fortas, which naturally raised questions inside the Internal Revenue Service about any income taxes involved, and that the justice had taken a trip to the financier's horse farm in Florida.[2]

But as Lambert continued to dig, the reaction of his sources told him even more than the substance of their comments. When government sources discovered that the queries concerned the legendary counselor behind the Johnson throne, they were "all but div[ing] under their desks." Having investigated the mob in the Pacific Northwest, fraudulent veterans' organizations, and even the finances of the great Lyndon Johnson, the reporter was accustomed to having to dig for a story. But he had never seen such reluctance by potential sources to speak. "Don't ask me any questions; don't even tell me anything," one fellow told him. "I don't want to know." Lambert did ask, though—and providing he got the right sort of help he would unravel the mystery.[3]

But not if Abe Fortas could help it. On Saturday, November 9, 1968, the outgoing attorney general phoned the justice to ask if he could come out to Fortas's fashionable Georgetown house to speak about a private matter. The night before, United States Attorney Robert Morgenthau had called Ramsey Clark from New York with the news that *Life* magazine was about to run a story on Fortas's financial connection to Wolfson. The news of the two men's personal contact did not come as a complete shock to Clark. Sometime earlier Fortas had spoken to him about Wolfson, making it apparent that they were acquainted. Clark could see that the justice was "fiercely loyal" to his friend, and that "it was a genuine feeling," as Fortas recounted how Wolfson in his view had been "mistreated" by the SEC and the courts. For Clark, though, this was just another example of a man who was noted for his devotion to his friends simply expressing his outrage over the course of events.[4]

Once more Clark had cause to regret the fact that no new FBI investigation had been run on Fortas when he was nominated to become chief justice. Like the American University disclosure, this new trouble was coming as "a complete surprise" to the Johnson administration.[5] The attorney general was "kind of disappointed about it, to say the least," but since he and the justice were friends and mutual admirers, he was ready to hear any explanation that Fortas might have to offer. After listening to Clark's warning at the house, Fortas phoned his secretary because she kept all of his financial books and records. Whether a man of Fortas's prodigious memory had actually put the entire connection with Wolfson out of his mind, including the transfer of twenty thousand dollars just twenty-three months before, or whether this whole scene was carried out for the benefit of the attorney general can never be known. Whatever the case, the news was better than could have been hoped. "Well, I paid that money back," Fortas proclaimed after listening to the voice at the other end of the phone line. "I decided that I couldn't do it."

It seemed to Clark that this was another of those paid lectureship arrangements reminiscent of the American University connection. Fortas's only fault here, to Clark's way of thinking, was continuing his active concern in the area of civil rights even to the point of maintaining associations from the high bench. "I guess[ed] he just didn't want to be out of it," he would explain later.[6] And this time Fortas seemed to have had the good sense to sever the relationship.

So with the administration in its last days, rather than pressing forward with an unseemly inquiry about a matter that seemed fully under control, Clark worked on polishing his tribute to Fortas on the occasion of the hanging of his portrait at Yale Law School just six days after their difficult meeting. (Six months later, though, when another phone call to the former attorney general from New York informed him that his earlier concern had been justified, he would have cause to regret one step not taken. Since he had not troubled the president with the rumor, Lyndon Johnson would read about it for the first time with the rest of America.)

*   *   *

By now, Abe Fortas had become a *cause célèbre* for the defeated liberal movement. And the gala evening in New Haven commemorating the unveiling of Fortas's official portrait at Yale Law School proved that fact. So many people had accepted the invitations to attend that the guests spilled out into the hallway of the law school.[7] Much later, some of the guests would reflect on how exceedingly difficult the evening must have been for the guest of honor. Only he knew how much there was left to hide and, most crucially, how close some people were to finding out the full truth about him.[8]

To all outward appearances, not even the prospect that his face might be smeared on the cover of *Life* in just three days could dampen Fortas's combative spirit on this occasion. "I am told that a few days ago a certain Senator was advised that the Yale Law School is going to hang Justice Fortas. He said, 'It's about time.' He said, 'It's the only good thing I have ever heard about that institution.' But I want to assure all of you that . . . I have discovered that a hanging is much to be preferred to a lynching." The audience roared with approval and applause.[9] However, one of Fortas's most popular jokes that evening, given the events that followed, would later be remembered with great irony. "As I look at that [picture]," Fortas concluded, "I just want to tell you, Dean, that any time that a substantial group in this Law School, say nine-tenths of the student body, disagrees with any of my votes on the Supreme Court, you are hereby authorized to turn my portrait to the wall."[10]

But as he stood at the podium, basking in the waves of glorious applause and looking at the portrait that would hang in a place of honor in the center of the law school library, Fortas could not have known the sad fate awaiting it. In just six short months, rather than being turned to the wall, it would instead be repeatedly moved farther and farther from the center of the library's traffic flow, until it was finally stashed in a side faculty lounge where only school meetings were held and no outsiders could see it to ask embarrassing questions. Then, one day—whether it was removed or just stolen nobody really knew—the picture would simply disappear from sight, never to be seen again.[11]

For now, though, all seemed well. When Clark and Fortas checked *Life* magazine the following week, the warning from New York seemed to have no merit—there was no article. With each passing issue, the danger seemed further and further removed. Finally, Clark just put the matter out of his mind.[12] But William Lambert didn't.

Once more, it was the well-intentioned, but ineffective, Paul Porter who unwittingly placed the justice in more danger. Following Ramsey Clark's suggestion to get in touch with *Life* magazine and explain that the Wolfson payment had been returned, Fortas had asked Porter to become his agent in the negotiations.[13] So, on December 10, Lambert spoke to the justice's former law partner, seeking confirmation of the few facts that he now had.[14] There was every reason for Porter, who much later would "assume personal responsibility" for the American University fiasco and who had also been so totally ineffective in his lobbying efforts during the Senate battle, to want to make amends here.[15]

Unfortunately, in displaying his usual hospitality as a raconteur, Porter accomplished two things—both of which damaged Fortas's chances for escape. First, he confirmed to Lambert that such a payment had been made by Wolfson, even offering a rough approximation of the size of the fee. Then Porter added that the money had been returned by the justice that same year. "Abe had a whole sackful of petitions for writs," he stated; "the business of the Court took so much of his time he couldn't do the work for the foundation." But Porter was vague as to the nature of this "work" and it was not clear to Lambert why Fortas could not have foreseen the time crunch just eleven months earlier.[16] So the meeting served only to pique the reporter's interest in the case further.

Lambert needed help, and Richard Nixon's men were only too happy to provide it. It did not take geniuses to see the delicate state of Fortas's political health. After the Senate debate the mere hint of one more skeleton in the justice's closet was all that was needed by the new administration to bring a flood of negative opinion crashing around him. Given the aura of mystery around Fortas, the 1968 revelations had seemed to confirm all of the public's worst fears as to his behavior. With people ready to believe *anything* now, this attitude, if properly tapped, could become fatal. And the Nixonians knew it.[17]

It was Fortas's bad luck that the assistant attorney general in charge of the Criminal Division of the Department of Justice for Richard Nixon—the agency investigating whether the justice had violated the Internal Revenue Code—was fifty-six-year-old Will Wilson, a man whose hostility toward Lyndon Johnson at that time may well have matched the level of the justice's devotion. Later, Fortas would understand that once again he had been caught in the backwash of Lyndon Johnson's accrued political enmities: "The real truth about this was that they were bound and determined to get me because of my association with Johnson. . . . They were going to get me."[18]

The story here was Wilson's unrequited political ambitions, and the perhaps justifiable impression that Lyndon Johnson had been responsible for his failures. The two men had first met back in 1948, when Wilson was the district attorney in Dallas and Johnson was first running for the Senate. Their contacts were limited until 1960 when Lyndon Johnson, in running for the vice presidency on a ticket with liberal John F. Kennedy, called on Wilson for help. With old friends in Texas so angry about Johnson's acceptance of the nomination, he was finding Democratic help in his home state, whose electoral votes he was expected to deliver, very hard to line up. But Wilson agreed at Johnson's personal request to become the state organizational chairman for the presidential campaign. And indeed, the Kennedy-Johnson ticket was able to carry the crucial state of Texas.[19]

For all of his efforts while other Texans sat out the campaign, actions that cost Wilson "many of [his] lifetime supporters," no real rewards were forthcoming from the new administration. So Wilson turned his attention to the state arena. After an unsuccessful race for Johnson's Senate seat, Wilson launched a drive for the governorship in 1962.

When word came out from Washington that Johnson's old friend Secretary of the Navy John Connally would be returning to his home state as one of the Democratic candidates, Wilson went to Washington to ask for the vice president's help in preventing this candidacy. Wilson argued that a number of prominent Texas Democrats had gone out on a limb for the liberal Democratic presidential ticket, and, whether anything was said or not, Connally's entry in the race would make it appear as though the administration was supporting a candidate against those initial allies.

Despite Wilson's most persuasive appeals, Johnson said that while he "hoped Connally wouldn't make the governor's race," he had no control over his actions. "I didn't really believe that at the time," states Wilson.[20] So the friendship between Lyndon Johnson and Will Wilson ended. As did the latter's state political career, with his defeat at the hands of Connally. "I was mad at the time," Wilson confessed later, "but that's long since gone." Of course, Wilson's generous spirit may well have been nurtured by the events that transpired in the next presidential administration.

Thanks to Richard Nixon's team, good things started to happen for Wilson in 1969. In return for supporting Republican John Tower for a Senate seat in Texas, Wilson was appointed to the Justice Department.[21] It seemed to be a good match. Wilson appeared to have the sort of zealous attitude that John Mitchell wanted. "Let me have this job," the Texan said in his interview, "and I'll guarantee you that organized crime in America will be gone in six months!" To which Mitchell later responded, "The distinguished former Texas attorney general has a big surprise in store for him."[22] But the big surprise would be Mitchell's, as Wilson would help to ensure that a Supreme Court justice would be gone in six months—and a close friend of Lyndon Johnson's at that.

Wilson got his chance when he invited William Lambert to his office on April 10, 1969. The reporter had put aside his investigation of Fortas until April 1, when the Supreme Court had announced that it was refusing to hear Louis Wolfson's appeal, thereby upholding his criminal conviction. Once more, Lambert was intrigued when he noted that Fortas had refused to sit on the case, indicating to him that there was some kind of connection to Wolfson. (Ironically, since the court never announces why a justice has declined to sit on a case, Lambert did not realize that Fortas's action here stemmed from the fact that Wolfson's attorneys were from the justice's old law firm. Lacking that understanding, Lambert was free to assume that the action had to do with the financial relationship between the two men.) By this time, though, all that Lambert had uncovered were the dates of the financial transactions, and rumors that the financier had dropped the justice's name to investigating authorities.

The conversation with Wilson lasted about forty minutes, with Lambert doing most of the talking.[23] When he first heard about Fortas's potential difficulties, Wilson later candidly confessed, he "was excited about the prospect. I knew what kind of a potential coup we had. In all candor, we wanted Fortas off the Court."[24] Wilson realized that this might be a quick and convenient way of keeping the new president's promises to change the direction of the court. So he launched his own investigation of Fortas, making the matter a top priority for the Justice Department.

For the next two weeks Lambert unsuccessfully tried in every way possible to get confirmation of his story from either Fortas or Wolfson. Fortas cavalierly responded to the reporter's request for an interview by writing, "Since there has been no impropriety, or anything approaching it in my conduct, no purpose would be served by any such meeting."[25]

Fortas refused to speak to the reporter at that time for good reason. Just as Lambert was closing in on the justice, the law was closing in on Wolfson. And the financier was seeking help from his prominent friends. Since one of those friends not only served on the Supreme Court but also retained close connections to the retired president in Texas, Wolfson had a special favor to ask. "Abe, I want you to do something for me," he wrote on April 11. "I cannot go to prison right now; if you could do anything to get me a Presidential pardon—have President Johnson call Mr. Nixon."[26] It was, Wolfson later told Fortas, "the only time I ever asked you for one thing." So he expected help—but none was forthcoming.[27] Wolfson could not have known that, given the timing, the idea of Fortas doing *anything*, let alone undertaking a quixotic quest for a pardon, on his behalf at that time was unthinkable.

But just about this time, in the words of one archivist, "something very odd" *was* done in the Johnson Library in Austin, Texas. Most extraordinarily, while the library's thirty-one million documents were being categorized, all of the Wolfson letters—the originals and all copies—were pulled out of the various locations in the White House Central Files and put into a single folder. Then the newly created file was lost. (Not until it was requested by a researcher sixteen years later would an alert archivist rediscover it.)[28]

It is hard to know precisely who, or what, motivated this effort to purge the Johnson White House files of any connection to Louis Wolfson. In and of itself, the file of over two dozen letters and memos seems relatively harmless. In fact, a number of the letters make it clear that while the financier had once lived near Senator Johnson's home in Georgetown, the personal relationship was not close at all.[29] Perhaps it was felt that letters showing a campaign contribution of one thousand dollars from Wolfson, combined with letters detailing the repeated efforts of the Wolfson family to secure assistance in handling his legal problems, would be embarrassing.[30] Or perhaps someone concluded that a 1966 letter from the now-embattled justice to Johnson on Wolfson's Merritt-Chapman and Scott company activities relating to civil rights, and a letter from Wolfson to Fortas about their meeting in January 1967 in Miami, seemed to portray just the sort of cozy relationship that, if it surfaced in response to inquiries by government and press investigators, would prove to be just one more embarrassment for Fortas.[31] For whatever reason, these materials would not come to light during the controversy.

Meanwhile, Wolfson's pleas for help in Washington did not stop with Fortas. He wrote to Florida Senator Spessard Holland and "several other lawmakers" asking for help in approaching Richard Nixon for a presidential pardon. Normally Holland, one of the ultraconservative southern Democrats who provided the crucial swing votes in the Senate for the Nixon administration, could have expected a swift audience with the president. But this time the request was denied. And all John Mitchell would tell Holland was that "clarifying developments would make clear why it was unwise for Mr. Nixon to become involved."[32]

But William Lambert did not have reason to be as confident about the course of events as Mitchell. Without a confirming second source or some verifying documents, it would be impossible for *Life* to run the story.[33] And no one in a position to know seemed willing to help the reporter. No one, that is, except for Will Wilson, who had both the legal clout and the inclination to use it.

Following the conversation with Lambert, the assistant attorney general made himself the point man in the early effort to end the public career of Lyndon Johnson's closest friend on the Supreme Court.[34] But even in conducting his own parallel investigation, Wilson found it difficult to confirm and expand on the *Life* reporter's information. This was the first that he had heard about Fortas's problems, even though Johnson administration holdover Fred Vinson, Jr., was still in the Justice Department winding up the Democrats' business. As enticing as the news was, the Nixon people had more than enough to keep them busy without adding this new investigation to the agenda.[35] So Wilson passed Lambert's information on the Fortas-Wolfson connection along to Attorney General John Mitchell. Since Mitchell was also hearing about the matter for the first time, he, in turn, began to keep President Nixon informed as well.[36]

It was clearly up to the Nixon Justice Department to lead the investigation, since Wilson had understood Lambert to say that, despite all of his efforts, there was not enough evidence to proceed into print. The key, the Nixonians knew, lay in compelling Louis Wolfson to provide testimony against Fortas. So John Mitchell launched a series of conferences with William Bittman, the convicted man's attorney. A tough "law enforcement–minded attorney," Bittman had made his reputation in the Justice Department in the prosecution of Jimmy Hoffa and was seen by the Nixonians as an exceedingly hard bargainer.

At the time, wanting to appear completely nonpartisan in their involvement in this case, the Nixon people led the press to believe that they had "flatly refused any promise of leniency for Wolfson—either now or later." In fact, just the opposite was true. Bittman was negotiating for a plea bargain involving Mitchell's intervention in the New York indictments and other problems, in return for Wolfson's full statement about his relationship with Fortas.[37]

Wilson and Mitchell quickly realized, though, that even if they were so inclined, such a deal was nearly impossible for them to accept. First, there was really very little left for them to offer Wolfson. After the refusal of the Supreme Court to review his case, Wolfson was scheduled to enter jail on April 25 on the Continental Enterprises case and had already been sentenced in the Merritt-Chapman case pending further appeals.[38]

Even more difficult for the Justice Department officials were the problems of dealing with Robert Morgenthau, the ultratough prosecuting United States attorney in New York. It is not surprising that Morgenthau's office had been unimpressed by rumors that a Supreme Court justice might well intervene personally in the Wolfson case. The son of Henry Morgenthau, Jr., who had served as secretary of the Treasury under Franklin D. Roosevelt, the U.S. attorney had already prosecuted such luminaries as the chairman of the New York Stock Exchange, Truman Bidwell, and a former dean of the Harvard Law School and chairman of the Securities and Exchange Commission, James Landis.[39] And though it had been in power less than half a year, the Nixon Justice Department was already having trouble "getting along" with Morgenthau.

Thinking that Bittman could not have known of this problem, but was well aware of Morgenthau's toughness, Wilson and Mitchell decided to run a bluff. They used the prosecuting attorney's toughness as a wedge, telling Bittman that he could either deal with them or take his chances with Morgenthau. After "two or three" conferences, the two sides "reached an understanding." The result would be a statement given by Wolfson given to the FBI after the *Life* magazine article was published. Of course, Richard Nixon was fully informed about all of these matters. After all, as Wilson later put it, "Fortas was in the enemy camp."[40]

The exact details of the deal are not known, but what is known is that after serving only nine months of an eighteen-month sentence, Wolfson was released from prison.[41] Whatever the arrangement, though, Wolfson later complained that the Justice Department's side had not been fulfilled. It could well have been that the financier expected to be paroled a few months earlier. However, that application had been denied. (The Justice Department had promised that it would use its "good offices" to intercede with the United States attorney in New York, Wilson would later explain, but when it was over Wolfson did not think "our offices were good enough.")[42]

Though Wolfson would not speak to either the Justice Department or Lambert until after the *Life* article's publication, he did give an interview to *The Wall Street Journal* shortly before entering prison, which served only to add some fuel to the fire. The lead sentence was enough to pique everyone's interest: "If Louis Wolfson is to be believed, he could have obtained a Presidential pardon last December, sparing him the anguish of a prison sentence." According to the convicted man, he was assured of such assistance "from somebody who is as close as anybody could be" to Lyndon Johnson.[43] But Wolfson added that he had refused the offer because "he didn't want any favors" (no doubt a surprise to both Fortas and Senator Holland).[44]

Wilson continued his own investigation, but by late April he knew little more than Lambert.[45] Meanwhile, the reporter's attempts to get confirmation had stalled out, and his April 30 press deadline, nearly six months to the day from the first tip on the story, was looming large. He had only one hope for the story—Nixon's Department of Justice.

In the weeks that followed, Democrats would charge that the Nixon administration "may have helped" *Life* magazine in the production of the damaging Fortas piece. Though Lambert, trying to protect the identities of his sources, was understandably silent, this charge was indeed true.[46]

Lambert returned to the office of a senior Justice Department official and told him that he still needed confirmation of the story. When assistance was not immediately forthcoming, the reporter pressed: "I will not run the story unless I have confirmation of it." So, even though Justice Department files about an ongoing investigation are confidential, the official confirmed the story. This was all that Lambert needed to proceed. With that, the Nixon Justice Department had now become an accomplice in the production of the story.[47]

In point of fact, the Justice Department official's confirmation was almost completely groundless. Because of the ineffectiveness of the government's investigation of Fortas and the deal with Wolfson's attorney, the department had yet to see the actual documents about which Lambert was reporting, and had not yet spoken to Wolfson himself. The Nixon official knew, though, that confirming the story anyway would ensure its publication. And, as it turned out, it was the publication of Lambert's piece that helped to set in motion the next phase of the government's investigation. But Lambert could not have known that when he felt secure in proceeding with his scoop.

Up to this point, even with the press and the Justice Department closing in, Fortas had been the picture of cool confidence. Just over two weeks earlier he had been at a White House dinner with Richard Nixon honoring the retiring chief justice, and jokingly remarked to the press corps shivering from the air conditioning, "The Republicans may have turned on the lights, but they turned off the heat." Then the night prior to the release of the *Life* article, even knowing that rumors as to its imminent publication were flying all around official Washington, the embattled justice had whiled away the evening hours at a charity dance.[48]

When the Lambert piece was released to the news media on May 4, it indicated the incomplete state of the reporter's knowledge about the Fortas-Wolfson relationship. But even this sketchy information was more than enough to cripple the Supreme Court justice once more. The six-page revelation, provocatively entitled "Fortas of the Supreme Court: A Question of Ethics," opened with huge portraits of the principals in the story, captioned "The Justice . . . and the Stock Manipulator." The story revealed only the bare essentials of the arrangement—the single payment of twenty thousand dollars from the Wolfson Family Foundation to Fortas, expressly provided for work on "educational and civil rights projects." "Whatever services he may or may not have rendered in this respect," Lambert then noted, "Justice Fortas's name was being dropped in strategic places by Wolfson and [his partner Buddy] Gerbert in their effort to stay out of prison. That this was done without his knowledge does not change the fact that his acceptance of the money, and other actions, made the name-dropping effective."[49] After reporting that the money had been returned, Lambert was careful to indicate that "by that time Wolfson and Gerbert had been twice indicted on federal criminal charges." Then, using a diary entry format to indicate the dates of the various transactions and meetings with Fortas in relationship to Wolfson's work, all that was left was for Lambert to ask, "Aside from legal advice [to the trustees on civil rights projects, as Fortas's wife had explained], what manner of counseling service could Fortas perform for the foundation that would justify a twenty thousand dollar fee? In the light of other recorded foundation expenditures, the amount seems generous in the extreme.''[50]

Given the chance by Lambert to respond in the piece to the charges, Fortas wrote the reporter a letter that conceded little: ''My only 'association' with Mr. Wolfson had to do with conversations beginning when I first met him in 1965, in which he told me of the program of the Wolfson Family Foundation in Jacksonville to promote racial and religious understanding and co-existence and to provide financial assistance, on a non-denominational basis, to candidates for the clergy.'' While nothing was admitted about any financial connection between them, the justice did recall his visit to Wolfson's ''famous horse farm'' and attendance at a meeting of the family's foundation in June of 1966. However, he added, ''I did not, of course, participate in any of Mr. Wolfson's business or legal affairs during that visit, nor have I done so at any time since I retired from law practice.''

After he read the article for the first time when it was released to newsmen on Sunday, May 4, 1969, Fortas's sense of cool did not desert him. But other old and dangerous habits reappeared. Since judicial propriety required that the publication of the article be answered, Fortas changed his strategy from one of denial to one of evasion. Perhaps thinking back to his past as a Washington lawyer, where he had been able to find the technical loopholes and write clients out of trouble, Fortas tried to do that for himself. But in so doing he made the same two mistakes that had haunted him in the 1968 confirmation battle. First, he gambled that the subsequent investigations would fail to corroborate Lambert's charges. But even worse, he told less than the whole truth—cynics might say he just plain lied. Here, once more, Fortas failed to understand that the reporters would continue to dig until they found the full story. And in this case their instincts were right.

The inadequacy of the normally eloquent Fortas's ''explanatory'' press statement now served only to encourage them. ''Since I became a member of the Court: (1) I have not accepted any fee or emolument from Mr. Wolfson or the Wolfson Family Foundation or any related person or group,'' he began. Perhaps to the lawyer in Fortas the payment from Wolfson had not been ''accepted,'' in that it was no longer in his possession, but at the very least it had been ''held'' for a period of nearly a year. Then, while it may not have been a ''fee,'' in that it was not payment for services rendered, it had certainly been given in anticipation of work to be done in the future.[51] And Fortas knew that without the actual contract letter, no one would know that this payment, whatever one might call it, was supposed to be only the first of many.

Regardless of whether they knew all the facts, reporters were still able to see the loopholes and contradictions in Fortas's defense of himself. Just four paragraphs later in the statement, the justice wrote, "In 1966, in the hope that I would find time and could undertake, consistently with my Court obligations, research functions, studies and writings connected with the work of the foundation, the Wolfson Family Foundation *tendered a fee to me*. Concluding that I could not undertake the assignment, I returned the fee with my thanks [italics added]." It is hard to know whether it was worst for the justice to give the impression that people were just throwing money at him, to neglect to explain that it had taken eleven months to return the fee, or to contradict his own denial that he had received payment. So apparent was the contradiction that it became the focal point of Fred Graham's piece in *The New York Times* the following day.[52]

Fortas was no more honest when it came to discussing his relationship with Louis Wolfson personally. After explaining that the "tender of the fee" had not been motivated by the expectation of legal help, and that he had not "communicated with any official" with respect to the financier's cases or the chances for a pardon, the justice added, "At no time have I given Mr. Wolfson or any of his family, associates, foundations or interests any legal advice or services, since becoming a member of the Court." Even if Wolfson had done all of the talking, at the very least the two men had still had "legal discussions"—but that was not what Fortas chose to deny.[53] (Later even Fortas himself would concede in speaking to Wolfson that a contrary conclusion could easily be drawn about their relationship: "Now, in some of these letters that I wrote you and in many of the letters you wrote me there are long discussions or short discussions of the SEC problems and this and that and what goes on. [And others] would construe some of the things that I wrote to you as being legal work . . . although it did not amount to a damn thing.")

But Fortas vastly overestimated the benefits of his making any statement in his own defense. It would not matter to the American public whether a monetary payment, whatever its kind, had been returned or not. The mere appearance of a Supreme Court justice taking money even for an hour under such circumstances was damaging. Even worse, after the American University scandal of just seven months earlier, the public was prepared to believe almost anything regarding Abe Fortas and money.

"I guess I have made full disclosure," he had said in 1968, challenging the Senate Judiciary Committee to find more. With this new statement Fortas was saying the same thing to the press and the Justice Department in 1969. And once more, he was safe only so long as people did not discover his secret—the Wolfson letters and contract.

The Justice Department let it be known that it was not about to give up the search. As if to prove that fact, word came that Arnold and Porter was now under federal investigation concerning allegations of delaying the production of evidence in a case. While the Nixon administration dutifully expressed embarrassment at the timing of the story, there was no question that by leaking a secret grand jury investigation of an action taken two years after Fortas had left the firm, John Mitchell and company were turning up the heat on the justice one notch at a time.[54]

With the publication of Lambert's piece, a "tide of indignation and revulsion" swept over Washington's high political circles.

The questions from the press were predictable. "Serious questions of propriety are raised by the financial relationships of Associate Justice Abe Fortas. . . . It is doubtful that any judge, particularly one sitting on the highest court, should have substantial outside involvements in any area of private remuneration," editorialized *The New York Times*.[55] "The situation in which Justice Abe Fortas finds himself is, or should be, a source of acute embarrassment to him," added the *Washington Star*.[56] And, saying that his action with Wolfson had "irreparably harmed his usefulness on the high court," the *Los Angeles Times* called for Fortas's resignation.[57] Soon, *The Washington Post*, the *Chicago Tribune*, and the *New York Daily News* would demand the same.

Even more predictable were the gleeful calls for resignation from the justice's opponents of the previous year. Strom Thurmond said Fortas should consider whether "the faith of the people in the integrity of the Supreme Court would be better served by his resignation." Robert Griffin said the *Life* article "raises most serious questions which need to be resolved." Congressman H. R. Gross of Iowa bluntly labeled Fortas "a glorified fixer" and called for his impeachment if he failed to resign. Senator John Williams of Delaware, while offering a bill revoking the tax-exempt status of any foundation offering money to sitting public officials, said, "There is no excuse for the members of the Supreme Court to accept these outside legal fees on the basis of financial need."[58]

Predictably, Fortas's once-burned allies in the Senate seemed to be among the angriest following his explanation. In the Senate dining room, William Proxmire threw his arms up in the air and exclaimed, "I can't understand it. I just can't. What does he need that $20,000 for? He's a wealthy man. His wife has a lucrative law practice. They have no children to educate, to send through college. Why did he do it?"[59] A poll by *The New York Times* could find *no* Democrats in Congress now supporting Fortas. Indeed, one observer recalls that with only one exception, Fortas's Senate supporters from the previous year's confirmation fight were so angry that they would not even discuss his name any longer. The one senator who was talking used the occasion to utter nothing but obscenities and threats against the justice.[60] Even Thurman Arnold now said, "Thank God that he didn't get to be Chief Justice."[61] All the early signs following the *Life* article pointed to the justice's being in deep, deep trouble.

Old habits die hard, though, and Fortas still felt confident that he could rescue his good name. So, after falsely proclaiming his innocence in public, the justice made his second self-destructive move, which, while totally in character, caught even John Mitchell by surprise.

"Fortas wants to come see me," exclaimed a puzzled Mitchell to Will Wilson, explaining that the justice had just phoned to ask for an appointment. It was so typical of the Washington-lawyer-on-the-court, who believed that he could solve everything with a few mellow words in private conference. But the move baffled the Justice Department officials. Here was the same foolishness that had led Fortas to face the Senate Judiciary Committee in his own defense so confidently the summer before. But just as on that occasion, the justice was doing the equivalent of putting a loaded gun to his head and asking his enemies whether they cared to pull the trigger.

In fact, Fortas could not have picked a worse time to approach Mitchell, who was now dealing from a position of great strength. With the publication of the *Life* magazine piece on Monday, May 5, the Internal Revenue Service stepped up its investigation by issuing a subpoena that day for the Wolfson Family Foundation records relating to the relationship between Fortas and Wolfson. The delivery of six documents to the revenue agents on May 6, portions of which were then transcribed for the attorney general, and one of which was the actual

Fortas-Wolfson contract letter, gave Mitchell more than enough evidence to put Fortas in jeopardy.[62] It was *this* material that the senior Justice Department official had implied was in the department's file when he confirmed Lambert's initial story, thus ensuring the publication that made further revealing investigation possible. Now, though, the only question was what to do with the actual packet of material.

Meanwhile, Washington was afire with rumors about Fortas. In a meeting on May 6, congressional leaders asked Mitchell, "Are there more developments in the Fortas matter than have come to light in the *Life* article?" He responded from across the cabinet table with a simple, but ominous, "Yes." That same day Spessard Holland's unsuccessful lobbying effort on behalf of Wolfson found its way into print, and the public once again began to smell blood. At the same time, overlooking his Justice Department's complicity in all of this, Richard Nixon maintained a superficially reserved public posture, pleading with congressional leaders not to do "something rash" by prematurely discussing impeachment (thus planting the idea in their minds).[63]

Knowing all of this, Wilson gave Mitchell the proper advice regarding any thought of a meeting with Fortas. "John, I don't think that's a good idea," he offered. "I've been a prosecutor too long not to know that you don't want a personal relationship" with the object of an investigation. Indeed, forgetting the personal politics for the moment, the mere hint of a private conference with the justice during an ongoing inquiry was certain to blow up in the Nixonians' faces. But the call from Fortas had forced their hand. So Wilson came up with the idea that many others would later credit to Richard Nixon. Reasoning that it was proper to speak to the *attorney* of the man in trouble, Wilson suggested that the person most analogous to Fortas's attorney now would be Earl Warren. So he convinced Mitchell that someone from the Justice Department should go see the chief justice and reveal the fruits of their investigation. Of course, both men realized that such a meeting would serve not only to blunt Fortas's exculpatory efforts, but also perhaps prod the court to do something about its errant member.[64]

Without question, Fortas's "Mr. Fix It" attempt served only to speed up the building pressure against him. For no one on the court could have been less receptive to Mitchell's news than Earl Warren. Warren had already shown his distaste for noncourt activities by his unequivocal Shermanesque withdrawal from consideration for a presidential nomination in 1956 ("God couldn't draft him," one justice said) and his great reluctance to head the Kennedy assassination investigation in 1963.[65] Now, even with scandal surrounding one of his allies on the Court, the chief justice refused to become involved. In fact, by one former law clerk's account, he was "very disappointed in it and disillusioned by it."[66]

When John Mitchell met covertly with Earl Warren at 11:30 on the morning of Wednesday, May 7, he carried with him a packet of documents in a carefully sealed envelope.[67] The contents of this envelope have been the subject of speculation for years—certain circles in Washington even suggesting that some of the material contained allegations of Communist activities by Fortas during the New Deal. Later, it was rumored that to avoid press leaks the items were kept under Mitchell's "personal lock and key," never transferred to the general department files, and taken with him when the administration abruptly ended.[68] (Even Fortas believed this story, later telling Wolfson, "The whole thing has been sealed in the Department of Justice so that it will not get out. Justice has got it all buttoned up.")[69]

But no one had counted on Chief Justice Warren's reaction. Realizing the historical importance of these materials, before transmitting the original documents back to the attorney general with a cover letter implying that he had kept no file on the issue, Warren had made copies of everything on the Supreme Court's single overworked photocopying machine. Those copies, containing the answers to one of the remaining mysteries from this tragic episode, remained sealed in the chief justice's files until a decade after his death.[70]

The surprising thing about these documents is how remarkably little the Justice Department knew about Fortas's connection with Louis Wolfson three days *after* the *Life* magazine article had been published. This was true despite the fact that the article had gone into print based on the department's confirmation of the validity of its contents.

What the Nixonians had, though, was more than enough to damage Abe Fortas's credibility with the chief justice seriously. The entire five-page packet handed to Warren by Attorney General Mitchell consisted of the transcriptions of six documents—portions of the minutes from two Wolfson Family Foundation meetings and four letters between Fortas and Wolfson. At first glance, the sum total of this meager file seemed only to detail the establishment of the consulting relationship between the two men. As such, all the file did was confirm the earlier charges by Lambert.[71] But it was the final document in the packet that had caused the attorney general to gasp when he saw it for the first time just hours before this meeting, and no doubt had the same effect on the ultra-ethical chief justice.[72]

The government investigators had finally discovered the formal contract letter. Just so Warren would not miss the best part, someone had thoughtfully drawn two highlighting lines in the margin next to the fifth paragraph. For the first time, the chief justice now knew that the twenty-thousand-dollar payment was not a one-time deal, but was to recur yearly for the rest of Fortas's life *and that of his wife.* Not even the note at the bottom of the transcription indicating that this arrangement had been "cancelled" could mitigate the shocking questions raised by this new evidence.[73]

Despite all of Mitchell's dramatic evidence, there was something very encouraging about it for the chief justice. First, there was no question now that long ago Fortas had indeed canceled the arrangement and returned the money. Then, too, there was not one shred of evidence that Fortas had done anything improper by way of intervening in the legal troubles of Wolfson. But Warren knew that action now had to be taken.

For his part, Fortas was confidently counting on the fact that the Justice Department could not add to the evidence file, and was telling friends, "I'm going to ride this thing out."[74] For a while, this must have seemed to him to be a pretty good gamble. Mitchell never would discover an equally damaging letter from Wolfson to Fortas dated January 11, 1967. Written a full month after the justice had unilaterally ended their agreement, the letter discussed the unproductive meeting between them in Miami that month.[75] Had the Justice Department found this document, it might well have had reason to doubt that the agreement had ever really been canceled and might have been able to ask even more embarrassing questions.

However, the strength of the evidence against Fortas was not the most important factor now. Rather, it was the *manner* in which the investigative material was used that would be the key to fulfilling Richard Nixon's promise. John Mitchell, spurred into action by Fortas's own suicidal blunder, had already discovered that in dealing with Earl Warren. Even if Louis Wolfson did not confirm their suspicions that the justice had actively intervened in the criminal investigation, the right pressure might be brought to bear to ensure Fortas's departure from the Court.

By now, the Nixon administration had developed allies everywhere in pressuring Fortas. For the remainder of the week, the justice tried to maintain a public posture of joking confidence about his problems. Seeing no reason to curtail his heavy speaking schedule, on May 8 he journeyed to Boston's Northeastern University to speak to thirteen hundred people on "The Generation Gap." It was a curious subject for the man whose best friend in the White House had been victimized by this phenomenon. The auditorium was packed, the klieg lights were burning, and the news media's still and movie cameras were in evidence everywhere. Meanwhile the center of attention innocently looked around the room and joked, "I can't imagine why all this interest." But others could—and they wanted some answers. Since under the ground rules of the lecture no one was permitted to ask about the Wolfson scandal, a crowd of reporters surrounded Fortas's car as he left the hall, shouting out questions. "No, no, no," answered their target.[76]

As Fortas prepared for his next lecture, reports circulated that the Supreme Court itself had asked Fortas for an explanation. The truth, though, was that the chief justice had decided on a different course of action. Given what he had seen already, Warren could only assume that more information was now in the hands of the Nixon administration and would soon surface. Moreover, he knew that the investigation, which by its very existence was potentially devastating to the court's prestige, would continue. Unless, of course, something was done to stop it. And that something, Warren knew, was nothing less than a resignation. So he decided to move his colleague in that direction.

Thinking that the matter could be handled privately with a little conversation between gentlemen, Warren asked Hugo Black to speak with their embattled colleague. Only if Fortas called first, was Black's answer. (Warren's choice of a messenger here—Fortas's worst enemy on the court—may well have been a not-so-subtle indication to the junior justice as to what the chief wanted to happen.) When Fortas called the Blacks' residence at 8 A.M. on Saturday, May 10, it was quickly apparent, contrary to all outward appearances of confidence, how devastated he was by these attacks. Black's wife, Elizabeth, barely recognized the "hurt, weak voice" on the phone asking for her husband. No longer the superconfident presidential counselor, Fortas sounded to her like a "broken-hearted sick man" who, reeling under the effects of repeated assaults on his character, had not slept in a long time.

If Fortas was looking for support from Hugo Black, and if Warren was hoping Black would deliver a harsher message, both men were to be disappointed. Black's sense of compassion moved him to mix his signals. When he met Fortas two hours later at the court building, it quickly became apparent that Black was just as fastidious about the ethics of the court as Earl Warren. Having once plotted to get Fortas *on* the court, Black now started out the meeting by trying to get him *off* it. Elizabeth Black recorded in her diary that her husband was "sick about this whole mess." Were it his choice, Black said to Fortas, he would resign to preserve the reputation of the court. But Fortas resisted now for a curious reason. A resignation, he said, would only mean more embarrassing hearings and "it would kill" his wife. Black, of course, well knew that this was the same Carolyn Agger who had originally opposed her husband's ascension to the court, and perhaps it was not she but Fortas himself who would feel destroyed. Still, Black said that he found the argument to be persuasive, and now told Fortas that perhaps he should stay and fight.

For two hours the men talked, with Black now acting as Fortas's attorney in assessing the damage. If no new evidence against Fortas came out, Black concluded, he would not have to worry about facing either an impeachment or a criminal proceeding. But there *was* something more, Fortas finally confessed. After he heard about the lifetime nature of the Wolfson contract, Black recognized what had to be done. Tell the press yourself, he advised Fortas. After all, the initial payment had been returned and the agreement had been canceled.[77]

But Fortas had a different idea. He decided to keep it secret. Had he acted immediately after speaking with Black, there might have been a chance to save whatever was left of his good name. However, too much in Fortas's past character was coming back to haunt him now. Once more, there was the confidence, or perhaps the hope, that nothing more could be discovered. The same hesitancy that had been so evident during earlier transitional stages in his career reappeared. And, whether born of confidence or confusion, Fortas's inaction now doomed him.

While Fortas debated his course of action, he could not have known that his fate was being sealed in a Florida prison. For just minutes after the conclusion of his meeting with Hugo Black, representatives of the Justice Department were talking to Louis Wolfson. And twenty-four hours later, *Newsweek* would report on the secret meeting between Mitchell and Warren.

Rather than worry, Fortas tried to bury his troubles in more work— keeping to his hectic speaking schedule. But now solace was becoming harder and harder to find. He gave his generation gap lecture to an audience in the Richmond Public Forum, carefully announcing that the speaking fee was being donated to a scholarship fund at the University of Virginia Law School. But this time Fortas got a firsthand demonstration of his own topic. As he was about to speak, one young man yelled, "Honest Abe!"—to the titters and laughter of some in the audience.[78]

Things were going no better for him on Capitol Hill. The attacks in Congress were escalating, but now they came from longtime supporters. On May 10, Senator Walter Mondale of Minnesota became the first Democratic member of Congress to call openly for Fortas's resignation. This was followed later by an angrier call from one of Fortas's most vocal supporters in 1968 on the Senate Judiciary Committee, Joseph Tydings, who said to his colleagues, "The confidence of our citizenry in the federal judiciary must be preserved. Mr. Justice Fortas must resign. He must resign immediately."[79] On May 11, Congressman H. R. Gross announced that he had prepared articles of impeachment, and the House Judiciary Committee chairman, Emanuel Celler of New York, called for "some further explanation." By the twelfth, when the Fortas speechmaking road show made a stop in his hometown of Memphis, rumors began flying around the Hill that Fortas was about to resign.[80] These reports were considered to be so reliable that Arizona Senator Paul Fannin announced that he was canceling plans to urge an investigation of the justice.

But, perhaps even more embarrassingly for Fortas, the calls for resignation started coming from members of his own profession. Letters, copies of which were sent to the chief justice, were arriving from judges on the lower federal courts, telling, not asking, this member of their superior tribunal to resign, and do so with dispatch. The time had come, they said, to think of the good of the institution itself.[81]

Sadly, Fortas still seemed incapable of action, even though the reasons for movement were certainly there. It was one thing to face hostility from politicians and the press—Fortas had been accustomed to that all his life. It was another thing to face a lack of support from his own brethren. In the face of these compelling pressures, he did nothing.

Instead, Fortas still had some fight, or rather hope, left in him. He was willing to gamble that the Nixonians would find nothing more. Just as in the 1968 confirmation battle, he underestimated his opposition.

The Nixonians had their man on the ropes, and they were not about to give up now. They hoped that the deal with attorney William Bittman had ensured that Louis Wolfson would now provide all that was needed to keep the heat on Fortas, and perhaps finish him entirely. But

Wolfson proved at first glance to be a big disappointment to the Justice Department.

With Nixon and the Department of Justice brass at Key Biscayne, Florida, for the weekend of May 9, Will Wilson and FBI agents Charles Bolz and Carter Billings flew to the federal prison camp at Eglin Air Force Base in Florida for a chat with the financier.[82] As agreed, upon first meeting him in the stark conference room at the prison, they served Wolfson with a subpoena giving the witness no choice but to respond to questions under oath, a point that was carefully made in the statement itself. Wolfson then, as arranged, proceeded to recount the entire history of his relationship with Fortas.

On its face, the statement taken from Louis Wolfson in Florida appeared to be nine pages of legal dynamite. The secrecy surrounding this document, then and now, had always led people to expect the worst in terms of its revelations about Fortas.[83] Later, Tennessee Senator Albert Gore would charge that the Justice Department used this material to "intimidate" and "blackmail" Fortas into resigning.[84] And the Justice Department, the White House, and the FBI remained silent, thus fueling even more speculation.

However, as bad as things were for Fortas, the statement by Wolfson was actually much more to his benefit than anyone has previously thought. Most of the statement served only to verify the account in Lambert's article, while sketching in a few additional details here and there. One new claim, for instance, was Wolfson's statement that he had warned Fortas about his legal troubles' being "a lot more serious than I had previously been led to believe by my attorneys and associates" *before* they had formalized their financial arrangement.[85] But for the most part, the account gave little more than a verifiable context to all of the documents that the Justice Department already had in its possession.

The key to the entire questioning, though, came down to what Fortas had actually *done* for Wolfson, specifically on his SEC and other legal troubles. This was the evidence that the Nixonians most needed, since the actual minutes of the foundation meeting attended by Fortas seemed to verify his account that his role had been a compensated "research function." So they put the question to the convicted financier.[86]

Wolfson's answer, though, was a major disappointment to the Nixonians. Fortas had not even raised a finger to help him. To be sure, Fortas had held the hand of the man who was promising him a fortune in twenty-thousand-dollar installments. In their initial meeting, Wolfson had received assurances from the justice that "the Securities and Exchange Commission investigation appeared to involve technical violations and that nothing of a serious nature would develop as a result of the investigation." Then, during their Ocala meeting in June 1966, Fortas had "again assured [Wolfson] that [he] need not worry since he still felt that these were technical violations," while also "indicat[ing] that he had or would contact Manuel Cohen of the Securities and Exchange Commission regarding this matter." But for the Nixonians, this language was too vague. An effort by Fortas to "contact" SEC Chairman Cohen could range from a request for help down to a simple inquiry about the proceedings.

It all came down, then, to the final meeting between the two men before Wolfson had gone to jail. Because the letter from Wolfson to Fortas dated January 11, 1967, had been missed by the Justice Department officials, they were learning for the first time about this meeting between the two men in the Hotel Deauville in Miami.[87] It was at that time, with the SEC indictments against Wolfson pending, that Fortas had been left with the simple choice of either offering help or stepping aside. When Wolfson again expressed his "complete dissatisfaction" with the manner in which the cases had been handled, Fortas only "agreed that [Wolfson] had not been treated fairly and expressed indignation at the Securities and Exchange Commission actions in not giving [him] a hearing as previously promised."

But had Fortas actually phoned Lyndon Johnson, Ramsey Clark, SEC Chairman Cohen—whom Fortas later claimed credit for having appointed—or anyone else on Wolfson's behalf?[88] Had he done anything more than offer a few words of support to a friend in trouble on a couple of occasions? In short, had Fortas actually broken the law and tried in any way to influence the case? Wolfson's answer to the FBI agents was unequivocal: Fortas had *"made no offer of assistance nor did he indicate he would do anything one way or the other in connection with this matter* [italics added]."[89]

If this was the smoking gun anticipated by the Justice Department, and speculated about over the years since then, it was filled mostly with blanks.

Wolfson, under oath, had cleared Fortas—most emphatically—of any complicity in his legal proceedings. All the justice had ever done was to accept and then return a payment, which constituted his agreement to and then cancellation of a long-term consultation. If Fortas was guilty of anything, one would think upon reading this document, it was of insensitivity to the Caesar's-wife appearance demanded of a judge as opposed to his old role of Washington lawyer. Or, if one wanted to make a less charitable charge, he was guilty of outright stupidity, combined with some amount of greed, in agreeing to take the money. But Wolfson had made it eminently clear that Fortas was not guilty of one thing—involvement in the financier's legal affairs from the bench. So, naturally, given the way politics and the press work, that was what the charge became.

By the time the government agents had finished typing up the statement and obtaining Wolfson's signature and handwritten corrections, it was early evening. The group immediately phoned Deputy Attorney General Richard Kleindienst at the Florida White House. So, within hours after the meeting with Wolfson, the Nixon high command knew that help in nailing Fortas would have to come from other quarters.[90]

Even though the Wolfson statement was a disappointment to the Nixon administration, it knew how political hardball could be played. It did not matter *what* Wolfson had said; the mere fact that *he* had said it was important. The only question was how best to use the new "evidence."

The Nixon administration decided to put even more pressure on Fortas by working on the rest of the court. Back in Washington, any hope that Earl Warren might have harbored for the controversy to blow over ended at 6:10 P.M. on the evening of May 12. Sol Lindenbaum, from the attorney general's office, handed him another sealed manila packet labeled ominously PERSONAL AND CONFIDENTIAL: FOR EYES ONLY OF THE CHIEF JUSTICE.

As Warren flipped through the contents of the packet, it did not take him long to discover that all but two of the documents were merely the originals of the transcribed materials left with him by John Mitchell the previous week. But this time the attorney general had also included a letter confirming the cancellation of the agreement and, of course, a copy of Wolfson's statement to the FBI. There could be no doubt now in the chief justice's mind that Mitchell was on top of a rapidly unfolding investigation.[91]

Then, too, there was the press offensive, where the administration was scoring some direct hits. Whether intending that the information reach the press or just to keep allies in Congress informed, the president and his people personally told certain members of Congress about Mitchell's visit with Warren.[92] Sam Shaffer of *Newsweek* soon learned about it, and in an exclusive release on May 12 was able to offer both an account of the meeting and the ominous warning from Mitchell to

Warren that he had "far more serious evidence" against Fortas than any information made public thus far. The implication was that it would come out unless the justice withdrew.[93] This story allowed Mitchell, after first carefully checking with Earl Warren, to twist the screws further by confirming the rumor with a suitably vague reference to his actions: "At my request, the Chief Justice was kind enough to see me in his chambers Wednesday, May 7, 1969, at 11:30 A.M. As a courtesy to the Chief Justice, I felt it incumbent upon me to inform him of certain information known by me which might be of aid to him."[94] Now everyone was just dying to know what that "far more serious" "certain information" happened to be.

The press and the public appeared ready to believe almost anything that was printed about the new "evidence." In a matter of days, the Justice Department would ominously warn *The Washington Post,* which was reported to be in possession of the "certain information," that to print it was a violation of federal law in revealing "secret" grand jury evidence.[95] It mattered little that *The Washington Post* denied ever having the documents in question, for the mere threat by the Justice Department was taken as another sign that there was even *more* damaging evidence in the Fortas file. People would never know that just the opposite was true.[96] For someone had already fired the fatal shot.

Before the bullet hit, though, it was time for Fortas to face his colleagues. The chief justice had decided to place all the Justice Department material before the whole court in a conference at 11 A.M. on the May 13. By that time, Fortas had just about decided to resign from the court. It is hard to know which straw broke his back. Fortas himself was unclear on the exact moment of decision, later saying that "the days have merged." Perhaps it was the embarrassment of having to face all of his brethren in conference. Perhaps it was the new evidence now in Warren's possession that came directly from Louis Wolfson, with the prospect that unless something was done quickly it too might leak out, further staining Fortas's name and reputation. Or perhaps, as Paul Porter later reported, it just was time for the man who had never really wanted to be on the court in the first place to take the opportunity to return to private life. "I have had it. To hell with it," Fortas told him.[97]

But before arriving at a final decision, Fortas wanted to make a full and complete statement to his brethren. He at least owed them that. He did so, he later reported, "not because the Court had any jurisdiction or any power in the matter, but because the Court is a sacred institution—like a collegium."[98]

The conference went about as well as one could expect for a discussion between a condemned man and his co-workers. According to all accounts, Warren simply laid out all of the evidence provided him by John Mitchell for the other members of the court to see. Fortas himself gave an oral explanation of his connection to Wolfson, and was careful to reaffirm that he had paid all of the money back.[99] And, according to Justice Douglas's recollection, he also "explained that while he had done nothing improper, he thought that in view of the outcry in the press, it would be in the best interests of the court for him to resign."[100] But the move had come too late to save what remained of Fortas's professional reputation.

Ironically, it may have been William O. Douglas who was inadvertently responsible for Fortas's indecisive moves at this time. Throughout the controversy, Fortas had been without the benefit of advice from his sage mentor, who was in Brazil lecturing at the Cándido Mendes legal institute.[101] The embattled justice had decided, he later told a reporter, to hold off resigning and releasing a full explanation to the press until Douglas and the other justices returned to Washington from a court recess. It was a decision that he later said had been "a mistake." Fortas explained, "Instead of being so damn duty-stricken, it would have been better to have quickly made a detailed public statement." Or, he might have added, a more truthful one earlier on.[102]

Douglas later wrote in his memoirs his account of those dark days on the court. By the time he had returned, "the hounds were in full pursuit." Thereafter, Douglas writes, "I sat up with him two nights, serving as a sounding board. . . . I urged Abe not to resign, though parts of the press were demanding it. At first Abe agreed with me, but he quickly changed. I saw him the next night and he was then resolved to resign. My son Bill was with me and he too pleaded with Abe not to resign. 'Blood will taste good to this gang. And having tasted it, they will want more,' my son said. I told Abe that if he decided to resign, to do so on his timetable, not on someone else's."[103]

The only problem with this very dramatic and oft-repeated account is that, according to Fortas, it never happened.[104] "It's an absolute fabrication . . . absolute crap," he later commented. "You have to remember that at the time Douglas wrote that he was a very sick man. He didn't know what he was doing or what he was saying." While the two justices did meet, Fortas recalled, and some of these words might well have been spoken, it was in a radically different context. *After* Fortas had made up his own mind to resign, Douglas came in to speak with him for just fifteen minutes. "I wish you wouldn't resign," he said. What did not need to be said between the two men was that Douglas himself was quite obviously in the on-deck circle for this new vicious game, with his liberal philosophy and his similar consulting relationship with the Parvin Foundation, which had raised such a flap in 1966.[105] "But Bill," Fortas responded, "it's too late. You should've told me earlier. I might have acted differently." Indeed, he might well have stuck it out a bit longer, for as Fortas explained, "I resigned to save Douglas."[106]

But given the course of events over the next several days, it seems probable that a more timely plea by Douglas would only have delayed the inevitable.[107] After facing his colleagues, Fortas sat down to offer the general public a full and final explanation of his reasons for now resigning from the court. Saying that he did not want the court to "continue to be subjected to extraneous stress which may adversely affect the performance of its important functions," Fortas devoted four pages to restating the explanation that Wolfson had already provided the government of the course of their relationship.

There was, however, one crucial difference between the two accounts, one for which no confirming letter had been found by the government. Fortas pointed out that he had resigned from the foundation on June 21, 1966, six months before he returned the twenty-thousand-dollar payment. As he explained, "There were two reasons for this decision: My work for the Court was much heavier than I had anticipated and my idea of the amount of time I would have free for non-judicial work had been a substantial overestimate. I had also learned shortly before informing the Foundation of my decision to terminate the arrangement, that the SEC had referred Mr. Wolfson's file to the Department of Justice for consideration as to criminal prosecution."

Fortas then said he kept the initial payment in anticipation of "completing the projects for the year." Whether he actually performed any real service will never be known. Fortas then explained that once the Wolfson indictments had been handed down in the fall of 1966, "I concluded that, because of the developments which had taken place, the service which I had performed should be treated as a contribution to the Foundation, and the money was returned." Even at this late date, the explanation for why Fortas had kept the money long after the arrangement's cancellation, and a minimum of two months after the second indictment had been issued, seemed less than satisfactory.

Then came the crucial denial: As Wolfson had secretly told the Justice Department, Fortas had not intervened in the cases in any way, shape, or form. "Since becoming a member of the Court, I have not, at any time, directly or indirectly, received any compensation from Mr. Wolfson or members of his family or any of his associates for advice, assistance or any reason whatever, except the Foundation fee which was returned. Since I became a member of the Court, Mr. Wolfson on occasion would send me material relating to his problems, just as I think he did to many other people, and on several occasions he mentioned them to me, *but I have not interceded or taken part in any legal, administrative or judicial matter affecting Mr. Wolfson or anyone associated with him* [italics added]."[108]

Nevertheless, Fortas knew that he had to go. As he later told Ben Bradlee of *The Washington Post,* "There wasn't any choice for a man of conscience."[109] So he explained in concluding his statement to the court, "There has been no wrongdoing on my part. There has been no default in the performance of my judicial duties in accordance with the high standards of the office I hold. So far as I am concerned, the welfare and maximum effectiveness of the Court to perform its critical role in our system of government are factors that are paramount to all others. It is this consideration that prompts my resignation which, I hope, by terminating the public controversy, will permit the Court to proceed with its work without the harassment of debate concerning one of its members."[110] Seeking to persuade the chief justice of the justification for his work with Wolfson, Fortas added to his statement to the court a private communication to Warren. "Perhaps this will make things a little clearer," he wrote, enclosing an article by Jim Bishop entitled "Wolfson's Hidden Heart," which recounted many of the financier's compassionate charitable activities.[111]

As he finished the statement, Fortas could be pleased that all of the pieces of the puzzle seemed to fit together. The only problem was that the shrouds of mystery had so clouded the public's mind already that no one would believe him. He had simply procrastinated too long. More important, he had failed to release the last bombshell—the lifetime financial contract.

So others did it for him.

As he ate breakfast on May 15, Fortas thought that he had at least a few more hours of peace left in his life. After the White House had received his resignation letter at 5:30 P.M. the day before, word came back to the court that Richard Nixon had temporarily shelved acting on it in favor of other business. That evening he announced yet another plan to end the Vietnam War, proposing a withdrawal of troops within twelve months, and he wanted the news to focus there. So Fortas was told that the resignation would not be formally accepted and released to the press until noon on the fifteenth.

Fortas's expectation of one last morning of relative solitude, however, was shattered by that day's *Los Angeles Times*. Paired with an account of the Nixon speech was another headline that screamed out at him: $20,000-A-YEAR LIFETIME OFFER TO FORTAS TOLD: PRISON STATEMENT TO FBI BY WOLFSON SAYS JURIST AGREED TO TAKE RETAINER.

As one might expect, what was reported was *not* the financier's unmistakable absolution of Fortas's role in his legal affairs. Instead, the story revealed to the public for the first time that Wolfson had spoken to the authorities and exposed the lifetime contract with the justice. But the scoop did not end there: "Some documents said to be in the possession of the government, plus Wolfson's statement to FBI agents last week, *are being interpreted by Justice Department officials to mean that Fortas appeared to be willing to assist Wolfson* in a Securities and Exchange Commission investigation of the financier [italics added]."[112] Of course, no such documents existed. And how the Justice Department "interpreted" what Fortas "appeared to be willing" to do was the weakest sort of indictment. Furthermore, in his statement to the FBI from the Florida prison, Wolfson himself had said that Fortas had "made no offer of assistance nor did he indicate he would do anything one way or the other in connection with this matter." Yet none of these comments found their way into the article. Fortas had done nothing.[113] Wolfson knew that he had done nothing.[114] The Justice Department now knew that he had done nothing. But the press, and hence the public, now believed otherwise. In Washington, he who leaks to the press first gets to determine its direction.

Fortas's gamble had failed. Not only had the last secret been discovered, but it had also been leaked in a manner guaranteed to ruin whatever might have been left of a tattered reputation. It must have seemed to Fortas as if his last ally in the world had deserted him.

For the man whose trademark was coolness under fire, it was the last straw. In the words of the chief justice, Fortas "became overwrought," and immediately breached protocol in authorizing the announcement of his resignation to the press before it had been formally accepted by the White House. "In his troubled state of mind," Earl Warren later explained to the president, Fortas did what "he would not have been moved to do . . . under normal conditions." And it took Nixon a full hour to react with a one-sentence acknowledgment. His promise to the voters had been fulfilled—at Abe Fortas's expense.[115]

The dramatic and unprecedented resignation from the court of one of the New Deal liberals' brightest stars struck different people in different ways.

The reaction of members of the press was predictably intrusive. What would he do now? they asked. "The only offer I've gotten so far is [from violinist Alexander Schneider] to be a second-fiddle player. I don't think I can practice that much any more," he responded.[116] But most expected he would return to his old law firm, Arnold and Porter. Had there been a conspiracy to remove him? they wondered. "It's just as if an automobile hit me as I stepped off the curb. I wouldn't think the driver is a fiend or an evil man. I'm not the kind of man who looks for that kind of thing."[117]

The chief justice did not quite know how to handle the situation. He was caught in a quandary between his compassion for a friend and his strong reverence for the ethics of the court. Slowly Warren had labored over his public reaction to the resignation, writing draft after draft. An early draft was much more charitable and defensive: "On behalf of the Court, I would like to express the sadness we feel on Justice Fortas' leaving us. Most of us have had the great privilege of serving with him for the past four years. During that time, he proved himself to be a learned, fair and able jurist with a deep compassion for the law and his fellow man. His decision to resign, which I know was motivated purely by his concern for the Court as an institution, is regretted not only by the Justices but by all of the personnel." Then, perhaps with Hugo Black in mind, the chief thought better of the final clause and substituted for it: "is characteristic of his devotion to it."[118] However, Warren could not bring himself to release this statement, instead relying on a much simpler and more formal declaration.[119]

Thereafter Warren tried to ease the psychological trauma for his former colleague as much as possible. When a ceremony commemorating the retirement of the chief justice was held, and Fortas chose not to attend, Mrs. Warren sent a note indicating that she and her husband were thinking of the fallen justice. Then a week later, Mrs. Warren continued the tradition of sending a "justice's birthday cake" to Fortas on the occasion of his fifty-ninth birthday.[120]

The Fortas law clerks, whose careers depended for the present on the luster of their boss, were naturally bewildered. Before resigning he had called them together, but instead of speaking about their fate preferred to reminisce about happier days when he had been the twenty-three-year-old "symbol of the New Deal."[121] Thereafter, it was left to the clerks and the office staff to box up all of the papers and documents for shipment to the Yale library. One court observer at the time recalled the sadness of peeking into a half-open door to see one of the Fortas law clerks, Martha Field, sitting morosely in the half-empty office on one of the rungs of a stepladder, surrounded by piles of books and partially filled boxes.[122]

Fortas's friends thought of ways to offer their support and cheer. A former secretary of health, education, and welfare, Wilbur Cohen, labored for four nights over a simple two-line sympathy card and then gave up. Instead, Cohen, an avid stamp collector, found several select stamps with violins on them and sent them to Fortas.[123] Meanwhile, several of Fortas's musician friends, including Isaac Stern, raced to his Georgetown home, where they played for days. "Playing the fiddle," Fortas later told a journalist, "takes out every unpleasant emotion I have."[124]

But of all the reactions to the political death of Abe Fortas, none was more profound than that of the former president now living in virtual political exile, supervising his partially constructed library in Austin, Texas. When word of the justice's troubles first reached Lyndon Johnson, together with the stories showing that the discovery of the problems dated back to his administration, he was completely surprised. All that he could do now was ask his former attorney general Ramsey Clark "why hadn't [he] told him." (Not even Clark would be able to re-create in his own mind why he had kept it secret.)[125]

And the man who felt at least partially responsible for the political attacks could think of only one more thing to do. Sadly, he dialed his old friend and personal attorney, Donald S. Thomas. Could Thomas go for a little drive around town? So the former president came by in his large convertible at midmorning and they drove around until two or three in the afternoon. Unlike the other times, though, when Johnson had used such occasions to remember his glorious past, now he was using the occasion to forget. They didn't say much to each other about the problems in Washington. Words at a time like that between old friends were not necessary. But after a while Johnson allowed himself to reflect briefly on Fortas's fate: "You know—you can't walk away from the obligations of these friendships that you've accumulated—the dependencies of people."[126] It was a telling epitaph, for few men had benefited more from those "obligations of friendship" felt by Abe Fortas than Lyndon Johnson. And few men knew better the price that had been paid as a result.

XXV

THE
LAST DAYS
OF ABE FORTAS

The meeting seemed improbable enough to be the stuff of fiction. But it was all too real. A full eleven years had passed since the judicial career of Abe Fortas had been sacrificed to fulfill promises made by Richard Nixon. On that day Abe Fortas was enjoying a few moments of solitude, nursing a drink at the bar of Washington's exclusive Sulgrave Club. Looking down the bar rail he noticed an old friend, a building contractor named Malcolm Price, sitting next to a gnarled, well-tanned man with his back to Fortas. When Fortas nodded in his direction, it occurred to Price that perhaps his out-of-town guest might want to meet yet another of the famous personages around Washington. So Price said, "Abe, this is Will Wilson from Texas."

Price was puzzled when the two men said nothing to each other. Instead, they half-smiled, nodded, and looked away.[1] It was the first and only time the two old adversaries met.

A lot had happened since they had been like gunfighters facing each other at ten paces. And it was not clear which man, reflecting on all that had happened, had more reason to be bemused by the innocent faux pas.

During his years as a political exile in Washington, Fortas had had the satisfaction of seeing Wilson's efforts on Nixon's behalf fail to win any of his enemies everlasting happiness as public servants. One by one, Fortas had watched his opponents fall.

But first, they had tried to harass him further. Wilson and Mitchell, not content with his resignation from the Supreme Court, had looked further into Fortas's case, searching for more scandals to pin on him. All their efforts resulted in, however, was an admission that their case had been pretty weak all along. Their next target was William O. Douglas. They developed a file on his financial involvement with the Parvin Foundation, an organization established to promote international peace and understanding by Albert Parvin, a Los Angeles businessman with ties to Las Vegas gambling interests. Three years earlier it had been discovered that Douglas was taking a twelve-thousand-dollar annual retainer from the foundation, while serving as its president. However, not even the threat of impeachment fazed Douglas now, in 1969. He resigned from the foundation and he faced the Nixonians down. "[House minority leader Gerald] Ford took the material we gave him and screwed it up. Ford blew it," Wilson would later lament.[2]

The American Bar Association also took action in the days surrounding the resignation. After twice praising the merits of Fortas for judicial appointments, the Committee on Professional Ethics of the ABA launched an investigation of the new charges. In a private opinion it was argued that Fortas had, by his involvement with Wolfson, violated eight separate articles of the Canons of Judicial Ethics written in 1924, especially Canon Four, which says that "a judge's official conduct should be free from impropriety, and the appearance of impropriety."[3] Then, three months later, the ABA began an effort that would in three years result in an entirely revised code of judicial conduct (which seemed no clearer than the earlier version).[4]

Meanwhile, the Department of Justice was having difficulty filling Fortas's seat on the court. Any promise to Strom Thurmond, perceived or expressed, was seemingly fulfilled when, after three months of deliberation, an eminently capable Fourth Circuit Court of Appeals judge from South Carolina, Clement F. Haynsworth, Jr., was nominated to replace Fortas. However, in a fit of piety over judicial ethics and of power over a sitting president, the Senate refused to confirm the appointment, ostensibly because the nominee had failed to recuse himself in a minor case involving a company in which he still owned stock. (In reality, as a Republican southerner, perceived to be a conservative, Haynsworth was bound to face opposition from the still smarting Democratic majority.)[5] Years later, even *The Washington Post,* which had opposed the nomination, had to admit that Haynsworth would have been a fine justice.[6]

Then the Nixonians would then turn to G. Harrold Carswell, on the Fifth Circuit Court of Appeals. Though John Mitchell would crow that Carswell was "almost too good to be true," the Senate found that he was too bad to be believed, after digging up significant allegations of racial insensitivity on the bench.[7] Finally, after a vacancy of thirteen months, the administration successfully filled the seat with a scholarly judge from Minnesota, Harry A. Blackmun. Ironically, Blackmun eventually turned out to be much more liberal than the "strict constructionist" the Nixon camp would have liked. Fortas could rest assured that his debacle had gained the Nixonians little with respect to his own seat.

Then there was the problem faced by Will Wilson himself. Two years after Fortas's resignation, Wilson found himself in a similar quagmire. One of his old law clients came under investigation by the Justice Department and the SEC for a number of financial transaction. Though Wilson claimed that he had properly recused himself from any consideration of the case, questions were raised when the man was not only provided with a grant of immunity on the criminal charges, but also given an extremely light sentence on other charges brought by the SEC. So Texas Democratic Congressman Henry Gonzalez raised the connection in repeated speeches on the House floor. As the attacks continued, just as with Fortas, it was a stalemated situation for Wilson. His enemies could not prove any wrongdoing, but his friends could not disprove it either. So Wilson, too, was forced to resign.[8]

In the end, Fortas had the pleasure of watching his two other nemeses, Richard Nixon and John Mitchell, go down to disgrace. While Nixon was being driven from office and Mitchell fought against going to jail, Fortas seemed so delighted by these events that he temporarily came out of his self-imposed exile of public silence to comment upon them. It was his version of "Look who's laughing now." Fortas suggested, apparently with tongue firmly in cheek, that Congress grant immunity to Nixon if he should decide to resign. He called it a type of "plea bargaining in advance," which was designed to remove any "hesitation" Nixon felt about resigning.[9] In writing later for the more sedate law-journal crowd, Fortas was even less charitable in discussing the Watergate episode, which he labeled "a national disaster": "Watergate was more than a series of incredible assaults upon our political process; it was more than a series of patently lawless acts of a base, criminal nature. Watergate was the ugly excrescence of a theory of government which asserts the supremacy of the Presidency over the Congress and the law of the land. . . . This is an intolerable theory for a democratic society. . . . By the grace of God and good fortune, we have been saved—this time."[10]

Since not everybody reads the law journals, Fortas did a reprise for *The New York Times*. This time he set out after Nixon personally: "However well-motivated the President may be, or however unaware he may be of the implications of his actions, the net effect of his actions has been an attempted constitutional coup d'etat: a fundamental alteration—a subversion—of our basic constitutional structure." Then Fortas reminded his readers, "A President is accountable for criminal acts, if he has committed them, like any other citizen. He may be removed from office."[11] It seemed only fair; after all, this was nothing more than what the Nixonians had been saying about Fortas in 1969.

The last years of Abe Fortas's private life were no easier than the last years of his public life. Following the court resignation, Fortas had been living in virtual exile, or in a life of "low profile," depending how one looked at it. No one wanted him. "Whatever he says," one old friend later told a reporter, "I know the Supreme Court affair left him crushed. He felt very ill-used. It doesn't surprise me that he would have a much quieter life now. People don't make new friends so easily in their late 60's, especially people like Abe, and many of his old friends have passed on. I guess he's kind of isolated now. He really had quite a fall from glory."[12]

Not even his old legal allies offered a safe haven. Fortas's old law firm, the one he and Thurman Arnold and later Paul Porter had built from scratch, refused to take him back. Late in his life, Paul Porter was still trying to protect his old friend—just as unsuccessfully as before—by saying that Fortas had refused to join the firm. He "wouldn't come back to this place," Porter explained, because it was "too damn big."[13] But Fortas's friends, such as William O. Douglas, knew the truth—that the firm had "turned him down." And the journalists who looked into it soon told the whole world.[14]

The precise reasons for the rejection were not clear. It was said that some in the firm wanted no part of their former partner now that he was "soiled goods."[15] However, one of the firm's senior men later took pains to explain to a writer that this was not the case: "It was a *mutual* agreement. It was discussed, very quietly, and both Abe and the firm sort of let it slide."[16] But another man who had been in the firm at the time saw it quite differently: "There was very strong feeling about Abe at the time, so much so that everyone knew there was a good chance of a lot of the best lawyers splitting off into a new firm if Abe came back. Fortas had his boys, guys he'd personally taught, who were in their late 30's when he left. They figured the Supreme Court was a lifetime appointment, and they began to play a more important part in dealing with the clients, Fortas's clients. Four years later, there's the Wolfson scandal, and the lawyers have to confront the possibility of Fortas coming back. They know he's not great about sharing power, and they think he'll stultify their professional growth if he comes back and takes the clients over again." No doubt these younger partners also recalled all too vividly how Fortas had once lorded over them, driving them fiercely to achieve his version of perfection. With Fortas's wife still in the firm heading its tax division, it made the situation all the more uncomfortable.[17]

But the exact reason for his failure to return did not matter much. Even though no formal vote was taken about Fortas's reentry, since he forestalled it with the decision to open his own office, he clearly knew the score. And that did not sit well with the man who had fallen from grace. "I never saw Fortas so sick, and so furious over anything as he was that summer after the law firm refused to take him back," said former Douglas law clerk Bernard Jacob. "He was really furious."[18]

Fortas went in other directions. He asked former senator Wayne Morse, the man he had once opposed in the Interior Department and who had been so helpful in the Senate confirmation fight, to go into practice with him. But Morse turned him down as well.[19] Finally, Fortas got together with an attorney from Chicago, Howard Koven, rather than with someone established in the capital, and opened what he called a "small, small" law firm in Georgetown, geographically removed from the playing fields of Washington's most powerful lawyers, which he had once roamed.[20] Located on the second floor above a bank in a complex of shops and offices, the office was an exclusive sort of place; if you had to ask where it was, you did not belong there. One entered a door behind the bank, climbed a set of stairs, and came face to face with the only visible sign of the firm's existence—a well-secured door and a four- by six-inch gold-plated sign reading simply FORTAS AND KOVEN.

From this office Fortas took on the role of behind-the-scenes legal counselor "dispensing advice and strategy" on antitrust and securities matters to some of his old clients. He told reporters that he was just trying to "enjoy life, do some good, and have some fun."[21] The word from his associates was that Fortas still had incredible stamina, working late into the evening on a case while fighting off a case of Brazilian flu.[22] The rumors from others in town, though, were that times were pretty tough for a while and the class of Fortas's clientele was not what he once would have accepted.[23] And it was said that his income was only about half of what it had been in his glory days at Arnold, Fortas and Porter.[24]

Sadly, it was not just his fellow lawyers who shunned Fortas. Scholars as well were trying to avoid mentioning his name in their work. Departures from the Supreme Court are normally greeted by waves of articles from scholars attempting to stake out new territory for research, but Fortas's exit was greeted with virtual silence. The Warren Court had created a legal revolution and it seemed that Fortas's ex-colleagues on that court were receiving all the attention that was their due. In the five years following Hugo Black's resignation from the Supreme Court, twenty-five law journal pieces were written on his career. Seven articles were written in the same period on the departed John Harlan, and eleven pieces on Earl Warren appeared in a three-year period. But in the thirteen years from the time of Fortas's resignation until his death, only one journal article was written on him—and that was more on the year when he had been appointed to the court than on the man himself.[25]

Other publications on Fortas did not please him at all, and he struggled to save what remained of his tattered reputation. The one book on Fortas that appeared—concentrating on aspects of the resignation—worried him enough that he publicly threatened a libel suit.[26] And in late 1974, *Newsweek* did a sort of "Where is he now?" piece on Fortas for its "Update" section. After recounting his demise, the piece described his new office as a "second floor walk-up." The insinuation that Fortas had fallen from his opulent offices at Arnold, Fortas and Porter, not to mention the Supreme Court building, to the equivalent of a small, unfurnished cold-water flat in a New York tenement did not sit well with him. "You've seen the furniture in that office you described," Fortas said sharply to reporter Stephan Lesher over the phone. "My *furniture* there could buy and sell you."[27] For now Fortas, like Greta Garbo, would have preferred it if everyone had just left him alone.

Generally, Fortas tried to maintain a very low profile in the early years off the court. However, law review articles allowed him to comment on antitrust law, civil liberties, the patent system, and criminal justice.[28] Meanwhile, one by one, his old friends died, allowing him to eulogize them publicly. One of these losses for Fortas was his greatest political ally. Just days after Lyndon Johnson would have left office had he served out a second full presidential term, the big man's heart gave out. In an impassioned eulogy in *The New York Times,* Abe Fortas paid tribute to his old friend. "Let us continue," he and Hubert Humphrey had written for the new president in his first speech to Congress. Now, nearly every paragraph by Fortas contained the phrase "Let us remember." "Let us remember Lyndon Johnson's greatness. Let us remember his love for people. . . . Let us remember the fullness of his understanding of his nation, of its roots, its meaning, its mission. Let us remember that he was determined that his nation should fulfill and not frustrate its destiny. . . . Above all, let us remember that he was a large man, of enormous strength and intense dedication. He was a man alive, vital, eager, restless, warm, and passionate. He was American. He was America's frontier, without which America is just another tired, retreating society, headed toward mankind's end and not toward the fulfillment of its dream. Let us not lose our way. Let us honor him by continuing the ascent which he began."[29]

Still, nothing that Fortas could do would keep people from also remembering the stain on his judicial career. And the old New Deal liberal crowd still had not forgiven him for his money-making legal career or his role in the Vietnam War.[30] As those from the New Deal era died off, people busied themselves with making unfavorable comparisons. Paul Porter's choking to death on a piece of lobster at the Palm restaurant in Washington in late 1975 seemed to them to contrast appropriately with the quiet death of the true-blue New Dealer Clifford Durr that same year. Fortas eulogized Durr at a memorial service in a voice so choked with sorrow and emotion, as he mournfully recounted their battles against Jesse Jones in World War II, that one had to wonder whether the eloquent speaker would be able to finish. "Like all of you and like many thousands of others, I loved Cliff Durr. Like millions of others, I am deeply indebted to him. I am deeply indebted to him for enrichment of my life. I am deeply indebted to him for a model, a model of what it is to be a man. To be a man of compassion, a man of understanding, a man of unshakable idealism, who, nevertheless, turned his formidable talents to the accomplishment of practical results."[31] Clearly, Fortas fancied himself to be in this mold as well.

Others, however, did not see it quite that way. Perhaps without intending to, one of the later speakers contrasted Durr with men like Fortas who had seemed to desert the orthodoxy of the New Deal for the golden path of a lucrative corporate law practice. Durr had been offered "the opportunity to capitalize in his law practice on his valuable experience and prestige as a member of the Federal Communications Commission. A financial fortune was easily within his grasp. His sense of integrity would not permit it. His early Calvinistic training shaped his character. What does it profit a man to gain a fortune and lose his own soul? Cliff unhesitatingly chose to abide by the biblical injunctions. 'Do not lay up for yourselves' treasure only where moths and rust could consume, and as thieves break in and steal, but lay up for yourselves treasure in heaven, where neither moth nor rust consume, and where thieves do not break in and steal.' The value of treasure is there where your heart be also."[32]

In 1977, just when things seemed to be quieting down for Fortas, disaster struck once more. Bob Woodward of *The Washington Post* came into possession of a transcript of a conversation which took place between Fortas and Louis Wolfson just after the latter's release from jail six years earlier, which had been recorded without the lawyer's knowledge. Fortas had asked for the meeting in an effort to influence the nature of the financier's upcoming press conference explaining their personal relationship. The release of their letters would be "very bad for me," Fortas explained. "If you release those, I tell you that you will inadvertently and unwittingly be doing me harm. . . . Things are quiet now and I have reached a point where I think I can resume my life."[33] While Fortas rewrote Wolfson's intended press release, arguing that certain things would make a "bad headline," his lack of skill in judging the press did him in again. By attempting to control the nature of the conference, which got only minor play in the press, Fortas set himself up for an even bigger fall when the transcript itself became a front-page story and once more brought the Wolfson problems to the forefront.

Richard Nixon, on the other hand, proved more resilient and resourceful in recovering his good name. Public careers in America are never permanently ruined—they just await the passage of time, the forgiveness of a forgetful public, and either revisionist historians or "retrospectively rediscovering" journalists to revive them. After Nixon was pardoned by President Ford for any and all offenses, the American people proved once more either their charity or their forgetfulness. Nixon had lasted long enough to plot his return to grace carefully. He gave a series of paid interviews with David Frost, published his memoirs and books on foreign policy, and gave political speeches before select gatherings of wealthy Republican supporters. By 1980, the conversion was complete. Aided by the inauguration of a Republican in the White House and a Republican Senate, Nixon was now seen as the elder statesman of the GOP—consulted by the nation's new leaders, questioned by the news media, and glorified by buildings named for him in various locations. Not even a damning book challenging his lifetime commitment to veracity, or the truckload of books analyzing Watergate, seemed to affect him now. In 1986, Newsweek would put Nixon on a cover proclaiming "He's Back: The Rehabilitation of Richard Nixon."[34]

Fortas was not so lucky. For a while it seemed that his public career was slowly making its way along the same comeback trail. After Watergate, some even began to wonder, with considerable justification, whether Fortas himself had been one of the first victims of the Nixon White House "enemies list."[35] And journalists began to wonder, "Where is Fortas now?"[36] Tamar Lewin wrote a moving account, describing him as a "balding, elderly man" who every day "[leaves] the big yellow house near Dumbarton Oaks formal gardens and makes his way past Georgetown's fancy homes to M Street, where he enters an unmarked door behind a modest two-story bank."[37]

Nineteen eighty-one seemed to be Fortas's year for coming out. He appeared before a federal commission that was investigating whether Japanese American victims of the World War II internment camps should be compensated.[38] Then, with the appointment of Sandra Day O'Connor to the Supreme Court and the anticipation of her questioning by the Senate Judiciary Committee, the man who had faced its wrath in 1968 was asked to appear on PBS's The Lawmakers program. In commenting on the confirmation process, Fortas made it clear that he knew its hazards all too well: "The confirmation process is an important process . . . and the appearance before the [Judiciary] Committee is . . . not like going on a picnic. There's tension about it. You never know whether it's going to be an objective and intelligent experience, or whether it is going to be an attempt by one or more members of the committee to run a lynching party."[39]

It was the first time anyone could remember since the resignation that Fortas had appeared for a public interview on television. With the ice now broken, Fortas interviews appeared in the newspapers more and more often over the next several months. In late January 1982, the fiftieth anniversary of Franklin Roosevelt's first election to the presidency allowed Fortas to join a number of others in offering their reminiscences of the man and the era.[40] Then came an article in *The New York Times* about the "High Court Alumni"—Fortas, Arthur Goldberg, and Potter Stewart—which outlined their activities in private practice.[41]

Fortas was coming back. Privately, too, he had decided to be a little more forthcoming about some of those sensitive subjects, including his relationship with Lyndon Johnson and his resignation, with visitors. One day he spoke with an inquiring visitor about his role with Lyndon Johnson, the standards of behavior for members of the court, and the Wolfson connection—all previously taboo subjects. The bitterness was still there, however. When Senator John McClellan, one of Fortas's Dixiecrat tormenters, was mentioned, all the former justice would spit out was "That son-of-a-bitch!"

He regretted nothing, Fortas said on that occasion, puffing on his Kent III cigarettes. He had been needed by his president, and thus the nation. "There were times when [Lyndon Johnson] called me when he needed my counsel, I admit that." Fortas spoke of the Vietnam War meetings, and the Sunday night when he had been called to the White House to advise on the Detroit riots. His actions had not been so different from the behavior of many of his predecessors during times of national crisis. But he made it clear that he had become a puritan in spirit concerning the ethics of the court. "I think the question really is, 'Shall we allow these events to pollute the clear stream of judicial prestige?'" While he wouldn't want to "try and completely restrict members of the Court from any political involvement whatsoever," he warned that "the form is the key." The "tricky part" for Fortas was whether outside work by a justice was "likely to involve you in undesirable relationships." Perhaps his years in self-imposed exile had led him to think differently about his life, or maybe he had been telling the truth when he once characterized his service to Johnson as more a duty than a pleasure.[42]

Only one event could make Fortas's comeback complete. Like getting back on a horse that had thrown him to demonstrate that he had not lost his courage and skill, Fortas's reappearance before the Supreme Court, the scene of some of his greatest triumphs and certainly of his greatest humiliation, was now viewed by everyone as evidence of his final "coming out." The newspapers had carefully noted it back in 1970 when he had filed his first case with the court involving a patent dispute (ironically, appealing a decision against his client by Homer Thornberry).[43] When asked by a reporter whether the justices would allow him to present a case before them, Fortas cited the precedent of Charles Evans Hughes. Hadn't he left the court to run for the presidency and later argued before his former brethren? But then Fortas added, "his eyes growing large and sad": "Yes, but I resigned."[44] Since that case was not granted a review by the court, there was no need for further debate on that issue.

Finally, in late March 1982, Fortas got his opportunity. It was fitting that the case that marked his return to the high court involved Puerto Rico. That gentle island, which had helped Fortas make his reputation in the Interior Department as a young man, and had helped him to start his career in private legal practice as a middle-aged man, was now providing him with a ride back to glory one final time as an old man.

It was a media event. The reporters took the opportunity to once more rehash the accounts of the Wolfson scandal. Fortas, though, preferred to speak about life in private practice. Such a legal appeal was "my bag," he told The New York Times, adding that he would continue to work "until my clients retire me or the Lord retires me." Did he have any apprehension over this first appearance before his former colleagues? "Whenever I argue before a court," he answered, "it's a period of tension in which you work pretty hard to get ready for the argument."[45]

The case involved a dispute between two of Puerto Rico's political parties over the manner in which vacancies in the island's legislature were filled following the death of a sitting member. Could the deceased member's own party appoint a successor, or were new open elections necessary? Fortas defended the position that the vacancy should be filled by internal party appointment.

Fortas's first appearance before the high court in thirteen years made it clear that he had lost none of his spellbinding oratorical skills.[46] Before the argument began, William Brennan's normally impassive face "burst into a broad, beaming smile" when he saw his old colleague at the counsel's table.[47] On its face, the argument seemed to present some difficult philosophical dilemmas for Fortas, since he seemed to be opposing the same right to vote that from the bench he had once tried to preserve. In fact, the opposing counsel cited against him the "one man, one vote" Reynolds v. Sims case, which the Warren Court had decided.[48] Since the opposing counsel was skewered with questions, there was every reason for Fortas to expect similar treatment from the court. Instead, the justices just listened to his entire argument without significant comment or questions.

As it turned out, Fortas had lost nothing of his skill at finding the jugular in the case. Using the nature of federalism—a prime concern of the Burger Court—and lecturing on the history of the "special and unique status in the American system" of Puerto Rico, Fortas pulled the rug from under his opposition. Puerto Rico's autonomy needed to be preserved, he argued. "It would be highly advantageous and highly desirable [for the United States to defer to the island's] unique status, its cultural background, its history, [and] its difference."[49] In this case, Fortas seemed to be arguing, special elections could mean violence on the island. When his allotted thirty minutes had expired, Fortas said simply, "Thank you very much. It has been a great pleasure and an honor to be here." The pictures of a smiling Fortas leaving the Supreme Court building in triumph, with his wife at his side, showed how pleased he was with his performance.

But a balding, disbarred attorney who was then working as the chairman of Global Research International was not so enraptured. And he seemed a bit bewildered when he ran into a reporter who had once covered his actions in government service. "Hey," murmured John Mitchell derisively, "did you see who argued in the Court yesterday?"[50]

Fortas would never know that he had won his final legal battle.[51] Almost two weeks later, on April 5, he was dead—a burst aortic valve had ended his comeback. Ironically, the eulogies that Fortas had not received when he left the court now came in bunches. They were somewhat strained, however, as writers looked for ways to explain the tragedy of his public career, or simply ignored its disastrous end entirely. *The New York Times* and *The National Law Journal* titled their pieces "The Reluctant Justice" and focused on the "contradictions" and "complexities" in the man who had seen his place in history destroyed after being forced onto the court against his will by his presidential friend.[52] *The Washington Post,* and columnist Anthony Lewis, however, preferred to concentrate on the "courage in hard times" that Fortas had exhibited in defending the victims of McCarthyism in the 1950's. "There were no people in town any stronger than [Fortas, Arnold and Porter], and nobody stood as high as Abe," it was said.[53]

The later law journal eulogies were more effusive. Former justice Arthur Goldberg called the man who had succeeded him on the court "an outstanding jurist and a great American."[54] Supreme Court colleague William J. Brennan, Jr., remembered Fortas as being "among those rare individuals possessed of the energy and ability to forge several distinguished careers in one lifetime. . . . The work, career and character of this scholarly, gentle, quiet-spoken and unfailingly courteous man exemplified the judicial role at its best. He richly earned the high respect in which he was held by all who were privileged to know him."[55]

Of all the comments on the tragedy of Abe Fortas's public career, perhaps the most fitting and accurate epitaph was supplied by the man himself. "The greatest fear . . . is of dying on the Court," Fortas had said in reflecting on his ill-fated career just months before his death. And he should have known. Fortas had already faced this mortality three times in his life—once psychologically just after his court appointment, again professionally in the 1968 Senate confirmation battle, and then historically in 1969 with the Wolfson scandal. Now it seemed possible that the pressures of preparing for his reappearance before the Supreme Court in 1982 had killed him one final time. If so, in "dying on the Court" this time, Fortas had finally died in triumph.

EPILOGUE:
A POLITICAL
AUTOPSY OF
ABE FORTAS

Who or what killed the public career of Abe Fortas?

That is the question that haunted me in researching and writing this book. To some extent it haunts me still. Was Lyndon Johnson correct in saying, "I ruined his life"? Was Fortas correct in saying of the Nixon forces, "They had [my seat] promised"? Were court observers correct in thinking that Fortas had done himself in? The incidents recounted in this book bring us closer to an understanding of the answers not just for Fortas, but for the Supreme Court as a whole.

Among those who have tried to conduct "political autopsies" of Abe Fortas's public career, there are nearly as many theories as there are people who have explored the topic. For some, this was just a case of avarice—a man taking twenty thousand dollars a year because he thought he could get away with it.[1] In that respect, they say, Fortas was not only greedy, but not nearly as smart as he thought he was. Reflecting an entire school of thought, Joseph Kraft saw it as a case of hubris—too much pride and confidence that he could get his enemies before they got him. Geoffrey Cowan saw it as a case of indiscretion—a man who never took the rules seriously and got caught.[2] Mary McGrory blamed it all on Fortas's relationship with Lyndon Johnson, who unwittingly delivered the justice to his enemies. Meanwhile, reporters David Broder and Robert Shogan saw larger themes in the controversy. To Broder, Fortas's fate represented the fall of New Deal liberalism, and the idea that those who made the rules were no longer permitted to bend them to their own advantage. For Shogan, Fortas was crushed by the failure of institutions—a vulnerable court caught in the war between the president and Congress.[3]

While all of these views have some surface explanatory power, they do not reveal what actually did Fortas in. Greed, ambition, normative insensitivity, occasional dishonesty, and overconfidence are not normally fatal diseases in Washington. If they were, the city would now be empty. These qualities were just contributing causes to his demise. In actuality, there were much larger forces at work that were well beyond his, or anyone else's, control. Abe Fortas's fate was sealed the day he was forced onto the court. And after the terrible fight of 1968, his reputation was such that even the slightest new allegation would be believed and would finish him. The problem was that Fortas became the wrong man, in the wrong place, at the wrong time.

Abe Fortas's life and career were filled with contradictions. By his own admission the man who coolly counseled others in times of crisis could not seem to make up his mind about his own career at similar turning points. The man who is remembered by friends for countless kindnesses made an equal number of enemies who were waiting for their chance in 1968 and 1969. The man who was constantly concerned about the "appearances" presented by his clients' actions did not seem to realize the way his own behavior would appear to the general public. Here was a man who was put on the Supreme Court by Lyndon Johnson to change the face of constitutional law by the force of his analytical brilliance and his eloquence. Instead, he is remembered as the man who spurred the American Bar Association to change its code of judicial ethics. And finally, here was a man who was expected to carry forward the torch of the Warren Court, and instead is remembered as the person responsible for extinguishing its flame. With his departure, and the subsequent ascensions of Harry Blackmun and Warren Burger, to be then followed by the appointments of Lewis Powell and William Rehnquist, the course of constitutional law was altered toward conservatism for the rest of the twentieth century.

Yet Fortas paid a far greater price for his "transgressions" than seems justified, given the circumstances. His offenses, according to journalist Victor Navasky in the early 1970's, were considered to be fourfold: "Washington is an ungenerous town. Some of its younger inhabitants consider Abe Fortas a 'war criminal' because he has not yet repudiated the hawkish advice he allegedly gave LBJ on the war. Liberals blame him for consulting with the President at all, and for the indiscretion that caused him to resign, thereby upsetting the balance of the old Warren Court in Nixon's favor . . . [and] public interest lawyers consider Fortas's greatest sin to be the work he did on behalf of such clients as Philip Morris cigarettes before he arrived on the Court."[4] In fact, while it is true that he advised the president on the Vietnam War, it was more as a friend counseling on public relations than as a general plotting military strategy. While it is true that he was involved in advising Lyndon Johnson, the relationship was not unlike those that other justices maintained with other presidents. But Louis Brandeis, Felix Frankfurter, William O. Douglas, Fred Vinson, and Roger Taney were not caught, and Fortas was. While it is true that he was involved with Louis Wolfson, the contact was limited and soon terminated. Furthermore, William O. Douglas's financial involvement with the Parvin Foundation made it clear that Fortas was not alone in taking this course. Finally, while it is true that Fortas made a fortune in practicing corporate law and counseling the former enemies of the New Deal, his *pro bono* work during the McCarthy period and in the *Gideon* case cannot be ignored.

That Fortas made mistakes is undeniable. It was not just what Fortas did, but how and when he did it. Tom Wolfe wrote about "the right stuff," and Fortas certainly had that as a lawyer. But he did not have it as a judge. The intellect was certainly there, but not the temperament. Being a judge requires that one be removed from the political fray, out of the action. This preserves both the independence of the entire institution and the reflective detachment necessary to fulfill the adjudicative role. Fortas never came to this understanding. Rather than changing his manner of action and ethical code once on the court, he continued to follow the same standards that had previously guided his legal career. And that got him into trouble. But the major mistake that Fortas made was one of a man seemingly panicked by the prospect of "dying on the Court," after being forced to take the post by someone more certain than he in a moment of weakness.

In many ways, what began for me as a "murder mystery" in which the victim was a man's public career became instead a "murder-suicide." Whatever others perpetrated upon Fortas he could have prevented with a different attitude and set of actions. He created his own vulnerabilities and set himself up for a fall. How different would his life have been if he had been stronger in critical periods and resisted

Lyndon Johnson's "charms" in 1965? How different would his life have been if he had adopted the strict code of Earl Warren and Hugo Black against political involvement from the bench? How different would his life have been if he had seen the obvious dangers in his relationship with Louis Wolfson? How different would his life have been if he had decided not to face the Senate questioners in 1968, as others were counseling? How different would his life have been if he had not withheld, first from the White House and then from the press and the nation, crucial facts about his actions until after his enemies released the material to their own advantage? And how different would his life have been if he had not tried to cut one last deal with John Mitchell, this time triggering his own downfall? All in all, how different would his life have been if this child of the New Deal had not cockily ignored the fact that the rules he had once helped to fashion governed him as well?

While these "roads not taken" made Abe Fortas more vulnerable to attack, it took the actions of others to bring about his fall. Everyone in Washington has a skeleton in the closet and hopes it will stay hidden. Why was it Fortas's unlucky fate to have his vulnerabilities totally exposed? What was it that created this unlikely circumstance in the pre-Watergate days, before the press viewed the skewering of a public figure as a national sport? Why, in the end, did his opponents succeed?

In the end, the answer lies not in the *actions* of any of his opponents, but the *timing* of their attack. The truth is that the forces that did Abe Fortas in were much greater than any one individual. Fortas was caught in a riptide of history, and no matter how strong his swimming skills, there was no possibility of escape. His fate was beyond his control in 1968 and 1969 because the nation was at what might be called a "triple critical period" in its history. Politics has a certain set of natural, though intermittent, rhythms of its own. Much as in the biorhythm theory, which charts the individual's cyclical passages from positive to negative on intellectual, emotional, and physical scales, certain political cycles can be tracked as well.

There are periodic shifts in the institutional, political, and generational relationships in Washington.[5] Institutionally, there is always a struggle between the president and Congress for power to set the political agenda. Generally, either the chief executive or Congress has more power, and the other is destined to follow until the hierarchical nature of the relationship changes.[6] Politically, there is a seesawing relationship between the conservatives and the liberals, with one side leading and the other following at any given time. When this balance shifts in other nations, it is called a revolution; here it is just called an election. And finally, generationally, it is axiomatic that just as all the rest of us are born, grow old, and die, so do politicians. At certain points in our history, certain groups of politicians who have dominated the national scene will grow old together and the task of governing will be passed on to a set of younger people. When any one of these shifts occurs, there is instability—new issues arising, new relationships developing, new arguments beginning, new alignments coalescing—and when two or three of them occur at the same time, there can be chaos.

There was chaos in 1968 and 1969. Institutionally, Congress was signaling that it was beginning to take power back from the "imperial presidency," which had kept the nation in a nearly constant state of undeclared executive war in Korea and Vietnam. The first signals of this change came in 1968 with the unexpected Senate changes in the White House's Omnibus Crime Control Act and the increasing attacks on the administration's Vietnam policy. Then came the three rejections of presidential nominations to the Supreme Court—Fortas, Clement Haynsworth, and G. Harrold Carswell. Eventually there were enough votes to force a withdrawal from Vietnam, set new limits on the presidential warmaking and budget-making powers, and even topple a president over the Watergate episode. From that time until the reign of Ronald Reagan it seemed as though Congress was dominant (though providing no more effective leadership). In many ways, then, the battle over Abe Fortas in 1968 was one of the earliest skirmishes in this new trend.

From a political standpoint, the shift of power was especially evident in 1968. With the election of Richard Nixon as president in the fall, which seemed almost preordained after the assassination of Robert Kennedy, eight years of Democratic liberal rule was about to end. In the coming years, the sixty-seven Democratic votes in the Senate would dissipate to the point that the Republicans could take majority control of the institution in 1980. In anticipation of Nixon's win in 1968, Senate conservatives from the South and the Republican party would have held up almost any Supreme Court nomination by Lyndon Johnson in the hope that they could control the seat in the fall.

Finally, there was the generational shift of power. Lyndon Johnson's public career was ending, and soon he would be joined on the sidelines by the two "whales" who had been the cornerstones of the defense effort—Everett Dirksen and Richard Russell. None of those in the outgoing generation were able or even willing, given the diminution of their own power, to help Fortas in the Senate fight. And no one from the incoming generation, with the exception of Phil Hart, wanted to be tainted by the issue.

If one was to name the disease that killed Abe Fortas, then, it would have to be classified as political progeria—a kind of premature aging. In the end, just as Lyndon Johnson had understood, Fortas became inextricably linked with the Texan's dying presidency. So closely were they linked that LBJ's vulnerabilities became Fortas's, and the president's political death was matched by the justice's. Because of the combination of circumstances, vulnerabilities, and bad luck, Fortas aged and died politically before his time. At age fifty-nine, just when he should have been coming into his prime in Washington with the rest of his generation, his career ended so suddenly that he went out with the older generation. It is ironic that the whiz kid who had always been the youngest member of his crowd was destined to suffer such a fate. The young man on the fast track became the middle-aged man careening off it, while the plodders his age maintained their slower pace to the top.

Should we care about this tragedy? Can it happen again? The answer to both questions is yes. Those political rhythms that swept up Abe Fortas and transformed his career are always with us. In fact, there is evidence that we may now be heading into, or have already entered, another unstable "triple critical period" in the late 1980's and early 1990's. Institutionally, congressional actions such as the Gramm-Rudman budget bill and the Nicaraguan aid fights evidence a new willingness to counteract the strong presidential drives of Ronald Reagan. Politically, Reagan's final term and the delicate balance of power in the Senate make life increasingly dicey as the conservatives and liberals hash out new programs. The political pendulum seems to be swinging, but yet to be determined is its new direction—remaining with the conservatives in power, or back to the liberals. Until then issues such as Social Security revision, tax reform, and budget limits can be solved only by searches for bipartisan compromises removing the issues from the political agenda for the moment. Finally, generationally, the world of Ronald Reagan and Thomas P. "Tip" O'Neill is about to give way to a much younger generation. No better evidence of this could be seen than the replacement of eighty-year-old Melvin Price by forty-six-year-old Les Aspin on the House Armed Services Committee. One must also mention three men in their early forties: William Gray, on the House Budget Committee; Richard Gephardt, chairman of the House Democratic Caucus; and Joseph Biden, chairing the Senate Judiciary Committee.

As a result of the instability produced by these shifts, in 1987 the nation relived some of the experiences of 1968. And it was conservative jurist Robert Bork who paid the price. The first indication of these changes came in 1984, when the nomination of Edwin Meese for attorney general was held up for months. Ironically enough, the same Strom Thurmond who had destroyed Abe Fortas, acting in 1984 in his capacity as chairman of the Senate Judiciary Committee, defused the Meese matter by delaying the final hearings and vote until after the presidential election. Then, in a move strongly reminiscent of Earl Warren's timely retirement in 1968, Warren Burger announced in the early summer of 1986 that he was resigning as chief justice to head the bicentennial celebration effort. While Burger denied having any political motives in handing the nomination to a Republican president, his disclaimer was hard to believe.

In seeking to fill the vacancy, the conservatives showed they had learned much from the experience of Lyndon Johnson in 1968. The resignation was irrevocable, and there was no delay in announcing Justice William Rehnquist as Burger's replacement. Still, the opposing alliance of Democrats and liberal Republicans put up a vigorous fight. Now it was Rehnquist who endured sixteen hours of questioning, to the dismay of Judiciary Committee Chairman Thurmond and Senator Orrin Hatch, who were now saying from the conservative side that the quizzing was unfair. In the end, though, Rehnquist was not nearly so vulnerable as Fortas—facing only comparatively minor charges of a discriminatory clause in his house deed and allegations that he had opposed minority voter registrations in Arizona over a decade earlier. After threatening to withhold on the basis of executive privilege some Justice Department memos written by Rehnquist in his capacity as assistant attorney general, the Reagan administration diverged from the Johnson White House's "no defense" strategy for Fortas to make the material available. In the end, only thirty-three negative votes could be mustered against the nomination.

In this fight, however, both sides had learned some valuable lessons. It was now Robert Bork's turn to be thrust into the cauldron. In November 1986, the Democrats had regained control of the Senate, taking fifty-four seats. This, in turn, gave them control over the Judiciary Committee now chaired by Delaware's Joe Biden. When Lewis Powell resigned from the Supreme Court at the end of the term in June 1987, Bork, a judge on the U.S. Court of Appeals for the District of Columbia, was nominated to fill the seat. A former professor at Yale Law School and a man with preeminent legal qualifications, Bork immediately faced a firestorm of liberal criticism because of the staunch conservative and "self-restraint" philosophies contained in his opinions and his writings.

The moves that followed seemed almost scripted, but the roles were reversed. Strom Thurmond, not Phil Hart, was now the man calling for speedy Senate deliberations. Joe Biden, not Sam Ervin, was now the man figuring out how to delay the Judiciary Committee proceedings. Howard Baker, now chief of staff for Ronald Reagan, was defending the president's right to have the justice he wanted. Robert Byrd, now the majority leader of the Senate, was defending the idea of fairness in considering the nomination. And now it was the liberal interest groups that were mounting the opposition. Soon the chant was heard, "Delay, delay, and more delay"—but now it was the liberals, not the conservatives, who were trying to stop the clock. All of the political rules were changing. Even the participants could sense this fact. "This is a bizarre year. It is going to go down like 68," said Joe Biden after Bork's failed confirmation and the withdrawal of the nomination of the next candidate, Douglas Ginsburg, [only] without the sense of tragedy, but the same sense of the unexpected." This time the liberals won. But for the conservatives, it was a bitter pill to swallow. They claimed that Bork's was the first modern nomination to the Supreme Court rejected for ideological reasons.

Had he been alive, Abe Fortas could have told them how wrong they were.

NOTES

ABBREVIATIONS
USED IN THE NOTES

AF	Abe Fortas
AFP	Abe Fortas Court Papers, Sterling Library, Yale University
AI	author interview
COHC	Columbia Oral History Collection, Columbia University
FDRL	Franklin D. Roosevelt Presidential Library, Hyde Park, N.Y.
JFKL	John F. Kennedy Presidential Library, Boston
JFK/OH	Oral History Collection, John F. Kennedy Library
LBJ	Lyndon Baines Johnson
LBJL	Lyndon Baines Johnson Presidential Library, Austin, Tex.
LBJ/OH	Oral History Collection, Lyndon Baines Johnson Library
LOC	Library of Congress, Manuscripts Division
NYT	*New York Times*
OH	oral history
RFK/OH	Robert F. Kennedy Oral History Collection, John F. Kennedy Library
WOD	William O. Douglas

PROLOGUE

1. AI, Harry Middleton, 10/26/82, Austin, Tex.
2. *Ibid.*

CHAPTER I
DOUGLAS'S WHIZ KID

1. Fred Graham, "The Many-Sided Justice Fortas," *New York Times Magazine*, 6/4/67, p. 89.
2. Charles Seib and Alan Otten, "Abe, Help!—LBJ," *Esquire*, June 1965, p. 147. The basic facts of Fortas's early life have been laid out in a variety of places. Unless otherwise noted, my account benefited from the following: "Abe Fortas," *Current Biography, 1966* (New York: H. W. Wilson

Co., 1966), pp. 100–103; Fred Graham, "Abe Fortas," in Leon Friedman and Fred Israel, *The Justices of the United States Supreme Court, 1789–1969* (New York: Chelsea House, 1980), Vol. IV, pp. 3016–17; *NYT*, 4/7/82, pp. 1, 15; *NYT*, 5/16/69, p. 20; *NYT*, 7/29/65, pp. 1, 13 and *NYT*, 4/7/82, pp. A1, 12; Robert Shogan, *A Question of Judgment: The Fortas Case and the Struggle for the Supreme Court* (Indianapolis: Bobbs-Merrill Co., 1972), pp. 30–31; and "Chief Confidant to Chief Justice," *Time* 7/5/68, pp. 14–15.

3. Shields McIlwaine, *Memphis Down in Dixie* (New York: E. P. Dutton and Co., 1948), p. 266.

4. *Ibid.*, pp. 27–28.

5. Seib and Otten, "Abe, Help!," p. 147.

6. Shogan, *Question of Judgment*, p. 31.

7. McIlwaine, *Memphis*, pp. 29–30, confirmed by an examination of the public portion of Fortas's student file at Yale Law School.

8. Shogan, *Question of Judgment*, p. 31.

9. *Ibid.*

10. The list of Fortas's undergraduate accomplishments comes from his school file at Yale Law School.

11. AF, LBJ/OH, pp. 36–37.

12. The account of the differences between the two law schools is drawn from Thomas Emerson, COHC, pp. 111–14, 128–29, and Frank R. Strong, "Reminiscences of Yale Law School of Fifty Years Ago," *Yale Law Report*, Spring/Summer 1982, pp. 14–17. For a broader perspective on the differences, see also Robert Stevens, *Legal Education in America from the 1850's to the 1980's* (Chapel Hill, N.C.: University of North Carolina Press, 1983), and Laura Kalman, *Legal Realism at Yale, 1927–1960* (Chapel Hill, N.C.: University of North Carolina Press, 1986).

13. Transcript, "Justice Abe Fortas 'Hanging,'" 11/15/68, Yale Law School, Office of Alumni Relations, pp. 13–14 (Presentation Transcript). My thanks to alumni relations director Gloria McHugh for providing this transcript.

14. Beverly Smith, "Uncle Sam Grows Younger," *American Magazine*, February 1934, p. 63.

15. Presentation Transcript, Yale Law School, p. 13.

16. Shogan, *Question of Judgment*, p. 32.

17. For a general perspective on the problems of Jews entering the legal field, see Jerold S. Auerbach, *Unequal Justice: Lawyers and Social Change in Modern America* (New York: Oxford University Press, 1976), Chaps. V, VI, VII.

18. See Thomas Emerson, COHC, pp. 13–16. The same decisions and pressures were faced by Louis Brandeis and Felix Frankfurter. For more on the effects of the Boston community on Brandeis, see the still seminal Alpheus Thomas Mason, *Brandeis—a Free Man's Life* (New York: Viking, 1946), and Allon Gal, *Brandeis of Boston* (Cambridge, Mass.: Harvard University Press, 1980). For a fascinating account of the effect of Boston on the psychological makeup of Frankfurter, see H. N. Hirsch, *The Enigma of Felix Frankfurter* (New York: Basic Books, 1981).

19. Presentation Transcript, Yale Law School, p. 11.

20. *Ibid.*, p. 10.

21. Yale Law School Catalog, 1931–1932, pp. 30–31, 55.

22. Account of the law review competition from Thomas Emerson, COHC, pp. 140–41.

23. Making this election even more remarkable was the fact that Fortas won none of the academic prizes for performance in his first-year classes, moot court, or examinations. (Yale Law School Catalog, 1931–1932.)

24. Grades are from Yale Law School faculty meeting notes, 9/27/32, Sterling Library, Yale University. Description and account of the awarding of the prizes from the Yale Law School Catalog, 1932–1933.

25. A good account of the professors at Yale Law School can be found in Thomas Emerson, COHC, pp. 117–34. The material on Hamilton comes from an interview with Creekmore Fath, 3/10/83, Austin, Tex. For more on Thurman Arnold, see Louis Cassels, "Arnold, Fortas, Porter and Prosperity," *Harper's Magazine*, November 1951, pp. 63–64, and William O. Douglas, *The Autobiography of William O. Douglas: Go East Young Man—The Early Years* (New York: Random House, 1974), pp. 167–69.

26. Douglas's Yale salary from a memo, "Pre-War Faculty Expenditures—Law School," 7/9/45, Charles Seymour Presidential Papers, Box 96, Sterling Library, Yale; Douglas, *Go East*, pp. 127–75; James Simon, *Independent Journey: The Life of William O. Douglas* (New York: Harper and Row, 1980), pp. 100–14.

The $25,000 figure is from AI, Judge Charles Wyzanski, 1/13/77, Richmond, Virginia. James

Simon says that the figure was $20,000 (Simon, *Independent Journey*, p. 110). Douglas himself put the figure at $25,000. (Douglas, *Go East Young Man*, p. 164).

27. On Douglas's teaching skills and the development of the business-law curriculum see Emerson, COHC, pp. 123–24; Kalman, *Legal Realism*, pp. 113, 138, and 78–144 generally; Douglas, *Go East*, p. 173; and Simon, *Independent Journey*, pp. 126, 131. More evidence of this effort comes from letters written when Fortas eventually took over the development of the course, while Douglas was in Washington. See, e.g., AF to WOD, 4/30/36; WOD to AF, 6/8/36; and WOD to Charles Clark, 6/8/36, William O. Douglas Papers, Box 30, LOC.

28. Douglas, *Go East*, p. 164.

29. *Ibid.*, p. 174.

30. WOD to James Landis, 7/11/34, Douglas Papers, Box 6, LOC.

31. WOD to Donald Slesinger, 7/27/32, Douglas Papers, Box 8, LOC.

32. Abe Fortas, "Wage Assignments in Chicago—*State Street Furniture Co.* v. *Armour & Co.*," *Yale Law Review*, Vol. 1933, p. 526.

33. Years later, one of Fortas's former colleagues at Yale, Fleming James, would say that the piece was "an excellent piece of scholarship . . . [and] a thing that I really admire." (Presentation Transcript, Yale Law School, pp. 8–9.)

34. Eugene Rostow, "Professor Fortas—A Student's Reminiscence," *Yale Law Report*, Vol. 12, No. 1, Fall 1965, p. 2.

35. Others have frequently reported that Fortas graduated first in his class. See, e.g., Smith, "Uncle Sam Grows Younger," p. 63, and *NYT*, 5/16/69, p. 20. While the formal record of class averages is closed, a letter from law school dean Ashbel Gulliver to President Charles Seymour, when Fortas was being considered for a teaching job at Yale in 1945, states that he was graduated second in his class. It is reasonable to expect that this letter was written on the basis of an examination of the actual class averages. See Gulliver to Seymour, 9/26/45, Seymour Presidential Papers, Box 94, Sterling Library, Yale.

36. *NYT*, 5/16/69, p. 20.

37. Yale Law School Catalog, 1931–1932 and 1933–1934.

38. Yale Law School faculty meeting notes, 1/19/33 and 2/9/33; salary figure comes from Charles Clark to Charles Seymour, 4/22/33, James Angell Presidential Papers, Yale Law School folder, Box 120, Sterling Library, Yale.

39. For more, see Auerbach, *Unequal Justice*, pp. 130–231.

40. Walter H. Pollak to WOD, 12/21/32, Douglas Papers, Box 7, LOC. See also WOD to Emory Buckner, 12/13/32, Douglas Papers, Box 2, LOC.

41. Ashbel Gulliver to Charles Seymour, 9/26/45, Seymour Presidential Papers, Box 94, Sterling Library, Yale.

42. WOD to Mark May, 6/9/33, and May to WOD, 6/10/33, Douglas Papers, Box 2, LOC.

43. WOD to H. J. Ostrander, 7/19/33, Douglas Papers, Box 2, LOC.

44. For an excellent study of the purpose and operation of the AAA, see Peter Irons, *The New Deal Lawyers* (Princeton, N.J.: Princeton University Press, 1982), Chaps. 6, 7.

45. George N. Peek with Samuel Crowther, *Why Quit Our Own* (New York: D. Van Nostrand Company, Inc., 1936), p. 20.

46. Irons, *New Deal Lawyers*, pp. 126–28.

47. Katie Louchheim, ed., *The Making of the New Deal: The Insiders Speak* (Cambridge, Mass.: Harvard University Press, 1983), p. 220.

48. Shogan, *Question of Judgment*, p. 39.

49. Smith, "Uncle Sam Grows Younger," p. 62.

50. Howard Tolley, COHC, p. 229, and Louchheim, *Making of the New Deal*, pp. 220–221.

51. For an example of this attitude, see Samuel Bledsoe, COHC, pp. 258–59.

52. Smith, "Uncle Sam Grows Younger," p. 122. This ability to simplify the difficult concepts of law and explain them in language everyone could understand was noticed by others. A later law partner, Howard Koven, said, "The essential thing about [Abe] is that he can take any legal question, not just one about securities, and reduce it to understandable language." (Tamar Lewin, "Fortas Lies Low," *National Law Journal*, 12/3/79, p. 27.)

53. AF, Lawrence Fly project, COHC, pp. 1–6. See also Louchheim, *Making of the New Deal*, p. 221; Irons, *New Deal Lawyers*, pp. 138–40; and Smith, "Uncle Sam Grows Younger," p. 122.

54. Thurman Arnold, Lawrence Fly project, COHC, pp. 1–2.

55. *Ibid.*, p. 2, and Irons, *New Deal Lawyers*, p. 139.

56. Jerome Frank, COHC, p. 150, and Smith, "Uncle Sam Grows Younger," p. 122.

57. This account relies on AF, Lawrence Fly project, COHC, pp. 1–6, and Irons, *New Deal Lawyers*, pp. 142–44.

58. *Newsweek*, 7/8/68, p. 17; see also Lewin, "Fortas Lies Low," p. 27.

59. AF to WOD, 4/30/36; AF to WOD, 6/5/36; WOD to Charles Clark, 6/8/36; WOD to AF, 6/8/36; WOD to AF, 11/27/36, Douglas Papers, Box 30, LOC.

60. Course description comes from Yale Law School Catalog, 1936–1937.

61. AF curriculum vitae, undated, in 1946, School of Law, Office of the Dean Papers, Abe Fortas Folder, Box 69, Sterling Library, Yale; Ashbel Gulliver to Charles Seymour, 9/26/45, Seymour Presidential Papers, Box 94, Yale.

62. For more on Douglas's position in this field of study, see Joel Seligman, *The Transformation of Wall Street: A History of the Securities and Exchange Commission and Modern Corporate Finance* (Boston: Houghton Mifflin Co., 1982), pp. 71–72, 110–11.

63. Abe Fortas, "William O. Douglas: A Eulogy," *Yale Law Journal*, Vol. 89, No. 4, March 1980, p. 615; Presentation Transcript, Yale Law School, pp. 26–27.

64. Charles Clark to Charles Seymour, 6/15/34, Angell Presidential Papers, Box 121, law school faculty folder, Sterling Library, Yale. Account of the "get ahead" game is found in Douglas, *Go East*, pp. 168–69, and Simon, *Independent Journey*, pp. 117–18.

65. Charles Clark to Charles Seymour, 6/15/34, Angell Presidential Papers, Box 121, law school faculty folder, Sterling Library, Yale. Independent evidence of this impression is provided by Fortas's search for a job in Washington; see WOD to James Landis, 7/11/34, Douglas Papers, Box 6, LOC. Douglas relays this information in the context of recommending that Landis interview Fortas for a position in the newly established Federal Trade Commission. In a letter to Douglas on 7/13/34, Landis agrees to the interview. (Douglas Papers, Box 6, LOC.) All of this worried the dean, who was trying to plan his faculty for the upcoming year. See Clark to James Angell, 5/18/34, Angell Presidential Papers, Box 121, Sterling Library, Yale.

66. Seligman, *Transformation of Wall Street*, pp. 109–12; Simon, *Independent Journey*, pp. 139–50.

67. WOD to AF, 10/8/34, Douglas Papers, Box 30, LOC.

68. Jerome Frank, COHC, p. 150.

69. On the salary negotiations and the confusion of the dean and the faculty as to whether Fortas would return, talks that were mediated by Douglas in many instances, see Charles Clark to WOD, 9/13/34, Douglas Papers, Box 2, LOC. The salary figure for Fortas from the AAA differs from the four thousand dollars reported by Robert Shogan (*Question of Judgment*, p. 37). It is possible that after the experience of the previous year, Fortas got a raise to sixty-six hundred dollars, or that his job classification had been changed with a concomitant increase in salary.

   On the debate within the Yale faculty over the Washington commuting crowd, see Kalman, *Legal Realism*, pp. 120–44. The noncommuters criticized their governmentally involved colleagues for missing classes and diverting too much of their energies from teaching and researching. The commuters, on the other hand, argued that the practical governmental experience gave them rich new materials for the classroom.

70. For more, see Irons, *New Deal Lawyers*, Chaps. 7, 8.

71. *Ibid.*; see also Gardner Jackson, COHC, pp. 506–9.

72. One of Douglas's first instructions was to send Fortas to the financial expert Max Lowenthal for help. (See WOD to Lowenthal, 11/19/34, Douglas Papers, Box 12, LOC.) In his autobiography, Douglas explains that he went on leave for a semester from Yale Law School when he went to Washington with the SEC. (See Douglas, *Go East*, p. 258.) Indeed, the Yale records show that he continued to receive his fifteen-thousand-dollar annual salary, taking a leave only in the second term of 1935–1936 (except for expenses to supervise graduate students working with him), and the second term of 1936–1937. (Memorandum, "School of Law Leaves of Absence Granted Since 1931," Seymour Presidential Papers, Box 94, Sterling Library, Yale.) In the Douglas Papers, Box 30, LOC, is a folder labeled "Protective Committee Study—Confidential File," which has a great number of letters from Fortas to Douglas illustrating the degree of long-distance control that Douglas could exert over the agency through his young lieutenant.

73. WOD to AF, 10/8/34, Douglas Papers, Box 30, LOC. Fortas's original salary on the Protective Committee was fifty-six hundred dollars, though Douglas was repeatedly trying to get it raised, first to sixty-four hundred and then to eight thousand. See memorandum, Protective Committee Study Staff, undated, Douglas Papers, Box 30, LOC; "Memorandum to the Securities and Exchange Commission Re—Protective Committee Study," 11/26/34, and WOD to James Landis, 10/15/35, Douglas Papers, Box 12, LOC.

74. AF to WOD, 10/8/34, and Jerome Frank to WOD, 10/8/34, Douglas Papers, Box 30, LOC.
75. WOD to AF, 10/8/34, Douglas Papers, Box 30, LOC. See also WOD to AF, 10/8/34, and WOD to AF, 10/9/34, Douglas Papers, Box 30, LOC.
76. Jerome Frank to WOD, 10/8/34, Douglas Papers, Box 30, LOC.
77. WOD to Jerome Frank, 10/10/34, and Frank to WOD, 10/11/34, Douglas Papers, Box 30, LOC.
78. AF to WOD, undated but noted as being written "about 10/12/34," Douglas Papers, Box 30, LOC.
79. WOD to AF, 10/15/34; WOD to Jerome Frank, 10/16/34; and WOD to Frank, 10/20/34; Douglas Papers, Box 30, LOC.
80. WOD to Wes Sturges, 10/19/34, and Sturges to Frank, 10/31/34, Douglas Papers, Box 30, LOC; WOD to Sturges, 11/5/34, Douglas Papers, Box 9, LOC.
81. Jerome Frank to WOD, 11/3/34, and WOD to Frank, 11/5/34, Douglas Papers, Box 30, LOC.
82. WOD to Wes Sturges, 11/5/34, Douglas Papers, Box 30, LOC.
83. Jerome Frank to Rexford Tugwell, 8/14/47, Rexford Tugwell Papers, Box 4, FDRL.
84. Conversation with Raoul Berger, July 26, 1987, State College, Pa.
85. *U.S.* v. *Butler* 297 U.S. 1 (1936).
86. See Louchheim, *Making of the New Deal,* p. 224. It should be noted here that Alger Hiss recalled to one historian that the only person who had ever discussed Communism with him while he was working in the government in the 1930's was Abe Fortas. (Allen Weinstein, *Perjury: The Hiss-Chambers Case* [New York: Alfred A. Knopf, 1978], p. 209.)
87. AI, Arthur "Tex" Goldschmidt, 6/10/84, Durham, N.Y.
88. Boxes 11 and 30 in the Douglas papers, LOC, are filled with daily letters, sometimes in several different mailings each day between the two men. See e.g., AF to WOD, 3/20/35, 3/21/35, 3/23/35, 3/28/35, 3/29/35, 4/2/35, 4/3/35, 4/4/35, 4/10/35, 4/18/35, 4/29/35, 4/30/35; and WOD to AF, 3/22/35, 4/9/35, 4/11/35, 4/18/35, 4/19/35, 4/26/35, 5/1/35, Douglas papers, Box 30, LOC. For a general account of the reports, see Simon, *Independent Journey,* pp. 148–50.
89. See, e.g., telegrams, AF to WOD, 6/12/35, and WOD to AF, 8/23/35, Douglas Papers, Box 30, LOC.
90. For details, see Seligman, *Transformation of Wall Street,* pp. 110–11, and Simon, *Independent Journey,* pp. 142–50.
91. Simon, *Independent Journey,* pp. 149–50.
92. See Charles Clark to James Angell, 5/17/35; Clark to Angell, 5/20/35; AF to Clark, 5/20/35; Clark to Charles Seymour, 6/18/35; Seymour to Angell, 7/1/35, Angell Presidential Papers, Box 121, law school faculty folder, Sterling Library, Yale; memorandum, "School of Law Leaves of Absences Granted Since 1931," Seymour Presidential Papers, Box 94, law school faculty folder, Sterling Library, Yale; and Yale Law School faculty meeting notes, 5/16/35 and 5/29/35, Sterling Library, Yale.
93. Memorandum, AF to James Landis, 1/13/36, Douglas Papers, Box 30, LOC.
94. Malvina Stephenson, "Fortas Always Has Had One Vote of Confidence," 10/15/68, Women's News Service, housed in files of *Washington Star,* Martin Luther King Library, Washington, D.C.; Dorothy McCardle, "Mrs. Fortas, Nee Agger, Smokes Out Tax Laws," *Washington Post,* 3/22/64; *Washington Star,* 10/10/66; and "Smoke Signals," *Washington Star,* 7/8/68, also housed in *Washington Star* morgue, M.L.K. Library, Washington, D.C.
95. Yale Law School Catalog, 1936–1937, p. 45.
96. WOD to Arlene B. Hadley, 7/14/36, Douglas Papers, Box 23, LOC.
97. AF to WOD, 6/5/36, Douglas Papers, Box 16, LOC.
98. Charles Clark to James Angell, 1/30/36, Angell Presidential Papers, Box 121, law school faculty folder, Sterling Library, Yale.
99. *Ibid.*
100. For more on Yale Law School's troubles at the time, see Kalman, *Legal Realism,* pp. 115–44.
101. WOD to Charles Clark, 5/27/36, Douglas Papers, Box 23, LOC; AF to WOD, 11/20/36, Douglas Papers, Box 23, LOC; AF to WOD, 1/16/37, Douglas Papers, Box 16, LOC; and WOD to AF, 1/21/37, Douglas Papers, Box 16, LOC.
102. AF to WOD, 11/20/36, Douglas Papers, Box 23, LOC. See also AF to WOD, 4/30/36, Douglas Papers, Box 16, LOC.
103. See Charles Clark to Edgar Furniss, 1/14/38, Seymour Presidential Papers, Box 94, law school faculty folder, Sterling Library, Yale, and Dorothy McCardle, "Mrs. Fortas, Nee Agger, Smokes Out Tax Laws," *Washington Post,* 3/22/64, in *Washington Star* morgue, M.L.K. Library, Washington, D.C.
104. Yale Law School faculty meeting notes, 10/28/37 and 1/27/38, Sterling Library, Yale, and AF to

Charles Clark, 1/13/38, Seymour Presidential Papers, Box 94, law school faculty folder, Sterling Library, Yale.

105. AF to WOD, 12/30/37, Douglas Papers, Box 16, LOC, and Charles Clark to Edgar Furniss, 1/14/38, Seymour Presidential Papers, Box 94, law school faculty folder, Sterling Library, Yale.
106. Louchheim, *Making of the New Deal*, p. 223.
107. Seligman, *Transformation of Wall Street*, pp. 122–23 and Chap. 6 generally.
108. Memorandum by Roy Smith, "Re: Adequacy of Administration of the Utilities Division," 11/15/38; Jerome Frank to Robert Healy, 11/22/38; "Memorandum re the Legal Work of the Utilities Division and Recommendation for Changes in the Supervision Thereof," 11/28/38; Frank to Healy, 12/27/38; and Frank to Healy and Smith, 12/30/38, Jerome Frank Papers, Box 26, Sterling Library, Yale.
109. Roy Smith to Jerome Frank, 11/2/38, and Robert Healy to Frank, 12/5/38, Frank Papers, Box 26, Sterling Library, Yale.
110. Stewart Alsop and Robert Kintner, "Startling New Technique in Government-Business Relations Lies Behind Naming of Utility Head," *Washington Star*, 10/8/38, Frank Papers, Box 26, Sterling Library, Yale.
111. Jerome Frank to WOD, 10/12/38; Roy Smith to Robert Healy, 10/14/38; "Memorandum by Gesell re Victor Emanuel," 11/15/38; Frank to Healy and Smith, 12/29/30; "Facts Concerning Emanuel, Brought Out in Hearings, Which Facts Roy Smith Did Not Call to the Commission's Attention When Emanuel's Election Was Being Considered by the Commission," undated, Frank Papers, Box 26, Sterling Library, Yale.
112. Jerome Frank to Robert Healy and Roy Smith, 12/29/38, Frank Papers, Box 26, Sterling Library, Yale.
113. AI, AF, 8/7/81, Washington, D.C.; Diaries of Harold Ickes, 12/29/41, Harold Ickes Papers, LOC.
114. "Memorandum by Commissioners Edward Eicher and Frank re Roy Smith," 4/1/39, and WOD to Roy Smith, 4/4/39, Frank Papers, Box 26, Sterling Library, Yale. Smith to WOD, 4/11/39; Eicher to WOD, 4/11/39; WOD to commission, 4/12/39; Jerome Frank to Robert Healy, 4/12/39; copies of commission meeting notes, April 4–13, 1939; Frank to Healy, 5/4/39; and Frank, memorandum for the files, 5/9/39, Frank Papers, Box 26, Sterling Library, Yale University.

CHAPTER II
ICKES'S FIELD MARSHAL

1. For more on Ickes's psychological makeup and background, see Graham White and John Maze, *Harold Ickes of the New Deal: His Private Life and Public Career* (Cambridge, Mass.: Harvard University Press, 1985). This book's almost sole reliance on Ickes's diaries, however, to the exclusion of the massive collection of his papers housed in the Library of Congress, makes one anxiously await the forthcoming definitive study of Ickes's life by Linda J. Lear of George Washington University.
2. AI, AF, 8/7/81, Washington, D.C.; William O. Douglas, *The Autobiography of William O. Douglas: Go East Young Man—The Early Years* (New York: Random House, 1974), p. 465. Harold Ickes had been given the responsibility for supervising this agency.

   Douglas was always looking out for Fortas's next career move. Frequently, he wrote to law school deans and professors investigating possibilities for Fortas to resume his teaching career. See WOD to Harry Shulman, 5/13/40; Shulman to WOD, 5/17/40; WOD to Leon Green, 5/11/40; Green to WOD, 5/16/40; WOD to Karl N. Llewellyn, 6/9/45; WOD to Max Radin, 6/18/45, William O. Douglas Papers, Box 327, LOC.
3. Diaries of Harold Ickes, unpublished version, 4/8/39, Harold Ickes Papers, LOC (hereinafter Ickes Diaries). This quote comes from a duplicate of many of the diary entries concerning Fortas that can be found in a memorandum that was compiled and entitled "Abe Fortas," undated, p. 1, Box 464, Ickes Papers (hereinafter Ickes "Fortas" memo).
4. *Newsweek*, 7/5/43, p. 52.
5. AF to R. N. Elliott, 4/22/40, LBJA Famous Names Files, Box 4, LBJL.
6. This account of the struggle relies on the excellent study by Linda J. Lear, "The Struggle for Control of National Power Policy, 1941–1943," unpublished paper presented at the Western History Association Meeting, Salt Lake City, Utah, 10/14/83. See also Ickes Diaries, 4/16/41, in Ickes "Fortas" memo, LOC.

7. Ickes Diaries, 4/16/41, in Ickes "Fortas" memo, pp. 1–2, LOC. For an account of the takeover of the Cohen position, see also Ickes Diaries, 2/16/41, pp. 5210–11, LOC.

8. Ickes Diaries, 4/20/41, pp. 5396–97, LOC.

9. AI, Arthur "Tex" Goldschmidt, 6/10/84, Durham, N.Y. See also Ickes Diaries, 6/26/42, in Ickes "Fortas" memo, LOC.

10. Ickes Diaries, 5/23/41, in Ickes "Fortas" memo, p. 2, LOC.

11. This term comes from Arthur "Tex" Goldschmidt's view of how he and Fortas saw themselves in working in the government. (AI, Goldschmidt, 6/10/84, Durham, N.Y.) Goldschmidt adds: "Fortas was so self-assured he felt he could take on any subject and master it given a reasonable period of time."

12. See Lear, "National Power Policy," generally, and Ickes Diaries, 4/19/42, pp. 6544–47, LOC.

13. For more on Jones, see Gerald T. White, *Billions for Defense: Government Financing by the Defense Plant Corporation During World War II* (Birmingham, Ala.: University of Alabama Press, 1980), p. 13.

14. AI, Arthur "Tex" Goldschmidt, 6/10/84, Durham, N.Y.

15. White, *Billions for Defense*, Chap. 2, has more details on this effort.

16. Clifford Durr, COHC, pp. 65–86, has a fine account of the details of this dispute. Fortas considered this to be one of the truly remarkable fights of his governmental career, as indicated by his glowing eulogy of Durr thirty-five years later, which contained an account of this fight. (Tape of Durr Eulogy, 6/12/75, Audio and Visual Materials Collection, LBJL.)

17. White, *Billions for Defense*, p. 43; Clifford Durr, COHC, p. 72.

18. Clifford Durr, COHC, p. 78.

19. AI, Virginia Durr, 3/3/83, Austin, Tex.

20. *Ibid.*

21. Ickes Diaries, 8/27/41, 9/5/41, 9/8/41, and 9/20/41, pp. 5853–54, 5872–74, 5877–78, 5897, LOC.

22. For more on this incident, see Clifford Durr, COHC, pp. 79–80.

23. Ickes Diaries, 12/29/41, in Ickes "Fortas" memo, p. 2, LOC.

24. The position was formally offered to Fortas on May 28, the letter of nomination was made on June 13, and he was sworn in on June 24. The quote indicating FDR's concern with Fortas's religion is from the Ickes Diaries, 5/31/42, p. 6661, LOC. For more on this career move, see Ickes Diaries, 5/28/42, 5/31/42, 6/13/42, 6/24/42, and 6/26/42, pp. 6605–77, LOC. After the appointment was made, Fortas, who was very anxious lest something might go wrong with the promotion, wrote to Douglas and thanked him profusely for his assistance in the matter. (AF to WOD, 6/15/42, Douglas Papers, Box 327, LOC.)

25. "How long . . ." is from *Time*, 6/29/42, p. 19; "bat boy . . ." is from *Newsweek*, 7/5/43, p. 52.

26. Ickes Diaries, 6/26/42, in Ickes "Fortas" memo, pp. 6–7, LOC.

27. For more on the state of Ickes's mental health, see White and Maze, *Harold Ickes*, generally.

28. AF to Bernard Baruch, 8/21/42, Office Files of Undersecretary Abe Fortas, 1942–1946, records of the Department of the Interior, RG 48, Box 2, National Archives, Washington, D.C. (hereinafter AF Undersecretary Files).

29. Walter Gellhorn, COHC, pp. 467–80.

30. *Ibid.*, pp. 473–84, confirmed by a review of the AF Undersecretary Files in the National Archives.

31. This list, which will be amplified upon below, was developed from a review of the AF Undersecretary Files and the accounts in the Diaries of Harold Ickes.

32. Walter Gellhorn, COHC, pp. 474–75.

33. AF to Harold Ickes, 10/2/42, AF Undersecretary Files, Box 2, National Archives.

34. Francis Biddle, *In Brief Authority*, (New York: Doubleday and Co., 1962), p. 176.

35. Ickes Diaries, 2/26/45, in Ickes "Fortas" memo, p. 42, LOC. As will be explained below, Ickes was not at all pleased with Fortas's attendance at this meeting without his knowledge. He was even less pleased to discover that Fortas had attended as a substitute for Ickes after the secretary had refused to attend.

36. For more, see *Newsweek*, 6/28/43, pp. 48–50, and 7/5/43, p. 52; Ickes Diaries, 3/6/43, 6/20/43, 6/26/43, and 7/4/43, pp. 7524–955, LOC.

37. Harold Ickes, unpublished "Cabinet Memoirs," "John L. Lewis and Coal" chapter, pp. 48–52, Ickes Papers, Boxes 436–41, LOC. See also Ickes Diaries, 6/12/43, LOC.

38. Rexford Tugwell, *The Stricken Land: The Story of Puerto Rico* (New York: Doubleday and Co., 1947), p. 511. Confirmed by an examination of the Puerto Rico files in the Rexford Tugwell Papers, Box 20, and the unpublished Tugwell Diary for 1942 in Box 18 of the same collection, at the

Franklin D. Roosevelt Library. See, e.g., Rexford Tugwell Diary, 7/11/42, 11/10/42, 12/5/42, 12/16/42, 2/4/43, 5/25/43, 5/26/43, 7/16/43, 9/10/43, 9/16/43, 12/14/43, and 10/24/43, Tugwell Papers, Box 18, FDRL. See also Tugwell to AF, 9/14/43, Tugwell Papers, Box 20. Also Thomas Karsten to Tugwell, 5/3/43; Karsten to Tugwell, 4/21/44; and Karsten to Tugwell, 7/21/44, Tugwell Papers, Box 6, FDRL.

39. Tugwell, *Stricken Land,* p. 347.

40. *Newsweek,* 7/5/43, p. 52.

41. *Ibid.*

42. For more descriptions of Lyndon Johnson, see Robert Caro, *The Years of Lyndon Johnson: The Path to Power* (New York: Vintage Press, 1983), pp. 265, 457, and *passim*; Merle Miller, *Lyndon: An Oral Biography* (New York: Ballantine Books, 1980), *passim*; and Ronnie Dugger, *The Politician: The Life and Times of Lyndon Johnson* (New York: W. W. Norton and Co., 1982), *passim.*

43. Harold Ickes and countless others claimed at one time or another to have introduced Fortas and Johnson. However, over the years, Fortas himself had no doubt that it was Arthur Goldschmidt who had done so. (See Fred Rodell, ''The Complexities of Abe Fortas,'' *New York Times Magazine,* 8/25/68, p. 25, confirmed by interviews with AF, 8/7/81, Washington, D.C., and Goldschmidt, 6/10/84, Durham, N.Y.)

The precise date of this introduction has been lost in the mists of time. It seems likely that the year was 1939, because as of October 1938 Goldschmidt was still carefully identifying Abe Fortas's governmental position when mentioning his name in letters to Lyndon Johnson. (See Goldschmidt to LBJ, 10/18/38, LBJ/House of Representatives files, Box 170, LBJL.)

44. For a fine account of this seductive manner with Rayburn, see Caro, *Path to Power,* Chap. 18.

45. AI, Walter Jenkins, 11/3/82, Austin, Tex.

46. For more, see Katie Louchheim, ed., *The Making of the New Deal: The Insiders Speak* (Cambridge, Mass.: Harvard University Press, 1983), *passim.*

47. AI, Elizabeth Wickenden Goldschmidt and Arthur ''Tex'' Goldschmidt, 6/9/84, Durham, N.Y.

48. *Ibid.*

49. AI, Creekmore Fath, 3/10/83, Austin, Tex.

50. AI, Elizabeth Wickenden Goldschmidt and Arthur ''Tex'' Goldschmidt, 6/9/84, Durham, N.Y.

51. AI, Mary Rather, 11/12/82, Gonzalez, Tex.

52. AF to LBJ, 11/29/40; LBJ to AF, 12/3/40; AF to LBJ, 12/28/45; AF to LBJ, 12/19/49; AF to LBJ, 12/29/50; and LBJ to AF, 12/15/45, LBJA Selected Names, Fortas folder, Box 18, LBJL. See also Paul Porter to LBJ, 1/1/44, LBJA Famous Names Files, Paul Porter folder, Box 7, LBJL.

53. For more on this episode, and its importance in Johnson's political career, see Caro, *Path to Power,* pp. 459–66, which was used as the basis for this account.

54. AF to LBJ, 1/29/43 and 2/27/43, AF Undersecretary Files, Box 2, National Archives.

55. AF to LBJ, 6/23/43, AF Undersecretary Files, Box 2, National Archives.

56. AF to LBJ, 7/2/43; LBJ to AF, 6/28/43; AF to LBJ, 6/23/43; AF to LBJ, 7/23/43; AF to Ralph Davies, 7/5/43; and AF to Davies, 7/2/43. AF Undersecretary Files, Box 2, National Archives.

57. LBJ to AF, 10/5/43, AF Undersecretary Files, Box 2, National Archives.

58. AF to LBJ, 10/13/43, and LBJ to AF, 10/14/43, AF Undersecretary Files, Box 2, National Archives.

59. Bryan Spires to AF, 10/19/43, AF Undersecretary Files, Box 2, National Archives.

60. AF to LBJ, 10/23/43, and AF to Bryan Spires, 10/23/43, AF Undersecretary Files, Box 2, National Archives.

61. Ickes Diaries, 10/28/40 and 6/28/41, pp. 4855–56, 5668, LOC.

62. This account relies on Rowland Evans and Robert Novak, *Lyndon B. Johnson: The Exercise of Power* (New York: New American Library, 1966), pp. 13–14. For more extensive accounts, see Miller, *Lyndon,* pp. 94–106, and Caro, *Path to Power,* pp. 675–740.

63. Alvin Wirtz to LBJ, 6/20/44; a copy of the *writ of mandamus* suit in this case, *Stanford* v. *Butler,* is attached to a letter from Wirtz to LBJ, 6/14/44, LBJA Selected Names, Alvin Wirtz folder, Box 37, LBJL.

64. AI, Arthur ''Tex'' Goldschmidt, 6/10/84, Durham, N.Y.; AI, Mary Rather, 11/12/82, Gonzalez, Tex.

65. AI, Walter Jenkins, 11/3/82, Austin, Tex. For more on the view of the Washington politicians toward this group, see the unpublished Diaries of Henry Wallace, COHC, pp. 2989–92.

66. See ''Report by C. B. Baldwin on Democratic National Convention, 1944,'' written on 2/27/51, and reproduced in the Diaries of Henry Wallace, COHC, p. 3383ff.

67. There was a charge that Fortas had convinced Harold Ickes to come out against Wallace. Much later,

Wallace came to doubt that particular charge. (Wallace Diary, COHC, p. 4107.) For more evidence that this group was indeed working on Douglas's behalf in the 1944 election, however, see a letter talking about "the abortive Bill Douglas-for-President" campaign: Robert W. Kenny to AF, 2/13/52, Douglas Papers, Box 327, LOC. See also Benjamin Sonnenberg to AF, 6/12/45, Douglas Papers, Box 327, LOC.

68. "An Unwanted Secretary," *Washington Times Herald*, Oscar Cox Papers, Abe Fortas file, Box 11, FDRL. The piece does not name the offended undersecretary, but Cox, who was in a position to know, with his wartime contacts in the government, wrote on the article that it was indeed Fortas.

69. For more, see Ickes Diaries, 7/30/43, in Ickes "Fortas" memo, pp. 8–9, LOC.

70. The observation comes from a conversation with James H. Rowe, Jr., who cited the case of his law partner, Joseph Fanelli, who left Fortas's employ in the Interior Department a few months after he had started. (Author's conversation, Rowe, 3/3/83, Austin, Tex.)

71. Ickes to AF, 5/19/43, and AF to Ickes, 5/22/43, Ickes Papers, Box 161, LOC. See also Ickes Diaries, 11/16/44 and 1/7/45, pp. 9338, 9466–67, LOC.

72. Ickes Diaries, 8/6/43, LOC. See also *Washington Post*, 8/31/65, and memo from AF to Ickes, 6/19/43, Ickes Papers, Box 148, LOC.

73. Wayne Morse to FDR, 6/4/43, attached to a series of White House memos headed by a memo for William H. Davis from FDR, 6/4/43, OF 4451, Box 1, FDRL. This Morse letter responds to a memorandum from Fortas to FDR, 6/3/43, OF 4451, Box 1, FDRL. For more, see Ickes Diaries, 8/27/43, LOC. Copies of most of the letters in this incident can also be found in the Ickes Papers, Box 148, LOC.

74. "I considered your . . ." is from AF to Morse, 6/5/43, OF 4451, Box 1, FDRL. "After I am convinced . . ." is from Morse to Marvin McIntyre, 6/6/43, OF 4451, Box 1, FDRL. Both letters are also quoted in *Washington Post*, 8/31/65, p. A10.

75. Wayne Morse to AF, 6/7/43, OF 4451, Box 1, FDRL, also quoted in *Washington Post*, 8/31/65.

76. *Washington Post*, 8/31/65, p. A10. A copy of this letter from Fortas could not be found in the files in either the Library of Congress or the Roosevelt presidential library.

77. Dr. Benjamin Rones, "Resume of Mr. Abe Fortas," 11/15/43, Ickes Papers, Box 161, LOC. An undated letter from Fortas to Ickes from this period and in this same box makes many of the same points.

78. *Time*, 9/20/43, p. 21.

79. AF to Harold Ickes, 8/31/43, Ickes Papers, Box 161, LOC. See also Ickes Diaries, 5/7/43 and 5/11/43, in Ickes "Fortas" memo, p. 8, LOC.

80. A full account of this fight can be found in the Ickes Diaries, 9/12–10/18/43, pp. 8170–252, LOC. See also Ickes to Frank Knox, 11/9/43, Ickes Papers, Box 161, LOC.

81. Walter Gellhorn, COHC, pp. 409, 466–68.

82. Ickes Diaries, 8/30/43, in Ickes "Fortas" memo, p. 9, LOC.

83. The evidence for this statement, building on the observation of Fortas during his switch from the AAA to the SEC, comes from a variety of sources. Fortas's letters to Ickes and other friends from the period, and Ickes's scores of diary entries on Fortas, are filled with descriptions of the young man's ailments, his need for rest, and his uncertainty at career turning points, many of which are cited below. Even the press noticed it, but did not tie the ailments to critical career periods. After the big coal-mine fight with Lewis, one journalist reported that Fortas was "dog tired and down with a bad cold." Fortas is said to have told Ickes at the time: "If we keep on having coal strikes every 30 days we're simply not going to be able to stay on our feet." (*Newsweek*, 7/5/43, p. 52.) Harold Ickes was very troubled by this frailty of his undersecretary. In 1943, during a dispute over Fortas's draft status, Ickes wrote that he had contracted the flu, "looked terrible," and "really had the appearance of an anxious, ill man." Ickes records that another mutual friend, Eliot Janeway, thought that Fortas was on the verge of "a nervous or physical breakdown of a serious nature." (Ickes Diaries, 12/19/43, p. 8470, LOC.) By the end of the war Ickes had concluded in his diary, "[Fortas] had decided that he ought to go away for a couple of weeks to get back on his feet again and I made no objection although it seems to me that Fortas is a little soft." (Ickes Diaries, 11/4/45, pp. 10096–97, LOC.) Friends and acquaintances also noticed these traits. (AI, Virginia Durr, 3/3/83, Austin, Tex.) "Abe had a touch of hypochondria," adds Arthur "Tex" Goldschmidt. (AI, Goldschmidt, 6/10/84, Durham, N.Y.) Interestingly, Owen Lattimore also speaks of the terrible cold Fortas was fighting during the "terrible strain" of his handling of the case against Joseph McCarthy. See Lattimore, *Ordeal by Slander* (Boston: Little, Brown and Co., 1950), pp. 51, 53.

84. AF to WOD, 6/15/42, Douglas Papers, Box 327, LOC. Ickes put it almost the same way in reflecting on Fortas's dilemmas over both whether to leave the Interior Department in 1945 and whether to go

into the service in 1943. "Fortas has put me through a repetition of what he did when I was in the Navy one moment and out the next. In those days he seemed utterly incapable of making up his mind and taking a firm position." (Ickes Diaries, 12/21/45, in Ickes "Fortas" memo, LOC.)

85. James H. Rowe, Jr., LBJ/OH, II, p. 4.

86. Frank Peckham, Local Draft Board No. 1 to Harold Ickes, 10/13/43, Ickes Papers, Box 161, LOC.

87. Ickes Diaries, 9/5/43 and 9/7/43, pp. 8139–53, LOC.

88. AF to Harold Ickes, 11/4/43, and Ickes to Frank Knox, 11/9/43, Ickes Papers, Box 161, LOC.

89. AI, AF, 8/7/81, Washington, D.C.

90. Ickes Diaries, 11/7/43–11/21/43, pp. 8320–74, LOC.

91. Ickes Diaries, 11/7/43, p. 8334, LOC.

92. Ickes Diaries, 11/7/43, p. 8337, LOC.

93. AF to Harold Ickes, 11/15/43, Ickes Papers, Box 161, LOC.

94. Harold Ickes to AF, 11/17/43 and 9/2/43, Ickes Papers, Box 161, LOC.

95. Fortas described his experiences in a number of letters home. See AF to Jane Dahlman Ickes, 11/25/43; AF to Harold Ickes, 12/3/43; AF to Harold Ickes, dated only "Tuesday"; AF to Harold Ickes, dated only "Saturday," Ickes Papers, Box 27, LOC. See also AF to WOD, 11/26/43, and AF to WOD, 12/6/43, Douglas Papers, Box 327, LOC.

96. AF to WOD, 11/26/43, Douglas Papers, Box 327, LOC.

97. Ibid., and AF to WOD, 12/6/43, Douglas Papers, Box 327, LOC.

98. Ickes Diaries, 12/11/43, pp. 8432–33, LOC.

99. Ickes Diaries, 2/12/44, LOC.

100. AF to WOD, 11/26/43, Douglas Papers, Box 327, LOC. Once more, the reason for Fortas's thinking that he should leave governmental service was the delicate state of his health.

101. Ickes Diaries, 12/19/43, p. 8470, LOC. See also 12/26/43, pp. 8490–91, in the Ickes Diaries.

102. Even after he had decided to return to Interior, Fortas wanted Ickes to arrange a meeting for him with the president. Indicating his anxious state of mind at the time, Fortas wanted to be reassured that the president wanted him back. See AF to Harold Ickes, 12/21/43; Ickes to AF, 12/24/43; and Ickes to AF, 12/28/43, Ickes Papers, Box 161, LOC. William O. Douglas also passed along the message to Ickes that Fortas wanted, and needed, to be reassured by the president personally, before returning to the government. (Ickes Diaries, 12/26/43, pp. 8490–91, LOC.)

103. AF to Harold Ickes, 12/21/43, Ickes Papers, Box 161, LOC.

104. AF to WOD, 11/26/43, Ickes Papers, Box 161, LOC. However, his letter to Douglas in the same file, dated 12/6/43, still indicates a great deal of uncertainty by Fortas about his decision.

105. For more on this terrible event in United States history, see Peter Irons, Justice at War: The Story of the Japanese American Internment Cases (New York: Oxford University Press, 1983), passim.

106. AF to Dillon Myer, 3/31/44, AF Undersecretary Files, Box 1, National Archives.

107. AF to Fiorello La Guardia, 4/11/44, and La Guardia to Harold Ickes, 4/21/44, AF Undersecretary Files, Box 1, National Archives.

108. AF to John J. McCloy, 6/16/44, and AF to McCloy, 6/21/44, Ickes Papers, Box 380, LOC.

109. AF to Harold Ickes, 5/16/44, Ickes Papers, Box 380, LOC; Shogan, Question of Judgment, p. 53.

110. AF to Harold Ickes, 3/9/44, and Dillon Myer to Ickes, 3/9/44, Ickes Papers, Box 380, LOC.

111. Harold Ickes to AF, 4/24/44, Ickes Papers, Box 161, LOC.

112. AF to Harold Ickes, 4/12/44, and AF to Ickes, 4/8/44, Ickes papers, Box 161, LOC.

113. White and Maze, Harold Ickes, p. 8. For more on the hiring of detectives and the development of files against Ickes's enemies, see Walter Gellhorn, COHC, pp. 473–75, 497–98.

114. AF to Harold Ickes, 4/12/44, Ickes Papers, Box 161, LOC.

115. Ickes Diaries, 4/18/44, in Ickes "Fortas" memo, pp. 21–22, LOC.

116. Ickes Diaries, 5/7/44, in Ickes "Fortas" memo, pp. 39–40, LOC.

117. Harold Ickes to AF, 4/24/44, Ickes Papers, Box 161, LOC.

118. Ickes Diaries, 4/23/44, p. 8813, LOC. The general account is based on Harold Ickes, unpublished "Cabinet Memoirs," "John L. Lewis and Coal" chapter, Ickes Papers, Boxes 436–41, LOC.

119. NYT, 9/20/44, p. 38. This charge was leveled in a seven-hundred-word telegram that was drafted by Lewis and the United Mine Workers to be sent to Ickes, and was then released to the press. The message was sent in response to an unsigned telegram from the Interior Department to the union imploring it not to strike for the duration of the war.

120. Ickes Diaries, 4/23/44, p. 8815, LOC. This seems to have been the starting point of what turned out to be a justifiable paranoia on Ickes's part about Fortas's activities within the department.

121. See Ickes Diaries, 11/16/44 and 1/7/45, pp. 9338, 9467–68, LOC. See also Harold Ickes to AF, 5/19/43, and AF to Ickes, 5/22/43, Ickes Papers, Box 161, LOC.

122. Ickes Diaries, 8/11/44, p. 9164, LOC.

123. Ickes Diaries, 8/27/44, pp. 9197–98, LOC.

124. Characterization of the early relationship can be found in Ickes Diaries, 4/8/39, in Ickes "Fortas" memo, LOC.

125. Ickes Diaries, 11/26/44, p. 9360, LOC.

126. Ickes Diaries, 11/26/44, p. 9361, LOC.

127. *Ibid.*

128. Ickes Diaries, 12/19/44, in Ickes "Fortas" memo, p. 41, LOC.

129. Ickes Diaries, 1/6/45, in Ickes "Fortas" memo, pp. 41–42, LOC.

130. Ickes Diaries, 1/15/45, in Ickes "Fortas" memo, p. 42, LOC.

131. Ickes Diaries, 2/26/45, in Ickes "Fortas" memo, p. 42, LOC.

132. Ickes Diaries, 3/2/45, 3/4/45, 3/10/45, 3/17/45, and 3/31/45, pp. 9565–9634, LOC.

133. Ickes Diaries, 7/21/45, p. 9897, LOC.

134. Ickes Diaries, 9/2/45, p. 9970, LOC.

135. *Ibid.*

136. See AF to WOD, 6/27/45; AF to WOD, 7/30/45; AF to WOD, 8/6/45; Edwin D. Dickinson to AF, 6/22/45; AF to Dickinson, 6/27/45; WOD to Karl N. Llewellyn, 6/9/45; WOD to Max Radin, 6/18/45, Douglas Papers, Box 327, LOC. As of the 8/6/45 letter, Fortas was still wishing that Yale would make an offer for him to return. He seemed very reluctant to relocate on the west coast.

137. Ashbel Gulliver to Charles Seymour, 9/26/45, Charles Seymour Presidential Papers, Box 94, Sterling Library, Yale.

138. Wes Sturges to A. H. Williams, 3/11/46, School of Law, Office of the Dean Collection, Box 69, Sterling Library, Yale.

139. In April 1940, the school was considering hiring three new professors from a list of twelve names. Fortas came out a paltry eighth in a polling of the Board of Permanent Officers. The nature of the voting chart showed why. While several of those polled had Fortas in the highest, "strongly favored" category, an equal number put him in the lowest category of "strongly opposed." So there was the same sharp division of opinion over Fortas then that had dogged him throughout his career. (See Ashbel Gulliver to Members of Board of Permanent Officers, 4/16/40, Walton Hamilton Papers, University of Texas Library, Austin, Tex.) In the end, one of the men hired for the post ranked below Fortas in the ratings. (Irene Till to Walton Hamilton, 5/24/40, Hamilton Papers.) This outcome thoroughly annoyed William O. Douglas, who complained to the dean about a report he had heard that Fortas had been passed over for another candidate. Douglas told a story about how Louis Brandeis personally had selected Fortas to continue the work on railroad monopolies at Yale that the justice and Douglas had begun. (WOD to Harry Shulman, 5/13/40, and Shulman to WOD, 5/17/40, Douglas Papers, Box 327, LOC.)

140. Ashbel Gulliver to Charles Seymour, 10/11/45, Seymour Presidential Papers, Box 96, Sterling Library, Yale.

141. *Ibid.*

142. Thurman Arnold, *Fair Fights and Foul: A Dissenting Lawyer's Life* (New York: Harcourt, Brace, and World, 1951), pp. 188–90; Abe Fortas, "Thurman Arnold and the Theatre of the Law," *Yale Law Journal,* Vol. 79, 1970, p. 990; and see *United States* v. *Pullman Co.,* 64 F. Supp. 108 (1947).

143. AF to WOD, 7/30/45, Douglas Papers, Box 327, LOC.

144. Arnold, *Fair Fights and Foul,* p. 190.

145. Ickes Diaries, 10/13/45, p. 10058, LOC.

146. Ickes Diaries, 12/15/45 and 12/23/45, pp. 10188–206, 10213, LOC.

147. This account is based on: Malvina Stephenson, "Fortas Always Has Had One Vote of Confidence," 10/15/68, Women's News Service, unpublished article in files of the *Washington Star,* Martin Luther King Library, Washington, D.C.; "Smoke Signals," *Washington Star,* 7/8/68; *Washington Star,* 9/4/67; Daisy Cleland, "Love for Law and a Good Cigar," *Washington Star,* 7/22/65; Dorothy McArdle, "Mrs. Fortas, Nee Agger, Smokes Out Tax Laws," *Washington Star,* 3/22/64, all housed in *Washington Star* morgue, M.L.K. Library, Washington, D.C.

148. Ickes Diaries, 11/4/45, pp. 10096–97, LOC.

149. The resignation letter was promised to Ickes on December 11, and the secretary is not clear on whether it was delivered on either the twentieth or the twenty-sixth. See Ickes Diaries, 12/23/45 and 12/29/45, 10202–24, LOC.

150. Wes Sturges to AF, 12/20/45, School of Law, Office of the Dean Collection, Box 69, Sterling Library, Yale.

151. Excerpt from Lewis broadcast, 12/18/45, filed in Seymour Presidential Papers, Box 94, Sterling Library, Yale.

152. Ashbel Gulliver to Charles Seymour, 1/5/46, Seymour Presidential Papers, Box 94, Sterling Library, Yale.

153. Henri Brown to Charles Seymour, 1/4/46; H. LeRoy Whitney to Seymour, 1/9/46; Untitled and undated description sheet of all three men; John Dempsey to Seymour, 1/10/46; Charles Fay to Seymour, 1/11/46, Seymour Presidential Papers, Box 94, Sterling Library, Yale.

154. Charles Seymour to Wes Sturges, 1/10/46; Seymour to Charles Fay, 1/16/46; Sturges to Seymour, 1/11/46, Seymour Presidential Papers, Box 94, Sterling Library, Yale.

155. Jerome Frank to AF, 12/20/45, James Angell Presidential Papers, Box 120, Sterling Library, Yale; Wes Sturges to AF, 12/20/45, Seymour Presidential Papers, Box 94, Sterling Library, Yale.

156. Ickes Diaries, 12/21/45, in Ickes "Fortas" memo, LOC.

157. Ickes Diaries, 1/12/46, pp. 15–18, LOC.

158. Ickes Diaries, 1/19/46 and 1/20/46, pp. 2–9 LOC.

159. Ickes Diaries, 1/26/46, p. 4, LOC.

160. Victor Navasky, "In Washington, You Just Don't Not Return a Call from Abe Fortas," *New York Times Sunday Magazine*, 8/1/71, p. 28.

161. Ickes Diaries, 12/9/44, pp. 9209–10, LOC.

162. Ickes Diaries, 2/10/46, p. 14, LOC.

163. Senate Hearings, "Nomination of Edwin W. Pauley for Appointment as Undersecretary of the Navy," United States Senate Report of Proceedings, Committee on Naval Affairs, 2/20/46, Vol. 7, pp. 1189–94, Senate Historical Office, Washington, D.C.

164. *Ibid.*

165. *Ibid.*

166. Ickes Diaries, 2/24/46, pp. 3–4, LOC.

167. Ickes Diaries, 2/24/46, pp. 4–5, LOC.

Chapter III
The Legal Gunslinger

1. Horace Busby, "Remembering LBJ—Warts and All," *Washington Post*, 3/29/83.

2. Abe Fortas, "Thurman Arnold and the Theatre of the Law," *Yale Law Journal*, Vol. 79, 1970, pp. 990–91.

3. See Warner Gardner to Rexford Tugwell, 3/8/46, and AF to Tugwell, 2/19/46 (two letters), Rexford Tugwell Papers, Box 27, FDRL.

4. Rexford Tugwell Diaries, 2/14/46 and 2/16/46, Tugwell Papers, Diary for January–June, 1946, Box 19, FDRL.

5. AF to Rexford Tugwell, 2/19/46; draft agreement between R. G. Tugwell and Arnold and Fortas, undated; AF to Tugwell, 2/26/46 (confirming the signing of this agreement); Tugwell to AF, 2/28/46 (on billing of expenses for the first Fortas trip to Puerto Rico); Warner Gardner to Tugwell, 3/8/46, Tugwell Papers, Box 27, FDRL.

6. Warner Gardner to Rexford Tugwell, 3/8/46, quoting letter from AF to Tugwell, 3/13/45, Tugwell Papers, Box 27, FDRL. Letter is also found in Office Files of Undersecretary Abe Fortas, 1942–1946, Box 10, RG 48, National Archives.

7. *Ibid.*, and Rexford Tugwell to Warner Gardner, 3/11/46, Tugwell Papers, Box 27, LOC. This entire matter so angered Harold Ickes that after Fortas had deserted him on the Pauley matter, he wrote about it in his newspaper column. See Harold Ickes, "Writer Charges Law Partners Picked Davis for Interior's Island Division Post," *Washington Post*, 10/1/47, housed in the *Washington Post* morgue, Washington, D.C.

8. There are numerous accounts of Arnold's life, each one more hilarious than the last. This version benefited from Louis Cassels, "Arnold, Fortas, Porter and Prosperity," *Harper's Magazine*, November 1951, pp. 62–64; Joseph Goulden, *The Superlawyers: The Small and Powerful World of the Great Washington Law Firms* (New York: Weybright and Talley, 1971), pp. 110–43; Jonathan Cottin, "Washington Pressures: Law Firm with Big-Name Clients is a Mover and Shaker in Nation's Capital," *National Journal*, 1/8/72, pp. 44–56; Thurman Arnold, *Fair Fights and Foul: A Dissenting Lawyer's Life* (New York: Harcourt, Brace, and World, 1951), *passim;* and William O. Douglas, *The*

Autobiography of William O. Douglas: Go East Young Man—The Early Years (New York: Random House, 1974), pp. 167–69, 423–25.

9. Cassels, "Arnold, Fortas, Porter and Prosperity," p. 63.

10. *Ibid.*

11. AI, Creekmore Fath, 3/10/83, Austin, Tex.

12. For more on Porter, see Cassels, "Arnold, Fortas, Porter and Prosperity," pp. 64–65; Goulden, *The Superlawyers*, pp.110–43; Paul Porter, LBJ/OH, *passim*; Clifford Durr, COHC, pp. 179–82; Paul Porter, Lawrence Fly project, COHC, *passim*.

13. Clifford Durr, COHC, p. 182.

14. Clifford Durr, COHC, pp. 179–80.

15. Cottin, "Washington Pressures," p. 49; see also Goulden, *The Superlawyers*, p. 122.

16. Fred Rodell, "The Complexities of Mr. Justice Fortas," *New York Times Magazine*, 7/28/68, p. 13.

17. Fred Graham, "Fortas, High Court Nominee, Leaving Law Firm That Is a Capital Byword," *NYT*, 8/8/65, p. 40; see also Cassels, "Arnold, Fortas, Porter and Prosperity," p. 68, and Fortas, "Thurman Arnold," p. 994.

18. Fortas, "Thurman Arnold," p. 991.

19. Cassels, "Arnold, Fortas, Porter and Prosperity," p. 67. For more on Washington lawyers as a breed, see Goulden, *The Superlawyers, passim;* Joseph Kraft, "The Washington Lawyers," *Harper's Magazine*, Vol. 228, No. 1367, April 1964, pp. 103–5; Martin Mayer, *The Lawyers*, (New York: Harper and Row, 1967); Lee Loevinger, "A Washington Lawyer Tells What It's Like," *George Washington Law Review*, Vol. 38, 1969–1970, pp. 531–45; and "They Build a Bridge to Washington," *Business Week*, 4/23/66, pp. 87–100. For a fine in-depth look at a single such lawyer, see Robert Pack, *Edward Bennett Williams for the Defense* (New York: Harper and Row, 1983).

20. Cassels, "Arnold, Fortas, Porter and Prosperity," p. 69.

21. Fred Lazarus to LBJ, 6/24/68, Files Pertaining to Abe Fortas and Homer Thornberry, Box 4, LBJL.

22. Lists of the clients of Arnold, Fortas and Porter have been developed in a variety of locations: Cottin, "Washington Pressures," pp. 46 and 44–56 generally; Cassels, "Arnold, Fortas, Porter and Prosperity," pp. 62–70; Andrew Kopkind and James Ridgeway, "Law and Power in Washington," *Hard Times*, No. 36, June 16–23, 1969, pp. 1–4; and Andrew Kopkind, "Fortas and the Power Game," *New Statesman*, 6/6/69, pp. 339–40.

23. Fortas, "Thurman Arnold," p. 1002. On other occasions, though, Fortas took a slightly different slant on the issue of clients and the law. Once he told an after-dinner group: "There are few things in a lawyer's life more rewarding than a substantial corporation whose officers are threatened with criminal prosecution. Here we have an ideal combination: a long purse, moral indignation, a protracted trial and a reasonable amount of fear." (E. W. Kenworthy, "From a Shoe Store to Legal Fame and Wealth," *NYT*, 5/16/69, p. 20.)

24. Cottin, "Washington Pressures," pp. 45–47; Charles Seib and Alan Otten, "Abe, Help!—LBJ," *Esquire*, June 1965, pp. 86–87; *NYT*, 8/8/65, p. 40; Anthony Lewis, *Gideon's Trumpet* (New York: Vintage Press, 1964), p. 53; and Goulden, *The Superlawyers*, pp. 119–20.

25. There are as many accounts of Fortas's income in his law practice as there are of Fortas's life. Fred Graham says that it was $150,000. (See Graham, "Fortas, High Court Nominee, Leaving Law Firm That Is a Capital Byword," *NYT*, 8/8/65, p. 40.) *Time* magazine says that the Fortases earned a combined income of $200,000 to $250,000. (*Time*, 8/6/65, p. 24.) Andrew Kopkind and James Ridgeway say that in 1965 Fortas's partnership was worth $325,000, and Carolyn Agger's was worth $216,000. (Kopkind and Ridgeway, "Law and Power in Washington," p. 1.) Robert Shogan says that Fortas earned $200,000 in 1964, while his wife took in another $100,000. (Shogan, *A Question of Judgment: The Fortas Case and the Struggle for the Supreme Court* (Indianapolis: Bobbs-Merrill Co., 1972), p. 192.) Finally, Fred Rodell says that Fortas's income in private practice was "four to five times" his judicial salary of $39,500. (Fred Rodell, "The Complexities of Mr. Justice Fortas," *New York Times Magazine*, 7/28/68, p. 64.)

26. There are as many accounts of the Fortas's lavish lifestyle as there are accounts of the Fortases. On the lifestyle, see Lewis, *Gideon's Trumpet*, pp. 52–53; Merle Miller, *Lyndon: An Oral Biography* (New York: Ballantine Books, 1980), pp. 586–87; *Time*, 8/6/65, p. 24; *Time*, 7/5/68, pp. 13, 16; Malvina Stephenson, "Fortas Always Has Had One Vote of Confidence," 10/15/68, Women's News Service, unpublished article in files of *Washington Star*, Martin Luther King Library, Washington, D.C.; AI, confidential source, 11/8/82, Austin, Tex.

27. Clifford Durr, COHC, p. 180; AI, confidential source, 11/8/82, Austin, Tex.

28. AI, Joseph L. Rauh, Jr., 7/9/79, Washington, D.C.

29. Milton Freeman, "Abe Fortas: A Man of Courage," *Yale Law Journal*, Vol. 91, 1982, p. 1052.

30. AI, Scott Powe, 11/8/82, Austin, Tex.

31. AI, Gloria McHugh, 7/15/83, New Haven, Conn.

32. Seib and Otten, "Abe, Help!—LBJ," p. 147.

33. *NYT*, 7/29/65, pp. 1, 13.

34. Anthony Lewis, "A Tough Lawyer Goes to the Court," *New York Times Magazine*, 8/8/65, p. 52. For more on the split in Fortas's personality, see Rodell, "Complexities of Mr. Justice Fortas," p. 13.

35. AI, Arthur "Tex" Goldschmidt, 6/10/84, Durham, N.Y.

36. Victor Kramer, ed., *Selections from the Letters and Legal Papers of Thurman Arnold* (Washington, D.C.: Merkle Press, 1961), p. 61.

37. Arnold, *Fair Fights and Foul*, p. 205.

38. For more on this incident and the general role of Arnold, Fortas and Porter during this dark period, see Kramer, "Wit and Wisdom of Arnold," pp. 67–68; Freeman, "Abe Fortas," p. 1055; Bert Andrews, *Washington Witch Hunt* (New York: Random House, 1948); Arnold, *Fair Fights and Foul*, pp. 204–27; Anthony Lewis, "Courage in Hard Times," *NYT*, 4/22/82; Goulden, *The Superlawyers*, pp. 119–21; and Cassels, "Arnold, Fortas, Porter and Prosperity," pp. 65–67.

39. Freeman, "Abe Fortas," pp. 1055, 1057.

40. Address by Abe Fortas to the *Yale Law Journal* banquet, 4/2/66, Tom Clark Papers, University of Texas Law School, Austin, Tex.

41. Arnold, *Fair Fights and Foul*, pp. 206–7; Cassels; "Arnold, Fortas, Porter and Prosperity," p. 67; Freeman, "Abe Fortas," 1055–56.

42. Owen Lattimore, *Ordeal by Slander* (Boston: Little, Brown and Co., 1950), p. 37 and *passim*.

43. Shogan, *Question of Judgment*, p. 62. Cottin, "Washington Pressures," *passim*, and Goulden, *The Superlawyers*, pp. 110–43, both indicate how this became a particular style of the Arnold, Fortas and Porter film.

44. Lattimore, *Ordeal by Slander*, pp. 1–50, 201; Drew Pearson, *Diaries: 1949–1959*, Tyler Abell, ed. (New York: Holt, Rinehart and Winston, 1974), p. 48.

45. Lattimore, *Ordeal by Slander*, pp. 37–38, 52–53, 111–12.

46. Lattimore, *Ordeal by Slander*, pp. 59–60 and 50–145 generally; also David Oshinsky, *A Conspiracy So Immense: The World of Joe McCarthy* (New York: Free Press, 1983), p. 147, and Thomas C. Reeves, *The Life and Times of Joe McCarthy: A Biography* (New York: Stein and Day, 1982), *passim*.

47. Lattimore, *Ordeal by Slander*, pp. 112–13, 115, 145; Reeves, *Life and Times of Joe McCarthy*, pp. 272, 296.

48. Lattimore, *Ordeal by Slander*, p. viii; Arnold, *Fair Fights and Foul*, pp. 214–27; Freeman, "Abe Fortas," pp. 1058–59. While Arnold remembers the hearings as being twelve days long, I have relied on Freeman's account. On the cost of the trials, see *NYT*, 8/8/65, p. 40.

49. Anthony Lewis, "Courage in Hard Times," *NYT*, 4/22/82, p. A31.

50. According to Joseph Goulden, who is very skeptical about the firm's reasons for taking such cases, some suspect these cases were carefully selected for their publicity value. (Goulden, *The Superlawyers*, pp. 120–22.) It was reputedly Sun Oil that was lost as a client. For another cynical view of the firm's motivation here, see Kopkind and Ridgeway, "Law and Power in Washington," p. 1. For the view of corporate practice as being treasonous to the New Deal, see Navasky, "Don't Not Return a Call," p. 32.

51. Cf. Freeman, "Abe Fortas," p. 1055, and Cassels, "Arnold, Fortas, Porter and Prosperity," p. 67.

52. Clifford Durr, COHC, pp. 220–21.

53. Willard Van Dyke, COHC, pp. 333–34.

54. Cassels, "Arnold, Fortas, Porter and Prosperity," p. 67.

55. Fortas himself gave an excellent account of this case in a speech for the Conference on Insanity and the Law, University of Chicago Law School, 2/28/55, entitled "Durham's Case: Mad or Bad?," William O. Douglas Papers, Box 327, LOC. For two more-accessible accounts, see Fred Graham, "Abe Fortas," in Leon Friedman and Fred Israel, *The Justices of the United States Supreme Court, 1789–1969*, Vol. IV (New York: Chelsea House, 1971), pp. 3015–16, and Shogan, *Question of Judgment*, pp. 74–75.

56. The version that follows relies on the best account of the case, which can be found in Anthony Lewis, *Gideon's Trumpet* (New York: Vintage Books, 1964), *passim*.

57. *Betts* v. *Brady*, 316 U.S. 455 (1942).

58. Abe Fortas, LBJ/OH, p. 9. Fortas makes this point to differ from the account in Lewis's book at pp. 118–38.

59. William O. Douglas, *The Autobiography of William O. Douglas: The Court Years, 1939–75* (New York: Random House, 1980), p. 187.
60. Lewis, *Gideon's Trumpet*, pp. 171–72.
61. *Ibid.*, p. 174.
62. *Gideon* v. *Wainwright*, 372 U.S. 335 (1963).
63. AI, AF, 8/7/81, Washington, D.C.
64. AI, Dagmar Hamilton, 10/14/82, Austin, Tex.

CHAPTER IV

FAVORS

1. Merle Miller, *Lyndon: An Oral Biography* (New York: Ballantine Books, 1980), p. 161.
2. *The New York Times* reported in 1965 that it was William O. Douglas who had brought Fortas into the 1948 litigation. However, in a letter to the justice, an angry Fortas recalled vividly that it was Wirtz who had done so. (See AF to WOD, 3/2/65, William O. Douglas Papers, Box 327, LOC.) See also AF, LBJ/OH, p. 5, and Abe Fortas, "The President, the Congress, and the Public: The Lyndon B. Johnson Presidency," in Kenneth Thompson, ed., *The Virginia Papers on the Presidency*, Vol. X (Lanham, Md.: University Press of America, 1982), p. 13.
3. Fortas, "The President, the Congress, and the Public," p. 13.
4. Fortas himself realized this fact. See Fortas, "The President, the Congress, and the Public," *passim.* This can be confirmed by a review of the Fortas materials in the Johnson Library, which are cited below, and interviews with mutual acquaintances—e.g., AI, Walter Jenkins, 11/3/82, Austin, Tex.; AI, Donald Thomas, 11/16/82, Austin, Tex.; and AI, Warren Woodward, 11/9/82 (by phone), Dallas, Tex.
5. Aside from a number of general accounts on the Johnson election to the Senate, the secondary source material for this version includes Miller, *Lyndon*, pp. 141–67, and Alfred Steinberg, *Sam Johnson's Boy: A Close-up of the President from Texas* (New York: Macmillan Co., 1968), pp. 229–72.
6. AI, Donald Thomas, 11/16/82, Austin, Tex.
7. *Ibid.*
8. Paul Porter, LBJ/OH, p. 13; Marshall McNeil, "How Fortas Gave LBJ His Senatorial Start," *Washington Post*, 8/3/65, housed in the *Washington Post* morgue, Washington, D.C.
9. AI, Walter Jenkins, 11/3/82, Austin, Tex.; Miller, *Lyndon*, p. 160.
10. AI, Walter Jenkins, 11/3/82, Austin, Tex.
11. AF, LBJ/OH, p. 6.
12. Paul Porter, LBJ/OH, I, p. 13.
13. Miller, *Lyndon*, p. 161.
14. AI, Mary Rather, 11/12/82, Gonzalez, Tex.
15. AF, LBJ/OH, p. 6.
16. AI, Mary Rather, 11/12/82, Gonzalez, Tex.
17. James H. Rowe, Jr., LBJ/OH, pp. 22–23.
18. Paul Porter, LBJ/OH, p. 13.
19. *Ibid.*, p. 14.
20. Here I rely on the account of a witness who was a pool reporter at the time: Marshall McNeil, "How Fortas Gave LBJ His Senatorial Start," *Washington Post*, 8/3/65, housed in the *Washington Post* morgue, Washington, D.C. While Paul Porter (LBJ/OH, p. 15) says that the hearing was in open court, it seems likely that the single judge involved, Justice Black, would choose to hear the arguments in the more intimate surroundings of his private office.
21. Fortas, "The President, the Congress, and the Public," p. 13; Paul Porter, LBJ/OH, p. 15.
22. The account that follows relies on McNeil, "How Fortas Gave LBJ His Senatorial Start," *Washington Post*, 8/3/65, housed in the *Washington Post* morgue, Washington, D.C.
23. *Ibid.*
24. *Ibid.*
25. Paul Porter, LBJ/OH, p. 15; Miller, *Lyndon*, p. 162.
26. LBJ to AF, 10/1/48, LBJA Selected Names Files, Box 18, LBJL.
27. AI, Walter Jenkins, 11/3/82, Austin, Tex.
28. Transcript of an interview with Richard Russell, "Richard Russell: Georgia Giant," 1970, WSB-TV,

Documentary No. 3, p. 25 (hereinafter WSB-TV Transcript); Douglas Kiker, "Russell of Georgia: The Old Guard at its Shrewdest," *Harper's Magazine,* September 1966, p. 106.

29. Kiker, "Russell of Georgia," p. 104; Meg Greenfield, "The Man Who Leads the Southern Senators," *The Reporter,* 5/21/64, p. 20.

30. William Darden, LBJ/OH, p. 8.

31. WSB-TV Transcript, No. 3, p. 21.

32. William Jordan, LBJ/OH, p. 5.

33. William Darden, LBJ/OH, p. 4.

34. Greenfield, "Man Who Leads the Southern Senators," p. 20.

35. Wayne Kelley, "How Russell Helped LBJ to Presidency," *Atlanta Journal and Constitution Magazine,* 6/30/68, pp. 7, 21.

36. Harry McPherson, LBJ/OH, p. 31.

37. Kelley, "How Russell Helped LBJ," p. 20.

38. Rowland Evans and Robert Novak, *Lyndon B. Johnson: The Exercise of Power* (New York: New American Library, 1966), p. 50.

39. *Ibid.,* p. 51.

40. Greenfield, "Man Who Leads the Southern Senators," p. 20–21.

41. Kelley, "How Russell Helped LBJ," pp. 20–21. Two other articles by Kelley are very useful for discovering the relationship between LBJ and Russell. See "Senator Russell Vows to Speak His Mind," *Atlanta Journal and Constitution Magazine,* 2/4/68, pp. 8–9, 22–23, and "A Conversation with Richard Russell," *Atlanta Magazine,* 12/68, pp. 1–5.

42. Harry McPherson, LBJ/OH, pp. 31–34. For an engaging account of this fight, see Walter Murphy, *Congress and the Court* (Chicago: University of Chicago Press, 1962).

43. Kelley, "How Russell Helped LBJ," p. 21; Greenfield, "Man Who Leads the Southern Senators," pp. 20–21.

44. Kelley, "How Russell Helped LBJ," p. 21.

45. See Elizabeth Goldschmidt, LBJ/OH, *passim;* AI, Arthur "Tex" Goldschmidt, 6/10/84, Durham, N.Y.

46. Robert Caro, *The Years of Lyndon Johnson: The Path to Power* (New York: Vintage Books, 1981), p. 177; Miller, *Lyndon,* pp. 212–14; Evans and Novak, *Lyndon B. Johnson,* pp. 106–22.

47. Richard Tanner Johnson, *Managing the White House: An Intimate Study of the Presidency* (New York: Harper and Row, 1974), p. 173.

48. Miller, *Lyndon,* p. 212.

49. These impressions are drawn from my observation of Fortas during my 8/7/81 interview with him in Washington, D.C.

50. AI, Walter Jenkins, 11/3/82, Austin, Tex.; AI, Arthur "Tex" Goldschmidt, 6/10/84, Durham, N.Y.

51. AI, Mildred Stegall, 11/16/82, Austin, Tex.; confirmed in AI with Walter Jenkins, 11/3/82, Austin, Tex.

52. AI, Walter Jenkins, 11/3/82, Austin, Tex.

53. *Ibid.*

54. *Ibid.*

55. *Ibid.*

56. The term comes from Steinberg, *Sam Johnson's Boy,* p. 323.

57. AI, Sim Gideon, 11/15/82, Austin, Tex. These sentiments were echoed in interviews with Walter Jenkins, 11/3/82 and Mildred Stegall, 11/16/82, Austin, Tex.

58. Steinberg, *Sam Johnson's Boy,* p. 323.

59. Miller, *Lyndon,* p. 82.

60. Elizabeth Goldschmidt, LBJ/OH, I, pp. 24–25.

61. AI, Walter Jenkins, 11/3/82, Austin, Tex.

62. *Ibid.* Others used much the same language—e.g., AI, Warren Woodward, 11/9/82 (by phone), Dallas, Tex.

63. AI, Sim Gideon, 11/15/82, Austin, Tex.

64. AI, Donald Thomas, 11/16/82, Austin, Tex.

65. AI, Warren Woodward, 11/9/82 (by phone), Dallas, Tex.

66. One is left to wonder whether Johnson saw Wirtz as having originally tapped Fortas for this role by insisting initially that he be brought into the 1948 litigation. That early recommendation and confidence could only have been confirmed by Johnson's own observations of Fortas's actions in that crisis and later on.

67. Fred Rodell, "The Complexities of Mr. Justice Fortas," *New York Times Magazine*, 7/28/68, p. 12.

68. LBJ to AF, 10/26/55, 11/3/55, and 8/24/56, Senate Masters, 1955 and 1956 folders, LBJL.

69. LBJ to AF, 8/24/56, Senate Masters, 1956 folder, LBJL.

70. *Ibid.*

71. Memorandum of conversation with Abe Fortas, by Walter Jenkins, 10/26/56, LBJA Selected Names Files, Fortas folder, LBJL.

72. AF to LBJ, undated; AF to LBJ, 3/27/59; AF to LBJ, 1/15/59; AF to LBJ, 10/28/58; and AF to LBJ, 7/22/58, Senate Masters, 1958 and 1959 folders, LBJL. AF to LBJ, 7/30/58, LBJA Selected Names Files, Box 18, LBJL.

73. AI, Donald Thomas, 11/16/82, Austin, Tex.

74. *Ibid.* See also AF to Walter Jenkins, 3/27/59, U.S. Senate 1949–61, Box 661, LBJL, and AF to LBJ, 8/9/56, LBJA Selected Names Files, Box 18, LBJL.

75. See AF to Walter Jenkins, 3/27/59, U.S. Senate 1949–61, Box 661, LBJL, on Fortas's recommendation of Stuart Rothman as general counsel for the National Labor Relations Board. And see AF to Jenkins, 7/25/60, Senate Files, Box 1193, LBJL, on Fortas's recommendation for Robert Bicks as assistant attorney general.

76. AF to Walter Jenkins, 8/1/55; AF to Jenkins, 6/8/55; "Brief on Section 7 of the bill to amend the fair labor standards act of 1938"; and Jenkins to LBJ, 6/6/55, LBJA Selected Names Files, Box 18, LBJL.

77. Phone message memorandum, undated; action memorandum, 7/23/58; and memorandum from AF to LBJ, 7/22/58, U.S. Senate 1949–61, Box 587, LBJL.

78. Walter Jenkins to LBJ, 8/18/58, Senate Masters, 1958 folder, LBJL. The Senate bill Fortas was pushing, S4129, was allowed to die in lieu of the identical House bill, H13666. This bill became PL 85-894.

79. Charles Seib and Alan Otten, "Abe, Help!—LBJ," *Esquire*, June 1965, pp. 88, 147.

80. Memorandum of phone conversation with Abe Fortas, by Walter Jenkins, 5/21/60, Senate Masters, 1960 folder, LBJL.

81. Memorandum of phone conversation with Abe Fortas, by Walter Jenkins, 6/3/60, Senate Masters, 1960 folder, LBJL.

82. AF to Walter Jenkins, 7/8/60, Senate Masters, 1960 folder, LBJL.

83. AF to Walter Jenkins, 7/25/60, Senate Masters, 1960 folder, LBJL.

84. Walter Jenkins to AF, 8/6/60, Senate Masters, 1960 folder, LBJL.

85. Walter Jenkins to LBJ, 9/27/60, VP Recommendations Files, LBJL.

86. George Reedy, *Lyndon B. Johnson: A Memoir* (New York: Andrews and McMeel, 1982), p. 127.

87. Press release, White House, 3/6/61, WHCF, FG 731, JFKL.

88. Seib and Otten, "Abe, Help!—LBJ," p. 148.

89. Memorandum of phone call, Mildred to vice president, 6/13/63, Senate Masters, 1963 folder, LBJL.

90. Seib and Otten, "Abe, Help!—LBJ," p. 147.

91. Meeting notes, 4/11/61, President's Committee on Equal Employment, 1/20/61–6/15/61, WHCF, FG 731, JFKL.

92. Harris Wofford, RFK/OH, p. 126; George Weaver, RFK/OH, p. 25; and Hobart Taylor, RFK/OH, p. 7, JFKL.

93. Hobart Taylor, RFK/OH, p. 13, JFKL.

94. Conversation with Floyd Feeney, 1/9/87, Davis, Calif.

95. Harris Wofford, RFK/OH, *passim*, JFKL; Steinberg, *Sam Johnson's Boy*, p. 561.

96. JFK to AF, 6/22/62, WHCF, FG 642, JFKL.

97. AF, LBJ/OH, p. 15.

98. Seib and Otten, "Abe, Help!—LBJ," p. 149.

99. Memorandum, AF to Pierre Salinger, 10/5/61, WHCF, Box 506, JFKL; see also program and list of attendees, WHCF, Box 28, JFKL.

100. AF, LBJ/OH, pp. 15–17. See also AF to Jay Gildner, 1/10/62, WHCF, PR12, JFKL.

101. This is said based on an examination of both the presidential files in the Kennedy Library and the vice presidential files in the Johnson Library. Exceptions to this rule came, however, when the actions of the administration affected Fortas's law work. In 1961 he praised the Kennedy administration's executive memorandum on the status of Puerto Rico in United States government agencies. Then in 1963 Fortas was asked by the deputy special counsel to the president, Myer Feldman, to analyze the White House's formula for approval of a proposed merger between American Airlines and Eastern Airlines. (See "Memorandum for the Heads of the Executive Departments and Agen-

cies,'' 7/25/61, WHCF, Box 941; AF to Lee White, 7/26/61, WHCF, Box 941; and AF to Feldman, 6/12/63, WHCF, Box 29, JFKL.)

102. Miller, *Lyndon*, pp. 361–66, was used as a basis for this account.

103. AF, LBJ/OH, p. 21; Miller, *Lyndon*, p. 362.

104. Miller, *Lyndon*, pp. 364–65; George Reedy, LBJ/OH, III, pp. 37–38. For more, see Steinberg, *Sam Johnson's Boy*, pp. 595–602.

105. Bobby Baker, *Wheeling and Dealing: Confessions of a Capitol Hill Operator* (New York: W. W. Norton and Co., 1978), p. 160. There is some dispute about who was in Fortas's office during the time of Kennedy's assassination. The same claim is also made by former secretary of the navy Fred Korth, who remembers consulting Fortas at that time about his own legal problems. Given the delay between the announcements about the president's shooting and his actual death, it is possible that both men's recollections are correct. (See Fred Korth, LBJ/OH, p. 28.)

106. Baker, *Wheeling and Dealing*, p. 160.

107. Steinberg, *Sam Johnson's Boy*, p. 612.

108. Seib and Otten, ''Abe, Help!—LBJ,'' p. 87.

109. AF, LBJ/OH, p. 21.

Chapter V
''Presidential Adviser, Washington''

1. AF, LBJ/OH, pp. 22–23.

2. The words from the first encounter of the two men after the assassination are from Fred Rodell, ''The Complexities of Mr. Justice Fortas,'' *New York Times Magazine*, 7/28/68, p. 65. As Rodell was an intimate of Fortas, the first words of that encounter were well within his field of knowledge, and his account seems thoroughly consistent with the nature of the Fortas-Johnson relationship at that time.
     There is considerable controversy, however, about the location of this conversation. An oft-told tale, which is repeated in Rodell, claims that Johnson phoned Fortas from Air Force One on his way back to Dallas asking the attorney to meet him at Andrews Air Force Base. (See Eric Goldman, *The Tragedy of Lyndon Johnson* [New York: Alfred A. Knopf, 1969], p. 39.) On the other hand, Alfred Steinberg writes that Johnson ''missed'' seeing Fortas upon landing at the base. (See Steinberg, *Sam Johnson's Boy: A Close-up of the President from Texas* [New York: Macmillan Co., 1968], p. 611.) However, this account could not be confirmed either by an examination of the files in the Kennedy and Johnson presidential libraries, or by discussions with people who observed the president's actions, and others who were familiar with the president's actions, on the plane. Accordingly, I am relying on the account of Fortas himself, who had a clear recollection of the meeting taking place the following morning in the EOB.

3. LBJ used precisely the same language with at least two men. (AI, Walter Jenkins, 11/3/82, and Donald Thomas, 11/16/82, Austin, Tex.)

4. Rex Lee, ''In Memoriam: Abe Fortas,'' reprinted from the solicitor general's remarks before the Supreme Court of the United States during the Special Session in memory of Justice Fortas on December 13, 1982, *Supreme Court Historical Society Yearbook*, 1983, p. 8.

5. Interview with James Jones, by John Ben Sutter, in Sutter, ''The Advisory Relationship of Justice Abe Fortas to President Lyndon B. Johnson,'' unpublished master's thesis, Baylor University, 1983, p. 112.

6. AI, Donald Thomas, 11/16/82, Austin, Tex.

7. William Manchester, *The Death of a President, November 20–November 25, 1963* (New York: Harper and Row, 1967), pp. 458–59.

8. *Ibid.*, pp. 472, 630.

9. The first mention of Fortas's role with the Warren Commission appears to be in Manchester's *Death of a President* (pp. 458–59). Manchester, however, says that Fortas ''played an unknown but vital role in the Commission's investigation.'' Perhaps the vagueness of this statement led later writers to surmise that Fortas had proposed the commission. (See *NYT*, 7/29/65, p. 13, and Charles Seib and Alan Otten, ''Abe, Help!—LBJ,'' *Esquire*, June 1965, p. 87.) Even Fortas's friend Fred Rodell said that ''it has been reported'' that Fortas was involved here, perhaps even in the selection of the personnel involved. (Rodell, ''The Complexities of Mr. Justice Fortas,'' p. 65.) Alfred Steinberg also claims that Fortas initiated the idea of the national investigatory commission and selected all of

the major figures who would serve on it. (Steinberg, *Sam Johnson's Boy,* p. 625.) The record is further confused by the fact that Fortas himself later claimed, contrary to the contemporaneous written record in the Johnson Library files, that the investigatory commission had been his idea. (Merle Miller, *Lyndon: An Oral Biography* [New York: Ballantine Books, 1980], p. 422.)

10. James H. Rowe, Jr., LBJ/OH, II, p. 33.

11. See George Reedy, *The Twilight of the Presidency* (New York: World, 1970), *passim,* and Doris Kearns, *Lyndon Johnson and the American Dream* (New York: New American Library, 1970), *passim.*

12. Transcript of phone conversation with Abe Fortas, by Walter Jenkins, 11/25/63, Executive Box FG1, LBJL. Whether this was Fortas's initial belief, or one adopted in response to a request by Lyndon Johnson, is not known. Given the nature of their working arrangement at the time, it seems likely that the idea was originally the president's. In his conversations with those outside the White House, however, Fortas gave the impression that he was speaking for himself only.

13. *Ibid.* Another interesting question in this incident is whether, once the president decided to have a federal commission, Fortas then turned around and advised him on how to accomplish it. Did he, then, in fact help to select the members of the commission? Once again, Fortas himself claimed that he had suggested Earl Warren as chairman of the commission. (Miller, *Lyndon,* p. 422.) If so, there is no record of this advice presently available in the Johnson Library, and no transcript has been released, if any exists, of the two men's conversations at that time. All that can be said definitively, then, is that contrary to other accounts, Fortas opposed the initial creation of the Warren Commission and acted on the president's behalf in trying to convince others to adopt the same view.

14. Interview with James Jones, in Sutter, "Fortas to LBJ," pp. 96–97.

15. AF to Adolf Berle, 5/27/64, Adolf Berle Papers, Box 220, FDRL.

16. Abe Fortas, "The President, the Congress, and the Public: The Lyndon B. Johnson Presidency," in Kenneth Thompson, ed., *The Virginia Papers on the Presidency,* Vol. X (Lanham, Md.: University Press of America, 1982), p. 14.

17. *Ibid.,* p. 15, has an account of this dinner. The date was confirmed by an examination of the Johnson presidential diaries.

18. Miller, *Lyndon,* p. 411.

19. Fortas, "The President, the Congress, and the Public," p. 15.

20. *Ibid.*

21. Miller, *Lyndon,* p. 411; Seib and Otten, "Abe, Help!—LBJ," pp. 88, 147.

22. Miller, *Lyndon,* p. 411; Steinberg, *Sam Johnson's Boy,* p. 625.

23. Tom Wicker, *JFK and LBJ: The Influence of Personality on Politics* (New York: Penguin Books, 1968), p. 168.

24. Steinberg, *Sam Johnson's Boy,* p. 627; Jack Bell, *The Johnson Treatment: How Lyndon B. Johnson Took Over the Presidency and Made It His Own* (New York: Harper and Row, 1965), p. 24.

25. This conclusion is drawn from an examination of Fortas's handwritten draft of the speech, "Remarks of the President Before a Joint Session of Congress, House Chamber—Capitol," 11/27/63, Statements File, Folder 1, Box 89, LBJL, and a comparison with the final draft in *NYT,* 11/28/63, p. 20.

26. Sorensen's draft speech, written 11/26/63, can be found in "Remarks of the President Before a Joint Session of Congress, House Chamber—Capitol," 11/27/63, Statements File, Folder 1, Box 89, LBJL.

27. Fortas, "The President, the Congress, and the Public," pp. 17–18.

28. *NYT,* 11/28/63, p. 20, and Miller, *Lyndon,* p. 412, contain this final speech wording. While the predominant thrust of this language is Fortas's, a comparison with the earlier speech draft indicates that his language was changed only slightly for stylistic improvement.

29. *Ibid.*

30. *NYT,* 11/28/63, p. 20.

31. Duplicate accounts of this meeting were given by two sources: AI, Donald Thomas, 11/16/82, Austin, Tex., and AI, Waddy Bullion, 11/10/82, Dallas, Tex.

32. AI, Donald Thomas, 11/16/82, Austin, Tex.

33. *Ibid.*

34. The rules for such an instrument were relatively straightforward. The president was not to know how his businesses were being operated as long as he held elective office. At the end of the fiscal year, his accountants would receive only enough financial information to fill out his tax returns.

   As it turned out, liquid cash for household expenses was not going to be a problem. Several years earlier, Don Thomas explained to the assembled group at The Elms, the Johnsons' broadcasting company had adopted a salary continuation plan in anticipation of the retirement of its president,

Jesse Kellam, who was known not to have much in reserve for his final days. The idea was that any officer of the corporation would continue to receive a full salary for a period of time equal to the number of years of service in the company after the adoption of the plan. Since the plan was already in place, it meant that the company would be supporting the Johnsons with substantial financial payments throughout this presidency. (AI, Donald Thomas, 11/16/82, Austin, Tex.)

35. Seib and Otten, "Abe, Help!—LBJ," p. 87.

36. AI, Waddy Bullion, 11/10/82, Dallas, Tex. For more on how LBJ continued to run his financial affairs even with the blind trust, see Steinberg, *Sam Johnson's Boy*, p. 627, and Robert A. Caro, *The Years of Lyndon Johnson: The Path to Power* (New York: Vintage Press, 1981), pp. xxii–xxiii. Caro promises more on this subject in his forthcoming volumes.

37. AI, Donald Thomas, 11/16/82, Austin, Tex.

38. AI, Waddy Bullion, 11/10/82, Dallas, Tex.

39. Nothing was done about the surplus funds from the radio and cable company, however, because that was separate property owned only by Mrs. Johnson.

40. AI, Donald Thomas, 11/16/82, Austin, Tex.

41. AI, Arthur "Tex" Goldschmidt, 6/10/84, Durham, N.Y.

42. David Halberstam argues that the fact that Fortas was tied only to Johnson and no other politician in Washington made him even more attractive to the president as being *his* man. Indeed, unlike other prominent Washington lawyers who have served as advisers to several administrations, this was Fortas's only real fling in the White House. (See Halberstam, *The Best and the Brightest* [New York: Fawcett World Library, 1972], p. 715.) Later, one attorney at Arnold and Porter would reflect on his colleague's actions during this period and tell a reporter, "People there practically lost track of [Fortas]. He was living on the telephone or at the White House." (Robert Shogan, *A Question of Judgment: The Fortas Case and the Struggle for the Supreme Court* [Indianapolis: Bobbs-Merrill Co., 1972], p. 96.)

43. AI, AF, 8/7/81, Washington, D.C.

44. *Ibid.*

45. AI, Arthur "Tex" Goldschmidt, 6/10/84, Durham, N.Y.

46. AI, AF, 8/7/81, Washington, D.C. At times, Fortas said, he and Clifford would be brought in together and asked to debate both sides of a given topic. Clifford, on the other hand, recalls these occasions slightly differently. While he does recall that the two men were being phoned separately on the same issues, and that on occasion they were brought to the White House together for consultations with the president, Clifford does not recall that it was "a practiced policy" for the two men to debate both sides of an issue before Johnson. "That was not our function," adds Clifford. Instead, issues were raised for the two men to discuss, while the president just sat and listened. If there were disagreements on issues, they would come out in the course of the discussions. (Clark Clifford, LBJ/OH, IV, p. 7, and II, p. 4.)

47. James H. Rowe, Jr., LBJ/OH, II, p. 32.

48. AI, George Christian, 11/11/82, Austin, Tex.

49. Clark Clifford, LBJ/OH, IV, p. 7.

50. One such list contained Fortas's marginal comments on plans for the "Commission on Registration and Voting Participation," the "President's Advisory Commission on Narcotic and Drug Abuse," and campaign financing. (See memo, Lee C. White to LBJ, 12/6/63, Ex FG/RS/Pr 18, Box 9, LBJL.

51. See AF to LBJ, undated; Walter Jenkins to AF, 11/28/63, plus attached memo from Reedy to LBJ, undated; and AF to LBJ, 12/1/63, Files Pertaining to Abe Fortas and Homer Thornberry, Box 1, LBJL (hereinafter Fortas-Thornberry Files).

52. *Ibid.*

53. AF to LBJ, 12/1/63, Diary Backup, Box 2, LBJL.

54. Memo, "The Presidential Succession," undated, Fortas-Thornberry Files, Box 1, LBJL.

55. Memo, AF to LBJ, undated, Fortas-Thornberry Files, Box 1, and memo, Walter Jenkins to LBJ, 12/8/63, FG 1, LBJL.

56. "Bob" to LBJ, 12/1/63, Diary Backup, Box 2, plus White House Diary entry for December 1; AF to Walter Jenkins, 12/24/63, Fortas-Thornberry Files, Box 1; and memo, AF to LBJ, re: foreign aid, 12/24/63, Legislation Files, Box 57, LBJL.

57. To this point, Fortas had only suggested that the president use "charts and graphs" in the speech. See Walter Jenkins to LBJ, 12/8/63, Ex FG 1; Jenkins to AF, 12/10/63, Fortas-Thornberry Files, Box 1; and AF to LBJ, 1/29/64, Fortas Name File, Box 1, LBJL.

The account of the meeting that follows comes from a set of meeting notes now in the possession of Walter Rostow, 12/23/63, Austin, Tex. The other quotations are taken from the account of the meeting by Eric Goldman, in *The Tragedy of Lyndon Johnson* (New York: Alfred A. Knopf, 1955), pp. 41–42, 129.

58. President's personal autograph file record, 1/21/64, White House photo collection. Other autographed pictures were sent on 12/21/63 and 12/23/63, and two were sent on 12/24/63.

59. The "certain assignments" phrase comes from Fortas's letter explaining why he was resigning from Bobby Baker's case. (See *Washington Post,* 12/3/63 and 12/4/63, A6, A10; *NYT,* 12/3/63, p. 36; and *Washington Star,* 12/3/63 and 12/4/63, housed in *Washington Star* morgue, Martin Luther King Library, Washington, D.C.)

60. AI, confidential source, 11/8/82, Austin, Tex.

61. *Ibid.* The growth in the size of the Arnold, Fortas and Porter law firm can be charted from a review of the yearly editions of the *Martindale-Hubbell* law directory.

62. Elizabeth Brenner Drew, "A Quiet Victory for the Cigarette Lobby," *Atlantic Monthly,* Vol. 216, No. 3, September 1965, p. 77. This article contains perhaps the best account of Fortas's work for the tobacco industry.

63. For other fine accounts of Fortas's work in this area, see Joseph Goulden, *The Superlawyers: The Small and Powerful World of the Great Washington Law Firms* (New York: Weybright and Talley, 1971), pp. 131–32; Victor Navasky, "In Washington, You Just Don't Not Return a Call from Abe Fortas," *New York Times Magazine,* 8/1/71, p. 32; and Andrew Kopkind and James Ridgeway, "Law and Power in Washington," *Hard Times,* No. 36, June 16–23, 1969, p. 3.

64. Drew, "A Quiet Victory," p. 77.

65. Robert Sherrill, *The Accidental President* (New York: Grossman, 1967), p. 151; Kopkind and Ridgeway, "Law and Power in Washington," p. 3.

66. Memo, Marvin [Watson] to LBJ, 7/30/65, Ex Gen FG 535/A, Box 360, LBJL.

67. See, AF to LBJ, 1/6/64, answered by O'Brien to LBJ, 1/10/64, Fortas-Thornberry Files, Box 1, LBJL.

68. AF to Walter Jenkins, 1/24/64, Fortas-Thornberry Files, Box 1, LBJL.

69. AF to Jack Valenti, 2/20/64, Fortas-Thornberry Files, Box 1; AF to Walter Jenkins on Republican James P. Mitchell, 7/11/64, Fortas-Thornberry Files, Box 1; AF to Ralph Dungan on Joan Raushenbush, 8/25/64, John Macy Office Files, Fortas folder; and Valenti to LBJ, 12/28/64, Fortas-Thornberry Files, Box 2, LBJL.

   Also, for a superb account of the multitiered Johnson personnel process in this period, on which my account relies, see Richard L. Schott and Dagmar S. Hamilton, *People, Positions and Power: The Political Appointments of Lyndon Johnson* (Chicago: University of Chicago Press, 1983), pp. 1–34. The counts of contacts and phone calls between Fortas and LBJ come from the White House Presidential Diary in LBJL.

70. AF to Bill Moyers, 1/21/64; AF to Walter Jenkins, 7/10/64; Jack Valenti to Ralph Dungan, 2/13/64; and Dungan to Mr. Clinton, 2/13/64, Fortas Name File, LBJL. Mildred to Jenkins (on AF call), 5/2/64, Fortas-Thornberry Files, Box 1, LBJL. Valenti to LBJ (on AF call), 8/24/64, and AF to Valenti, 1/31/64, Confidential File, Name File, Box 3, LBJL.

71. AF to Walter Jenkins, 9/19/64, Fortas-Thornberry Files, Box 1, and Jenkins to AF, 10/3/64, Fortas Name File, LBJL.

72. Jack Valenti to LBJ (on AF call) 8/24/65; AF to LBJ (on presidential cultural program), 3/10/64; and Valenti to AF, 12/3/64, Fortas Name File, LBJL. AF to Walter Jenkins, 3/23/64, Fortas-Thornberry Files, Box 1, LBJL.

73. Walter Jenkins to LBJ (on AF call), 3/12/64, Fortas-Thornberry Files, Box 1, LBJL. See also Jack Valenti to AF, 11/24/64, and Valenti to LBJ, 12/1/64, Fortas Name File, LBJL. (Here AF was recommending Joan Braden for the Kennedy Center board, because Jackie Kennedy very much wanted the selection to be made.)

74. AF to Jack Valenti, 11/16/64, Fortas Name File, LBJL.

75. See, for example, Fortas's recommendation of a businessman with the requisite skills to do both, in his opinion, a man named Richard Cudahy. (AF to Jack Valenti, 12/7/64, Fortas-Thornberry Files, Box 1, and Valenti to John Macy, 12/10/64, Fortas Name File, LBJL.)

76. AF to John Macy, 11/16/64, undated, 12/19/64, 12/28/64, 1/15/65, 1/28/65, 1/30/65, 2/2/65, 2/12/65, 2/24/65, 3/9/65, 3/13/65, 4/10/65, 6/10/65, 6/24/65; and AF to Nicholas deB. Katzenbach, 3/15/65, with a copy to John Macy, John Macy Office Files, Fortas folder, LBJL.

77. This account is based on Schott and Hamilton, *People, Positions and Power,* pp. 59–64; plus material not used in the book and shared with me in a discussion with Dagmar Hamilton, 3/1/82, Austin,

Tex. My thanks are offered here for the assistance and encouragement of Ms. Hamilton here and throughout the project.

78. AF to Walter Jenkins, 2/7/64 (with memorandum for the special counsel draft attached), and AF to Jenkins, 2/12/64, Fortas-Thornberry Files, Box 1, LBJL.

79. Memorandum opinion of Arnold, Fortas and Porter, 2/17/64, Fortas-Thornberry Files, Box 1, LBJL; Steinberg, *Sam Johnson's Boy*, p. 630.

80. Memo, AF to LBJ, 12/9/64, Clark Clifford Name File; AF to LBJ, 2/12/64, and AF to Bill Moyers, 2/25/65, Fortas-Thornberry Files, Box 1; memo, MJDR to LBJ, undated, Diary Backup, Box 1; and Lee White to LBJ, 6/21/65, Fortas Name File, LBJL.

81. AF to LBJ, memo re: removal power, 6/15/65, Fortas-Thornberry Files, Box 1; and Jacobsen to LBJ, 7/6/65, Legislative Background Files, Box 6, LBJL. Here Fortas took the hard-line Johnson stance, contrary to the advice of the attorney general. He argued that the man could be removed at the president's "pleasure" rather than for "cause" (which did not include a disagreement over policy).

82. Mrs. Lyndon Baines Johnson, *A White House Diary* (New York: Holt, Rinehart and Winston, 1970), p. 627; Shogan, *Question of Judgment*, p. 97; Sutter, "Fortas to LBJ," pp. 51–55; Goldman, *Tragedy of LBJ*, p. 39; and Fortas, LBJ/OH, pp. 15–17.

83. AF interview in 1976, by John Ben Sutter, in Sutter, "Fortas to LBJ," p. 56.

84. August Heckscher to AF, 1/7/64; memo, AF to Messrs. Battle, Salinger, and Stern, 1/31/64; and AF to Myer Feldman, 6/17/64, Fortas Name File, LBJL.

85. Bill Moyers to AF, 3/17/65; AF to Myer Feldman, 3/30/64; and AF to Roger Stevens, 11/23/64, Fortas Name File, LBJL. AF to Jack Valenti, 8/3/64, Fortas-Thornberry Files, Box 1, LBJL. See also Fortas, LBJ/OH, p. 18.

86. See Walter Jenkins to LBJ, 11/24/63; AF to Jack Valenti, 1/14/65; LBJ to Luis Muñoz-Marin, 8/24/64; Valenti to LBJ, 12/12/64; Marvin Watson to LBJ, 5/10/65; McGeorge Bundy to AF, 6/25/65; and AF to Valenti, 6/30/65, Fortas Name File, LBJL. AF to Walter Jenkins, 2/4/64; AF to LBJ, 2/4/64; AF to Valenti, 1/14/65; AF to Bundy, 6/21/65; and AF to Valenti, 6/30/65, Fortas-Thornberry Files, Box 1, LBJL. Mary White to ———, 1/29/65, with "Memorandum Re: Scheduled Conference Between LBJ and Governor of Puerto Rico" (envelope shows this was sent by AF to George Reedy initially with the intention of educating the new president about the island in a four-page memo), and Marvin Watson to LBJ, 2/8/65, Diary Backup, LBJL.

87. Interview with James Jones, by John Ben Sutter, in Sutter, "Fortas to LBJ," p. 105.

88. Theodore White, *The Making of the President, 1964* (New York: Atheneum, 1965), p. 367ff.

89. AF to LBJ, 8/18/64, Fortas-Thornberry Files, Box 1, LBJL; Bill Moyers to LBJ, 9/3/64, and AF to Moyers, 9/4/64, Fortas Name File, LBJL.

90. Arthur Schlesinger, Jr., *Robert Kennedy and His Times* (New York: Ballantine, 1978), p. 715; Evans and Novak, *Lyndon B. Johnson*, pp. 445–48.

91. Many accounts have been given of this incident, so I will concentrate on the new information gleaned about Fortas's role in it. For more on the general background, though, see Seib and Otten, "Abe, Help!—LBJ," pp. 86–87; Evans and Novak, *Lyndon B. Johnson*, pp. 479–80, and White, *Making of the President, 1964*, pp. 386–89.

92. AI, Mildred Stegall, 11/16/82, Austin, Tex.; AI, Liz Carpenter, 11/1/82, Austin, Tex.; Clark Clifford, LBJ/OH, II, pp. 13–14; George Reedy, LBJ/OH, IV, pp. 3–8; Elizabeth Wickenden Goldschmidt, LBJ/OH, I, p. 92; George Reedy, *Lyndon B. Johnson: A Memoir* (New York: Andrews and McMeel, 1982), p. 37; Miller, *Lyndon*, pp. 486–88; *NYT*, 11/26/85, p. B14.

93. Shogan, *Question of Judgment*, p. 101, citing Fortas's own testimony before the Senate Judiciary Committee.

94. This account is based on the entries for that date in the presidential diaries in LBJL. The account differs from that of others who claim that Fortas made his moves without first consulting Johnson. (See Seib and Otten, "Abe, Help!—LBJ," pp. 86–87, and Shogan, *Question of Judgment*, pp. 101–3.)

95. AI, Liz Carpenter, 11/1/82, Austin, Tex.

96. AI, Mildred Stegall, 11/16/82, Austin, Tex.

97. Shogan, *Question of Judgment*, p. 116, citing Fortas's own testimony before the Senate Judiciary Committee.

98. AI, Liz Carpenter, 11/1/82, Austin, Tex.

99. AI, Mildred Stegall, 11/16/82, Austin, Tex.

100. Memorandum, Walter Jenkins to LBJ (shorthand notes of phone conversation with AF that have been transcribed by LBJL staff), 5/11/64, Fortas-Thornberry Files, Box 1, LBJL.
101. *Ibid.*
102. Seib and Otten, "Abe, Help!—LBJ," p. 88.
103. *NYT*, 5/17/69, p. 16; Shogan, *Question of Judgment*, pp. 100, 221–22. The presidential diary for that date in the Johnson Library shows that the meeting lasted from 9:45 to 12:30 P.M.
104. A copy of the listing can be found in Fortas-Thornberry Files, Box 3, LBJL.

CHAPTER VI
THE DAVIDSON OPERATION

1. The account in this chapter relies on a voluminous memorandum from John Bartlow Martin to Secretary Rusk et al., 5/26/65, which was an NSF history of the Dominican crisis in 1965 (hereinafter, Martin, NSF History) and another narrative chronology sent from Benjamin Reed to McGeorge Bundy, 5/7/65 (both in National Security File, NSC History, Dominican Crisis 1965, Box 7, LBJL). See also "Chronology of Dominican Crisis—1965," undated, National Security File, NSC History, Dominican Crisis 1965, Box 8, LBJL (hereinafter NSC History).
   While there are many books on this crisis, this chapter benefited from John Bartlow Martin, *Overtaken by Events: The Dominican Crisis from the Fall of Trujillo to the Civil War* (New York: Doubleday, 1966); Abraham Lowenthal, *The Dominican Intervention* (Cambridge, Mass.: Harvard University Press, 1972); Tad Szulc, *Dominican Diary* (New York: Delacorte Press, 1965); and George W. Ball, *The Past Has Another Pattern: Memoirs* (New York: W. W. Norton and Co., 1982), pp. 326–31.
2. AI, Thomas Mann, 11/19/82, Austin, Tex. See also Ball, *Past Has Another Pattern*, p. 329.
3. This count was made for the period 4/25–5/11/65 in the White House Diaries, and is confirmed in a memorandum from MJDR [Juanita Roberts] to LBJ, 5/12/65, NSF Aides Files, Box 3, LBJL. This secretarial count was done at the request of the president. The count for the period 5/11–5/20 was then taken from the White House Diaries as well.
4. Ball, *Past Has Another Pattern*, p. 327.
5. AI, Thomas Mann, 11/19/82, Austin, Tex.
6. AF, LBJ/OH, p. 26.
7. These transcripts of conversations between Thomas Mann and LBJ, which for the first time help to illuminate Abe Fortas's plans and actions during this period, are contained in a personal memoir written by, and in the possession of, Mr. Mann. My sincere thanks go to him for sharing them with me. This conversation took place on 4/28/65 (hereinafter Mann Transcripts).
8. Mann Transcripts, 4/30/65, Austin, Tex.
9. Martin, NSF History, p. 69.
10. Mann Transcripts, 5/1/65, Austin, Tex.
11. AI, Thomas Mann, 11/19/82, Austin, Tex.
12. McGeorge Bundy to LBJ, 5/1/65, opened by governmental classification review and unfiled in LBJL.
13. LBJ, notes of telephone conversation with AF, 5/1/65, Diary Backup, Box 16, LBJL.
14. McGeorge Bundy to LBJ, 5/1/65, LBJL.
15. McGeorge Bundy to LBJ, 5/3/65, NSF Aides Files, Box 3, LBJL.
16. Mann Transcripts, 5/5/65, Austin, Tex.
17. Memo by Len Meeker, legal adviser for the Department of State, "Legal Basis For United States Actions in the Dominican Republic," 5/7/65, NSC History, Box 7, LBJL.
18. AF to McGeorge Bundy, 5/6/65 (commenting on an early draft of the Meeker document), NSC History, Box 7, LBJL.
19. Mann Transcripts, 5/9/65, Austin, Tex.
20. *Ibid.*
21. The code name that is used comes from the entries of the period in the official White House Diaries, during the period 5/13–5/17/65, LBJL. As will be outlined below, there was incredible confusion over the precise code name being used by Fortas.
22. McGeorge Bundy to LBJ, 5/12/65 and 5/13/65, McGeorge Bundy Memos to the President, Box 3, LBJL. See also White House Diaries, 5/13–5/17/65, LBJL, for evidence of secretarial confusion.
23. McGeorge Bundy, handwritten notes of White House meetings on 5/14/65, NSC History, Box 11,

LBJL. Another series of notes by Bundy on later meetings, which were opened through governmental classification rereview procedures, display the same uncertainty. See Bundy, White House meeting notes, 5/15–5/17/65, LBJL.

24. Martin, *Overtaken by Events*, p. 679; Ball, *Past Has Another Pattern*, p. 329.

25. Untitled note by AF to White House, undated but circa 5/20/65, attached to untitled White House document, 5/20/65; also similar document dated 5/13/65, McGeorge Bundy Memos for the President, Box 3, with identical copies in NSF Aides Files, Box 3, LBJL.

   Time magazine perpetuated the problem by referring to rumors of the "J. B. Davidson" mission. ("Chief Confidant to Chief Justice," *Time*, 7/5/68, p. 16.)

26. AF, LBJ/OH, p. 27.

27. McGeorge Bundy to LBJ, 5/13/65, National Security File, Country File, Dominican Republic, Box 51, "Davidson" folder, LBJL. Special thanks go to Dave Humphrey of the Johnson Library staff for helping me locate these materials. After the initial clues to this operation by Fortas from his oral history and the *Time* magazine hint, all efforts to locate written materials on the operation in the various library "country files" and "crisis files" failed. Interestingly, as Humphreys discovered, it was the White House staff's decision to file the materials in a special folder under the code name of the operation that threw us off. Much of the material in this thick folder still remains classified by the government.

28. McGeorge Bundy to LBJ, 5/12/65, Bundy Memos to the President, Box 3, LBJL.

29. Untitled document dated 5/20/65, but apparently written by both Bosch and Fortas (as Mr. Davidson), 5/13/65, Bundy Memos to the President, Box 3, LBJL.

30. Message dictated by Fortas (as Mr. Davidson) to White House staff on the phone, 5/13/65, Bundy Memos to the President, Box 3, LBJL.

31. The account below is based on the handwritten notes of the meeting by McGeorge Bundy, 5/14/65, NSC History, Box 11, LBJL. Present at the meeting were Ball, Bundy, Mann, LBJ, Jack Hood Vaughn, Kennedy Crockett, Cyrus Vance, Robert McNamara, Bill Moyers, Admiral William F. Raborn, Jr., and Richard Helms.

32. *Ibid.*

33. *Ibid.*

34. AF, LBJ/OH, p. 30.

35. Martin, NSF History, LBJL.

36. Jack Valenti to LBJ, 5/27/65, Ex ND 19/CO 62, LBJL.

37. McGeorge Bundy to LBJ, 6/11/65, Cable #1427, with attached draft memo to Ellsworth Bunker from the State Department, NSC Files, Dominican Republic, declassified by the government on rereview and unfiled, LBJL.

38. *Ibid.* The actual cable sent to Texas has not yet been declassified by the government. The description, however, is based on a confidential source who viewed the document. The mere debate between Fortas and the foreign policy machinery over the cable, paralleling the debate over the legal adviser's memo, is instructive as to the advisory relationships involved in the Dominican Republic crisis, and around the president generally.

39. Mann Transcripts, 7/12/65, Austin, Tex.

40. Memo by Thomas Mann for the file, "The Bundy-Mann Mission," 7/12/65, NSC History, Box 7, LBJL.

41. McGeorge Bundy to LBJ, 7/13/65, NSF Aides Files, Box 4, LBJL.

42. AI, Thomas Mann, 11/19/82, Austin, Tex.

43. Mildred Stegall to Cartha D. DeLoach, 5/10/65, John Macy Office Files, Fortas folder, LBJL; *Washington Post*, 2/3/65, p. D15.

44. *Washington Post*, 2/3/65, p. D15. See also Charles Seib and Alan Otten, "Abe, Help!—LBJ," *Esquire*, June 1965, p. 87; AF, LBJ/OH, p. 24; and Lyndon B. Johnson, *The Vantage Point: Perspectives of the Presidency, 1963–1969*, (New York: Holt, Rinehart and Winston, 1971), p. 545. Fortas also refers to the refusals during this period in his later letter declining a Supreme Court appointment. (See AF to LBJ, 7/19/65, Fortas Name File, Box 1, LBJL.)

45. Seib and Otten, "Abe, Help!—LBJ," p. 87.

46. For more on Frankfurter's motivations and actions in his relationships with FDR, see See Bruce Allen Murphy, *The Brandeis-Frankfurter Connection: The Secret Political Activities of Two Supreme Court Justices* (New York: Oxford University Press, 1982). My analysis of Fortas's motivations is in agreement with that of others before me. See Robert Shogan, *A Question of Judgment: The Fortas Case and the Struggle for the Supreme Court* (Indianapolis: Bobbs-Merrill Co., 1972), p. 105, and Doris Kearns, *Lyndon Johnson and the American Dream* (New York: New American Library, 1976), p. 324.

47. Seib and Otten, "Abe, Help!—LBJ," p. 87.

CHAPTER VII
THE AMBUSH

1. A copy of the photo can be found in the White House photograph collection at LBJL. The story as to its inscription is in Abe Fortas, "The President, the Congress and the Public: The Lyndon B. Johnson Presidency," in Kenneth W. Thompson, ed., *The Virginia Papers on the Presidency*, Vol. X, (Lanham, Md.: University Press of America, 1982), p. 26.
2. James H. Rowe, Jr., LBJ/OH, I, pp. 27–28.
3. George Ball, *The Past Has Another Pattern: Memoirs* (New York: W. W. Norton and Co., 1982), p. 437.
4. Lyndon B. Johnson, *The Vantage Point: Perspectives of the Presidency, 1963–1969* (New York: Holt, Rinehart and Winston, 1971), p. 545.
5. AI, Walter Jenkins, 11/3/82, Austin, Tex.
6. This portion of the story is drawn from the memoirs of John Kenneth Galbraith. See Galbraith, *A Life in Our Times: Memoirs* (New York: Ballantine Books, 1981), p. 455, and pp. 455–57 generally.
7. *Ibid.*, p. 456. Galbraith's view as to Goldberg's actual positive attitude toward his job will be confirmed by a discussion of various memoranda outlined in the chapter below.
8. *Ibid.*
9. Johnson, *Vantage Point*, p. 26.
10. Earl Warren, *The Memoirs of Earl Warren* (New York: Doubleday and Co., 1977), pp. 356–58.
11. Of course, not every justice observed this stricture. In fact, very few did. On the Warren Court alone, two justices—Felix Frankfurter and William O. Douglas—were among the most extrajudicially active members of the court ever. But Warren saw it differently. So, when his name was bandied about in 1956 as a possible candidate, Warren told reporters that he was opposed to being even considered. See Bruce Allen Murphy, *The Brandeis-Frankfurter Connection: The Secret Political Activities of Two Supreme Court Justices* (New York: Oxford University Press, 1982), appendix, and an unpublished and untitled biographical essay on Warren by Martin Agronsky, Earl Warren Papers, Box 6, LOC.
12. AI, Walter Jenkins, 11/3/82, Austin, Tex.; Johnson, *Vantage Point* pp. 26–27; Warren, *Memoirs*, p. 358.
13. Warren, *Memoirs*, p. 358.
14. Johnson, *Vantage Point*, p. 544.
15. Mrs. Lyndon Baines Johnson, *A White House Diary* (New York: Holt, Rinehart and Winston, 1970), p. 299.
16. *Ibid.*, pp. 299–300.
17. Robert Shogan, *A Question of Judgment: The Fortas Case and the Struggle for the Supreme Court* (Indianapolis: Bobbs-Merrill Co., 1972), p. 110; "Lawyer and Friend," *Time*, 8/6/65, p. 24; Merle Miller, *Lyndon: An Oral Biography* (New York: Ballantine Books, 1980), pp. 586–91. For more on the Fortases' rich lifestyle, see Chap. III, "The Legal Gunslinger," nn. 25, 26.
18. AI, AF, 8/7/81, Washington, D.C.
19. Johnson, *White House Diary*, p. 304; see also annual listings in the *Martindale-Hubbell* law directory.
20. Johnson, *White House Diary*, p. 304.
21. *Ibid.*, p. 300. For more on Agger's reactions here, see the chapter below.
22. Henry J. Abraham, *Justices and Presidents: A Political History of Appointments to the Supreme Court*, 2nd ed. (New York: Oxford University Press, 1985), p. 279.
23. Johnson, *Vantage Point*, p. 544.
24. Memo by Jack Valenti, "Summary of Conversation with Arthur Goldberg," undated, Confidential Office Files, Goldberg Folder, LBJL. Valenti goes on to quote Goldberg as saying, "But if [the] President wants him in [the] UN, he will do it." This memo confirms Goldberg's own account as to his reluctance to leave in Herbert Y. Schandler, *The Unmaking of a President: Lyndon Johnson and Vietnam* (Princeton, N.J.: Princeton University Press, 1977), p. 238, n. 2.
25. Quoting Goldberg himself, Shogan, *Question of Judgment*, p. 107.
26. Quoting Goldberg himself, Schandler, *Unmaking of a President*, p. 238, n. 2.
27. Valenti, "Summary of Conversation with Arthur Goldberg," undated, Confidential Office Files, Goldberg Folder, LBJL; Johnson, *Vantage Point*, p. 545.
28. On the offer of the vice presidency: AI, Bill Moyers, 4/12/86, Hempstead, N.Y., confirming AI,

confidential source, 11/6/82, Austin, Tex. On the offers of return to the court, see Abraham, *Justices and Presidents,* pp. 279–80; Shogan, *Question of Judgment,* pp. 107–8; Bernard Schwartz, *Super Chief: Earl Warren and His Supreme Court—A Judicial Biography* (New York: New York University Press, 1983), pp. 583–85, 720.

29. The story comes from a speech by Bill Moyers titled "Second Thoughts," 4/11/86, delivered at a conference on "Lyndon Baines Johnson: A Texan in Washington," Hofstra University, Hempstead, N.Y.

30. AI, Bill Moyers, 4/12/86, Hempstead, N.Y.

31. See Chap. X, "Lyndon's First String Man." The same observation has been made by others; see David Halberstam, *The Best and the Brightest* (New York: Random House, 1972), pp. 714–16, and Townsend Hoopes, *The Limits of Intervention: An Inside Account of How the Johnson Policy of Escalation in Vietnam Was Reversed* (New York: David McKay Co., 1969), p. 185.

32. Paul Porter, LBJ/OH, I, p. 29; confirmed by White House Diaries, 7/19/65, LBJL.

33. White House Diaries, 7/20/65, LBJL. Arthur Goldberg's formal letter of resignation, an explanatory letter to his colleagues on the court, and the president's acceptance of the resignation did not come until six days later. See Goldberg to LBJ, 7/26/65, and LBJ to Goldberg, 7/26/65, Ex Gen FG 535/A, Box 360, LBJL; and Goldberg to the Court, 7/26/65, Hugo Black Papers, Box 60, LOC.

34. White House Diaries, 7/20/65, LBJL.

35. *Ibid.* The diaries show that there were three calls to Valenti. It is not clear which one actually connected.

36. Valenti, "Summary of Conversation with Arthur Goldberg," undated, Confidential Office Files, Goldberg Folder, LBJL. See also LBJ reminiscences for his memoirs, 6/24/68, with attached secretarial memorandum from the diaries confirming Galbraith's recollections, Confidential Office Files, Goldberg Folder, LBJL.

37. AF to LBJ, 7/19/65, quoted in full in Johnson, *Vantage Point,* pp. 544–45; with original document to be found in Files Pertaining to Abe Fortas and Homer Thornberry, Box 1, LBJL (hereinafter, Fortas-Thornberry Files).

38. But in this case, like Chief Justice Warren, he understood perfectly once he heard what had happened with the president. See Hugo L. Black and Elizabeth Black, *Mr. Justice and Mrs. Black: The Memoirs of Hugo L. Black and Elizabeth Black* (New York: Random House, 1986), p. 118.

39. Hugo Black to Earl Warren, 8/3/65 (with explanatory note by Black for his own files), Black Papers, Box 59, LOC. See also Black and Black, *Memoirs,* pp. 118–19.

40. WOD to LBJ, 7/21/65, Ex Gen FG 535/A, Box 360, LBJL.

41. Johnson, *White House Diary,* p. 304.

42. For more on Wolfson's charitable endeavors, see Chap. VIII, "Dying on the Court," and Shogan, *Question of Judgment,* pp. 188–91.

43. Shogan, *Question of Judgment,* pp. 190–91; AI, confidential source, 3/22/82, Cambridge, Mass.

44. See affidavit taken by FBI from Louis Wolfson, 5/10/69, Eglin Air Force Base, Fla., attached to materials titled "Personal and Confidential: For Eyes Only of the Chief Justice," 5/12/69, Warren Papers, Box 353, LOC (hereinafter Wolfson Affidavit), and Bob Woodward, "Fortas Tie to Wolfson Is Detailed," *Washington Post,* 1/23/77, pp. 1, A12 (hereinafter Woodward Transcript).

45. Wolfson Affidavit, Warren Papers, Box 353, LOC.

46. *Ibid.,* and Woodward Transcript, p. A12.

47. Memorandum for the president by Attorney General Nicholas deB. Katzenbach, 7/22/65, Ex Gen 535/A, Box 360, LBJL (copy can also be found in Ramsey Clark Papers, LBJL).

48. McGeorge Bundy to LBJ, 7/20/65, NSF Aides Files, Box 4, LBJL.

49. William O. Douglas, *The Autobiography of William O. Douglas: The Court Years, 1939–1975* (New York: Random House, 1980), p. 318.

50. John MacKenzie, *The Appearance of Justice* (New York: Charles Scribner's Sons, 1974), p. 18.

51. Shogan, *Question of Judgment,* p. 111.

52. Interview with James Jones in 1977, by John Ben Sutter, in Sutter, "The Advisory Relationship of Justice Abe Fortas to President Lyndon B. Johnson," unpublished master's thesis, Baylor University, 1983, p. 73.

53. Pearson report quoted in *National Review,* 8/10/65, p. 676. Fortas's call is reported in Black and Black, *Memoirs,* p. 119. Fortas told Black that he was pushing for the appointment of Walter Shaefer, chief justice of Illinois.

54. *Washington Post,* 7/29/65, p. 8.

55. "Report of Job for Fortas Still Persists," *Washington Post,* 7/28/65, housed in the *Washington Post* morgue, Washington, D.C.

56. This account relies on the story of a reporter who was present at the conference: James Deakin, *Straight Stuff: The Reporters, The White House and the Truth* (New York: William Morrow and Co., 1984), p. 237.

57. On the president's meeting with AF, see White House Diaries, 7/27/65, LBJL. On LBJ's prospective offer of the chief justiceship down the road, see Schwartz, *Super Chief*, p. 584. And on Fortas's backing of Schaefer, see Black and Black, *Memoirs*, p. 119.

58. Memorandum for the president, from Attorney General Nicholas deB. Katzenbach, 7/22/65, Ex Gen 535/A, Box 360, LBJL.

59. LBJ to WOD, 7/28/65, Ex Gen FG 535/A, Box 360, LBJL.

60. Transcript of interview of McGeorge Bundy in "Vietnam: A Television History," WGBH, "LBJ Goes to War," 10/18/83, pp. 18–19.

61. Nina Totenberg, "Abe Fortas in Private Life: Pessimistic," *National Observer*, 11/2/70, p. 14; see also *NYT*, 7/29/65, pp. 1, 13.

62. *Ibid.*

63. Califano to LBJ, undated, Fortas-Thornberry Files, Box 1; cf. the final nomination remarks by LBJ, undated, Office Files of Horace Busby, Box 43, LBJL.

64. Norman Diamond, "Abe Fortas: Practicing Lawyer," *Yale Law Report*, Spring/Summer 1982, p. 11.

65. Paul Porter, LBJ/OH, I, p. 30.

66. White House Diaries, 7/28/65, LBJL; Totenberg, "Fortas: Pessimistic," p. 14.

67. This account relies on the vast number of other accounts of this encounter between LBJ and AF: Paul Porter, LBJ/OH, I, p. 30; Fortas, LBJ/OH, p. 25; AI, Abe Fortas, 8/7/81, Washington, D.C.; Johnson, *Vantage Point*, p. 544; Miller, *Lyndon*, p. 587; Douglas, *Court Years*, pp. 318–19; Schwartz, *Super Chief*, p. 584–85; Shogan, *Question of Judgment*, pp. 111–12; Totenberg, "Fortas: Pessimistic," p. 14; and Black and Black, *Memoirs*, pp. 118–19.

68. Shogan, *Question of Judgment*, p. 111; Johnson here is using the arguments that Lady Bird Johnson first heard from Fortas and jotted in her diary (see Johnson, *White House Diary*, p. 304).

69. Black and Black, *Memoirs*, p. 119.

70. Miller, quoting Marianne Means, *Lyndon*, p. 587.

71. AF, LBJ/OH, p. 25.

72. *Washington Post*, 7/29/65, p. 8.

73. *NYT*, 7/29/65, p. 12.

74. For the White House version of events, see *NYT*, 7/29/65, pp. 1, 13, and Deakin, *Straight Stuff*, p. 237.

75. *NYT*, 7/29/65, p. 13.

76. Hugh Jones, "The Defeat of the Nomination of Abe Fortas as Chief Justice of the United States," unpublished Ph.D. dissertation, Johns Hopkins University, 1976, p. 43.

77. Shogan, *Question of Judgment*, p. 113; Schwartz, *Super Chief*, p. 584.

78. Jones, "Defeat of Abe Fortas," p. 43; Shogan, *Question of Judgment*, p. 113.

79. Conversation with Douglass Cater, 4/12/86, Hempstead, N.Y.

80. For more on Agger's unhappiness about the appointment, see Paul Porter, LBJ/OH, I, p. 31; Shogan, *Question of Judgment*, p. 113; and Schwartz, *Super Chief*, p. 584. Also, AI, Marquis and Jane Childs, 11/4/82, Austin, Tex., and AI, Virginia Durr, 3/3/83, Austin, Tex.

81. Paul Porter, LBJ/OH, I, p. 30.

82. Douglas, *Court Years*, pp. 318–19.

83. Paul Porter, LBJ/OH, I, p. 31.

84. White House Diaries, 7/28/65, LBJL; AI, Walter Jenkins, 11/3/82, Austin, Tex.; Paul Porter, LBJ/OH, I, p. 31.

85. AI, Mildred Stegall, 11/16/82, Austin, Tex.

86. Paul Porter, LBJ/OH, I, p. 31.

87. Jones, "Defeat of Abe Fortas," pp. 28–29.

88. Douglas, *Court Years*, p. 319.

89. Paul Porter, LBJ/OH, I, pp. 31–32.

90. WOD to Hugo Black, 8/1/65, quoted in Schwartz, *Super Chief*, p. 584. Original letter can be found in the Black Papers, Box 59, LOC.

91. Hugo Black to WOD, 8/3/65, Black Papers, Box 59, LOC.

92. Black and Black, *Memoirs*, pp. 120–21.

93. AF to Hugo Black, 8/11/65, Black Papers, Box 59, LOC.

94. *Ibid.*

95. "Nominations of Abe Fortas and Homer Thornberry," Hearings Before the Committee on the Judiciary, United States Senate, 90th Congress, 2nd Session, 7/11–7/23/68, pp. 124–25.
96. Douglas, *Court Years*, p. 319.
97. Totenberg, "Fortas: Pessimistic," p. 14.

CHAPTER VIII
DYING ON THE COURT

1. This account comes from the following sources: memo for the brethren by Earl Warren, 9/27/65, Hugo Black Papers, Box 59, LOC; Memo, John Davis to AF, undated, Black Papers, Box 59, LOC; and Hugo L. Black and Elizabeth Black, *Mr. Justice and Mrs. Black: The Memoirs of Hugo L. Black and Elizabeth Black* (New York: Random House, 1986), pp. 125–26.
2. White House Photograph File, LBJL.
3. For more on the quiet of the job, see John A. Jenkins, "The Partisan: A Talk with Justice Rehnquist," *New York Times Magazine*, 3/3/85, p. 100. The view of the court as separate law firms comes from Justice John Harlan, quoted in David M. O'Brien, *Storm Center: The Supreme Court in American Politics* (New York: W. W. Norton and Co., 1986), pp. 122–24. Fortas personally agreed with this view (AI, AF, 8/7/81, Washington, D.C.).
4. AF to LBJ, 7/29/65, Files Pertaining to Abe Fortas and Homer Thornberry, Box 1, LBJL (hereinafter Fortas-Thornberry Files); president's notation on note from AF to LBJ, 10/7/65, Fortas-Thornberry Files, Box 1, LBJL.
5. McGeorge Bundy, 8/4/65; "Draft Memorandum on the Obligations of Presidential Appointments with Respect to Privileged Information," 8/4/65; and memo, Bundy to LBJ, "Administration Policy on Books and Articles by Those Who Leave Us," 8/12/65, NSF Memos to the President, Vol. 143, LBJL. Bundy had drafted the original memo for use in the next meeting with Fortas and Clifford. The second memo has a series of questions and answers attached to it for use in a future news conference.
   This was not Fortas's only work for the president during this period. He also offered a recommendation for the D.C. Court of General Sessions. See AF to John Macy, 8/10/65, John Macy Office Files, Fortas Folder, LBJL.
6. White House Diaries, 10/12–10/15/65, LBJL.
7. For more on LBJ's physical condition, see Vaughn Davis Bornet, *The Presidency of Lyndon B. Johnson* (Lawrence, Kans.: University Press of Kansas, 1983), p. 293.
8. AI, AF, 8/7/81, Washington, D.C.
9. *Ibid.*
10. *Ibid.*
11. *Ibid.*
12. See Fred Graham, "The Many-Sided Justice Fortas," *New York Times Magazine*, 6/4/67, p. 98. See also Victor Navasky, "In Washington, You Just Don't Not Return a Call from Abe Fortas," *New York Times Magazine*, 7/1/71, p. 32.
13. A count taken from the White House Diaries, LBJL, in the period from 8/1/64 to 7/31/65 shows that there were 221 phone calls between the two men, and twenty-three private meetings (along with thirty-five meetings with others). The day with fourteen calls was 4/30/65.
14. White House Diaries, LBJL.
15. There were a total of eighty-two phone calls in the year after Fortas was sworn in on the court. (White House Diaries, LBJL.)
16. *New Republic*, 8/21/65, pp. 7–8.
17. For more on Fortas's views of the differences between practicing law and judging, see his speech to the American College of Trial Lawyers, delivered 8/3/68, copy in Fortas-Thornberry Files, Box 2, LBJL.
18. AF to Hugo Black, 2/27/66, Hugo Black Papers, Box 59, LOC.
19. *Rosenblatt* v. *Baer*, 383 U.S. 75 (1966). For more on the outcome and Fortas's views in this case, and those cited below, see Chap. IX, "Mr. Justice Fortas," and Chap. XXIII, "The 'Fortas Under the Fortas'?"
20. *U.S.* v. *Yazell*, 382 U.S. 359 (1966).
21. *U.S.* v. *Speers*, 382 U.S. 266 (1965).
22. *Shuttlesworth* v. *Birmingham*, 382 U.S. 87 (1965).

23. Navasky, "Don't Not Return a Call," p. 32.

24. AI, AF, 8/7/81, Washington, D.C.

25. *Ibid.*

26. Biographical Sketch of Louis Wolfson, John Macy Office Files, Box 653, LBJL. One of the best published sketches of Wolfson can be found in Robert Shogan's *A Question of Judgment: The Fortas Case and the Struggle for the Supreme Court* (Indianapolis: Bobbs-Merrill Co., 1972), pp. 185–91.

27. Stanley Penn, "Industrialist, Facing a Year in Jail Friday, Turns Cold Shoulder Toward Wall Street," *Wall Street Journal,* 4/22/69, p. 40; Richard Phalon, "Wolfson Is Indicted in Sales of Stock," *NYT,* 9/20/66, pp. 1, 63.

28. Jim Bishop, "Wolfson's Hidden Heart," 1969, found in Earl Warren Papers, Box 352, LOC.

29. Paul Porter, LBJ/OH, I, p. 39.

30. Affidavit taken from Louis Wolfson by FBI at Eglin Air Force, Fla., 5/10/69, attached to paper labeled "Personal And Confidential: For Eyes Only of the Chief Justice," 5/12/69, Warren Papers, Box 353, LOC (hereinafter Wolfson Affidavit), confirms Shogan, *Question of Judgment,* p. 192. This is the first time that these documents are being revealed in print. The reason for this fact and the interesting history behind them are detailed below in Chap. XXIV, "Death on the Supreme Court." See also note 43 *infra.*

31. Wolfson Affidavit, LOC; Shogan, *Question of Judgment,* p. 195; and an invitation to the event can be found in the Fortas Name File, 1965 folder, LBJL.

32. Bob Woodward, "Fortas Tie to Wolfson Is Detailed," *Washington Post,* 1/23/77, pp. 1, 12 (hereinafter Woodward Transcript).

33. Wolfson Affidavit, LOC; Woodward Transcript, p. 12.

34. The Wolfson Affidavit, LOC, confirms that Fortas offered this view. In the Woodward Transcript, Fortas is quoted as saying, "Lou, I still think this is a technical matter and I have not changed my opinion and I have not heard anything different." See also Shogan, *Question of Judgment,* p. 195.

35. Wolfson Affidavit, LOC.

36. AI, AF, 8/7/81, Washington, D.C.

37. Author's conversation with Douglass Cater, 4/12/86, Hempstead, N.Y.

38. Author's conversation with Adam Yarmolinsky, 4/12/86, Hempstead, N.Y.

39. Wolfson Affidavit, LOC.

40. William Lambert, "Fortas of the Supreme Court: A Question of Ethics," *Life,* Vol. 66, 5/9/69, p. 36; *Newsweek,* 5/19/69, p. 29.

41. "Memorandum Concerning the Honorable Fred Korth," undated, Fortas-Thornberry Files, Box 1, LBJL. For more on Korth's problems, see *Newsweek,* 11/4/63, p. 27, and *Time,* 6/14/63, p. 25.

42. More on this connection appears in Chap. XXIV, "Death on the Supreme Court."

43. "Excerpts from Minutes of Special Meeting of Board of Trustees of the Wolfson Foundation," 12/28/65, by E. B. Gerbert, attached to note reading "Papers delivered to the Chief Justice by Attorney General Mitchell—5/7/69—11:30 A.M.," with the full document attached to paper labeled "Personal And Confidential: For Eyes Only of the Chief Justice," Warren Papers, Box 353, LOC. Like the affidavit above, this is the first time that these documents revealing the financial relationship between the two men have been revealed in print.

44. Louis Wolfson to AF, 1/3/66 and 1/10/66, attached to paper labeled "Personal and Confidential: For Eyes Only of the Chief Justice," Warren Papers, Box 353, LOC.

45. The contract letter is Louis Wolfson to AF, 2/1/66, attached to paper labeled "Personal and Confidential: For Eyes Only of the Chief Justice," Warren Papers, Box 353, LOC.

46. AF to Jack Valenti, 1/17/66, enclosing with it the resolution adopted 5/31/55, EXHU, Box 1, LBJL.

47. Interview of James Jones in 1977, by John Ben Sutter in Sutter, "The Advisory Relationship of Justice Abe Fortas to President Lyndon B. Johnson," unpublished master's thesis. Baylor University, 1983, p. 90.

48. AI, AF, 8/7/81, Washington, D.C.

49. Telegram, Hayes Redmon to Bill Moyers, 11/24/65, and Jake [Jacobsen] to Mr. Justice [Fortas], 11/27/65, Fortas-Thornberry Files, Box 1, LBJL.

50. Memo, AF to LBJ, 11/29/65, Fortas-Thornberry Files, Box 1, LBJL.

51. AF to LBJ, 11/29/65, Fortas-Thornberry Files, Box 1, LBJL.

52. Harry McPherson to LBJ, 12/1/65, Office Files of Harry McPherson, Box 52, LBJL; Jake Jacobsen to LBJ, 12/8/65, Fortas Name File, 1966, LBJL.

53. Harry McPherson to LBJ, 4/14/66; S. Dillon Ripley, memorandum for the president, 4/12/66; Harry McPherson, memo for the president, 5/10/66; and Harry McPherson, memo for the president, 5/16/66, Office Files of Harry McPherson, Box 52, LBJL.

54. Harry McPherson to LBJ, 5/20/66, Office Files of Harry McPherson, Box 52, LBJL.

55. White House Diaries, LBJL.

56. White House Diaries, LBJL. For a shorthand version of diary entries on many of the meetings between Fortas and LBJ, see untitled and undated list of meetings in Fortas-Thornberry Files, Box 1, LBJL.

57. AF to Jack Valenti, 1/17/66, ExHO, Box 1, LBJL.

58. AF to Jack Valenti, 1/28/66, Fortas-Thornberry Files, Box 1, LBJL.

59. This action is contrary to Fortas's later portrayals of his work in the White House. He claimed to the Senate Judiciary Committee that he never volunteered anything to the president. See Chapter XVI below, "The Battle of Capitol Hill."

60. Douglass Cater to Secretary [Anthony] Celebrezze, 6/7/65, Fortas Name File, 1965 folder, LBJL.

61. *Ibid.*, and AF to LBJ, 2/10/66, Fortas-Thornberry Files, Box 1, LBJL.

62. LBJ to AF 2/18/66, Ex and Gen FG 535, Box 359, LBJL.

63. "Memorandum for Mr. Popple," 3/16/66, Ex and Gen FG 535, Box 359, LBJL.

64. Marvin Watson to LBJ, 8/19/66, and Joseph Clark to Mike Manatos, 8/18/66, Diary Backup, Box 43, LBJL.

65. Charles Maguire to Robert Kintner, 8/23/66, Diary Backup, Box 43, LBJL.

66. Marvin Watson, "Memorandum for the President Concerning Animal Welfare Bill Signing Wednesday," 8/23/66, Diary Backup, Box 43, LBJL. The changes here from the original version of the memo are clearly marked on the original document. A "1" was written next to Fortas's name, and on the previous page markings were made to show how far up on the memo the justice's comments should now be placed.

67. Robert Kintner to Marvin Watson, 8/23/66, Diary Backup, Box 43, LBJL.

68. The list of names for the signing at twelve noon on 8/24/66 can be found in Diary Backup, Box 43, LBJL.

69. Richard Pious, "Congress, the Organized Bar, and the Legal Services Program," *Wisconsin Law Review*, Vol. 1972, No. 2, p. 434. After this speech, Fortas was contacted once again for help in doubling the budget of the legal services program. It is not clear whether he once again proceeded on that basis.

70. Harry McPherson to LBJ, 7/21/66 and 7/22/66; and remarks by LBJ entitled "To the People of the Commonwealth of Puerto Rico," 7/22/66, Office Files of Harry McPherson, Box 52, LBJL.

71. Unless otherwise noted, the following account is drawn from a much fuller account of the investigation by Robert Shogan. (Shogan, *Question of Judgment*, Chap. 7.) It is my purpose here not to repeat that work, but instead to focus on materials that have only recently come to light.

72. Woodward Transcript, p. 12.

73. *Ibid.*

74. *Ibid.*, and Shogan, *Question of Judgment*, p. 200.

75. Woodward Transcript, p. 12.

76. *Ibid.*

77. Shogan, *Question of Judgment*, pp. 203–6.

78. Woodward Transcript, p. 12; confirmed by Wolfson Affidavit.

79. This account comes from Shogan, *Question of Judgment*, pp. 210–12.

80. From the explanatory letter by AF to Earl Warren, 5/14/69, in Shogan, *Question of Judgment*, Appendix B, p. 281.

81. Paul Porter, LBJ/OH, I, p. 39.

82. AF to Louis Wolfson, 12/15/66, attached to paper labeled "Personal and Confidential: For Eyes Only of the Chief Justice," Warren Papers, Box 353, LOC.

83. Paul Porter, LBJ/OH, I, p. 29. See also Fred Rodell, "The Complexities of Mr. Justice Fortas," *New York Times Magazine*, 7/28/68, p. 65.

84. Fred Graham, "The Many-Sided Justice Fortas," *New York Times Magazine*, 6/4/67, p. 92.

85. AI, AF, 8/7/81, Washington, D.C.

86. Navasky, "Don't Not Return a Call," p. 28.

87. Louis Wolfson to AF, 1/11/67, Johnson Social Files, LBJL.

88. Wolfson Affidavit, LOC.

89. *Ibid.*

90. The outcome of this error will be detailed in Chap. XXIV, "Death on the Supreme Court."

CHAPTER IX
MR. JUSTICE FORTAS

1. *Newsweek,* 8/16/65, p. 85. Since this is a political biography of Justice Fortas, I will not devote a great deal of space to his actual judicial decisions. The relatively few opinions in his brief judicial career also seem to justify this option. However, in this chapter, Chap. XXIII, and a section in Chap. XVIII, I intend to give the reader a broad overview of where Fortas appeared to be heading in his judicial philosophy before his resignation from the court.

   In writing these chapters I greatly benefited from the initial observations of Dean Alfange, Jr., of the University of Massachusetts, Dagmar Hamilton of the University of Texas, and two research assistants, Linda Mandel and Bruce Bauman.
2. Anthony Lewis, "A Tough Lawyer Goes to the Court," *New York Times Magazine,* 8/8/65, p. 66.
3. *Business Week,* 7/31/65, p. 19.
4. Henry J. Abraham, *Justices and Presidents* (New York: Oxford University Press, 1974), p. 246.
5. 372 U.S. 335 (1963).
6. Fred Rodell, "The Complexities of Mr. Justice Fortas," *New York Times Magazine,* 7/28/68, pp. 67–68.
7. Abe Fortas, "Mr. Justice Douglas," *Yale Law Journal,* Vol. 73, No. 6, May 1964, p. 918.
8. Rodell, "Complexities of Fortas," p. 63.
9. AI, AF, 8/7/81, Washington, D.C.
10. *Ibid.*
11. Rodell, "Complexities of Fortas," p. 68.
12. Hugo Black, *A Constitutional Faith* (New York: Alfred A. Knopf, 1968), p. 66.
13. For more on Black's jurisprudence, see his article "The Bill of Rights," *New York University Law Review,* Vol. 35, April 1960. An excellent analysis of the justice's views can also be found in James Magee's *Mr. Justice Black: Absolutist on the Court* (Charlottesville, Va.: University of Virginia Press, 1980).
14. Black, *Constitutional Faith,* p. 14.
15. *Adamson* v. *California,* 332 U.S. 46 (1947), p. 92, citing *Federal Power Commission* v. *Pipeline Co.,* 315 U.S. 575, 599, 601.
16. Fortas, "Equal Rights—for Whom?," *New York University Law Review,* Vol. 42, May 1967, p. 411.
17. AI, Benno Schmidt, 5/12/84, Philadelphia.
18. David J. Danelski and Jeanne C. Danelski, "Leadership in the Warren Court," paper delivered at the 1986 Annual Meeting of the American Political Science Association, Washington, D.C., p. 15. Compilations of voting agreement scores are extrapolated from the yearly summaries by the *Harvard Law Review* for the court years 1965, 1966, and 1967. The summaries are based only on cases with full-opinion decisions that dispose of issues on the merits. See *Harvard Law Review,* Vol. 80, 1966, p. 147; Vol. 81, 1967, p. 131; and Vol. 82, 1968, p. 307.
19. *U.S.* v. *Grinnell Corp.,* 384 U.S. 563, at 591 (1966); *U.S.* v. *Pabst Brewing Company,* 384 U.S. 546, at 562 (1966).
20. *Giles* v. *Maryland,* 386 U.S. 66, at 100 (1967).
21. Lyle Denniston, "Fortas Philosophy Emerging as Middle of Road Liberal," *Washington Star,* 5/21/67, housed in *Washington Star* morgue, Martin Luther King Library, Washington, D.C.
22. John MacKenzie, "Two Judicial Decisions Affect Rights of Defendants," *Washington Post,* 3/2/66, p. 2.
23. Fred Graham, "The Many-Sided Justice Fortas," *New York Times Magazine,* 6/4/67, p. 92.
24. Fred Graham, "Abe Fortas," in Leon Friedman and Fred Israel, *Justices of the United States Supreme Court, 1789–1978,* Vol. V (New York: Chelsea House, 1980), pp. 3018–19.
25. AI, Benno Schmidt, 5/12/84, Philadelphia.
26. Victor Navasky, "In Washington, You Just Don't Not Return a Call From Abe Fortas," *New York Times Magazine,* 8/1/71, p. 32.
27. Abe Fortas, "Dangers to the Rule of Law," *American Bar Association Journal,* Vol. 54, October 1968, p. 957.
28. Abe Fortas, *Concerning Dissent and Civil Disobedience* (New York: Signet Books, 1968), p. 18.
29. *Ibid.,* p. 19.

30. Rodell, "Complexities of Fortas," p. 67.

31. *Schmerber* v. *California*, 384 U.S. 757, at 779 (1966).

32. Rodell, "Complexities of Fortas," p. 67.

33. Fortas, *Civil Disobedience*, p. 33.

34. *Ibid.*, p. 18.

35. *Ibid.*, pp. 39–40.

36. The one exception to this rule, which is based on a comparison of the White House Diary record in the Johnson Library and the meeting times of the Supreme Court, was in early 1968 in response to an emergency call by Lyndon Johnson. See Chap. XX. The "bleary-eyed" quote is from Robert Shogan, *A Question of Judgment: The Fortas Case and the Struggle for the Supreme Court* (Indianapolis: Bobbs-Merrill Company, 1972), pp. 134–35.

37. 394 U.S. 705 (1969).

38. *Baltimore and Ohio Railroad* v. *U.S.*, 386 U.S. 372, at 478 (1967). The analysis of Fortas's views in the business area benefited from Linda Mandel, "Abe Fortas in Business: 'Neither an Activist Nor a Liberal Be,'" unpublished senior honors thesis, Penn State University, Fall 1985.

39. *U.S.* v. *Speers*, 382 US 266, at 279-80 (1965).

40. For more on Black's self-perceived role on the court, see the definitive work on the Warren Court: Bernard Schwartz, *Super Chief: Earl Warren and His Supreme Court—A Judicial Biography* (New York: New York University Press, 1983), Chaps. 14, 15.

41. AF to William Brennan, 12/14/65; Brennan to AF, 12/6/65; and Harlan to AF, 1/6/66, *Yazell* case folder, AFP. The incident was reported initially by Fred Graham in "The Many-Sided Justice Fortas," p. 93.

42. *U.S.* v. *Yazell*, 382 US 341, at 351 (1966).

43. AF to William Brennan, 12/14/65, *Yazell* case folder, AFP.

44. Hugo L. Black and Elizabeth Black, *Mr. Justice and Mrs. Black: The Memoirs of Hugo L. Black and Elizabeth Black* (New York: Random House, 1986), p. 131.

45. 382 U.S. 341, at 361 (1966).

46. Since Fortas could not get the votes of a majority of his colleagues, the final result was a plurality opinion speaking for the court.

47. Schwartz, *Super Chief*, p. 608.

48. Earl Warren to AF, 1/12/66, Earl Warren Papers, LOC.

49. 383 U.S. 131, at 167 (1966).

50. *Ibid.*, at 168.

51. *Washington Post*, 2/24/66, pp. 1, 6.

52. 384 U.S. 563 (1966); 384 U.S. 597 (1966), pp. 1, 6.

53. 384 U.S. 563, at 576 (1966).

54. *Ibid.*, at 587.

55. *Ibid.*

56. Showing the influence of one of his old Yale mentors and law partners, Fortas no doubt got the image from the classic *The Symbols of Government*, written by Thurman Arnold (New Haven: Yale University Press, 1935). In imploring the social sciences to become more empirical and pragmatic, Arnold argued through the image of the Procrustean bed that society was taking outworn symbols and distorting them in an effort to explain reality.

57. One is left to wonder whether this excessive concern with the integrity and health of the whole body is in any way related to the frequent health problems and occasional psychosomatic illnesses that friends observed in Fortas in times of stress.

58. 384 U.S. 563, at 592 (1966).

59. *Ibid.*, at 596.

60. 384 U.S. 597, at 618–19 (1966).

61. *Ibid.*, at 621, 625.

62. *Ibid.*, at 634.

63. *Ibid.*, at 621, 635.

64. John MacKenzie, "High Court Decisions Make It Tough on Mergers," *Washington Post*, 7/31/66, p. K1.

65. This case is also interesting in that Fortas's desire to be involved in the decision here impelled him to override his own ethical standards. Normally careful about recusing himself from cases in which friends or former law partners were either representing the litigants or were themselves the litigants, Fortas in this instance overlooked the fact that his former law partner Thurman Arnold had filed a "friend of the court" brief. Indicating Fortas's normal behavior, journalist Victor Navasky quotes an

Arnold and Porter lawyer as saying: "Fortas was meticulous on the conflict point. Every session he'd send over the entire Supreme Court docket to make sure we were not related to any of the cases, and if we were he disqualified himself." (Navasky, "Don't Not Return a Call," p. 32.)

66. 383 U.S. 541 at 555 (1966).
67. *Ibid.*, at 555–59.
68. *Ibid.*, at 561.
69. *NYT*, 6/22/66, p. 19.
70. *Newsweek*, 7/4/66, p. 19.
71. *U.S. News and World Report*, 7/14/66, p. 14.
72. Rodell, "Complexities of Fortas," p. 67.
73. 385 U.S. 374, at 412 (1967).
74. Fortas was speaking to financier Louis Wolfson, after all the events of his public life had transpired, and unknown to him the conversation was being secretly recorded. Bob Woodward, "Fortas Tie to Wolfson Is Detailed," *Washington Post*, 1/23/77, p. A12.
75. Navasky, "Don't Not Return a Call," p. 32.
76. Graham, "Many-Sided Justice," p. 87.
77. *Washington Post*, 4/28/66, pp. 1, 9. The high point in the debate came when Nixon erred in his citation of a California case, only to be quickly corrected by Chief Justice Warren, also a California attorney, who was no fan of Nixon's. The attorney was embarrassed for a moment by the correction, but then went on to finish his argument.
78. Fortas draft opinion, dated 6/8/66, as quoted in Schwartz, *Super Chief*, p. 643.
79. Fortas draft opinion, 6/8/66, Tom Clark Papers, University of Texas Law School, Austin, Tex.
80. Nina Totenberg, "Behind the Marble, Beneath the Robes," *New York Times Magazine*, 3/16/75, p. 62.
81. Hugo Black to AF, 6/16/66, and handwritten on note from AF, "Memorandum for the Brethren re: No. 562—*Time Inc.* v. *Hill*," 6/14/66, Hugo Black Papers, Box 396, LOC.
82. AF, memo for the conference, 6/16/66, Clark Papers, University of Texas Law School.
83. Black and Black, *Memoirs*, pp. 150–51.
84. Black, memorandum for the conference, 10/17/66, Clark Papers, University of Texas Law School.
85. Black and Black, *Memoirs*, p. 153.
86. 385 U.S. 374, at 380–91 (1967). The actual test is drawn from *New York Times* v. *Sullivan*, 376 U.S. 254 (1964).
87. 385 U.S. 374, at 411–12 (1967).
88. Fortas argued that the plaintiffs should have won even under the majority's standard. For him, the instruction that called for a finding of "fiction" in the original New York trial was the same as a finding of "reckless falsity," which was now being required by the Supreme Court. Fortas could see no practical difference between the two, and so voted for the Hills.
89. Fortas conference notes, 12/5/66, AFP; confirming account in Schwartz, *Super Chief*, pp. 636–37. For the switched vote, see William Brennan to conference, 12/6/66, AFP.
90. Byron White to AF, 12/6/66, AFP.
91. Hugo Black to AF, 12/8/66, AFP.
92. Hugo Black to conference, 12/6/66, AFP; Black and Black, *Memoirs*, p. 156.
93. Black, memo for the conference, 12/7/66, AFP; Schwartz, *Super Chief*, pp. 636–37; Black and Black, *Memoirs*, pp. 156–57.
94. 385 U.S. 231, at 243. Fortas later argued that this was a "state mechanism for *total* disregard of the principle of one man, one vote" (p. 246).
95. *Ibid.*, at 249.
96. Black and Black, *Memoirs*, p. 157.
97. *Ibid.*
98. *Ibid.*

CHAPTER X
LYNDON'S FIRST STRING MAN

1. "Chief Confidant to Chief Justice," *Time*, 7/5/68, p. 14.
2. Doris Kearns, *Lyndon Johnson and the American Dream* (New York: New American Library, 1976), pp. 351–52; Stanley Karnow, *Vietnam: A History* (New York: Viking Press, 1983), p. 488.

3. Karnow, *Vietnam*, p. 488.

4. See Karnow, *Vietnam*, p. 420, for one of those exaggerated accounts. My analysis of the number of contacts between Fortas and LBJ comes from the White House Diaries, LBJL.

5. LBJ to AF, 2/15/67, Fortas Name File, 1967 folder, LBJL.

6. Memos, Joe Califano to LBJ, 2/12/67, and Jim Gaither to Califano, 2/11/67, Files Pertaining to Abe Fortas and Homer Thornberry, Box 1, LBJL (hereinafter Fortas-Thornberry Files).

7. Joe Califano to LBJ, 6/7/67, Fortas Name File, 1967 folder, LBJL.

8. AF to LBJ, 8/28/67, Fortas-Thornberry File, Box 1, LBJL.

9. James H. Rowe, Jr., LBJ/OH, IV, p. 1.

10. Bill Moyers to McGeorge Bundy, 4/27/64, C.F. CO 312, LBJL.

11. It was the precise wording of the announcement that enabled Johnson to convince Fortas to come over to the White House on the day of his appointment to the court. For more, see Chap. VII "The Ambush." As for Fortas's role in the creation of the statement, William O. Douglas quotes Lyndon Johnson as saying to Fortas: "This Vietnam statement *that you approved* says fifty thousand boys are going to Vietnam—perhaps to die" (italics mine). Douglas, *The Autobiography of William O. Douglas: The Court Years, 1939–1975* (New York: Random House, 1980), p. 319.

12. AI, Thomas Mann, 11/19/82, Austin, Tex.

13. AI, Arthur "Tex" Goldschmidt, 6/10/84, Durham, N.Y.

14. Zbigniew Brzezinski, LBJ/OH, p. 24.

15. AI, AF, 8/7/81, Washington, D.C.

16. *Ibid.*

17. David Halberstam, *The Best and the Brightest* (New York: Fawcett World Library, 1972), p. 715. Others in the administration certainly saw him as a hawk. (Conversations with Townsend Hoopes, 4/11/86, and Harry McPherson, 4/10/86, Hempstead, N.Y.) See also Karnow, *Vietnam*, p. 420, and Larry Berman, *Planning a Tragedy: The Americanization of the War in Vietnam* (New York: W. W. Norton and Co., 1982), p. 121.

18. For more on the strategy behind the bombing pause, see Karnow, *Vietnam*, pp. 481–84; Lyndon B. Johnson, *The Vantage Point: Perspectives of the Presidency, 1963–1969* (New York: Holt, Rinehart and Winston, 1971), pp. 232–41; Townsend Hoopes, *The Limits of Intervention: An Inside Account of How the Johnson Policy of Escalation in Vietnam Was Reversed* (New York: David McKay Co., 1969), pp. 48–50; and Herbert Y. Schandler, *The Unmaking of a President: Lyndon Johnson and Vietnam* (Princeton, N.J.: Princeton University Press, 1977), pp. 33–38.

19. For more, see fn. 30 *infra*.

20. Unless otherwise noted here and below, all of the quotations from this meeting come from the copious notes taken at the time by Jack Valenti, 12/18/65, Meeting Notes File, Box 1, LBJL.

21. The description of LBJ's appearance here comes from Karnow, *Vietnam*, p. 481.

22. All quotes from Jack Valenti's notes of the meeting, 12/18/65, Meeting Notes File, Box 1, LBJL.

23. Merle Miller, *Lyndon: An Oral Biography* (New York: Ballantine Books, 1980), p. 630.

24. Schandler, *Unmaking of a President*, p. 190, and Chester L. Cooper, *The Lost Crusade* (New York: Dodd, Mead, 1970), pp. 295–96, 391.

25. Douglas, *The Court Years*, p. 188. Given the way this story is reported, this could well have been an account of the December 18 meeting, but probably it was not. Douglas lists the Joint Chiefs of Staff as being present at this meeting. There were indeed a number of other meetings with Fortas, Clifford, McNamara, and members of the high military command present, among them: 4/4/66, 6/21/66, 10/18/67, 11/2/67, and 12/5/67. Based on the written and unpublished accounts of the 12/18/65 meeting and other such meetings, though, it is easy to believe that McNamara made such a statement after one of them.

26. Cooper, *Lost Crusade*, p. 391.

27. Halberstam, *Best and the Brightest*, pp. 758–59.

28. The same irony was seen by others; see Halberstam, *Best and the Brightest*, pp. 714–16, and Hoopes, *Limits of Intervention*, p. 185.

29. Memorandum for the record, typed by Nell Yates, 1/11/66, compared to AF handwritten revisions of speech draft, undated, in Statements Files, Box 172, LBJL.

30. Hoopes, *Limits of Intervention*, p. 217. Curiously, after the book was published Fortas saw Hoopes at a dinner party in 1971 and, after praising the book in general, added, "But you were wrong about one thing; I did not *advise* LBJ." Even then, Fortas was trying to hide the nature of his true relationship with the former president. (Author's conversation with Hoopes, 4/11/86, Hempstead, N.Y.)

31. Karnow, *Vietnam*, p. 512.

32. Polls cited in Kearns, *Lyndon Johnson*, p. 352.

33. *Ibid.*, p. 330.
34. The quotations below are from AF to LBJ, undated, "Public Relations Activities," National Security File, Vietnam Country File, Box 99, 7E, (1)b 9/67–10/67, LBJL.
35. *Ibid.* See notations of staff written on the memo upon receipt.
36. For more on McNamara's change of heart, see Schandler, *Unmaking of a President*, p. 64, and Karnow, *Vietnam*, pp. 485, 498–501.
37. Johnson, *Vantage Point*, p. 372. For more on the "Tuesday Lunch" meetings, see an excellent article: David Humphrey, "Tuesday Lunch at the Johnson White House: A Preliminary Assessment," *Diplomatic History*, Winter 1984, pp. 81–101.
38. Memo, Robert McNamara to LBJ, 11/1/67, quoted in Johnson, *Vantage Point*, p. 372.
39. Johnson, of course, was well aware of the hawkish views of Fortas, Rostow, and Clifford. Taylor, former chairman of the Kennedy administration's Joint Chiefs of Staff, and Johnson's ambassador to Saigon in July 1965 during the first huge troop escalation, could certainly be expected to mirror their views.
40. White House Diaries, 11/2/67, LBJL.
41. Unless otherwise indicated, quotations below are taken from a set of newly declassified meeting notes by Jim Jones for the president, 11/2/67, Meeting Notes File, Box 2, LBJL.
42. Walt Rostow to LBJ, 11/2/67, Rostow Memoranda No. 23, Meeting Notes File, Box 2, LBJL.
43. Walt Rostow to LBJ, 11/3/67, President's Appointment File, LBJL.
44. Jim Jones for the president, 11/2/67, Meeting Notes File, Box 2, LBJL. Later, Clark Clifford would significantly change the course of his thinking on Vietnam. Clifford claimed in a later article that the change in his attitude had come at this time: "I returned home [from a visit to the Pacific allies seeking more troop support in late summer 1967] puzzled, troubled, concerned. Was it possible that our assessment of the danger to the stability of the Southeast Asia and the Western Pacific was exaggerated? Was it possible that those nations which were neighbors of Vietnam had a clearer perception of the tides of world events in 1967 than we? Was it possible that we were continuing to be guided by judgments that might once have had validity but were now obsolete? In short, although I still counted myself a staunch supporter of our policies, there were nagging, not-to-be-suppressed doubts in my mind." (Clark Clifford, "A Viet Nam Reappraisal: The Personal History of One Man's View and How It Evolved," *Foreign Affairs*, Vol. 47, No. 4, July 1969, pp. 601–22.) Whatever private doubts he might have had, Clifford was not expressing them in this forum, or in his upcoming memorandum on this question to the president responding to McNamara's memo. (Clifford to LBJ, 11/7/67, National Security File, Aides' Files, Memos to the President, Walt Rostow, Vol. 49, LBJL.) Also, others in the administration still saw Clifford as a devout hawk based on his statements and writings at the time. (AI, Walt Rostow, 11/19/82, Austin, Tex.)
45. Emphasis added. AF to LBJ, 11/5/67, National Security File, Vietnam Country File, 1967–1968, Box 127, LBJL.
46. AF to LBJ, 11/5/67, as quoted in Johnson, *Vantage Point*, p. 374; original found in National Security File, Vietnam Country File, 1967–1968, Box 127, LBJL.
47. Quoted from LBJ's speech to meeting of Jewish Labor Committee, 11/9/67, Statements of LBJ, Box 252, LBJL. The letter quoted by the president is AF to LBJ, 11/9/67, Statements of LBJ, Box 252, LBJL, and Files Pertaining to Abe Fortas and Homer Thornberry, Box 1, LBJL (hereinafter Fortas-Thornberry Files).
48. LBJ to AF, 11/15/67, Fortas-Thornberry Files, Box 1, LBJL.
49. Kearns, *Lyndon Johnson*, p. 351.
50. Karnow, *Vietnam*, p. 547. The broadcast was on 2/27/68.
51. George Ball, *The Past Has Another Pattern* (New York: W. W. Norton and Co., 1982), p. 407; Schandler, *Unmaking of a President*, p. 258.
52. As the days wound down now to the end of Johnson's presidency, as marked by his March 31 speech that he would not run for reelection, this became more and more true.
53. Douglas, *The Court Years*, pp. 336–37.
54. Helen Gahagen Douglas, LBJ/OH, II, p. 13.
55. AF to LBJ, 2/19/68, Fortas-Thornberry Files, Box 1, LBJL.
56. AF to LBJ, 2/9/68, Fortas Name File, 1968 folder, LBJL.
57. White House Diaries, LBJL. See also Schandler, *Unmaking of a President*, pp. 106–9.
58. AF to LBJ, 2/19/68 (sent along to the White House on 3/12/68), Fortas-Thornberry Files, Box 1, LBJL. Copy also located in Clark Clifford Papers, Box 1, "National Objectives, Resources and Strategy vis-a-vis SEA [1]," LBJL.
59. *Ibid.*

60. Clark Clifford's notation on AF memo to LBJ, 2/19/68, Clifford Papers, Box 1, "National Objectives, Resources and Strategy vis-a-vis SEA [1]," LBJL.

61. A comparison of the White House Diary entry for 3/12/68 and the schedule for the court's oral argument shows that the White House meeting with Fortas did not end until 10:12 A.M., and the oral argument in the liability case *Elisha Edwards* v. *Pacific Fruit Express Co.* had already begun its oral arguments at 10:00. Fortas had the option of later participating in the decision in this case, and chose to do so. While Bob Woodward and Scott Armstrong in *The Brethren* (New York: Avon Books, 1979), p. 146 footnote, claim that Fortas missed even court decision conferences to go to the White House, this could not be confirmed. It is true that on several occasions Fortas went to the White House on days when court conferences would have been held, but his visits were late enough in the day so that the conferences would have been over. (See White House Diary entries for 5/26/67, 3/22/68, and 4/5/68. The first two are afternoon meetings on Fridays, when conferences would have been held by the court, and the third date is a call to the White House for help in handling the Washington riots.) Furthermore, a comparison of the court's schedule and the White House Diary entries for meetings with Fortas present shows that Fortas missed no other work because of calls to the White House. Fortas's own notes show that he missed a conference on 10/18/68, but there is no indication from the White House files that it was presidential work that caused him to do so. (See Fortas Supreme Court files, Yale University.) What is impossible to discover is how many times calls from the White House interrupted Fortas's work on the court, or the toll taken on his energy level from all of the work. Robert Shogan quotes Fortas's law clerks as saying that it was quite extensive. (Shogan, *Question of Judgment*, pp. 134–35.)

On the meeting itself, see Hoopes, *Limits of Intervention*, p. 182.

62. Arthur Schlesinger, *Robert Kennedy and His Times* (New York: Ballantine Books, 1978), p. 915.

63. Hoopes, *Limits of Intervention*, p. 184.

64. *Ibid.*, pp. 198–200; Schandler, *Unmaking of a President*, pp. 256–58; Karnow, *Vietnam*, pp. 484–91.

65. Hoopes, *Limits of Intervention*, pp. 184–85, 205.

66. White House Diaries, 3/15/68, LBJL.

67. Johnson, *Vantage Point*, p. 408.

68. Hoopes, *Limits of Intervention*, p. 185.

69. *Ibid.*, p. 206.

70. Schandler, *Unmaking of a President*, p. 248.

71. *Ibid.*, p. 249.

72. McGeorge Bundy to LBJ, 3/22/68, Diary Backup, Box 95, LBJL.

73. McGeorge Bundy, memo to the president, 3/22/68, Diary Backup, Box 95, LBJL.

74. Unless otherwise noted, these and other quotes below are taken from untitled notes of the meeting on 3/20/68, Meeting Notes File, Box 2, LBJL.

75. Johnson, *Vantage Point*, p. 412.

76. *Ibid.*, pp. 412–13.

77. Notes of meeting on 3/20/68, Meeting Notes File, Box 2, LBJL.

78. McGeorge Bundy, memo for the president, 3/22/68, Diary Backup, Box 95, LBJL.

79. Notes of luncheon meeting, 3/22/68, Meeting Notes File, Box 2, LBJL.

80. Johnson, *Vantage Point*, p. 413.

81. George Christian, notes of luncheon meeting, 3/22/68, Meeting Notes File, Box 2, LBJL.

82. An excellent and full account of Clifford's motivations and actions here can be found in his *Foreign Affairs* piece. See Clifford, "A Viet Nam Reappraisal," *passim*.

83. According to the entry in the White House Diary for that day, the meeting began at 1:15 P.M. and Fortas did not arrive until 2:50 P.M., with lunch beginning at 3:15 P.M.

84. Quoting Walt Rostow, Schandler, *Unmaking of a President*, p. 262.

85. Summary of notes of the meeting on 3/26/68, by McGeorge Bundy, 3/26/68, Meeting Notes File, Box 2, LBJL.

86. Tom Johnson to president, 3/27/68, Diary Backup, Box 93, LBJL.

87. Johnson's own meeting notes, undated, Meeting Notes File, Box 2, LBJL.

88. *Ibid.*, and McGeorge Bundy meeting notes, 3/26/68, Meeting Notes File, Box 2, LBJL.

89. The following are from a summary of meeting notes, 3/26/68, Meeting Notes File, Box 2, LBJL. The full notes of this meeting have not yet been released. Until they are, we cannot be sure of the exact order of the speakers. Hoopes gives the impression that Bradley, Murphy, and Fortas responded immediately. (Hoopes, *Limits of Intervention*, p. 216.) However, these notes do not reflect that order (though they do confirm Hoopes's account of a sharp exchange between Fortas and Dean

Acheson). So I have chosen to present the views in the order reflected in the summary of the notes in the Johnson White House file, on the assumption that this order is correct, or so close to correct as not to change the context of the discussion.

90. Summary of meeting notes, 3/26/68, Meeting Notes File, Box 2, LBJL.
91. *Ibid.*
92. Marvin Kalb and Elie Abel, *Roots of Involvement: The U.S. in Asia, 1784–1971* (New York: W. W. Norton and Co., 1971), p. 248.
93. Summary of meeting notes, 3/26/68, Meeting Notes File, Box 2, LBJL.
94. McGeorge Bundy to president, 3/27/68, Fortas Name File, 1968 folder, LBJL.
95. Johnson, *Vantage Point,* p. 418.
96. Abe Fortas, "The President, the Congress, and the Public: The Lyndon B. Johnson Presidency," in Kenneth Thompson, ed., *The Virginia Papers on the Presidency,* Vol. X (Lanham, Md.: University Press of America, 1982), p. 29.
97. *Ibid.*
98. For more, see Clifford, "A Viet Nam Reappraisal," *passim,* and Schandler, *Unmaking of a President,* pp. 121–290.
99. Memo, Jim Jones to president, 3/31/68, Fortas Name File, 1968 folder, LBJL.
100. Luncheon speech notes, 5/28/68, Diary Backup, Box 101, LBJL.
101. Memorandum, Joseph Califano to president, 7/23/68, Fortas Name File, Box 1, LBJL.
102. Memo, Joseph Califano to AF, 5/9/68, Confidential File, Name File, Box 3, LBJL.
103. Memo, Joseph Califano to AF, 5/9/68, Confidential File, Name File, Box 3, LBJL.
104. Memo, Joseph Califano to AF, 5/9/68, Confidential File, FG 400–FG 600, Box 34, LBJL.
105. White House photo, in Fortas Name File, 1968 folder, LBJL.

CHAPTER XI
A WHALE, A MINNOW, AND A PHONE BOOTH

1. In beginning this portion of the book, it is a pleasure to acknowledge a large intellectual debt. Students of the 1968 confirmation fight over Abe Fortas are indebted to two scholars whose efforts to unravel this mystery came years ago in the form of unpublished Ph.D. dissertations. These fine efforts, undertaken without the benefit of access to the Johnson White House papers, or to other private collections of papers that were not open at the time, provided many of the clues for later study in my examination of these files. (See Hugh Jones, "The Defeat of the Nomination of Abe Fortas as Chief Justice of the United States," unpublished Ph.D. dissertation, Johns Hopkins University, 1976, and John L. Massaro, "Advice and Dissent: Factors in the Senate's Refusal to Confirm Supreme Court Nominees, with Special Emphasis on the Cases of Abe Fortas, Clement F. Haynsworth, Jr., and G. Harold Carswell," unpublished Ph.D. dissertation, Southern Illinois University, 1972.) Scholarship is a building-block process, and without these two cornerstone studies, especially the timely interviews by Professor Hugh Jones of Senate sources, it is probable that much valuable information would have been lost to the mists of time. My thanks also to Professor Jones, now in the Political Science Department at Shippensburg State College of Pennsylvania, for sharing some of his original files and his insights with me, as I was completing this study. Professor Massaro later went to the files of the Johnson White House and published a study based on his dissertation work. My intellectual differences with some of his conclusions will be outlined in the notes below. See Massaro, "LBJ and the Fortas Nomination for Chief Justice," *Political Science Quarterly,* Vol. 97, No. 4, Winter 1982–83, pp. 603–21. See also Massaro, "'Fortascast': Dark Clouds over President Ford's Forthcoming Supreme Court Nominations," *Federal Bar Journal,* Vol. 34, No. 4, Fall 1975, pp. 257–78. Also useful on this episode was Donald G. Tannenbaum, "Presidential Nominations: The Record of Lyndon B. Johnson," unpublished paper delivered at the Northeast Political Science Association, November 18–20, 1982.

   This initial chapter of the 1968 story builds on the information in the two dissertations, the published and unpublished articles, and useful and informative accounts in several other sources, which were also written without access to White House documents that have only recently been made available: Samuel Shaffer, *On and Off the Floor: Thirty Years as a Correspondent on Capitol Hill* (New York: Newsweek Books, 1980), Chap. 5; "Sen. Robert Griffin: A Power in Washington?," *Detroit Scope Magazine,* 11/2/68, pp. 10–11; and "Sen. Griffin Wins Once Lonely Battle to Block Court

Change," *Chicago Tribune*, 10/3/68, p. 2. The story of the phone booth and Ms. Updike is taken from Shaffer, *On and Off the Floor*, pp. 80–82, and Jones, "Defeat of Abe Fortas," pp. 104–5.

2. Memo, Jim Jones to president, 6/11/68, ExFG 535, LBJL.

3. Transcript of 7/31/68 news conference by the president, *U.S. News and World Report*, 8/12/68, p. 65. It is possible that Johnson suspected this to be the reason for the meeting request based on phoned information from Fortas, but the written record does not indicate so.

4. Memo for the record by James Jones, 6/13/68, Ex and Gen FG 535/A, Box 360, LBJL.

5. Bernard Schwartz, *Super Chief: Earl Warren and His Supreme Court—A Judicial Biography* (New York: New York University Press, 1983), pp. 680–82.

6. Benno Schmidt, COHC, p. 71.

7. The news conference took place on 7/31/68. A partial transcript was reprinted in *U.S. News and World Report*, 8/12/68, p. 65. This story is reminiscent of the strategy used by Johnson in misleading the reporters on the initial appointment of Fortas to the Supreme Court.

8. Earl Warren, LBJ/OH, pp. 31–32.

9. WOD to LBJ, 6/18/68, Warren Christopher Name File, LBJL.

10. For more on the Fortas-Warren agreement scores, see Chap. IX, "Mr. Justice Fortas." On Warren's views about his replacement, see Schwartz, *Super Chief*, p. 720.

11. An excellent description of the mechanics and history of the Supreme Court appointment process can be found in Henry J. Abraham, *Justices and Presidents: A Political History of Appointments to the Supreme Court*, 2nd ed. (New York: Oxford University Press, 1985), *passim*.

12. Earl Warren to LBJ, 6/13/68, Ex FG 535/A Box 360, LBJL.

13. Earl Warren to LBJ, 6/13/68, Ex FG 535/A Box 360, LBJL (emphasis added).

14. Earl Warren, LBJ/OH, p. 30.

15. There seems to be no typical pattern as to whether presidents wait until they have a replacement name in mind before announcing a vacancy. But that was not why Johnson decided to hold up the announcement, as explained below.

16. LBJ to Earl Warren, 6/26/68, and Fortas draft letter, 6/24/68, Ex FG 535/A Box 360, LBJL.

17. As will be indicated below, the chief justice was well aware of the reasons for this strategy and concurred in its operation. However, in a press conference, he refused to divulge that awareness publicly. See "Earl Warren Talks About the 'Warren Court,'" *U.S. News and World Report*, 7/15/68, pp. 62–64.

18. Fortas explains his lack of desire for the post in a letter to Adolf Berle, 10/16/68, Adolf Berle Papers, Box 221, FDRL.

19. *Wall Street Journal*, 6/14/68, p. 1.

20. "Sen. Robert Griffin: A Power in Washington?," *Detroit Scope Magazine*, 11/2/68, p. 10.

21. Anonymous source quoted in Jones, "Defeat of Abe Fortas," p. 281.

22. The material on Griffin's life and career comes from several sources: "Robert P. Griffin," in *Leaders in Profile: The United States Senate*, George Douth (New York: Sperr and Douth, 1975), pp. 327–35; Paul Delaney, "Author of Antibusing Proposal Robert Paul Griffin," *NYT*, 2/26/72, p. 33; Marjorie Hunter, "Leading Fortas Foe Robert Paul Griffin," *NYT*, 9/28/68, p. 30.; and Walter Rugaber, "Romney Appoints Griffin to Senate," *NYT*, 5/12/66, p. 26. For more on the coup in the House, see Robert Peabody, *Leadership in Congress* (Boston: Little, Brown and Co., 1976), pp. 100–148.

23. Marjorie Hunter, "Leading Fortas Foe Robert Paul Griffin," *NYT*, 9/28/68, p. 30.

24. Anonymous source quoted in Jones, "Defeat of Abe Fortas," p. 281.

25. There is some dispute about the starting date of the Griffin opposition effort. This account relies on the interviews conducted with Griffin's legislative assistant, and the conclusions of Hugh Jones ("Defeat of Abe Fortas," pp. 76, 92). Months after this incident, another version of Griffin's early moves in the controversy was published that seemed intended to give the senator an appearance of nonpartisanship in engaging in the fight. It was reported that Griffin had heard a report of the resignation plan on the radio while driving to work on the twenty-first, a full week later, and that same morning he decided to deliver a blistering opposition speech to the Senate opposing *any* Supreme Court appointment by this president. There seems little doubt that this incident occurred as well, but the interviews by Jones, as well as common sense, indicate that a senator would not make such a move without some indication that he would have the support of several of his colleagues. Griffin, having started a week earlier than the public later believed, was reasonably sure of getting the support because his effort was now well under way. For the other versions, see "Sen. Griffin Wins Once Lonely Battle to Block Court Change," *Chicago Tribune*, 10/2/68, p.2, and *Newsweek*, 10/28/68, p. 48.

Any doubt about this start-up date seemingly has to be resolved in favor of the earlier date when one observes that the chronology of the fight put out by Griffin's own office *also* lists the *Wall Street*

Journal article on the fourteenth as being the starting point. It is at this point that the senator began speaking to his Republican colleagues to form a rump caucus of rebels. See "Chronology: Events Relating to Supreme Court Nominations," compiled by Jack Hushen, press secretary for Senator Robert Griffin, Files Pertaining to Abe Fortas and Homer Thornberry, Box 2, LBJL (hereinafter Fortas-Thornberry Files).

For more evidence on this point see footnote 92 in Chapter XIV: The Scarlett Letter.

26. For more on the early effort, see *Newsweek*, 10/28/68, p. 48; "Sen. Griffin Wins Once Lonely Battle to Block Court Change," *Chicago Tribune*, 10/3/68, p. 2; Jones, "Defeat of Abe Fortas," p. 76ff. and n. 172; and "Sen. Robert Griffin: A Power in Washington?," *Detroit Scope Magazine*, 11/2/68, pp. 10–11.

27. Harry McPherson, "The Senate Observed: A Recollection," *Atlantic*, May 1972, p. 82.

28. After the assassination of Democrat Robert F. Kennedy, the Republicans' number in the Senate would increase to thirty-seven with the addition of his replacement, Charles Goodell.

29. The "flexibility" quote comes from Charles Roberts, "The Other Ev Dirksen," *Newsweek*, 6/16/69, pp. 26, 27–28. In general, this account of Everett Dirksen comes from a variety of overlapping sources: Edward L. Schapsmeier and Frederick H. Schapsmeier, *Dirksen of Illinois: Senatorial Statesman* (Urbana, Ill.: University of Illinois Press, 1985), Chaps. 8–11; Charles and Barbara Whalen, *The Longest Debate: A Legislative History of the 1964 Civil Rights Act* (Cabin John, Md.: Seven Locks Press, 1985), pp. 150–57; Neil MacNeil, *Dirksen: Portrait of a Public Man* (New York: World Publishing Co., 1970), Chap. 13; Everett Dirksen, LBJ/OH, *passim*; Jack Valenti, LBJ/OH, V, pp. 10–13; Ben Bagdikian, "The Oil Can Is Mightier than the Sword," *New York Times Magazine*, pp. 30–88; "Everett Dirksen: American Original," *Time*, 9/19/69, pp. 25–26; Milton Viorst, "Honk, Honk, the Marigold," *Esquire*, October 1966, pp. 116–84; and Paul O'Neil, "Grand Old King of the Senate," *Life*, 3/26/65, pp. 88–112.

30. Bagdikian, "The Oil Can," pp. 31, 34.

31. *Ibid.*, p. 31.

32. Everett Dirksen, LBJ/OH, p. 4.

33. Lyndon Baines Johnson, *The Vantage Point: Perspectives of the Presidency, 1963–1969* (New York: Holt, Rinehart and Winston, 1971), p. 158.

34. Roberts, "The Other Ev Dirksen," p. 26.

35. *Ibid.*

36. Jack Valenti, LBJ/OH, V, pp. 11–12.

37. Whalen and Whalen, *The Longest Debate*, pp. 132–33.

38. *Ibid.*, pp. 185–86. The Whalens argue that Dirksen never actually changed his opinion on this matter because he was negotiating with the White House behind the scenes. Others all look at Dirksen's public position, and say there was a definite shift of opinion by the senator. See, e.g., Schapsmeier and Schapsmeier, *Dirksen of Illinois*, pp. 153–61.

39. *NYT*, 6/27/68, p. 30.

40. Schapsmeier and Schapsmeier, *Dirksen of Illinois*, p. 207; MacNeil, *Dirksen*, p. 328.

41. Henry J. Abraham, *Justices and Presidents: A Political History of Appointments to the Supreme Court*, 2nd ed. (New York: Oxford University Press, 1985), pp. 16–17.

42. Richard Harris, *Decision* (New York: E. P. Dutton and Co., 1971), p. 180.

43. The account of this conversation comes from Everett Dirksen, LBJ/OH, pp. 12–14.

44. *Ibid.*

45. For more on the negotiations over Goldberg's resignation, see untitled memo from Goldberg presumably to LBJ, 4/23/68; George Christian to president, 12/8/67; George Christian to president, 12/7/67; Drew Middleton, "Goldberg's Future," *NYT*, 12/6/67; Drew Pearson and Jack Anderson, "Goldberg Probably Will Be Next to Go," *Washington Post*, 12/6/67; and George Sherman, "McNamara, Now Goldberg," *Washington Star*, 12/8/67, copies of all three articles and the memos in Arthur Goldberg Office Files, LBJL.

Among the reasons listed by Goldberg for leaving were: "I don't want the impression left I am hanging around for reappointment to the Supreme Court. That is not good for the President, the country or me." (4/23 memo) This seems to confirm the earlier account that Goldberg's move to the UN was made with the implication that one day he would return to the court. (See Chap. VII, "The Ambush.")

46. *Wall Street Journal*, 6/28/68, p. 1; *Washington Post*, 6/25/68, p. 1.

47. "Chronology: Events Relating to Supreme Court Nominations," compiled by Jack Hushen, press secretary for Senator Robert Griffin, Fortas-Thornberry Files, LBJL.

48. Everett Dirksen, LBJ/OH, pp. 12–13; "Chronology: Events Relating to Supreme Court Nomina-

tions,'' compiled by Jack Hushen, press secretary for Senator Robert Griffin, Fortas-Thornberry Files, LBJL.

49. *Washington Post*, 6/22/68, p. A8.

50. Brennan was confirmed by the Senate in 1957, after being given a recess appointment in 1956 and having his name resubmitted to the Senate the following year. Stewart was appointed to the court in a recess appointment in 1958, and then resubmitted and confirmed in 1959.

51. Memorandum, Sol Lindenbaum to attorney general, 6/24/68, Fortas-Thornberry Files, Box 2, LBJL.

52. For more on the problems faced by Lewis Strauss, who was renominated for the position after originally serving in a recess appointment capacity, see "Strauss Nomination," *Congressional Quarterly Almanac*, 1959, pp. 665–69; "When Strauss Was Defeated: Both Sides of the Argument," *U.S. News and World Report*, 6/29/59, pp. 62–63; John L. Steele, "Passions and Stratagems in the Fall of Strauss," *Life*, 6/29/59, pp. 28–29; "The Storm over Strauss," *Newsweek*, 6/15/59, pp. 27–28; "In Public, In Private," *Newsweek*, 6/29/59, pp. 24–25; *Time*, 6/29/59, pp. 8–10; and Richard Pfau, *No Sacrifice Too Great: The Life of Lewis L. Strauss* (Charlottesville, Va.: Univ. of Virginia Press, 1984), *passim*.

53. Warren Christopher, "Memorandum for Honorable Larry Temple, Special Assistant to the President, re: The Fortas and Thornberry Nominations," 12/20/68, Fortas-Thornberry Files, Box 3, LBJL (hereinafter, Department of Justice Chronology).

54. Cf. LBJ's account of appointment in his July 31 news conference (which is reprinted in *U.S. News and World Report*, 8/12/68, p. 65) with Department of Justice Chronology, LBJL, and Ramsey Clark, LBJ/OH, I, pp. 18–19. On the lack of consultation with Mansfield, see Jones, "Defeat of Abe Fortas," pp. 61–62, 86. Jones finds no lack of precedent for this failure to inform the Democratic leadership of the upcoming nomination, but the lack of full consultation bothers Massaro. See Massaro, "LBJ and the Fortas Nomination," *passim*.

55. Ramsey Clark, LBJ/OH, I, p. 19. While the FBI records on Fortas still remain sealed, there is no indication from any of the available files in the Johnson Library that an investigative report, other than the 1965 "name check" report in Chap. VI ("The Davidson Operation"), was ever done on the justice.

56. This portrait is based on a number of sources: AI, Homer Thornberry, 11/17/82, Austin, Tex.; Thornberry, LBJ/OH, *passim*; *NYT*, 6/27/68, p. 30; *Time*, 7/5/68; p. 15.

57. Homer Thornberry, LBJ/OH, pp. 5–6.

58. Ramsey Clark, memorandum for the president, 6/24/68, Ex and Gen FG 535, Box 359, LBJL.

59. AI, Larry Temple, 11/15/82, Austin, Tex.

60. "Chronology: Events Relating to Supreme Court Nominations," compiled by Jack Hushen, press secretary for Senator Robert Griffin, Fortas-Thornberry Files, LBJL.

61. Hugh Jones, "Defeat of Abe Fortas," p. 104.

62. Shaffer, *On and Off the Floor*, p. 82. The remainder of the story that follows about the phone booth and Chief Justice Warren relies on Shaffer, pp. 79–94, and Jones, "Defeat of Abe Fortas," pp. 104–5. Warren was no doubt referring to Dirksen's role in the late 1950's and middle 1960's in the efforts to overturn Supreme Court decisions, especially in the areas of voter representation and apportionment and school prayer, by legislative enactments. For more on this, see Walter Murphy, *Congress and the Court* (Chicago: University of Chicago Press, 1962).

63. Allan Nevins, *The War for the Union*, Vol. III, *The Organized War* (New York: Charles Scribner's Sons, 1971), p. 111 and *passim*. See also Bruce Catton, *Glory Road: The Bloody Route from Fredricksburg to Gettysburg* (New York: Doubleday and Co., 1952).

CHAPTER XII
LET'S MAKE A DEAL

1. Democrat Robert F. Kennedy of New York had been killed earlier that month, leaving only ninety-nine sitting members in the Senate. His replacement, Republican Charles Goodell, would be in place for the final vote on the Fortas confirmation.

2. This calculation is taken from a summary chart in the *Congressional Quarterly*, 11/1/68, p. 2990. Those southern Democratic senators voting 75 percent of the time with the conservative coalition are considered by this chart to be Dixiecrats.

3. Harry McPherson, "The Senate Observed: A Recollection," *Atlantic Monthly*, May 1972, p. 79.

4. *NYT*, 3/20/86, p. D23.

5. *Newsweek*, 3/3/86, p. 71.

6. *NYT*, 2/20/86, p. D23.

7. George Douth, "James O. Eastland," *Leaders in Profile: The United States Senate* (New York: Sperr and Douth, 1975), p. 356. See also Robert G. Sherrill, "James Eastland: Child of Scorn," *Nation*, 10/4/65, pp. 184–95.

8. Lyndon Baines Johnson, *The Vantage Point: Perspectives of the Presidency, 1963–1969* (New York: Holt, Rinehart and Winston, 1971), p. 547.

9. *Newsweek*, 3/3/86, p. 71.

10. Arthur M. Schlesinger, Jr., *Robert Kennedy and His Times* (New York: Ballantine Books, 1978), pp. 331 and 330–332 generally.

11. James O. Eastland, LBJ/OH, pp. 17–18.

12. Johnson, *Vantage Point*, p. 545; also AI, Homer Thornberry, 11/17/82, Austin, Tex.

13. This account relies on AI, Larry Temple, 11/15/82, Austin, Tex.; and Samuel Shaffer, *On and Off the Floor: Thirty Years as a Correspondent on Capitol Hill* (New York: Newsweek Books, 1980), pp. 82–83.

14. The Department of Justice and the president also understood those problems. A list showing the difficulty of confirmation of appointments in this situation was sent by Sol Lindenbaum to the attorney general, 6/24/68, Files Pertaining to Abe Fortas and Homer Thornberry, Box 2, LBJL (hereinafter Fortas-Thornberry Files). See also memo, Jim Gaither to Joe Califano, 6/24/68, Fortas-Thornberry Files, Box 1, LBJL.

15. A copy of the memo with these numbers is from Warren Christopher to Larry Temple, 9/9/68, Fortas-Thornberry Files, Box 3, LBJL. The calculations were done by the Department of Justice based on an untitled and undated memorandum, Fortas-Thornberry Files, Box 3, LBJL. Though the president was apprised of these numbers, he chose to ignore them in this fight.

16. Before the fight even began, the White House searched for ways to secure the support of the Jewish Republican senator from New York, Jacob Javits. (Memo, Tom [Johnson] to Willie Day, 6/24/68, Fortas-Thornberry Files, Box 6, LBJL.)

17. While Shaffer says that one of Dirksen's concerns was his reelection chances, and the possible opposition of young Democratic challenger Adlai Stevenson III, this could not be confirmed by the documents or interview sources. However, while Dirksen's seat seemed relatively safe at the time, it is interesting to note that Stevenson did not run against the senior senator, instead waiting to take the seat after Dirksen's death in 1971. (Shaffer, *On and Off the Floor*, p. 83.)

18. The account of this meeting comes from AI, Larry Temple, 11/15/82, Austin, Tex., confirming the report by Shaffer, *On and Off the Floor*, pp. 82–83.

19. See, *inter alia*, *Albertson* v. *SACB*, 382 U.S. 70 (1965), and *U.S.* v. *Robel*, 389 U.S. 258 (1967).

20. This history of the agency is drawn from Edward L. Schapsmeier and Frederick H. Schapsmeier, *Dirksen of Illinois: Senatorial Statesman* (Urbana, Ill.: University of Illinois Press, 1985), pp. 190–92; *New Republic*, 6/8/68, p. 8; and *Newsweek*, 7/15/68, p. 28. As late as February 1968, Everett Dirksen was still urging others, such as a man named Robert Morris, for appointment to the SACB. See Marvin Watson to Dirksen, 2/6/68, Ex FG 285, LBJL.

21. Schapsmeier and Schapsmeier, *Dirksen of Illinois*, p. 192.

22. At the time, the White House was well aware that each man had very good reasons for taking his respective position on this issue. However, it did not seem to want to be drawn into the fight if it could be avoided. (AI, Larry Temple, 11/15/82, Austin, Tex.)

23. Fred Graham, "Low-Key and Liberal," *New York Times Magazine*, 4/2/67, p. 31.

24. Harry McPherson, LBJ/OH, VIII, pp. 8–9.

25. Larry Temple, LBJ/OH, VII, p. 8.

26. *Ibid.*, p. 7.

27. AI, Larry Temple, 11/15/82, Austin, Tex.; see also Temple LBJ/OH, III, pp. 27–30.

28. Graham, "Low-Key and Liberal," p. 135. And on "thinking about Ramsey . . ." see Harry McPherson, LBJ/OH, VIII, p. 10.

29. This account relies on AI, Larry Temple, 11/15/82, Austin, Tex. The date can be confirmed in the White House Diaries, LBJL.

30. *Ibid.*

31. "Sen. Robert Griffin: A Power in Washington?," *Detroit Scope Magazine*, 11/2/68, p. 10.

32. *Newsweek*, 7/15/68, p. 27.

33. *Washington Star*, 7/3/68, p. 1; *Washington Post*, 7/3/68, p. 1.

34. Shaffer, *On and Off the Floor*, pp. 84–85.

35. Warren Christopher, "Memorandum for Honorable Larry Temple, Special Assistant to the President, re: The Fortas and Thornberry Nominations," 12/20/68, Fortas-Thornberry Files, Box 3, LBJL (hereinafter Department of Justice Chronology).

36. Mike Manatos to LBJ, 6/25/68, Fortas-Thornberry Files, Box 4, LBJL.

37. Hugh Jones, "The Defeat of the Nomination of Abe Fortas as Chief Justice of the United States," unpublished Ph.D. dissertation, Johns Hopkins University, 1976, p. 212.

38. Mike Manatos to LBJ, 6/25/68, Fortas-Thornberry Files, Box 1, LBJL.

39. Department of Justice Chronology, LBJL.

40. Shaffer, *On and Off the Floor*, p. 84.

41. *Ibid.*

42. AI, Homer Thornberry, 11/17/82, Austin, Tex.; cf. with Johnson, *Vantage Point*, p. 545.

43. AI, Homer Thornberry, 11/17/82, Austin, Tex.; "Chief Confidant to Chief Justice," *Time*, 7/5/68, p. 15.

44. AI, Homer Thornberry, 11/17/82, Austin, Tex.

45. *Ibid.*; Department of Justice Chronology, LBJL; James O. Eastland, LBJ/OH, pp. 17–18; Johnson, *Vantage Point*, pp. 546–47.

46. Mike Manatos to LBJ, 6/26/68, Fortas-Thornberry Files, Box 4, LBJL.

47. Johnson, *Vantage Point*, p. 547.

48. James O. Eastland, LBJ/OH, pp. 17–18.

49. Transcript of Presidential Press Conference No. 128, 6/26/68, Fortas-Thornberry Files, Box 1, LBJL.

50. The statement had been reworded to say that this opposition was "no reflection on any individuals involved." This was done to overcome possible objections that a former congressional colleague, Thornberry, and a man of such a fine legal reputation, Fortas, were being unjustly slandered. See Shaffer, *On and Off the Floor*, pp. 84–85, and "Chronology: Events Relating to Supreme Court Nominations," compiled by Jack Hushen, press secretary to Senator Robert Griffin, Fortas-Thornberry Files, Box 2, LBJL. See also "Attempt to Stop Fortas Debate Fails by 14-Vote Margin," *Congressional Quarterly Almanac*, 1968 Vol., pp. 531–32. The eighteen Republican signers were Gordon Allott (Colo.), Howard Baker (Tenn.), Wallace Bennett (Utah), Frank Carlson (Kans.), Norris Cotton (N.H.), Carl Curtis (Nebr.), Paul Fannin (Ariz.), Hiram Fong (Hawaii), Robert Griffin (Mich.), Clifford Hansen (Wyo.), Len Jordan (Idaho), Jack Miller (Iowa), Thruston Morton (Ky.), Karl Mundt (S.D.), George Murphy (Calif.), Strom Thurmond (S.C.), John Williams (Del.), and Milton Young (N.D.).

51. A summary of the three major TV news broadcasts that day can be found in Bob Fleming to LBJ, 6/26/68, Fortas-Thornberry Files, Box 6, LBJL.

52. Joe Califano to LBJ, 6/26/68, Califano: Memos to File, Box 18, LBJL.

53. LBJ note to himself, attached to memo, Joe Califano to LBJ, 6/26/68, Fortas-Thornberry Files, Box 6, LBJL.

54. Mike Manatos to LBJ, 6/26/68, Fortas-Thornberry Files, Box 6, LBJL.

CHAPTER XIII
THE EMPIRE STRIKES BACK

1. *Congressional Record*, 6/26/68, p. 18790.

2. The rule for invoking cloture, which would end a filibuster, has changed. In 1968, one needed two thirds of those senators present and voting to invoke cloture. In effect, this often meant sixty-seven votes, as cloture votes carry such importance that often all of the senators are present for the counting. Now, to make invoking cloture easier, the rule has been changed so that one needs three fifths of the constitutional size of the Senate, or sixty votes, to accomplish the feat.

3. *Wall Street Journal*, 6/28/68, p. 8.

4. *NYT*, 6/27/68, p. 30.

5. *Washington Star*, 6/27/68, p. 1.

6. For more on the presidential motivations in making such selections, see Henry J. Abraham, *Justices and Presidents: A Political History of Appointments to the Supreme Court*, 2nd ed. (New York: Oxford University Press, 1985), *passim*.

7. AI, George Christian, 10/31/82, Austin, Tex.

8. *Washington Star*, 6/28/68, p. 1.

9. Mike Manatos to LBJ, 6/26/68, Files Pertaining to Abe Fortas and Homer Thornberry, Box 6, LBJL (hereinafter Fortas-Thornberry Files).

10. Mike Manatos, LBJ/OH, p. 16ff.; Harold Barefoot Sanders, LBJ/OH, p. 35ff.

11. AI, Larry Temple, 11/15/82, Austin, Tex.

12. *Ibid.*

13. *Ibid.*, and AI, George Christian, 11/11/82, Austin, Tex.

14. Paul Porter, LBJ/OH, I, pp. 33–35.

15. The details of this seminar have been pieced together from W. Carey Parker to Warren Christopher (plus attachments), received 9/24/68, Warren Christopher Papers, Box 2, LBJL; Paul Porter speech draft, "The American University Teaching Seminar"; B. J. Tennery to Paul Porter, 11/2/67 (plus attachment); and "Proposal for: Institute on Law and the Social Environment," undated, Paul Porter Papers, Box 5, LBJL.

16. Memorandum, AF to Paul Porter, undated, Porter Papers, Box 3, LBJL.

17. *Ibid.*

18. Letter to author from Sam Ervin, 6/19/84.

19. Mike Manatos to LBJ, 6/26/68, Fortas-Thornberry Files, Box 6, LBJL.

20. *Wall Street Journal,* 6/28/68, p. 8.

21. Warren Christopher, "Memorandum for Honorable Larry Temple, Special Assistant to the President, re: The Fortas and Thornberry Nominations," 12/20/68, Fortas-Thornberry Files, Box 3, LBJL (hereinafter Department of Justice Chronology).

22. Jim Jones to LBJ, 6/27/68, with attached Senate head count, 6/27/68, Fortas-Thornberry Files, Box 3, LBJL.

23. Harold Barefoot Sanders to LBJ, 6/28/68, Fortas-Thornberry Files, Box 6, LBJL; untitled head count, Fortas-Thornberry Files, Box 1, LBJL.

24. Harold Barefoot Sanders to LBJ, 6/27/68, Harold Barefoot Sanders Papers, Box 24, LBJL.

25. Mike Manatos to LBJ, 6/27/68, Fortas-Thornberry Files, Box 1, LBJL.

26. Dick Darling to Doug Nobles, 6/27/68, Fortas-Thornberry Files, Box 1, LBJL.

27. Memo of phone call from Abe Fortas, 6/27/68, Fortas-Thornberry Files, Box 4, LBJL.

28. Harold Barefoot Sanders to LBJ, 6/27/68, Fortas-Thornberry Files, Box 4, LBJL.

29. Larry Levinson to LBJ, "A Four-Part Dialogue," 6/28/68, Fortas-Thornberry Files, Box 1, LBJL.

30. *Washington Post,* 6/29/68, p. A6.

31. "Chronology: Events Relating to Supreme Court Nominations," compiled by Jack Hushen, press secretary for Senator Robert Griffin, Fortas-Thornberry Files, Box 2, LBJL (hereinafter Griffin Chronology). See also *NYT,* 6/28/68, p. 1.

32. Hugh Jones, "The Defeat of the Nomination of Abe Fortas as Chief Justice of the United States," unpublished Ph.D. dissertation, Johns Hopkins University, 1976, p. 208; Robert Griffin, LBJ/OH, I, pp. 7–14.

33. Robert Griffin, LBJ/OH, I, pp. 12–13.

34. Paul Porter, LBJ/OH, I, p. 36.

35. *Ibid.*, p. 36–37.

36. Harold Barefoot Sanders to LBJ, 6/29/68, plus attached statement by George Meany, Sanders Papers, Box 24, LBJL.

37. Untitled memo on the efforts of Clarence Mitchell and Andy Biemiller, 6/29/68, Ex and Gen 535/A, Box 360, LBJL.

38. Joe Califano to LBJ, 6/29/68, and Ernie Goldstein to LBJ, 7/8/68, Fortas-Thornberry Files, Box 5, LBJL.

39. Harold Barefoot Sanders to LBJ, 7/1/68, Sanders Papers, Box 24, LBJL.

40. Judge David Dyer to Senator George Smathers, 7/1/68; Judge John Brown to Larry Temple, 7/10/68; Larry Temple to LBJ (on Judge Minor Wisdom's view), 7/10/68; Judge Minor Wisdom to LBJ, 7/1/68; Judge John Brown to James O. Eastland, 7/10/68; Judge Wade McCree, Jr., to Philip Hart, 7/1/68; Judge Joe Fisher to Ralph Yarborough, 7/2/68; Judge W. M. Taylor to Yarborough, 7/2/68; Judge Adrian Spears to Yarborough, 7/2/68, Fortas-Thornberry Files, Box 2, LBJL. This lobbying effort by the judiciary was arranged by the White House; see memo, Harold Barefoot Sanders to LBJ, 6/29/68, Fortas-Thornberry Files, Box 4, LBJL.

41. Mike Manatos to LBJ, 6/28/68, Fortas-Thornberry Files, Box 1, LBJL.

42. Irv Sprague to Barefoot Sanders, 6/28/68, Fortas-Thornberry Files, Box 4, LBJL; two untitled memos, 6/28/68, Fortas-Thornberry Files, Box 7, LBJL; *Washington Star,* 7/3/68, p. 1.

43. Jim Gaither to Joe Califano, 6/29/68, Fortas-Thornberry Files, Box 1, LBJL; untitled memo on efforts of Clarence Mitchell and Andy Biemiller, 6/29/68, Ex and Gen 535/A, Box 360, LBJL.

44. Untitled memo on Ellender, undated, Fortas-Thornberry Files, Box 7, LBJL; two memos, Larry Temple to LBJ, 6/29/68, Fortas-Thornberry Files, Box 1, LBJL.

45. Larry Temple to LBJ, 7/1/68, and two memos, Jim Gaither to Joe Califano, 7/1/68, Fortas-Thornberry Files, Box 4, LBJL; James Ling to John Tower, 7/1/68, Porter Papers, Box 6, LBJL. See also Gaither to Califano, 7/2/68, Fortas-Thornberry Files, Box 4, LBJL.

46. Ernie Goldstein to LBJ, 7/8/68, Fortas-Thornberry Files, Box 5, LBJL.

47. George Reedy to LBJ, 7/2/68, Fortas-Thornberry Files, Box 4, LBJL.

48. Mike Manatos to LBJ, 6/28/68, Fortas-Thornberry Files, Box 4, LBJL.

49. Mike Manatos to LBJ, 6/28/68, Fortas-Thornberry Files, Box 5, LBJL.

50. Untitled memo on Ellender, undated, Fortas-Thornberry Files, Box 7, LBJL.

51. Senate head counts, 6/28/68 and 6/29/68, Fortas-Thornberry Files, Box 1, LBJL; Harold Barefoot Sanders to LBJ, 6/28/68, Fortas-Thornberry Files, Box 6, LBJL.

52. AI, Larry Temple, 11/15/82, Austin, Tex. The actual memo can be found attached to memo, Larry Temple to LBJ, 6/28/68, which is covered by memo, Ramsey Clark to LBJ, 6/28/68, Fortas-Thornberry Files, Box 1, LBJL.

53. *Ibid.*

54. See note on top of memo, Harry McPherson to LBJ, 6/28/68, Fortas-Thornberry Files, Box 1, LBJL; unpublished and untitled extracts of Fortas book, *Concerning Dissent and Civil Disobedience,* Fortas-Thornberry Files, Box 7, LBJL; AI, Larry Temple, 11/15/82, Austin, Tex.; and Larry Temple, LBJ/OH, I, pp. 26–29.

55. Mike Manatos to LBJ, 6/29/68, Fortas-Thornberry Files, Box 6, LBJL.

56. Joe Califano to LBJ, 6/29/68 (plus attached news article on Griffin), Fortas-Thornberry Files, Box 4, LBJL.

57. Untitled sheaf of Fortas notes to Paul Porter, undated, Porter Papers, Box 3, LBJL.

58. *Ibid.*, and AI, Larry Temple, 11/15/82, Austin, Tex.

59. Ernie Goldstein to Larry Temple and LBJ, 6/29/68, with attached letter from I. L. Kenen to "Dear Friend," 6/28/68; and untitled memo on contacts, 6/28/68, Fortas-Thornberry Files, Box 6, LBJL.

60. Robert Shogan, *A Question of Judgment: The Fortas Case and the Struggle for the Supreme Court* (Indianapolis: Bobbs-Merrill, 1972), p. 156.

61. Irv Sprague to Barefoot Sanders, 6/28/68, Fortas-Thornberry Files, Box 4, LBJL.

62. Memo on phone call of Gene Wyman, 6/28/68, Fortas-Thornberry Files, Box 7, LBJL.

63. Joe Califano to LBJ, 6/29/68, Fortas-Thornberry Files, Box 1, LBJL.

64. Later, Smathers would phone the White House and ask for time with the president to speak about "3 or 4 personal items," but it is not known whether they were linked to the involvement in this dispute. The precise motivation for Smathers's involvement here remains one of the mysteries of the dispute. Interestingly, the senator's involvement at the end of the debate would prove to be very different from his early efforts on behalf of the White House.

65. Warren Christopher to Larry Temple, 6/28/68 (with attached memo on Thornberry), Warren Christopher Papers, Box 1, LBJL.

66. A copy of the memo titled "The Illustrative Decisions of Judge Thornberry in the Field of Law Enforcement" can be found in the Christopher Papers, Box 1, LBJL. A note at the top of the memo indicates that copies were delivered to Abe Fortas, Paul Porter, and Senator Smathers's office, as well as to Larry Temple at the White House.

67. *Congressional Record,* 7/1/68, p. 19535.

68. Baker's statement is found at *Congressional Record,* 7/1/68, p. 19543 (emphasis added); the letter is Charles Fairman to Warren Christopher, 6/30/68, Fortas-Thornberry Files, Box 2, LBJL.

69. Warren Christopher to Larry Temple, 7/3/68, Fortas-Thornberry Files, Box 2, LBJL.

70. *Ibid.*

71. Justice Department Chronology, LBJL.

72. Copies of this correspondence—Horace Gray to Theodore Roosevelt, 7/9/02 and Roosevelt to Gray, 7/11/02—can be found attached to memo from Warren Christopher to Larry Temple, 7/5/68, in the Fortas-Thornberry Files, Box 2, LBJL.

73. Warren Christopher to Wayne Morse, 7/9/68, Christopher Papers, Box 1, LBJL; *Congressional Record,* p. 20877.

74. Joe Califano to LBJ, 7/2/68 (plus attachments), Fortas-Thornberry Files, Box 4, LBJL; *Congressional Record,* pp. 20284–85.

75. *Washington Post,* 7/2/68, p. 1.

76. Fred Graham, "Subversives Unit Is Asked to Cite 7," *NYT,* 7/2/68, p. 16; Griffin Chronology, LBJL.

77. Griffin Chronology, LBJL.
78. This incident was reported in several places, with the quote combining two of those reports that dovetail: *Newsweek*, 7/15/68, p. 27, and "Sen. Robert Griffin: A Power in Washington?," *Detroit Scope Magazine*, 11/2/68, p. 10. See also *Washington Post*, 7/3/68, p. A11.
79. "Sen. Robert Griffin: A Power in Washington?," *Detroit Scope Magazine*, 11/2/68, p. 10.
80. *NYT*, 3/21/68, p. 43; the account of the article's use is from Everett Dirksen, LBJ/OH, pp. 10–11.
81. Memo, Norma Arata to Dorothy Territo, 7/2/68, Fortas Finding Aid File, Fortas-Thornberry Files, Box 6, LBJL.
82. Memo, Norma Arata to Dorothy Territo, 7/29/68, Fortas-Thornberry Files, Box 6, LBJL. These documents were organized and divided up, and became the Fortas-Thornberry Files, which have been so useful in this part of the book.
   The Kennedy memo can be found at LBJ order to secretary, 4/1/66, plus attached memo from Liz [Carpenter] to LBJ, 4/1/66, White House Famous Names File, Robert Kennedy folder, Box 6, LBJL.

CHAPTER XIV
THE SCARLETT LETTER

1. White House Diaries, 7/3/68, LBJL. Also AI, Larry Temple, 11/15/82, Austin, Tex.
2. William Jordan, LBJ/OH, I, p. 18.
3. Larry Temple, LBJ/OH, I, pp. 37–38; AI, Larry Temple, 11/15/82, Austin, Tex.; White House Diaries, 7/3/68, LBJL.
4. Larry Temple, LBJ/OH, I, pp. 37–38.
5. *Ibid.*, p. 17.
6. Douglas Kiker, "Russell of Georgia, the Old Guard at Its Shrewdest," *Harper's Magazine*, September 1966, pp. 102 and 101–6 generally. See also Meg Greenfield, "The Man Who Leads the Southern Senators," *The Reporter*, Vol. 30, 5/21/64, pp. 17–21.
7. *Congressional Record*, 1/25/71, p. 405.
8. *Ibid.*, p. 421.
9. *Ibid.*
10. The first quote is from William Jordan, LBJ/OH, I, p. 14; the second quote is from Powell Moore, LBJ/OH, I, p. 10.
11. Larry Temple, LBJ/OH, I, p. 18.
12. Wayne Kelley, "Senator Russell Vows to Speak His Mind," *Atlanta Journal and Constitution Magazine*, 2/4/68, p. 8.
13. Powell Moore, LBJ/OH, I, p. 11.
14. *Ibid.* For more on the split, see "Richard B. Russell: A Georgia Giant," interview by WSB/TV, pp. 19–27; copy deposited in Richard B. Russell Library, Athens, Ga.
15. Wayne Kelley, "How Russell Helped LBJ to Presidency," *Atlanta Journal and Constitution Magazine*, 6/30/68, p. 21.
16. William Jordan, LBJ/OH, p. 14.
17. Kiker, "Russell of Georgia," pp. 102–3.
18. Herman Talmadge, OH, Russell Library, Athens, Ga., p. 24; *NYT*, 6/17/65, p. 22.
19. Kiker, "Russell of Georgia," p. 106.
20. *Congressional Record*, 4/10/67, pp. 8854–55.
21. *Congressional Record*, 7/10/67, p. 18093; Kelley, "Russell Vows to Speak," p. 9.
22. Powell Moore, LBJ/OH, I, p. 8; Congressional Record, 7/10/68, pp. 18093–97.
23. Greenfield, "The Man Who Leads," p. 17.
24. Gerald Siegel, LBJ/OH, IV, p. 16.
25. Powell Moore, LBJ/OH, I, pp. 14–15.
26. Quoted in letter from Warren Christopher to Wayne Morse, 7/27/68, Warren Christopher Papers, Box 1, LBJL.
27. For more on the appointment process at the lower federal court level, see Sheldon Goldman and Thomas Jahnige, *The Federal Courts as a Political System*, 3rd ed. (New York: Harper and Row, 1985), Chap. 3, and Harold W. Chase, *Federal Judges: The Appointing Process* (Minneapolis: University of Minnesota Press, 1972). A fine new study on this appointment process during the Johnson

years is Neil D. McFeeley, *Appointment of Judges: The Johnson Presidency* (Austin, Tex.: University of Texas Press, 1987).

28. Herman Talmadge, OH, Russell Library, Athens, Ga., p. 20.

29. This portion of the story relies on the accounts in the oral histories of Alexander Lawrence, Jr., *passim*; Lawton Miller Calhoun, pp. 19A–19B; and Herman Talmadge, pp. 20–21, Richard B. Russell, Jr., Library, Athens, Georgia.

30. Richard Russell to LBJ, 5/20/68, and see biographical summary of Lawrence, Ex FG 530/ST1-42, Box 355, LBJL. See also Russell to LBJ, 2/13/68, John Macy Office Files, Box 329, LBJL. The Lawrence sections of the appointment folders in these locations are filled with important and relevant documents on this controversy.

31. Marvin Watson to Larry Temple, 3/4/68, WHCF Name File, Alexander Lawrence folder, LBJL.

32. Larry Temple, summary of the status of judicial appointments, 3/19/68, Office Files of Larry Temple, Box 1, LBJL.

33. Tom Johnson to Jim Jones, 5/7/68 (with attachment), Ex FG 530/ST1-42, Box 355, LBJL. See also editorial, *Atlanta Constitution*, 3/30/68, copy in Ex FG 530/ST1-42, LBJL.

34. Herman Talmadge, OH, Russell Library, Athens, Ga., pp. 21–22. See also untitled memo on Lawrence from Russell staff, sent to White House on 5/7/68, attached to Tom Johnson to Jim Jones, 5/7/68, Ex FG 530/ST1-42, Box 355, LBJL.

35. The Lawrence speech is reprinted in *Congressional Record*, 2/2/59, pp. 1539–41.

36. *Ibid.*, p. 1539.

37. *Atlanta Constitution*, 3/29/68 and 3/30/68, copies of articles in Ex FG 530/ST1-42, LBJL.

38. Telegram, NAACP of Georgia (represented by Sherman Roberson and Julius C. Hope) to LBJ, 4/3/68, attached to memo, John Macy to Roberson, 4/15/68, John Macy Office Files, Box 329, LBJL.

39. Marvin Watson to Larry Temple, 4/4/68, WHCF Name File, Alexander Lawrence folder, LBJL.

40. Richard Russell to Frank Scarlett, 4/2/68, Series I, DI, Russell Library, Athens, Ga.

41. *Atlanta Journal*, 3/29/68, copy of article in Ex FG 530/ST1-42, LBJL.

42. Arthur Schlesinger, Jr., *Robert Kennedy and His Times* (New York: Ballantine Books, 1978), pp. 330–37.

43. *Ibid.*; also author's conversation with Ramsey Clark, 4/11/86, Hempstead, N.Y.

44. Richard Russell to LBJ, 5/20/68, Ex FG 530/ST1-42, LBJL.

45. Larry Temple, LBJ/OH, I, pp. 16–17.

46. AI, Judge Harold Barefoot Sanders, 11/9/82, Dallas, Tex.

47. Larry Temple, LBJ/OH, I, pp. 19–20.

48. Lawton Calhoun, OH, Russell Library, Athens, Ga., pp. 19A–19B; Powell Moore, LBJ/OH, I, p. 20 (and see I, pp. 16–21, generally); Jim Jones to Richard Russell, 5/2/68, Ex FG 530 ST1-42, Box 355, LBJL; memo, Jones to Juanita Roberts, 7/2/68, Ex FG 530 ST1-42, Box 355, LBJL.

49. Tom Johnson to Jim Jones, 5/7/68, Ex FG 530 ST1-42, Box 355, LBJL.

50. Ramsey Clark to LBJ, 5/13/68, Ex Gen FG 530, Box 530, LBJL.

51. Editorial, *Atlanta Journal*, 3/29/68, copy in Ex FG 530 ST1-42, Box 355, LBJL.

52. Ramsey Clark to LBJ, 5/13/68, Ex Gen FG 530, Box 355, LBJL.

53. *Ibid.*

54. Larry Temple to LBJ, 5/20/68, FG 530 ST10, LBJL.

55. Richard Russell to LBJ, 5/20/68, Ex FG 530/ST1-42, LBJL.

56. Larry Temple, LBJ/OH, I, p. 22; AI, Larry Temple, 11/15/82, Austin, Tex.

57. Tom Johnson to Jim Jones, 5/22/68, Office Files of Larry Temple, Box 1, LBJL; Tom Johnson to Jim Jones, 5/24/68, WHCF Name File, Alexander Lawrence folder, LBJL; Tom Johnson to Larry Temple, Ex FG 530/ST1-42, LBJL.

58. LBJ to Richard Russell, 7/2/68, Office Files of Larry Temple, Box 1, LBJL.

59. Tom Johnson to LBJ, 5/28/68, and packet of materials covered by Tom Johnson to LBJ, 6/7/68, Ex FG 530/ST1-42, LBJL.

60. Richard Russell to LBJ, 6/14/68, John Macy Office Files, Box 329, LBJL.

61. Tom Johnson to LBJ, 6/11/68, Ex FG 530/ST1-42, LBJL; Tom Johnson to Juanita Roberts, 6/24/68, FG 530/ST10, LBJL.

62. Richard Russell to LBJ, 7/1/68, and LBJ to Russell, 7/3/68, Office Files of Larry Temple, Box 1, LBJL.

63. Larry Temple, LBJ/OH, I, p. 24.

64. Herman Talmadge, OH, Russell Library, Athens, Ga., p. 21; Alexander Lawrence, Jr., OH, Russell Library, Athens, Ga., pp. 4–6.

65. AI, Larry Temple, 11/15/82, Austin, Tex.; Larry Temple, LBJ/OH, I, pp. 28–29.
66. Larry Temple, LBJ/OH, I, pp. 28–29.
67. AI, Larry Temple, 11/15/82, Austin, Tex.; memo, Larry Temple to LBJ, 7/1/68, Office Files of Larry Temple, Box 1, LBJL.
68. *Ibid.*
69. AI, Larry Temple, 11/15/82, Austin, Tex.
70. *Ibid.*
71. *Ibid.*, and author's conversation with Ramsey Clark, 4/11/86, Hempstead, N.Y.
72. Larry Temple, LBJ/OH, I, pp. 32–33.
73. Richard Russell to LBJ, 7/1/68, Office Files of Larry Temple, Box 1, LBJL.
74. Larry Temple, LBJ/OH, I, pp. 33–35. No hard evidence could be discovered either to connect the two events in Johnson's mind, or to explain why Russell now believed that there had been a connection in the first place. As explained in the text, there was no reason for Johnson to worry about such a quid pro quo. As for Russell's belief, it could just have been the view of a sick and dying man seeking to explain why he could not get what he wanted from the White House as quickly as he wanted it. Johnson himself remained convinced that the story had been planted in Russell's mind by the nomination opponents. (Temple, LBJ/OH, I, p. 34.)
75. Tom Johnson to Larry Temple, 7/2/68, and Jim Jones to Juanita Roberts, 7/2/68, Ex FG 530/ST1-42, LBJL.
76. Harry McPherson to LBJ, 7/2/68, Office Files of Larry Temple, Box 1, LBJL. Also useful for this section were the many drafts produced by the White House team for the response to Senator Russell.
77. Larry Temple to LBJ, 7/2/68, Diary Backup, Box 71, LBJL.
78. LBJ to Richard Russell, 7/3/68, Fortas-Thornberry Files, Box 5, LBJL; Larry Temple, LBJ/OH, I, p. 38.
79. LBJ to Richard Russell, 7/3/68, Fortas-Thornberry Files, Box 5, LBJL.
80. Mike Manatos to LBJ, 7/9/68, Ex FG 530/ST1-42, Box 355, LBJL.
81. Larry Temple, LBJ/OH, I, pp. 36–37; Tom Johnson to LBJ, 7/12/68, Diary Backup, Box 108, LBJL.
82. Powell Moore, LBJ/OH, p. 17.
83. AI, Homer Thornberry, 11/17/82, Austin, Tex. The White House Diaries in Austin indicate that the dinner was on the evening of 7/12/68.
84. No one raised a single objection to the conditional nature of the resignation letter at any point during this process. In fact, Scarlett used the same language as the White House's earlier response to the resignation of Earl Warren, saying that his resignation was made "subject to the appointment and qualification of his successor."
85. An interesting question is whether the objections would have been heard had the nomination been sent to the Senate much earlier, when the objecting groups would have been able to focus their full energies on the Senate Judiciary Committee rather than the White House and the Department of Justice.
86. Wayne Kelley, "Conversation with Richard Russell," *Atlanta Magazine*, December 1968, copy supplied by Russell Library, Athens, Ga.
87. AI, George Christian, 11/11/82, Austin, Tex.; see also Powell Moore, LBJ/OH, I, p. 10.
88. William Darden, LBJ/OH, pp. 23–24.
89. Powell Moore, LBJ/OH, I, pp. 28–29.
90. *Ibid.*, pp. 29–30; William Darden, LBJ/OH, I, p. 24; Herman Talmadge, OH, Russell Library, Athens, Ga., p. 25.
91. Powell Moore, LBJ/OH, I, pp. 27–28; AI, Homer Thornberry, 11/17/82, Austin, Tex. Copies of the editorials castigating Lawrence and a review of his record in his later obituary can be found in Ex FG 530 ST/1-42, Box 355, LBJL.

   For a different interpretation of this same controversy, see John Massaro, "LBJ and the Fortas Nomination for Chief Justice," *Political Science Quarterly*, Vol. 97, No. 4, Winter 1982–83, pp. 603–21. Massaro argues that Johnson did not consult widely enough with members of the Senate to ensure the confirmation's success. I argue that the consultation process was fine, but circumstances changed and so did the arrangements various senators had made with the president.
92. Griffin himself remembers that the conversation with Russell took place on the phone, with him on his way home to Michigan for the July 4 holiday and Russell in Winder, Ga. (Robert Griffin, LBJ/OH, I, p. 9.) And Robert Shogan, relying on the account of fellow reporter Samuel Shaffer, repeats the story. (Robert Shogan, *A Question of Judgment: The Fortas Case and the Struggle for the Supreme Court* [Indianapolis: Bobbs-Merrill Co., 1972], p. 159.) In fact, the Office Diaries of Richard Russell show that both men were in D.C. at the time, and the conversation took place there. Moreover, Powell Moore remembers the conversation, as he came into the office after the two men had talked and found

Senator Griffin "in a big grin." (Powell Moore, LBJ/OH, I, p. 21.) It is possible that the two men spoke about this issue again on the phone, but there seems little doubt that the formal deal was consummated in the Russell Senate office.

93. Jones, "Defeat of Abe Fortas," p. 119.

CHAPTER XV
THE HOLY WAR

1. Mike Manatos to LBJ, 7/2/68, Files Pertaining to Abe Fortas and Homer Thornberry, Box 2, LBJL (hereinafter, Fortas-Thornberry Files).
2. Memo of taped conversation from Arlington, Va., location, 7/3/68, attached to memo, Larry Temple to Mike Manatos, 7/10/68, Fortas-Thornberry Files, Box 5, LBJL.
3. The document is dated 7/6/68, Paul Porter Papers, Box 3, LBJL.
4. Merle Miller, *Lyndon: An Oral Biography* (New York: Ballantine Books, 1980), p. 590. The identity of the senator who made the statement was discovered by Hugh Jones, who shared it with the author in a conversation, 7/23/87, Shippenburg, Pa.
5. The column appeared in *Washington Post*, 7/9/68, p. B11.
6. Harry McPherson to LBJ, 7/11/68, Fortas-Thornberry Files, Box 5, LBJL.
7. Memo, Ernie Goldstein to LBJ, 7/8/68, Fortas-Thornberry Files, Box 5, LBJL.
8. Edwin Weisl to Joe Califano, 7/8/68, Fortas-Thornberry Files, Box 5, LBJL.
9. Joe Califano to LBJ, 7/2/68, Fortas-Thornberry Files, Box 4, LBJL; Califano to Leo Janos, 7/2/68, Fortas-Thornberry Files, Box 4, LBJL; Richard Lippes to Dan Levitt, undated, Porter Papers, Box 3, LBJL.
10. Speech, forwarded by Warren Christopher to Larry Temple, 7/1/68, Ex Gen FG 535/A, Box 360, LBJL. The speech was delivered by Mike Mansfield on 7/2/68; see *Congressional Record*, 7/2/68, p. 19633.
11. The speech was finished and dated 7/3/68, and can be found in the Porter Papers, Box 2, LBJL, and *Congressional Record*, 7/8/68, p. 20143.
12. Dick Darling to Doug Nobles, 6/28/68, Fortas-Thornberry Files, Box 1, LBJL.
13. Mike Manatos to LBJ, 7/2/68, and Jim Gaither to Joe Califano, 7/2/68, Fortas-Thornberry Files, Box 4, LBJL.
14. AI, Larry Temple, 11/15/82, Austin, Tex.
15. Larry Temple to LBJ, 7/2/68, Fortas-Thornberry Files, Box 2, LBJL.
16. AI, Larry Temple, 11/15/82, Austin, Tex.
17. Larry Temple to LBJ, 7/1/68, Fortas-Thornberry Files, Box 4, LBJL. Johnson did not give the speech, and McClellan did not vote for Fortas. Whether giving the speech would have turned that around is not known, but extremely doubtful given the events that followed.
18. Harry McPherson to LBJ, 7/2/68, Fortas-Thornberry Files, Box 4, LBJL.
19. Harry McPherson to Mike Manatos, reporting on the actions of Doug Wynn, 7/2/68, Fortas-Thornberry Files, Box 7, LBJL; Mike Manatos to LBJ, 7/2/68, Ex Gen FG 535/A, Box 360, LBJL.
20. Doug Nobles to Marvin Watson, 7/9/68, and Marvin Watson to LBJ, 7/31/68, Fortas-Thornberry Files, Box 7, LBJL.
21. "Earl Warren Talks About the 'Warren Court,'" *U.S. News and World Report*, 7/15/68, pp. 62–64.
22. *Ibid.*
23. Ernie Goldstein to LBJ, 7/8/68, Fortas-Thornberry Files, Box 5, LBJL.
24. Jim Gaither to Joe Califano, 7/2/68, Fortas-Thornberry Files, Box 4, LBJL.
25. Like the general public, and the other members of the Senate, they had no knowledge at this point of the meeting between Griffin and Russell.
26. Mike Manatos to LBJ, 7/9/68, Fortas-Thornberry Files, Box 2, LBJL.
27. Mike Manatos to Abe Ribicoff, 7/3/68, Ex LE/NR, Box 142, LBJL.
28. Jim Gaither to Joe Califano, 7/2/68, and Mike Manatos to LBJ, 7/2/68, Fortas-Thornberry Files, Box 4, LBJL.
29. Jim Jones to LBJ, 7/9/68, Fortas-Thornberry Files, Box 5, LBJL.
30. Samuel Shaffer, *On and Off the Floor* (New York: Newsweek Books, 1980), p. 90.
31. Harry McPherson to LBJ, 7/10/68, Office Files of Harry McPherson, Box 53, LBJL.
32. *Washington Post*, 7/10/68, copy found in Fortas-Thornberry Files, Box 1, LBJL; *Congressional Record*, 7/10/68, p. 20482.

33. Warren Christopher, "Memorandum for Honorable Larry Temple, Special Assistant to the President, re: The Fortas and Thornberry Nominations," 12/20/68, Warren Christopher Papers, Box 3, LBJL.
34. AI, Larry Temple, 11/15/82, Austin, Tex.
35. Larry Temple, LBJ/OH, I, p. 42.
36. *Ibid.*, p. 43.
37. *Ibid.*, p. 42; AI, Larry Temple, 11/15/82, Austin, Tex.

CHAPTER XVI
THE BATTLE OF CAPITOL HILL

1. "Nominations of Abe Fortas and Homer Thornberry," Hearings Before the Committee on the Judiciary, United States Senate, 90th Congress, 2nd Session, 7/11–7/23/68 (Washington, D.C.: U.S. Government Printing Office, 1968), p. 103 (hereinafter Confirmation Hearings).
   The title of the chapter is taken from a phrase in *Business Week*, 9/7/68, p. 29.
2. Larry Temple, LBJ/OH, VI, p. 3.
3. Ernie [Goldstein] to White House (on Dave Brody), undated, Files Pertaining to Abe Fortas and Homer Thornberry, Box 3, LBJL (hereinafter Fortas-Thornberry Files).
4. Joe Califano to LBJ, 7/10/68, Fortas-Thornberry Files, Box 5, LBJL. A note on this document indicates that the message was relayed to Fortas himself.
5. Two undated and untitled lists of questions labeled only "For Senator Smathers," Paul Porter Papers, Box 2, LBJL.
6. See the memo on excerpts from Walter Murphy's book, *Elements of Judicial Strategy*, 7/12/68, Fortas-Thornberry Files, Box 2, LBJL.
7. AI, Larry Temple, 11/15/82, Austin, Tex.; AI, Judge Harold Barefoot Sanders, 11/9/82, Dallas, Tex.
8. Tom Johnson to Jim Jones, dated only "filed 7/17/68," and LBJ to William Gossett, 7/12/68, Fortas-Thornberry Files, Box 5, LBJL.
9. AI, Larry Temple, 11/15/82, Austin, Tex.; AI, Judge Harold Barefoot Sanders, 11/9/82, Dallas, Tex. See also Harold Barefoot Sanders, LBJ/OH, III, pp. 21–23, 29.
10. Diaries of Harold Ickes, 6/27/41, Harold Ickes Papers, LOC. Also mentioned in memo, "Abe Fortas," undated, p. 2, Ickes Papers, Box 464, LOC.
11. AI, Arthur "Tex" Goldschmidt, 6/10/84, Durham, N.Y.
12. For more, see Owen Lattimore, *Ordeal by Slander* (Boston: Little, Brown and Co., 1950), *passim*.
13. Confirmation Hearings, p. 168; Fortas repeats this quotation and says that these claims are "still exaggerated." The original version of the quote is taken from Robert Shogan, *A Question of Judgment: The Fortas Case and the Struggle for the Supreme Court* (Indianapolis: Bobbs-Merrill Co., 1972), p. 116.
14. Shogan, *Question of Judgment*, p. 115.
15. Ernie [Goldstein] to LBJ, 7/12/68; Joe Califano to LBJ, 7/12/68; and Mike Manatos to LBJ, 7/15/68, Fortas-Thornberry Files, Box 2, LBJL.
16. The term comes from *Newsweek*, 7/15/68, pp. 27–28.
17. "Chronology: Events Relating to Supreme Court Nominations," compiled by Jack Hushen, press secretary to Senator Robert Griffin, Fortas-Thornberry Files, Box 2, LBJL (hereinafter Griffin Chronology).
18. Confirmation Hearings, pp. 19–20.
19. *Ibid.*, p. 25. My count of Ervin's breaking of vows agrees with that of Hugh Jones. See Jones's "The Defeat of the Nomination of Abe Fortas as Chief Justice of the United States," unpublished Ph.D. dissertation, Johns Hopkins University, 1976, p. 166.
20. *Baltimore Sun*, 7/15/68, p. A3.
21. Albert Gore to LBJ, 7/11/68, Fortas-Thornberry Files, Box 4, LBJL; Robert Byrd to LBJ, 7/12/68, Ex Gen FG 535, Box 359, LBJL.
22. *Congressional Record*, 7/12/68, pp. 20981–83.
23. Confirmation Hearings, p. 46.
24. *Ibid.*, pp. 51–54; *NYT*, 7/13/68, p. 1; Warren Christopher, "Memorandum for Honorable Larry Temple, Special Assistant to the President, re: The Fortas and Thornberry Nominations," 12/20/68, Warren Christopher Papers, Box 3, LBJL (hereinafter Justice Department Chronology).

25. Warren Christopher to Larry Temple, 7/12/68, Fortas-Thornberry Files, Box 2, LBJL; Confirmation Hearings, p. 54; Justice Department Chronology, LBJL.

26. Confirmation Hearings, p. 58; "Attempt to Stop Fortas Debate Fails by 14-Vote Margin," *Congressional Quarterly Almanac,* 1968 Vol., p. 534 (hereinafter *CQ* Chronology).

27. Confirmation Hearings, p. 49.

28. *New York Times Magazine,* 6/4/67, p. 92.

29. "Chief Confidant to Chief Justice," *Time,* 7/5/68, p. 14.

30. Justice Department Chronology, LBJL.

31. Untitled memo to the Justice Department researchers, 7/16/68, Joe Califano Papers, Box 22, LBJL.

32. AI, Homer Thornberry, 11/17/82, Austin, Tex.

33. For more on this, see Jones, "Defeat of Abe Fortas," pp. 144–45, and Confirmation Hearings, pp. 89–97.

34. On the reactions to the timing of Fortas's book and his appearance on the *Today* show, see Jones, "Defeat of Abe Fortas," pp. 74, 144–47.

35. Others who see it as the turning point include Shogan, *Question of Judgment,* pp. 262–77; Bernard Schwartz, *Super Chief: Earl Warren and His Supreme Court—A Judicial Biography* (New York: New York University Press, 1983), p. 721; and Robert Griffin, in *Chicago Tribune,* 10/3/68, p. 2.

36. Confirmation Hearings, pp. 100–103.

37. Mike Manatos to LBJ, 7/15/68, Fortas-Thornberry Files, Box 2, LBJL. For more on Eastland's enigmatic efforts in running these hearings, see Oswald Johnston, "Eastland Plays Crucial Role in Fortas-Thornberry Vote," *Baltimore Sun,* 7/15/68, pp. 1, 3.

38. Confirmation Hearings, pp. 102–3.

39. AF to LBJ, 10/27/67, Fortas Name File, 1967 folder, LBJL.

40. AF to LBJ, 12/13/66, Fortas Name File, 1966 folder, LBJL.

41. Jack Valenti to LBJ, 9/29/65, Fortas Name File, 1965 folder, LBJL; Harry McPherson to LBJ, 10/8/65, John Macy Office Files, Fortas folder, LBJL. Fortas recommended Harris Weinstein for the D.C. Public Service Commission and favored men named Kaplowitz and Neff for the vacancy as chairman of the Tariff Commission.

42. For more on the personnel appointment process in the Johnson administration and Fortas's role in it, see Richard L. Schott and Dagmar S. Hamilton, *People, Positions and Power: The Political Appointments of Lyndon Johnson* (Chicago: University of Chicago Press, 1983), Chap. I and generally, and Emmette S. Redford and Marlan Blissett, *Organizing the Executive Branch: The Johnson Presidency* (Chicago: University of Chicago Press, 1981), *passim.*

43. Lou Schwartz to John Macy, 5/10/66, John Macy Office Files, Fortas folder, LBJL.

44. AF to Robert Kintner, 5/25/66, Name File, C. Davidson folder, LBJL; Kintner to John Macy, 8/2/66, John Macy Office Files, Fortas folder, LBJL.

45. Lou Schwartz, memorandum for the files, 1/25/66, John Macy Office Files, Fortas folder, LBJL; AF to LBJ, 2/23/66, Ex FG 233, LBJL; Robert Kintner to LBJ, 5/5/66, Diary Backup, Box 81, LBJL; Marvin Watson to LBJ, 5/12/66, Fortas Name File, 1966 folder, LBJL.

46. Robert Kintner to John Macy, 2/9/67, John Macy Office Files, Fortas folder, LBJL.

47. John Macy to AF, 4/1/67, John Macy Office Files, Fortas folder, LBJL.

48. AF to John Macy, 10/19/67, John Macy Office Files, Fortas folder, LBJL.

49. The Fortas quote is from Confirmation Hearings, p. 103; the Moyers story is from a conversation between the author and Bill Moyers, 4/10/86, Hempstead, N.Y.

50. The Fortas quote is from Confirmation Hearings, p. 103; Fortas's actual role with Bress begins with Marvin Watson to LBJ, 9/1/65, WHCF Name File, David Bress folder, LBJL.

51. Drew Pearson to LBJ, 3/16/67, and Warren Christopher to Larry Temple, 4/30/68, Ex FG 530/ST1-42, Box 355, LBJL; White House biographical sheet on Bress, WHCF Name File, David Bress folder, LBJL.

52. Marvin Watson to David Bress, 8/4/67, Office Files of Larry Temple, Box 1, LBJL.

53. The Fortas statement is from Confirmation Hearings, p. 103; AF to LBJ, 10/15/65, Fortas Name File, 1965 folder, LBJL.

54. This story has been developed from a large number of unpublished documents: AF to John Macy, 11/30/65; Macy to AF, 12/13/65; LBJ to Jack Valenti, note on memo from Valenti to LBJ, 2/25/66, John Macy Office Files, Fortas folder, LBJL. AF to Valenti, 2/23/66, and Ramsey Clark to Valenti, 2/28/66, John Macy Office Files, Ramsey Clark folder, LBJL; Valenti to WOD and Valenti to AF, 3/25/66; AF to LBJ, 3/30/66; WOD to LBJ, 3/29/66, Ex FG 530/ST1-42, LBJL. WOD to LBJ, 9/15/67, WHCF Name File, Allan Hart folder, LBJL. Ramsey Clark to LBJ, re: new judgeships on

the Ninth Circuit Court of Appeals, 6/17/68, Office Files of Larry Temple, Box 1, LBJL. See also *NYT*, 2/20/66, p. 48.

55. Jack Valenti to LBJ, 3/29/66, John Macy Office Files, Fortas folder, LBJL.

56. AF to LBJ, 7/20/67, Ex Gen FG 505, Box 352, LBJL.

57. Larry Temple to LBJ, 4/8/68, Ex FG 530/ST1-42, Box 355, LBJL.·

58. See also Larry Temple to LBJ, 4/3/68, Office Files of Larry Temple, Box 1, LBJL.

59. Larry Temple to LBJ, 3/19/68, Office Files of Larry Temple, Box 1, LBJL.

60. Ramsey Clark to LBJ, 6/17/68, and Warren Christopher to Larry Temple, 9/3/68, Office Files of Larry Temple, Box 1, LBJL.

61. The Eastland-Fortas exchange is at Confirmation Hearings, pp. 103–4. The actual events are drawn from memo, Joe Califano to LBJ, 5/23/67, LE/PL 2, LBJL.

62. The White House Diaries, LBJL, indicate that the meeting went from 4:50 to 5:43 P.M.

63. The Fortas statement is from Confirmation Hearings, p. 104. The actual actions are from AF, LBJ/OH, p. 31; Shogan, *Question of Judgment*, p. 140; White House Diaries, 1/4–1/5/66, LBJL; and Andrew Kopkind, "Fortas and the Power Game," *New Statesman*, 6/6/69, pp. 339–40.

64. White House Diaries, LBJL. The issues are reviewed in memo, Joe Califano to LBJ, 3/7/67; Willard Wirtz to LBJ, 3/6/67; and Wilfred Rommel to Califano, 4/18/67, WHCF, Ex LE/LA 2-1, Box 135, LBJL.

65. Memo, Gardner Ackley to Larry Levinson, 4/8/67, Legislative Background, Rail Strike Settlement, Box 1, LBJL.

66. Summary from LBJ speech to Congress, draft, 5/1/67, Legislative Background, Rail Strike Settlement, Box 1, LBJL.

67. A record of this meeting, labeled "Memorandum for the Record re: Meeting on the Impending Railroad Strike and Other Labor Matters," 4/10/67, is attached to a memo from Joe Califano to Juanita Roberts, 4/11/67, and was newly released for this project. It is now filed in Diary Backup, 4/9/67, Box 60, LBJL. This account also benefited from AI, Judge Harold Barefoot Sanders, 11/9/82, Dallas, Tex.

68. Larry Levinson for the record, 4/10/67, Diary Backup, Box 60, LBJL.

69. Draft message for the president, 5/10/67, Fortas-Thornberry Files, Box 1, LBJL.

70. A copy of this statement is attached to a memo from Joe Califano to LBJ, 4/10/67, Fortas-Thornberry Files, Box 1, LBJL.

71. Joe Califano to LBJ, 4/10/67, Fortas-Thornberry Files, Box 1, LBJL.

72. Wire, Joe Califano to LBJ, 4/24/67, Ex LE/LA, Box 135, LBJL.

73. White House Diaries, 5/2/67, LBJL.

74. Joe Califano to LBJ, 5/1/67, Legislative Background, Rail Strike Settlement, Box 1, LBJL.

75. Memo, Joe Califano to Willard Wirtz, 7/14/67, Fortas-Thornberry Files, Box 1, LBJL.

76. Draft message to Congress, 5/1/67, Legislative Background, Rail Strike Settlement, Box 1, LBJL.

77. The Fortas-Eastland exchange is at Confirmation Hearings, p. 104. Rauh's statement is from AI, Joseph L. Rauh, Jr., 7/9/79, Washington, D.C.

78. The Fortas-Eastland exchange is at Confirmation Hearings, pp. 104–5; Fortas's recollection about Johnson's call is from AI, AF, 8/7/81, Washington, D.C.

79. "Chief Confidant to Chief Justice," *Time*, 7/5/68, p. 76. (It became so well known that Fortas had this group that musicians in town would phone at times to volunteer to fill any empty seats as replacements. One day a female attorney called to volunteer her talents as a violinist, but Fortas, thinking that she was looking for a job as a law clerk, asked what law school she had attended. "George Washington University," she responded. "Not good enough," Fortas responded sharply; "we have people from much better law schools working here in the office as law clerks.")

80. "Final Report of Cyrus Vance, Special Assistant to the Secretary of Defense, Concerning the Detroit Riots," enclosed in Vance, LBJ/OH, LBJL (hereinafter Vance Report).

81. "The Detroit Riots Chronology," Diary Backup, Box 71, LBJL.

82. AI, AF, 8/7/81, Washington, D.C.; confirms the account of Joe Califano in Shogan, *Question of Judgment*, p. 140.

83. Vance Report, LBJL.

84. AI, AF, 8/7/81, Washington, D.C.

85. Cf. *ibid.* with Confirmation Hearings, pp. 104–5.

86. U.S. Constitution, Article IV, Section 4.

87. *Ibid.*, Article II, Section 3. For more on the meaning of this phrase, see Edward S. Corwin, *The*

Constitution and What It Means Today, rev. by Harold W. Chase and Craig R. Ducat, 1978 ed. (Princeton, N.J.: Princeton University Press, 1978), pp. 191–92, 267.

88. Romney telegram, 7/24/67, Diary Backup, Box 71, LBJL.

89. Lyndon Johnson, *The Vantage Point: Perspectives of the Presidency, 1963–1969* (New York: Holt, Rinehart and Winston, 1971), p. 168.

90. Tom Johnson, notes of meeting, 7/24/67, Diary Backup, Box 71, LBJL.

91. Detroit Riots Chronology. While the witnesses' accounts are vague as to exactly which statement Fortas produced, the likelihood that it was the justice's work that produced the official White House statement is due to the short period of time involved in its creation, and the accounts of the presence of Fortas at those meetings and times. According to one White House chronology, the governor's wire having arrived at 10:58 A.M., the president's reply was prepared by 11:05 A.M. These seven minutes coincided with the meeting described in the text. (Detroit Riots Chronology.) Then, as described below, the responding telegram was available for the president to read to his advisers at the Cabinet Room meeting at 11:23 A.M. (See notes of second meeting by George Christian, 7/24/67, memo for president, Diary Backup, Box 71, LBJL.) Furthermore, this statement was, according to all the records available, the only statement that came out of the White House that early in the day. So it would have been the most obvious matter for Fortas's attention, given the situation. Regardless, as outlined below, the final product from the White House still strongly bore the imprint of the advising Justice Fortas.

92. George Christian, notes of second meeting on Detroit riots, 11:15 A.M., 7/24/67, in memo for the president, Diary Backup, Box 71, LBJL.

93. Telegram, LBJ to George Romney, 7/24/67, Diary Backup, Box 71, LBJL.

94. For more on this, see Cyrus Vance, LBJ/OH, pp. 30–42, and the collection of UPI dispatches in Diary Backup, Box 71, LBJL.

95. Cyrus Vance, LBJ/OH, p. 34; UPI dispatches, Diary Backup, Box 71, LBJL.

96. Vance Report, in Vance, LBJ/OH, pp. 10–11.

97. White House Diaries and White House Picture Files, LBJL.

98. According to the White House diary, among the participants were Secretaries Wirtz, McNamara, and Fowler, as well as Gardner Ackley, Arthur Okun, Charles Schultze, Joe Califano, and David Ginsburg.

99. For some reason the message was never sent. (Harry McPherson to LBJ, 7/24/67, with attached telegram from LBJ to Governor Roberto Sanchez-Vilella, 7/24/67, Office Files of Harry McPherson, Box 53, LBJL.) It was not uncommon for the president's men to "clear" with Fortas the wording of such Johnson messages for various occasions on the island. Such would be the case several months later when a congratulatory telegram in honor of the birthday of former Puerto Rico governor Luis Muñoz-Marin was cleared with Fortas by McPherson before being sent. (McPherson to LBJ, 3/21/68, Office Files of Harry McPherson, Box 53, LBJL.)

100. According to the White House Diary, Fortas left at 12:45 A.M. the next day. For more on the president's activities, see "The President's Schedule," 7/24/67, memo, Diary Backup, Box 71, LBJL.

101. See "The President's Schedule," 7/24/67, memo, Diary Backup, Box 71, LBJL.

102. The White House Diary indicates that the meeting included McNamara, J. Edgar Hoover, Secretary of the Army Stanley Resor, and others. For more, see Johnson, *Vantage Point*, p. 170.

103. List, "Troop Requests by Governors to Suppress Domestic Violence," NSF History, Dominican Crisis 1965, Box 7, LBJL.

104. United States Code, Title 10, Chapter 15, Sections 331, 333, 334, Diary Backup, Box 72, LBJL.

105. According to the Detroit Riots Chronology, LBJL, they were looking at a copy from the FDR Presidential Papers.

106. For more on Johnson's attitudes toward FDR, see William Leuchtenburg, *In the Shadow of FDR: From Harry Truman to Ronald Reagan* (Ithaca, N.Y.: Cornell University Press, 1983), *passim*.

107. Detroit Riots Chronology, LBJL.

108. This section of the account relies on Tom Johnson, notes of Detroit riot meetings, 7/25/67, Diary Backup, Box 71, LBJL.

109. Executive Order issued on 7/24/67, cited in Detroit Riots Chronology.

110. Author's conversation with Harry McPherson, 4/10/86, Hempstead, N.Y.

111. LBJ press statement, Diary Backup, Box 71, LBJL.

112. Tom Johnson, notes of Detroit riot meetings, 7/25/67, Diary Backup, Box 71, LBJL.

113. White House Diaries, LBJL.

114. "Chief Confidant to Chief Justice," *Time*, 7/5/68, p. 16.

115. Confirmation Hearings, p. 106.

116. *Ibid.* See the headlines on 7/17/68 editions of *NYT, Washington Post,* and *Washington Star*; AI, Larry Temple, 11/15/82, Austin, Tex.; AI, Judge Harold Barefoot Sanders, 11/9/82, Dallas, Tex.
117. *Washington Post,* 7/17/68, p. 1.
118. Mike Manatos to LBJ, 7/16/68, Fortas-Thornberry Files, Box 2, LBJL.
119. *Washington Post,* 7/17/68, p. 1.

CHAPTER XVII

THE TRIAL OF EARL WARREN'S COURT

1. Hugh Jones, "The Defeat of the Nomination of Abe Fortas as Chief Justice of the United States," unpublished Ph.D. dissertation, Johns Hopkins University, 1976, p. 156.
2. John Herbers, "Senator Ervin Thinks the Constitution Should Be Taken Like Mountain Whiskey—Undiluted and Untaxed," *New York Times Magazine,* 11/15/70, p. 112.
3. "Nominations of Abe Fortas and Homer Thornberry," Hearings Before the Committee on the Judiciary, United States Senate, 90th Congress, 2nd Session, 7/11–7/23/68 (Washington, D.C.: U.S. Government Printing Office, 1968), pp. 109–11 (hereinafter Confirmation Hearings).
4. *Ibid.,* pp. 113–15.
5. *Ibid.,* pp. 115–16.
6. John Corry, "Strom's Dirty Movies," *Harper's Magazine,* December 1968, p. 38; Richard Harris, *Decision* (New York: E. P. Dutton and Co., 1971), p. 16.
7. George Douth, *Leaders in Profile: The United States Senate* (New York: Sperr and Douth, 1975), pp. 318–23.
8. Jones, "Defeat of Abe Fortas," p. 279.
9. Mike Manatos to LBJ, 7/16/68, Files Pertaining to Abe Fortas and Homer Thornberry, Box 2, LBJL (hereinafter Fortas-Thornberry Files).
10. The Ervin-Fortas exchange is at Confirmation Hearings, p. 122; the source of Hart's information is in Larry Temple to Everett Dirksen, 7/16/68, Fortas-Thornberry Files, Box 2, LBJL.
11. Confirmation Hearings, p. 124.
12. *Ibid.*
13. *Ibid.,* pp. 124–25.
14. *Ibid.,* p. 125.
15. The case was *Textile Workers Union of America* v. *Darlington Manufacturing Co.,* 380 U.S. 263 (1965). Ervin represented the Darlington firm, and won at the court-of-appeals level. However, the Supreme Court vacated the decision and remanded the case for further proceedings.
    For more on Ervin's hostile reaction to that loss, and the White House's knowledge of that fact, see Larry Temple, LBJ/OH, VI, p. 3; AI, Larry Temple, 11/15/82, Austin, Tex.; Paul Porter, LBJ/OH, I, pp. 27–40; and Larry Temple to LBJ, 7/2/68, Fortas-Thornberry Files, Box 2, LBJL.
16. Confirmation Hearings, p. 125.
17. The account of the reaction of Fortas and the committee room audience comes from the *Washington Star* and the *Baltimore Sun.* See Oswald Johnston, "Consulted by Johnson, Fortas Says," *Baltimore Sun,* 7/17/68, pp. 1–2, and Lyle Denniston, "Ervin Blasts Decisions of Fortas and the Court," *Washington Star,* 7/17/68, pp. 1, 10.
18. John MacKenzie, "Fortas Proud of Role as a Johnson Adviser," *Washington Post,* 7/17/68, p. 1.
19. Fred Graham, "Fortas Testifies He Rebuked Critic of War Spending," *NYT,* 7/18/68, pp. 1, 20.
20. Warren Christopher to LBJ, 7/12/68, attached to excerpts from Walter Murphy's book *Elements of Judicial Strategy,* Fortas-Thornberry Files, Box 2, LBJL. See also memo, "Supreme Court Justices as Presidential Advisers," 7/16/68, Paul Porter Papers, Box 6, LBJL.
    Some of this research work was being done by Justice Fortas and his law clerks, and then sent over to the Department of Justice to help in its endeavors. Such a memo was done by Fortas and his clerks on the confirmation records of previous Supreme Court appointments, then was sent over to the Department of Justice by Fortas's clerks. At the end of the seven-page memo, Fortas wrote that he was still checking into unpublished sources for more information. This material was then packaged by the Justice Department into its own work, and sent to the White House for use with members of the Senate. See memo, Warren Christopher to Martin Richman, 7/8/68, attached to memo from AF and his law clerks, "Nominations to the Supreme Court That Were Not Confirmed by the Senate," undated, Warren Christopher Papers, Box 1, LBJL.
    Graham's piece is in *New York Times Magazine,* 6/4/67, p. 26ff.

21. Fred Graham, "Fortas Testifies He Rebuked Critic of War Spending," *NYT*, 7/18/68, pp. 1, 20.
22. *Ibid.*
23. Confirmation Hearings, pp. 167–68.
24. See p. 1 of the 7/18/68 editions of *NYT, Washington Post,* and *Baltimore Sun.*
25. The interviews by Hugh Jones at the time support this conclusion. See Jones, "Defeat of Abe Fortas," p. 159.
26. Here, without saying so, Hart was relying on information provided him by the White House. See Confirmation Hearings, pp. 169–70.
27. Confirmation Hearings, pp. 170–72. *Warden* case citation is 387 U.S. 294 (1967).
28. Larry Temple to LBJ, 7/13/68, Fortas-Thornberry Files, Box 2, LBJL; Warren Christopher to Temple, 7/13/68, Christopher Papers, Box 1, LBJL.
29. Confirmation Hearings, pp. 172–73. The *Powell* case dealt with the Sixth Amendment right to counsel in the Scottsboro Boys case, in which several black young men were accused of rape. The ultraconservative court ruled that in cases involving circumstances like this one, an accused must be provided with counsel for the trial. See 287 U.S. 45 (1932).
30. Confirmation Hearings, p. 173.
31. Don Oberdorfer, "Ex-Democrat, Ex-Dixiecrat, Today's 'Nixiecrat,'" *New York Times Magazine,* 10/6/68, p. 84.
32. This section on Thurmond comes from a number of sources: Oberdorfer, "Ex-Democrat, Ex-Dixiecrat," pp. 54–85; David Bruck, "Strom Thurmond's Roots," *New Republic,* Vol. 186, 3/3/82, pp. 15–23; "The Senator from South Carolina," *Time,* 2/2/62, p. 15; Stephen Chapman "Strom's Law," *New Republic,* Vol. 183, 12/6/80, pp. 11–12; Franklin Ashley, "South Carolina," *New Republic,* Vol. 179, 3/4/78, pp. 28–30; William Chapman, "The Legend of Strom Thurmond," *Progressive,* Vol. 33, January 1969, pp. 32–34; "Hon. Strom Thurmond Does It," *Newsweek,* 9/13/71, pp. 19–20; Douth, *Leaders in Profile,* pp. 596–607; Lewis Chester, Godfrey Hodgson, and Bruce Page, *An American Melodrama: The Presidential Campaign of 1968* (New York: Viking Press, 1969), pp. 476–81.
33. *Ibid.*
34. Oberdorfer, "Ex-Democrat, Ex-Dixiecrat," p. 84; Chester et al., *American Melodrama,* p. 480.
35. Oberdorfer, "Ex-Democrat, Ex-Dixiecrat," p. 37.
36. *Ibid.,* p. 56.
37. *Ibid.,* p. 37; Chester et al., *American Melodrama,* p. 479.
38. 391 U.S. 99 (1968).
39. *The Washington Post* (7/19/68, pp. 1–2) called this "one of the session's few light moments." See Confirmation Hearings, pp. 175–77.
40. The exchange between Fortas and Hruska is at Confirmation Hearings, pp. 178 and 177–80 generally. Thurmond's comment comes from one of Hugh Jones's interviews; see Jones, "Defeat of Abe Fortas," p. 284.
41. The description of the scene is from Oswald Johnston, "Fortas Gives Defense of Court Record," *Baltimore Sun,* 7/19/68, p. 1, and John MacKenzie, "Fortas Berated for Two Hours," *Washington Post,* 7/19/68, p. 1.
42. Confirmation Hearings, p. 181. For press reaction, see Fred Graham, "Thurmond Prods Fortas to Reply," *NYT,* 7/19/68, p. 16.
43. Oswald Johnston, "Fortas Gives Defense of Court Record," *Baltimore Sun,* 7/19/68, p. A4.
44. Confirmation Hearings, pp. 182–83.
45. *Ibid.,* pp. 184–89; *Fortson* case citation is 385 U.S. 231 (1966).
46. Thurmond could not have known that this case was a particularly sore spot for the justice, having been part of the cause of his early break with Justice Hugo Black. Instead, Thurmond continued to try to characterize Fortas incorrectly as being the same kind of liberal as Black and William O. Douglas. For more, see Chap. IX, "Mr. Justice Fortas."
47. Confirmation Hearings, p. 189.
48. 383 U.S. 663 (1966); see also Confirmation Hearings, p. 189.
49. Confirmation Hearings, pp. 189–90; *Baker* case citation is 369 U.S. 186 (1962); *Reynolds* citation is 377 U.S. 533 (1964).
50. Confirmation Hearings, p. 190.
51. *Ibid.,* pp. 190–91.
52. *Ibid.,* p. 191. This record was corrected from the original version, which was reported identically in the newspapers of the next day. I have relied on those eyewitness accounts for the first line in the quotation. See John MacKenzie, "Fortas Berated for Two Hours," *Washington Post,* 7/19/68, p. 1;

Fred Graham, "Thurmond Prods Fortas to Reply," *NYT,* 1/19/68, p. 16; and Oswald Johnston, "Fortas Gives Defense of Court Record," *Baltimore Sun,* 7/19/68, p. A4.

53. For more on Thurmond's other attacks against the court, mostly involving its civil rights decisions, see Oberdorfer, "Ex-Democrat, Ex-Dixiecrat," *passim,* and Jones, "Defeat of Abe Fortas," p. 189.

54. Confirmation Hearings, pp. 101–2.

55. *Ibid.,* p. 192.

56. 391 U.S. 510 (1968); see Confirmation Hearings, pp. 198–99.

57. For more on Eastland here, see Oswald Johnston, "Eastland Plays Crucial Role in Fortas-Thornberry Vote," *Baltimore Sun,* 7/15/68, pp. 1, A5.

58. *Ibid.*

59. Confirmation Hearings, pp. 211–13.

60. *Ibid.,* p. 214.

61. An account of Fortas's reaction is in Lyle Denniston, "Thurmond Challenges Justice on Decisions," *Washington Star,* 7/19/68, p. A8.

62. Confirmation Hearings, pp. 214–15.

63. *Ibid.,* p. 215.

64. *Ibid.,* pp. 218–19.

65. Lyle Denniston, "Thurmond Challenges Justice on Decisions," *Washington Star,* 7/19/68, p. A8.

66. Confirmation Hearings, pp. 219–20.

67. *Ibid.,* pp. 226–28.

68. *NYT,* 7/20/68, p. 26.

69. *Jewish Week,* 8/1/68, copy in Porter Papers, Box 5, LBJL.

70. The McClellan-Fortas exchange is at Confirmation Hearings, p. 230; for more on this proposal and the White House's reaction to it, see memo, Joe Califano to LBJ, 11/12/66, WHCF, Ex LE/FG/HS, Box 45, LBJL; *Congressional Quarterly,* 6/30/67, p. 1108.

71. Harry McPherson, LBJ/OH, IV, p. 39.

72. *Ibid.*

73. *Ibid.,* and memo, Joe Califano to LBJ, 11/12/66, WHCF, Ex LE/FG/HS, Box 45, LBJL.

74. Teletype, Joe Califano to LBJ, 11/12/66, WHCF, Ex LE/FG/HS, Box 45, LBJL.

75. Memo of phone message from AF to LBJ, by White House secretary Juanita Roberts, 1/10/67, Statements File, box 226, LBJL; the timing of the plan comes from a memo for the files, by James C. Gaither, "Summary Description of the Safe Streets and Crime Control Act of 1968," 11/15/68, Legislative Background, Safe Streets Act, Box 1, LBJL.

76. Joe Califano to AF, 2/6/67, FG 535/A, Box 360, LBJL; phone message from AF to LBJ, 2/6/67, Diary Backup, Box 54, LBJL.

77. For Fortas's advice, see memo, Joe Califano to LBJ, 2/24/67, WHCF Ex LE/FG/HS, Box 45, LBJL.

78. Unsigned memo identified by markings of White House secretaries as connected to Fortas, 11/6/67, Fortas Name File, 1967 folder, LBJL; wire, Larry Levinson to Jim Jones, 12/27/67, WHCF Ex LE/FG/HS, Box 45, LBJL; text of signing statement as written, Ex Sp2-3/1963/JL, Box 124, LBJL; text of signing statement as spoken was reported in *Washington Post,* 12/28/67, pp. 1, A11.

79. AF memo signed only as "A.," titled "Crime Message," undated, Legislative Background, Safe Streets Act, Box 5, LBJL. See also a typed draft of Fortas's handwritten comments, undated, and the presidential speech draft with another set of Fortas's handwritten comments thereon, 2/5/68, Ex SP 2-3/1967/JL, Box 124, LBJL.

80. Memo, "Muriel" to Joe Califano, 2/6/68, Ex SP 2-3/1967/JL, Box 124, LBJL.

81. Confirmation Hearings, p. 230. Fortas's statement about the Omnibus Crime Bill was reported in Fred Graham, "Fortas Condemns Columbia Protest," *NYT,* 5/24/68, p. 33.

82. The exchange between Thurmond and Fortas is at Confirmation Hearings, p. 234. See *NYT,* 7/20/68, p. 26, and *Washington Star,* 7/20/68, housed in *Washington Star* morgue, Martin Luther King Library, Washington, D.C. Also, copies of the *Salt Lake Tribune* editorial printed the day after Fortas's testimony ended on 7/19/68 can be found in the Fortas-Thornberry Files, Box 2, LBJL.

83. These editorials all appeared on 7/18/68. See, e.g., *Washington Post,* 7/18/68, p. A2.

84. Handwritten memo labeled only "Cloakroom comment," dated only "filed 7/25/68," Ramsey Clark Papers, Box 47, Supreme Court (Warren, Fortas, Thornberry) 6/68 folder, LBJL.

85. The wording of and facts surrounding the tip are from Jones, "Defeat of Abe Fortas," p. 265, n. 41. The timing of the actual tip is hard to pin down. Jones says in his account that the tip came in "early July," and earlier in my account I have relayed Dirksen's recollection that the newspaper item was spotted earlier. However, another account, which details the role of Robert Griffin, indicates that the tip came in on the final day of the hearings, which seems credible given the manner in which the

controversy developed. See "Sen. Griffin Wins Once Lonely Battle to Block Court Change," *Chicago Tribune*, 10/3/68, p. 2. For more on the development of Griffin's strategy, see "Sen. Robert Griffin: A Power in Washington?," *Detroit Scope Magazine*, 11/2/68, pp. 10–11.

86. Samuel Shaffer, *On and Off the Floor: Thirty Years as a Correspondent on Capitol Hill* (New York: Newsweek Books, 1980), p. 90; "Sen. Griffin Wins Once Lonely Battle to Block Court Change," *Chicago Tribune*, 10/3/68, p. 2; "Sen. Robert Griffin: A Power in Washington?," *Detroit Scope Magazine*, 11/2/68, pp. 10–11; "Battle of Capitol Hill" phrase is from *Business Week*, 9/7/68, p. 29.

Chapter XVIII
Porn Wars

1. The opening scene is from John Corry, "Strom's Dirty Movies," *Harper's Magazine*, December 1968, p. 30.
2. *Ibid.* See also *Time*, 8/2/68, p. 19; the account of the movie brought by Clancy can be found in Judge Hauk's opinion, which is cited in "Nominations of Abe Fortas and Homer Thornberry," Hearings Before the Committee on the Judiciary, United States Senate, 90th Congress, 2nd Session, 7/11–7/23/68 (Washington, D.C.: U.S. Government Printing Office, 1968), p. 295 (hereinafter Confirmation Hearings).
3. *Life*, 9/27/68, p. 8.
4. Corry, "Strom's Dirty Movies," p. 30.
5. AI, Homer Thornberry, 11/17/82, Austin, Tex.
6. Confirmation Hearings, pp. 291–97.
7. *Ibid.*, p. 103.
8. *Ibid.*, p. 296.
9. *Ibid.*, p. 305.
10. *Ibid.*, pp. 312–13.
11. Corry, "Strom's Dirty Movies," p. 32.
12. Confirmation Hearings, p. 358.
13. Confirmation Hearings, p. 359.
14. McClellan's reaction is in Joe Califano to LBJ, 7/24/68, Memos of Joseph Califano, Box 22, LBJL.
15. Memo, Fred Drogula to Warren Christopher, "Re: Conversation with Senator Hart on July 24 Re Fortas Nomination," 7/24/68, Warren Christopher Papers, Box 1, LBJL; Larry Temple to LBJ, 7/24/68, Files Pertaining to Abe Fortas and Homer Thornberry, Box 7, LBJL (hereinafter Fortas-Thornberry Files).
16. Mike Manatos to LBJ, 7/25/68, Fortas-Thornberry Files, Box 2, LBJL.
17. Memo, Joe Califano to LBJ, 7/24/68, Fortas-Thornberry Files, Box 4, LBJL. Also indicated in two Senate head counts by the White House during those days: Fortas-Thornberry Files, Box 2, LBJL.
18. Senate head counts by White House, two dated 7/15/68 and one dated 7/16/68, Fortas-Thornberry Files, Boxes 2 and 7, LBJL.
19. The time pressure on Phil Hart was certainly clear in his letter to Warren Christopher pleading for help. See Hart to Christopher, 8/7/68, Christopher Papers, Box 1, LBJL. For more on this, see the text below on Hart's National Press Club speech.
20. Memo, Joe Califano to LBJ, 7/24/68, Fortas-Thornberry Files, Box 4, LBJL.
21. "Fleshing Out the Case," *Newsweek*, 8/12/68, p. 28.
22. *Washington Post*, 9/15/68, p. 24.
23. Samuel Shaffer, *On and Off the Floor: Thirty Years as a Correspondent on Capitol Hill* (New York: Newsweek Books, 1980), p. 92. The case involved was *Jacobs* v. *New York*, 388 U.S. 431 (1967). For more on the use of the films, see "Fleshing Out the Case," *Newsweek*, 8/12/68, p. 28.
24. Shaffer, *On and Off the Floor*, pp. 90–92. For more on the role of Strom Thurmond in this episode, see Hugh Jones, "The Defeat of the Nomination of Abe Fortas as Chief Justice of the United States," unpublished Ph.D. dissertation, Johns Hopkins University, 1976, pp. 251–52. The account of the black-and-white photographs is from AI, Hugh Jones, 7/23/87, Shippensburg, Pa.
25. *Congressional Record*, 8/1/68, p. 10014.
26. Corry, "Strom's Dirty Movies," p. 35.
27. *Congressional Record*, 7/26/68, pp. 23487–88.

28. Shaffer, *On and Off the Floor*, p. 91.

29. "Fleshing Out the Case," *Newsweek*, 8/12/68, p. 28; Corry, "Strom's Dirty Movies," p. 30.

30. The memo is attached to another memo, Warren Christopher to Everett Dirksen, 7/27/68, Christopher Papers, Box 1, LBJL.

31. Larry Temple to LBJ, 7/26/68, Fortas-Thornberry Files, Box 2, LBJL; Warren Christopher to Everett Dirksen, 7/27/68, attached to Justice Department memo titled "Memorandum Re the Views of Justice Fortas on Obscenity," Christopher Papers, Box 2, LBJL.

32. Warren Christopher, "Memorandum for Honorable Larry Temple, Special Assistant to the President, re: The Fortas and Thornberry Nominations," 12/20/68, Christopher Papers, Box 3, LBJL (hereinafter Justice Department Chronology).

33. *Congressional Record*, 10/1/68, p. 28928; also Corry, "Strom's Dirty Movies," p. 34.

34. A copy of this constituent letter, dated 7/25/68, can be found in Fortas-Thornberry Files, Box 2, LBJL.

35. AF to John Harlan, 7/24/68, as quoted in David O'Brien, *Storm Center: The Supreme Court in American Politics* (New York: W. W. Norton and Co., 1986), p. 92.

36. AF to Earl Warren, 7/25/68, Earl Warren Papers, Box 352, LOC; also partially quoted in O'Brien, *Storm Center*, p. 92.

37. *Ibid.*

38. Survey of the White House Diaries, 7/19–10/2/68, LBJL. Fortas spoke with the president only eleven times, met with him only once in the Cabinet Room, and attended only one social dinner. However, the conversations and meetings with the president's aides, both in person and on the phone, to discuss the course of the Senate fight would not have been recorded in this diary.

39. Joe Califano to LBJ, 7/23/68, Fortas Name File, 1968 folder, LBJL.

40. Joe Califano to LBJ, 7/26/68, Fortas Name File, 1968 folder, LBJL.

41. A copy of the picture in the brochure is attached to a memo: Charles Maguire to LBJ, 7/27/68, Fortas-Thornberry Files, Box 7, LBJL.

42. *New York*, 7/22/68, p. 17.

43. One of the places where the charges appeared: Edith Kermit Roosevelt, "The Abe Fortas Controversy," syndicated column, copy in Fortas-Thornberry Files, Box 2, LBJL.

44. Jones, "Defeat of Abe Fortas," pp. 240, 265; "Sen. Griffin Wins Once Lonely Battle to Block Court Change," *Chicago Tribune*, 10/3/68, p. 2.

45. Memo, Mike Manatos to LBJ, 7/29/68 (two memos passed between the men on this date on this issue), Fortas-Thornberry Files, Box 2, LBJL.

46. Excerpts are from Robert Griffin's remarks to the National Press Club, 7/30/68, copy in Paul Porter Papers, Box 3, LBJL.

47. Morton Mintz, "Griffin Says 40 Ready to Block Vote on Fortas," *Washington Post*, 7/31/68.

48. Larry Temple to LBJ, 7/25/68 and 7/26/68, Fortas-Thornberry Files, Box 2, LBJL.

49. George Reedy to LBJ, 7/30/68, Fortas-Thornberry Files, Box 7, LBJL. See also Shaffer, *On and Off the Floor*, pp. 90–92; "Sen. Robert Griffin: A Power in Washington?," *Detroit Scope Magazine*, 11/2/68, pp. 10–11; the counts from the senators' files on the issue come from Jones, "Defeat of Abe Fortas," pp. 243–53.

50. *NYT*, 7/25/68, pp. 1, 23.

51. Justice Department Chronology, LBJL.

52. Harold Barefoot Sanders to LBJ, 7/29/68, Harold Barefoot Sanders Papers, Box 25, LBJL; Sanders to LBJ, 7/30/68, Fortas-Thornberry Files, Box 2, LBJL.

53. *Newsweek*, 7/29/68, p. 21.

54. As the fight went on, the White House began to realize that it might well be fighting a numbers battle, with the rebels having to produce only enough votes to keep a filibuster going. Faced with the challenge of producing an absolute majority vote, and taking the time to deal with the hit-and-run tactics of the rebels, the White House continued now to search for new options.

55. *Congressional Record*, 8/2/68, p. 24893.

56. *Ibid.*, pp. 24932–37, for a copy of the entire speech. For more on Ervin's constitutional amendment, see *Congressional Record*, 7/23/68, p. 22836.

57. Untitled handwritten memo, AF to Paul Porter, 8/1/68, Porter Papers, Box 3, LBJL. See also Porter to Joe Ball, 7/30/68, Porter Papers, Box 3, LBJL.

58. Memo, Joe Califano to LBJ, 8/1/68, Fortas-Thornberry Files, Box 5, LBJL; Dan Levitt to Paul Porter, 8/1/68, Porter Papers, Box 3, LBJL.

59. Transcript of ABA meeting, 8/2/68, Christopher Papers, Box 2, LBJL; Justice Department Chronology, LBJL.

60. *Time,* 8/2/68, p. 19.
61. Copies were sent by Porter to, among others, Edward Morgan of the Public Broadcast Library, Erwin Canham of the *Christian Science Monitor,* James Reston of *The New York Times,* Roscoe Drummond at the National Press Building, Marquis Childs of the *St. Louis Dispatch,* John Steele of Time-Life; Richard Wilson of the *Des Moines Register and Tribune,* Alan Barth of *The Washington Post,* William White of United Features Syndicate, Carl Rowan of the *Chicago Daily News,* Robert Donovan of the *Los Angeles Times,* and Ralph McGill of the *Atlanta Constitution.* (8/1/68, Porter Papers, Box 5, LBJL.)
62. A transcript of the speech, delivered by Fortas on 8/3/68, is in Fortas-Thornberry Files, Box 2, LBJL.
63. Thurman Arnold to AF, 8/2/68, Fortas-Thornberry Files, Box 5, LBJL.
64. For Arnold's change of heart, see Shogan, *Question of Judgment,* p. 262.
65. Paul Porter to Tom Mulroy, 8/16/68, and Porter to James Jones, 8/7/68, Porter Papers, Box 5, LBJL.
66. James J. Kilpatrick, "Proposal Suggested to Save Time in Fortas Argument," *Washington Star,* 8/13/68, copy in Fortas-Thornberry Files, Box 6, LBJL.
67. For more, see *Roth* v. *United States,* 354 U.S. 476 (1957).
68. *Ginzburg* v. *New York,* 390 U.S. 629, 630 (1968).
69. The ambivalence of Fortas is evident in the notes of the judicial conference on this case in his court papers, Sterling Library, Yale University.
70. 390 U.S. 629 at 673 (1968).
71. *Ibid.,* pp. 674–75.
72. *Ibid.,* pp. 671–75.
73. AF to WOD, 4/15/66, William O. Douglas Papers, *Ginzburg* v. *United States* folder, LOC. See also Bernard Schwartz, *Super Chief: Earl Warren and His Supreme Court—A Judicial Biography* (New York: New York University Press, 1983), pp. 619, 652–56.
74. *Book Named "John Cleland's Memoirs of a Woman of Pleasure"* v. *Massachusetts,* 383 U.S. 413 (1966).
75. See AF to WOD, 4/15/66, Douglas Papers, *Ginzburg* v. *United States* folder, LOC. The citation of the *Ginzburg* case is 383 U.S. 463 (1966). While Fortas claims credit for selling Brennan, the eventual writer of this opinion, on the "pandering" formula, Bernard Schwartz argues that the man who originally suggested this approach to Fortas was Earl Warren. (Schwartz, *Super Chief,* p. 621.) This chain of the development of the idea makes some sense in that the first to suggest the "pandering" notion in print was Warren in his concurring opinion in *Roth.* For more on Warren's attitudes on the case, see Schwartz, *Super Chief,* pp. 219–21, 621–22.
76. AF to WOD, 4/15/66, Douglas Papers, *Ginzburg* v. *United States* folder, LOC. Fortas was writing in response to an article he had seen on the holding in the case in *The New Yorker,* 4/9/66, p. 31.
77. See a redraft of Fortas's judicial opinion in *Redrup* v. *New York,* 3/31/67, Tom Clark Papers, University of Texas Law School, Austin, Tex. This early draft, which as is explained below in the text was never publicly issued, relies largely on a memo Fortas sent to the brethren on 4/13/66 (also in Clark Papers), laying out his overall philosophy on a series of obscenity cases then before the court.
78. *Ibid.*; see also letter, AF to John Harlan, 4/8/68, AFP, Sterling Library, Yale University.
79. This untitled and undated letter, clearly written in Fortas's hand, can be also identified as his by the other drafts of the letter that are attached to this document in the files. One of these documents also identifies the original version of the memo as being Fortas's. Porter Papers, Box 2, LBJL.
80. One man who was especially unhappy with Fortas's defense was his former mentor, William O. Douglas. See WOD to Fred Rodell, 7/27/68, Fred Rodell Papers, Haverford College.
81. See the series of drafts of Williams's letter to the *Washington Star* editorial board, dated 8/14/68 and 8/15/68, attached to Fortas's handwritten early draft of the letter, Porter Papers, Box 2, LBJL; another copy of a Williams draft is in the Porter Papers, Box 6, LBJL; a final version of the letter is in the Fortas-Thornberry Files, Box 2, LBJL.
    The letter was published in the *Washington Star,* 8/23/68, p. A-12.
82. See "Memorandum re the Views of Justice Fortas on Obscenity," undated, attached to letter from Warren Christopher to Phil Hart, 9/3/68, Christopher Papers, Box 2, LBJL. The crucial arguments on the *Schackman* case appear at the end of this memo.
    As noted, this is the memo that was hand-delivered to Senator Dirksen at his request by the Justice Department on 7/27/68, but Dirksen did nothing with it. See Christopher to Dirksen, 7/27/68, Christopher Papers, Box 1, LBJL. The memo was then sent to Hart in early September to help in the preparation of a speech he was to give before the National Press Club.
83. See p. 2 of an early version of Williams's letter, on which is written "strike out per Justice Fortas' instructions," Porter Papers, Box 2, LBJL; and p. 2 of another early draft of Williams's letter, where

the passage is struck out and in handwriting in the margin it is noted: "Justice Fortas called and said to strike this as Hart's memo was not printed in record." (Porter Papers, Box 6, LBJL.)

84. The final version of the letter, Edward Bennett Williams to *Washington Star*, dated 8/15/68, Fortas-Thornberry Files, Box 2, LBJL.

85. As noted above, the Williams-Fortas letter was printed by the *Washington Star* (although, of course, not indicating Fortas's co-authorship, as it was not known), 8/23/68, p. A12.

   For more on the relationship between Fortas and Williams, which was close for a time although they grew apart, see Robert Pack, *Edward Bennett Williams for the Defense* (New York: Harper and Row, 1983), pp. 359–60.

86. Buckley, "Obscenity Ruling Needs Explaining," *Washington Star*, 8/21/68.

87. Untitled and undated memo, AF to Paul Porter, Porter Papers, Box 3, LBJL.

88. Untitled memo, AF to Paul Porter, 8/1/68, Porter Papers, Box 3, LBJL.

89. The original draft of the memo, as written on 8/20/68, can be found in the Porter Papers, Box 6, LBJL. For more on the strategy as to its release, see letter, Dean Joseph O'Meara to William D. Rogers (of Arnold and Porter), 8/22/68, Porter Papers, Box 6, LBJL. The letter was printed in the *Washington Post*, 9/11/68, p. A18.

90. "Fleshing Out the Case," *Newsweek*, 8/12/68, p. 28. The article was referring to events taking place before the Senate adjournment.

91. Lyndon B. Johnson, *The Vantage Point: Perspectives of the Presidency, 1963–1969* (New York: Holt, Rinehart and Winston, 1971), p. 547.

Chapter XIX
A Policy of Silence

1. *NYT*, 7/25/68, p. 23.

2. Cf. *NYT*, 6/27/68, p. 21, and *NYT*, 7/18/68, p. 20. Later, see Don Oberdorfer, "Nixon Draws Big Turnout in Chicago," *Washington Post*, 9/5/68, pp. 1, 4.

3. Eugene Bogan to Jack Miller, 7/16/68, Paul Porter Papers, Box 6, LBJL.

4. Eugene Bogan to Paul Porter, 7/16/68, Diary Backup, Box 19, LBJL; *NYT*, 7/18/68, p. 20.

5. *Washington Post*, 7/31/68, p. 1.

6. Robert Allen and John Goldsmith, "Fight on Fortas to Go On," syndicated column, copy in Files Pertaining to Abe Fortas and Homer Thornberry, Box 6, LBJL (hereinafter Fortas-Thornberry Files).

7. The full text of the platform can be found in *Congressional Quarterly*, 8/9/68, p. 2130.

8. Mike Manatos to LBJ, 7/29/68, Fortas-Thornberry Files, Box 2, LBJL; Ernie [Goldstein] to White House, filed 7/29/68, Fortas-Thornberry Files, Box 7, LBJL.

9. *Washington Post*, 8/4/68, p. A5.

10. For more on this, see Lewis Chester, Godfrey Hodgson, and Bruce Page, *An American Melodrama: The Presidential Campaign of 1968* (New York: Viking Press, 1969), pp. 458–66.

11. The term comes from the *NYT* report on Nixon's campaign (9/6/68, p. 1), in which it was reported that Nixon used the same policy of silence on the issues of Vietnam and Mayor Richard Daley's handling of the Democratic party convention.

12. Chester et al., *An American Melodrama*, p. 462.

13. The transcript of this meeting was released long after the convention. ("How Nixon Sees the Presidency," *U.S. News and World Report*, 8/19/68, p. 38.)

14. Chester et al., *An American Melodrama*, p. 465.

15. *Congressional Quarterly*, 8/9/68, p. 2138.

16. *Newsweek*, 8/19/68, p. 13.

17. This was certainly the assessment of one of the aides of Senator Robert Griffin at the time. See Hugh Jones, "The Defeat of the Nomination of Abe Fortas as Chief Justice of the United States," unpublished Ph.D. dissertation, Johns Hopkins University, 1976, p. 201.

18. *NYT*, 7/25/68, p. 23.

19. Robert Allen and John Goldsmith, "Fight on Fortas to Go On," syndicated column, copy in Fortas-Thornberry Files, Box 6, LBJL.

20. *Ibid.*

21. Untitled memo from AF to Paul Porter, 8/1/68, Porter Papers, Box 3, LBJL.

22. *Ibid.*

23. *NYT*, 7/24/68, p. 1; *NYT*, 7/25/68, p. 1. For more on O'Dwyer's attacks, see *NYT*, 9/11/68, p. 33, and *NYT*, 9/14/68, p. 17.

24. Untitled memo from AF to Paul Porter, 8/1/68, Porter Papers, Box 3, LBJL.

25. This section on Javits comes from a number of sources: *Newsweek*, 3/17/86, p. 23, and *Washington Post*, 3/8/86, pp. 1, A5.

26. Untitled memo from AF to Paul Porter, 8/1/68, Porter Papers, Box 3, LBJL.

27. Paul Porter to Mr. Lazarus, 8/1/68, Porter Papers, Box 5, LBJL.

28. Ernie [Goldstein] to LBJ, undated, Fortas-Thornberry Files, Box 3, LBJL.

29. George Reedy to LBJ, 7/26/68, Fortas-Thornberry Files, Box 7, LBJL; *NYT*, 7/27/68, p. 1.

30. *NYT*, 7/25/68, p. 23.

31. Paul Porter to Mr. Lazarus, 8/1/68, Porter Papers, Box 5, LBJL.

32. AF to Paul Porter, undated, Porter Papers, Box 6, LBJL.

33. Paul Porter to Bernard Segal, 9/5/68, Porter Papers, Box 5, LBJL.

34. George Reedy to LBJ, 8/22/68, Fortas-Thornberry Files, Box 2, LBJL.

35. Ernie [Goldstein] to LBJ, undated, Fortas-Thornberry Files, Box 3, LBJL; Paul Porter to Walter Thayer, 8/20/68, Porter Papers, Box 5, LBJL.

36. See Hugh Jones, "Defeat of Abe Fortas," pp. 208–9, citing interview with Howard Baker.

37. AI, Homer Thornberry, 11/17/82, Austin, Tex.; White House Diaries, 8/27/68, LBJL; Johnson, *Vantage Point*, pp. 543–47.

38. Previous accounts of this episode have answered both yes and no as to whether a formal deal was made between Nixon and the conservatives. No hard evidence could be found during this study to support either side conclusively. However, as the text indicates, this was a case where the deal, if there ever was one, did not need to be expressed formally for everyone to understand what the outcome of events would be if they progressed in a certain direction. For the view that there was a deal, see Sidney Asch, *The Supreme Court and Its Great Justices* (New York: Arco Publishing Co., 1971), pp. 34, 236; and John Ehrlichman, *Witness to Power: The Nixon Years* (New York: Pocket Books, 1982), pp. 92–93, says that the opposition by the conservatives was "at Nixon's urging." However, after his study, Hugh Jones concluded that "the opposite was true" and Nixon had tried to stay clear of the controversy for a long time. See Jones, "Defeat of Abe Fortas," pp. 208–11.

39. Author's conversation with Ramsey Clark, 4/11/86, Hempstead, N.Y.

40. Paul Porter to Edwin Weisl, 8/20/68, Porter Papers, Box 5, LBJL.

41. While various letters by Porter during the period from mid-August to early September kept changing the numbers involved, a letter by him to Mrs. Bernard Segal, dated 9/3/68, claimed that the endorsement letter had been signed by 424 law school professors, from 61 law schools, covering all 50 states. (Porter Papers, Box 6, LBJL.) Copies of the kit can be found in Fortas-Thornberry Files, Boxes 8 and 9, LBJL.

42. This poll was cited by Senator Phil Hart in his speech to the National Press Club on 9/4/68.

43. While these letters fill Boxes 5 and 6 in the Porter Papers, LBJL, it is impossible to know whether any of them had any effect on the actions of their recipients. See, e.g., Paul Porter to William Gossett, 8/20/68, Porter Papers, Box 5, LBJL.

44. Paul Porter to William P. Rogers, 8/22/68, and Porter to Bernard Segal, 9/5/68, Porter Papers, Box 5, LBJL.

45. Don Oberdorfer, "Nixon Draws Big Turnout in Chicago," *Washington Post*, 9/5/68.

46. Paul Porter to Thruston Morton, 9/4/68, Porter Papers, Box 5, LBJL.

47. Thruston Morton to Paul Porter, 9/9/68, Porter Papers, Box 6, LBJL.

48. Jim Jones to LBJ, 9/6/68, Fortas-Thornberry Files, Box 7, LBJL.

49. Untitled memo for the White House files, 9/10/68, Fortas-Thornberry Files, Box 3, LBJL.

50. *Ibid.*

51. Max Frankel, "Humphrey Scores the Same Nixon," *NYT*, 9/14/68, p. 1.

52. Chester et al., who were covering the campaign closely, saw no such deal. They say that Nixon was leading Thurmond to think that he had a role to play in the choice of the vice president, but that Nixon had been leaning toward Agnew all along. His effort with Thurmond, then, was to execute a forced choice. See Chester et al., *An American Melodrama*, pp. 459–60.

53. Marjorie Hunter, "Fortas Refuses to Appear Again in Senate Inquiry," *NYT*, 9/14/68, pp. 1, 17.

54. *Ibid.*

55. Jones, "Defeat of Abe Fortas," p. 262.

56. For an example of the fortunes shifting to Griffin's side, see the comments of the new senator from New York, Charles Goodell: *NYT*, 9/25/68, p. 27.

57. *NYT*, 9/15/68, p. 76.

58. *NYT*, 9/14/68, p. 17.
59. *Congressional Record*, 9/13/68, p. 26797.

CHAPTER XX

THE ICEBERG BELOW

1. A copy of this speech by Senator Phil Hart, delivered on 9/4/68 to the National Press Club in Washington, D.C., is filed in the Warren Christopher Papers, Box 2, LBJL.
2. "Sen. Robert Griffin: A Power in Washington?," *Detroit Scope Magazine*, 11/2/68, pp. 10–11.
3. Hugh Jones, "The Defeat of the Nomination of Abe Fortas as Chief Justice of the United States," unpublished Ph.D. dissertation, Johns Hopkins University, 1976, p. 240.
4. *Ibid.*, pp. 239–43; "Sen. Robert Griffin: A Power in Washington?," *Detroit Scope Magazine*, 11/2/68, pp. 10–11; "Sen. Griffin Wins Once Lonely Battle to Block Court Change," *Chicago Tribune*, 10/3/68, p. 2.
5. Larry Temple to LBJ, 7/25/68, and Temple to ――――, 7/26/68, Files Pertaining to Abe Fortas and Homer Thornberry, Box 2, LBJL (hereinafter Fortas-Thornberry Files).
6. Warren Christopher to Larry Temple, 8/5/68, Fortas-Thornberry Files, Box 2, LBJL. The signers of the document were Senators Phil Hart, Thomas Dodd, Edward Kennedy, Joseph Tydings, Birch Bayh, Quentin Burdick, and Hugh Scott. A copy of the Thornberry report is attached to memo, Fred Drogula to Warren Christopher, 7/31/68, Christopher Papers, Box 2, LBJL.
7. Phil Hart to Warren Christopher, 8/7/68, and Christopher to Fred Drogula, 8/8/68, Christopher Papers, Box 2, LBJL.
8. Cary Parker to Warren Christopher (with attached informative memo), 8/15/68, Christopher Papers, Box 2, LBJL. The attached memo—titled "The Excellence of Fortas," by Phil Hart, 8/15/68—had clearly been drafted by the Justice Department.
   On 9/3/68, Warren Christopher sent Hart a copy of the memo on obscenity, the court, and Fortas titled "Memorandum re the Views of Justice Fortas on Obscenity," which had been delivered to Senator Dirksen in late July but not used then. (Christopher Papers, Box 2, LBJL; also Larry Temple to Everett Dirksen, plus attached obscenity memo, 7/27/68, Christopher Papers, Box 1, LBJL.)
   This blitz did not stop with the delivery of the speech. On 9/13/68, the Justice Department sent Hart another memo, titled "Questions on Obscenity," with a series of rhetorical questions to be used with colleagues on the various obscenity cases that had been raised in the hearings. (Christopher Papers, Box 2, LBJL.)
9. Speech by Senator Phil Hart, 9/4/68, Christopher Papers, Box 2, LBJL. See also memo, Cary Parker to Warren Christopher, 8/15/68 (with a note explaining who to send the information to in Hart's office, and the speech draft with Hart's by-line on it attached), Christopher Papers, Box 2, LBJL.
10. Speech by Senator Phil Hart, 9/4/68, Christopher Papers, Box 2, LBJL. The Fortas allies were still confused about the strength of their support in the legal community. Porter was now claiming in some letters, one to Joseph Yanich on 9/6/68, to have the support of 480 law school deans and professors from 68 schools. (Paul Porter Papers, Box 5, LBJL.) In the speech, though, Hart had been claiming two days earlier to have the support of "more than 500" such people for the nomination.
11. *Ibid.* The editorials had been sent to Hart at his request attached to a memo by Dorothy Page, 8/29/68, Porter Papers, Box 5, LBJL.
12. *Ibid.* The memo that was the basis for this remark came from the White House after being transferred in a memo from the Justice Department: Warren Christopher to Larry Temple, 8/24/68, Christopher Papers, Box 2, LBJL.
13. *Ibid.*
14. Harold Barefoot Sanders to LBJ, 9/4/68 (reporting on the meeting schedule), and Sanders to LBJ, 7/30/68 (speculating on the vote agreement predictions), Fortas-Thornberry Files, Box 2, LBJL.
15. *Time*, 9/20/68, pp. 28–29; Harold Barefoot Sanders to LBJ, 9/4/68, Harold Barefoot Sanders Papers, Box 22, LBJL; Marjorie Hunter, "Johnson Told Hope of a Fortas Victory Is Fading in Senate," *NYT*, 9/6/68, pp. 1, 21.
16. Marjorie Hunter, "Johnson Told Hope of a Fortas Victory Is Fading in Senate," *NYT*, 9/6/68, pp. 1, 21.
17. "Attempt to Stop Fortas Debate Fails by 14-Vote Margin," *Congressional Quarterly Almanac*, 1968 Vol., p. 535 (hereinafter *CQ* Chronology); Robert Albright, "LBJ Scores Tactics of Fortas Foes," *Washington Post*, 9/7/68, pp. 1, A4.

18. *CQ* Chronology, p. 535.

19. *Ibid.* This was the strategy that had been suggested originally by Abe Fortas to Paul Porter, and was then passed along by the Porter operation to the White House. See Chap. XIII, "The Empire Strikes Back," and Chap. XV, "The Holy War."

20. Robert Albright, "LBJ Scores Tactics of Fortas Foes," *Washington Post*, 9/7/68.

21. *Ibid.*

22. The head count memo, with the instructions for Temple, is dated 9/9/68 and found in Fortas-Thornberry Files, Box 3, LBJL.

23. Harold Ickes, unpublished "Cabinet Memoirs," untitled section on the Division of Territories and Islands, Reel 5, pp. 79–80, Harold Ickes Papers, LOC. Eventually Gruening was absent, but indicated publicly that he would have voted against Fortas. While the White House staff later found out that Gruening held a grudge against Fortas (though it was never clear whether they knew the real cause of those feelings), the senator himself denied to a researcher that this was his motivation. See Jones, "Defeat of Abe Fortas," pp. 321, 353.

24. Harry McPherson to Mike Manatos, 9/10/68, Fortas-Thornberry Files, Box 3, LBJL; Marvin [Watson] to Larry Temple, 9/3/68, Fortas-Thornberry Files, Box 7, LBJL; Jim Jones to LBJ, on phone call of Palmer Hoyt, 9/3/68, Fortas-Thornberry Files, Box 3, LBJL.

25. Charles Roos, "Too Lenient Judges Criticized by Allott," *Denver Post*, reprinted in "Nominations of Abe Fortas and Homer Thornberry," Part 2, Hearings Before the Committee on the Judiciary, United States Senate, 90th Congress, 2nd Session, 9/13–9/16/68 (Washington, D.C.: U.S. Government Printing Office, 1968), p. 1359 (hereinafter Confirmation Hearings II).

26. Confirmation Hearings II, p. 1358.

27. UPI report, filed 9/7/68, copy in Fortas-Thornberry Files, Box 7, LBJL.

28. As will be explained below, the Allott story differed from the news reporter's account. "I never said [Fortas] wrote an amendment, that is the reporter's interpretation of it," Allott later explained to the Senate Judiciary Committee. (Confirmation Hearings II, p. 1358.)

29. Joe Califano to the files, 10/15/66, Diary Backup, Box 47, LBJL.

30. Memos, Larry Temple to LBJ, 6/5/68, and DeVier Pierson to LBJ, 6/5/68, Diary Backup, Box 102, LBJL.

31. Fortas list of names to Jim Jones, 6/5/68, White House Famous Names, Box 6, LBJL. Only two of Fortas's suggestions were included on the final list: attorney Albert Jenner of Illinois and court of appeals judge Leon Higgenbotham.

32. Fortas's draft of speech, titled "Address to the Nation," attached to memo from AF to Jim Jones, on his list of possible crime commission members, 6/5/68, White House Famous Names files, Box 6, LBJL; also untitled instruction memo typed by White House secretary, from Jim Jones to unnamed source, presumably Fortas, on LBJ's instructions for revising the speech, 6/5/68, 4:30 P.M., also attached to another copy of memo from AF to Jones on list of commission members, 6/5/68, Diary Backup, Box 101, LBJL.

33. Harry McPherson, *A Political Education* (Boston: Little, Brown and Co., 1972), p. 381.

34. Larry Levinson to LBJ, 6/6/68, Ex LE/JL3 1/1/68, Box 80, LBJL.

35. Memo, MJDR [secretary Juanita Roberts] to LBJ, 9/7/68, Fortas-Thornberry Files, unfiled as was opened for this project by library rereview process, LBJL.

36. Robert Griffin to Judiciary Committee, 9/9/68, copies in Fortas-Thornberry Files, Box 3, LBJL; Confirmation Hearings II, pp. 1369–70.

37. Edith Kermit Roosevelt, "The Abe Fortas Controversy," *Philadelphia Bulletin*, Porter Papers, Box 3, LBJL. For more on this, see Chap. XVIII, "Porn Wars."

38. The president's instructions appear on the copy of the memo from Robert Griffin to Judiciary Committee, 9/9/68, Fortas-Thornberry Files, Box 3, LBJL.

39. White House Diaries, 1/12/66, LBJL.

40. Various drafts of Fortas's version of this State of the Union address, along with the many drafts of others, can be found in the 1966 State of the Union address folder, one subfolder of which is titled "1/12/66 Annual Message to the Congress on the State of the Union—Changes Made by Pres. Johnson, Justice Fortas, Clark Clifford" (containing 115 pages of these revisions), Presidential Statements File, Boxes 172 and 173, LBJL. Many of these drafts are untitled, and identifiable only by Fortas's handwriting on the typed copy. One draft is attached to a "Memorandum for the Record" in which she notes, "Changes made by Justice Abe Fortas," to help the staff identify the source of the changes on that draft. One of these drafts contains both Fortas's stylistic revisions on the typed version and many sheets of lined yellow paper on which he had handwritten large portions of a new address for the president to deliver. This handwritten material was then typed by the staff and also appears in

the files melding the two early versions for the president's consideration.

The various versions of the speech show that Fortas took part in the drafting process from start to finish. Not only did he help to write early drafts of the speech, but one bold typed copy of the final version of the speech that the president would read in his actual delivery to the Congress also has Fortas's handwritten revisions.

41. White House Picture File, LBJL.
42. *CQ* Chronology, p. 535.
43. Warren Christopher, "Memorandum for Honorable Larry Temple, Special Assistant to the President, re: The Fortas and Thornberry Nominations," 12/20/68, Christopher Papers, Box 3, LBJL (hereinafter Justice Department Chronology).
44. Memo, Larry Temple to LBJ, 9/10/68, Fortas-Thornberry Files, Box 7, LBJL.
45. Justice Department Chronology, LBJL.
46. Robert Albright, "Committee to Vote on Fortas," *Washington Post,* 9/12/68, p. 1.
47. Memo, Harold Barefoot Sanders to LBJ, 9/11/68, Sanders Papers, Box 25, LBJL; Robert Albright, "Committee to Vote on Fortas," *Washington Post,* 9/12/68, p. 1.
48. Phil Hart to Judiciary Committee, 9/11/68, copy in Fortas-Thornberry Files, Box 3, LBJL.
49. Proposed letter from Phil Hart to Senator James Eastland, marked as received over the phone by Warren Christopher on 9/11/68, attached to memo, Larry Temple to LBJ, 9/11/68, Fortas-Thornberry Files, Box 3, LBJL. The letter had already been signed by Senators Hart, Edward V. Long, Edward Kennedy, Birch Bayh, Quentin Burdick, Joseph Tydings, George Smathers, and Hugh Scott. Dodd's signature would not have been needed the day before, as this group constituted a majority of the committee that had considered the nomination to this point. However, as will be explained below, that afternoon Howard Baker of Tennessee was added to the committee under less than clear circumstances, making the total membership of the committee seventeen members and changing the number of signers necessary to make a majority of the group.
50. The instructions from LBJ for Rowe to see Dodd are handwritten on a memo from Larry Temple to LBJ, 9/11/68, Fortas-Thornberry Files, Box 3, LBJL. The report on the visit by Rowe and the continuing efforts to woo Dodd are in memo, Temple to LBJ, 9/12/68, Fortas-Thornberry Files, Box 7, LBJL. Other material on the lobbying efforts of the labor unions are in the congressional contacts reports from Harold Barefoot Sanders to the White House, dated 9/11/68, 9/12/68, and 9/13/68, Sanders Papers, Box 25, LBJL.
51. An undated draft of the letter from AF to the Judiciary Committee can be found in the Fortas-Thornberry Files, Box 3, LBJL. Larry Temple indicated in his message to the president on the letter that he was concerned with the tenor of the second half of the letter.
52. Larry Temple to LBJ, 9/12/68, Fortas-Thornberry Files, Box 17, LBJL.
53. Justice Department Chronology, LBJL.
54. Larry Temple to LBJ, 9/12/68, Fortas-Thornberry Files, Box 17, LBJL; Bernard Segal to Paul Porter, 9/12/68, Porter Papers, Box 6, LBJL, discusses Segal's letter to Senator Scott dated 9/10/68.
55. DeVier Pierson to LBJ, 9/11/68, Fortas-Thornberry Files, Box 7, LBJL.
56. *Ibid.*; typed chronology of the development of the legislation for Secret Service protection of presidential candidates, titled "History of Preparation of Amendments for Secret Service Protection of Candidates and Assistance from other Agencies to Secret Service on Protective Functions," Fortas-Thornberry Files, Box 7, LBJL; Larry Temple to ———, 9/10/68, Fortas-Thornberry Files, Box 3, LBJL.
57. Joseph Barr to LBJ, 9/11/68 (transmitting the chronology of the development of this legislation to the White House), and Charles Murphy to DeVier Pierson, 9/11/68, Fortas-Thornberry Files, Box 7, LBJL.
58. Memo for the president from ——— (reporting on the comments of Joseph Barr in reaction to the charges), 9/12/68, JL6 General, Box 41, LBJL.
59. According to the White House Diaries, LBJL, meetings on Vietnam took place on May 25 and 28, the LBJ school meeting was on May 28, and a luncheon of aides, businessmen, and Texas friends of LBJ on May 16 was also a discussion of the future of the LBJ Library.
60. DeVier Pierson to LBJ, 5/27/68, 5/29/68, and 6/5/68, Fortas-Thornberry Files, Box 7, LBJL; DeVier Pierson to LBJ, 6/5/68, Diary Backup, Box 102, LBJL; Larry Temple to LBJ, 6/5/68, Diary Backup, Box 102, LBJL.
61. DeVier Pierson to LBJ, 9/11/68, Fortas-Thornberry Files, Box 7, LBJL.
62. Harold Barefoot Sanders to LBJ, 9/12/68, Fortas-Thornberry Files, Box 3, LBJL.
63. Joe Califano to LBJ, 9/12/68, and press release from the Lawyers Committee on Supreme Court Nominations, 9/12/68, Fortas-Thornberry Files, Box 1, LBJL.

Chapter XXI
The Trial of Abe Fortas

1. For a wonderful brief account of how Johnson achieved this title, see Doris Kearns, *Lyndon Johnson and the American Dream* (New York: New American Library, 1976), Chap. 4.

2. Precisely dating this fascinating sheet of paper, attached to one of the undated Senate head counts in the Fortas-Thornberry Files (Box 7), is impossible. In this case, the head count was an anticipated one, labeled "Cloture Vote for the Week of September 30," and was stapled to another head count labeled 9/6/68. (There were in fact only minor differences between the results of the two counts.) A note at the top of the initial head count in LBJ's handwriting indicates that it was taken sometime after 9/10/68. The fact that Everett Dirksen is still listed as being "for" the nomination indicates that it was taken before 9/28.

   However, the precise date for this undated piece of paper, which formed the basis for LBJ's strategy, is not so important. In fact, the numbers of votes and the names of those senators who were crucial were fairly set by early September, and would vary little for the remainder of the month. Thus the strategy for the White House would remain the same. For more on this, see Senate head counts, 9/6/68, 9/11/68, and 9/25/68, Files Pertaining to Abe Fortas and Homer Thornberry, Box 3, LBJL (hereinafter Fortas-Thornberry Files).

3. Hugh Jones, "The Defeat of the Nomination of Abe Fortas as Chief Justice of the United States," unpublished Ph.D. dissertation, Johns Hopkins University, 1976, p. 258. On the deal to put Baker on the Judiciary Committee, the information is from AI, Hugh Jones, 7/23/87, Shippensburg, Pa.

4. Jones, "Defeat of Abe Fortas," pp. 235, 239–40, 263, 265; "Sen. Griffin Wins Once Lonely Battle to Block Court Change," *Chicago Tribune,* 10/3/68, p. 2.

5. Robert Albright, "Committee to Vote on Fortas," *Washington Post,* 9/12/68, pp. 1, A10.

6. Jones, "Defeat of Abe Fortas," pp. 258–59.

7. *George Washington University Hatchet,* 9/19/68, Vol. 65, No. 2, Paul Porter Papers, Box 5, LBJL. The appearance by Fortas was eventually canceled because of the confirmation controversy.

8. *Ibid.* The money requested was five hundred dollars plus expenses, said to be used by the senator for the printing of his weekly newsletter and any other printing costs not covered by the government. In the end, without collecting his usual fee of five hundred dollars, Thurmond did speak to the group on December 6, 1967, on the U.S. involvement in Vietnam. See *Washington Post,* 9/20/68, p. A7.

9. The early part of this account comes from Paul Porter's report to the donors for the Fortas seminar. See Porter to Benjamin Sonnenberg, 9/17/68 and 9/26/68; Porter to Maurice Lazarus, 9/17/68 and 9/26/68; Porter to Troy V. Post, 9/17/68 and 9/26/68; Porter to Gustave Levy, 9/17/68 and 9/26/68; and Porter to Paul D. Smith, 9/17/68 and 9/26/68, Porter Papers, Box 5, LBJL.

10. Fortas's handwritten corrections appear on p. 7 of an early draft of Dean Tennery's remarks to the Judiciary Committee, labeled only "Revised 9/13/68," Porter Papers, Box 5, LBJL.

11. Dean B. J. Tennery to Paul Porter, 11/2/68, Porter Papers, Box 5, LBJL.

12. Abe Krash to Paul Porter, 11/20/68, and Porter to AF, 12/14/68, Porter Papers, Box 5, LBJL.

13. Paul Porter to AF, 12/14/68 (with a copy of the new seminar proposal and proposed budget attached, as well as one of the confirming letters from Tennery to Porter, 11/2/67), Porter Papers, Box 5, LBJL.

14. This paragraph relies on the proposal for creating the institute, titled "Proposal for: Institute on Law and the Social Environment," labeled as being sent to Fortas, Porter Papers, Box 5, LBJL. An initial copy of this proposal, with a projected budget of only twenty-five thousand dollars, was forwarded to Paul Porter by Dean Tennery. (See Tennery to Porter, 11/2/67, with attachment, Porter Papers, Box 5, LBJL.) Porter was unhappy with the idea, and told Fortas that he was having Abe Krash in the Arnold and Porter office revise it. (Porter to AF, 12/14/68, Porter Papers, Box 5, LBJL.) Porter appears to have been unhappy with this draft as well. The final author of the proposal, then, is unclear, and unstated on the actual document. It seems probable, though, that if Porter did not write it himself, he played a large role in the drafting process. Two open questions that remain are what role Fortas himself might have played in the drafting process of this document, and who suggested the huge increase in the projected budget.

15. Paul Porter to Benjamin Sonnenberg, 2/8/68; Porter to Troy V. Post, 2/1/68; Porter to Gustave Levy, 2/2/68 and 2/23/68; Porter to Paul D. Smith, 2/2/68; Porter to Maurice Lazarus, 2/9/68; Porter to Dean B. J. Tennery, 2/23/68, Porter Papers, Box 5, LBJL. See also the testimony of Dean Tennery

for more on these financial negotiations: "Nominations of Abe Fortas and Homer Thornberry," Part 2, Hearings Before the Committee on the Judiciary, United States Senate, 90th Congress, 2nd Session, 9/13–9/16/68, (Washington, D.C.: U.S. Government Printing Office, 1968), pp. 1286–1306 (hereinafter Confirmation Hearings II).

16. Dean B. J. Tennery to Maurice Lazarus, 2/15/68; Tennery to Gustave Levy, 2/29/68; Tennery to John Loeb, 2/15/68; Paul D. Smith to Paul Porter, 2/12/68; and Tennery to Troy V. Post, 2/15/68, Porter Papers, Box 5, LBJL.

17. John Corry, "Strom's Dirty Movies," *Harper's Magazine,* December 1968, p. 40.

18. Tennery's opening statement appears in Confirmation Hearings II, pp. 1286–90. Since this testimony does not differ appreciably from the statement that Fortas revised and approved, it is clear that this is the way the justice, and by implication Paul Porter, wanted the dean to testify. (See Tennery draft testimony, labeled only "Revised 9/13/68," Porter Papers, Box 5, LBJL.) This account, of course, differs from that of Porter, who claims that the impetus for developing and funding the seminar came from him. In fact, he "assume[d] personal responsibility" for that problem. (See Porter, LBJ/OH, pp. 33–36.) Tennery explains in his statement that the initial negotiations with Fortas for the seminar began between the two of them the previous fall when the justice was agreeing to give the Mooers Lecture at American University, and that he then went out with the "good offices" of Porter to raise the funds. (The lecture was delivered on 3/20/68.) (Confirmation Hearings II, pp. 1289–90.)

As explained in the text and notes above, while both men were involved in the development of the seminar, and it is quite possible that Tennery, as he explains in his statement, first thought of and even discussed in generalities the prospect of continuing the work with Fortas during his Mooers Lecture the previous year, the written record clearly indicates that the lead role in the seminar's development and funding process was Porter's.

19. Tennery draft testimony, labeled only "Revised 9/13/68," Porter Papers, Box 5, LBJL. This version squares with the dean's testimony as it was actually delivered to the Judiciary Committee. See Confirmation Hearings II, pp. 1289–90.

20. It is clear at least from the proposal for the seminar that a much larger role was envisioned for Fortas, not only in the conduct of the seminar, but in the development of the entire institute. See "Proposal for: Institute on Law and the Social Environment," Porter Papers, Box 5, LBJL, p. 3.

21. An untitled and handwritten student evaluation of the course is filed in Porter Papers, Box 3, LBJL. Another description of the course appears in "Background of the Fortas Lectures," *Washington Star,* 9/15/68, housed in *Washington Star* morgue, Martin Luther King Library, Washington, D.C. One member of the class described it as a "seminar in the true sense. . . . I wouldn't call any of it a lecture. The vast majority of the time was spent in conversations between the students and Fortas and in conversations between the students themselves." The account also indicates that about six of the class members took approximately thirty minutes apiece to deliver reports on their seminar papers to the class. While this is also a common practice in advanced seminars, it is clear from the tone of this article that the reporter was surprised at the apparently low level of involvement by Fortas in the course. The reporter does quote another student as saying, however, that "Fortas dominated the discussions but not to the extent of lecturing. He posed the questions, gave the direction, and provided a summary."

22. W. Carey Parker to Warren Christopher, labeled only "Received 9/24/68" (with several attachments—an index of materials used by Fortas in preparing the course, the three reading lists and bibliography, dated 6/4/68, 6/18/68, and 7/9/68, and a syllabus prepared after the course by one of the students, Ronald Elberger), Warren Christopher Papers, Box 2, LBJL.

23. Paul Porter, LBJ/OH, pp. 34–35.

24. "Justice Fortas at American University," memo prepared by the Justice Department and sent to Phil Hart, and memo, Warren Christopher to Larry Temple, 9/26/68, Christopher Papers, Box 2, LBJL. See also similar claims by Paul Porter in a letter to Clark Clifford, saying that Fortas would edit and reedit his teaching materials and syllabi. (Porter to Clifford, 9/26/68, Porter Papers, Box 5, LBJL.) See also a draft of a letter for the *New York Times* editorial page (intended to be signed by Dean Tennery), and a speech draft for the Senate floor from the Porter operation, titled "The American University Teaching Seminar," Porter Papers, Box 5, LBJL.

25. Tennery told the committee that he had written his testimony that day. (Confirmation Hearings II, p. 1286.) Hugh Jones explains how much time the committee is supposed to have in receiving copies of planned testimony. (Jones, "Defeat of Abe Fortas," p. 263 and n. 20.)

26. Confirmation Hearings II, p. 1289.

27. *Ibid.,* pp. 1290–91.

28. *Ibid.,* p. 1295.

29. *Ibid.*, p. 1307.

30. The charge was leveled by Senator McClellan; see Confirmation Hearings II, p. 1351.

31. Jones, "Defeat of Abe Fortas," pp. 241–42; Robert Shogan, *A Question of Judgment: The Fortas Case and the Struggle for the Supreme Court* (Indianapolis: Bobbs-Merrill Co., 1972), p. 185.

32. Pearson did eventually vote against cloture as predicted.

33. Thruston Morton, LBJ/OH, pp. 20–22. Hugh Jones discovered that Senator Morton was one of those who had heard Allott's story privately before the actual public testimony and was "annoyed by this story of blatant violation of the 'tripartite' principle of government." (Jones, "Defeat of Abe Fortas," p. 322.)

34. Harry McPherson to Mike Manatos, 9/20/68, Fortas-Thornberry Files, Box 3, LBJL; Thruston Morton, LBJ/OH, p. 22.

35. Richard Harris, *Decision* (New York: E. P. Dutton, 1971), p. 135.

36. Thruston Morton, LBJ/OH, p. 22.

37. *Congressional Record*, 10/1/68, p. 28929.

38. The movement of three senators to the opposition side is recorded in an undated head count, Ernie [Goldstein] to White House, Fortas-Thornberry Files, Box 3, LBJL. Notification of Richard Russell's actual switched vote comes in a letter from Russell to LBJ, 9/26/68, Fortas-Thornberry Files, Box 3, LBJL. Russell's statement that Lawrence was the cause of the shift in his vote is in Wayne Kelley, "A Conversation with Richard Russell," *Atlanta Magazine*, December 1968, copy in Richard Russell Library, Athens, Ga.

39. Lyle Denniston, "Call Source of AU Fund Improper," *Washington Star*, 9/14/68, p. 1.

40. Lyle Denniston, "Letter Ties Meetings to Vietnam War," *Washington Star*, 9/15/68, pp. 1, 4.

41. One of the journalistic accounts that came out on the seminar and Fortas's role in it, was "Background of the Fortas Lectures," *Washington Star*, 9/15/68, housed in the *Washington Star* morgue, M.L.K. Library, Washington, D.C.

    Draft speech, "The American University Teaching Seminar," Porter Papers, Box 5, LBJL. According to a letter from Edward Levi to Everett Dirksen, other prominent dual careerists on the court of appeals were Calvert Magruder, Jerome Frank, Walter Schaefer (the man whom Fortas touted for the seat on the Supreme Court that Fortas eventually got in 1965), and Roger Traynor. (Levi to Dirksen, 9/25/68, Porter Papers, Box 3, LBJL.)

42. Paul Porter to Clark Clifford, 9/24/68, Porter Papers, Box 5, LBJL; draft of letter to *NYT* editors, Porter Papers, Box 3, LBJL (not published.)

43. Draft speech, "The American University Teaching Seminar," Porter Papers, Box 5, LBJL. Albert Gore delivered this speech to the Senate on 9/30/68. (See *Congressional Record*, pp. 28780–83.) Paul Porter made slight revisions in the text of the speech, along the lines of some suggestions made by Warren Christopher. (See Porter to Mary Lee, 9/25/68, and Porter to Christopher, 9/25/68, Porter Papers, Box 5, LBJL.) In a letter to Clark Clifford, Porter says that he prepared this position paper, and drafts of it clearly show evidence of his handwriting on them. (Porter to Clifford, 9/24/68, Porter Papers, Box 5, LBJL.) A copy of this position paper was then sent to a professor of law at Chicago University, Edward Levi. (Porter to Levi, 9/23/68, Porter Papers, Box 5, LBJL.) He was sufficiently convinced by the account to write to Everett Dirksen that it "would appear" that the justice had not known the source of the funds. (Levi to Dirksen, 9/25/68, Porter Papers, Box 3, LBJL.)

44. The materials that came from the Fortas office are headed by a memo from W. Carey Parker to Warren Christopher, marked "received 9/24/68." See also a memo from Parker to Christopher, 9/25/68, and a memo from Christopher to Larry Temple, 9/26/68, saying that Christopher had sent the material along to Senator Phil Hart that day. The speech was never given. (All of these materials are in the Christopher Papers, Box 2, LBJL.)

45. See Paul Porter to Maurice Lazarus, 2/9/68; Porter to Gustave Levy, 2/9/68; and Porter to Troy V. Post, 2/7/68, Porter Papers, Box 5, LBJL. In the latter two letters, Porter says that he has told Fortas of his correspondents' participation. In letter to Lazarus, and a letter from Porter to John Loeb (2/14/68, Porter Papers, Box 5, LBJL), Porter says that he will inform Fortas of their contributions. There is no question that Fortas knew about the nature and size of the projected honorarium, based on these letters and his closeness to Porter. At the time, there was no reason for him not to know.

46. Undated note, AF to Paul Porter, Porter Papers, Box 3, LBJL.

47. Shaidell's testimony appears in Confirmation Hearings II, pp. 1311–16. Hart's reading of the obscenity memo into the record is in Confirmation Hearings II, pp. 1312–15.

48. Hart's reading into the record of the O'Meara letter, which as explained earlier was drafted by the Porter operation (see Chap. XVIII, "Porn Wars"), is in Confirmation Hearings II, pp. 1315–16.

49. Warren Christopher, "Memorandum for Honorable Larry Temple, Special Assistant to the President,

re: The Fortas and Thornberry Nominations,'' 12/20/68, Christopher Papers, Box 3, LBJL (hereinafter Justice Department Chronology).

50. Young was being counted in this fashion on both the revised 9/6/68 head count and the private handwritten list attached to it by LBJ, Fortas-Thornberry Files, Box 3, LBJL. Mike Manatos to LBJ, 9/16/68, has the evidence of the promised walkout by Young. (Fortas-Thornberry Files, Box 3, LBJL.)

51. "On Capitol Hill with Senator Young—A Personal Report to the People of North Dakota,'' 9/18/68, cited in Jones, "Defeat of Abe Fortas,'' p. 271.

52. Jones, "Defeat of Abe Fortas,'' pp. 250, 271. Jones cites the report of a "close associate'' of Young as the actual reason for the switched vote.

53. *Congressional Record*, 9/16/68, p. 26870.

54. *NYT*, 9/17/68, p. 3.

55. Marvin Watson to Larry Temple, 9/20/68, Fortas-Thornberry Files, Box 7, LBJL.

56. Confirmation Hearings II, p. 1349. This testimony that Fortas was reported by Barr to have "cleared'' the amendment was, of course, different from the earlier news account that Allott was going to say that he "wrote'' the legislation. Allott, however, blamed this erroneous report on a misunderstanding by the reporter at the time. (Confirmation Hearings II, p. 1358.)

57. Confirmation Hearings II, p. 1357; Thruston Morton, LBJ/OH, p. 22.

58. Harris, *Decision*, p. 164.

59. Harry McPherson to Mike Manatos, 9/20/68, Fortas-Thornberry Files, Box 3, LBJL.

60. Justice Department Chronology, LBJL. Jones found some indications that the pornography issue had increased the flow and virulence of the negative constituent mail to some senators. (See Jones, "Defeat of Abe Fortas,'' p. 247.) An examination of the Senate files of other participants in this fight, however, indicates that the same was not true in all offices. Despite a claim by Richard Russell that obscenity was having an effect on his constituents, an examination of his office files from this period indicates that the voters in his state were far more concerned with Fortas's alleged "Communist'' leanings. Obscenity did not seem to be a real factor in the Dirksen files. And the files of Senator Phil Hart show that the voters in his state were more concerned with his reasons for supporting this nomination when he had once voiced opposition to recess appointments. Since this was not a recess appointment, it was hard to see how the voters made this connection in their minds, and Hart told them so. (Examinations of the Senate office files of Everett Dirksen, Everett Dirksen Library, Pekin, Ill.; Richard Russell, Richard B. Russell Library, Athens, Ga.; and Phil Hart, whose files are now at the University of Michigan, Ann Arbor, Mich.)

61. Confirmation Hearings II, pp. 1364–72. Griffin simply inserted his memo from 9/9/68 to Senator Eastland, seeking to have the Judiciary Committee re-open the hearings.

62. Confirmation Hearings II, pp. 1368–69.

CHAPTER XXII
THE VERDICT

1. Mike Manatos to LBJ, 9/16/68, Files Pertaining to Abe Fortas and Homer Thornberry, Box 3, LBJL (hereinafter Fortas-Thornberry Files).

2. "Fortas Class Substitute Says He Filled in Free,'' *Washington Post*, 9/17/68, p. A6.

3. *NYT*, 9/18/68, p. 1.

4. *Congressional Record*, 9/17/68, pp. 27105–6.

5. *Ibid.*, p. 27109.

6. Edward V. Long of Missouri was absent, but later recorded his vote in favor.

7. This was listed as Executive Report Number 8, portions of which are cited in "Attempt to Stop Fortas Debate Fails by 14-Vote Margin,'' *Congressional Quarterly Almanac*, 1968 Vol., p. 536 (hereinafter CQ Chronology).

8. Hugh Jones, "The Defeat of the Nomination of Abe Fortas as Chief Justice of the United States,'' unpublished Ph.D. dissertation, Johns Hopkins University, 1976, p. 292.

9. George Reedy to LBJ, 9/20/68, Fortas-Thornberry Files, Box 7, LBJL.

10. Warren Christopher to Larry Temple, 9/16/68 (with attached memo), Fortas-Thornberry Files, Box 3, LBJL.

11. Typed oral instructions from LBJ to Larry Temple, 9/16/68, Fortas-Thornberry Files, Box 3, LBJL.

12. The document is dated 9/5/68, and is filed in Fortas-Thornberry Files, Box 8, LBJL.

13. Harold Barefoot Sanders to Andrew Biemiller, 9/13/68, Fortas-Thornberry Files, Box 3, LBJL.

14. The material was released by the committee on 9/18/68 in New York City (copy in Fortas-Thornberry Files, Box 3, LBJL).

15. "Fortas Is Favored in Poll; Anti-Semites Seen Active," *New York Law Journal*, 9/19/68, p. 1.

16. Robert Albright, "Fortas Foe Decries Hint of Bigotry," *Washington Post*, 9/21/68, p. 1.

17. Jones, "Defeat of Abe Fortas," p. 375. See also Robert Shogan, *A Question of Judgment: The Fortas Case and the Struggle for the Supreme Court* (Indianapolis: Bobbs-Merrill Co., 1972), p. 185.

18. This document was discovered by Hugh Jones in the Judiciary Committee files in the National Archives that were open to him at the time, but are now closed. (Jones, "Defeat of Abe Fortas," p. 365.) Jones reports that this letter was "presumably" sent to all of the senators on the Judiciary Committee. He also reports that the reaction of John Holloman, the chief counsel of the Judiciary Committee during the fight, when provided with a copy of the letter by Jones, was "I wish we had not missed this one." (Jones, "Defeat of Abe Fortas," pp. 374–75.)

19. The source of this tip remains a mystery. The only people who had reason to know about this connection were the lawyers for Wolfson, the star witness Alex Rittmaster, and lawyers in the office of the U.S. attorney for the Southern District of New York, Robert M. Morgenthau. The Morgenthau office had stumbled upon the connection in successfully prosecuting Louis Wolfson in two trials for conspiracy to violate the securities laws, selling unregistered securities, perjury, and filing misleading annual company reports. Wolfson had yet to be sentenced in one of the cases. The first case, connected with Continental Enterprises, was that in which Wolfson was found guilty of conspiracy and of selling unregistered stocks. Though he was sentenced to a year in prison and fined $100,000, Wolfson's conviction was sustained after the Supreme Court refused to hear the case. In the other case, related to Merritt-Chapman, in which Wolfson was convicted of conspiracy, perjury, and filing misleading annual reports, and for which he was eventually sentenced in December of 1968 to an additional eighteen months in jail, the conviction was ultimately reversed in the U.S. Court of Appeals. (For more, see Shogan, *Question of Judgment*, pp. 213–14.)

At the time, the knowledge by the authorities of the connection between Wolfson and Fortas was very sketchy. Relying on the testimony of their star witness, Alex Rittmaster, the chief financial adviser to Wolfson, government investigators had learned only that Fortas was connected closely enough to the financier to have spoken with him on the phone, invited him to a cocktail party, and traveled to Florida for a meeting of the Wolfson Family Foundation. The implication was felt to be clear enough among Wolfson's inner circle that Fortas had been helpful in offering legal advice and might well even intervene in the case. Moved by that prospect, the government's investigating attorney, Michael F. Armstrong, had developed, along with others in his office, more on the connection in case the justice planned to appear at the trial. All they discovered, though, was that Fortas had indeed gone to Florida in mid-June, which happened to have been shortly after Wolfson's case was referred to the Justice Department by the SEC. (See Shogan, *Question of Judgment*, Chap. 7, especially pp. 206–10.)

Because Fortas had never been publicly involved with either of Wolfson's trials, this information remained buried in Morgenthau's office files. But how far it got into the various rumor circles is not known. Regardless, someone who knew, or guessed quite correctly, was trying to get that piece of dynamite into the hands of the people in Washington who could put it to best use in opposing Fortas.

20. See Warren Weaver, Jr., "G.O.P. Aware in Campaign of Fortas's Tie to Wolfson," *NYT*, 5/23/69, pp. 1, 26. As this story indicates, the means by which Javits was made aware of the Fortas problem is hazy and Byzantine. Since Alex Rittmaster, the star witness for the U.S. prosecution team against Louis Wolfson, was the source of the allegations surrounding Fortas, his attorney, Norman Ostrow, was well aware of the story. Ostrow happened to be a member of the prominent New York law firm of Rogers and Wells. One of the name partners of the firm, William P. Rogers, was then one of Richard Nixon's closest campaign advisers and would soon become his secretary of state. When the other name partner in the firm, John Wells, heard about the connection between Fortas and Wolfson, he then informed John Trubin, one of Jacob Javits's law partners and a co-director of the senator's reelection campaign.

From then on the story becomes more unclear. The *NYT* account is hazy about the actual nature of the warning that was thus passed to the Javits campaign operation, and then to Javits himself. Originally, Trubin told the reporter that Wells had explained the full nature of what was then known about the Fortas-Wolfson connection to him (including the Fortas trip to Florida). Upon being re-interviewed, though, and after having spoken to Wells, Trubin told the reporter that he was now "willing to accept what he [Wells] now recalls to me as being fact." The account by Wells to the reporter was:

"All I told him [Trubin] was not to get too far out in front in defending Fortas." Despite the fact that Javits himself told the reporter that he did not recall any such episode, there seems little doubt from his actions during the Senate fight that he had some reason for holding back, other than just the politics of the battle itself. The key point in this *NYT* account is that a key aide to Javits, and most probably Javits himself, had been given at least some minimal warning about Fortas's connection to Wolfson. It seems highly likely that this warning was the reason for the senator's relative silence throughout the fight, which so disappointed the White House.

My account in the text relies for the first phrase on the recollection of Mr. Wells himself, and for the second phrase on the recollection of Mr. Trubin after his recollection was refreshed by the conversation with Wells.

21. *Ibid.*
22. Jones, "Defeat of Abe Fortas," p. 365. Jones also cites the persuasive reasoning on this question of a Democrat: "You can be sure that if the opponents of Fortas had this information, they would have used it."
23. Larry Temple to Mike Manatos, 9/25/68, (with head count attached), Fortas-Thornberry Files, Box 3, LBJL.
24. Harold Barefoot Sanders to Larry Temple, 9/14/68 (with the 9/11/68 head count attached), Fortas-Thornberry Files, Box 3, LBJL.
25. Mike Manatos to LBJ, 9/25/68, FG 535/A, Box 360, LBJL.
26. *Congressional Record*, 9/24/68, p. 28113.
27. *Ibid.*
28. Warren Christopher, "Memorandum for Honorable Larry Temple, Special Assistant to the President, re: The Fortas and Thornberry Nominations," 12/20/68, Warren Christopher Papers, Box 3, LBJL (hereinafter Justice Department Chronology).
29. *CQ* Chronology, pp. 531, 536–38. See also Jones, "Defeat of Abe Fortas," p. 315, in which Jones questions Mansfield's tactics.
30. Conversation between author and Hugh Jones, revealing his research on the 1968 confirmation battle, 7/23/87, Shippensburg, Pa.
31. Justice Department Chronology, LBJL.
32. Edward L. Schapsmeier and Frederick H. Schapsmeier, *Dirksen of Illinois: Senatorial Statesman* (Urbana, Ill.: University of Illinois Press, 1985), p. 195; "Chronology: Events Relating to Supreme Court Nominations," compiled by Jack Hushen, press secretary for Senator Robert Griffin, Fortas-Thornberry Files, Box 2, LBJL (hereinafter Griffin Chronology). See also Fred Graham, "Subversives Unit Is Asked to Cite 7," *NYT*, 7/2/68, p. 16.
33. 391 U.S. 510 (1968).
34. Robert Albright, "Fortas Bid Dealt Blow by Dirksen," *Washington Post*, 9/28/68, p. 1; *CQ* Chronology, p. 538. The announcement from Dirksen came on 9/27/68. Dirksen explained his switch in full on 10/1/68; see *Congressional Record*, pp. 11687–88.
35. AI, Larry Temple, 11/15/82, Austin, Tex.
36. Justice Department Chronology, LBJL.
37. Joe Califano to LBJ, 10/1/68, FG 535/A, Box 360, LBJL.
38. The speeches by both senators were given on 10/1/68: Hart's is at *Congressional Record*, p. 28926, and Griffin's at *Congressional Record*, pp. 28929–30. See also *CQ* Chronology, p. 538.
39. The vote appears at *Congressional Record*, October 1, 1968, p. 28933. As of 9/25/68, Bible was listed by the White House as "against us on cloture, but he has had a hard fight in Nevada [for reelection] and might be induced to stay there." (See memo, Mike Manatos to LBJ, 9/25/68, Ex and Gen 535/A, Box 360, LBJL.)
40. Frank Church joined with Morse in providing the affirmative vote in this pair. Since it was a cloture vote, requiring a two-thirds vote, it took two senators to offset the negative vote of Gruening.
41. The first indication of this came in a Senate head count on the cloture issue, 9/25/68, attached to memo, Larry Temple to attorney general, 9/25/68, Fortas-Thornberry Files, Box 3, LBJL.
42. In the end, of the eighteen names on the original list, only "6 or 7" of which LBJ had thought he could count on at that moment, the White House would get only ten supporting votes. Of course, one of those, John Sherman Cooper of Kentucky, was gone from that moment on and would vote against confirmation of the nominations.
43. Jones, "Defeat of Abe Fortas," pp. 319–20, 352.
44. On Hill's early position, see Joe Califano to LBJ, 6/29/68, Fortas-Thornberry Files, Box 1, LBJL; Harry McPherson to Mike Manatos, 7/2/68, Fortas-Thornberry Files, Box 4, LBJL; and Ernie [Goldstein] to White House, undated but sent circa 7/10/68, Fortas-Thornberry Files, Box 7, LBJL.

See also the Senate head counts dated 6/27 (Hill is "solidly right"), 7/1 (Hill is "right?"), 7/3 (Hill is a "?"), 7/9 (Hill is "probably wrong"), 7/15 (Hill is "wrong?"), and 7/16 (Hill is back to "right?"), Fortas-Thornberry Files, Boxes 3 and 4, LBJL.

45. The contact was Mary Lasker. See Jim Jones to White House, 7/9/68, Fortas-Thornberry Files, Box 5, LBJL.

46. The indication that Hill might be willing to deal is in Harry McPherson to Mike Manatos, 7/2/68, Fortas-Thornberry Files, Box 4, LBJL.

The new Senate head counts are dated 7/24 (Hill is "no") and 8/13 (Hill is "hard against"), Fortas-Thornberry Files, Box 3, LBJL. By the middle of September, the White House would discover that the Steelworkers were bringing heavy pressure to bear on Hill.

The idea on the Hill-Burton Act is in an untitled, handwritten set of notes, marked "Sept. 6 address by Segal," Fortas-Thornberry Files, Box 3, LBJL.

47. The quote is taken from the official White House statement. This quotation is exactly the same as Fortas's untitled and undated, handwritten early draft of the statement. That draft was attached to another draft by Ramsey Clark, which was passed on to the president by Larry Temple with the recommendation that the Clark draft be used because of its greater eloquence. Johnson ordered that the two drafts be combined, and the paragraph quoted in the text is the only portion of the final statement issued by the White House on 10/10/68 that comes from the Fortas draft. All of these materials are attached to memo, Larry Temple to LBJ, 10/7/68, Fortas-Thornberry Files, Box 3, LBJL.

48. *Congressional Record*, 10/2/68, p. 29152.

49. Doris Kearns, *Lyndon Johnson and the American Dream* (New York: New American Library, 1976), p. 237.

50. Mrs. Lyndon Baines Johnson, *A White House Diary* (New York: Holt, Rinehart and Winston, 1970), Book V, pp. 712–13.

Chapter XXIII
The "Fortas Under the Fortas"?

1. Bernard Schwartz, *Super Chief: Earl Warren and His Supreme Court—A Judicial Biography* (New York: New York University Press, 1983), p. 721.

2. Ernest Gruening to LBJ, 10/2/68; memo, Charles S. Murphy to LBJ, 10/3/68; W. DeVier Pierson to LBJ, 10/3/68; and W. DeVier Pierson to LBJ, 10/5/68, Ex and Gen FG 535, LBJL. See also Schwartz, *Super Chief*, pp. 723–25, for negotiations by Johnson and Nixon with Earl Warren.

3. Schwartz, *Super Chief*, pp. 723–25.

4. Paul Porter, LBJ/OH, p. 37.

5. Fred Rodell to WOD, 8/16/68, William O. Douglas Papers, Box 367, LOC.

6. Paul Porter, LBJ/OH, p. 37; AI, Arthur "Tex" Goldschmidt, 6/10/84, Durham, N.Y.; William O. Douglas, *The Autobiography of William O. Douglas: The Court Years, 1939–1975* (New York: Random House, 1980), p. 359.

7. *NYT*, 10/4/68, p. 53.

8. AF to Adolf Berle, 10/16/68, Adolf Berle Papers, FDRL.

9. WOD to Fred Rodell, 10/7/68, Fred Rodell Papers, Haverford College.

10. Paul Porter to Troy V. Post, 10/15/68, and Porter to Palmer Hoyt, 10/9/68, Paul Porter Papers, LBJL.

11. WOD to Fred Rodell, 7/27/68, Rodell Papers, Haverford College.

12. Fred Rodell to WOD, 8/16/68, Douglas Papers, Box 367, LOC. The article is Rodell, "The Complexities of Mr. Justice Fortas," *New York Times Magazine*, 7/28/68, p. 12–68.

13. Rodell, "Complexities of Fortas," p. 63.

14. Extrapolation made from the annual Supreme Court review in "The Supreme Court, 1968 Term," *Harvard Law Review*, Vol. 83, 1969, p. 279.

15. Rodell, "Complexities of Fortas," p. 67. For more on this view of Fortas's jurisprudential philosophy, see Ronald Jay Heckert, "Justice Fortas and the First Amendment," unpublished Ph.D. dissertation, State University of New York at Albany, 1973, Chap. II.

16. *St. Amant* v. *Thompson*, 390 U.S. 727, at 734 (1968).

17. *Schmerber* v. *California*, 384 U.S. 757, at 779 (1966).

18. "A murder trial—indeed any criminal proceeding—is not a sporting event," Fortas wrote in *Giles* v. *Maryland*, 386 U.S. 66, at 102 (1967).

19. *Powell* v. *Texas*, 392 U.S. 514, 567 (1968).

20. *Warden* v. *Hayden*, 387 U.S. 294, at 312 (1966).

21. *United States* v. *Wade*, 388 U.S. 218, at 261 (1967).

22. *Ibid.*, at 262.

23. *Gilbert* v. *California*, 388 U.S. 263, at 291 (1967).

24. 387 U.S. 1, at 28 (1966).

25. *Bloom* v. *Illinois*, 391 U.S. 194, at 214–15 (1968).

26. *Ibid.*, 391 U.S. 194, at 214 (1968).

27. *Avery* v. *Midland County*, 390 U.S. 474 (1968); *Kirkpatrick* v. *Preisler*, 394 U.S. 526 (1968); *Wells* v. *Rockefeller*, 394 U.S. 542 (1969).

28. 390 U.S. 474, at 496–97 (1967).

29. 386 U.S. 372 (1967).

30. *Ibid.*, at 464.

31. *Ibid.*, at 478.

32. "Supreme Court, 1968 Term," *Harvard Law Review*, p. 279.

33. *Epperson* v. *Arkansas*, 393 U.S. 97 (1968).

34. Schwartz, *Super Chief*, pp. 754–55.

35. 393 U.S. 97, at 103 (1968).

36. *Ibid.*, at 114.

37. 393 U.S. 503, at 509 (1969).

38. *Ibid.*

39. "The Court's holding . . ." is from 393 U.S. 503, at 515; "School discipline . . ." is from the same case at 524–26.

40. *Ibid.*, at 513.

41. As for the claims by the state that the arrests came from the failure of the demonstrators to disperse upon command, Warren said simply that the convictions were clearly based on the nature of the demonstration itself, and not on the disobedience of the police. See 394 U.S. 111, at 111–13 (1969).

42. WOD, note for the file, "No. 60," undated, Douglas Papers, Box 1431, LOC. Thanks go to Professor John Muller of Luther College for initially pointing out the location of this document.

43. AF to WOD, 1/21/67, Douglas Papers, Box 1431, LOC.

44. WOD, note for the file, "No. 60," undated, Douglas Papers, Box 1431, LOC. A copy of the Black draft can be found in the *Gregory* v. *Chicago* folder, 1/15/69, AFP.

45. AF draft opinion, "February ——," *Gregory* v. *Chicago* folder, AFP.

46. 394 U.S. 111, at 125–26 (1969).

47. WOD to Earl Warren, 3/5/69, Douglas Papers, Box 1431, LOC.

48. WOD, note for the file, "No. 60," undated, Douglas Papers, Box 1431, LOC.

49. *Foster* v. *California*, 394 U.S. 440, at 442 (1969).

50. *Ibid.*, at 443.

51. *Ibid.*, at 448.

52. *Ibid.*, at 450 (emphasis added).

53. *Fortner Enterprises* v. *U.S. Steel*, 394 U.S. 495, at 524 (1969) (emphasis added).

54. *Snyder* v. *Harris*, 394 U.S. 332, at 346 (1969).

55. *Street* v. *New York*, 394 U.S. 576, at 616 (1968).

56. *Ibid.*, at 617.

57. *Gunn* v. *Committee to End the War*, AF draft opinion, 5/7/69, AFP.

58. AF draft opinion, *Brandenburg* case file, "April ——," AFP. For more on the "clear and present danger" test, see *Abrams* v. *United States*, 250 U.S. 616 (1919); *Schenck* v. *United States*, 249 U.S. 47 (1919); and *Debs* v. *United States*, 249 U.S. 211 (1919). The best articulation of this test can be found in the concurring opinion by Holmes and Brandeis in *Whitney* v. *California*, 274 U.S. 357 (1927). See also Richard Polenberg, *Fighting Faiths: The Abrams Case, the Supreme Court, and Free Speech* (New York: Viking Press, 1988).

59. See *Dennis* v. *United States*, 341 U.S. 494 (1951).

60. 395 U.S. 444, (1969).

61. Hugo Black to AF, 4/15/69, and AF to Black, 4/30/69, *Brandenburg* case file, AFP.

62. John Harlan to AF, 4/15/69, *Brandenburg* case file, AFP. The two cases were *Younger* v. *Harris* and *Samuels* v. *Mackell*.

63. The later drafts indicating Brennan's authorship can be found in the *Brandenburg* case folders in the Brennan, Douglas and Warren papers, all in the Library of Congress. Thanks go to Professor Scott Powe of the University of Texas Law School for initially suggesting this avenue of research, by

sharing with me his hunch that there might be a connection between Fortas's resignation and the unusually long *per curiam* opinion in this case.

64. Victor Navasky, "In Washington, You Just Don't Not Return a Call from Abe Fortas," *New York Times Magazine*, 8/1/71, p. 33.

65. Bob Woodward, "Fortas Tie to Wolfson Is Detailed," *Washington Post*, 1/23/77, p. A12. Fortas is speaking here to financier Louis Wolfson. Whether Fortas had any evidence of his own for this charge is not known. While this theory has a great deal of plausibility given the events that transpired in 1968, and such an arrangement has long been suspected by others since Nixon's appointment of South Carolinian Clement F. Haynsworth, Jr., to replace Fortas, no evidence could be found conclusively proving this connection. It may well have been one of those "deals" in Washington that did not need to be put into words, but was understood by all of the parties involved. (One of the speculative accounts can be found in Sidney Asch, *The Supreme Court and Its Great Justices* [New York: Arco Publishing Co., 1971], pp. 34, 236.)

Chapter XXIV
Death on the Supreme Court

1. John Kifner, "Chance Remark Led Reporter to Disclosures in Fortas Case," *NYT*, 6/17/69, p. 16. In writing this account I am indebted to reporter Robert Shogan for his excellent contemporaneous investigative reporting and his in-depth chronological work on the events surrounding this incident in his book *A Question of Judgment: The Fortas Case and the Struggle for the Supreme Court* (Indianapolis: Bobbs-Merrill Co., 1972), especially Chaps. 1, 7, 8. While much new evidence on this controversy has come to light since this account, and was discovered in the course of researching this book, placing all of this new evidence into the proper context would not have been as easy without access to this earlier work. Much of the evidence that Shogan uncovered at the time would have been lost.

This new account will not try to duplicate that earlier effort. Instead, I will seek to build on that base using the new evidence that has come to light since. As will be articulated in the text below, among the new information gleaned for this account, two key packets of evidence that everyone thought lost forever were the actual documents that the Justice Department used in investigating the Fortas case, and in its later negotiations with the Supreme Court. This latter packet was the long-fabled "file" on Fortas, which in the end was used to force his resignation from the court. It was said that Attorney General John Mitchell had locked the documents in his personal safe, and it was long assumed that they had been destroyed when the administration ended. (See Fred Graham and Max Frankel, two articles under the single title "Subpoenaed Fortas Data Locked Up by Mitchell," *NYT*, 5/18/69, pp. 1, 54, 56.) Even Fortas thought the material was lost forever, telling Louis Wolfson: "The whole thing has been sealed in the Department of Justice so that it will not get out. . . . Justice has got it all buttoned up." (Bob Woodward, "Fortas Tie to Wolfson Is Detailed," *Washington Post*, 1/23/77, pp. 1, 12 (hereinafter Woodward Transcript). (See also Shogan, *Question of Judgment*, pp. 248–54.)

I was fortunate enough to find those actual documents in the recently opened papers of Chief Justice Earl Warren, and am revealing them for the first time in this book. (In fact, as indicated in the notes, these documents were also used for detailing the early Fortas-Wolfson connection in Chap. VIII: "Dying on the Court.") While much of the speculation that appeared in the press at the time, and in the Shogan book, about the nature of these documents was accurate, there was one very important omission (due to the inability to examine one of the documents closely). Furthermore, it was impossible to know the nature of the full extent of the documents that were being used by the Justice Department, and the timing of their discovery. (For example, rumors floated around Washington, undoubtedly fueled by the vague nature of the Justice Department's claims as to the extent of the material, that the file also contained information about Fortas's alleged connection to the Communist party. This was not true, as the file concentrated solely on his relationship with Louis Wolfson.) Finally, without access to this information, it was impossible to understand the strategy used by the Justice Department during this controversy, and the role of the materials in executing this strategy. In short, I will divert from the less argumentative, reportorial approach of others in the past to make a very specific argument, based on this new information, about the Nixon administration's role in bringing about the resignation of Abe Fortas from the bench.

2. John Kifner, "Chance Remark Led Reporter to Disclosures in Fortas Case," *NYT*, 6/17/69, p. 16.

3. *Ibid.*

4. Author's Conversation with Ramsey Clark, 4/11/86, Hempstead, N.Y. See also Ramsey Clark, LBJ/OH, pp. 19–20. Clark could not recall the exact chronology or context of the conversation, just that it had been sometime during the 1968 Senate confirmation battle. Whatever the timing, this was long after the point when the Justice Department could have helped Wolfson. So it was not an effort by Fortas to influence the case, but only a personal conversation. Thus, it apparently breached no canon of judicial ethics.

5. Ramsey Clark, LBJ/OH, p. 19.

6. *Ibid.*, p. 20.

7. Author's conversation with Gloria McHugh, 7/15/83, Yale Law School, New Haven, Conn.

8. *Ibid.*

9. Transcript, "Justice Abe Fortas 'Hanging,'" 11/15/68, Yale Law School, Office of Alumni Relations, New Haven, Conn.

10. *Ibid.*

11. Author's conversation with Gloria McHugh, 7/15/83, confirmed by a librarian in the law school library, Yale Law School, New Haven, Conn.

12. However, had the attorney general been inclined to inquire, he would have discovered that the government's investigation of the Wolfson Foundation was not at a stage that would have told him any more than he had learned from Morgenthau by the time Clark formally left office. See Shogan, *Question of Judgment*, Chaps. 7, 8.

13. Shogan, *Question of Judgment*, p. 223.

14. James Wechsler, "Footnotes to the Fortas Case," copy in Hugo Black Papers, Box 159, LOC; Shogan, *Question of Judgment*, pp. 222–23.

15. Paul Porter, LBJ/OH, p. 33.

16. William Lambert, "Fortas of the Supreme Court: A Question of Ethics," *Life*, 5/9/69, p. 36.

17. A fine early piece on the complicity of the Nixon administration in the resignation of Abe Fortas, to which I am indebted in the early formulation of my own argument, is Sheldon Goldman, "The Fortas Resignation Reconsidered," unpublished. Professor Goldman ingeniously examines just the timing of the release of information to the newspapers to make his argument about the Nixon administration's lead role in this outcome.

18. Woodward Transcript, p. 12. I agree with this conclusion, as outlined below. Shogan also takes this tack, arguing that Wilson "was also said to be deeply resentful of Lyndon Johnson." (*Question of Judgment*, p. 226.)

19. Will Wilson, LBJ/OH, pp. 10–11.

20. *Ibid.*, pp. 21–22. Years later, after Johnson was out of office and Wilson's career had taken a turn for the better, he became a bit more forgiving. Wilson said that it might have been that the Kennedys were using Connally as a foil in the state of Texas to pose a rival power to Lyndon Johnson himself. (AI, Will Wilson, 11/2/82, Austin, Tex.)

21. Richard Kleindienst, *Justice: The Memoirs of an Attorney General* (Ottawa, Ill.: Jameson Books, 1985), p. 138.

22. *Ibid.*

23. AI, Will Wilson, 11/2/82, Austin, Tex.; *Washington Post*, 5/16/69, p. 1; Shogan, *Question of Judgment*, pp. 225–26. These sources all agree that Lambert had developed the story on his own to that point and was mainly informing Wilson of things he had not known about Fortas to that point.

24. AI, Will Wilson, 11/2/82, Austin, Tex.

25. Lambert, "Fortas of the Supreme Court," p. 33.

26. Woodward Transcript, p. 12.

27. *Ibid.* According to this account, Wolfson later claimed in the transcript that Milton Freeman, one of his lawyers from Arnold and Porter, and a former law partner of Fortas's, had called him, saying: "Listen, you understand you will get a letter—formal letter—but you can rest assured that your friend [Fortas] is going to help you any way he can with the former President."

28. Author's conversation with LBJL Archivist Claudia Anderson, 4/15/85, after the file was located in response to my request. Although Ms. Anderson had been on the archival staff at that time, neither she nor any others in the library who had been on the staff at that time could remember seeing this file or explain its history. Consequently, it is impossible to know precisely when the materials were refiled and removed, or by whom. Knowing this would help to reveal whether the materials were removed in response to a phone call from Fortas, at the behest of the president himself, or for some

other reason. One wonders, though, how history might have been changed if Fortas and Wolfson had been as successful in burying their own correspondence.

29. More than once, Wolfson and his family found it necessary in their letters to Johnson to re-introduce themselves. They often did so by recalling the time that the Johnson family servant, Zephyr Wright, had slipped on the ice and broken her leg in front of the Wolfsons. This provided the occasion for the two families to meet and converse. Then, on another occasion, when Wolfson sent the then vice president a telegram of support, the secretaries were asked to find out the identity of the sender. All that LBJ could remember at the time was that perhaps Wolfson had been connected to the city's rapid transit company at one time (which he had). See Louis Wolfson to Lady Bird Johnson, 1/26/65 and 10/6/65, White House Social File, Alpha File, Box 2117, LBJL; and Wolfson to Edwin Weisl, 7/23/64, WHCF, Wolfson Name File, LBJL. See also Wolfson to LBJ, 3/22/62, with attached instructions from LBJ for response, WHCF, Wolfson Name File, LBJL.

30. M. Clements Tomberlin to Richard Maguire, 10/4/65; Eugenia Sapp to Marvin Watson, 10/7/65; Marvin Watson to Louis Wolfson, 10/9/65; Mrs. Manfred Rechtschaffen to Linda Bird Johnson, 10/12/67; Mrs. Louis Wolfson to LBJ, 1/7/68; and Mrs. Louis Wolfson to Ramsey Clark, 2/1/68 (containing an affidavit from a cardiologist, Harold Rand, attesting to the severe damage to Wolfson's health caused by further actions against him), WHCF, Wolfson Name File, LBJL.

31. AF to Jack Valenti, 1/17/66 (plus attached note from Valenti to LBJ, dated 1/18/66, and excerpts of minutes of Board of Directors meeting of the Merritt-Chapman and Scott Corporation), 5/31/55, ExHU, Box 1, LBJL.

32. *Washington Post,* 5/16/69, p. 1.

33. *Ibid.,* and Shogan, *Question of Judgment,* pp. 114–25.

34. AI, Will Wilson, 11/2/82, Austin, Tex.

35. Kleindienst, *Justice,* p. 115.

36. This account is based on an interview with Will Wilson (11/2/82, Austin, Tex.). Shogan (*Question of Judgment,* pp. 226–37) has an early version of these negotiations, but Wilson's account years later is much richer in detail. Thus, we are now able to know more specifics about the Justice Department's negotiations with Wolfson's attorney, and the Nixon administration's motivations at this point. (See also *Los Angeles Times,* 5/15/69, p. 1.) After the interview, Wilson, who had not seen Shogan's book, kindly consented to read those portions of the book concerning his role in this matter, and he confirmed nearly all of that account. The corrections that he then offered are incorporated into this new account.

37. AI, Will Wilson, 11/2/82, Austin, Tex.

38. *Ibid.*; Paul Porter, LBJ/OH, p. 37; *Washington Star,* 11/12/70, p. 1; Shogan, *Question of Judgment,* pp. 213–14, 224–25. (It would be late the following year before the U.S. Court of Appeals ordered a retrial in the Merritt-Chapman case.)

39. For more on Morgenthau's career, see *NYT,* 6/17/85, p. B1, and 3/24/85, p. E6. See also Shogan, *Question of Judgment,* p. 205.

40. AI, Will Wilson, 11/2/82, Austin, Tex. This is the first time that the details of these conversations have been revealed in print. Combined with the documentary evidence discussed below, these actions show quite clearly the complicity of the Nixon administration's Justice Department in actively attempting to develop evidence against Fortas. Certainly, the development of that evidence against a sitting government official of any kind who is suspected of violating the law is justifiable and a part of the department's role. However, as will be discussed below, it is the later use of that evidence that is open to question. The subsequent actions show that other motivations were at work in the Justice Department at that time.

The timing of these conversations—before the *Life* magazine piece was published—differs from Shogan's account. He states that the conversations with Bittman were not launched until after the publication of the piece. (Shogan, *Question of Judgment,* p. 228.) Since both of our accounts rely on some of the same sources, the discrepancy can be easily explained. At the time of the publication of Shogan's book, in 1971, the Nixon administration was still in power. Certainly those officials would not have wanted to make it appear that this was a partisan attack, which of course it was, by acknowledging they had made any kind of a deal with Wolfson in return for his help on Fortas. In fact, press accounts at that time quoted administration officials who went to great pains to deny any connection or partisan motivations here. Some of those accounts denied that the negotiations had even occurred. But the negotiations, with their concomitant partisan motivations, did occur.

One correction was made in Wilson's account. On two occasions he expressed to the author his belief that the Justice Department had spoken to Wolfson *before* the publication of the *Life* article. This would have given the Justice Department even more evidence against Fortas at an earlier time.

However, subsequently discovered evidence confirms the earlier reports that the conversation between Wolfson and the Justice Department occurred after the publication of the article. (AI, Will Wilson, 11/2/82 and 11/4/82 [by phone], Austin, Tex., cf. footnotes 68, 82 *infra*.)

41. Wolfson was released on 1/26/70.

42. AI, Will Wilson, 11/2/82, Austin, Tex. See also Shogan, *Question of Judgment*, p. 253.

43. Stanley Penn, "Industrialist, Facing a Year in Jail Friday, Turns Cold Shoulder Toward Wall Street," *Wall Street Journal*, 4/22/69, p. 40.

44. Shogan, *Question of Judgment*, p. 228. Shogan correctly points out that this position is inconsistent with Wolfson's efforts, almost simultaneous with this article, to mobilize congressional support for himself to influence Richard Nixon, using people such as Florida's Spessard Holland.

45. Shogan, *Question of Judgment*, p. 227.

46. No evidence was offered at the time that the Nixon administration was connected to the *Life* piece, though. See, e.g., *NYT*, 5/18/69, p. 54.

47. AI, Will Wilson, 11/2/82, Austin, Tex.

48. Shogan, *Question of Judgment*, pp. 7, 25.

49. Lambert, "Fortas of the Supreme Court," pp. 32–37, especially p. 32.

50. *Ibid.*, p. 36.

51. A copy of Fortas's statement, issued on 5/4/69, can be found in Shogan, *Question of Judgment*, pp. 277–78. Perhaps the words *advance payment* or *stipend* might have been a more apt description. A lawyer might call the payment a "consideration," fulfilling the legal requirements of a contract. Whatever one calls it, though, money changed hands.

52. *Ibid.*; see also Fred Graham, "*Life* Says Fortas Received and Repaid a Wolfson Fee," *NYT*, 5/5/69, pp. 1, 22.

53. *Ibid.*

54. The Fortas statement is from Woodward Transcripts, p. 12. The account of the Justice Department probe is in *NYT*, 5/7/69, p. 1.

55. *NYT*, 5/6/69, p. 46.

56. *Washington Star*, 5/7/69.

57. *Los Angeles Times*, as quoted in *NYT*, 5/6/69, p. 27.

58. *NYT*, 5/6/69, p. 27.

59. Samuel Shaffer, *On and Off the Floor: Thirty Years as a Correspondent on Capitol Hill* (New York: Newsweek Books, 1980), p. 93.

60. Author's conversation with Hugh Jones, 7/23/68, Shippensburg, Pa.

61. Shogan, *Question of Judgment*, p. 262.

62. Malvern B. Fink to J. Garcia and Gordon Chapman, 5/6/69, attached to series of documents headed by memo from attorney general to chief justice, but listed as being "delivered to the Chief Justice May 12, 1969—6:00 P.M. by Mr. Sol Lindenbaum of the Attorney General's office," and labeled "The Chief Justice, Supreme Court, Personal and Confidential: For Eyes Only of the Chief Justice," Earl Warren Papers, Box 353, LOC (hereinafter Chief Justice Eyes Only Packet). This is one of the packets of material presumed lost that were discovered in the course of this research and are discussed in n.1, above.

Later it was reported, no doubt as a result of government accounts seeking to prove the reluctant nonpartisan nature of the investigation, that the Justice Department had launched this subpoena only *after* its May 8 conversation with Louis Wolfson. This account made it appear as though the words of the financier himself had inexorably led the investigators to the new evidence. (See *Los Angeles Times*, 5/15/69, p. 1.) Even the account of the Wolfson meeting itself was wrong. The conversation with the federal agents actually took place two days later, on Saturday, May 10. In fact, though, the newly discovered evidence makes it clear that from the first day after the release of the Lambert article, the government had successfully compelled the production of the documents necessary to prove the relationship between Fortas and Wolfson—and then some.

63. *NYT*, 5/7/69, p. 25; *Washington Post*, 5/16/69, p. 1.

64. AI, Will Wilson, 11/2/82, Austin, Tex. To the best of the author's knowledge, this is the first time this phone call has been revealed in print. Previously, it was thought that the events that followed came as a result of a meeting between Mitchell and Richard Nixon. It was believed that they concocted the master plan to put pressure on the court and the chief justice, and thus on Fortas, by having Mitchell make his visit to Earl Warren. (Shogan, *Question of Judgment*, pp. 252–53; *Newsweek*, 5/19/69, p. 29.) While this meeting undoubtedly took place, and such a discussion is probable, in fact the triggering event was the phone call from Fortas himself, and the master strategy

was already set in the Justice Department before any meeting took place between Mitchell and Nixon.

65. For more on this, see Chap. VII, "The Ambush," as well as Bruce Allen Murphy, *The Brandeis-Frankfurter Connection: The Secret Political Activities of Two Supreme Court Justices* (New York: Oxford University Press, 1982), appendix, and Bernard Schwartz, *Super Chief: Earl Warren and His Supreme Court—A Judicial Biography* (New York: New York University Press, 1983), pp. 493–96. See also an untitled biographical article on Earl Warren by Martin Agronsky, Warren Papers, Box 6, LOC.

66. Benno Schmidt, COHC, pp. 216–17.

67. Packet of papers headed by note reading, "Papers delivered to the Chief Justice by Attorney General Mitchell—May 7, 1969—11:30 A.M.," Warren Papers, Box 353, LOC. Richard Kleindienst describes the process that the Justice Department went through in delivering the documents in his book *Justice*, p. 115.

68. *NYT*, 5/18/69, p. 54.

69. Woodward Transcript, p. 12.

70. Earl Warren to John Mitchell, 5/14/69, Warren Papers, Box 353, LOC.

71. See "Excerpts from Minutes of Special Meeting of Board of Trustees of the Wolfson Family Foundation, Inc.," 12/28/65; Louis Wolfson to AF, 1/3/66; AF to Wolfson Family Foundation, 1/10/66; Wolfson Family Foundation, Inc., to AF, 2/1/66; excerpt from the minutes of a board meeting of the Wolfson Family Foundation, 6/15/66; and AF to Wolfson Family Foundation, 12/15/66, composing the packet of papers headed by note reading, "Papers delivered to the Chief Justice by Attorney General Mitchell—May 7, 1969—11:30 A.M.," Warren Papers, Box 353, LOC (hereinafter Mitchell's Fortas File).

72. See Shogan, *Question of Judgment*, p. 246, for the account of Mitchell's reaction to the packet of papers.

73. Letter, Wolfson Family Foundation, Inc., to AF, 2/1/66, Mitchell's Fortas File.

74. *Newsweek*, 5/19/69, p. 29.

75. Louis Wolfson to AF, 1/11/67, White House Social File, Alpha File, Box 2117, LBJL.

76. Don Oberdorfer, "The Gathering of the Storm That Burst upon Abe Fortas," *Washington Post*, 5/16/69, pp. 1, 10. See also John MacKenzie, "Speech by Fortas Skirts Furor over Wolfson Fee," *Washington Post*, 5/16/69.

77. This account relies on the memoirs of Elizabeth Black, in her 5/7–5/15/69 diary entries. See Hugo L. Black and Elizabeth Black, *Mr. Justice and Mrs. Black: The Memoirs of Hugo L. Black and Elizabeth Black* (New York: Random House, 1986), pp. 298–301.

78. Don Oberdorfer, "The Gathering of the Storm That Burst upon Abe Fortas," *Washington Post*, 5/16/69, pp. 1, 10.

79. Shaffer, *On and Off the Floor*, p. 93.

80. Don Oberdorfer, "The Gathering of the Storm That Burst upon Abe Fortas," *Washington Post*, 5/16/69, pp. 1, 10.

81. Judge Walter Mansfield to AF, 5/13/69, and Judge Inzer B. Wyatt to AF, 5/13/69, Warren Papers, Box 353, LOC.

82. AI, Will Wilson, 11/2/82, Austin, Tex., confirmed by date of 5/10/69 on sworn affidavit of Louis Wolfson, given to FBI agents Charles Bolz and Carter G. Billings at Eglin Air Force Base, Fla., part of the Chief Justice Eyes Only Packet, LOC (hereinafter Wolfson Affidavit.)

The precise date of this encounter is a matter of contention. All of the newspapers at the time reported that the conversation with Wolfson had occurred on Thursday, May 8. (See, e.g., Don Oberdorfer, "The Gathering of the Storm That Burst upon Abe Fortas," *Washington Post*, 5/16/69, pp. 1, 10.; *NYT*, 5/18/69, p. 54; and *Los Angeles Times*, 5/15/69, p. 1.) Shogan may well have relied on these accounts in writing that the encounter had taken place on Thursday, listing it in a typographical error as May 9, a mistake that is corrected on the following page. (See Shogan, *Question of Judgment*, pp. 253–54.)

Besides the fact that the newly discovered Wolfson Affidavit is dated May 10, Will Wilson has a very clear recollection that the conversation took place while the rest of the president's team, and Nixon himself, were at the Florida White House in Key Biscayne. That occurred during the weekend, beginning May 9.

83. Shogan, *Question of Judgment*, pp. 253–54.

84. *NYT*, 5/18/69, p. 54.

85. This quote and the account that follows are from the Wolfson Affidavit, LOC.

86. "Minutes of Special Meeting of Board of Trustees," 6/15/66, Chief Justice Eyes Only Packet, LOC.

87. Louis Wolfson to AF, 1/11/67, White House Social Files, Alpha File, Box 2117, LBJL.

88. Woodward Transcript, p. 12.

89. Wolfson Affidavit, LOC.

90. AI, Will Wilson, 11/2/82, Austin, Tex.

91. The summary of material is based on an examination of the Chief Justice Eyes Only Packet, which consists of the Wolfson Affidavit (Malvern B. Fink to J. Garcia and Gordon Chapman, 5/6/69); "Minutes of Special Meeting of Board of Trustees [of the Wolfson Family Foundation]," 12/28/65; Louis Wolfson to AF, 1/3/66; AF to Wolfson Family Foundation, Inc., 1/10/66; Louis Wolfson to AF, 2/1/66 (the actual contract letter in full, which is marked "cancelled"); "Minutes of Special Meeting of Board of Trustees [of the Wolfson Family Foundation]," 6/15/66; and AF to Wolfson Family Foundation, Inc., 12/15/66.

Shogan says that more letters were taken by subpoena from Wolfson's files. That seems unlikely now, for Mitchell certainly would have sent them on to Earl Warren at this time. (See Shogan, Question of Judgment, p. 253.)

92. Shogan, Question of Judgment, pp. 251–52.

93. "Justice Abe Fortas on the Spot," Newsweek, 5/19/69, pp. 29–30. While the article did not appear until May 19, word about Shaffer's report was leaked out prior to the publication of the article (thus allowing the Justice Department to respond). See Washington Post, 5/16/69, p. 10, and Shogan, Question of Judgment, p. 252.

94. Mrs. McHale to Chief Justice Warren, 5/12/69, Warren Papers, Box 353, LOC; Washington Star, 5/12/69, p. 1; Washington Post, 5/13/69, p. 1.

95. NYT, 5/18/69, p. 54.

96. Washington Post, 5/17/69, p. 1.

97. Paul Porter, LBJ/OH, p. 37.

98. Washington Post, 5/16/69, pp. 1, 9, 10.

99. Schwartz, Super Chief, p. 761.

100. William O. Douglas, The Autobiography of William O. Douglas: The Court Years, 1939—1975 (New York: Random House, 1980), p. 359.

101. Ibid., p. 358.

102. Washington Post, 5/16/69, p. A9, reprinted in U.S. News and World Report, 5/26/69, p. 33.

103. Douglas, The Court Years, p. 358.

104. This Douglas account is repeated in a number of places: Washington Post, 5/16/69, pp. 1, 10; Shogan, Question of Judgment, p. 256; Schwartz, Super Chief, p. 761; and James Simon, Independent Journey: The Life of William O. Douglas (New York: Harper and Row, 1980), p. 396. My account is from an interview with Fortas, 8/7/81, Washington, D.C.

105. AI, AF, 8/7/81, Washington, D.C. For more on Douglas's troubles with the Parvin Foundation, see Simon, Independent Journey, pp. 392–99, and Philip J. Cooper, "Justice Douglas and Administrative Law," unpublished Ph.D. dissertation, Syracuse University, 1978.

106. AI, AF, 8/7/81, Washington, D.C. Not only is Fortas's account more believable, given the relative states of the health of the two sources, but the dates of events at the time seem to support his account. Douglas agrees that Fortas announced his intention to resign in the Supreme Court conference on May 13. So sitting up two nights with Fortas would have placed him in Washington on May 11. However, by other accounts in the press, Douglas was in Brazil at the time giving his lectures. (See NYT, 5/6/69, p. 27, and Washington Post, 5/6/69, p. 1.) Also, had Douglas been in town earlier, it seems likely that Warren would have called an earlier meeting of the Supreme Court conference.

107. Bernard Schwartz argues that had Fortas stayed on, it seems likely that Warren would have been compelled by his own sense of ethics to force a resignation by his colleague. (See Schwartz, Super Chief, pp. 761–62.)

108. Fortas's resignation letter to Chief Justice Earl Warren, dated 5/14/69, is reprinted in Shogan, Question of Judgment, pp. 279–82 (hereinafter Fortas Resignation Letter).

109. Washington Post, 5/16/69, p. 1.

110. Fortas Resignation Letter.

111. Located in Warren Papers, Box 353, LOC.

112. Los Angeles Times, 5/15/69, p. 1.

113. Wolfson Affidavit.

114. *Ibid.*, supported by Woodward Transcript, p. 12.

115. Earl Warren to Richard M. Nixon, 5/16/69, Warren Papers, Box 353, LOC. The chronology of events can be found in *Washington Post*, 5/16/69, pp. 1, 10.

116. *Newsweek*, 5/26/69, p. 33; *Washington Post*, 5/16/69, p. A9.

117. *Washington Post*, 5/16/69, p. 1.

118. The statement as revised is dated 5/14/69, and is in the Warren Papers, Box 353, LOC.

119. "Statement by Chief Justice Warren," 5/15/69, Warren Papers, Box 353, LOC.

120. AF to Nina Warren, 6/11/69 and 6/19/69, Warren Papers, Box 353, LOC; AF to Adolf Berle, 10/16/68, Adolf Berle Papers, Box 221, FDRL.

121. Shogan, *Question of Judgment*, p. 260.

122. Author's conversation with Dagmar Hamilton, 10/14/83, Austin, Tex.

123. AI, Wilbur Cohen, 10/22/82, Austin, Tex.

124. Nina Totenberg, "Abe Fortas in Private Life: Pessimistic," *National Observer*, 11/2/70, p. 14.

125. Ramsey Clark, LBJ/OH, p. 20.

126. AI, Donald Thomas, 11/16/82, Austin, Tex.

Chapter XXV
The Last Days of Abe Fortas

1. AI, Will Wilson, 11/2/82, Austin, Tex.

2. *Ibid.* For more on the Douglas impeachment effort, see James Simon, *Independent Journey: The Life of William O. Douglas* (New York: Harper and Row, 1980), pp. 391–412.

3. Fred Graham, "Abe Fortas," in Leon Friedman and Fred Israel, eds., *The Justices of the United States Supreme Court, 1789–1978: Their Lives and Major Opinions* (New York: Chelsea House, 1980), Vol. V, p. 3027; commentary by Professor Bernard E. Jacob, 4/10/86, Lyndon Baines Johnson Conference, Hofstra University, Hempstead, N.Y.

4. In fact, the two events were coincidental. This study had begun five years before to update the old Canons of Ethics. See John P. MacKenzie, *The Appearance of Justice* (New York: Charles Scribner's Sons, 1974), p. 166.

5. For more, see *ibid.*; Richard Harris, *Decision* (New York: E. P. Dutton and Co., 1971); and John L. Massaro, "Advice and Dissent: Factors in the Senate's Refusal to Confirm Supreme Court Nominees, with Special Emphasis on the Cases of Abe Fortas, Clement F. Haynsworth, Jr., and G. Harrold Carswell," unpublished Ph.D. dissertation, Southern Illinois University, 1975.

6. Karlyn Barker, "Haynsworth: Rebuilding a Reputation," *Washington Post*, 4/9/79, p. 1. This piece denies that Haynsworth was the choice of Thurmond for the seat, but the senator certainly did not disapprove of his conservative philosophy on the bench.

7. Henry J. Abraham, *Justices and Presidents: A Political History of Appointments to the Supreme Court* (New York: Oxford University Press, 1985), pp. 16–17.

8. AI, Will Wilson, 11/2/82, Austin, Tex.; Richard Kleindienst, *Justice: The Memoirs of an Attorney General* (Ottawa Ill.: Jameson Books, 1985), pp. 139–40.

9. Warren Weaver, "Fortas Suggests a Bill to Give Immunity to Nixon If He Resigns," *NYT*, 1/13/74, p. 55. See also Fortas's "Mr. Nixon and the Constitution," *NYT*, 7/28/74, p. 17.

10. Abe Fortas, "The Constitution and the Presidency," *Washington Law Review*, Vol. 49, 1974, pp. 1010–11.

11. *NYT*, 7/28/74, p. 17.

12. Tamar Lewin, "Fortas Lies Low," *National Law Journal*, 12/3/79, p. 27. See the shorter version of this piece at Tamar Lewin, "Abe Fortas Today: A 'Lawyer's Lawyer,'" *Washington Post*, 12/16/79, p. B5.

13. Paul Porter, LBJ/OH, p. 41.

14. WOD to Fred Rodell, 9/15/69, Fred Rodell Papers, Haverford College.

15. For more on this, see Lewin, "Fortas Lies Low," p. 27; Victor Navasky, "In Washington, You Just Don't Not Return a Call from Abe Fortas," *New York Times Magazine*, 8/1/71, p. 7ff.; and Nina Totenberg, "Abe Fortas: Pessimistic," *National Observer*, 11/2/70, p. 14; also confidential source, 11/8/82, Austin, Tex.

16. Joseph C. Goulden, *The Superlawyers: The Small and Powerful World of the Great Washington Law Firms* (New York: Weybright and Talley, 1971), p. 112.

17. Lewin, "Fortas Lies Low," p. 27; *Newsweek*, 10/14/74, p. 10.

18. Author's conversation with Bernard E. Jacob, 4/10/86, Hempstead, N.Y.

19. WOD to Fred Rodell, 9/15/69, Rodell Papers, Haverford College. Robert Pack reports that Edward Bennett Williams had wanted to add Fortas to his law firm, but, upon hearing the objections of the younger lawyers in his firm, chose not to finalize the deal. See Robert Pack, *Edward Bennett Williams for the Defense* (New York: Harper and Row, 1983), p. 360.

20. "Fortas Plans New Law Firm," *Washington Post*, 4/12/70, p. 3.

21. *Ibid.*, and Lewin, "Fortas Lies Low," pp. 1, 27.

22. Lewin, "Fortas Lies Low," pp. 1, 27.

23. Confidential source, 11/8/82, Austin, Tex.

24. *Newsweek*, 10/14/74, p. 10.

25. L. M. Roth, "Remembering 1965: Abe Fortas and the Supreme Court," *Mercer Law Review*, Vol. 28, Summer 1976, pp. 961–76.

26. Maxine Cheshire, "Book about Fortas," *Washington Post*, 2/8/72, p. B3.

27. My thanks to Steve Lesher for sharing this story with me. The *Update* piece, titled "An Opinion from Abe Fortas," can be found in *Newsweek*, 10/14/74, p. 10.

28. Abe Fortas, "The Patent System in Distress," *Idea*, 1971, pp. 571–79; Abe Fortas, "The Frontier Between the Antitrust Law and the Securities Markets," *Illinois Bar Journal*, September 1972, pp. 24–31; Abe Fortas, "Criminal Justice 'Without Pity,'" *Trial Lawyers Quarterly*, Summer 1973, pp. 9–14; Abe Fortas, "The U.S. Investment Environment: The Legislative and Regulatory Framework," *Conference Board Record*, August 1974, pp. 27–30; Abe Fortas, "Strengthening Government to Cope with the Future," *New Republic*, 11/9/74, pp. 34–35; Abe Fortas, "The Case Against Capital Punishment," *New York Times Magazine*, 1/28/77, pp. 9–29; Abe Fortas, "The Press's Integrity Is on the Line, Too," *Center Magazine*, March/April 1979, p. 44.

29. *NYT*, 1/25/73, p. 39.

30. For more on the nature of these charges, see Navasky, "You Just Don't Not Return a Call," p. 32.

31. Transcription of a tape of the Durr eulogy, Washington, D.C., 6/12/75, LBJL. For more on Porter's death, see his obituary at *NYT*, 11/27/75, p. 36.

32. Tape of Durr eulogy, Washington, D.C., 6/12/75, LBJL. The speaker was unidentified except as a judge on the Fifth Circuit Court of Appeals. The actual biblical passage, located at Matthew 6:19–21, is different from the paraphrased version used in this speech.

33. Bob Woodward, "Fortas Tie to Wolfson Is Detailed," *Washington Post*, 1/23/77, pp. 1, 12.

34. *Newsweek* was not unusual in this regard. More and more, the tenor of the daily newspaper press coverage was to portray Nixon as a "senior statesman" being consulted by the Reagan administration.

35. To the best of the author's knowledge, this idea was first put forward by Professor Sheldon Goldman. This was done not only in an unpublished piece, "The Fortas Resignation Reconsidered," but also Sheldon Goldman and Thomas Jahnige, *The Federal Courts as a Political System* (New York: Harper and Row, 1976), pp. 12–14.

36. See, e.g., Lewin, "Fortas Lies Low," pp. 1, 27.

37. *Ibid.*

38. *Washington Post*, 7/15/81, p. 5. The appearance was before the Commission on Wartime Relocation and Internment of Civilians.

39. Transcript of PBS TV program, *The Lawmakers*, 9/10/81, p. 3.

40. *Washington Post*, 1/24/82, p. H5.

41. David Shribman, "High Court Alumni: Hard at Work," *NYT*, 3/22/82, p. 6.

42. The comment on McClellan is from AI, AF, 8/7/81, Washington, D.C.

43. "Fortas Files 1st Case in High Court," *Washington Post*, 9/19/70, p. A6.

44. Nina Totenberg, "Abe Fortas in Private Life: Pessimistic," *National Observer*, 11/2/70, p. 14.

45. *NYT*, 3/14/82, p. 33. The case was *Rodriguez et al.* v. *Popular Democratic Party et al.*, 457 U.S. 1 (1982). Argued on 3/22/82, it was decided by the court on 6/7/82.

46. The account below relies on Jim Mann, "The Court Hears One of Its Own," *American Lawyer*, June 1982, p. 46.

47. *Ibid.* See also "Abe Fortas Returns to Court After Dozen Years' Absence," *Washington Post*, 3/23/82, p. A5.

48. *Ibid.*, p. 46.

49. *Ibid.*

50. *Ibid.*

51. The case was decided on June 7, 1982, with the court taking Fortas's view that the Puerto Rico law

that vested in the political party the initial authority to appoint an interim replacement for a vacated seat in the island's House of Representatives, or Senate, did not violate the U.S. Constitution.

52. *NYT*, 4/7/82, p. 1, 15, 22; *National Law Journal*, 4/19/82, p. 10.

53. *Washington Post*, 4/7/82, p. 24; Anthony Lewis, "Courage in Hard Times," *NYT*, 4/22/82, p. 31.

54. Arthur Goldberg, "Dedication: A Tribute to Justice Abe Fortas," *Hastings Constitutional Law Quarterly*, Spring 1982, pp. 459–61.

55. William J. Brennan, Jr., "Abe Fortas," *Yale Law Journal*, Vol. 91, No. 6, May 1982, pp. 1049–51.

EPILOGUE
A POLITICAL AUTOPSY OF ABE FORTAS

1. This is probably the most popular theory about the fall of Abe Fortas. See, e.g., Andrew Kopkind, "Fortas and the Power Game," *New Statesman*, 6/6/69, pp. 339–40.

2. Joseph Kraft, "Importance of Fortas Case Bears on New Appointees," *Washington Post*, 5/8/69; Joseph Kraft, "The Reason Why," *Washington Post*, 5/18/69; Geoffrey Cowan, book review of Joseph Goulden's *The Superlawyers* and Robert Shogan's *Question of Judgment*, *NYT*, 5/28/72, VII, p. 1. See also Marquis Childs, "Fortas's Acts Flout Tradition, Could Harm Court's Reputation," *Washington Post*, 5/12/69.

3. Mary McGrory, "The Fortas Affair," *Washington Star*, 7/21/68; with which Marquis Childs agrees, in "Fortas Case Carries a Lesson for All Presidents to Come," *Washington Post*, 5/19/69. David Broder, "Fortas Case Demonstrated a Corrupt Strain in Liberalism," *Washington Post*, 5/20/69, p. 21; Robert Shogan, *A Question of Judgment: The Fortas Case and the Struggle for the Supreme Court* (Indianapolis: Bobbs-Merrill Co., 1972), pp. 262–75.

4. Victor Navasky, "In Washington, You Just Don't Not Return a Call from Abe Fortas," *New York Times Magazine*, 8/1/71, p. 32.

5. The elements of this theory first came to me after reading a David Broder column detailing the generational shifts of political figures in Congress. The piece was titled "Power Shift to a New Generation on the Hill, *Washington Post*, 1/9/85, p. A21."

6. This theory was first advanced by Woodrow Wilson in his *Congressional Government* (Boston: Houghton Mifflin, 1885).

7. Robert Kaiser, "Nominee's Downfall Reflects Conflicts in American Culture," *Washington Post*, 11/8/87, p. 19.

SELECTED BIBLIOGRAPHY

MANUSCRIPT COLLECTIONS AND ORAL HISTORIES

Columbia University, New York, Butler Library. Manuscripts Division. Columbia Oral History Collection. Thurman Arnold Memoirs (Lawrence Fly project); Simon Bessie Memoirs; Samuel Bledsoe Memoirs; Clifford Durr Memoirs; Thomas Emerson Memoirs; Abe Fortas Memoirs (Lawrence Fly project); Jerome Frank Memoirs; Walter Gellhorn Memoirs; Gardner Jackson Memoirs; Paul Porter Memoirs (Lawrence Fly project); Benno Schmidt Memoirs; Howard Tolley Memoirs; Willard Van Dyke Memoirs.

Everett Dirksen Library, Pekin, Ill. Everett Dirksen Senatorial Papers.

Harvard University, Cambridge, Mass. Houghton Library, Henry Wallace Unpublished Diary and Papers (on microfilm.)

————. Law School Library. Manuscripts Division. Felix Frankfurter Court Papers.

————. Law School Library. Manuscripts Division. James Landis Papers.

Haverford College, Haverford, Pa. Manuscripts Division. Fred Rodell Papers.

Lyndon Baines Johnson Presidential Library, Austin, Tex. Manuscripts Division. Warren Christopher Papers.

————. Ramsey Clark Papers.

————. Files Pertaining to Abe Fortas and Homer Thornberry.

————. Lyndon Baines Johnson Oral History Collection. George Ball Memoirs; Joseph Barr Memoirs; Lucius D. Battle Memoirs; Kenneth M. Birkhead Memoirs; George R. Brown Memoirs; Zbigniew Brzezinski Memoirs; Raymond E. Buck Memoirs; William P. Bundy Memoirs; Cecil E. Burney Memoirs; Joseph A. Califano Memoirs; Jerome P. Cavanagh Memoirs; Oscar L. Chapman Memoirs; George E. Christian Memoirs; Warren M. Christopher Memoirs; Ramsey Clark Memoirs; Tom C. Clark Memoirs; Clark Clifford Memoirs; John Crooker, Sr., Memoirs; Lloyd N. Cutler Memoirs; William H. Darden Memoirs; Charles C. Diggs, Jr., Memoirs; Everett Dirksen Memoirs; Helen Gahagan Douglas Memoirs; Clifford and Virginia Durr Memoirs; Virginia Durr Memoirs; James O. Eastland Memoirs; Allen J. Ellender Memoirs; Courtney A. Evans Memoirs; Adrian S. Fisher Memoirs; Abe Fortas Memoirs; James C. Gaither Memoirs; W. Sim Gideon Memoirs; Irving Goldberg Memoirs; Arthur and Elizabeth Goldschmidt Memoirs; Elizabeth Wickenden Goldschmidt Memoirs; E. Ernest Goldstein Memoirs; Robert P. Griffin Memoirs; Ernest Gruening Memoirs; Robert Hardesty Memoirs;

Theodore Hesburgh Memoirs; Luther H. Hodges, Sr., Memoirs; Welly K. Hopkins Memoirs; Jake Jacobsen Memoirs; Sam Houston Johnson Memoirs; Luther E. Jones, Jr., Memoirs; William H. Jordan, Jr., Memoirs; William J. Jorden Memoirs; Nicholas deB. Katzenbach Memoirs; Fred Korth Memoirs; Gene Latimer Memoirs; William Lewis Memoirs; Gale McGee Memoirs; Harry McPherson Memoirs; Warren Magnuson Memoirs; Mike Manatos Memoirs; Thomas Mann Memoirs; Stanley Marcus Memoirs; Sherwin J. Markman Memoirs; Leonard Marks Memoirs; Thurgood Marshall Memoirs; John Bartlow Martin Memoirs; A. S. "Mike" Monroney Memoirs; Booth Mooney Memoirs; Powell Moore Memoirs; Thruston Morton Memoirs; Frank E. Moss Memoirs; Dorothy J. Nichols Memoirs; Matthew Nimetz Memoirs; Covey T. Oliver Memoirs; Frank "Posh" Oltorf Memoirs; Eugene C. Patterson Memoirs; Claiborne Pell Memoirs; Paul A. Porter Memoirs; Ben H. Powell, Jr., Memoirs; Mary Rather Memoirs; Joseph L. Rauh, Jr., Memoirs; George Reedy Memoirs; John P. Roche Memoirs; Mitchell Rogovin Memoirs; Eugene V. Rostow Memoirs; Walt W. Rostow Memoirs; Elizabeth Rowe Memoirs; James H. Rowe, Jr., Memoirs; Harold Barefoot Sanders Memoirs; Gerald Siegel Memoirs; Margaret Chase Smith Memoirs; Roger L. Stevens Memoirs; Robert S. Strauss Memoirs; Herman E. Talmadge Memoirs; Hobart Taylor, Jr., Memoirs; Willie Day Taylor Memoirs; Larry Temple Memoirs; Homer Thornberry Memoirs; Strom Thurmond Memoirs; Jack Valenti Memoirs; Cyrus R. Vance Memoirs; Fred M. Vinson, Jr., Memoirs; Robert E. Waldron Memoirs; Earl Warren Memoirs; Edwin L. Weisl, Jr., Memoirs; Edwin L. Weisl, Sr., Memoirs; Lee C. White Memoirs; Roy Wilkins Memoirs; A. M. "Monk" Willis Memoirs; Will Wilson Memoirs.

————. Lyndon Baines Johnson Prepresidential Papers

————. Lyndon Baines Johnson Presidential Papers

————. John Macy Office Files

————. Paul Porter Papers

————. Harold Barefoot Sanders Papers

————. Mildred Stegall Office Files

————. Larry Temple Papers

John F. Kennedy Presidential Library, Boston. Manuscripts Division. John F. Kennedy Oral History Collection. Bernard Boutin Memoirs, Fowler Hamilton Memoirs, John Macy Memoirs, Clarence Mitchell Memoirs, Francis Sayre Memoirs, Hobart Taylor Memoirs, George Weaver Memoirs, Roy Wilkins Memoirs, Harris Wofford Memoirs.

————. John F. Kennedy Presidential Papers.

————. Robert F. Kennedy Oral History Collection. Robert F. Kennedy Memoirs.

————. Harris Wofford Papers.

Library of Congress, Washington, D.C. Manuscripts Division. Hugo Black Papers.

————. William Brennan Papers.

————. Emanuel Celler Papers.

————. Benjamin V. Cohen Papers.

————. Thomas Corcoran Papers.

————. William O. Douglas Papers.

————. Felix Frankfurter Papers.

————. Fred Graham Papers.

————. Learned Hand Papers.

————. Harold Ickes Unpublished Diary and Papers.

————. Earl Warren Papers.

National Archives, Washington, D.C. Agricultural Adjustment Administration Official Papers, Record Group 145.

————. Office Files of Undersecretary Abe Fortas, 1942–46, Record Group, 48.

Franklin D. Roosevelt Library, Hyde Park, N.Y. Manuscripts Division. Adolf Berle Papers.

————. Francis Biddle Papers.

————. Oscar Cox Papers.

————. Wayne Coy Papers.

————. Gardner Jackson Papers.

————. Isadore Lubin Papers.

————. Franklin D. Roosevelt Presidential Papers.

————. Charles Taussig Papers.

————. Rexford Tugwell Unpublished Diary and Papers.

University of Georgia, Athens, Ga. Richard B. Russell Memorial Library. Manuscripts Division. Richard B. Russell, Jr., Oral History Collection. Lawton Calhoun Memoirs, Alexander Lawrence Memoirs, Herman Talmadge Memoirs.

————. Richard B. Russell, Jr., Senatorial Papers

University of Michigan, Ann Arbor, Mich. Michigan Historical Collections. Philip Aloysius Hart Senatorial Papers.

University of Texas, Austin, Tex. Law School. Manuscripts Division. Tom Clark Papers.

————. Walton Hamilton Papers.

Yale University, New Haven, Conn. Sterling Library. Manuscripts Division. James R. Angell Yale University Presidential Papers.

————. Chester Bowles Papers.

————. *Brown* v. *Board of Education* Papers.

————. Charles E. Clark Papers.

————. John Collier Papers.

————. Abe Fortas Court Papers.

————. Jerome Frank Papers.

————. Max Lerner Papers.

————. Charles Seymour Yale University Presidential Papers.

————. Henry L. Stimson Papers.

————. Yale University School of Law Papers.

SELECTED BOOKS, DISSERTATIONS, AND MASTER'S THESES

Abraham, Henry J. *Justices and Presidents: A Political History of Appointments to the Supreme Court.* 2nd edition. New York: Oxford University Press, 1985.

Amrine, Michael. *This Awesome Challenge: The Hundred Days of Lyndon Johnson.* New York: G. P. Putnam's Sons, 1964.

Anderson, Patrick. *The President's Men: White House Assistants of Franklin D. Roosevelt, Harry S. Truman, Dwight D. Eisenhower, John F. Kennedy and Lyndon B. Johnson.* New York: Doubleday and Co., 1968.

Andrews, Bert. *Washington Witch Hunt.* New York: Random House, 1948.

Arnold, Thurman. *Fair Fights and Foul: A Dissenting Lawyer's Life.* New York: Harcourt, Brace and World, 1951.

Asch, Sidney H. *The Supreme Court and Its Great Justices.* New York: Arco Publishing Co., 1971.

Auerbach, Jerold S. *Unequal Justice: Lawyers and Social Change in Modern America.* New York: Oxford University Press, 1976.

Baker, Bobby, and Larry L. King. *Wheeling and Dealing: Confessions of a Capitol Hill Operator.* New York: W. W. Norton and Co., 1978.

Baker, Leonard. *The Johnson Eclipse.* New York: Macmillan Co., 1966.

Baker, Liva. *Miranda: Crime, Law and Politics.* New York: Atheneum Publishers, 1983.

Ball, George. *The Past Has Another Pattern.* New York: W. W. Norton and Co., 1982.

Bell, Jack. *The Johnson Treatment: How Lyndon B. Johnson Took Over the Presidency and Made It His Own.* New York: Harper and Row, 1965.

Berman, Larry. *Planning a Tragedy: The Americanization of the War in Vietnam.* New York: W. W. Norton and Co., 1982.

Biddle, Francis. *In Brief Authority.* New York: Doubleday and Co., 1962.

Black, Hugo L. *A Constitutional Faith.* New York: Alfred A. Knopf, 1968.

———— and Elizabeth Black. *Mr. Justice and Mrs. Black: The Memoirs of Hugo L. Black and Elizabeth Black.* New York: Random House, 1986.

Blum, John Morton, ed. *The Price of Vision: The Diary of Henry A. Wallace, 1942–1946.* Boston: Houghton Mifflin Co., 1973.

Bornet, Vaughn Davis. *The Presidency of Lyndon B. Johnson.* Lawrence, Kans.: University of Kansas Press, 1983.

Califano, Joseph A., Jr. *A Presidential Nation.* New York: W. W. Norton and Co., 1975.

Caro, Robert. *The Years of Lyndon Johnson: The Path to Power.* New York: Alfred A. Knopf, 1982.

Chase, Harold W. *Federal Judges: The Appointing Process.* Minneapolis: University of Minnesota Press, 1972.

Chester, Lewis; Godfrey Hodgson; and Bruce Page. *An American Melodrama: The Presidential Campaign of 1968.* New York: Viking Press, 1969.

Christian, George. *The President Steps Down: A Personal Memoir of the Transfer of Power.* New York: Macmillan Co., 1970.

Clancy, Paul R. *Just a Country Lawyer: A Biography of Senator Sam Ervin.* Bloomington, Ind.: Indiana University Press, 1974.

Cooper, Chester L. *The Lost Crusade.* New York: Dodd, Mead and Co., 1970.

Cooper, Philip J. "Justice Douglas and Administrative Law." Unpublished Ph.D. dissertation. Syracuse University, 1978.

Divine, Robert, ed. *Exploring the Johnson Years.* Austin, Tex.: University of Texas Press, 1981.

Douglas, William O. *The Autobiography of William O. Douglas: Go East Young Man—The Early Years.* New York: Random House, 1974.

————. *The Autobiography of William O. Douglas: The Court Years, 1939–1975.* New York: Random House, 1980.

Douth, George. *Leaders in Profile: The United States Senate.* New York: Speer and Douth, 1972.

Dugger, Ronnie. *The Politician: The Life and Times of Lyndon Johnson. The Drive for Power— from the Frontier to Master of the Senate.* New York: W. W. Norton and Co., 1982.

Ehrlichman, John. *Witness to Power: The Nixon Years.* New York: Pocket Books, 1982.

Ervin, Sam. *Preserving the Constitution: The Autobiography of Senator Sam Ervin.* Charlottesville, Va.: Michie Co., 1984.

Evans, Rowland, and Robert Novak. *Lyndon B. Johnson: The Exercise of Power.* New York: New American Library, 1966.

Ewald, William Bragg, Jr. *Who Killed Joe McCarthy?* New York: Simon and Schuster, 1984.

Fortas, Abe. *Concerning Dissent and Civil Disobedience.* New York: Signet Books, 1968.

Fritschler, A. Lee. *Smoking and Politics: Policymaking and the Federal Bureaucracy.* 3rd edition. Englewood Cliffs, N.J.: Prentice-Hall, 1983.

Galbraith, John Kenneth. *A Life in Our Times.* New York: Ballantine Books, 1981.

Goldman, Eric F. *The Tragedy of Lyndon Johnson.* New York: Alfred A. Knopf, 1969.

Goulden, Joseph C. *The Superlawyers: The Small and Powerful World of the Great Washington Law Firms.* New York: Weybright and Talley, 1971.

Graff, Henry F. *The Tuesday Cabinet: Deliberation and Decision on Peace and War Under Lyndon B. Johnson.* Englewood Cliffs, N.J.: Prentice-Hall, 1970.

Grossman, Joel B. *Lawyers and Judges: The ABA and the Politics of Judicial Selection.* New York: John Wiley and Sons, 1965.

Halberstam, David. *The Best and the Brightest.* New York: Random House, 1966.

Haley, J. Evetts. *A Texan Looks at Lyndon: A Study in Illegitimate Power.* Canyon, Tex.: Palo Duro Press, 1964.

Harris, Joseph P. *The Advice and Consent of the Senate.* Los Angeles: University of California Press, 1953.

Harris, Richard. *Decision.* New York: E. P. Dutton and Co., 1971.

Heckart, Ronald Jay. "Justice Fortas and the First Amendment." Unpublished Ph.D. dissertation. State University of New York at Albany, 1973.

Hoopes, Townsend. *The Limits of Intervention*. New York: David McKay Co., 1969.

Hughes, Emmet John. *The Living Presidency: The Resources and Dilemmas of the American Presidential Office*. New York: Coward, McCann and Geoghegan, 1972.

Ickes, Harold L. *The Secret Diary of Harold L. Ickes*, 3 vols. New York: Simon and Schuster, 1954.

Irons, Peter H. *The New Deal Lawyers*. Princeton, N.J.: Princeton University Press, 1982.

———. *Justice at War: The Story of the Japanese American Internment Cases*. New York: Oxford University Press, 1983.

Isaacson, Walter, and Evan Thomas. *The Wise Men: Six Friends and the World They Made*. New York: Simon and Schuster, 1986.

Johnson, Lyndon Baines. *The Vantage Point: Perspectives of the Presidency, 1963–1969*. New York: Holt, Rinehart and Winston, 1971.

Johnson, Mrs. Lyndon Baines. *A White House Diary*. New York: Holt, Rinehart and Winston, 1970.

Johnson, Richard Tanner. *Managing the White House: An Intimate Study of the Presidency*. New York: Harper and Row, 1974.

Johnson, Sam Houston. *My Brother Lyndon*. New York: Cowles Book Co., 1969.

Jones, Hugh. "The Defeat of the Nomination of Abe Fortas as Chief Justice of the United States." Unpublished Ph.D. dissertation. Johns Hopkins University, 1976.

Kalb, Marvin, and Elie Abel. *Roots of Involvement: The U.S. in Asia, 1784–1971*. New York: W. W. Norton and Co., 1971.

Kalman, Laura. *Legal Realism at Yale, 1927–1960*. Chapel Hill, N.C.: University of North Carolina Press, 1986.

Karnow, Stanley. *Vietnam: A History*. New York: Viking Press, 1983.

Katcher, Leo. *Earl Warren: A Political Biography*. New York: McGraw-Hill, 1967.

Kearns, Doris. *Lyndon Johnson and the American Dream*. New York: Harper and Row, 1976.

Kelly, Robert. *Court of Reason: Robert Hutchins and the Fund for the Republic*. New York: Free Press, 1981.

Kelly, Tom. *The Imperial Post: The Meyers, the Grahams, and the Paper That Rules Washington*. New York: William Morrow and Co., 1983.

Kleindienst, Richard. *Justice: The Memoirs of an Attorney General*. Ottawa, Ill.: Jameson Books, 1985.

Kohlmeier, Louis M., Jr. *"God Save This Honorable Court."* New York: Charles Scribner's Sons, 1972.

Kramer, Victor. *Selections from the Letters and Legal Papers of Thurman Arnold*. Washington, D.C.: Merkle Press, 1961.

Lasky, Victor. *It Didn't Start with Watergate*. New York: Dial Press, 1977.

Lattimore, Owen. *Ordeal by Slander*. Boston: Little, Brown and Co., 1950.

Leuchtenburg, William E. *In the Shadow of FDR: From Harry Truman to Ronald Reagan*. Ithaca, N.Y.: Cornell University Press, 1983.

Levy, Leonard. *Against the Law: The Nixon Court and Criminal Justice*. New York: Harper Torchbooks, 1974.

Lewis, Anthony. *Gideon's Trumpet*. New York: Vintage Books, 1964.

Lewy, Guenter. *America in Vietnam*. New York: Oxford University Press, 1978.

Louchheim, Katie, ed. *The Making of the New Deal: The Insiders Speak*. Cambridge, Mass.: Harvard University Press, 1983.

McFeeley, Neil D. *Appointment of Judges: The Johnson Presidency*. Austin, Tex.: University of Texas Press, 1987.

MacKenzie, John P. *The Appearance of Justice*. New York: Charles Scribner's Sons, 1974.

MacNeil, Neil. *Dirksen: Portrait of a Public Man*. New York: World Publishing Co., 1970.

McPherson, Harry. *A Political Education.* Boston: Little, Brown and Co., 1972.

Magee, James J. *Mr. Justice Black: Absolutist on the Court.* Charlottesville, Va.: University of Virginia Press, 1980.

Manchester, William. *The Death of a President.* New York: Harper and Row, 1967.

Martin, John Bartlow. *Overtaken by Events.* New York: Doubleday and Co., 1966.

Massaro, John L. "Advise and Dissent: Factors in the Senate's Refusal to Confirm Supreme Court Nominees, with Special Emphasis on the Cases of Abe Fortas, Clement F. Haynsworth, Jr., and G. Harrold Carswell." Unpublished Ph.D. dissertation. Southern Illinois University, 1975.

Miller, Merle. *Lyndon: An Oral Biography.* New York: Ballantine Books. 1980.

Miller, Nathan. *FDR: An Intimate Biography.* New York: New American Library, 1983.

Murphy, Bruce Allen. *The Brandeis/Frankfurter Connection: The Secret Political Activities of Two Supreme Court Justices.* New York: Oxford University Press, 1982.

O'Brien, David. *Storm Center: The Supreme Court in American Politics.* New York: W. W. Norton and Co., 1986.

Oshinsky, David M. *A Conspiracy So Immense: The World of Joe McCarthy.* New York: Free Press, 1983.

Pack, Robert. *Edward Bennett Williams for the Defense.* New York: Harper and Row, 1983.

Pfau, Richard. *No Sacrifice Too Great: The Life of Lewis L. Strauss.* Charlottesville, Va.: University of Virginia Press, 1984.

Pritchett, C. Herman. *Constitutional Civil Liberties.* Englewood Cliffs, N.J.: Prentice-Hall, 1984.

Redford, Emmette S., and Marlan Blissett. *Organizing the Executive Branch: The Johnson Presidency.* Chicago: University of Chicago Press, 1981.

Reedy, George. *The Twilight of the Presidency.* New York: World Publishing Co., 1970.

———. *Lyndon B. Johnson: A Memoir.* New York: Andrews and McMeel, 1982.

Reeves, Thomas C. *The Life and Times of Joe McCarthy: A Biography.* New York: Stein and Day, 1980.

Roberts, Charles. *LBJ's Inner Circle.* New York: Delacorte Press, 1965.

Schandler, Herbert Y. *The Unmaking of a President: Lyndon Johnson and Vietnam.* Princeton, N.J.: Princeton University Press, 1977.

Schapsmeier, Edward L., and Frederick H. Schapsmeier. *Dirksen of Illinois: Senatorial Statesman.* Urbana, Ill.: University of Illinois Press, 1985.

Schlesinger, Arthur M., Jr. *A Thousand Days.* Boston: Houghton Mifflin Co., 1965.

———. *Robert Kennedy and His Times.* New York: Ballantine Books, 1978.

Schott, Richard L., and Dagmar S. Hamilton. *People, Positions and Power: The Political Appointments of Lyndon Johnson.* Chicago: University of Chicago Press, 1983.

Schwartz, Bernard. *Super Chief: Earl Warren and His Supreme Court—A Judicial Biography.* New York: New York University Press, 1983.

Seligman, Joel. *The Transformation of Wall Street: A History of the Securities and Exchange Commission and Modern Corporate Finance.* Boston: Houghton Mifflin Co., 1982.

Shaffer, Samuel. *On and Off the Floor: Thirty Years as a Correspondent on Capitol Hill.* New York: Newsweek Books, 1980.

Sherrill, Robert. *The Accidental President.* New York: Grossman Publishers, 1967.

Shogan, Robert. *A Question of Judgment: The Fortas Case and the Struggle for the Supreme Court.* Indianapolis: Bobbs-Merrill Co., 1972.

Sidey, Hugh. *A Very Personal Presidency: Lyndon Johnson in the White House.* New York: Atheneum Publishers, 1968.

Simon, James. *In His Own Image: The Supreme Court in Richard Nixon's America.* New York: David McKay Co., 1974.

———. *Independent Journey: The Life of William O. Douglas.* New York: Harper and Row, 1980.

Steinberg, Alfred. *Sam Johnson's Boy: A Close-Up of the President from Texas*. New York: Macmillan Co., 1968.

Sutter, John Ben. "The Advisory Relationship of Justice Abe Fortas to President Lyndon Baines Johnson." Unpublished master's thesis. Baylor University, 1983.

Taylor, Maxwell D. *Swords and Plowshares*. New York: W. W. Norton and Co., 1972.

Thies, Wallace J. *When Governments Collide: Coercion and Diplomacy in the Vietnam Conflict, 1964–1968*. Los Angeles: University of California Press, 1980.

Thompson, Kenneth W., ed. *The Virginia Papers on the Presidency*, Vol. X. Lanham, Md.: University Press of America, 1982.

Valenti, Jack. *A Very Human President*. New York: W. W. Norton and Co., 1975.

Warren, Earl. *The Memoirs of Chief Justice Earl Warren*. New York: Doubleday and Co., 1977.

Weaver, John D. *Warren: The Man, the Court, the Era*. Boston: Little, Brown and Co., 1967.

Weinstein, Allen. *Perjury: The Hiss-Chambers Case*. New York: Alfred A. Knopf, 1978.

Whalen, Charles, and Barbara Whalen. *The Longest Debate: A Legislative History of the 1964 Civil Rights Act*. Cabin John, Md.: Seven Locks Press, 1985.

White, G. Edward. *Earl Warren: A Public Life*. New York: Oxford University Press, 1982.

White, Graham, and John Maze. *Harold Ickes of the New Deal: His Private Life and Public Career*. Cambridge, Mass.: Harvard University Press, 1985.

White, Theodore. *The Making of the President 1964*. New York: Atheneum Publishers, 1964.

White, William S. *The Professional Lyndon B. Johnson*. Boston: Houghton Mifflin Co., 1964.

Wicker, Tom. *JFK and LBJ: The Influence of Personality upon Politics*. New York: Penguin Books, 1968.

Woodward, Bob, and Scott Armstrong. *The Brethren: Inside the Supreme Court*. New York: Avon Books, 1979.

AUTHOR'S NOTE
AND
ACKNOWLEDGMENTS

This volume is a continuation of a journey that began for me fourteen years ago in graduate school at the University of Virginia. There, my mentor, Henry J. Abraham, suggested that I look into the topic of extrajudicial activities of Supreme Court justices. As I examined what little literature existed on the topic at the time, I was puzzled by the constant comparisons of the revered Louis D. Brandeis and Felix Frankfurter, who represented for many the "paragons of judicial virtue," with the sometimes brutally criticized Abe Fortas, who represented for these same people a judge who had become tainted by his involvement in politics. These comparisons puzzled me greatly because I was also finding hints in that same literature that Brandeis and Frankfurter might well have been heavily involved in private politicking while serving on the Supreme Court. I was also fascinated because I still remembered the problems that Abe Fortas had had with the United States Senate at the time of my political awakening in high school in 1968. So I was left with two unresolved questions: Were Brandeis and Frankfurter really all that different from Abe Fortas in their off-the-bench activities? And did Fortas get a raw deal in 1968?

My first book, *The Brandeis/Frankfurter Connection: The Secret Political Activities of Two Supreme Court Justices,* was an attempt to answer both questions. If I could show that the two presumed judicial saints, Brandeis and Frankfurter, had been involved in politics, then it could be assumed that nearly all members of the court did likewise. In turn, then, Abe Fortas's reputation would be somewhat defended. My purpose in this volume had simply been to expose the political lives of two justices and leave it to the reader to decide whether that made him or her uncomfortable. In a world where there are few judicial norms, it is left to the citizenry to decide what is right and what is wrong. With that in mind, I included an appendix illustrating the incredible range of political activities undertaken by other justices, so as not to leave the reader with the impression that Brandeis and Frankfurter had been alone in the extent of their involvement.

Once that book was written, however, I still felt that my journey was incomplete. By finding that other members of the court had been involved in politics, I still had not proven that Abe Fortas could be defended for his extrajudicial political activities. The time had come, I concluded, to examine the life of Fortas in general, and the controversy surrounding his nomination to the chief justiceship in 1968 in particular. With that in mind, thanks to the efforts of my great friend and colleague Professor Arthur Goldschmidt, Jr., I was able to interview Fortas on August

7, 1981. My purpose was twofold: to speak with him about the topic of extrajudicial activities, and to inform him about my intention to write on his life next. What ensued remains one of the most interesting periods of my life. Fortas was in a very expansive mood, saying, "Well, I think there are certain things that should be known for history." With that, he began to speak on a subject that he had specifically avoided with other researchers—his personal and political relationship with Lyndon Baines Johnson. The account that he gave was so interesting, and so different from what had been portrayed in the literature, that it cried out for further investigation.

But there was more. In the middle of this conversation, almost entirely out of context, Fortas began speaking in a sad voice about the isolation felt by members of the court. As I explain in the text, it was then that he spoke about "dying on the court." Then suddenly he said, "That's why I got involved with the children. That's why I got involved with that board." The topic came up so suddenly and disappeared so quickly that it was a long while before I realized that he had touched on the subject that I had thought was absolutely forbidden in our conversation—the Louis Wolfson relationship. Toward the end of our talk, Fortas granted me permission to see his Supreme Court papers at Yale University, saying, "I haven't any idea what is there; we just boxed all the papers up in 1969 and sent them to New Haven." Since at the time the papers were closed to all researchers until the year 2000, no one had any idea what was there. So Fortas added, "Come back when you've taken a look and let me know if you find anything interesting." I greatly looked forward to having another chat with him, to show Fortas what he already knew: that he had gotten a very raw deal. But the fates were not to allow it, as he died suddenly in April of the following year.

My course, though, was already set. The phrase that kept rolling around in my head was his "dying on the court." In a very real sense, I realized, Fortas *had* "died" on the court, and not just in the way that he understood. This man of mystery had watched his career go down in flames, and neither he nor any of his friends seemed able to prevent it. So another question was added to my agenda: Who or what killed the public life of Abe Fortas? For me, what had begun as a judicial biography now became something of a murder mystery. And because of Fortas's conscious efforts to cover his trial by destroying papers, for a while it seemed like the answers would remain forever clouded in mystery.

My research trip to the Johnson Library at Austin, Texas, proved to me that the book I now wanted to write could be done. In searching through papers that had been slotted for destruction, the files pertaining to Abe Fortas's and Homer Thornberry's nominations, I saw two things clearly. First, an account of the relationship between Fortas and Johnson, one that many thought could never be written, was now possible. But more than that, it seemed to me that the detailed records of the White House efforts to secure confirmation of Fortas and Thornberry were the stuff that novels are made of. For me, it seemed just as interesting as Allen Drury's classic *Advise and Consent*, made even more so by the fact that it was *real* and that real people's lives had been changed and even destroyed. Then I was struck by the fact that in this one fight not only had Fortas's life been irrevocably altered, but so had the history of the entire Supreme Court and of constitutional law for the rest of this century. I began to understand that Fortas's public career had only formally died when he resigned from the court in 1969, although that is the only incident in his life that many people now remember. The seeds of his destruction had been sown in that 1968 confirmation battle, and the results were inevitable thereafter. I remain convinced that at an opportune time, when Fortas thought he could be replaced by a like-minded jurist, he would have left the court on his own.

The toughest part of the project, though, was the writing. I had gone into the book with the intention of defending Fortas, and I still thought that Fortas deserved defending. Yet, like all human beings, he had done some things that were not within the rules, and that in the end left him vulnerable. How does one sort out what caused a man's demise when there are so many different reasons, all of them sharing some of the blame or credit? With that in mind, perhaps too early one morning, partially in a fit of desperation and partially in a moment of inspiration, I decided to conduct what I called my own political autopsy of Abe Fortas. The results of that investigation appear in the Epilogue of this book. As I tried the idea out on various classes and audiences over the years, though, I kept seeing some of the same trends that had led to the destruction of Fortas recurring in our own political scene. So, like any good academic trying to give his research modern relevance for bored students, I kept warning audiences that "the same thing that happened to Fortas may very well happen to someone else very soon."

When I was walking around in the Central Pennsylvania Festival of the Arts in July 1987 in State College, Pennsylvania (a place where sometimes *The New York Times* does not arrive because bad weather prevents the trucks from getting over the mountains), and saw a booth surrounded by people signing petitions against Robert Bork's appointment to the Supreme Court, I knew that the "next time" had arrived. Bork, like Fortas, in part fell victim to shifting political winds. Twenty years from now, if the Reagan administration is as good about saving every scrap of paper as the Johnson administration was, some researcher will be just as excited and happy in doing a study of the Bork battle as I have been in studying Fortas. I wish that person the best of luck.

But as I said at the beginning, this journey is still continuing. Much work remains to be done on the topic of the extrajudicial side of judges, and the role of the judiciary in the political system. In 1969, a new chief justice, Warren Burger, came to his post openly wishing that his court would not return to its mythical "monastic life." Whatever one thinks of Burger's jurisprudence, he will go down in history as one of the most politically active chief justices since William Howard Taft for his laudable efforts to improve the financial and work situation of the federal judiciary. The extent, effect, and advisability of his other political actions, not related to such lobbying, remains to be investigated. Perhaps because of those efforts and that attitude, though, it is now common for justices to give provocative speeches, some even attempting to explain the meaning of judicial opinions that have been issued by the court, and others commenting on the qualities of a sitting president or a prospective colleague. The new chief justice, William Rehnquist, has already written a book, and two other justices are reported to be in the process of writing their memoirs, something that is not unprecedented but certainly indicates a liberalization in the political ethical standards of the court. Will there soon come a time when a sitting justice, perhaps because of his or her own inclinations or perhaps because of bad timing, faces the same kind of hostility that Fortas faced because of private political actions? I think it is quite likely. Will the court survive that encounter, and if it does, will it be the same type of institution? Only time will tell. Until then, the path that took me through the lives of Brandeis, Frankfurter, and Fortas clearly impels me to grapple with these questions. I look forward to the next stage of this journey.

Completing the fascinating exploration of Fortas's life would not have been possible without the help of a great many friends. I must single out first and foremost the outstanding staff of the Lyndon Baines Johnson Presidential Library in Austin, Texas, under the enlightened directorship of Harry Middleton. One has a very real sense of being on the edge of historical research in examining documents from times as recent as the 1960's and 1970's. Material is not yet opened, and one is never sure if it even exists. One's only guides through this maze are the archivists who are accomplishing Herculean tasks in trying to meet all the demands on their time. The type of book that I have done would simply not have been possible without the patient and intelligent efforts of each member of this highly skilled and professional staff. I am particularly indebted to Claudia Anderson, Gary Gallagher (now a colleague here at Penn State), Linda Hanson, Tina Lawson, and Nancy Smith. Dave Humphrey was particularly helpful in guiding me through the maze of searches for Fortas's foreign policy work. Finally, I would especially like to thank Mike Gillette, who heads one of the finest oral history collections anywhere, for his efforts to make my sailing easier at every stage of the research.

I would also like to thank several friends in Austin, one of the most hospitable places I have ever visited, for making me feel so welcome: Larry and Louann Temple, Dagmar and Bob Hamilton, Walt and Elspeth Rostow, and Liz Carpenter. They all went out of their way to make a lonely traveler feel very welcome.

The staffs of a great many other libraries were equally professional and helpful in guiding my research. My gratitude goes to the staffs and archivists of the Library of Congress (especially Charles Kelly and Gary Kohn), the Sterling Library at Yale University, the National Archives, the Columbia Oral History Collection, the Harvard Law School (especially the wonderful Erika Chadbourn), the John F. Kennedy Presidential Library, the Franklin D. Roosevelt Library, and the Richard Russell Library (particularly Sheryl Vogt). Examining some of these collections was made possible by permissions that I would also like to acknowledge gratefully: Abe Fortas (for his court papers), William Brennan (for his court papers), Hugo L. Black, Jr., and Mrs. Elizabeth Black (for Hugo Black's papers), and Kathleen Winsor (for Paul Porter's papers). Finally, I would like to thank the staff of the Penn State Pattee Library, which has helped me throughout the project in a variety of ways.

Since so much of what Fortas did was on the phone and in person, it was necessary to supplement the documentary evidence and the rich oral history collections on the period with personal interviews. I would like to offer my thanks to all of those cited in the notes to the book who took time out of their busy schedules to tell me what they could.

Research of this sort is always very expensive, and I am deeply indebted to a number of people who helped to defray some of the financial burden with monetary grants. Early on in the work, grants from the Pennsylvania State University Institute for the Arts and Humanistic Studies, from then university provost (and now president of the University of Rhode Island) Edward T. Eddy's Fund for Academic Excellence, and from Liberal Arts College Dean Stanley Paulson's Dean's Research Fund got me under way. I was further aided by a generous grant from the Lyndon Baines Johnson Foundation, and a small typing grant from the Penn State liberal arts research dean, Joseph Michaels.

Sanity tests are in order for those who read early versions of the manuscript, which was at one point three times longer than the final draft. Instead, I would like to offer these people my deepest thanks for showing me ways to cut, and errors that I had made. James Milholland was incredibly kind and insightful in reading the early manuscript and offering line-by-line editing suggestions. Dean Alfange, Jr., was equally insightful and pleaded with me to add more on Fortas's court career to the manuscript. As so often is the case, I argued at the time that he was wrong, and soon concluded that he was right. Bernard Schwartz was very kind in taking the time from his incredibly productive writing schedule to examine the manuscript, and his suggestion on the need for more court material was equally correct. The manuscript also benefited from the suggestions of Maria Benecki, Kenneth Martin, Patricia G. Wright, Deborah Welch Wright, and one anonymous reviewer (who suggested the subtitle of the book).

I would also like to thank Arthur Goldschmidt, Jr., for his early help in seeing Fortas, and for his constant support throughout the endeavor. Professors Dagmar Hamilton and Hugh Jones were especially generous in sharing the fruits of their own research at different points in the project. Charles Franzetta also gets my thanks for his calls every few days just to see if I was still alive (there were times when I did not know for sure). Thanks finally to Paul Drager, Phil Jacobson, and Marty and Ruth Orland for providing shelter and friendship on various research trips.

Melanie Romig deserves a special mention for her unbelievable energy in typing and formatting the huge manuscript repeatedly. I would also like to thank the exemplary staff here at Penn State for countless favors: Virginia Struble, Judy Zanot, Vicki Norton, Anne Stevens, Claire Kreider, and Shirley Rader.

The more lost I got at points in this project, the more I realized how well I had been trained to finish it. I will always be grateful to my mentor at the University of Virginia, Henry J. Abraham, for initially sending me on this journey, and for his constant support throughout. With that, and the support of three other formative influences in my life—Professors Dean Alfange, Jr., Robert J. Harris, and Sheldon Goldman—my life was made easier. I only wish that Edward Allen Hendrick, who used to hold up Arthur Schlesinger's Age of Roosevelt series and say, "You can do that," had lived to see what his grandson was able to accomplish. As always, I was supported spiritually by my parents, Mr. and Mrs. Alfred E. Coe, and my parents-in-law, Mr. and Mrs. Harold Wright.

Two department heads—John D. Martz and Trond Gilberg—have been very supportive of my writing efforts, and I wish to thank my colleagues in the Political Science Department for their congeniality. I would like to add a special word of thanks to James Eisenstein for always being there, and *never* telling me that I was right. My students, to whom I have expressed many of the theories and thoughts and much of the information in this book, have also been incredibly interested in the progress of my work. A number of them have done a variety of chores over the course of the project, and I wish to acknowledge their efforts especially: Eileen Mallon, Janice Bole, Chris Shaw, Nancy Kurland, Theresa Bakner, Mary Patricia Callahan, Phil Jacobson, Lisa Reid, Stu Feldman, Mary Sotis, Karl Klein, Linda Mandel, and Bruce Bauman.

It is a pleasure to thank the staff of William Morrow and Company for their efforts on this project. They have exhibited a level of professionalism that is unprecedented in my experience. I am more grateful than I can say to a remarkable editor, Maria Guarnaschelli. She knew instinctively when to leave me alone, and when to throw me a lifeline. I am not certain that this project could have been completed without her sensitive companionship on it. I am certain that it would have not been the same book had it not been for her enthusiasm and her intensive editing effort. The book was also greatly improved by the highly professional copy editing of Bruce Giffords and proofreading of Kathleen Morahan. They were able to find errors and inconsistencies that had eluded me through countless drafts. Thanks are also due to Dennis Combs for his tireless efforts on a variety of tasks.

The picture section would not have been possible without the efforts of Sally Evans, Mary Ann Ferrarese, Lois Long, and E. Philip Scott. My thanks are extended to all of them.

It is also a pleasure finally to be able to thank in public my agent, Gerard F. McCauley. Throughout the project he has been a beacon of light in the murky world of publishing, and performed services far beyond that of an ordinary agent. The friendship of Gerry and his wife, Kirsten, has meant a lot to me throughout this effort.

How does one properly thank his family for the support they have provided on a six-year journey? My children, Emily and Geoffrey, aged six and three, have been a true joy to watch growing up, but there were times when I was so busy on this book that I feared I would hear the words "Bruce, come on down and see Emi off to college now!" Still, they are incredibly forgiving of the time demands placed on their father, and very understanding of his frequent preoccupation. In fact, had it not been for Geoff's weekly visits to gymnastics class, I might never have made it out of the house at all. Emily told me the reason she was so forgiving of an occasionally absent father: "Dad, whatever you write, just be sure to put my name in it." I did, honey.

The reason that these children are so well adjusted, and that I am still sane, is Carol Lynn Wright. An attorney by trade, but an editor and psychiatrist by avocation, my wife has made all things seem possible throughout this effort. Fighting with her over how to word a thought in the book has become one of the major joys in my life. In fact, there is a fifty-fifty chance that she may have rewritten this acknowledgment to her. I cannot say enough about what she means to my life, and how much she makes me want to improve as a writer and as a human being. Her warmth, affection, cheerfulness, optimism, and knowledge have been absolutely indispensable for me.

Thanks finally to the Coca-Cola Company for restoring the original formula to the shelves and keeping me awake. And thanks to Joe Paterno's Nittany Lions for constantly keeping me entertained.

BRUCE ALLEN MURPHY
State College, Pennsylvania
March, 1987

INDEX

ABOUT THE AUTHOR

Bruce Allen Murphy received his B.A. in political science from the University of Massachusetts at Amherst and his Ph.D. in government at the University of Virginia, where he studied with Professor Henry J. Abraham. He is now a professor of political science at Penn State University, where he teaches on constitutional law, the American presidency, and American government. He has conducted research in the areas of judicial ethics and the political role of judges, and his first book was the critically acclaimed *The Brandeis-Frankfurter Connection: The Secret Political Activities of Two Supreme Court Justices*. Born and raised in New England, he and his wife, Carol L. Wright, and their two children, Emily and Geoffrey, now live in State College, Pennsylvania.